Wendt / Wendt

New Artificial Intelligence Act

New Artificial Intelligence Act

A Practitioner's Guide

edited by

Janine Wendt
Domenik H. Wendt

2026

BECK • HART • NOMOS

Published by
Nomos Verlagsgesellschaft mbH & Co. KG, Waldseestraße 3-5, 76530 Baden-Baden, Germany,
email: service@nomos.de

Co-published by
Verlag C.H.Beck oHG, Wilhelmstraße 9, 80801 München, Germany,
email: bestellung@beck.de

and

Hart Publishing, Kemp House, Chawley Park, Cumnor Hill, Oxford, OX2 9PH, United Kingdom,
online at: www.hartpub.co.uk

Published in North America by Hart Publishing,
An Imprint of Bloomsbury Publishing 1385 Broadway, New York, NY 10018, USA
email: mail@hartpub.co.uk

ISBN 978 3 7560 0666 3 (NOMOS Print)
ISBN 978 3 7489 3999 3 (NOMOS ePDF)
ISBN 978 3 406 82048 9 (C.H.BECK)
ISBN 978 1 5099 9402 1 (HART)

First Edition 2026

Foreword

The Artificial Intelligence Act (AI Act) establishes the first legal framework for the development, placing on the market, and use of artificial intelligence (AI) in the European Union (EU). The EU regulation is the world's first comprehensive set of rules that attempts to keep the application of AI within the bounds of product safety law while also safeguarding fundamental rights.

The basic idea behind the AI Act is a horizontal regulatory approach. This is accompanied by a risk-based differentiation of the intensity of intervention by AI systems. This risk-based differentiation is fundamentally technology-neutral and based on the area of application of an AI system. Depending on the risk profile of the application scenario, a four-tier regulatory framework applies, distinguishing between unacceptable risk, high risk, transparency risk, and minimal risk. The AI Act standardizes numerous compliance requirements, particularly for providers and deployers of so-called high-risk AI systems. It also sets standards for general-purpose AI (GPAI).

The AI Act also forms the basis for a new supervisory regime that relies on cooperation between authorities at EU level and in the EU Member States. The EU Commission, with its affiliated AI Office, is taking control of GPAI and formulating guidelines for certain aspects of the AI Act. Other supervisory activities will be carried out by national authorities.

The AI Act is supplemented by harmonized standards. These are intended to help implement the compliance requirements in AI systems. These standards are currently being developed by the CEN-CENELEC Joint Technical Committee 21 (JTC 21) Artificial Intelligence at EU level.

Since the AI Act came into force on 1.8.2024, the new law on artificial intelligence in the EU has developed dynamically. The legal framework for AI systems and AI models Act has taken shape. The EU Commission's guidelines on AI systems and prohibited practices, which have been published in the meantime, specify the requirements of the AI Act. A living repository is intended to provide guidance on the implementation of measures to ensure the necessary AI competence. The provisions of the AI Act on GPAI models are accompanied by the AI Office's first practical guide (Code of Practice for General-Purpose AI Models). The EU Commission has also developed further guidelines for providers of these models. Additional provisions on the new supervisory system have been created via a new delegated act. Case law is also increasingly dealing with AI systems and AI models and the regulatory requirements to be observed in this regard.

This handbook is intended to provide clear and quick access to the complex new regulatory system. We have therefore endeavored to break down the sometimes complex requirements into a readable format. The primary goal is to provide a basic understanding of the new regulatory framework. This book does not aim to provide a detailed examination of the individual requirements of the AI Act.

The subject matter regulated by the AI Act, AI, is also not yet an everyday topic. For this reason, the technological basics are discussed at the beginning of this book to the extent that they are necessary for understanding the requirements of the AI Act.

In addition to the provisions of the AI Act, this handbook also outlines the basic aspects of copyright and liability law that must be observed when using AI systems and models.

In order to facilitate access to the relevant legal requirements, we have reproduced the AI Act, together with explanatory notes and appendices, in the book in consultation with the publisher. In addition, we have compiled a list of sources with links to the individual texts in the chapter 'Overview: Legal sources, administrative practice, and standards'. The overview also includes a list of standards published to date by the CEN-CENELEC Joint Technical Committee 21 (JTC 21) Artificial Intelligence.

We would like to thank Beck/Hard/Nomos, in particular Dr. Marco Ganzhorn, whose tireless efforts were a major motivation for this book.

This is the first edition of the handbook. We have compiled it with the greatest possible care. Should you notice any errors while reading, we would be grateful for any helpful comments.

Janine and Domenik Wendt, August 2025

CONTENTS

Abbreviations

AG	Amtsgericht (German District Court)
AGI	Artificial General Intelligence
AI	Artificial Intelligence
AIGO	Working Party on AI Governance
AILD	Artificial Intelligence Liability Directive
API	Application Programming Interface
arg.	argument
Art.	Article(s)
BB	Betriebs-Berater (journal)
BGB	Bürgerliches Gesetzbuch (German Civil Code)
BIFOLD	Berlin Institute for the Foundations of Learning and Data
CCTV	Closed-Circuit Television
CEN	European Committee for Standardization
CENELEC	European Committee for Electrotechnical Standardization
CEO	Chief Executive Officer
cf.	see, compare
CR	Computer und Recht (journal)
CRP	Concept Relevance Propagation
DL	Deep Learning
DMA	Digital Markets Act
DPIA	Data Protection Impact Assessment
DPO	Data Protection Officer
e.g.	for example
EC	European Community
ECB	European Central Bank
ECJ	European Court of Justice
ECLI	European Case Law Identifier
EEC	European Economic Community
ENISA	European Union Agency for Cybersecurity
ESCB	European System of Central Banks
et al.	and others
ETSI	European Telecommunications Standards Institute
EU	European Union
EuCML	Journal of European Consumer and Market Law
EUR	Euro(s)
EuR	Europarecht (journal)
EuroHPC	European High Performance Computing Joint Undertaking
EuZW	Europäische Zeitschrift für Wirtschaftsrecht (journal)

FLOP	Floating Point Operation
GDPR	General Data Protection Regulation
GenAI	Generative Artificial Intelligence
GPAI	General Purpose Artificial Intelligence
GPDP	Garante per la Protezione dei Dati Personale
GPT	Generative Pre-Trained Transformer
GRUR	Gewerblicher Rechtsschutz und Urheberrecht (journal)
GRUR-Prax	Gewerblicher Rechtsschutz und Urheberrecht – Praxis im Immaterialgüter- und Wettbewerbsrecht (journal)
GSZ	Zeitschrift für das gesamte Sicherheitsrecht (journal)
HD	High Definition
HdB	Handbuch (handbook)
HHI	Herfindahl-Hirschman Index
HLEG	High-Level-Expert Group
HMD	Head-Mounted Display
HR	Human Resources
i.e.	that is
IEC	International Electrotechnical Commission
IIC	International Review of Intellectual Property and Competition Law
IMCO	Committee on Internal Market and Consumer Protection (European Parliament)
IP	Internet Protocol
IPPR	Institute for Public Policy Research
ISO	International Organization for Standardization
IST	Implementing Technical Standards
ITRE	Industry, Research and Energy
JTC	Joint Technical Committee
JURI	Committee on Legal Affairs
LAION	Large-scale Artificial Intelligence Open Network
LG	Landgericht (German Regional Court)
LIBE	Committee on Civil Liberties, Justice and Home Affairs (European Parliament)
lit.	literature
LLC	Limited Liability Company
LLM	Large Language Model
MIS	Management Information System
ML	Machine Learning
MMR	Multimedia und Recht (journal)
mn.	margin number(s)

NAI	Network Access Identifier
NANDO	New Approach Notified and Designated Organisations
NJW	Neue Juristische Wochenschrift (journal)
NLF	New Legislative Framework
no.	number(s)
NVwZ	Neue Zeitschrift für Verwaltungsrecht (journal)
NZA	Neue Zeitschrift für Arbeits- und Sozialrecht (journal)
OECD	Organisation for Economic Co-operation and Development
OJ	Official Journal of the European Union
OLG	Oberlandesgericht (German Higher Regional Court)
p.	page(s)
para.	paragraph(s)
PhD	Doctor of Philosophy
PLD	Programmable Logic Device
RDi	Recht Digital (journal)
rec.	recital(s)
et seq.	and the following
SME	Small and Medium-sized Enterprise
SSI	Supplemental Security Income
subpara.	subparagraph(s)
TDM	Text and Data Mining
TFEU	Treaty on the Functioning of the European Union
UK	United Kingdom
UrhG	Urheberrechtsgesetz (German Act on Copyright and Related Rights)
US	United States (of America)
USD	United States Dollar
v	versus
VO	Verordnung (Regulation)
VPN	Virtual Private Network
WTO	World Trade Organization
XAI	Explainable Artificial Intelligence
ZEuP	Zeitschrift für Europäisches Privatrecht (journal)
ZfDR	Zeitschrift für Digitalisierung und Recht (journal)
ZUM	Zeitschrift für Urheber- und Medienrecht (journal)

§ 1
Introduction

Literature: *Altenburg, Nadia/Scherr, Julius*, Artificial intelligence in law in 2024 – Quo vadis? LTZ 2024, 34; *Ammann, Thorsten/Pohle, Jan*, KI-Verordnung – Was bisher geschah und jetzt zu tun ist, CB 5/2024, 137; *Antweiler, Dario/Beckh, Katharina/Chakraborty, Nilesh/Giesselbach, Sven/Klug, Katrin/Rüping, Stefan*, Natural Language Processing in der Medizin, Whitepaper Fraunhofer IAIS, April 2023; *Asenger, Hüveyda*, Künstliche Intelligenz im Strafverfahren und Fairness, InTeR 3/2023, 134; *Ashkar, Daniel/Schröder, Christian*, Das Gesetz über künstliche Intelligenz der Europäischen Union (KI-Verordnung), BB 2024, 771; *Bachgrund, Richard/Nesum, Long/Bernstein, Max/Burchard, Christoph* – Das Pro und Contra für Chatbots in Rechtspraxis und Rechtsdogmatik, CR 2/2023, 132; *Batista, Patricia*, ChatGPT versus Arbeitsrecht – Leistungserbringung mithilfe von Sprachmodellen, LTZ 2024, 118; *Baumgartner, Ulrich/Brunnbauer, Jonas H./Cross, Samuel*, Anforderungen der DS-GVO an den Einsatz von Künstlicher Intelligenz, MMR 2023, 543; *Becker, Daniel/Feuerstack, Daniel*: Der neue Entwurf des EU-Parlaments für eine KI-Verordnung, MMR 2024, 22; *Berz, Amelie/Engel, Andreas/Hacker, Philipp*: Generative KI, Datenschutz, Hassrede und Disinformation – Zur Regulierung von KI-Meinungen, ZUM 2023, 586; *Biermann, Friedrich G.*, Wissenszurechnung und Künstliche Intelligenz, 2022; *Binder, Nadja/Egli, Catherine*, Umgang mit Hochrisiko-KI-Systemen in der KI-VO, MMR 2024, 626; Birska, Sylwia/Röver, Timo: Künstliche Intelligenz in der Prävention, ARP 2024, 21; *Blasek, Katrin*: KI-Regulierung in der Volksrepublik China, RDi 2023, 557; *Bomhard, David/Siglmüller, Jonas*, AI Act – das Trilogergebnis, RDi 2024, 45; *Bomhard, David/Siglmüller, Jonas*, Europäische KI-Haftungsrichtlinie, RDi 2022, 506; *Borges, Georg*, Liability for AI Systems Under Current and Future Law, CRi 1/2023, 1; *Borges, Georg*, Der Begriff des KI-Systems. Tatbestandsmerkmale und Auslegungsansätze, CR 11/2023, 706; *Botta, Jonas*, (K)ein Recht auf Behandlung mit KI? – Access to intelligent medical devices, ZfPC 2024, 42; *Botta, Jonas*, Die Förderung innovativer KI-Systeme in der EU, ZfDR 2022, 391; *Brollo, Fernanda/Dabla-Norris, Era/de Mooij, Ruud/Garcia-Macia, Daniel/Hanappi, Tibor/Liu, Li/Nguyen, Anh. D. M.*, Broadening the Gains from Generative AI: The Role of Fiscal Policies, IMF study of 17.6.2024, SDNEA2024002; *Buchalik, Barbara/Gehrmann, Mareike Christine*, From zeros and ones to paragraphs: Der AI Act, ein Rechtscode für Künstliche Intelligenz, CR 3/2024, 145; *Burchardi, Sophie*, Risikotragung für KI-Systeme EuZW 2022, 685; *Busche, Daniel*, Einführung in die Rechtsfragen der künstlichen Intelligenz, JA 2023, 441; *Buxmann, Peter/Schmidt, Holger*, Grundlagen der Künstlichen Intelligenz und des Maschinellen Lernens, in Buxmann, Peter/Schmidt, Holger (eds.), Künstliche Intelligenz, 2019; *Chibanguza, Kuuya/Steege, Hans*, Die KI-Verordnung – Überblick über den neuen Rechtsrahmen, NJW 2024, 1769; *Conrads, Markus/Schweitzer, Sascha*: Einsatz Künstlicher Intelligenz im Vertrags-, Wirtschafts- und Arbeitsrecht, NJW 2023, 2809; *Dix, Alexander/Seyerlein-Klug, Annegrit*, EAID: Exportschlager AI Act – Setzt die EU einen weltweiten Standard für die KI-Regulierung? ZD-Aktuell 2024, 04506; *Ebert, Andreas/Busch, Philip/Spiecker gen. Döhmann, Indra/Wendt, Janine*, Roboter im Supermarkt, ZfPC 2023, 16; *Ensthaler, Jürgen*, Zum neuen Verhältnis zwischen Rechtswissenschaft und Technik, ZRP 2022, 55; *Ensthaler, Jürgen*, Künstliche Intelligenz (KI) – einige Gedanken zu den vorhandenen und geplanten Schutzmaßnahmen, InTeR 1/24, 2; *Feuerstack, Daniel/Becker, Daniel/Hertz, Nora*, Die Entwürfe des EU-Parlaments und der EU-Kommission für eine KI-Verordnung im Vergleich, ZfDR 2023, 421; *Frost, Yannick/Steiniger, Manuela/Vivekens, Sabrina*, Take the risk or lose the chance? Essential questions that companies should consider from a legal perspective in the field of AI, MPR 2024, 4; *Gaub, Daniela/Kadler, Mathias*, Die Beeinflussung von menschlichem Verhalten durch Künstliche Intelligenz – Chance oder Gefahr? Rethinking Law 6.2022, 4; *Gengler, Eva*, Feministische Künstliche Intelligenz, Rethinking Law 6.2022, 32; *Gumpp, Tobias/Schneider, Marc Pierre*, Methoden der Künstlichen Intelligenz in der Rechtswissenschaft, ZfDR 2021, 155; *Haar, Tobias*, KI-Regulierung: Gelingt die Quadratur des Kreises? MMR 2023, 397; *Hacker, Philipp*: The regulation of ChatGPT et al. – ein europäisches Trauerspiel, GRUR 2023, 289; *Hacker, Philipp/Berz, Amelie*, Der AI Act der Europäischen Union – Überblick, Kritik und Ausblick, ZRP 2023, 226; *Hahn, Johanna*, Die Regulierung biometrischer Fernidentifizierung in der Strafverfolgung im KI-Verordnungsentwurf der EU-Kommission, ZfDR 2023, 142; *Hoeren, Thomas/Pinelli, Stefan*, Künstliche Intelligenz – Ethik und Recht, 2022; *Kerkmann, Christof/Scheuer, Stephan*, Das Microsoft-Prinzip, Handelsblatt vom 14./15./16.7.2023, 42; *Krüger, Daniel/Wagner, Susan*, Das Phänomen "Künstliche Intelligenz" aus regulatorischer und haftungsrechtlicher Sicht, ZfPC 2023, 124; *Kühling, Jürgen*, Der Einsatz von Künstlicher Intelligenz durch Unternehmen und Aufsichtsbehörden bei der Bekämpfung von Hassrede, ZUM 2023, 566; *Kumkar, Lea Katharina/Rapp, Julian Philipp*, Deepfakes, ZfDR 2022, 199; *Martini, Mario*, Blackbox-Algorithmus, 2019; *Martini, Mario/Wiesehöfer, Christine*, Auf dem Weg zur Regulierung von General-Purpose-AI – eine erste Bestandsaufnahme und Kritik der Regelungsentwürfe, NVwZ 1/2024, 1; *Meckel, Miriam/Steinacker, Léa*, Alles überall auf einmal, 2024; *Möller-Klapperich, Julia*, ChatGPT und Co. – aus der Perspektive der Rechtswissenschaft, NJ 2023, 144; *Prange, Hans Michael*, Datenschutz- und lauterkeitsrechtliche Kernfragen des Einsatzes Künstlicher

Intelligenz im Marketing, WRP 2024, 151; *Roth-Isigkeit, David*, Der risikobasierte Ansatz als Paradigma des Digitalverwaltungsrechts, MMR 2024, 621; *Russell, Stuart/Norvig, Peter*, Artificial Intelligence, 4th ed. 2021; *Schmid, Thomas/Hildesheim, Wolfgang/Holoyad, Taras*, Künstliche Intelligenz managen und verstehen, 2023; *Schwartmann, Rolf/Keber, Tobias/Zenner, Kai*, KI-Verordnung. Leitfaden für die Praxis, 2024; *Schürmann, Kathrin*, Datenschutz-Folgenabschätzung beim Einsatz Künstlicher Intelligenz, ZD 2022, 316; *Wendt, Domenik/Jung, Constantin*, Europäischer Rechtsrahmen für Künstliche Intelligenz (Teil I), LRZ 2021, 34; *Wendt, Janine/Wendt, Domenik*, Einigung auf Rechtsrahmen für Künstliche Intelligenz in der EU, ZfPC 2024, 86.

I. AI as a universal technology to be regulated

1 In recent years, AI has developed into a **universal technology**.[1] It has begun to slowly but irreversibly change our everyday and economic lives. The change is being driven by the promise **of increased productivity and efficiency** as well as cost reductions.

2 In fact, we are already encountering AI applications in many areas that deliver on this promise and improve our lives. The most striking upheavals are in key areas such as medicine.[2] Here, AI is making it possible to increase the accuracy of **predictions**[3] and thus make better decisions.[4] For example, an AI called Path-BigBird can process pathology reports and provide accurate information about a cancer in almost real time.[5] It is clear that these and similar AI applications rapidly accelerate **medical progress**.[6]

3 But we are also increasingly encountering AI applications in everyday life. Apple's **integration** of generative AI into devices such as smartphones, for example, is likely to lead to a rapid and comprehensive impact of AI on daily routines in private and professional environments. The integration of generative AI into Office solutions offered by Microsoft also promises fascinating progress. Further investment in data, skills and digitized workflows is still required to unlock the full potential of AI. Currently, 37 % of German companies surveyed in a study by the IW future panel state that they use AI. This usage rate is high compared to previous studies. The OECD recorded a rate of use of only 13.3 % in Germany in 2024. For Europe the EU Commission has identified a rate of just under 20 % in 2024. Compared to AI pioneers such as China, where 50 % of companies were already using AI in 2023, the share is still low.[7] However, AI is al-

[1] Roth-Isigkeit MMR 2024, 621 (621).

[2] Antweiler/Beckh/Chakraborty/Giesselbach/Klug/Rüping, Natural Language Processing in der Medizin, Whitepaper Fraunhofer IAIS 2023, https://newsletter.fraunhofer.de/public/a_14338_S4Jdz/file/data/4410_Fraunhofer_IAIS_Whitepaper_Clinical_NLP_Web.pdf.

[3] AI systems are already outperforming humans in the analysis of medical images, see Botta ZfPC 2024, 42 (42).

[4] See also the examples in Schürmann ZD 2022, 316 (317) and Botta ZfDR 2022, 391 (394).

[5] Chandrashekar/Lyngaas/Hanson/Gounley/Gao/Wu, JCO Clinical Cancer Informatics, https://doi.org/10.1200/CCI.23.00148.

[6] Frost/Steininger/Vivekens MPR 2024, 4 (6).

[7] See IW Future Panel: https://www.iwkoeln.de/fileadmin/user_upload/Studien/Report/PDF/2025/IW-Report_2025-KI-als-Wettbewerbsfaktor.pdf?utm_source=chatgpt.com as well as ifo Business Survey: https://www.ifo.de/fakten/2025-06-16/unternehmen-setzen-immer-staerker-auf-kuenstliche-intelligenz.

ready being used successfully in many companies today. Even a simple AI assistant such as Klarna Bank AB's chatbot conducts around 2.3 million customer conversations in a month. This is equivalent to the work of 700 full-time employees.[8] Thanks to the accuracy of the AI's responses, the number of repeated requests is said to have fallen by 25 %. An average conversation now only takes just under two minutes – compared to eleven minutes previously required by a human employee. The chatbot is also available around the clock in more than 35 languages.

What these successful AI applications also have in common is that they are all 4
still in the early stages of development. They have the **potential** to overcome global challenges and increase **innovation** and growth.[9]

At the same time, the rise of AI is triggering **fears.**[10] How will AI affect the labor 5
market? Will large sections of the working population lose their jobs?[11] Studies show: The greater the knowledge about AI, the greater the perceived threat.[12] A quote from Jensen Huang, CEO of Nvidia, fits in with this: "AI won't take your job. But, if you are not using AI, you are going to lose your job to somebody who uses AI".[13] This raises the question: How can we steer the development of AI in the right direction? How do we deal with the **risks**, undesirable side effects and **ethical dilemmas** – in everyday life, but also in business? How do we deal with self-driving cars, virtual medical assistants or **fake news**?[14]

The first AI Safety Report was published on 29.1.2025.[15] "With all the noise sur- 6
rounding AI, this report aims to provide policymakers with an evidence-based, balanced overview of the risks of AI and how to mitigate them,"[16] explained AI pioneer Yoshua Bengio, under whose leadership the nearly 300-page report was produced.[17] The Safety Report focuses on AI systems that can perform a wide range of tasks, so-called "general-purpose AI" (GPAI) (→ § 11 mn. 1). It impressively demonstrates how quickly this technology has developed. For example, the best models in scientific reasoning tests have leaped from "random guessing" to "PhD-level experts" in the space of 18 months.[18]

As its capabilities grow, so do the potential risks, including "large-scale impacts on 7
the labor market, AI-based hacker attacks or biological attacks" and even "a loss of control of general-purpose AI by society". The report also lists further challenges, including copyright issues, damage caused by fraud, privacy violations, distorted results and general reliability issues.[19] The focus is therefore on the question of the trustworthiness of AI systems.

---

[8] See also Batista LTZ 2024, 118 (118).

[9] Botta ZfDR 2022, 391 (392 et seq.).

[10] See only DIE ZEIT 14.3.2024, 12.

[11] Brollo/Dabla-Norris/deMooij/Garcia-Macia/Hanappi/Liu/Nguyen, Broadening the Gains from Generative AI: The Role of Fiscal Policies, IMF study of 17.6.2024.

[12] Buxmann FAZ 18.8.2025.

[13] Huang, Milken Institute Global Conference 2025 of 6.5.2025.

[14] Gaub/Kadler Rethinking Law 6.2022, 4 (5).

[15] International AI Safety Report – The International Scientific Report on the Safety of Advanced AI, 2025, https://www.gov.uk/government/publications/international-ai-safety-report-2025/international-ai-safety-report-2025.

[16] See https://yoshuabengio.org/2024/07/09/reasoning-through-arguments-against-taking-ai-safety-seriously/.

[17] https://arxiv.org/pdf/2501.17805.

[18] International AI Safety Report – The International Scientific Report on the Safety of Advanced AI, 2025, p. 42.

[19] Bachgrund/Nesum/Bernstein/Burchard CR 2/2023, 132 (135).

8 It is about the risk of **reinforcing** existing unconscious **prejudices**, for example in relation to gender or ethnic origin,[20] the violation of human rights or values such as the **protection of privacy**. There is also growing concern that AI systems will reinforce inequalities, **market concentrations** and digital divides.

9 In order to get the right answers to these questions, we need to take a close look at the opportunities and risks associated with the use of AI. **International cooperation** and joint solutions **are** needed to steer the development and use of AI in a way that benefits us all. Ultimately, it is the **responsibility of the legislature** to formulate clear boundaries and requirements to enable the use of human-centered, **trustworthy AI**.

10 The fact that the European Union (EU) is leading the way here with the Artificial Intelligence Act (AI Act) is courageous. With the AI Act, the EU has launched the world's **first comprehensive regulatory system for AI**.[21] In doing so, it is daring to introduce groundbreaking legislation that will have an impact on the global AI landscape and, in the best-case scenario, lead to a "**Brussels Effect**".[22] Despite the criticism of individual regulations, this drive deserves respect. Well-balanced rules will be needed at the latest when AI enters the mainstream of society. The AI Act, the first provisions of which have been in force since February 2025, was well timed for this moment.

II. Accelerating change through generative AI

11 With ChatGPT, the age of generative AI dawned at the end of 2022. Unlike regular machine learning, generative AI is not only able to independently find patterns in large data sets, but also to create new content such as texts, images, code, and more based on the identified relationships. This meant that dialog formats were now possible; the time had come when humans could talk to machines.[23] ChatGPT allowed AI to arrive in the middle of society. OpenAI published an early demo of the chatbot on 30.11.2022, which spread rapidly on social media due to its many possible applications. As an AI system, **ChatGPT** was based on the GPT-3 AI model, which had been developed two and a half years earlier. But it was the release of ChatGPT that marked the **decisive moment**, when it became clear to the general public just how influential this technology could become.[24] Just as the iPhone made the revolution of mobile access to information and services possible with its launch on 29.6.2007, the turn of the year 2022/2023 marks the turning point of AI.[25] Generative applications, for which ChatGPT has almost established itself as a generic name,[26] made the technology accessible to the general public.

---

[20] Feldkamp/Kappler/Poretschkin/Schmitz/Weiss ZfDR 1/2024, 60 (105, 112); Kuntz ZfPW 2022, 177 (178); Schürmann ZD 2022, 316 (321); Gaub/Kadler Rethinking Law 6.2022, 4 (6); Ibold GSZ 2024, 10 (13).

[21] See Wendt/Wendt ZfPC 2024, 86 (86); only China has also passed an AI law, although this only covers individual sectors and generative AI, see Hacker/Berz ZRP 2023, 226 (226); Blasek RDi 2023, 557 (557).

[22] Haar MMR 2023, 397 (397); Frost/Steininger/Vivekens MPR 2024, 4 (4); Dix/Seyerlein-Klug ZD-Aktuell 2024, 04506.

[23] Möller-Klapperich NJ 2023, 144 (144).

[24] See also Meckel/Steinacker, Alles überall auf einmal, 17; Baumgartner/Brunnbauer/Cross MMR 2023, 543 (543).

[25] Martini/Wiesehöfer NVwZ 2024, 137 (137).

[26] Altenburg/Scherr LTZ 2024, 34 (34).

Chatbots existed long before ChatGPT. The **GPT models** used in the chatbot have also existed in their various **iterations since June 2018.**[27] However, it was the combination of ChatGPT with the then **AI model GPT-3** that made it possible to draft an email, a LinkedIn post or even an entire essay, summarize a meeting that had just been held and reformulate a school report in the style of Shakespeare.[28] The improved version of the AI model GPT-3.5 used in ChatGPT, released in March 2023, finally attracted widespread attention. 12

User numbers for ChatGPT grew to one million people in just five days; after two months, 100 million people were already using the tool.[29] This is the **most rapid increase in access to an application** since the invention of the Internet.[30] 13

III. Developments in and around OpenAI

Interestingly, the discussion about the changes brought about by generative AI is not only taking place in the media and academia, but also in the company itself that triggered the " **ChatGPT moment**. In the US company **OpenAI**, a farce began to unfold in 2023, which will be briefly recounted here in view of the concerns behind it: Sam Altman, Ilya Sutskever, Elon Musk, Greg Brockman and a few others founded the non-profit organization "Open Artificial Intelligence" – OpenAI – in 2015. Their original goal was to develop open-source AI in a **non-profit organization**. However, as early as 2017, they realized that the financial resources for the development of AI systems could not be procured via the non-profit route. Altman initiated a change in strategy and founded a company under the umbrella of OpenAI in 2019 that was allowed to be profitable – OpenAI LLC. Altman becomes Chief Executive Officer, Musk leaves. New investors join, above all Bill Gates. Microsoft finances Altman's work.[31] It is also Altman who brings ChatGPT to the public, almost single-handedly starting a **hype.**[32] Together with Brockman, Altman becomes the **face of (generative) AI**. 14

The tide turns during the summer of 2023. Sutskever sees a danger in the rapid progress of artificial intelligence. He fears that a **superintelligence** could disempower humanity. To fight back, Sutskever founds an Alpha Taskforce and calls it the Superalignment Team – it is supposed to **contain** the **AI** and **bind it to rules**. But Altmann's work can no longer be contained. 15

Sutskever rallies the original OpenAI team behind him and **dismisses Altman** on 17.11.2023, stating in a public statement that he had not been open in his communication. In response, Brockman also resigned from his role as President of OpenAI. Shortly afterwards, Microsoft announced that Altman was moving to Microsoft, which had invested more than USD 10 billion in OpenAI at the time, to lead a new AI research team. When almost 800 OpenAI employees also threatened to leave for **Microsoft**, Sutskever gave up. OpenAI announces that it has succeeded in bringing Altmann back as CEO and Brockman as President. 16

A good four months later the story continues with another chapter. On 1.3.2024, Musk **filed a lawsuit** in the US **against OpenAI** as well as Altman and Brockman for 17

[27] See also the table in Conrads/Schweitzer NJW 2023, 2809 (2811).

[28] Meckel/Steinacker, Everything everywhere at once, 17.

[29] The telephone took around 75 years to reach this target, while WhatsApp took three and a half years, i.e. around 21 times as long, see the world of statistics and Haar MMR 2023, 397 (397).

[30] Haar MMR 2023, 397 (397).

[31] Kerkmann/Scheuer, Handelsblatt of 14./15./16.7.2023, 45 et seq.

[32] Birska/Röver ARP 2024, 21 (21).

breach of contract and breach of fiduciary duty. Musk argues that OpenAI has abandoned its original mission to develop artificial intelligence for the benefit of humanity. In the founding agreement, OpenAI was obliged to make its technology open source. Instead, OpenAI had switched to a profit-oriented model and degenerated into a de facto subsidiary of Microsoft. However, the "founding agreement" on which Musk's lawsuit is based does not appear to be a formal contract, but rather a sentiment based primarily on emails. In response to the allegations, OpenAI made public that Musk had supported the plans to found the for-profit company, and that he even wanted to lead it and merge it with Tesla.

18 The extent to which OpenAI will maintain its non-profit status, at least for its parent company, remains unclear. On 26.9.2024, the company announced that it will withdraw the majority stake from the umbrella organization, which controls the for-profit part of the company through the board of directors, and remove the cap on investor returns. On 5.5.2025, the company reversed its decision. Despite months of preparation, OpenAI surprisingly abandoned its plans to transform the company into a purely for-profit start-up. According to a report by the Bloomberg news agency, Microsoft raised concerns and prevented the transformation. Several investors shared Musk's concerns that, if focused solely on profit, the company could neglect precautions against negative, sometimes even dangerous consequences of AI.[33]

IV. Artificial General Intelligence (AGI)

19 Another point of attack in Musk's lawsuit concerns so-called **Artificial General Intelligence** (AGI) research.[34] As a very advanced development stage of artificial intelligence, Artificial General Intelligence is said to be characterized by the fact that it is able to solve or process very different tasks and situations without the help and control of a human being, just like "general common sense". In particular, the degree of autonomy is significantly increased compared to the currently predominant Narrow Artificial Intelligence (NAI) systems.[35] However, it is by no means clear which specific capabilities the term encompasses.[36] OpenAI recently presented a five-level classification system that maps progress towards AGI: At level 1 are chatbots with conversational capabilities, at level 2 problem solvers at PhD level referred to as reasoners, at level 3 autonomous agents that can perform actions, at level 4 the so-called innovators AI that invents things and at level 5 ultimately as AGI an organizer AI that can take over the work of an entire organization.[37] The statement of claim already refers to GPT-4 as an AGI, which can only correspond to the definition if interpreted very broadly. While the GPT-5, -4, -4o and -o1 models continue the trend of exponential improvement over previous versions and bring us closer to a future where AI seamlessly integrates into our daily lives, the reality is arguably less spectacular than the lawsuit suggests.

---

[33] Alvares de Souza Soares, Handelsblatt 6.5.2025.

[34] See also Haar MMR 2023, 397 (398).

[35] Cf. Keber/Zenner/Hansen/Schwartmann in: Schwartmann/Keber/Zenner Part 1, Chapter 2, para. 8; Hildesheim/Schmid/Holoyad, in: Schmid/Hildesheim/Holoyad, Künstliche Intelligenz – gestern, heute, morgen 3 (14).

[36] Hildesheim/Schmid/Holoyad, in: Schmid/Hildesheim/Holoyad, Künstliche Intelligenz – gestern, heute, morgen 3 (14).

[37] According to its own information, OpenAI is currently close to Level 2, see https://the-decoder.com/openai-unveils-five-level-ai-scale-aims-to-reach-level-2-soon/.

Q* is also mentioned, another AI model from OpenAI, which is said to be able to solve math problems at primary school level, which is not a matter of course for a language model. 20

American courts must now decide whether GPT-4, Q* or other models are actually already AGI. If GPT-4 was indeed already AGI, OpenAI should never have given Microsoft access to it. The founding statute of OpenAI stipulates that AGIs should be available to all mankind.[38] 21

However, Musk has already tried to delay the development of AI several times in the past: In March 2023, he published an open letter together with other big names in the tech industry in which they called for a pause in AI development.[39] "*Advanced AI can represent a profound change in the history of life on Earth. [It should be [planned and managed] with appropriate care,*" it says.[40] It was quickly suggested that concerns for humanity were joined by a desire to buy time in the competition for commercially successful AI systems.[41] In fact, shortly after signing the letter, Musk is said to have pushed ahead with his own **Large Language Model (LLM)** – the chatbot Grok from xAI. According to Musk, Grok is a chatbot that remains "based". It is expressly not intended to give only politically desired, i.e. "woken" answers and challenge OpenAI.[42] 22

V. Danger of disinformation

There is no doubt that the use of AI – especially in the context of **chatbots** and **deepfakes** – poses risks to humanity.[43] Under the title "AI as a Public Good: Ensuring Democratic Control of AI in the Information Space", the International Forum on Information and Democracy published a comprehensive study in February 2024[44], which deals with the **social risks of AI**. The more advanced capabilities and commercial spread of systems such as ChatGPT show their "increasing potential to **profoundly influence democratic processes**, including the information and communication space", it says. They therefore pose "significant challenges" that "require great attention". 23

Researchers Viviana Padelli, Kaye Celine Palisoc and Lia Chkhetiani found that a significant percentage of AI-driven **misinformation** is related to elections.[45] There are still many gaps in knowledge in this area, for example about the use of generative AI for **microtargeting** for the purpose of personalized voter manipulation.[46] Accordingly, AI companies are advised to involve independent researchers and civil society actors as part of an "**inclusive and participatory process**" and to set up procedures for risk mitigation and the systematic collection of user feedback and complaints. They should also cooperate with "trusted whistleblowers" and **inform users about the use of data.** 24

[38] See also Glauner in: Ebers/Quarch, Technische Grundlagen von generativen KI-Modellen, para. 58.

[39] Krüger/Wagner ZfPC 2023, 124 (124).

[40] Future of Life Institute 22.3.2023, https://futureoflife.org/open-letter/pause-giant-ai-experiments/.

[41] Zellinger Der Standard 5.3.2023; Armbruster FAZ 29.3.2023.

[42] Mey, Der Standard of 12.7.2025; Holtermann/Knees, Handelsblatt 7.2.2024.

[43] Berz/Engel/Hacker ZUM 2023, 586 (588); Kumkar/Rapp ZfDR 2022, 199 (200).

[44] Available at: https://informationdemocracy.org/wp-content/uploads/2024/03/ID-AI-as-a-Public-Good-Feb-2024.pdf.

[45] See also NewsGuard's study on the infiltration of chatbots (OpenAI's ChatGPT, You.com's Smart Assistant, xAI's Grok, Inflection's Pi, Mistral's Le Chat, Microsoft's Copilot, Meta AI, Anthropic's Claude, Google's Gemini and Perplexity's search engine) by Russian government propaganda, https://www.axios.com/2024/06/18/ai-chatbots-russian-propaganda.

[46] See Milne, University of Washington News 6.8.2025; Kühling ZUM 2023, 566 (567).

25 According to the study's recommendations, AI developers should be legally obliged to provide information about the **training data sets** for public review in an easily accessible and comprehensible manner. **Regular impact assessments** and a **systematic risk assessment** should also be regulated by law. Other recommendations include setting standards for the authenticity and origin of content as well as **transparency and labeling obligations**. The creation of a tailored **certification system** for AI companies is also suggested.

26 As we will see, the AI Act already covers all of these recommendations.

§ 2
AI – Attempts at a definition

Literature: *Altenburg, Nadia/Scherr, Julius*, Artificial intelligence in law in 2024 – Quo vadis? LTZ 2024, 34; *Ammann, Thorsten/Pohle, Jan*, KI-Verordnung – Was bisher geschah und jetzt zu tun ist, CB 5/2024, 137; *Asenger, Hüveyda*, Künstliche Intelligenz im Strafverfahren und Fairness, InTeR 3/2023, 134; *Ashkar, Daniel/Schröder, Christian*, Das Gesetz über künstliche Intelligenz der Europäischen Union (KI-Verordnung), BB 2024, 771; *Bachgrund, Richard/Nesum, Long/Bernstein, Max/Burchard, Christoph* – Das Pro und Contra für Chatbots in Rechtspraxis und Rechtsdogmatik, CR 2/2023, 132; *Batista, Patricia*, ChatGPT versus Arbeitsrecht – Leistungserbringung mithilfe von Sprachmodellen, LTZ 2024, 118; *Baumgartner, Ulrich/Brunnbauer, Jonas H./Cross, Samuel*, Anforderungen der DS-GVO an den Einsatz von Künstlicher Intelligenz, MMR 2023, 543; *Becker, Daniel/Feuerstack, Daniel*: Der neue Entwurf des EU-Parlaments für eine KI-Verordnung, MMR 2024, 22; *Berz, Amelie/Engel, Andreas/Hacker, Philipp*: Generative KI, Datenschutz, Hassrede und Disinformation – Zur Regulierung von KI-Meinungen, ZUM 2023, 586; *Biermann, Friedrich G.*, Wissenszurechnung und Künstliche Intelligenz, 2022; *Birska, Sylwia/Röver, Timo*: Künstliche Intelligenz in der Prävention, ARP 2024, 21; *Blasek, Katrin*: KI-Regulierung in der Volksrepublik China, RDi 2023, 557; *Bomhard, David/Siglmüller, Jonas*, AI Act – das Trilogergebnis, RDi 2024, 45; *Bomhard, David/Siglmüller, Jonas*, Europäische KI-Haftungsrichtlinie, RDi 2022, 506; *Borges, Georg*, Liability for AI Systems Under Current and Future Law, CRi 1/2023, 1; *Borges, Georg*, Der Begriff des KI-Systems. Tatbestandsmerkmale und Auslegungsansätze, CR 11/2023, 706; *Bostrom, Nick*, Superintelligenz, 2016; *Botta, Jonas*, (K)ein Recht auf Behandlung mit KI? – Access to intelligent medical devices, ZfPC 2024, 42; *Botta, Jonas*, Die Förderung innovativer KI-Systeme in der EU, ZfDR 2022, 391; *Buchalik, Barbara/Gehrmann, Mareike Christine*, Von Nullen und Einsen zu Paragrafen: Der AI Act, ein Rechtscode für Künstliche Intelligenz, CR 3/2024, 145; *Burchardi, Sophie*, Risikotragung für KI-Systeme, EuZW 2022, 685; *Busche, Daniel*, Einführung in die Rechtsfragen der künstlichen Intelligenz, JA 2023, 441; *Buxmann, Peter/Schmidt, Holger*, Grundlagen der Künstlichen Intelligenz und des Maschinellen Lernens, in Buxmann, Peter/Schmidt, Holger (eds.), Künstliche Intelligenz, 2019; *Conrads, Markus/Schweitzer, Sascha*: Einsatz Künstlicher Intelligenz im Vertrags-, Wirtschafts- und Arbeitsrecht, NJW 2023, 2809; *Dix, Alexander/Seyerlein-Klug, Annegrit*, EAID: Exportschlager AI Act – Setzt die EU einen weltweiten Standard für die KI-Regulierung? ZD-Aktuell 2024, 04506; *Ebers, Martin/Quarch, Benedikt*, Rechtshandbuch ChatGPT, 2024; *Ebert, Andreas/Busch, Philip/Spiecker gen. Döhmann, Indra/Wendt, Janine*, Roboter im Supermarkt, ZfPC 2023, 16; *Ensthaler, Jürgen*, Zum neuen Verhältnis zwischen Rechtswissenschaft und Technik, ZRP 2022, 55; *Ensthaler, Jürgen*, Künstliche Intelligenz (KI) – einige Gedanken zu den vorhandenen und geplanten Schutzmaßnahmen, InTeR 1/24, 2; *Feuerstack, Daniel/Becker, Daniel/Hertz, Nora*, Die Entwürfe des EU-Parlaments und der EU-Kommission für eine KI-Verordnung im Vergleich, ZfDR 2023, 421; *Floridi, Luciano*, On the Brussels-Washington -Consensus About the Legal Defnition of Artifcial Intelligence, Philos. Technol. 36, 87, 2023 https://doi.org/10.1007/s13347-023-00690-z; *Floridi, Luciano*, The European Legislation on AI: a Brief Analysis of its Philosophical Approach. Philos. Technol. 34, 215–222, 2021, https://doi.org/10.1007/s13347-021-00460-9; *Frost, Yannick/Steiniger, Manuela/Vivekens, Sabrina*, Take the risk or lose the chance? Essential questions that companies should consider from a legal perspective in the field of AI, MPR 2024, 4; *Gaub, Daniela/Kadler, Mathias*, Die Beeinflussung von menschlichem Verhalten durch Künstliche Intelligenz – Chance oder Gefahr? Rethinking Law 6.2022, 4; *Gengler, Eva*, Feministische Künstliche Intelligenz, Rethinking Law 6.2022, 32; *Gumpp, Tobias/Schneider, Marc Pierre*, Methoden der Künstlichen Intelligenz in der Rechtswissenschaft, ZfDR 2021, 155; *Haar, Tobias*, KI-Regulierung: Gelingt die Quadratur des Kreises? MMR 2023, 397; *Hacker, Philipp*: The regulation of ChatGPT et al. – ein europäisches Trauerspiel, GRUR 2023, 289; *Hacker, Philipp/Berz, Amelie*, Der AI Act der Europäischen Union – Überblick, Kritik und Ausblick, ZRP 2023, 226; *Hahn, Johanna*, Die Regulierung biometrischer Fernidentifizierung in der Strafverfolgung im KI-Verordnungsentwurf der EU-Kommission, ZfDR 2023, 142; *Jin, Junqi/Song, Chengru/Li, Han/Gai, Kun*, Real-Time Bidding with Multi-Agent Reinforcement Learning in Display Advertising 2018, DOI:10.1145/3269206.3272021; *Kerkmann, Christof/Scheuer, Stephan*, Das Microsoft-Prinzip, Handelsblatt vom 14./15./16.7.2023, 42; *Martini, Mario*, Blackbox-Algorithmus, 2019; *Martini, Mario/Wiesehöfer, Christine*, Auf dem Weg zur Regulierung von General-Purpose-AI – eine erste Bestandsaufnahme und Kritik der Regelungsentwürfe, NVwZ 1/2024, 1; *Meckel, Miriam/Steinacker, Léa*, Alles überall auf einmal, 2024; *Mühleis Niklas/Akinci, Nick*, Rechtsleitfaden KI im Unternehmen, 2024; *OECD*, Künstliche Intelligenz in der Gesellschaft, 2020; *Pesch, Paulina Jo/Böhme, Rainer*, Verarbeitung personenbezogener Daten und Datenrichtigkeit bei großen Sprachmodellen, MMR 2023, 917; *Polanyi, Michael*, The Tacit Dimension, 1966; *Prange, Hans Michael*, Datenschutz- und lauterkeitsrechtliche Kernfragen des Einsatzes Künstlicher Intelligenz im Marketing, WRP 2024, 151; *Russell, Stuart/Norvig, Peter*, Artificial Intelligence, 4th ed. 2021; *Schmid, Thomas/Hildesheim, Wolfgang/Holoyad, Taras*, Künstliche Intelligenz managen und verstehen, 2023; *Schwartmann, Rolf/Keber, Tobias/Zenner, Kai*, KI-

Verordnung. Leitfaden für die Praxis, 2024; *Schürrmann, Kathrin*, Datenschutz-Folgenabschätzung beim Einsatz Künstlicher Intelligenz, ZD 2022, 316; *Searle, John R.*, The Behavioral and Brain Sciences, Vol. 3/1980, 417; *Turing, Alan M.*, Computing Machinery and Intelligence, Mind 236/1950, 433; *Wendehorst, Christiane/Nessler, Bernhard/Aufreiter, Alexander/Aichinger, Gregor*, Der Begriff des "KI-Systems" unter der neuen KI-VO, MMR 2024, 605; *Wendt, Domenik/Jung, Constantin*, Europäischer Rechtsrahmen für Künstliche Intelligenz (Teil I), LRZ 2021, 34; *Wendt, Janine/Wendt, Domenik*, Einigung auf Rechtsrahmen für Künstliche Intelligenz in der EU, ZfPC 2024, 86.

I. Can machines think? The Turing test

1 In overviews[1], the development of the concept of AI regularly begins in 1950 with the **Turing test.**[2] With this test, the British mathematician Alan Turing formulated a procedure in 1950 to determine whether a computer, as a machine, has **the same thinking ability as a human being.**[3] Turing himself called the test the "Imitation Game". The procedure of the test was modified and simplified several times over the years, especially after Turing's early death in 1954, so that in its most common form it follows a **simple structure**: A human questioner holds a conversation with two interlocutors unknown to him via a keyboard and a screen, i.e. without visual or auditory contact. One interlocutor is a human, the other a machine. If, after intensive questioning, the interviewer cannot tell which of the two is the machine, the machine has passed the Turing test and is considered to be artificially intelligent. Turing assumed that by the year 2000 it would be possible to program computers in such a way that an average user would have a maximum of 70 % chance of successfully distinguishing between a human and a machine after "talking" to them for five minutes.[4] Since April 2023, the "**Human or not**" platform operated by the Tel Aviv-based company AI21labs, which describes itself as the "biggest Turing test of all time", has been putting this to the test.[5] In a browser-based self-test based on current large language models such as GPT-4 or Jurassic-2, the company analyzed 15 million conversations that took place on the website. 68 % of the human participants answered the question of whether they were communicating with an AI or a human correctly. The fact that Turing's prediction was not fulfilled can be seen as proof of the complexity of reproducing human intelligence.

[1] Buxmann/Schmidt, Artificial Intelligence, 3rd ed.
[2] For AI methods dating back to the 1930s, however, see Glauner in: Ebers/Quarch, Technische Grundlagen von generativen KI-Modellen, para. 2.
[3] Turing, Computing Machinery and Intelligence, 433.
[4] Turing, Computing Machinery and Intelligence, 442.
[5] S. https://humanornot.so.

II. Definitions matter: Development of the concept of artificial intelligence at the Dartmouth conference

The Turing test was followed in the 1950s by a series of other events in the further development of the term AI. The 1956 **Dartmouth Conference**,[6], which is considered the birth of artificial intelligence as a field of research and coined the term, stands out:[7] Under the full name Dartmouth Summer Research Project on Artificial Intelligence, it took place in the summer of 1956 at Dartmouth College in Hanover, New Hampshire. It was proposed, planned and carried out by John McCarthy, Marvin Minsky, Nathaniel Rochester (IBM) and Claude Shannon. In their proposal to the Rockefeller Foundation, in which they applied for a grant of USD 13,500 in August 1955, they formulated the **core elements** of an AI research project for the first time: 2

> "*We propose to hold a seminar on artificial intelligence with ten participants at Dartmouth College over two months during the summer of 1956. The seminar will be based on the assumption that, in principle, all aspects of learning and other features of intelligence can be described so precisely that a machine can be built to simulate these processes. We will try to find out how machines can be made to use language, make abstractions and develop concepts, solve problems of the kind currently reserved for humans, and improve themselves further. We believe that significant progress can be made in one or other of these problem areas if a carefully assembled group of scientists work together for a summer.*"[8]

Specifically, the following sub-topics should already be addressed: 3

How must a **computer** be programmed to use a **language**? What requirements must be placed on **neural networks** and their ability to **learn autonomously**? What considerations are relevant to the scope of a computing operation? How does the system deal with **randomness** and **creativity**?

Each of these questions still played a role in the draft AI Act (AI Act-D) 65 years later. 4

In between, there were many years in which the technical foundations of AI changed fundamentally. The so-called symbolic AI[9] and its logic-based systems, which were modeled on human thinking, were initially followed by a period of disillusionment in the 1970s, the "**AI winter**".[10] In the 1990s, the chess computer Deep Blue brought AI back to the fore. From 2011 onwards, significant progress was finally made in **machine learning**, a sub-area of AI based on a statistical approach (margin no. 24). As the modeling technology of machine learning became increasingly sophisticated, the ability of systems to derive forecasts from historical data improved. The term "**neural networks**" became established; it went hand in hand with the need for larger data sets and computing capacities.[11] 5

III. First modern definition of artificial intelligence by the OECD

The **OECD**'s definition of artificial intelligence proved to be another important milestone on the road to the AI Act. Based on the results of the OECD conference "AI: Intelligent Machines, Smart Policies" in October 2017 and subsequent discussions, the 6

[6] Busche JA 2023, 441 (441).
[7] For the history of development, see Buxmann/Schmidt, Künstliche Intelligenz, 3rd ed.
[8] McCarthy et al, funding application 1955, 1.
[9] Keber/Zenner/Hansen/Schwartmann in: Schwartmann/Keber/Zenner, AI Regulation, Part 1, Chapter 2, para. 2 et seq.
[10] OECD, Artificial intelligence in society, 20.
[11] See also Berz/Engel/Hacker ZUM 2023, 586 (587).

AI Group of Experts@the OECD (AIGO) developed a definition of AI that is **comprehensible**, technically correct and **technology-neutral.** This definition was revised and adapted in November 2023 and currently reads:

> *An AI system is a machine-based system that, for explicit or implicit objectives, infers, from the input it receives, how to generate outputs such as predictions, content, recommendations, or decisions that can influence physical or virtual environments. Different AI systems vary in their levels of autonomy and adaptiveness after deployment.*

7 The definition is deliberately open to the future.[12]

IV. Definition of artificial intelligence in the AI Act

1. Regulation in the AI Act itself

8 In its draft AI Act of 21.4.2021 (hereinafter AI Act-D), however, the EU Commission initially opted for a **very broad definition** of the term AI: According to Art. 3 para. 1 of the AI Act-D, **software** that has been developed using one or more of the techniques and concepts listed in Annex I and is capable of producing results such as content, predictions, recommendations or decisions that influence the environment with which it interacts, with regard to a set of objectives determined by humans, was also already considered an **AI system.**[13]

9 Annex I, which lists the techniques and concepts of AI, included, in addition to the concepts of **machine learning** mentioned under a), with supervised, unsupervised and reinforcement learning using a wide range of methods, including deep **learning**, under b) also already logic- and knowledge-based concepts, including knowledge representation, inductive (logic) programming, knowledge bases, inference and deduction engines, (symbolic) reasoning and expert systems, and finally even under c) **statistical approaches**, Bayesian estimation, search and optimization methods.

10 This broad opening of the term AI system rightly attracted **criticism** and was significantly narrowed down in the further legislative process, so that in the end a welcome approximation to the OECD definition updated in November 2023 and a focus on self-learning capabilities, which are referred to as autonomy and adaptiveness, was achieved.[14]

11 In the final version of the AI Act, an AI system is therefore "a **machine-based system** that is designed to **operate with** varying degrees of **autonomy** and that, once operational, can be **adaptive** and that derives outputs such as predictions, content, recommendations or decisions from the inputs received for explicit or implicit goals that may affect physical or virtual environments," Art. 3 No. 1 AI Act.

12 The aspects of **autonomy** and capability to infer are particularly important here. The concept of autonomy distinguishes the AI system from simple "if-then systems", which only generate what humans have previously defined through rules.[15] Recital 12 also clarifies that the term AI explicitly **does not include software** that automatically performs a task based on rules set by humans. Rather, AI systems act independently of human intervention, at least to a certain extent. This means that at least simple software models are excluded.[16] According to recital 12, the capability to infer is an

---

[12] Altenburg/Scherr LTZ 2024, 34 (38); Pesch/Böhme MMR 2023, 917 (919).
[13] Cf. Borges CR 11/2023, 706 (706); Hacker/Berz ZRP 2023, 226 (227).
[14] Wendehorst/Nessler/Aufreiter/Aichinger MMR 2024, 605 (606).
[15] Birska/Röver ARP 2024, 21 (21).
[16] Wendehorst/Nessler/Aufreiter/Aichinger MMR 2024, 605 (607).

essential feature of AI systems that enables them to draw conclusions. This ability refers to the process of obtaining results. On the other hand, the concept of adaptability refers to the ability of a system to learn, which enables it to change during its use. However, the adaptability of AI models currently on the market only exists during the training process of the model. As an AI system, they regularly have no ability to continue adapting their own parameters on the basis of new data after they have been placed on the market because the corresponding optimization functions are not included in the AI system.[17]

At the same time, the legislator defines **general purpose AI (GPAI) systems**. These are AI systems that are based on a **general purpose AI model (GPAI model)** (→ § 11 mn. 8) and have the ability to fulfill a variety of purposes, both for direct use and for integration into other AI systems (Art. 3 no. 66 AI Act). **13**

The orientation towards the established OECD definition increases the **international compatibility** of the Al Act.[18] On the other hand, the definition still raises questions[19] that have been addressed by the EU Commission in its **guidelines.**[20] **14**

2. Regulation in the Commission Guidelines

On 6.2.2025, the EU-Commission published guidelines for defining AI systems.[21] The guidelines identify seven core elements of the AI definition, which are weighted differently. The core elements are: **15**

- Machine-based system,
- Autonomy,
- Adaptiveness,
- Explicit and implicit AI system objectives,
- Ability to infer (= inferencing how to generate outputs),
- Outputs that can influence physical or virtual environments,
- Interaction with the environment.

According to the Commission guidelines, the elements of "autonomy" and "ability to infer" are also defining characteristics. An AI system within the meaning of the AI Act therefore only exists if it has both of these elements. The other characteristics may also be present, but are not required. The EU-Commission explains in its guidelines that the terms autonomy and inference go "hand in hand" and that the inference capacity of an AI system is the key to its autonomy.[22] **16**

So, from the EU Commission's perspective, an AI system can be approved if it is based on machine learning (supervised, unsupervised, and reinforcement learning) or logic- and knowledge-based approaches. In its guidelines, the EU Commission thus takes up ideas that were already contained in the original Annex I to the draft AI Act of 21.4.2021. However, according to the EU Commission, no AI system should be **17**

[17] Wendehorst/Nessler/Aufreiter/Aichinger MMR 2024, 605 (608).

[18] Wendehorst/Nessler/Aufreiter/Aichinger MMR 2024, 605 (606).

[19] Chibanguza/Steege NJW 2024, 1769 (1770).

[20] Wendehorst/Nessler/Aufreiter/Aichinger MMR 2024, 605 (605).

[21] Annex to the Communication to the Commission Approval of the content of the draft Communication from the Commission – Commission Guidelines on the definition of an artificial intelligence system established by Regulation (EU) 2024/1689 (AI Act) from 6.2.2025.

[22] Annex to the Communication to the Commission Approval of the content of the draft Communication from the Commission – Commission Guidelines on the definition of an artificial intelligence system established by Regulation (EU) 2024/1689 (AI Act) from 6.2.2025, No. 42.

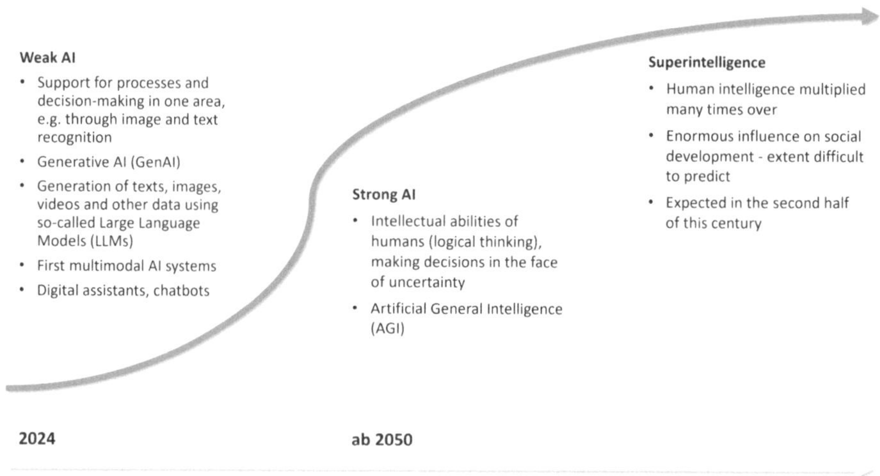

Figure 1: Development of AI

considered to exist in systems for improving mathematical optimization, nor in simple data processing, classical heuristics, or in the case of simple prediction systems.

18 This classification raises new questions in the EU Commission's guidelines. In connection with the distinction between machine learning (= AI) and statistical methods and mathematical optimization (= not AI), the question arises as to whether statistical analysis can become so complex that it should be classified as AI. Conversely, can machine learning be so simple that it no longer constitutes AI?

19 Further questions arise in connection with the so-called grandfathering rule. According to recital 12 of the AI Act and the EU Commission's guidelines, systems that have been "used in a consolidated manner for many years" do not constitute AI.[23] The grandfather clause contained in Article 111 para. 2 AI Act applies to these systems. This raises the question of whether this means that older systems are never AI.

V. Further development

20 With reference to the Turing test mentioned above (→ § 2 mn. 1), a distinction is generally made between three **development stages** of artificial intelligence:[24] We are currently in the **weak AI** phase.[25] Because weak AI is only capable of abstraction, it is primarily used in specific fields of application. It is not yet able to act outside of its context.[26] Nevertheless, it is already able to support humans in their decision-making. Weak AI already has the ability to recognize patterns. Voice or facial recognition systems that we use to unlock our smartphones (1:1 matching), for example, work reliably. We also already work well with digital assistants and chatbots in many places.[27]

---

[23] Annex to the Communication to the Commission Approval of the content of the draft Communication from the Commission – Commission Guidelines on the definition of an artificial intelligence system established by Regulation (EU) 2024/1689 (AI Act) from 6.2.2025, No. 15.

[24] The distinction between "weak" and "strong" AI goes back to Searle, Behavioral and Brain Sciences, 417, who, however, did not differentiate it much.

[25] Kuntz ZfPW 2022, 177 (183); otherwise Keber/Zenner/Hansen/Schwartmann in: Schwartmann/Keber/Zenner, AI Regulation, Part 1, Chapter 2, para. 8.

[26] Schürmann ZD 2022, 316 (316).

[27] Hahn ZfDR 2023, 142 (142); Schürmann ZD 2022, 316 (316).

A noticeable leap towards a **strong AI** is expected around the year 2050. This should be characterized by the fact that it approaches the intellectual abilities of humans, especially with regard to the ability to think logically and make decisions under uncertainty.[28] Strong AI should also be able to communicate with humans in natural language in such a way that it will no longer be possible to differentiate between humans and machines with regard to the Turing test. 21

Whether the further development of the strong AI will actually culminate in the danger of a **superintelligence** that is intellectually superior to humanity, develops its own consciousness and could subjugate or even wipe us out, as Sutskever has now also addressed in his own company Safe Superintelligence (SSI) (→ § 1 mn. 15), is questionable.[29] In April 2024, Musk predicted that AI would be more intelligent than the most intelligent human by 2026 at the latest.[30] This prediction did not go unchallenged.[31] 22

However, it is undisputed that generative AI has made a meteoric rise in recent years. Stanford University's **AI Index Report** has been examining how far it has come every year since 2017.[32] The latest report published in April 2025 shows that artificial intelligence already outperforms humans in many basic skills. However, complex logical thinking remains a challenge. AI models perform excellently in international math competitions, but still struggle with logic benchmarks such as PlanBench. They often fail to reliably solve logical tasks, even when there are proven correct solutions. This limits their effectiveness in demanding situations where precision is crucial, as explained in the report's second chapter (Technical Performance).[33] 23

However, according to a report in the Financial Times, if the announcements from OpenAI and Meta, among others, are correct, it will not be long before this threshold is crossed:[34] The latest generation of AI models such as Meta's Llama 3 or OpenAI's o1 can already perform **complex tasks** – especially the ability to plan and **assess consequences** – in a much more sophisticated way than before. 24

The currently ongoing next step in the development of AI applications are autonomous agents that can actively take control of the browser and execute commands independently. This would enable AI to take over our everyday to-dos on the internet, such as online shopping or booking trips. Both Microsoft and OpenAI, as well as Google, have recently introduced new functions for creating autonomous agents that are intended to replace "manual AI". 25

Instead of just generating content, AI should be able to take action based on screenshots: The agentic AI responds to commands by taking screenshots of what is on the computer screen and interpreting the images before finally taking an action such as clicking on a button. This means that agentic AI will once again significantly change the way AI is developed and used, as well as the impact it can have. New AI systems will be able to develop plans, solve problems and perform tasks autonomously in a range of other applications in which they are integrated. 26

---

[28] Asenger InTeR 3/2023, 134 (135).

[29] See also Hildesheim/Schmid/Holoyad, in: Schmid/Hildesheim/Holoyad, Künstliche Intelligenz – gestern, heute, morgen 3 (14 ff).

[30] Krichmayr, Der Standard 18.4.2024.

[31] See in summary Holzki/Bomke, Dumb as code? Wie viel Intelligenz wirklich in KI steckt, Handelsblatt 29.6.2024; see also Keber/Zenner/Hansen/Schwartmann in: Schwartmann/Keber/Zenner, AI Regulation, Part 1, Chapter 2, para. 8.

[32] S. https://aiindex.stanford.edu/report/.

[33] See https://hai.stanford.edu/assets/files/hai_ai_index_report_2025.pdf.

[34] Murgia/Criddle, OpenAI and Meta ready new AI models capable of "reasoning", Financial Times 9.4.2024.

27 The AI Act does not yet address the associated questions – such as that of meaningful human supervision when agentic AI systems autonomously perform tasks that have real world effects. Should there be actions that agentic AI systems are not allowed to perform? Data sources that are denied access? Is it feasible to conduct and continuously update traditional risk assessments for the myriad of multi-agent AI systems that could be embedded in all software applications?

VI. Polanyi Paradox

28 Overall, it can be said that AI-based systems are already **excellent autonomous learners** that are capable of surpassing human capabilities, at least in narrowly defined tasks. At the same time, however, the so-called Polanyi Paradox limits expectations regarding the capabilities of AI. The **Polanyi Paradox**, named after the British-Hungarian physicist Michael Polanyi,[35] is simply put: people know more than they can say. Our own abilities are largely beyond our explicit understanding. To put it more fully: many of our tasks are based on tacit, **intuitive knowledge** that is **difficult to automate**. Polanyi's paradox therefore always comes into play when a person has mastered something but cannot describe how they do it.

29 Polanyi thus distinguishes between **intuitive knowledge** and abstract knowledge. Only **abstract knowledge** is rule-bound and repeatable. Tacit knowledge is difficult to express formally because humans have developed the skills that constitute it through evolution. Therefore, it is hardly possible to train AI to perform tasks that require **tacit knowledge**.

30 At the same time, the **Polanyi paradox** is used by economists to explain why not all human occupations have been taken over by machines. If automation had not been limited to the abstract field of knowledge, machines would have taken over all human tasks and the number of jobs would have fallen sharply since the 1980s. However, automation has not led to this result because it requires the definition of precise rules to tell computers what tasks to perform.

VII. Sub-areas of AI

31 In their definitions of artificial intelligence, both the OECD and the EU focus on the element of **autonomy**, i.e. the self-learning behavior of AI (→ § 2 mn. 12, 15). This is made possible by the technologies of machine **learning** (ML) and, in particular, deep **learning** (DL).[36]

[35] Polanyi, The tacit dimension.
[36] See Altenburg/Scherr LTZ 2024, 34 (36); Dienes MMR 2024, 456 (459).

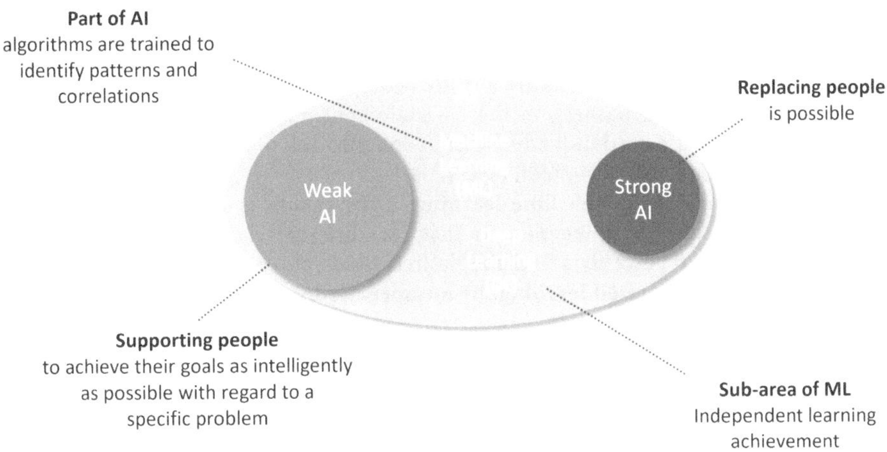

Figure 2: Weak and strong AI, ML and DL

32 Both terms form subsets of artificial intelligence, with **deep learning** in turn representing a subcategory of **machine learning.** What machine learning and deep learning have in common is that the AI processes data and improves with increasing experience without being explicitly programmed.[37] Machine learning algorithms enable AI not only to process data, but also to use it in such a way that the AI learns from it. It is therefore able to deliver more accurate results and becomes increasingly "intelligent" in its perception.[38]

Figure 3: AI, ML and DL

1. Machine learning

33 Machine learning describes an approach in which algorithms are trained to **find patterns and correlations** in large data sets and make decisions and predictions based on this analysis. In line with the **self-improving approach**, the applications

[37] Kuntz ZfPW 2022, 177 (185).
[38] Gumpp/Schneider ZfDR 2021, 155 (158).

for machine learning typically become more and more precise with ongoing use, and more specifically with the increasing availability of data.

34 Machine learning applications are already widespread; they are used in our homes, in our online shopping baskets, in the entertainment media and also in healthcare. The algorithms can be used individually or in combination to achieve the best possible accuracy with complex and unpredictable data.

35 Within the category of **machine learning**, a distinction is made between different types of machine learning models that use different algorithmic techniques.[39] Depending on the type of data and the desired result, three learning models can be differentiated: a) **supervised learning**, b) **unsupervised/partially supervised learning** and c) **reinforcement learning.**[40]

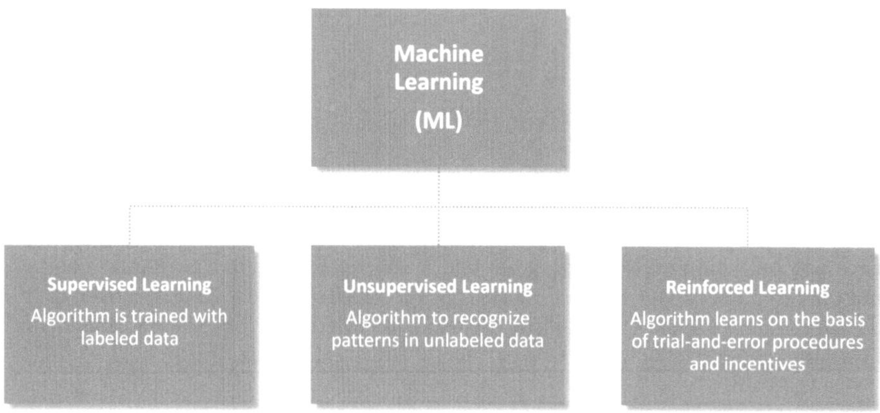

Figure 4: ML – Supervised, Unsupervised and Reinforced Learning

a) Supervised learning

36 **Supervised learning** is characterized by the fact that the AI learns on the basis of marked input and output data pairs in order to make the relationship between the inputs and the outputs comprehensible.[41] The **output**, i.e. the result, is labeled with a **desired value.**[42] Let's assume that the goal is for the AI to recognize the difference between the two dog breeds Dalmatian and French Bulldog.[43] In this case, a binary input data pair contains both an image of a Dalmatian and an image of a French bulldog, with the input data being paired with the correct output.[44]The system uses the annotations to learn a mapping from inputs to outputs, and then generalizes this to new, unseen data until it can finally determine the answer to the question about the dog breed on its own.[45]

[39] An overview of the range of machine learning methods can be found in Schmid/Hildesheim/Holoyad/Schumacher, in: Schmid/Hildesheim/Holoyad, Klassifizierung von KI-Methoden 93 (102); see also Wendehorst/Nessler/Aufreiter/Aichinger MMR 2024, 605 (609, 611).

[40] Glauner in: Ebers/Quarch, Technische Grundlagen von generativen KI-Modellen, para. 3.

[41] Russell/Norvig, 67; Dienes MMR 2024, 456 (459).

[42] Dienes MMR 2024, 456 (459).

[43] Greetings to Pepe and Samson.

[44] Russell/Norvig, 67.

[45] Pesch/Böhme MMR 2023, 917 (918 et seq.); Kuntz ZfPW 2022, 177 (183); Altenburg/Scherr LTZ 2024, 34 (36).

Supervised learning models can be found in many applications that we interact with every day, for example in **recommendation services for products**, but also in **traffic analysis apps** that predict the fastest route at different times of day. Other examples of AI systems based on supervised learning include diagnostic systems for medical devices that are trained on medical images labeled by human experts, and fraud detection systems that are trained on labeled transaction data. 37

b) *Non/partially supervised learning*

No answer key is used in **unsupervised learning**: The AI examines the input data, which is regularly unstructured, and begins recognizing patterns and correlations on its own.[46] Using various techniques such as clustering, dimensionality reduction, association rule learning, anomaly detection, or generative models, the system is trained to find patterns, structures, or relationships in the data without the result being explicitly specified. 38

This makes unsupervised learning similar to human perception in many respects. We humans also use intuition and experience to form categories and summarize individual things. The more examples we collect through our experience, the more precise our ability to categorize and identify becomes. For AI, the experience gathered can be equated to the amount of data that is entered and made available. Common examples of unsupervised learning applications are methods of **facial recognition** and gene sequence analysis. However, unsupervised learning is also used by pharmaceutical companies for drug discovery.

Similar **semi-supervised learning** refers to a machine learning model that combines large amounts of unstructured data with the input of small amounts of labeled data to **enhance data sets**. The small amount of labeled data serves as a kind of jump-start for the AI and can significantly improve **learning speed** and accuracy. A semi-supervised learning algorithm instructs the AI to analyze the labeled data for correlative properties that can be applied to the unlabeled data sets and raw data. 39

However, partially supervised learning in particular harbors risks resulting from the fact that **errors in the labeled data records** are learned and replicated by the system.[47] It is therefore particularly important to implement best practice protocols here. Semi-supervised learning is increasingly used in **language and linguistic analyses**, in **medical research**, such as the categorization of proteins.[48] 40

c) *Reinforcement learning*

Whereas in supervised learning, the AI receives the answer key and learns by finding correlations between all the correct results, reinforcement learning does not provide an answer key, but specifies a series of **permissible actions, rules and potential end states**. If the desired goal of the algorithm is fixed or binary, the AI is able to learn by example. In cases where the desired outcome is changeable, the model must learn through experience and reward. In reinforcement learning models, the "reward" is numerical and programmed into the algorithm as something the system wants to "capture". With the help of the **reward function**, the AI recognizes the value of a certain action. In this way, it imitates the learning process of a human being in 41

---

[46] Kuntz ZfPW 2022, 177 (185) with further references.

[47] S. https://www.molgen.mpg.de/3659531/MITPress--SemiSupervised-Learning.pdf.

[48] Antweiler/Beckh/Chakraborty/Giesselbach/Klug/Rüping, Natural Language Processing in der Medizin, Whitepaper Fraunhofer IAIS 2023, https://newsletter.fraunhofer.de/public/a_14338_S4Jdz/file/data/4410_Fraunhofer_IAIS_Whitepaper_Clinical_NLP_Web.pdf.

reinforcement learning: the model can be compared to teaching another person to play chess, for example. It would probably not be possible to show every potential move. Instead, people typically explain the rules and learners improve their skills through practice. The reward is not only to win the game, but also to capture the opponent's pieces.

42 In contrast to supervised learning, AI does not require any data in advance for reinforcement learning. The database is created through extensive **trial-and-error processes** within the simulation scenario itself.

43 Surprisingly, the areas of application for this advanced AI technology are quite practical: **applications for reinforcement learning** include automated price offers for buyers of online advertising (such as in the bidding process for display advertising at Chinese internet giant Alibaba)[49], the development of computer games and high-stakes stock market trading. Reinforced learning is also used to optimize traffic lights.[50]

2. Deep learning

44 **Deep learning** refers to a smaller subset within the category of machine learning. This type of machine learning is referred to as deep as it encompasses **many layers** of the **neural network.**[51]The depth makes it possible to capture intertwined patterns and representations in data. For this purpose, the deep neural networks "learn" an increasingly complex feature hierarchy from the training data, which makes them particularly powerful, especially for processing human language and image recognition.[52]The artificial neural network is roughly modeled on the neurons in a human brain.[53] The artificial neurons are called **nodes** and are grouped in several layers that work in parallel. When an artificial neuron receives a numerical signal, it processes it using mathematical methods and sends signals to the other neurons connected to it. In this way, neural networks simulate learning processes and continue to develop by constantly adjusting their internal parameters during training in order to make predictions or decisions. As in the human brain, neural reinforcement leads to improved pattern recognition, expertise and general learning.

45 To do this, a deep learning model that processes images of nature and searches for a Tricolor Dalmatian, for example, will recognize an animal in the first neural layer. As it moves through the neural layers, it first identifies a dog, then a Dalmatian and finally a Tricolor Dalmatian. Of course, these ideas of how an AI works are very simplified: while a simple artificial neural network consists of an **input layer**, several **hidden layers** and an **output layer**,[54] artificial neural networks are extremely complex in reality, which makes it difficult to interpret the individual decisions made by the AI.[55] In deep neural networks, it is considered almost impossible to understand how the model made a decision.

---

[49] Jin/Song/Li/Gai, 2018, DOI:10.1145/3269206.3272021.

[50] Cf. Fraunhofer Gesellschaft of 1.2.2022, https://www.fraunhofer.de/de/presse/presseinformationen/2022/februar-2022/kuenstliche-intelligenz-steuert-ampelanlagen.html.

[51] For use in image processing, see Meding in: Schwartmann/Keber/Zenner, AI Regulation, Part 1, Chapter 4, para. 3.

[52] Glauner in: Ebers/Quarch, Technische Grundlagen von generativen KI-Modellen, para. 15.

[53] Dienes MMR 2024, 456 (460); Russell/Norvig, 67.

[54] See also Kuntz ZfPW 2022, 177 (184).

[55] Dienes MMR 2024, 456 (459); Martini, Blackbox, 23 et seq.

46 The buzzword **black box** has emerged to describe the impenetrability and lack of transparency.[56] It runs counter to the principle of transparency, which the AI Act considers necessary for trustworthy AI. The aim of **explainable AI (XAI)** is to resolve this conflict. Explainable AI attempts to make decision-making processes comprehensible.

47 A milestone was reached at the end of 2023. For the first time, a research team from the Fraunhofer Heinrich Hertz Institute (HHI), the Technical University of Berlin and the Berlin Institute for the Foundations of Learning and Data (BIFOLD Institute) succeeded in tracing AI decisions in image recognition back to the most important factors that contributed to recognition – such as the Dalmatian's fur, eyes or snout. **Heatmaps** show where the model recognizes concepts and how it weights them. For dogs, the fur is most relevant.

48 The method known as **Concept Relevance Propagation** (CRP)[57] asks both: "Where is the AI looking?" and "What does it see there?" It can also be used to check whether the AI is using undesirable concepts to recognize an image – in other words, whether it is cheating. For example, some AI models only recognize a boat in an image if there is water at the bottom. They use the Kluger Hans method – named after the horse that was supposedly able to solve arithmetic problems, but instead reacted to its owner's impulses.

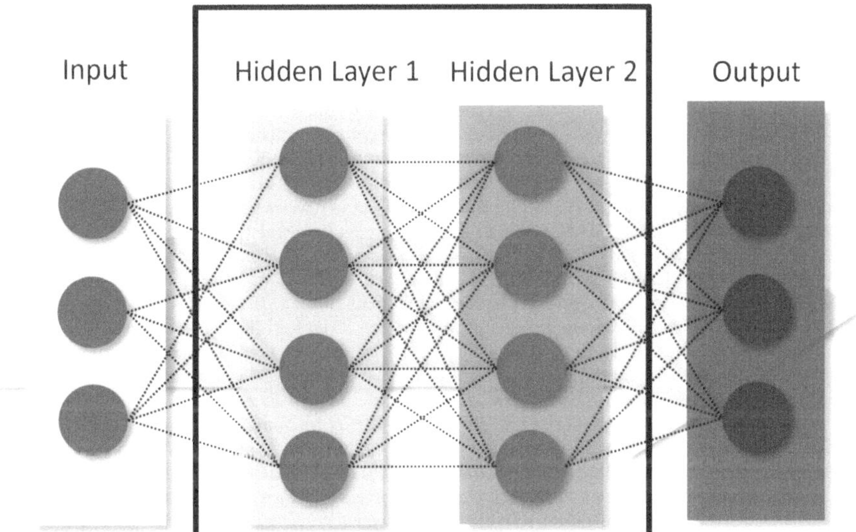

Figure 5: DL – principle of the black box

49 Examples of deep learning applications can be found in image classification, speech recognition and pharmaceutical analyses.[58]

[56] Martini, Blackbox, 44.
[57] https://www.hhi.fraunhofer.de/en/departments/ai/technologies-and-solutions/concept-relevance-propagation.html.
[58] Antweiler/Beckh/Chakraborty/Giesselbach/Klug/Rüping, Natural Language Processing in der Medizin, Whitepaper Fraunhofer IAIS 2023, https://newsletter.fraunhofer.de/public/a_14338_S4Jdz/file/data/4410_Fraunhofer_IAIS_Whitepaper_Clinical_NLP_Web.pdf.

§ 3
AI Act

Literature: *Altenburg, Nadia/Scherr, Julius*, Artificial intelligence in law in 2024 – Quo vadis? LTZ 2024, 34; *Ammann, Thorsten/Pohle, Jan*, KI-Verordnung – Was bisher geschah und jetzt zu tun ist, CB 5/2024, 137; *Asenger, Hüveyda*, Künstliche Intelligenz im Strafverfahren und Fairness, InTeR 3/2023, 134; *Ashkar, Daniel/Schröder, Christian*, Das Gesetz über künstliche Intelligenz der Europäischen Union (KI-Verordnung), BB 2024, 771; *Bachgrund, Richard/Nesum, Long/Bernstein, Max/Burchard, Christoph* – Das Pro und Contra für Chatbots in Rechtspraxis und Rechtsdogmatik, CR 2/2023, 132; *Batista, Patricia*, ChatGPT versus Arbeitsrecht – Leistungserbringung mithilfe von Sprachmodellen, LTZ 2024, 118; *Baumgartner, Ulrich/Brunnbauer, Jonas H./Cross, Samuel*, Anforderungen der DS-GVO an den Einsatz von Künstlicher Intelligenz, MMR 2023, 543; *Becker, Daniel/Feuerstack, Daniel*: Der neue Entwurf des EU-Parlaments für eine KI-Verordnung, MMR 2024, 22; *Berz, Amelie/Engel, Andreas/Hacker, Philipp*: Generative KI, Datenschutz, Hassrede und Disinformation – Zur Regulierung von KI-Meinungen, ZUM 2023, 586; *Biermann, Friedrich G.*, Wissenszurechnung und Künstliche Intelligenz, 2022; *Birska, Sylwia/Röver, Timo*: Künstliche Intelligenz in der Prävention, ARP 2024, 21; *Blasek, Katrin*: KI-Regulierung in der Volksrepublik China, RDi 2023, 557; *Bomhard, David/Siglmüller, Jonas*, AI Act – das Trilogergebnis, RDi 2024, 45; *Bomhard, David/Siglmüller, Jonas*, Europäische KI-Haftungsrichtlinie, RDi 2022, 506; *Borges, Georg*, Liability for AI Systems Under Current and Future Law, CRi 1/2023, 1; *Borges, Georg*, Der Begriff des KI-Systems. Tatbestandsmerkmale und Auslegungsansätze, CR 11/2023, 706; *Botta, Jonas*, (K)ein Recht auf Behandlung mit KI? – Access to intelligent medical devices, ZfPC 2024, 42; *Botta, Jonas*, Die Förderung innovativer KI-Systeme in der EU, ZfDR 2022, 391; *Buchalik, Barbara/Gehrmann, Mareike Christine*, Von Nullen und Einsen zu Paragrafen: Der AI Act, ein Rechtscode für Künstliche Intelligenz, CR 3/2024, 145; *Burchardi, Sophie*, Risikotragung für KI-Systeme, EuZW 2022, 685; *Busche, Daniel*, Einführung in die Rechtsfragen der künstlichen Intelligenz, JA 2023, 441; *Buxmann, Peter/Schmidt, Holger*, Grundlagen der Künstlichen Intelligenz und des Maschinellen Lernens, in Buxmann, Peter/Schmidt, Holger (eds.), Künstliche Intelligenz, 2019; *Conrads, Markus/Schweitzer, Sascha*: Einsatz Künstlicher Intelligenz im Vertrags-, Wirtschafts- und Arbeitsrecht, NJW 2023, 2809; *Dettling, Heinz-Uwe/Krüger, Stefan*, Erste Schritte im Recht der Künstlichen Intelligenz, MMR 2019, 211; *Dettlinger, Heinz-Uwe/Krüger, Stefan*, Erste Schritte im Recht der Künstlichen Intelligenz: Entwurf der "Ethik-Leitlinien für eine vertrauenswürdige KI", MMR 2019, 211; *Dix, Alexander/Seyerlein-Klug, Annegrit*, EAID: Exportschlager AI Act – Setzt die EU einen weltweiten Standard für die KI-Regulierung?, ZD-Aktuell 2024, 04506; *Ebert, Andreas/Busch, Philip/Spiecker gen. Döhmann, Indra/Wendt, Janine*, Roboter im Supermarkt, ZfPC 2023, 16; *Ensthaler, Jürgen*, Zum neuen Verhältnis zwischen Rechtswissenschaft und Technik, ZRP 2022, 55; *Ensthaler, Jürgen*, Künstliche Intelligenz (KI) – einige Gedanken zu den vorhandenen und geplanten Schutzmaßnahmen, InTeR 1/24, 2; *Feldkamp, Jakob/Kappler, Quirin/Poretschkin, Maximilian/Schmitz, Anna/Weiss, Erik*, Rechtliche Fairnessanforderungen an KI-Systeme und ihre technische Evaluation – Eine Analyse anhand ausgewählter Kreditscoring-Systeme unter besonderer Berücksichtigung der zukünftigen europäischen KI-Verordnung, ZfDR 1/2024, 60; *Feuerstack, Daniel/Becker, Daniel/Hertz, Nora*, Die Entwürfe des EU-Parlaments und der EU-Kommission für eine KI-Verordnung im Vergleich, ZfDR 2023, 421; *Frost, Yannick/Steiniger, Manuela/Vivekens, Sabrina*, Take the risk or lose the chance? Essential questions that companies should consider from a legal perspective in the field of AI, MPR 2024, 4; *Gaub, Daniela/Kadler, Mathias*, Die Beeinflussung von menschlichem Verhalten durch Künstliche Intelligenz – Chance oder Gefahr? Rethinking Law 6.2022, 4; *Gengler, Eva*, Feministische Künstliche Intelligenz, Rethinking Law 6.2022, 32; *Gumpp, Tobias/Schneider, Marc Pierre*, Methoden der Künstlichen Intelligenz in der Rechtswissenschaft, ZfDR 2021, 155; *Haar, Tobias*, KI-Regulierung: Gelingt die Quadratur des Kreises? MMR 2023, 397; *Hacker, Philipp*: The regulation of ChatGPT et al. – ein europäisches Trauerspiel, GRUR 2023, 289; *Hacker, Philipp/Berz, Amelie*, Der AI Act der Europäischen Union – Überblick, Kritik und Ausblick, ZRP 2023, 226; *Hahn, Johanna*, Die Regulierung biometrischer Fernidentifizierung in der Strafverfolgung im KI-Verordnungsentwurf der EU-Kommission, ZfDR 2023, 142; *Ibold, Victoria*, Künstliche Intelligenz im Sicherheitsrecht – Begründungsgebot quo vadis? GSZ 2024, 10; *Kerkmann, Christof/Scheuer, Stephan*, Das Microsoft-Prinzip, Handelsblatt of 14/15/16.7.2023, 42; *Martini, Mario*, Blackbox-Algorithmus, 2019; *Kilian, Matthias*, Weißer Rauch in Brüssel, EuZW 2024, 145; *Lachmayer, Konrad*, Grundrechtliche Implikationen von Videoaufzeichnungen im öffentlichen Raum, NLMR 2023, 203; *Martini, Mario/Wiesehöfer, Christine*, Auf dem Weg zur Regulierung von General-Purpose-AI – eine erste Bestandsaufnahme und Kritik der Regelungsentwürfe, NVwZ 1/2024, 1; *Meckel, Miriam/Steinacker, Léa*, Alles überall auf einmal, 2024; *Möslein, Florian*, Die normative Kraft des Ethischen – Ein Fallbeispiel zur Effektivität von Leitlinien für Künstliche Intelligenz, RDi 2020, 34; *Mühleis, Niklas/Akinci, Nick*, Rechtsleitfaden KI im Unternehmen 2024; *Orssich, Irina*, Das europäische Konzept für vertrauenswürdige Künstliche Intelligenz, EuZW 2022, 254; *Prange, Hans Michael*, Datenschutz- und lauterkeitsrechtliche

Kernfragen des Einsatzes Künstlicher Intelligenz im Marketing, WRP 2024, 151; *Rudkowski, Lena/ Wendt, Domenik/Block, Martina/Wettlaufer, Kai*, Einsatz Künstlicher Intelligenz bei der Begründung des Arbeitsverhältnisses, FA 2024, 126; *Russell, Stuart/Norvig, Peter*, Artificial Intelligence, 4th ed. 2021; *Schürrmann, Kathrin*, Datenschutz-Folgenabschätzung beim Einsatz Künstlicher Intelligenz, ZD 2022, 316; *Schwartmann, Rolf/Keber, Tobias/Zenner, Kai*, KI-Verordnung. Leitfaden für die Praxis, 2024; *Wendt, Domenik/Jung, Constantin*, Europäischer Rechtsrahmen für Künstliche Intelligenz (Teil I), LRZ 2021, 34; *Wendt, Janine/Wendt, Domenik*, Einigung auf Rechtsrahmen für Künstliche Intelligenz in der EU, ZfPC 2024, 86; *Zenner, Kai*, KI-Regulierung: ein Trilog unter großem Zeitdruck, RDV 2023, 340; *Zenner, Kai*, Die Ergebnisse der Trilog-Verhandlungen zur KI-Verordnung, RDV 2024, 58.

I. Initial situation

On 2.2.2024, the German Federal Ministry of Justice published a press release: "The Member States of the European Union have unanimously approved the Regulation laying down harmonized rules on artificial intelligence." This sentence was preceded by almost **three years of negotiations**, complex procedures and legal text work on a challenging subject.[1] 1

While the AI Act is celebrated by some as an outstanding achievement that came just in time, others see it as a **legislative intervention** that is unfavorably distorting or even **inhibiting** a development that is already not dynamic enough in Europe – with the result that AI development will be dominated even more by countries without regulation in the future.[2]

Of particular interest are the turning points that the original draft from April 2021 took until the version that the EU member states finally agreed on in the winter of 2023/2024 was available. It remains to be seen whether the final legal text 2

[1] Cf. also the ZEVEDI podcast "Digitalgespräch" episode 48, available at https://zevedi.de/digitalgespraech-048-domenik-wendt/; Buchalik/Gehrmann CR 3/2024, 145 (145).

[2] Hacker GRUR 2023, 289 (289); cf. also Zenner in: Schwartmann/Keber/Zenner, Part 2, Chapter 1, para. 1: "Overregulation".

has the potential to **play** a **pioneering role** in the regulation of artificial intelligence internationally.

II. Path to the AI Act

3

Figure 6: Timeline – development of the AI Act

1. General information

4 Three actors are involved in the legislative process at European level – the EU Commission, the EU Parliament and the Council of the European Union. The right of initiative lies solely with the **EU Commission**. Only the Commission can therefore initiate the legislative process by submitting a specific proposal for a legal act in the form of a directive or regulation. As a rule, the legal act is prepared by the EU Commission in several stages, for example through communications and a White Paper. The actual legislative process then begins with the submission of the concrete proposal.

2. Preliminary work

a) EU Parliament

5 On the part of the EU Parliament, an early report with recommendations on civil law regulations in the field of robotics from 2017[3] should be mentioned here first. This much-noticed but also much-criticized report included a proposal for the status of an **electronic person** for robots in order to "create a special legal status for robots in the long term […]", which would be responsible as an independent fictitious person for compensation for all damage caused by it.[4] This proposal has rightly **not** met with **approval**. It cannot be derived from the legal entity model, which implies the existence of humans behind a legal person, nor can it be reconciled with fundamental rights in the Union. The report is therefore rightly – in relation to the "e-person" proposed therein – only **an anecdote** today.

6 In 2019 and 2020, the EU Parliament adopted a number of further resolutions in which it identified and prioritized the need for regulation. Of particular note are the

[3] Report with recommendations to the EU Commission on civil law regulations in the field of robotics, (2015/2103(INL)) of 27.1.2017, para. 59 lit. f; see also P8_TA(2017)0051 Civil law regulations in the field of robotics – Resolution of the EU Parliament with recommendations to the Commission on civil law regulations in the field of robotics (2015/2103(INL)) of 16.2.2017, para. 59 lit. f.; Zenner in: Schwartmann/Keber/Zenner, Part 2, Chapter 1, para. 3.

[4] See Ensthaler ZRP 2022, 55 (56).

resolution on a comprehensive European industrial policy on artificial intelligence and robotics from February 2019,[5] and three resolutions with recommendations to the EU Commission from October 2020, firstly on the framework for the **ethical aspects** of artificial intelligence, robotics and related technologies,[6] secondly on the regulation of **civil liability** in the use of artificial intelligence[7] and thirdly on **intellectual property** rights in the development of AI technologies.[8]

b) EU Commission

As usual, the EU Commission has also prepared its proposal for a regulation over the years through various communications and consultation procedures.[9] 7

The relevant communications include, in particular, that of 25.4.2018,[10] in which the EU Commission outlines the objectives of the European AI initiative and attempts an **initial definition of an AI system**. Many of the objectives listed at the time, which included promoting the EU's technological performance, preparing for socio-economic changes in connection with AI and ensuring an appropriate ethical and legal framework, were also reflected in the later draft of the AI Act (AI Act-D). 8

With reference to ensuring an appropriate ethical and legal framework, the EU Commission also established a **High-Level Expert Group (HLEG)** in 2018, which drew up **ethical guidelines** for trustworthy AI.[11] In one of the guidelines, the HLEG sets out seven requirements for trustworthy AI that should be taken into account in the development, introduction and use of AI systems: 9

1) Priority of human action and human oversight,
2) Technical robustness and safety,
3) Privacy protection and data quality management,
4) Transparency,
5) Diversity, non-discrimination and fairness,
6) social and environmental well-being and
7) Accountability.

These results of the HLEG's work were also taken into account in the **AI White Paper**[12]. The AI White Paper already contained a basic plan for how AI should be regulated. In particular, the White Paper contains key basic ideas for the risk-based regula- 10

[5] Legislative resolution of the European Parliament on a comprehensive European industrial policy on artificial intelligence and robotics (2018/2088(INI)) of 12.2.2019, OJEU C 449, 23.12.2020, p. 37.

[6] EU Parliament legislative resolution on the framework for the ethical aspects of artificial intelligence, robotics and related technologies (2020/2012(INL)) of 20.10.2020, OJEU C 404, 6.10.2021, p. 63.

[7] Legislative resolution of the European Parliament on the regulation of civil liability for the use of artificial intelligence (2020/2014(INL)) of 20.10.2020, OJEU C 404, 6.10.2021, p. 107.

[8] Legislative resolution of the EU Parliament on intellectual property rights in the development of AI technologies (2020/2015(INI) of 20.10.2020, OJEU C 404 of 6.10.2021, p. 129; cf. on this Becker/Feuerstack MMR 2024, 22 (22).

[9] See, for example, Communication from the European Commission: Artificial Intelligence for Europe COM(2018) 237 final of 25.4.2018; Communication from the European Commission: Coordinated Plan for Artificial Intelligence, COM(2018) 795 final of 7.12.2018.

[10] Communication from the European Commission: Artificial Intelligence for Europe COM(2018) 237 final of 25.4.2018.

[11] Cf. High-Level Expert Group of the European Commission on Artificial Intelligence, Draft Ethics Guidelines for Trustworthy AI, of 18.12.2018; see Dettling/Krüger MMR 2019, 211 (211); High-Level Expert Group of the European Commission on Artificial Intelligence, Ethics Guidelines for Trustworthy AI, of 8.4.2019; see Möslein RDi 2020, 34 (35).

[12] EU Commission, White Paper: On Artificial Intelligence – a European approach to excellence and trust, COM(2020) 65 final; also Feuerstack/Becker/Hertz ZfDR 2023, 421 (421).

tory approach.[13] The **ethics guidelines** are also referred to in the later AI Act, for example in the area of **codes of conduct** (→ § 14 mn. 1 et seqq.).

3. Proposed regulation

11 The final draft regulation (AI Act-D)[14] is dated 21.4.2021. It is the cornerstone for the subsequent legal-political dialog and already contains many of the aspects regulated in the final version. The original draft of the regulation comprised **85 articles, 89 recitals and nine annexes.**

4. Trilogue negotiations

12 The next significant milestone in the legislative process after the draft regulation was the start of the so-called **trilogue negotiations.**[15]

a) General

13 The **trialogue**, which the EU itself refers to as **informal interinstitutional negotiations**, has established itself as a way of shortening the time-consuming legislative process at EU level, which consists of three readings and the back and forth of positions within certain deadlines. In the trialogue, representatives of the **EU Commission** and the **EU Parliament** (rapporteurs) meet with **representatives of the Council** (i.e. the member states) in order to agree on a legal text that is acceptable to all parties involved.

14 A **trilogue** can be held at any stage of the legislative process in order to clarify outstanding issues. It is chaired by the co-legislator hosting the meeting. The role of the **European Commission** is to mediate between the parties, although this role should not be confused with the use of the Conciliation Committee, which is a formal step in the ordinary legislative procedure after the second reading. In both cases, all three institutions mentioned above are represented, with the aim of reaching agreement on a joint text.

15 As the AI Act was of great interest to many EU parliamentarians as a **horizontal regulatory initiative**, the EU Parliament initially discussed which committee should be involved in the trilogue negotiations. Specifically, it was discussed whether the Internal Market Committee (IMCO – Internal Market and Consumer Protection) or the Civil Liberties Committee (LIBE – Civil Liberties, Justice and Home Affairs), the Legal Affairs Committee (JURI – Justice), the Industry Committee (ITRE – Industry, Research and Energy) or other committees should take the lead in the negotiations. In the end, the **EU Parliament** agreed on a **team of four**: the Industry and Legal Affairs Committees acted in an advisory capacity, while the Internal Market Committee and the Civil Liberties Committee took the lead in the **trilogue** on behalf of the EU Parliament.

b) Complications

16 Additional complications in the negotiations on the AI Act included the **time factor**, which was linked to the elections to the EU Parliament and did not allow for

---

[13] Roth-Isigkeit MMR 2024, 621 (621) is fundamental in this regard.

[14] Proposal for a Regulation laying down harmonized rules on Artificial Intelligence (Artificial Intelligence Act, COM/2021/206 final; see for example Orssich EuZW 2022, 254 (255 et seq.); Buchalik/Gehrmann CR 3/2024, 145 (145).

[15] Ashkar/Schröder BB 2024, 771 (772).

any delays.[16] The aim of every legislator should be to complete a legislative procedure once it has been started as an initiative within a **legislative period**. This was also the intention with the AI Act.

Secondly, the complexity of the legal policy issue had increased significantly during the ongoing negotiations. As already mentioned, the legislator had to react to the sudden emergence of **general purpose AI models** and systems based on them, such as ChatGPT, during the already advanced trilogue negotiations[17] (→ § 1 mn. 11). 17

There was also a great need for discussion regarding applications such as **real-time remote biometric identification** in publicly accessible areas for law enforcement purposes.[18] According to Art. 3 No. 41 AI Act, the term remote biometric identification generally refers to AI systems that serve the purpose of identifying natural persons without their active involvement and usually remotely by comparing their biometric data with the data stored in a reference database.[19] Identification is usually based on a person's face (**facial recognition**), but also by recognizing their gait (**gait recognition**).[20] If the capture, comparison and identification take place without delay, this constitutes real-time remote biometric identification in accordance with Art. 3 No. 42 AI Act. 18

The opportunities and risks of biometric identification were controversially discussed not only in the EU Parliament, but also among the member states.[21] Liberal and conservative currents in the EU Parliament had already strictly advocated a complete ban during the internal parliamentary negotiations. Only **ex-post use** to investigate particularly serious crimes should be permitted.[22] 19

Some **European governments**, on the other hand, wanted to reserve the use of these AI systems – also with a view to major events such as the Summer Olympics – in order to ensure the safety of participants. 20

The **compromise** that was reached in the trilogue now provides for a fundamental ban on real-time remote biometric identification, albeit with a few exceptions.[23] These include, for example, the targeted search for victims of kidnapping, human trafficking and sexual exploitation as well as the localization of missing persons. In addition, the use of such systems is permitted to avert a specific, significant and immediate threat to the life or physical integrity of natural persons or to avert an actual and present or foreseeable threat of a terrorist attack, Art. 5 para. 1 lit. h AI Act. The member states have the option of allowing further exceptions, as well as tightening the ban. 21

c) *Political agreement*

After tough negotiations and intensive preparatory negotiation steps, the political agreement was finally reached in the last planned time window in 2023.[24] 22

In the now famous **marathon session**, in which the legal act was discussed for up to 22 hours at a time from 6.12.2023 until the night of 9.12.2023, the aforementioned committees, two Commissioners and the Spanish Council Presidency, which negotiated on behalf of the Member States, including a large number of employees, attempted 23

16 Zenner RDV 2023, 340 (340).
17 Haar MMR 2023, 397 (398); Hacker/Berz ZRP 2023, 226 (226).
18 Frost/Steininger/Vivekens MPR 2024, 4 (9).
19 Lachmayer, NLMR 2023, 203 (204) is fundamental in this regard.
20 Hahn ZfDR 2023, 142 (145).
21 Martini NVwZ 2022, 30 (31); Ammann/Pohle CB 5/2024, 137 (139).
22 Ammann/Pohle CB 5/2024, 137 (139).
23 Hahn ZfDR 2023, 142 (145).
24 See also Zenner RDV 2024, 58 (58).

to agree on a direction, at least politically, on 21 points that were still contentious.[25] For many of these 21 points, it was possible to reach a final text in the trilogue and record it in writing. For some points, there was initially only a verbal agreement. Accordingly, the compromise reached was also referred to as **a handshake deal. There** was **no final document** at the time of the agreement; this was only compiled in parts from the various compromise texts afterwards.

24 The **recitals** to the AI Act were hardly negotiated at all in the trilogue. The original 85 articles of the regulation were initially preceded by 89 recitals, which were intended to explain the objectives of the regulation in more detail and facilitate the interpretation of the provisions in accordance with European law.

d) Subsequent technical negotiations

25 The subsequent **technical negotiations** were correspondingly relevant. At a technical level, what had been decided politically had to be formulated and clarified. The final text was agreed between the EU Commission, the European Parliament and the Council on 19.1.2024.[26] The EU Parliament approved the provisionally final version on 13.3.2024. Following an initial correction of the legal act, the Council adopted its decision on 21.5.2024. The final legal text now contains **113 articles, 180 recitals and 13 annexes**.

---

[25] Kilian EuZW 2024, 145 (145).
[26] Bomhard/Siglmüller RDi 2024, 45 (45).

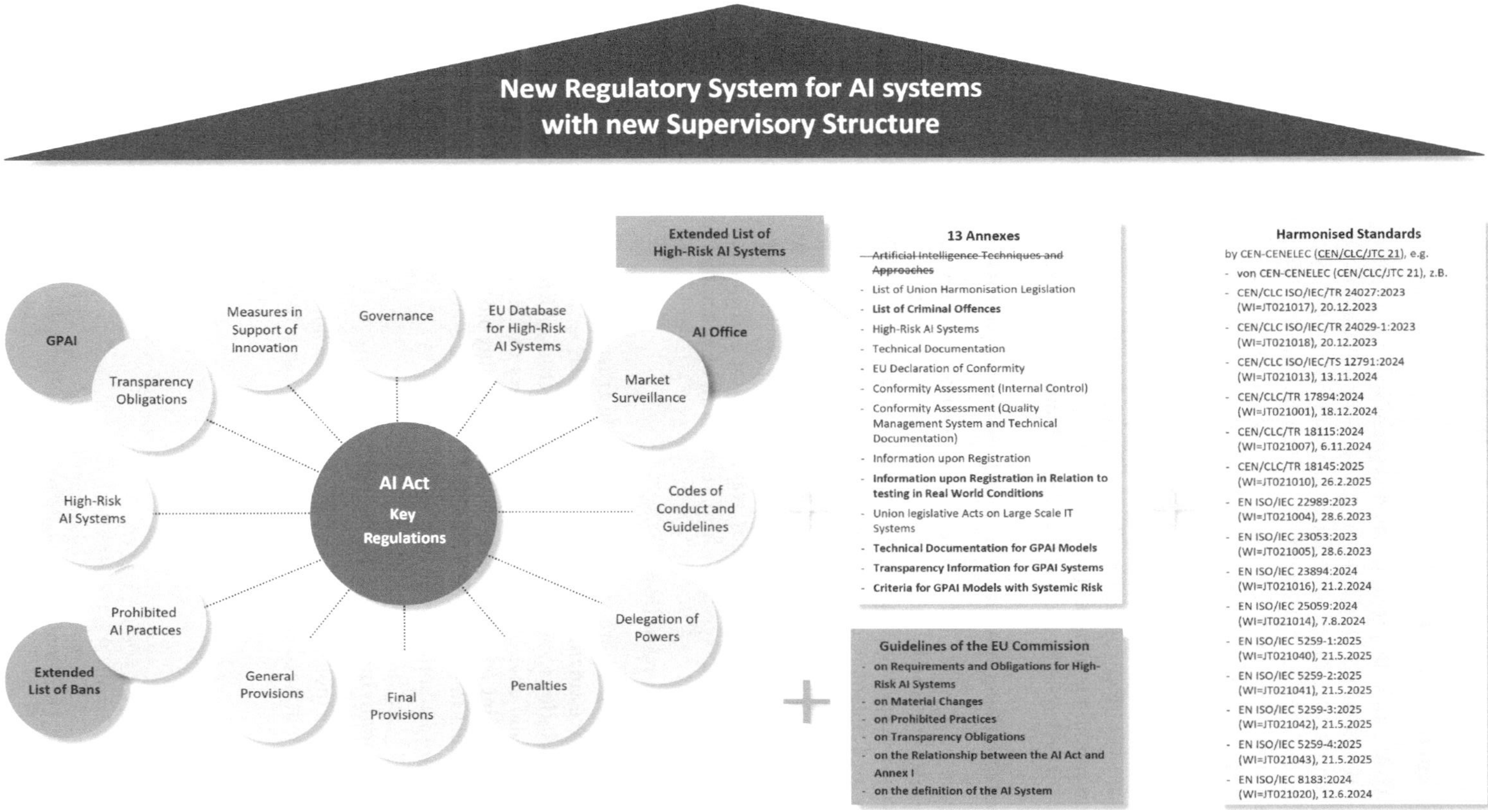

Figure 7: Key regulatory content of the AI Act

III. Objective of the AI Act

1. Strengthening trust in AI

26 The AI Act aims to promote the **acceptability** of AI. Ideally, risk-based regulation should strengthen people's **trust** in AI, leading to increased demand for AI applications. The increased demand will give providers access to larger markets.[27]

27 To this end, the AI Act essentially establishes **product safety requirements** for AI systems used in the EU.[28] Providers, developers, manufacturers and deployers of AI systems will have to meet requirements before the system is introduced so that the systems function in a controllable manner after market launch or are not introduced at all if the risks are too high.

28 The AI Act follows an **anthropocentric approach** that focuses on people and assigns AI the task of supporting them. This approach is based on the assumption that AI brings numerous benefits to humans, but can also harbor risks. It must therefore be ensured that AI systems are trustworthy and human-centered.

2. Safeguarding fundamental rights and transparency

29 The use of AI raises ethical questions. **Respect for human rights** and democratic values must therefore be at the heart of regulation. In particular, the AI characteristics of **opacity, complexity, data dependency** and **autonomous behavior** can lead to a violation of fundamental rights. The AI Act is intended to reduce or even eliminate these risks.[29]

30 There is also a risk that **biases** or distorted perceptions will be transferred from the analog to the digital world.[30] Decision-making by AI systems is regularly complex, meaning that their paths are not transparent and traceable. Here it is of central importance to develop systems whose results can be accounted for.

3. Investment promotion

31 National measures are needed to promote trustworthy AI systems, including **incentives for investment** in responsible AI research and development. In addition to technology solutions and large computing capacities, AI requires enormous amounts of data. A digital environment that enables access to data while ensuring a high level of **data protection** and privacy is therefore urgently needed. AI-friendly framework conditions can also support small and medium-sized enterprises in the introduction of AI and ensure a competitive environment.

4. Accompanying change in the workplace

32 However, it is not only the opaqueness of AI technology itself that causes people to have fears that need to be addressed by regulation. Many are also concerned about

---

[27] Ammann/Pohle CB 5/2024, 137 (137).

[28] Buchalik/Gehrmann CR 3/2024, 145 (145).

[29] Cf. critically Keber/Zenner in: Schwartmann/Keber/Zenner, Part 2, Chapter 1, para. 17.

[30] Feldkamp/Kappler/Poretschkin/Schmitz/Weiss ZfDR 1/2024, 60 (105, 112); Kuntz ZfPW 2022, 177 (178); Schürmann ZD 2022, 316 (321); Gaub/Kadler Rethinking Law 6.2022, 4 (6); Ibold GSZ 2024, 10 (13).

the changes to the world of work that AI will bring, as AI can change and often even replace human work.[31]

A study by the Institute for Public Policy Research (IPPR)[32] dated 27.3.2024 predicts that the use of AI in the next three to five years will initially jeopardize entry-level jobs and **administrative activities** such as database management or typical secretarial tasks. In the UK, this would affect around 11 % of the 22,000 different job profiles in the economy.[33] As AI continues to develop, this proportion could increase to 59 % if AI increasingly learns **more complex tasks**.[34] This second wave would then also affect activities that do not involve routine tasks. These include creating databases, **writing texts** or generating graphics. In this scenario, eight million jobs would become obsolete in the UK alone.[35] 33

However, the study also contrasts this scenario with a more optimistic forecast: According to this, AI would enrich companies, no jobs would be lost and gross domestic product would grow by 4 %.[36] Carsten Jung, economist at IPPR, is quoted in the article as saying that the generative AI that already exists will change the labor market enormously and could contribute to strong economic growth. Governments, employers and trade unions just need to [...] ensure that the technology is used correctly.[37] 34

This is precisely the aim of the AI Act. 35

IV. Regulatory approach of the AI Act

1. Horizontal

The AI Act essentially contains **product safety regulations** for AI systems that are used in the EU.[38] The idea behind it is that providers, developers, manufacturers and deployers of AI systems in particular should meet requirements before the system is introduced so that the systems function as controllably as possible after market launch or do not even reach the market if the risks are too high. To this end, the AI Act is based on a horizontal regulatory approach.[39] The EU Commission's proposal (AI Act-E) was already based on the idea that the regulation would have a **cross-sectoral** effect and not just cover individual sectors.[40] 36

This approach is not unproblematic in practice because the use of AI in the various **sectors** is extremely diverse and **entails different levels of risk**: In the transport sector, for example, autonomous vehicles with virtual driver systems, HD maps and optimized traffic routes promise benefits in terms of accessibility, safety, quality of life and the environment. In the healthcare sector, AI systems facilitate the diagnosis of diseases and the development of therapies and medicines. In digital security applications, AI systems are increasingly being used in real time for the automated 37

[31] Brollo/Dabla-Norris/deMooij/Garcia-Macia/Hanappi/Liu/Nguyen, Broadening the Gains from Generative AI: The Role of Fiscal Policies, IMF study of 17.6.2024.

[32] Jung/Srinivasa Desikan, Transformed by AI – how generative artificial intelligence could effect work in the UK, available at https://ippr-org.files.svdcdn.com/production/Downloads/Transformed_by_AI_March24_2024-03-27-121003_kxis.pdf.

[33] Jung/Srinivasa Desikan, Transformed by AI, 6, 15.

[34] Jung/Srinivasa Desikan, Transformed by AI, 7, 15.

[35] Jung/Srinivasa Desikan, Transformed by AI, 7.

[36] Jung/Srinivasa Desikan, Transformed by AI, 25.

[37] Jung/Srinivasa Desikan, Transformed by AI, 28.

[38] See only Orssich EuZW 2022, 254 (256).

[39] Cf. for example Wendt/Wendt ZfPC 2024, 86 (86).

[40] Orssich EuZW 2022, 254 (256).

detection of and defense against threats. In agriculture, AI applications monitor plant and soil health and provide crop yield forecasts. In the financial market, AI is used to detect fraud, assess creditworthiness, reduce customer service costs and automate trading. In marketing and advertising, AI helps to assess customer behaviour in order to personalize advertising, products and prices.[41]

2. Risk-based

38 Accordingly, the horizontal approach necessarily goes hand in hand with the second defining basic idea of the AI Act, namely that not all fields of application of AI are equally risky. In fact, the vast majority of AI systems currently on the market pose little or no risk.

39 In order to maintain proportionality and, in the spirit of **better regulation**, only intervene where regulation is absolutely necessary, the AI Act does not prescribe a uniform level of regulation. Instead, it establishes a **tiered system** that is based on the level of risk of the specific application and aligns the requirements with this.

40 **Risk** is defined in Art. 3 No. 2 AI Act as a combination of the likelihood of harm occurring and its severity. The legislator explicitly states in the recitals and Art. 1 AI Act that it wants to promote the introduction of human-centered and trustworthy AI and at the same time protect the **fundamental rights** (based on the **Charter of Fundamental Rights of the EU**), **health** and **safety** of EU citizens and enable **democratic control**. Putting this together, one could say that risk in the sense of the AI Act means the probability of a violation of these essential rights and protected interests in the EU as well as the potential harm to EU citizens.

41 The **risk-based regulatory approach**[42] can therefore be described as a **link between the intensity of the requirements and the level of risk**. The higher the risk associated with the use or placing on the market of an AI system, the higher the requirements for this system, including in terms of product safety, documentation and human monitoring.

42 Specifically, the tiered system is presented as a **pyramid** (→ § 5 mn. 1), which recognizes four levels of risk. At the **top of** the pyramid are the prohibited AI systems under Art. 5 AI Act. These are AI applications that the legislator classifies as so risky that their risk is unacceptable for the EU. They include the assessment of social behavior for public and private purposes (social scoring),[43] individual predictive policing or emotion recognition in the workplace[44] and in educational institutions, which is only permitted for medical or safety purposes.

43 The majority of the requirements of the AI Act address the **second-highest risk level** of so-called high-risk AI systems. To make the assessment easier for companies, a list of high-risk AI systems is attached to the AI Act itself. This list, consisting of regulatory examples, can be revised by the EU Commission in order to adapt it to current developments.

44 Not only **stand-alone AI** can fall into the high-risk category. AI systems that function, for example, as a safety component of a product that is itself covered by product safety sectoral legislation of the Union can also be classified as high-risk by the AI Act. In the assessment, the AI Act follows the sectoral legislation of the product

---

[41] Prange WRP 2024, 151 (151).

[42] Cf. for example Schwartmann/Köhler in: Schwartmann/Keber/Zenner, Part 2, Chapter 1, para. 51; Wendt/Wendt ZfPC 2024, 86 (86).

[43] Orssich EuZW 2022, 254 (257).

[44] See Rudkowski/Wendt/Block/Wettlaufer FA 2024, 126 (132 et seq.).

in which the AI has been incorporated in that it automatically assigns a high risk to the AI application if the host product is subject to third-party conformity assessment in accordance with the sectoral legislation.[45]

At the third level of the risk pyramid, disclosure obligations apply to AI applications with **transparency risk**; at the fourth level, there are no obligations, only a request for **voluntary self-commitment**. 45

The **basic idea** of the horizontal and risk-based regulatory approach has been pursued and **maintained** to the end. 46

3. Technology neutral

The AI Act also pursues a **technology-neutral approach**.[46] The focus is not on the AI system, but on the **risk potential of the specific application of** an AI system.[47] 47

This regulatory approach, which is convincing in itself, reaches its limits in the case of **AI systems and models with a general purpose**. By its very nature, **no specific application scenario** can be identified here (→ § 11 mn. 20). 48

V. Scope of application

1. Personal scope of application

According to Art. 2 para. 1 AI Act, the AI Act applies first and foremost to **providers** who place AI systems or AI models with a general purpose on the market in the EU, regardless of whether they are established in the Union or in a third country. In addition, the Regulation applies to **deployers** of AI systems that are established or located in the Union. Thus, while the term provider can refer to AI systems and general-purpose AI models, the deployer is always associated with an AI system, not an AI model. The AI model cannot be deployed; it is not a stand-alone operational unit, but only one element of the broader AI system (→ § 11 mn. 3).[48] 49

According to Art. 3 No. 3 AI Act, **providers** are natural or legal persons, authorities, institutions or other bodies that **develop** an AI system or model or have it developed and place it on the market or put it into operation under their own name or trademark, whether for a fee or free of charge. In contrast, natural or legal persons, authorities, institutions or other bodies that **use** an AI system under their own responsibility for their **professional activities** are deemed to be **deployers** in accordance with Art. 3 No. 4 AI Act.[49] 50

Classification as a provider therefore requires **proximity to the AI system**; participation in the development process is a prerequisite. However, it is sufficient for persons, authorities, institutions or other bodies to have an AI system developed for them and then place it on the market or put it into operation under their own name. Anyone who is not involved in the development process and uses an AI system for professional purposes is considered a **deployer**. Under the conditions of Art. 25 AI Act, deployers are exceptionally treated as providers (→ § 7 mn. 73).[50] AI systems that are 51

[45] Orssich EuZW 2022, 254 (258).

[46] Wendt/Wendt ZfPC 2024, 86 (86).

[47] See also Hacker GRUR 2023, 289 (290): "Not every screw has to meet the safety standards for space shuttles if it is only used for the next Ikea bed".

[48] Cf. rec. 12 AI Act.

[49] For possible demarcation problems, see Keber/Zenner in: Schwartmann/Keber/Zenner, Part 2, Chapter 1, para. 20.

[50] Still on the AI Act-E: Frank/Heine NZA 2023, 1281 (1283).

used in the context of a **private**, i.e. non-professional **activity**,[51] are not covered by the regulation in accordance with Art. 2 para. 10 AI Act.[52]

52 In addition to **providers** and **deployers**, the AI Act also applies to **importers** and **distributors** of AI systems as well as to **product manufacturers** who place on the market or put into service AI systems together with their product under their own name or trademark, as well as to authorized representatives of providers not established in the EU.

2. Spatial scope of application

53 The provision in Art. 2 para. 1 lit. a AI Act manifests the so-called **market place principle**, while the provision in Art. 2 para. 1 lit. b AI Act manifests the so-called **establishment principle**.[53] The most far-reaching inclusion is made in Art. 2 para. 1 lit. c AI Act, which also covers providers and deployers based in a **third country** if the AI system itself is used in the EU or the output is used in the EU. The aim of this **extraterritorial effect** is to ensure that providers and deployers such as OpenAI also comply with the rules of the AI Act.[54]

54 AI applications that do not even address the EU market are likely to be particularly interesting in this context. Evident questions arise here, also in connection with the **enforceability** of any sanctions.[55] The national supervisory authorities can only take action within the member state, the EU Commission only within the EU. The only way forward is therefore currently via **trade agreements**, arbitration tribunals and a **bilateral exchange** between the EU Commission and the respective government.

55 If, for example, the AI system of an American company that neither operates in Europe nor sells products or services here generates an output in the EU via data activities that in some way influences the population or even just individuals, it is included in the scope of the AI Act in this way. This means that the AI Act also applies to public and private actors outside the EU, provided that people in the EU are affected by the use of the AI system.

56 The starting point for this principle of **extraterritorial effectiveness** of the AI Act is essentially already outside of AI regulation: If a provider wants to operate in the European single market, it needs a so-called contact point in Europe, i.e. a representative of the company who can be contacted by the national supervisory authorities, but also by the EU Commission. The AI Act also provides for third-party providers to appoint an **authorized representative** in the European Union to ensure compliance with these regulations. This authorized representative takes on various tasks, including the review of technical documentation and cooperation with the AI Office and the national authorities. If he finds that the provider does not comply with the provisions of the AI Act, he must inform the AI Office and terminate his mandate.

57 In view of the extraterritorial effect, every company, regardless of whether it is of European origin or not, that launches or operates an AI system in Europe must fully comply with the AI Act. In this respect, the AI Act is based on the GDPR, the effect of which also extends beyond European borders. If the company does not comply with the obligation, it may not offer its products and services on the European internal market – at least in the final analysis. The **consequences** of the extraterritorial

---

[51] Cf. Frank/Heine NZA 2023, 1281 (1283).

[52] See also Block/Jung/Wendt CRi 2023, 97 (102).

[53] See also Keber/Zenner in Schwartmann/Keber/Zenner, Part 2, Chapter 1, para. 25 with reference to the provisions in Art. 3 (1) and (2) GDPR.

[54] Buchalik/Gehrmann CR 3/2024, 145 (147).

[55] Buchalik/Gehrmann CR 3/2024, 145 (147).

effect of the AI Act are particularly challenging for internet-based services, as it also affects providers that do not actively address the European market. These companies offer software-as-a-service solutions on English-only websites, for example, but are of course also found by customers from Europe who then subscribe to the service and pay by PayPal or credit card, for example. What leverage can these providers use to exclude the effect of the AI Act? Are they ultimately not allowed to accept credit card payments from people with a European credit card? Conversely, will companies outside Europe be blocked? It would be conceivable to **block access** to certain platforms. Ultimately, however, everyone is aware that the sites can still be accessed via simple detours, such as a VPN client. The idea of a complete blockade is therefore not very realistic.

This was also evident following the decision by the Garante per la Protezione dei Dati Personale (GPDP), i.e. the Italian data protection authority, on 31.3.2023, which **prohibited** OpenAI from **operating ChatGPT in Italy**. OpenAI responded by blocking access to IP addresses assigned to Italian users. Demand for VPN services that conceal their geographical origin is said to have reached record levels in Italy as a result.[56] **58**

Some of the major providers in the field of generative AI have already reacted to the extraterritorial effect of the AI Act: Open AI, as well as Google DeepMind and Antrophic, have stated that they will **not** make certain **products available** to the **European market** at all.[57] It remains to be seen whether these declarations can be dismissed as a tactical approach or whether the companies will ultimately actually forego 450 million potential European customers. **59**

A similar approach recently emerged in connection with the Digital Markets Act (DMA): Apple postponed the introduction of AI-based functions such as Apple Intelligence, iPhone Mirroring and SharePlay Screen Sharing in Europe, arguing that compliance with the interoperability requirements of the DMA would lead to security risks for user data.[58] In any case, it is remarkable that the European Union is acting very confidently here and has **significantly expanded** its **scope of action** by means of extraterritoriality. **60**

Overall, however, any regulation is most effective if it is **internationally** coordinated or at least **supported**. It remains to be seen how **acceptance of** the AI Act will develop. **61**

3. Material scope of application

AI systems (→ § 2 mn. 11) and certain AI models (→ § 2 mn. 13) are covered by the AI Act. **62**

AI systems that are placed on the market, put into service or used, with or without modification, solely for **military**, defense or **national security purposes** are exempt from the applicability of the AI Act pursuant to Art. 2 para. 3 subpara. 2 AI Act. In addition, Art. 2 para. 6 AI Act also exempts AI systems and AI models that are developed and put into operation solely for **scientific research** from the scope of application. The exemption extends to the **prototype development** that precedes the market launch, Art. 2 para. 8 AI Act. **63**

According to Art. 2 para. 12 subpara. 1 AI Act, the provisions of the AI Act also do not apply to AI systems that are available under **free** or **open source licenses**. The ex- **64**

---

[56] After OpenAI made improvements in the area of data protection, the IP block was ultimately lifted again after about a month, see Haar MMR 2023, 397 (398).

[57] Cf. Lawler The Verge 21.6.2024.

[58] On the Brussels Effect of the DMA, see Grzanna Tagesspiegel 28.6.2024.

ception in the material scope is intended to promote innovation by giving small, independent developers room to manoeuvre.

65 The AI Act only covers open source AI systems if they are placed on the market or put into service as high-risk AI systems, prohibited practices (Art. 5 AI Act) or AI systems with transparency risks (Art. 50 AI Act) (**backward exemption** in Art. 2 para. 12 subpara. 2 AI Act.[59] The AI Act leaves largely open when the **requirements** for a free or open-source licence are met. Recitals 102 to 104 merely highlight individual features of a free and open-source licence, in particular their potential to contribute to research and innovation and to open up growth opportunities for the European economic market.[60] Recital 102 clarifies that the licence must allow for the 'open sharing' of the model and 'free access, use, modification and redistribution' of the model 'or its modified versions' by users. If any of these rights (i.e. the right to access, use, modify and distribute) is missing, the licence cannot be considered free and open source. Recital 103 further specifies that AI components that are provided for a fee or otherwise monetised, including through the provision of technical support or other services, are not covered by the exceptions for free and open-source AI. No financial consideration may be required for access to, use, modification and distribution of the AI model. In this context, monetisation covers not only the provision of the model for a fee, but also other types of monetisation strategies.

66 – A more detailed interpretation of the requirements was provided by the European Commission's guidelines for providers of general-purpose AI models (GPAI guidelines), which were published on 18.7.2025.[61] In Chapter 4.2, they provide the criteria for the open source definition: In order to qualify for the open source exemption, an AI model must, in particular, be published under a free and open source licence that allows access, use, modification and distribution of the model, Art. 53 para 2 AI Act and Art. 54 para 6 AI Act. Free and open source is to be understood as a form of licensing that uses copyright to enable widespread distribution of the model and to create incentives for further development. According to Chapter 4.2.1. of the guidelines (**licence conditions**), in order to qualify, everyone must be allowed to modify the model and distribute it freely. Restrictions on non-commercial use are just as much an obstacle to open source privilege as prohibitions on the distribution of the model ('You may use the model, but not distribute it') and restrictions on use triggered by thresholds. Licensors may only impose security-oriented conditions that appropriately restrict use in areas where there is a significant risk to public safety or fundamental rights.

67 – According to Recital 103, the concept of monetisation plays a decisive role in determining whether the exceptions for open-source AI models apply. Chapter 4.2.2. of the guidelines (**Lack of monetisation**) specifies the concept and explains that the licence for the AI model must be freely available to everyone **without any payment requirements**. The term 'payment requirements' is to be understood in a broad sense. Technical support or other services that are inseparably linked to the model or its security and without which the model would not be accessible may also not be provided in return for payment. The non-monetisation requirement also covers compensation in the form of personal data: The protection of personal

---

[59] See also Keber/Zenner in Schwartmann/Keber/Zenner, Part 2, Chapter 1, para. 32.

[60] Recital 102.

[61] Annex to the Communication to the Commission Approval of the content of the draft Communication from the Commission – Guidelines on the scope of the obligations for general-purpose AI models established by Regulation (EU) 2024/1689 (AI Act) of 18.7.2025.

data is a fundamental right. It must not be treated as a commodity. Access to, use, modification or disclosure of a model that requires the collection or processing of personal data must therefore be treated in the same way as other monetisation strategies, unless the processing is strictly limited to the security of the model and does not aim to generate financial gain. The AI Act therefore does not consider Meta's Llama model to be an open source model. After all, users must provide their data in order to gain access. This violates the aspect of non-monetisation.

- According to Art. 53 para 2 and Art. 54 para 6 AI Act, the parameters of the model, including weights, information about the model architecture and information about model usage, must be made publicly available. Chapter 4.2.3 of the guidelines (**Public Availability of Parameters**) states that the information must be provided in a format and with a degree of clarity and specificity that enables access, use, modification and dissemination of the model. Specifically, information about the use of the model should include at least details of the input and output modalities, capabilities and limitations of the model. Information about the use of the model, on the other hand, should also include the technical means required to integrate the model into AI systems. This may also include the appropriate configuration for the intended use cases. The information must ensure that downstream providers of AI systems, developers and users can use the model for practical applications. 68

4. Temporal scope of application

The **temporal scope of application** is governed by Art. 113 AI Act. According to this, the provisions of the AI Act apply **in stages**. The prohibited AI practices pursuant to Art. 113 sentence 3 lit. a AI Act have already been applicable since 2.2.2025, with their date of application set at six months after the entry into force of the Regulation. 69

In a next step, the obligations for AI models and systems for general use pursuant to Art. 113 sentence 3 lit. b AI Act became applicable on 2.8.2025, i.e., 12 months after the AI Act entered into force. In view of the fact that the GPAI Code of practice (→ § 11 mn. 51) was not completed on time, the guidelines for providers of GPAI models were not published until 18.7.2025,[62] and the harmonised standards still pending (→ § 9 mn. 8), the Council of the EU has been considering postponing this deadline (so-called 'stop-the-clock' request). However, the EU Commission decided against a moratorium.[63]

A transition period of 24 months is provided for in the main part of the Regulation, including the high-risk systems listed in Annex III, Art. 113 sentence 2 AI Act. The majority of the AI Act will therefore enter into force on 2.8.2026. One year later, i.e., after 36 months, the obligations for high-risk systems listed in Annex I, for which other harmonization legislation already exists at EU level, will also become applicable, Art. 113 sentence 3 lit. c AI Act. 70

---

[62] Annex to the Communication to the Commission Approval of the content of the draft Communication from the Commission – Guidelines on the scope of the obligations for general-purpose AI models established by Regulation (EU) 2024/1689 (AI Act) of 18.7.2025.

[63] See EU Commission, Midday press briefing of 4.7.2025, https://audiovisual.ec.europa.eu/en/video/I-274901.

Figure 8: Temporal scope of application of the AI Act

§ 4
AI literacy

Literature: *Biedenkopf, Sebastian*, KI und die Kunst des Fragens, Der Aufsichtsrat 07–08/2024, 97; *Cipierre, Paula*, Konzepte zur Umsetzung von KI-Kompetenz im Unternehmen zwischen KI-VO und DS-GVO, RDV 5/2024, 261; *Delcker, Janosch*, Der Gedanken-Code 2024; *Fleck, Tilmann*, AI literacy als Rechtsbegriff. Anforderungen an die KI-Kompetenz nach Art. 4 KI-VO, KIR 3/2024. 99; *Fügener, Andreas/Grahl, Jörn/Gupta, Alok/Ketter* Wolfgang, Will Humans-in-the-Loop Become Borgs? Merits and Pitfalls of Working with AI, MIS Quarterly, 45(3), ssrn.com/abstract=3879937; *Goddard, Kate/Roudsari, Abdul/Wyatt Jeremy C.*, Automation bias: a systematic review of frequency, effect mediators, and mitigators, Journal oft he American Medical Informatics Association, 19(1), 121, doi.org/10.1136/amiajnl-2011-000089; *Jussupow, Ekaterina/Spohrer, Kai/Heinzl, Armin/Gawilitza Joshua*, Augmenting Medical Diagnosis Decisions? An Investigation into Physicians' Decision-Making Process with Artificial Intelligence, Information Systems Research, 32(3), 713, doi.org/10.1287/isre.2020.0980; *Klingbeil, Artur/Grützner, Cassandra/Schreck, Philipp*, Trust and reliance on AI – An experimental study on the extent and costs of overreliance on AI, Computers in Human Behavior (2024), doi: 10.1016/j.chb.2024.108352; *Leu, Don/Coiro, Julie/Kinzer, Charles/Castek, Jill/Henry, Laurie A.*, New Literacies: A Dual-Level Theory of the Changing Nature of Literacy, Instruction, and Assessment, Theoretical Models and Processes of Reading 2013; 1150; *Long, Duri/Magerko, Brian*, What is AI Literacy? Competencies and Design Considerations, CHI '20: Proceedings of the 2020 CHI Conference on Human Factors in Computing Systems, https://doi.org/10.1145/3313831.3376727; *Pinski, Marc/Benlian, Alexander*, AI Literacy for Users – A Comprehensive Review and Future Research Directions of Learning Methods, Components, and Effects, Computers in Human Behavior: Artificial Humans 2024; *Pinski, Marc/Benlian, Alexander*, AI Literacy – Towards Measuring Human Competency in Artificial Intelligence, Hawaii International Conference on System Sciences 2023; *Pinski, Marc/Hofmann, T./Benlian, Alexander*, AI Literacy for the Top Management: An Upper Echelons Perspective on Corporate AI Orientation and Implementation Ability, Electronic Markets 2024; *Pinski, Marc/Tarafdar Monideepa/Benlian Alexander*, Why Executives Can't Get Comfortable With AI, MIT Sloan Management Review, 2024; *Schwartmann, Rolf/Keber, Tobias/Zenner, Kai*, KI-Verordnung. Leitfaden für die Praxis, 2024.

I. Concept and general requirements

1 Article 4 of the AI Act introduces the previously unknown concept of AI literacy. It requires **providers and deployers** of AI systems to **take measures** to ensure that their personnel and other persons involved in the operation and use of AI systems on their behalf have a **sufficient level of AI literacy**.

2 In the definitions, Art. 3 No. 56 AI Act further specifies that literacy in relation to AI includes "*the skills, knowledge and understanding necessary to enable providers, operators and data subjects to make informed use of AI systems and to be aware of the opportunities and risks of AI and the possible harm it may cause, taking into account their respective rights and obligations under this Regulation*".

3 AI literacy is therefore made up of three essential elements:[1] **skills, knowledge and understanding.** The term "knowledge" encompasses both general and specific theoretical knowledge. The term "skills" refers to the practical application of knowledge, i.e., action. "Understanding" is when available information can be correctly classified in a given situation and effects can be assessed. Skills and understanding thus equally

[1] See also Fleck, KIR 2024, 99 (100): "Triad".

require knowledge. Ability applies to knowledge in practice; understanding denotes the correct conclusion based on knowledge.

4 According to recital 20, the aim of the provision is to familiarise providers, operators and other affected persons with the concepts needed to make informed decisions together with AI.

To this end, persons interacting with AI must also be aware of typical **automation biases**, Art. 14 para. 4 lit. b AI Act;[2] they must develop an understanding that humans tend to place **excessive trust** in results produced by AI systems, question them too rarely and, according to a study published in June 2025 by the Massachusetts Institute of Technology (MIT),[3] develop an AI dependency that reduces their own cognitive abilities.[4]

5 Art. 4 AI Act requires a "sufficient level" of AI literacy. The EU legislator has not created a rigid system of AI literacy requirements, but rather a **flexible one.** It allows for the tailoring of AI literacy to the practical needs of providers and operators and does not provide for a "one-size-fits-all" solution. The level of competence that is sufficient depends in particular on the AI system, its area of application and the users of the system. If a company provides its employees with an AI system for business use, it has a legal obligation to ensure that employees know and understand the workings of the specific technology to the extent that conscious application.[5] It is not about being able to technically understand every step, but rather to be familiar with the basic mechanisms of the AI application so that a sufficient understanding of the risks (including regulatory ones) is achieved.[6]

6 A sufficient understanding always requires a certain **minimum level of skills, knowledge and understanding.**[7] This minimum level can be described as **general AI literacy.** Divided into **core areas**, the necessary general AI literacy includes at least basic knowledge of AI models, data for AI, AI interfaces or surfaces, AI tools and the organizational environment of AI use.[8] The organizational environment also includes knowledge of the regulatory framework for AI systems.

7 Depending on the field of application of the AI system offered or operated, further skills and knowledge as well as a more profound understanding may be required in addition to general AI literacy. In these cases, a **specific AI literacy** is required that builds on the basic elements. At the latest when these are being trained, a distinction will have to be made between **expert systems** and **machine learning systems.**[9]

8 Overall, AI literacy can be understood as a **holistic human ability for human-AI interaction,**[10] which follows a hierarchical structure and differentiates between a general and a specific level of AI literacy.

---

[2] Jussupow et al., Information Systems Research, (32)3, 713; Goddard/Roudsari/Wyatt, Journal of the American Medical Informatics Association, 19(1) 121.

[3] Kosmyna et al., 'Your Brain on ChatGPT: Accumulation of Cognitive Debt when Using an AI Assistant for Essay Writing Task', https://doi.org/10.48550/arXiv.2506.08872.

[4] See Klingbeil/Grützner/Schreck, Computers in Human Behavior, 2024, doi: 10.1016/j.chb.2024.108352; Fügener et al., MIS Quarterly 45(3); Guijarro Santos ZfDR 1/2023, 23 (28).

[5] Schwartmann/Köhler in: Schwartmann/Keber/Zenner, 2nd part 1st chapter para. 55; Delcker, Gedanken-Code 167.

[6] Delcker, Gedanken-Code 167.

[7] Cf. also Cipierre RDV 2024, 261 (262 et seq.): "minimum knowledge"; Fleck, KIR 2024, 99 (101): "minimum standard".

[8] Pinski/Benlian, Computers in Human Behavior: Artificial Humans.

[9] Glauner, in: Ebers/Quarch, Technische Grundlagen von generativen KI-Modellen, mn. 2.

[10] Pinski/Benlian, Computers in Human Behavior: Artificial Humans.

II. Training measures

Based on the definition given in Art. 3 No. 56 AI Act, training should enable the groups of people listed in Art. 4 AI Act (staff and other persons) to use AI systems knowledgeably. The specific training measures to be taken depend on the general or specific level of AI literacy to be achieved, which in turn depends on the area of application of the AI application and the AI system used. 9

The specific **training measures** to be taken depend on the context and, in particular, on the specific AI system being used. As part of training to achieve general AI literacy, the above-mentioned **core areas** are to be taught first. The basic module includes, in any case, fundamental knowledge of AI systems and AI models, data for AI, AI interfaces or surfaces, AI tools, and the organizational and regulatory environment of AI use. 10

Training can be provided **internally** and **externally**.[11] **External training** can be provided, for example, through participation in specific **certificate courses.**[12] They can guarantee a secure, standardized AI literacy level for the basic module of the **tiered structure.**[13] 11

In any case, care must be taken to ensure that the content taught in the training concept sufficiently takes into account the company's individual needs. This applies all the more if the training is not merely geared towards acquiring general AI literacy, but is intended to go beyond the basic module and teach **specific AI skills.** In-house training courses will primarily be established here. 12

In view of the rapid development of AI systems, AI literacy is not something that can be acquired just once and for all time, but must be maintained and kept up to date in the long term. New technologies regularly and repeatedly transform previous literacies, continually redefining what it means to become literate.[14] Providers and deployers need to embrace that uncomfortable reality and prioritize developing AI literacy.[15] 13

In some cases, the creation of sufficient AI literacy is also seen as a **task for society as a whole**, requiring a coordinated approach by various actors (educational institutions, companies, political decision-makers and civil society).[16] This does not follow from Art. 4 AI Act. Nevertheless, the expected penetration of AI systems into society makes such a comprehensive requirement for AI literacy difficult to dispute. 14

III. AI Officer

The appointment of an in-house **AI officer** is seen as a strategic measure to centralize and promote AI expertise within the organization.[17] The AI officer can serve as a point of contact for all AI-related questions, monitor compliance with ethical guidelines and standards, and also ensure that education and training initiatives are implemented.[18] 15

---

[11] See also Fleck, KIR 2024, 99 (103 et seq.).
[12] Cf. also Martini/Wendehorst/Wendehorst KI-VO Art. 4(15).
[13] Cf. Martini/Wendehorst/Wendehorst KI-VO Art. 4(15).
[14] Leu et al., Theoretical Models 1150 (1160).
[15] Pinksi/Tarafdar/Benlian, MIT Sloan Management Review 2024.
[16] Cf. Martini/Wendehorst/Wendehorst KI-VO Art. 4 mn. 22 et seq.; Sorge, KIR 2024, 77 (77): "Part of school education".
[17] See Martini/Wendehorst/Wendehorst KI-VO Art. 4 mn. 15.
[18] Martini/Wendehorst/Wendehorst KI-VO Art. 4 mn. 18 et seq.

16 The AI Regulation does not explicitly require the appointment of a responsible person for specific tasks related to AI systems in companies. However, EU law provides for such responsible persons in other areas. For example, data protection law regulates the data protection officer (Art. 37 GDPR) and financial market law regulates specific key functions (compliance function, internal audit, actuarial function). In addition, the German Supply Chain Due Diligence Act, for example, recommends the appointment of a specific officer (human rights officer).

17 Even though there is no obligation to design and include the function of "AI officer" in the AI Act due to the lack of a corresponding requirement, practical considerations certainly speak in favor of introducing this function. It makes it possible to bundle responsibilities and competencies. Often, it may be in the interest of the company to expand the role of the data protection officer to include AI responsibilities.

IV. Living Repository

18 On 4.2.2025, the EU Commission published the first version of the Living Repository on AI Literacy. The compilation contains a collection of different implementation practices for ensuring AI-related skills. These were gathered as part of a survey. The list of practices included in the compilation is not exhaustive and will be updated regularly. The most recent update was made on 16.4.2025.

19 With the Living Repository, the EU Commission aims to provide examples of implementation practices for ensuring AI literacy within the meaning of Art. 4 AI Act. This is intended to promote learning and exchange between providers and deployers of AI systems on AI literacy.

The implementation practices listed are classified according to their degree of implementation (fully implemented, partially implemented, planned). The EU Commission emphasizes that the implementation of the initiatives contained in the repository does not constitute a presumption of compliance with the requirements of Art. 4 AI Act. The EU Commission does not therefore evaluate the implementation practices with their publication in the repository.

V. Specific requirements for national competent authorities

20 For national competent authorities within the meaning of Art. 70 et seq. AI Act (market surveillance authorities and notifying authorities), the requirements of Art. 70 para. 3 sentence 2 AI Act must also be observed (→ § 13 mn. 51). Accordingly, the employees of the national competent authorities must have an in-depth understanding of AI technologies, data and data processing, the protection of personal data, cybersecurity, fundamental rights, health and safety risks and knowledge of existing standards and legal requirements. In accordance with Art. 70 para. 3 sentence 3 AI Act, the individual contents of the AI literacy must be assessed once a year by the member states and updated if necessary.

§ 5
Risk levels

Literature: Block, Martina/Jung, Constantin/Wendt, Domenik, Requirements for "Legal Tech AI Systems" – Reflections on the negotiated AI Act with regard to Legal Technology using AI, CRi 2023, 97; *Brandão, Rodrigo/Arbix, Glauco*, Artificial Intelligence, Ethics and Public Policy – The Use of Facial Recognition Systems in Public Transport in the Largest Brazilian Cities, Journal of Service Science and Management, 2022, 15, 551; *Czaplicki, Kamil*, Use of Artificial Intelligence in Remote Biometric Identification Systems, GIS Odyssey Journal, 2023 3(2), 107; *Delcker, Janosch*, Der Gedanken-Code 2024; *Hahn, Johanna*, Die Regulierung biometrischer Fernidentifizierung in der Strafverfolgung im KI-Verordnungsentwurf der EU-Kommission, ZfDR 2023, 142; *Korte, Kai*, EU-Parlament: Für ein Verbot der automatisierten Gesichtsserkennung, ZD-Aktuell 2021, 05531; *Martini, Mario*, Gesichtserkennung im Spannungsfeld zwischen Sicherheit und Freiheit, NVwZ 2022, 30; *Mobilio, Giuseppe*, Your face is not new to me – Regulating the surveillance power of facial recognition technologies, Internet Policy Review, 2023 12(1); *Mund, Dorothea*, Das Recht auf menschliche Entscheidung – die Vorgaben des Grundgesetztes angesichts des Einsatzes Künstlicher Intelligenz bei der vollziehenden Gewalt, LTZ 2023, 85; *Paal, Boris/Hüger, Jakob*, Die KI-VO und das Recht auf menschliche Entscheidung, MMR 2024, 540; *Schindler, Stephan*, EU-Kommission: Draft Regulation on the Regulation of AI the End of Police Facial Recognition in Public Spaces?, ZD-Aktuell 2021, 05221; *Schwartmann, Rolf/Keber, Tobias/Zenner, Kai*, KI-Verordnung. Leitfaden für die Praxis, 2024; *Simmler, Monika/Canova, Giulia*, Gesichtserkennungstechnologie: Die "smarte" Polizeiarbeit auf dem rechtlichen Prüfstand, Sicherheit & Recht, (3) 2021, 105; *Tschorr, Sophie*, Regulierung der auf Biometrie basierenden KI-Systeme, MMR 2024, 304; *Wendt, Janine/Wendt, Domenik*, Einigung auf Rechtsrahmen für Künstliche Intelligenz in der EU, ZfPC 2024, 86.

The AI Act regulates **four risk categories**, which are based on the intended use of AI **in a technology-neutral manner** and form the well-known risk pyramid.[1] 1

The fifth category of **general-purpose AI systems and models** is outside this hierarchy. On the model side, it can in turn be divided into those AI models that pose a **systemic risk** due to their high-impact capabilities and those that do not. 2

[1] See Wendt/Wendt ZfPC 2024, 86 (86).

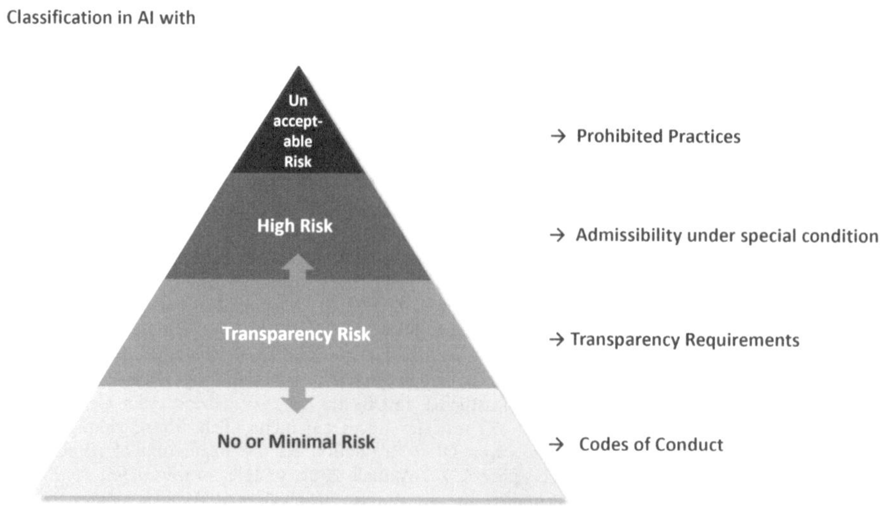

Figure 9: AI system – risk pyramid

I. Prohibited practices

1. Regulation in the AI Act

3 Prohibited practices are at the top of the risk pyramid. This is how European legislators refer to AI systems that pose **unacceptable risks** and therefore **may not be placed on the market**, put into operation or used in the EU.[2]

2. Specification in the Commission Guidelines

4 The first guidelines were issued on 4.2.2025, pursuant to Art. 96 para. 1 lit. b AI Act, on prohibited practices of artificial intelligence.[3] Here, it was particularly urgent to obtain clarity regarding applicability, as the bans have been directly applicable since 2.2.2025.

3. Specific prohibited practices

a) Subliminal influence

5 According to Art. 5 para. 1 lit. a AI Act, this includes AI systems that subliminally influence or deceive in order to significantly influence human behavior. The **manipulation** of AI systems is aimed at causing a person to make decisions that they would not otherwise have made and that could cause them or another person significant harm. The fundamental idea behind this prohibited practice is therefore to protect human autonomy and, in doing so, to give particular consideration to groups of people

---

[2] Ammann/Pohle CB 5/2024, 137 (139).

[3] Communication to the Commission Approval of the content of the draft Communication from the Commission – Commission Guidelines on prohibited artificial intelligence practices established by Regulation (EU) 2024/1689 (AI Act) und Annex to the Communication to the Commission Approval of the content of the draft Communication from the Commission – Commission Guidelines on prohibited artificial intelligence practices established by Regulation (EU) 2024/1689 (AI Act).

such as young people, who are particularly vulnerable and susceptible to exploitation.[4] The guidelines also mention hardware such as head-mounted displays (HMDs), which are used in connection with games in the metaverse, for example, and are even more intrusive and dangerous.[5]

6 Art. 5 para. 1 lit. a AI Act prohibits three alternative types of manipulative techniques: (1) subliminal techniques that are not accessible to the conscious mind, (2) deliberately manipulative techniques, and (3) misleading techniques.

7 According to the Commission guidelines, subliminal techniques can be both visual and auditory. Prohibited subliminal visual messages include text and images that are displayed so briefly that, although they are technically visible and can influence human behavior, they cannot be consciously perceived. Similarly, Article 5 para. 1 lit a AI Act prohibits the concealment of images in visual messages. Prohibited subliminal auditory influence, on the other hand, works, for example, through sounds that are so subtle or masked by other sounds that humans cannot consciously perceive them. Temporal manipulation, which influences the user's perception of time and creates a feeling of dependence, is also considered a subliminal technique.

8 An example of a misleading technique, on the other hand, is a chatbot that pretends to be a friend and imitates familiar voices. AI systems that temporarily cease undesirable behavior only to resume it once an observation period has ended also fall into this category.

b) Exploitation of the need for protection

9 The category of prohibited practices also includes AI systems that **exploit a person's** weakness or **vulnerability**, for example due to their age, disability or social or economic situation, Art. 5 para. 1 lit. b AI Act. This immediately brings to mind the tragic death of teenager Sewell Setzer in the US.[6] This group of AI systems is also prohibited because it significantly influences human behavior and is therefore at least reasonably likely to cause significant harm.

c) Social scoring

10 **Social scoring** is also prohibited, Art. 5 para. 1 lit. c AI Act. This refers to the placing on the market, commissioning or use of AI systems that classify human behavior on the basis of their social behavior or personal characteristics and make this "**social assessment**" the criterion for a disadvantage that is no longer related to the circumstances under which it was recorded (variant i), or that is unjustified or disproportionate with regard to social behavior (variant ii).

11 The proposals of the EU Parliament and the Council had initially limited the ban on social scoring to public authorities and private actors acting on behalf of public authorities. This restriction was not included in the final version of the AI Act.[7]

---

[4] Annex to the Communication to the Commission Approval of the content of the draft Communication from the Commission – Commission Guidelines on prohibited artificial intelligence practices established by Regulation (EU) 2024/1689 (AI Act), No. 59.

[5] Annex to the Communication to the Commission Approval of the content of the draft Communication from the Commission – Commission Guidelines on prohibited artificial intelligence practices established by Regulation (EU) 2024/1689 (AI Act), No. 66.

[6] Hunfeld, *Der Spiegel* from 29.3.2025, 50.

[7] Chibanguza/Steege NJW 2024, 1769 (1771).

d) Predictive policing

12 In the EU, the use of an AI system to carry out risk assessments of natural persons in order to predict the **likelihood of committing a criminal offense** or participating in a criminal activity is also prohibited, Art. 5 para. 1 lit. d AI Act. In other words, it is prohibited to make crime predictions linked to profiling, in which an AI system uses often historical socioeconomic data in conjunction with criminological theories to determine a risk value that measures the probability of a natural person committing a crime in the future. The ban applies regardless of whether the AI system evaluates the personality traits of only one natural person or a specific group of people (group profiling).[8] Personality traits include, for example, a person's nationality, place of birth or residence, marital status, number of children, level of debt, or choice of car.[9]

13 This prohibition does not extend to AI systems that are used to obtain a **second opinionon an assessment** already carried out by a human. They fall into the category of high-risk AI. The human assessment must be based on objective and verifiable facts related to the criminal activity.

e) Untargeted scraping of facial images

14 The prohibited practices also include the use of AI systems that create or expand **databases for facial recognition** by reading facial images from the internet or surveillance footage in an untargeted manner, Art. 5 para. 1 lit. e AI Act. Recital 43 of the AI Act justifies the ban with the "sense of mass surveillance" that would otherwise arise and the risk of "serious violations of fundamental rights, including the right to privacy."[10] The attribute "untargeted" limits the ban to AI systems that automatically extract data from various sources, including social media, via web crawlers, bots, or other means, and in doing so collect content indiscriminately "like a vacuum cleaner"[11] without targeting a specific person or group of people. In addition to collecting data from the internet, the ban also covers CCTV recordings, i.e., video surveillance material.

f) Emotion recognition in the workplace and in educational institutions

15 Another prohibited practice concerns AI systems for **inferring the emotions** of a natural person in the **workplace** and in **educational institutions**, Art. 5 para. 1 lit. f AI Act. Emotion recognition systems promise to read people's emotions by analyzing their bodies or behavior for biometric characteristics using AI. For example, facial expressions, movements and even voice colors can be recognized and evaluated for mood analysis.[12] This could give companies the opportunity to record the satisfaction

[8] Annex to the Communication to the Commission Approval of the content of the draft Communication from the Commission – Commission Guidelines on prohibited artificial intelligence practices established by Regulation (EU) 2024/1689 (AI Act), No. 194.

[9] Annex to the Communication to the Commission Approval of the content of the draft Communication from the Commission – Commission Guidelines on prohibited artificial intelligence practices established by Regulation (EU) 2024/1689 (AI Act), No. 198.

[10] Annex to the Communication to the Commission Approval of the content of the draft Communication from the Commission – Commission Guidelines on prohibited artificial intelligence practices established by Regulation (EU) 2024/1689 (AI Act), No. 223.

[11] Annex to the Communication to the Commission Approval of the content of the draft Communication from the Commission – Commission Guidelines on prohibited artificial intelligence practices established by Regulation (EU) 2024/1689 (AI Act), No. 228.

[12] Delcker, thought code 53.

of their employees using indicators. This method, also known as people analytics[13] is therefore also prohibited under the AI Act (in addition to the requirements of the GDPR). Recital 44 explains that the legislator has serious concerns about the scientific basis of these AI systems and doubts their reliability and the generalizability of their results. In addition, the recognition of emotions could be discriminatory and interfere with the right to privacy, human dignity, and freedom of thought. This is particularly dangerous in asymmetrical relationships, such as those typical in the workplace or in education, and is therefore prohibited.[14] The reference to educational institutions is broad and should be understood as meaning that there are no restrictions with regard to the type or age of pupils or students. A defining feature is that educational institutions can issue a certificate and participation is a prerequisite for obtaining it.[15]

For the ban to apply, it must be genuine emotion recognition, i.e., an AI system that derives emotions or intentions based on biometric data. The term "emotion" should be understood broadly here. Recital 18 of the AI Act cites happiness, sadness, anger, surprise, disgust, embarrassment, excitement, shame, contempt, satisfaction, and amusement as examples. The list is not exhaustive. Physical states such as pain or fatigue are not emotions. AI systems that detect and warn professional pilots or drivers when they are tired do not use emotion recognition,[16] as fatigue is purely a physical condition.[17] 16

Even the recording of easily recognizable expressions is not covered by the ban: Simply observing that a person is smiling does not constitute emotion recognition. A TV broadcaster may therefore use an AI system to measure how often a newsreader smiles.[18] However, AI systems that conclude that an employee is angry or frustrated based on the absence of a smile are using emotion recognition. The use of webcams in a call center to record employees' emotions is therefore prohibited. The only permitted use would be for personal training purposes, provided that the results are not passed on to HR managers.[19] 17

The prohibition in Article 5 para. 1 lit. f AI Act contains an explicit exception for emotion recognition systems used in the workplace or in educational institutions for medical or safety purposes. The exception must be interpreted narrowly in the interest of protecting fundamental rights.[20] General monitoring of employees' stress levels re- 18

[13] The Japanese supermarket chain Aeon, for example, uses artificial intelligence to check whether employees are smiling enough. The AI Mr. Smile uses image and sound recordings to evaluate 450 data points – e.g. facial expressions or the tone in which employees speak to customers, brandeins 9/2024.

[14] Annex to the Communication to the Commission Approval of the content of the draft Communication from the Commission – Commission Guidelines on prohibited artificial intelligence practices established by Regulation (EU) 2024/1689 (AI Act), No. 241.

[15] Annex to the Communication to the Commission Approval of the content of the draft Communication from the Commission – Commission Guidelines on prohibited artificial intelligence practices established by Regulation (EU) 2024/1689 (AI Act), No. 255.

[16] Annex to the Communication to the Commission Approval of the content of the draft Communication from the Commission – Commission Guidelines on prohibited artificial intelligence practices established by Regulation (EU) 2024/1689 (AI Act), No. 261.

[17] On the incident of the simultaneously sleeping pilots at Batik Air, see *FAZ* of 11.3.2024.

[18] Annex to the Communication to the Commission Approval of the content of the draft Communication from the Commission – Commission Guidelines on prohibited artificial intelligence practices established by Regulation (EU) 2024/1689 (AI Act), No. 249.

[19] Annex to the Communication to the Commission Approval of the content of the draft Communication from the Commission – Commission Guidelines on prohibited artificial intelligence practices established by Regulation (EU) 2024/1689 (AI Act), No. 254.

[20] Annex to the Communication to the Commission Approval of the content of the draft Communication from the Commission – Commission Guidelines on prohibited artificial intelligence practices established by Regulation (EU) 2024/1689 (AI Act), No. 256.

mains inadmissible, even for the purpose of preventing burnout. However, emotion recognition may be carried out for medical reasons to help students with autism.[21]

g) Biometric identification systems

19 After detailed discussion, AI systems used for **biometric categorisation** were also banned, Art. 5 para. 1 lit. g AI Act. They assign natural persons to groups based on their biometric data in order to draw conclusions about their race, political views, trade union membership, religious or ideological beliefs or sexual orientation. However, the filtering of data records based on biometric data in the area of **law enforcement** is still permitted.

20 The most controversial ban, for which it was also difficult to find a **compromise** in the trilogue, concerned the use of real-time remote biometric identification systems in publicly accessible spaces for law enforcement purposes, Art. 5 para. 1 lit. h AI Act.[22]

21 The solution to the conflict ultimately lay in opening up the ban for additional **exemptions at national level**, Art. 5 para. 5 AI Act. To this end, the member states define the requirements for applying for and granting the necessary authorizations and for the corresponding supervision. The EU Commission is informed of all exemptions. Conversely, the Member States may also adopt stricter legal provisions for the use of biometric remote identification systems, Art. 5 para. 5 sentence 5 AI Act.

22 The AI Act itself provides for a fundamental ban on the use of real-time remote biometric identification for law enforcement purposes in a **mediating position** in Art. 5 AI Act. These AI systems may only be used **in exceptional cases** if they are absolutely necessary for one of three objectives: The three objectives include as variant i) the targeted search for victims of **kidnapping**, human trafficking or sexual exploitation as well as the **search for missing persons**, variant ii) the averting of a concrete, significant and **immediate danger to the life** or physical integrity of natural persons or the at least foreseeable danger of a **terrorist attack**; (iii) the tracing or **identification of a suspected person** for the purposes of a criminal investigation, prosecution or execution of a sentence for specified criminal offenses punishable by at least four years' imprisonment in the Member State concerned.

23 The three exceptions to the prohibition are subject to further requirements[23], which include an assessment of the likelihood and extent of the harm that would arise if the AI system is not used, Art. 5 para. 2 AI Act. These consequences must be **weighed up** against the consequences of using the system for the rights and freedoms of all data subjects. The exceptions also require **proportionate safeguards**. Finally, the use of biometric real-time remote identification systems in publicly accessible areas may only be approved after a **fundamental rights impact assessment** has been carried out in accordance with Art. 27 AI Act.

24 Depending on the Member State, prior **authorization** is granted by a **judicial or independent administrative authority** upon reasoned request, Art. 5 para. 3 sentence 1 AI Act. The decision is binding. Only exceptionally, in duly justified urgent cases, can the use of the AI system begin without authorization, provided that the application is made immediately – within 24 hours at the latest, Art. 5 para. 3 sentence 2 AI Act. If

---

[21] Annex to the Communication to the Commission Approval of the content of the draft Communication from the Commission – Commission Guidelines on prohibited artificial intelligence practices established by Regulation (EU) 2024/1689 (AI Act), No. 263.

[22] See Kilian EuZW 2024, 145 (146); also in detail. Hahn ZfDR 2023, 142 (147).

[23] Cf. Ganter/Rembold in: Schwartmann/Keber/Zenner, Part 2, Chapter 1, para. 110 et seq.

the application is rejected, use must cease immediately and all data and results must be deleted, Art. 5 para. 3 sentence 3 AI Act.

Any use of a real-time biometric remote identification system in publicly accessible areas for law enforcement purposes must be notified to the competent **market surveillance authority** and the national **data protection authority**, Art. 5 para. 4 AI Act. 25

The national market surveillance authorities and the data protection authorities of the Member States that have been notified of the use of real-time biometric remote identification systems in publicly accessible spaces for law enforcement purposes in accordance with paragraph 4 shall submit annual reports on this use to the **European Commission**. For this purpose, the EU Commission shall provide the Member States and the national market surveillance and data protection authorities with a **template** containing information on the number of decisions of the competent judicial authorities or independent administrative authorities whose decision on applications for authorization is binding pursuant to Art. 5 para. 3 AI Act and their outcome. 26

The EU Commission **publishes annual reports** on the use of real-time biometric remote identification systems in publicly accessible spaces for law enforcement purposes, based on aggregated data from the Member States on the basis of the annual reports referred to in Art. 5 para. 6 AI Act, Art. 5 para. 7 AI Act. The annual reports may not contain sensitive operational data in connection with the associated law enforcement measures, Art. 5 para. 7 sentence 2 AI Act. 27

II. High-risk AI systems

Below the level of AI systems with unacceptable risk are the **AI systems with high risk**. These are the main focus of the AI Act. In practice, these are supposed to be a limited number of AI systems that have a potentially detrimental effect on people's safety or fundamental rights. In its draft regulation (AI Act-E), the EU Commission estimated that **5–15 % of applications** are **high-risk**.[24] A study of 106 AI systems in companies published by Applied AI in March 2023 found that 18 % of the group surveyed were high-risk.[25] In a related survey of 113 **AI start-ups**, 33 % of start-ups believed that their AI systems could be classified as high-risk.[26] 28

As the classification as high-risk AI has far-reaching consequences, Art. 6 AI Act initially sets out **classification requirements** for high-risk AI systems. Answering the question of whether a high-risk AI system exists is often complex in specific cases. The legislator has decided against an easily manageable legal definition and in favor of a **dynamic system for classifying** high-risk AI systems. 29

[24] Cf. Impact Assessment Accompanying the Proposal for a Regulation of the European Parliament and of the Council, available at https://eur-lex.europa.eu/legal-content/EN/TXT/?uri=CELEX%3A52021SC0631.

[25] Cf. study: AI Act: Classification of AI applications from a practical perspective, p. 12, available at https://www.appliedai.de/assets/files/AIAct_WhitePaper_DE-1_2024-03-04-123021_uwgf.pdf.

[26] AI Act Impact Survey, appliedAI Initiative, 2022, https://www.appliedai.de/hub/ai-act-impact-survey.

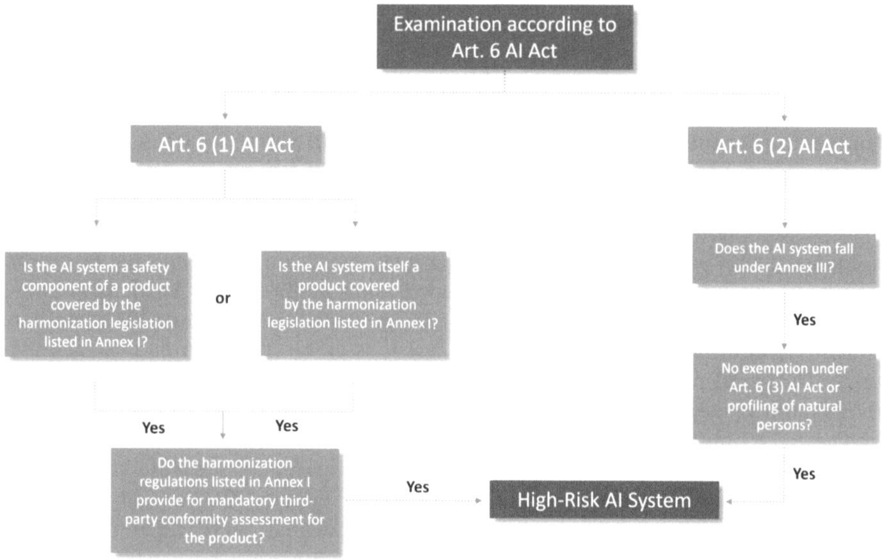

Figure 10: High-risk AI systems – review under Art. 6 AI Act

1. Product safety classification (reference to Annex I)

30 According to Art. 6 para. 1 AI Act, AI systems that serve as a safety component for a product that is already the subject of an EU legal act listed in Annex I Section A in accordance with the New Legislative Framework under product safety law (→ § 9 mn. 15), or that are themselves considered to be such a product, Art. 6 para. 1 lit. a AI Act.[27] These include machines, toys and medical devices, but also elevators, pressure equipment and radio equipment. The product of which the AI system is a safety component, or the AI system itself, must also undergo a conformity assessment by a third party with regard to placing on the market or putting into service in accordance with the Union harmonization legislation listed in Annex I, Art. 6 para. 1 lit. b AI Act.

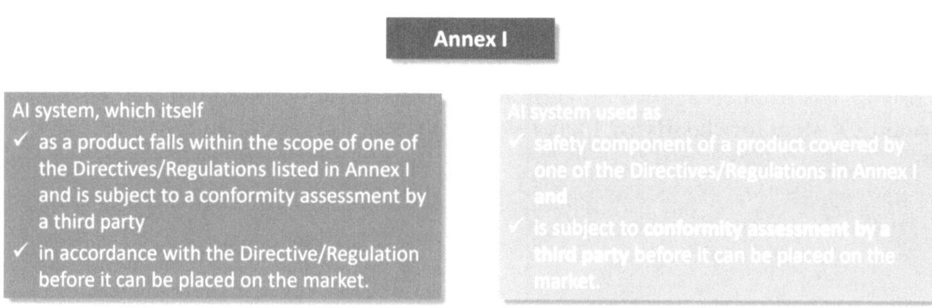

Figure 11: High-risk AI systems – Annex I

2. Independent classification (reference to Annex III)

31 However, as not all problematic areas of application of AI systems are subject to European product safety law, Art. 6 para. 2 classification as a high-risk AI system. **The**

[27] See Binder/Egli MMR 2024, 626 (627).

AI Act independently classifies this second group of AI systems as high-risk AI systems via Annex III due to their sensitive area of application.

The appendix breaks down the different areas in which the AI systems are used, namely 32

- Biometrics, insofar as their use is permitted under relevant Union or national law, No. 1,
- Critical infrastructure, No. 2,
- Education and vocational training, No. 3,
- Employment, personnel management and access to self-employment, No. 4,
- Accessibility and use of basic private and basic public services and benefits, No. 5,
- Law enforcement, insofar as their use is permitted under relevant Union or national law, No. 6,
- Migration, asylum and border control, insofar as their use is permitted under relevant Union or national law, No. 7 and
- Administration of justice and democratic processes, No. 8.

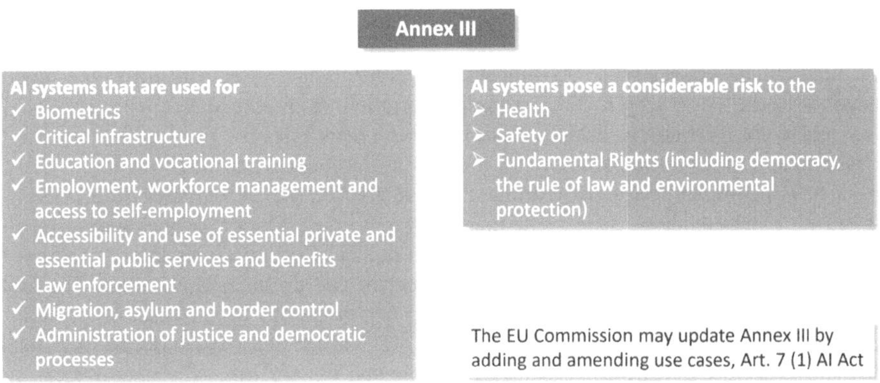

Figure 12: High-risk AI systems – Annex III

3. Exception/re-exception

By way of derogation from Art. 6 para. 2 AI Act, an AI system is not considered high-risk if it does not pose a significant risk of harm to the health, safety or fundamental rights of natural persons by, among other things, **not significantly influencing** the outcome of a **decision-making** process, Art. 6 para. 3 sentence 1 AI Act. 33

This is the case if one or more of the following conditions are met: The AI system is only intended to, 34

- to carry out a narrowly defined procedural task,
- to improve the result of a previously completed human activity,
- recognize decision patterns or deviations from previous decision patterns, and is not intended to replace or influence previously completed human judgment without appropriate human review; or
- carry out a preparatory task for an assessment that is relevant for the purposes of the use cases listed in Annex III, Art. 6 para. 3 sentence 2 AI Act.

35 The above-mentioned restrictions were imposed by the **EU Parliament** and the **Council**, which prevailed in the **trilogue.**[28] The EU Commission's original draft still classified all AI systems listed in Annex III of the AI Act as high-risk.[29] In the sense of a counter-exception, an AI system listed in Annex III is considered high-risk if it carries out **profiling** of natural persons, Art. 6 para. 3 sentence 3 AI Act. The AI Act defines the term profiling, with reference to the GDPR, as any type of automated processing of personal data that uses this data to analyze, evaluate or predict personal aspects. Personal aspects include, in particular, work performance, economic situation, health, reliability as well as behavior, whereabouts or upcoming relocation, Art. 3 no. 52 AI Act in conjunction with Art. 4 no. 4 GDPR.[30]

36 If, according to these criteria, a **provider** comes to the **conclusion** that its AI system listed in Annex III is nevertheless **not high-risk**, it must document its assessment and submit it to the national supervisory authority upon request, Art. 6 para. 4 sentences 1 and 3 AI Act. Only after the documentation has been completed may the system be placed on the market or put into operation. They are also subject **to** the **registration obligation** pursuant to Art. 49 para. 2 AI Act.

4. Specification in the Commission Guidelines

37 Pursuant to Art. 6 para. 5 AI Act, the EU Commission, after consulting the European AI Board (→ § 13 mn. 22), is to publish guidelines in accordance with Art. 96 AI Act and a comprehensive list of rules and counterexamples for the legally compliant classification of AI systems within 18 months of the AI Act entering into force. Art. 6 para. 5 AI Act refers to the provisions of Art. 96 AI Act, which regulates the EU Commission's competence to issue guidelines (→ § 13 mn. 6). The guidelines serve to provide greater legal clarity by giving insight into the EU Commission's interpretation of the AI Act in order to ensure its coherent, effective and uniform application. The first guidelines were issued on 4.2.2025 pursuant to Art. 96 para. 1 lit. b AI Act on prohibited practices of artificial intelligence (→ mn. 4).[31] Only two days later, on 6.2.2025, guidelines on the definition of AI systems followed (→ § 2 mn. 15).[32] Most recently, on 18.7.2025, the EU Commission published guidelines for providers of general-purpose AI models (GPAI guidelines).[33] Further guidelines are currently pending. The guidelines are always formally adopted by the EU Commission and are applicable from that point in time.

---

[28] See also Schwartmann/Köhler in: Schwartmann/Keber/Zenner, Part 2, Chapter 1, para. 126, 129 (Council).

[29] Ashkar/Schröder BB 2024, 771 (773).

[30] Cf. on the requirements of the AI Act and the GDPR in particular Paal/Hüger MMR 2024, 540 (542).

[31] COMMUNICATION TO THE COMMISSION Approval of the content of the draft Communication from the Commission – Commission Guidelines on prohibited artificial intelligence practices established by Regulation (EU) 2024/1689 (AI Act) und Annex to the Communication to the Commission Approval of the content of the draft Communication from the Commission – Commission Guidelines on prohibited artificial intelligence practices established by Regulation (EU) 2024/1689 (AI Act).

[32] Annex to the Communication to the Commission Approval of the content of the draft Communication from the Commission – Commission Guidelines on the definition of an artificial intelligence system established by Regulation (EU) 2024/1689 (AI Act).

[33] Annex to the Communication to the Commission Approval of the content of the draft Communication from the Commission – Guidelines on the scope of the obligations for general-purpose AI models established by Regulation (EU) 2024/1689 (AI Act).

5. Delegated acts

In addition, Art. 6 para. 6 and para. 7 AI Act empowers the EU Commission to issue **delegated acts** within the meaning of Art. 97 AI Act to amend the current classification conditions. 38

According to Art. 6 para. 6 AI Act, the EU Commission can adapt the regulations in Art. 6 para. 3 subpara. 2 AI Act by adding or changing conditions. According to Art. 6 para. 7 AI Act, **it** is **possible to delete** previously defined conditions. 39

The adoption of delegated acts must take account of **market developments** and **technological progress** and must **not reduce** the current **level of protection** with regard to health, safety and fundamental rights in the EU, Art. 6 para. 8 AI Act. 40

Art. 7 para. 1 AI Act also authorizes the EU Commission to add further use cases to the catalog of life circumstances or areas of application in Annex III or to amend the existing list. This allows the EU Commission to react flexibly to **technological progress** as required.[34] 41

III. AI systems with transparency risk

Below the level of **high-risk** AI systems in the **risk pyramid** are AI systems with a **transparency risk**. The European legislator recognizes this risk in AI systems that **interact directly with humans**. 42

In the pyramid that typically illustrates the risk-based regulatory approach, the transparency risk that Art. 50 AI Act addresses is regularly presented below the obligations for high-risk AI systems and is often referred to synonymously as **moderate or limited risk**.[35] This presentation is misleading in that the obligations for high-risk AI systems and the transparency obligations are **not** necessarily mutually **exclusive**: Providers and deployers of high-risk AI systems must also ensure that systems that come into contact with humans clearly disclose their AI nature. According to Art. 50 para. 5 AI Act, this information must be provided in clear and unambiguous language at the latest at **the time of the first interaction**, as barrier-free as possible. 43

(AI) **chatbots**, for example, are affected by the transparency risk. Within the meaning of Art. 50 para. 1 AI Act, they are intended as AI systems for direct interaction with natural persons (→ § 10 mn. 3). **Deepfakes** are also covered – i.e. image, audio or video content manipulated by AI that resembles existing persons, objects or events and falsely appears to a person to be truthful (→ § 10 mn. 5).[36] 44

IV. AI systems with no or minimal risk

At the lowest level of the risk pyramid are AI systems with no or at most **minimal risk**. The vast majority of AI systems currently and in future use in the EU are expected to fall within this risk level.[37] Typical examples are **AI-based video games** or **spam filters**. Legal tech AI systems are also likely to be AI systems with minimal risks.[38] Providers can develop and comply with voluntary codes of conduct for them (→ § 14 mn. 1). 45

---

[34] See also Schwartmann/Köhler in: Schwartmann/Keber/Zenner, Part 2, Chapter 1, para. 146.
[35] Chibanguza/Steege NJW 2024, 1769 (1773).
[36] Bock, Deepfakes, 25; Kumkar/Rapp ZfDR 2022, 199 (223).
[37] Ammann/Pohle CB 5/2024, 137 (137).
[38] See Block/Jung/Wendt CRi 2023, 97 (102 et seq.).

V. General-purpose AI systems (GPAI)

46 In the course of the trilogue, a further risk category has emerged in the form of general purpose AI (GPAI) systems.[39] A GPAI system is an **AI system that is based on a general purpose AI model** (GPAI model) and is capable of serving a **variety of purposes** both for direct use and for integration into other AI systems (Art. 3 para. 66 AI Act). What a GPAI model is, is defined in Art. 3 No. 63 AI Act. The obligations of providers of these models are governed by Art. 53 AI Act. GPAI models must be reviewed to determine whether they pose a **systemic risk** pursuant to Art. 51 para. 1 AI Act. In this case, providers are subject to further obligations under Art. 55 AI Act.

47 GPAI models can pose systemic risks if they **have** an **exceptionally high impact** or are widely used. Art. 3 para. 64 AI Act defines particularly high impact as capabilities that correspond to or exceed the most advanced AI models with a general purpose. Particularly powerful models, for example, can be misused for far-reaching cyberattacks.

48 In view of their initially unspecific area of application, it was not clear for a long time how these models should be regulated at all. Ultimately, a **graduated system** that differentiates between GPAI models with a lower risk and those with a systemic risk on the basis of **impact** was a compromise. Providers of systemic risk AI models are subject to further obligations (Art. 53 and Art. 55 AI Act).

49 With regard to the differentiation 'impact', it was decided to use **floating point operations (FLOPs)** as a basis. Art. 3 No. 67 AI Act defines floating point operations as arithmetic operations or assignments involving floating point numbers, which are a subset of real numbers typically represented on computers by the product of an integer with fixed precision and a fixed base with an integer exponent. The AI Act therefore focuses on how many calculations underlie the training of an AI model.

If the threshold of 10^{25} FLOPs is exceeded, a GPAI model is considered a model with systemic risk and is subject to additional requirements, Art. 51 para. 2 AI Act.

The focus on floating point operations has led to confusion and subsequent criticism. However, this was at least partly due to confusion between the terms **FLOPs** for floating point operations and **FLOPS** for floating point operations per second: The term FLOPS refers to the performance of a computer system based on the number of floating point calculations per second. The AI Act, on the other hand, refers solely to floating point operations (FLOPs) for classification purposes. It therefore only focuses on how many calculations were used to train the GPAI model. The performance of the computer used for this purpose, i.e., how many FLOPS it has, is initially irrelevant.

50 Models that remain below this level of impact are not subject to any additional requirements. This is likely to be particularly relevant for the systems currently being developed in the EU, such as Mistral AI in France. France in particular fought persistently in the trilogue to keep the regulation of GPAI at a level that would not hinder Mistral AI's competitiveness.[40] The surprise was correspondingly great when **Mistral AI** announced a multi-year partnership with Microsoft at the beginning of March 2024 to distribute its new Mistral Large language model via the company's Azure Cloud.[41]

51 Microsoft's investment of EUR 15 million, which will accompany the partnership, caused particular discussion. The deal once again led to the debate as to whether it is

[39] See also Ammann/Pohle CB 5/2024, 137 (142).
[40] Cf. Kilian EuZW 2024, 145 (146); Ammann/Pohle CB 5/2024, 137 (142).
[41] S. https://azure.microsoft.com/de-de.

even possible for Europe to create its own tech giants (not least in view of regulation). The underlying concern is that major US corporations are taking over promising European companies and that Europe runs the risk of **falling** even further and faster **behind the USA and China** in the age of AI.[42] These concerns were recently reinforced by the US announcement that it would invest US$500 billion in the Stargate project to build an AI infrastructure that would secure America's leading position. Almost at the same time, the Chinese AI model Deepseek caused a stir because it outperformed the leading American models in some benchmarks, and its launch is accordingly being described as the Sputnik moment of AI.[43]

Europe now seeks to counter concerns that it will be left behind in the global AI **52** race with a joint effort that can also focus strategically on alternative fields. Instead of entering into a competition for ever larger models, Europe could focus on innovative algorithms for smaller data sets.[44] Mistral AI, for example, has introduced Codestral 25.01, an open source model that sets new standards in code generation and, with its efficient use of resources, even outperforms OpenAI's o1 model with 95.3% accuracy in fill-in-the-middle tasks.

---

[42] The study "Large AI models for Germany" by the Academy for Artificial Intelligence in the German AI Association, from 2022, shows that 73 % of large basic models have been published by US companies since 2017, with China accounting for 15 %, see p. 56 of the study; Hacker/Berz ZRP 2023, 226 (226 et seq.).

[43] Voß, Der Deepseek-Schock, *Tagesspiegel* from 28.1.2025.

[44] Dehmel/Hecker KIR 2025, 215.

§ 6
Requirements for high-risk AI systems

Literature: *Biermann, Friedrich*, Wissenszurechnung und Künstliche Intelligenz, 2022; *Bomhard, David/Merkle, Marieke*, Regulation of Artificial Intelligence, EuCML 2021, 257; *Brockman, John*, Was sollen wir von Künstlicher Intelligenz halten? 2017; *Casper, Anna Felicitas*, Rechtliche Chancen und Grenzen der automatisierten Entscheidungsunterstützung und Entscheidungsfindung in der Medizin, 2024; *Daute, Ingvar/Sütthoff, Alicia*, Vereinbarkeit von Produktbeobachtungspflicht und Datenschutz beim autonomen Kraftfahrzeug, EuZW 2023, 500; *Denga, Michael*, Konformitätsbewertung von KI-Systemen, ZfPC 2023, 154; *Denga, Michael*, Unternehmenshaftung für KI – zur Konformitätsbewertung in Permanenz, CR 2023, 277; *Dienes, Jennifer*, Anforderungen an die menschliche Aufsicht über Künstliche Intelligenz, MMR 2024, 456; *Frank, Justus/Heine, Maurice*, Arbeitsrechtliche Dimension der KI-Verordnung, NZA 2024, 433; *Fuderer, Markus*, Doppelte Konformitätsbewertung bei KI-basierten Medizinprodukten?, MPR 2022, 121; *Gassner, Ulrich*, Menschliche Aufsicht über intelligente Medizinprodukte, MPR 2023, 5; *Gengler, Eva*, Feministische Künstliche Intelligenz, Rethinking Law 6.2022, 32; *Heil, Maria*, Die neue KI-Verordnung (E) – Regulatorische Herausforderungen für KI-basierte Medizinprodukte-Software, MPR 2022, 1; *Knappertsbusch, Inka*, Innovative HR-Lösungen durch KI: Potenziale und rechtliche Rahmenbedingungen, LTZ 2024, 40; *Krüger, Daniel/Wagner, Susan*, Das Phänomen "Künstliche Intelligenz" aus regulatorischer und haftungsrechtlicher Sicht, ZfPC 2023, 124; *Lachenmann, Matthias*, EU-Rat stimmt KI-Verordnung zu – neue Pflichten für Unternehmen, MMR-Aktuell 2024, 01359; *Lang, Flavia/Reinbach, Hubertus:* Künstliche Intelligenz im Arbeitsrecht, NZA 2023, 1273; *Langenbucher, Katja*, Diskriminierung bei der Vergabe von Verbraucherkrediten?, BKR 2023, 205; *Lingaht, Felix*, Organizational duties of the AG board of directors when using AI systems, JURA 2023, 940; *Malgieri, Gianclaudio/Pasquale, Frank*, Licensing high-risk artificial intelligence: Toward ex ante justification for a disruptive technology, Computer Law & Security Review, Volume 52, 2024, 105899; *Martini, Mario*, Blackbox Algorithmus – Grundfragen einer Regulierung Künstlicher Intelligenz, 2019; *Roos, Philipp/Weitz, Casper Alexander*, Hochrisiko-KI-Systeme im Kommissionsentwurf für eine KI-Verordnung, MMR 2021, 844; *Schwartmann, Rolf/Keber, Tobias/Zenner, Kai*, KI-Verordnung. Leitfaden für die Praxis, 2024; *Schulz-Große, Stefanie/Genske, Anna*, Auswirkungen der neuen KI-Verordnung auf den Behandlungsalltag – Datenschutzrechtliche Anforderungen und Sorgfaltspflichten der Behandelnden beim Einsatz von künstlicher Intelligenz zu Behandlungszwecken, GuP 2023, 81; *Ströbel, Lukas/Grau, Robert*, KI-gestützte Medizin-Apps. Legal challenges of an interdisciplinary product, ZD 2022, 599; *Thiermann, Arne/Böck, Nicole*, Künstliche Intelligenz in Medizinprodukten, RDi 2022, 333; *Veale, Michael/Zuiderveen Borgesius, Frederik*, Demystifying the Draft EU Artificial Intelligence Act, CRi (4)2021, 97.

1 High-risk AI systems are at the **heart of the AI Act**. The list of obligations for providers of these AI systems is extensive. Most of the requirements must be met before the system is placed on the market or put into operation:

2 Under Art. 16 AI Act, providers must ensure that their AI systems meet the requirements set out in Art. 8–15 AI Act before the AI system is launched on the market. According to the technology-neutral approach of the AI Act, the specific **purpose of** the AI system is always decisive.[1] At the same time, the provider must take into account the generally acknowledged state of the art with regard to AI-related technologies, Art. 8 para. 1 AI Act.

3 However, AI systems are often not designed as independent (**stand-alone**) **AI systems**, but are **embedded** in a product. If the AI system becomes part of a product that is subject to a product safety regulation under the New Legislative Framework,

[1] Schürmann ZD 2022, 316 (317).

providers must ensure that their product fully complies with all applicable requirements: **Compliance** must be established both with regard to the requirements of the AI Act and with regard to the parallel standards of the respective product safety law – such as the requirements for the safety of toys (Annex I Section A No. 2) or medical devices (Annex I Section A No. 11).[2]

In order to reduce the burden on providers and to create **consistency** in the test procedures and documentation, the AI Act allows the integration of the tests and records required by it into the procedures prescribed by the respective sector-specific product safety law (→ mn. 28). 4

The obligations that the AI Act imposes on high-risk AI systems include the following in the **second section** entitled "Requirements for high-risk AI systems" 5

- the establishment of a **risk management system** that must be applied, documented and maintained (Art. 9 AI Act),
- compliance with **data governance** (Art. 10 AI Act),
- the preparation of **technical documentation** (Art. 11 AI Act),
- enabling the **automatic recording of** events (logs) (Art. 12 AI Act),
- compliance with **transparency requirements** and provision of information to deployers (Art. 13 AI Act),
- enabling effective **human oversight** (Art. 14 AI Act) and finally the duty,
- an appropriate level of **accuracy, robustness and cybersecurity** (Art. 15 AI Act).

Art. 16 then begins the **third section,** which sets out obligations for providers and deployers of high-risk AI systems and other parties involved. The obligations of providers include, 6

- indicate the registered **trade name** or registered trade mark and their **contact address** (Art. 16 AI Act),
- have a **quality management system** (Art. 17 AI Act),
- the **documentation** and (Art. 18 AI Act)
- retain the **automatically generated logs** (Art. 19 AI Act),
- ensure that the AI system is subject to a **conformity assessment** (Art. 43 AI Act),
- to issue an **EU declaration of conformity** (Art. 47 AI Act),
- affix the **CE marking** (Art. 48 AI Act) and
- comply with the **registration obligations** (Art. 49 AI Act).

I. Risk management

For high-risk AI systems, a **risk management system** must be set up, used and maintained **throughout the life of the AI system** in accordance with Art. 9 AI Act. The legislator understands a risk management system to be a **continuous, iterative process** that is regularly reviewed and improved.[3] The risk management system should make it easier for the provider to assess the risks that typically arise from the use of the AI system. The scope of consideration initially extends to the use of the AI system in accordance with its **intended purpose.** The risk management system thus focuses on those risks that are known or at least foreseeable within the intended purpose of the 7

[2] Frost/Steininger/Vivekens MPR 2024, 4 (12).
[3] Hansen in: Schwartmann/Keber/Zenner, Part 2, Chapter 1, para. 282.

high-risk AI system and that affect health, safety or fundamental rights. At the same time, however, reasonably **foreseeable misuse** of the AI system must also be taken into account, i.e. those applications that may result from foreseeable human behavior or interaction with other systems, Art. 3 No. 13 AI Act.

The AI Act does not **specify** the **concrete design** and testing of the risk management system. It is the responsibility of the **harmonized standards** to define these (→ § 9 mn. 1). They will be developed by the organizations responsible for EU standardization, CEN (European Committee for Standardization) and CENELEC (European Committee for Electrotechnical Standardization), and are expected by the end of 2025. There are expected to be around 20 standards in total, with those for risk and quality management taking on an overarching function.

8 The risk management system also includes the provider's **product monitoring obligation**: According to Art. 72 AI Act, providers are obliged to keep an eye on their high-risk AI system even after it has been placed on the market. To this end, they must set up a compliance structure that is adequate for the high-risk AI system.

9 Overall, Art. 9 AI Act thus addresses those risks that can be avoided by ideally considering them during the development of the high-risk AI system (**compliance by design**) or by providing sufficient technical information to mitigate or eliminate them during the use of the AI system at the latest.

II. Data governance

10 High-risk AI systems are regularly based on models that are **trained, validated and tested** with **data**. This data must meet **quality criteria** that are specified in Art. 10 AI Act.

11 To ensure that the data records meet the requirements, they undergo a data governance or data management process. Its specific design must be **adequat**e for the intended purpose and thus the **risk propensity** of the AI system.

12 In any case, the **conceptual decisions** made with regard to the **training, validation and test data** used must be mapped in the data management process. Since at least the decisions on the training and validation data sets are already made at model level, the data governance obligations of the AI system provider and those of the AI model provider interlock here. The AI system provider is also dependent on the **information provided by the model provider** with regard to the origin of the data, its collection methods, suitability and the data preparation processes carried out, which include **annotation, labeling, cleansing and aggregation**. In return, the latter is obliged to provide it. If personal data is used, the original purpose of the data collection must be noted. The Higher Regional Court of Cologne considers the collection of 'public' personal data from social networks to be permissible.[4]

13 If, exceptionally, a high-risk AI system is not based on a trained AI model, the following requirements only apply to test data sets, Art. 10 para. 6 AI Act.

14 If **assumptions** were **formulated** on the basis of the data, these must also be stated.

15 An important part of assessing the suitability of a data set is examining the extent to which the data set **depicts and reproduces** possible **biases**.[5] Particularly critical are those biases that could affect the **health and safety** of individuals, have a negative im-

[4] OLG Köln of 23.5.2025 – 15 UKl 2/25, ECLI:DE:OLGK:2025:0523.15UKL2.25.00.
[5] Guijarro Santos ZfDR 1/2023, 23 (30).

pact on fundamental rights[6] or lead to prohibited **discrimination.**[7] The assessment is all the more relevant as the data outputs are reused and influence future applications.[8]

In addition to the mere identification, the legislator therefore requires measures to **prevent and mitigate identified biases**, the identification of relevant **data gaps** or deficiencies that prevent compliance with the AI Act and considerations as to how these gaps and deficiencies can be remedied. 16

In any case, the training, validation and test data sets must be relevant, **sufficiently representative** and **as error-free** and complete **as possible** with regard to the intended purpose. The requirement "as error-free as possible" was added in the trilogue at the request of the EU Parliament, as the EU Commission's original demand for complete freedom from errors had to be classified as unrealistic.[9] 17

In order to achieve the required degree of accuracy, suitable statistical characteristics must be used in advance. The data sets must **reflect** the **typical geographical, contextual, behavioral or functional conditions** in which the AI system will actually be used. 18

Where this is indispensable for the detection and correction of biases, providers may exceptionally process individual categories of personal data, provided that they take appropriate safeguards in favor of fundamental rights and freedoms. In particular, reasons must be given as to why **artificial or anonymized data** cannot be used effectively to detect and **correct the biases.** 19

In addition, the categories of personal data are subject to technical restrictions, including security and **data protection measures.** This includes **access restrictions and documentation obligations** in accordance with the GDPR,[10] the Directive on Data Protection in Criminal Matters[11] and the Data Protection Regulation.[12] 20

As soon as the goal of correcting a distortion or the end of the storage period for the personal data has been reached, the **data** must **be deleted.** 21

---

[6] Guijarro Santos ZfDR 1/2023, 23 (31).

[7] Cf. Langenbucher BKR 2023, 205 (206); Gengler Rethinking Law 6.2022, 32 (34); Knappertsbusch LTZ 2024, 40 (40); Lang/Reinbach NZA 2023, 1273 (1274).

[8] Wachter/Mittelstadt/Russell, Why fairness cannot be automated: Bridging the gap between EU non-discrimination law and AI, https://ssrn.com/abstract=3547922.

[9] See in this regard in detail. Feldkamp/Kappler/Poretschkin/Schmitz/Weiss ZfDR 1/2024, 60 (103).

[10] Regulation (EU) 2016/679 of the European Parliament and of the Council of 27.4.2016 on the protection of natural persons with regard to the processing of personal data and on the free movement of such data, and repealing Directive 95/46/EC (General Data Protection Regulation – GDPR), OJ L 119, 4.5.2016, pp. 1–88; for the relationship between the provisions of the GDPR and those of the AI Act, see OLG Cologne, 23.5.2025 – 15 UKI 2/25, ECLI:DE:OLGK:2025:0523.15UKL2.25.00.

[11] Directive (EU) 2016/680 of the European Parliament and of the Council of 27.4.2016 on the protection of natural persons with regard to the processing of personal data by competent authorities for the purposes of the prevention, investigation, detection or prosecution of criminal offences or the execution of criminal penalties, and on the free movement of such data, and repealing Council Framework Decision 2008/977/JHA, OJ L 119, 4.5.2016, pp. 89–131.

[12] Regulation (EU) 2018/1725 of the European Parliament and of the Council of 23.10.2018 on the protection of natural persons with regard to the processing of personal data by the Union institutions, bodies, offices and agencies and on the free movement of such data, and repealing Regulation (EC) No 45/2001 and Decision No 1247/2002/EC, OJ L 295, 21.11.2018, pp. 39–98.

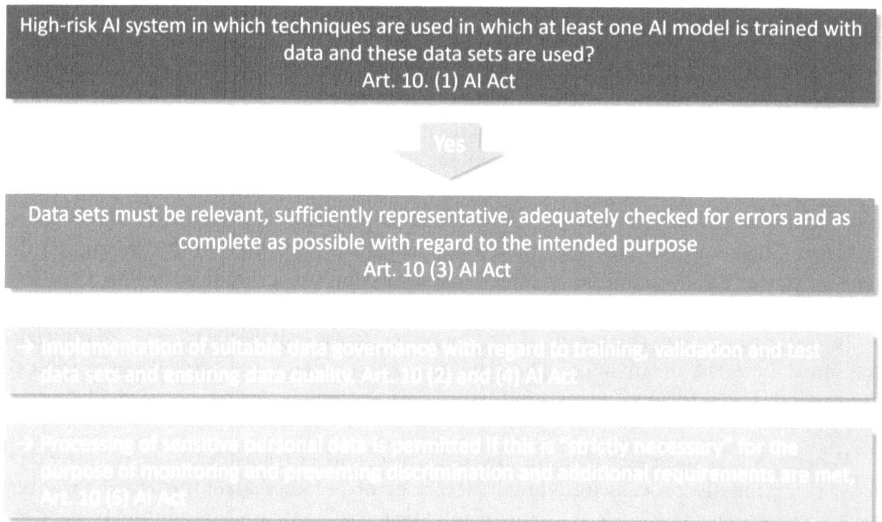

Figure 13: Data governance

III. Technical documentation

22 Art. 11 AI Act sets out requirements for the **technical documentation** of a high-risk AI system. The provider and deployer of the system can use the technical documentation to prove that the AI system meets the compliance requirements. This proof must be provided to the national supervisory authority[13], but the notified bodies also require the information.

23 The technical documentation is created for the first time **before** the AI system is **placed on the market**. It must be kept **up to date** during ongoing operation. With regard to the content requirements, Art. 11 AI Act stipulates that the technical documentation must contain at least the information listed in Annex IV in a clear and comprehensible form. The reference to Annex IV leads to very detailed requirements, which can be divided into **four basic categories. Firstly,** the Annex requires a general description of the AI system, including information on its intended purpose and how the AI system can be put into operation. If the AI system is part of a product, its external characteristics must be described.

24 As a **second category**, Annex IV requires a detailed description of the components of the AI system. This also includes the methods and steps for developing the AI, possibly using pre-trained systems. The general logic of the AI system and a description of the expected quality of the output also fall under this category.

25 The **third category** of Annex IV requires detailed information on the monitoring, functioning and control of the AI system, in particular with regard to its capabilities and performance limits. Finally, Annex IV requires extensive explanations on the suitability of the performance metrics for the specific AI system.

26 The EU Commission may **update Annex IV** by delegated act to ensure that the technical documentation always follows technological progress.

[13] See also Hansen in: Schwartmann/Keber/Zenner, Part 2, Chapter 1, para. 309.

As the requirements for technical documentation are quite extensive, small and medium-sized enterprises (**SMEs**), which also include **start-ups**, benefit from simplifications. They may provide the information in a simplified manner. However, they must use a form provided by the EU Commission when claiming the **privilege**. Its use creates desirable synergy effects, as it is also accepted by the notified bodies for conformity assessment. 27

There are also **simplifications** for high-risk AI systems that are embedded in a product that is regulated under product safety law in accordance with Annex I Section A of the AI Act (→ § 9 mn. 14). Providers of such a high-risk AI system only have to prepare a **single technical documentation**, which then covers all the information required by the AI Act and other information required under product safety law. 28

IV. Recording obligations

The recording obligations under Art. 12 AI Act require the **automated recording of** certain events: To an extent that is adequate for the intended purpose of the AI system, it must **record** all **situations** that pose a **risk to** the **health, safety** or **fundamental rights** of persons[14]. All events that lead to a **significant change in the AI system** must also be recorded. 29

In order to make it easier for providers of high-risk AI systems to fulfill their obligations under Art. 72 AI Act, Art. 12 AI Act also includes the **market surveillance** of AI systems after they have been placed on the market in the record-keeping obligation. Art. 72 AI Act obliges providers of high-risk AI systems not only to monitor the market for their systems on the market, but also to **document** the monitoring activities. 30

However, Art. 12 of the AI Act not only imposes obligations on providers, but also includes the **deployers** of AI systems via Art. 26 para. 6 AI Act. They too must retain the **logs automatically generated** by their high-risk AI system for an appropriate period of at least six months. 31

Biometric remote identification systems are explicitly covered: Their logging functions must at least capture the record of each period of use of the system including the date and time of the start and end of each use. In addition, the **reference database** with which the system compares the input data must be specified. In this context, the input data with which the query led to a match must also be recorded, as well as the identity of the persons who checked the result (→ mn. 53). 32

V. Transparency and provision of information to deployers

With its provisions, Art. 13 AI Act creates the **framework conditions that deployers need** in order to fulfill their obligations under Section 3 of the AI Act. After all, deployers need a range of information in order to be able to interpret and use the results of the AI system they use. 33

To this end, they are **dependent on the provider of** the AI system, who is obliged to provide transparency and information under Art. 13 of the AI Act: Providers must already **develop** high-risk AI systems in such a **transparent** manner that deployers are 34

[14] ISd Art. 3 No. 19 of Regulation (EU) 2019/1020 of 20.6.2019 on market surveillance and compliance of products and amending Directive 2004/42/EC and Regulations (EC) No. 765/2008 and (EU) No. 305/2011, OJ L 169, 25.6.2019, pp. 1 et seqq.

able to evaluate the results of the AI. Transparency must be established in a suitable manner.

35 Specifically, Art. 13 AI Act mentions **instructions for use,** which the provider must regularly make available **digitally**, and in any case **in an accessible form**. The instructions for use should contain the relevant information completely, precisely, correctly and clearly.

36 This abstract requirement includes at least the **name and contact details of the provider** and, if applicable, its authorized representative. With regard to the AI system, the **characteristics, capabilities** and **performance limits** must be specified.

37 The **characteristics** include the intended purpose, while the capabilities include the degree of accuracy, stating the relevant key figures. To determine the **performance limits,** the robustness and cybersecurity that have been tested and validated for the system must be specified, as well as all at least foreseeable circumstances that could influence the expected level. In addition to the intended use of the high-risk AI system, the consideration horizon must again include foreseeable misuse – at least if it poses risks to health, safety or fundamental rights.

38 If the information is required to interpret the results of the high-risk AI system, the instructions for use must also refer to the **technical capabilities** and the **training, validation and test data sets** used. The required computing and hardware resources, the expected lifetime of the high-risk AI system and all necessary maintenance and care measures must also be mentioned. This also includes **software updates.**

39 If it is already clear at the time of the initial conformity assessment that the high-risk AI system and its performance will undergo **subsequent changes**, the provider must already specify these in the instructions for use.

40 Finally, the instructions must provide information on the measures to be taken to ensure that the AI system can be **effectively supervised** by natural **persons.**

VI. Human oversight

41 High-risk AI systems must be accessible to effective human oversight, Art. 14 AI Act. This requirement must already be observed during development and therefore primarily addresses the **provider.**

42 Human oversight serves to **minimize risks** or, in the best case, to **prevent them,** Art. 14 para. 2 AI Act. To a certain extent, it is intended to act as a last line of defense against those risks to health, safety and fundamental rights that persist despite compliance with the other requirements for high-risk AI systems mentioned above.

43 Recital 27 states that the **ethics guidelines of the High-Level Expert Group** on Artificial Intelligence from 2019 already included the requirement of human oversight (→ § 3 mn. 9). Human action and human oversight means that an AI system is developed and used as an instrument that serves people, respects human dignity and personal autonomy and functions in such a way that it **can be adequately controlled** and supervised **by humans.** With regard to the substantive requirements for human oversight, the last half-sentence is likely to address the core element of the legislator's required understanding of the supervisor of the AI system, Art. 14 para. 4 lit. a AI Act.[15]

[15] See Dienes MMR 2024, 456 (456): "The legislative apprehension probably corresponds roughly to the quote from two AI computer scientists: "We may build them, but we don't understand them", with reference to Brockman/Kleinberg/Mullainathan, Künstliche Intelligenz, 96 and Martini, Blackbox, 44.

According to Art. 14 para. 3 AI Act, the required **level of** human oversight is risk-based and depends on the **degree of adaptability or autonomy** and the specific **area of application** of the high-risk AI system. In addition to the intended use of the AI system, the provider must also take into account reasonably foreseeable misuse when assessing the risk horizon, Art. 14 para. 2 AI Act. 44

From a technical point of view, human oversight can be carried out by means of **various precautions**. According to Art. 14 para. 3 lit. a AI Act, these can be built directly into the high-risk AI system. If a **human-machine interface** is not available, the provider must at least provide for those precautions that make human oversight possible, Art. 14 para. 3 lit. b AI Act. Implementation then takes place at the next stage of the value chain **by the deployer of** the AI system. To this end, the provider must prepare the high-risk AI system in such a way that the future supervisor is able to provide oversight, Art. 14 para. 4 sentence 1 AI Act. 45

The **implementation** of the preparations made by the provider is then carried out by the **deployer**, Art. 14 para. 3 lit. b AI Act. The deployer must take appropriate technical and organizational measures to ensure the use of the high-risk AI system in accordance with the attached instructions for use and other obligations and to appoint a natural person to supervise the AI.[16] In doing so, it must ensure that the supervisor appointed by it has the necessary **AI literacy** to fulfill the tasks assigned to it, Art. 26 para. 2, Art. 4 AI Act in conjunction with recital 91 (→ § 4 mn. 1). 46

The **requirements** for the necessary understanding of AI were **reduced** in the course of the legislative process:[17] While the EU Commission's original draft still stipulated that the supervisor must ultimately be able to "fully understand" the capabilities and limitations of the high-risk AI system,[18] the Council draft had already deleted the adverb. It only required an "understanding" of the capabilities and limitations of the high-risk AI system in order to properly monitor its operation.[19] The EU Parliament reduced the scope of understanding even further in its draft version[20] and demanded that the supervisor should "**know and sufficiently understand**" the relevant **capabilities and limitations** of the high-risk AI system while maintaining proportionality. The successive reduction of the required scope of understanding thus took place from a "full understanding" to a (simple) "understanding" to a (mere) "knowledge and sufficient understanding".[21] 47

As a result, the AI Act today requires that the AI system must be made available to the deployer in such a way that the **supervisors** are **reasonably and proportionately** able to **adequately** understand and **monitor** the relevant capabilities and limitations of the high-risk AI system, Art. 14 para. 4 lit. a AI Act. The importance of the **pragmatic restriction** to an appropriate level is reflected in the double use of the adverb. 48

However, adequate understanding also requires **AI literacy** pursuant to Art. 4 AI Act (→ § 4 mn. 1). This is to be understood as **corresponding specialist knowledge** that takes into account the technical knowledge, experience, education and training as well as the context in which the AI system is to be used and the persons (groups) for 49

---

16 Dienes MMR 2024, 456 (458).

17 Cf. in detail. Dienes MMR 2024, 456 (459).

18 Art. 14 para. 4 lit. a of the European Commission's draft, Proposal for a Regulation laying down harmonized rules on Artificial Intelligence, of 21.4.2021, COM(2021), 206 final.

19 Art. 14(4)(a) of the Draft Council of the European Union, General Approach to the Proposal for a Regulation laying down harmonized rules on Artificial Intelligence, 6.12.2022, 2021/0106(COD).

20 Art. 14(4)(a) of the European Parliament's draft, Amendments to the proposal for a Regulation laying down harmonized rules on Artificial Intelligence, 14.6.2023, P9_TA(2023)0236, available at: https://www.europarl.europa.eu/doceo/document/TA-9-2023-0236_DE.pdf.

21 Dienes MMR 2024, 456 (459).

whom it is to be used. The required competence is measured according to the complexity of the AI system. Finally, the supervising person must, among other things, understand its capabilities and limitations, for example in order to be able to **recognize malfunctions, anomalies and unexpected performance** and, if necessary, even remedy them, Art. 14 para. 4 lit. a AI Act.

50 The required knowledge could be acquired through special training or **courses** tailored to the AI used.[22]The required knowledge can also be ensured through the **cooperation** of several people with expertise in different fields.

51 In addition, the supervising persons must be aware of any **automation biases**. In other words, they must have developed an awareness of whether they are inclined to **place excessive trust** in the results produced by the AI system, Art. 14 para. 4 lit. b AI Act.[23] This is all the more important when high-risk AI systems provide information or recommendations on the basis of which natural persons make decisions.[24]

52 In order to be able to interpret the results of an AI system correctly, the supervisor should have knowledge of **current interpretation tools and methods** and use them, Art. 14 para. 4 lit. c AI Act. Of course, the supervisor can also come to the conclusion not to use the high-risk AI system in a certain situation or to disregard, override or even reverse the result, Art. 14 para. 4 lit. d AI Act. To this end, it must be able to intervene in the operation of the high-risk AI system and interrupt it by means of a "stop button" or similar and bring the system to a **safe standstill**, Art. 14 para. 4 lit. e AI Act.

53 For high-risk AI systems for **remote biometric identification**, Art. 14 para. 5 AI Act sets out separate requirements for human oversight: they must be designed in such a way that the deployer **does not make decisions based solely** on the **identification result** produced by the system. Instead, the identification must be **checked** and confirmed separately by at least two natural persons. Both persons must have the necessary competence, training and authorization to do so. As a counter-exception, the requirement of separate verification by at least two persons does not apply to those AI systems for real-time biometric identification that are used in law enforcement, migration, border control or asylum if this appears disproportionate under European or national law.

VII. Accuracy, robustness and cybersecurity

54 High-risk AI systems must be developed in such a way that they achieve an appropriate level of **accuracy, robustness and cybersecurity** and maintain this **throughout** their **lifecycle**, Art. 15 AI Act.

55 To determine the appropriate level of accuracy, the EU Commission will develop and publish **benchmarks and measurement methods**. This will be done in cooperation with relevant stakeholders and organizations. In particular, metrology and benchmarking authorities can be considered as designated organizations. The determined accuracy indicators are to be included in the **accompanying instructions of use** of the AI systems.

56 The **robustness** of a high-risk AI system refers to its **resilience to errors, faults or inconsistencies**. These can occur within the system, but also in interaction with natural persons or other systems. Robustness can be achieved through technical and

[22] Dienes MMR 2024, 456 (458).
[23] Cf. in detail. Guijarro Santos ZfDR 1/2023, 23 (28).
[24] For striking examples, see Guijarro Santos ZfDR 1/2023, 23 (28).

organizational measures. Technical redundancy, which regularly includes backup or fault tolerance plans, should be mentioned here in particular.

In the case of high-risk AI systems that **learn** after commissioning, the risk of **distorted feedback loops** must already be addressed during development. These must be accompanied by appropriate and suitable risk mitigation measures. 57

The requirement of **cybersecurity** demands that high-risk AI systems are designed to be resistant to attacks by third parties. The risk of system vulnerabilities being exploited by malicious third parties as a security hole to change the use, results or performance of the AI system must be minimized. 58

Technical solutions for dealing with AI-specific vulnerabilities include defending against attacks aimed at manipulating the training data set (**data poisoning**) or pre-trained components (**model poisoning**). 59

Attacks can also be carried out using **manipulated input data** that is intended to trick the model into making errors (hostile examples or model bypass). Here, too, preventive measures must first be taken to prevent attacks on confidential data or model deficiencies or to detect ongoing attacks, react to them and ultimately control and eliminate them. 60

The technical solutions for ensuring the cybersecurity of high-risk AI systems must be appropriate to the respective circumstances and risks. For high-risk AI systems that have been certified in accordance with the cybersecurity act[25] or for which a corresponding **declaration of conformity** has been issued, there is a presumption that they also meet all the cybersecurity requirements stipulated in Art. 15 AI Act, Art. 42 para. 2 AI Act. 61

[25] Regulation (EU) 2019/881 of the European Parliament and of the Council of 17.4.2019 on ENISA (the European Union Agency for Cybersecurity) and on Information and Communication Technology cybersecurity certification and repealing Regulation (EU) No 526/2013 (Cybersecurity Act), OJEU L 151, p. 15 of 7.6.2019.

§ 7
Obligations for high-risk AI systems

Literature: *Biermann, Friedrich*, Wissenszurechnung und Künstliche Intelligenz, 2022; *Blum, Benjamin/Rappenglück, Jakob*, Fine-Tuning of GPAI Models under the AI Regulation: A Regulatory Gap for Future Technology? CR 9/2024, 626; *Bomhard, David/Merkle, Marieke*, Regulation of Artificial Intelligence, EuCML 2021, 257; *Brockman, John*, Was sollen wir von Künstlicher Intelligenz halten? 2017; *Casper, Anna Felicitas*, Rechtliche Chancen und Grenzen der automatisierten Entscheidungsunterstützung und Entscheidungsfindung in der Medizin, 2024; *Daute, Ingvar/Sütthoff, Alicia*, Vereinbarkeit von Produktbeobachtungspflicht und Datenschutz beim autonomen Kraftfahrzeug, EuZW 2023, 500; *Denga, Michael*, Konformitätsbewertung von KI-Systemen, ZfPC 2023, 154; *Denga, Michael*, Unternehmenshaftung für KI – zur Konformitätsbewertung in Permanenz, CR 2023, 277; *Dienes, Jennifer*, Anforderungen an die menschliche Aufsicht über Künstliche Intelligenz, MMR 2024, 456; *Ebers, Martin/Quarch, Benedikt*, Rechtshandbuch ChatGPT, 2024; *Frank, Justus/Heine, Maurice*, Arbeitsrechtliche Dimension der KI-Verordnung, NZA 2024, 433; *Fuderer, Markus*, Doppelte Konformitätsbewertung bei KI-basierten Medizinprodukten?, MPR 2022, 121; *Gassner, Ulrich*, Menschliche Aufsicht über intelligente Medizinprodukte, MPR 2023, 5; *Heil, Maria*, Die neue KI-Verordnung (E) – Regulatorische Herausforderungen für KI-basierte Medizinprodukte-Software, MPR 2022, 1; *Krüger, Daniel/Wagner, Susan*, Das Phänomen "Künstliche Intelligenz" aus regulatorischer und haftungsrechtlicher Sicht, ZfPC 2023, 124; *Lachenmann, Matthias*, EU-Rat stimmt KI-Verordnung zu – neue Pflichten für Unternehmen, MMR-Aktuell 2024, 01359; *Lang, Flavia/Reinbach, Hubertus:* Künstliche Intelligenz im Arbeitsrecht, NZA 2023, 1273; *Lingaht, Felix*, Organisationspflichten des AG-Vorstands beim Einsatz von KI-Systemen, JURA 2023, 940; *Malgieri, Gianclaudio/Pasquale, Frank*, Licensing high-risk artificial intelligence: Toward ex ante justification for a disruptive technology, Computer Law & Security Review, Volume 52, 2024, 105899; *Martini, Mario*, Blackbox Algorithmus – Grundfragen einer Regulierung Künstlicher Intelligenz, 2019; *Roos, Philipp/Weitz, Casper Alexander*, Hochrisiko-KI-Systeme im Kommissionsentwurf für eine KI-Verordnung, MMR 2021, 844; *Schulz-Große, Stefanie/Genske, Anna*, Auswirkungen der neuen KI-Verordnung auf den Behandlungsalltag – Datenschutzrechtliche Anforderungen und Sorgfaltspflichten der Behandelnden beim Einsatz von künstlicher Intelligenz zu Behandlungszwecken, GuP 2023, 81; *Schwartmann, Rolf/Keber, Tobias/Zenner, Kai*, KI-Verordnung. Leitfaden für die Praxis, 2024; *Ströbel, Lukas/Grau, Robert*, KI-gestützte Medizin-Apps. Legal challenges of an interdisciplinary product, ZD 2022, 599; *Thiermann, Arne/Böck, Nicole*, Künstliche Intelligenz in Medizinprodukten, RDi 2022, 333; *Veale, Michael/Zuiderveen Borgesius, Frederik*, Demystifying the Draft EU Artificial Intelligence Act, CRi (4)2021, 97; *Wendt, Domenik*, Der AI Act: Compliance requirements for providers and deployers of AI systems, uj 2/2024, 42; *Witteler, Michael/Moll, Lucas*, Künstliche Intelligenz am Arbeitsplatz – Datenschutz und Rechte des Betriebsrats, NZA 2023, 327.

In contrast to the second section, the third section of the AI Act no longer focuses solely on the existence of a high-risk AI system, but differentiates between the categories of provider, deployer and other parties involved. The focus is on providers and deployers. As they are subject to different levels of obligation, it is important for the practical application of the requirements that they are assigned to one of the two groups of persons with legal certainty. 1

I. Obligations of the provider

According to Art. 3 No. 3 AI Act, a **provider** is a natural or legal person, authority, institution or other body that **develops** or has developed an **AI system** or an AI model with a general purpose and **places** it **on the market** or puts it into service **under its own name**. The AI Act does not differentiate between paid and unpaid providers. 2

Art. 16 AI Act provides an enumerated overview of the obligations of providers of high-risk AI systems. In order to enable the high-risk AI system to be attributed to the provider, Art. 16 AI Act obliges the provider to **indicate** its **name** or **company name** and a **contact address** on the AI system itself or, if this is not possible, on its packaging or in the accompanying documentation. 3

Subsequently, Art. 16 AI Act lists the **obligations for providers** that are contained in the following Art. 17–19, 43, 47 and 49 AI Act.[1] 4

1. Compliance by design approach

The list of obligations for providers of these AI systems is extensive. Some of the regulations explicitly require high-risk AI systems to be designed and developed in a certain way (see in particular Art. 13–15 AI Act). The AI Act thus addresses the familiar **compliance-by-design approach.**[2] The product – in this case the high-risk AI system – must therefore be designed in such a way that compliance violations do not occur or only occur with a reduced probability. 5

2. Quality management system

According to Art. 17 AI Act, the obligations of providers include the establishment of a quality management system. There are minimum requirements for the **quality management system**, including a compliance concept with regard to the conformity assessment procedure and the management of changes to the AI system. Inspection, testing and validation procedures before, during and after the development of the AI system are also an essential component. 6

If the relevant product safety legislation for the specific AI system does not cover all the requirements of the second section of the AI Act, the quality management system must explain how it will ensure that the high-risk AI system meets these requirements instead. 7

With regard to the training, validation and test data, the systems and procedures for **data management** that are used in the run-up to and for the purposes of placing the high-risk AI system on the market must also be mentioned. These include data collection, recording, analysis, labeling, storage, filtering, evaluation and aggregation. 8

Finally, **risk management systems** pursuant to Art. 9 AI Act and **market observation** pursuant to Art. 72 AI Act are also components of quality management. This se- 9

[1] Overview in Kremer/Haar in: Schwartmann/Keber/Zenner, Part 2, Chapter 1, para. 366.
[2] Wendt uj 2/2024, 42 (43).

ries also includes the procedure for reporting a serious incident, Art. 73 AI Act. The interrelationship is also **reflected** at the level of the **harmonized standards** (→ § 9 mn. 8), which will in future contain requirements for the specific design of the quality management system. The harmonized standards for risk and quality management are intended to have an overarching function.

10 Another component of the quality management system is the handling of **communication** with national **supervisory authorities, notified bodies**, other stakeholders, customers or interested parties in general.

11 Art. 17 AI Act provides a **graduated framework** for the implementation of the content requirements, which is based on the size of the provider's organization. The requirements for the quality management system are therefore based on a **proportionality test**. As the lowest limit, the level of protection required to ensure compliance of the high-risk AI systems with this regulation must be maintained.

12 If the provider of the high-risk AI system **already maintains a quality management system** in accordance with sector-specific legislation, the content required by the AI Act can become part of the existing quality management system.

13 If the provider of the high-risk AI system is a **financial institution** that is already subject to requirements in relation to internal corporate governance, the obligation to establish a quality management system is deemed to be fulfilled, Art. 17 para. 4 AI Act. Financial institutions in this sense are insurance companies and credit institutions, which are also covered by Annex III No. 5 lit. b and c AI Act. Only a **risk management system** in accordance with Art. 9 AI Act, a post-marketing **monitoring system** in accordance with Art. 72 AI Act and a **procedure for reporting serious incidents** in accordance with Art. 73 AI Act must also be set up.

3. Documentation keeping

14 Art. 18 AI Act requires providers of high-risk AI systems to **retain relevant documentation** for a **period of ten years** from the date of placing on the market or putting into service and to make it available to the competent authorities.

15 The documents include the **technical documentation** required by Art. 11 of the AI Act, as well as that relating to the quality management system in accordance with Art. 17 of the AI Act; also the documentation on any changes approved by notified bodies, including any decisions and other documents issued. Finally, the **declaration of conformity** must also be retained.

16 In the event that a provider or its established authorized representative goes **bankrupt** or ceases its activity before the end of the retention period, each Member State shall determine independently the conditions under which the documentation shall continue to be kept available for the national authorities.

17 If the provider is a **financial institution** (→ mn. 13) that is already subject to internal corporate governance requirements outside the AI Act, it may merge the documentation.

4. Automatically generated logs

18 According to Art. 19 AI Act, providers must also **retain** the **logs automatically generated** by their high-risk AI systems in accordance with Art. 12 para. 1 AI Act. This applies insofar as the logs are subject to the provider's control.

19 The logs must be kept for an appropriate period of time, which must be **at least six months**. The appropriateness is determined by the **purpose of** the high-risk AI system. If longer retention periods result from other EU regulations or requirements

of the Member States, in particular for the **protection of personal data**, these shall take precedence.

If the provider of the high-risk AI system is a **financial institution** that is already subject to **internal governance** legislation, the automatically generated logs can be stored again together with the rest of the documentation. 20

5. Corrective actions and duty of information

If the provider of a high-risk AI system believes or at least has reason to believe that a high-risk AI system it has placed on the market or put into service does not comply with the requirements of the AI Act, it must immediately take **corrective measures** in accordance with Art. 20 AI Act to **bring** the AI system **into compliance.** 21

If this is not successful, the system must **be recalled from the market** and deactivated. To this end, the provider must inform the distributors of the AI system in question as well as any deployers, the authorized representative and importers. 22

If the high-risk AI system poses a **risk to the health, safety or fundamental rights of** persons and the provider is aware of this risk, he must without delay – if necessary together with the deployer – carry out an investigation into the causes and inform the national authorities and, if applicable, the notified body that has issued a certificate under Art. 44 AI Act for the high-risk AI system of the nature of the non-compliance and of any relevant corrective measures already taken. 23

6. Cooperation with competent authorities

Art. 21 AI Act obliges providers of a high-risk AI system to provide the **competent authority, upon reasoned request,** with all information and documentation necessary to demonstrate the conformity of the high-risk AI system with the requirements set out in the second section of the AI Act. The evidence must be provided in a language that is easily understandable for the authority (→ mn. 62 et seq.) and that is one of the official languages of the EU institutions. 24

The information to be transmitted may also include the **automatically generated logs** of the high-risk AI system pursuant to Art. 12 para. 1 AI Act in the event of a justified request from a national competent authority, at least insofar as these are subject to the provider's control. 25

All information received by a **notified body** must be treated **confidentially** in accordance with Art. 78 AI Act. 26

7. Authorized representatives of the providers of high-risk AI systems

Providers from third countries must appoint an **authorized representative** who has an establishment in the EU before making a high-risk AI system available on the Union market. The authorized representative acts as a contact person for the competent authorities in addition to or instead of the provider. 27

His area of responsibility generally includes all issues relating to compliance with the AI Act. Specifically, the authorized representative performs his tasks in accordance with the **mandate** received from the provider; conversely, the provider must **enable** the authorized representative to perform the tasks. 28

For **transparency purposes**, the **order** must also be submitted to the market surveillance authorities on request. The subject of the mandate is at least the verification of the **EU** declaration of conformity including the adequacy of the conformity assessment procedure and the technical documentation according to Art. 11 AI Act. 29

30 For a period of **ten years after** the high-risk AI system **has been placed on the market** or put into service, the authorized representative must keep the **contact details** of the provider who appointed him. He must also keep a copy of the declaration of conformity, the technical documentation and, where applicable, the certificate issued by the notified body available for the national competent authorities or bodies.

31 Upon reasoned **request** from a national competent **authority**, the authorized representative shall provide it with all information and documents necessary to **demonstrate** the **conformity** of a high-risk AI system. This may also include the automatically generated logs, provided they are subject to the provider's control.

32 In general, the authorized representative must cooperate with the competent authorities if they **take measures** in connection with the high-risk AI system, for example to **reduce** the **risks** posed by it.

33 Finally, it may also be part of the agent's duties to fulfill the **registration obligations** under Art. 49 para. 1 AI Act or, if the registration is carried out by the provider itself, at least to **ensure** the **accuracy** of the information.

34 If the authorized representative has reason to believe that the provider is in breach of obligations under the AI Act, he must **terminate** the **contract** and immediately inform the **market surveillance authority** of the Member State in which he is located or established. If applicable, the **notified body** concerned must also be informed of the termination of the contract and the reasons for it.

II. Obligations of the deployer

35 According to Art. 3 No. 4 AI Act, a **deployer** is a natural or legal person, public authority, agency or other body that **uses** an **AI system under its authority**. The criterion for use under one's own authority is often justified by the fact that the deployer acts on its own account or at its own risk.[3] If an AI system is used at the workplace at the employer's instigation, the employer is the deployer.[4] However, if an employee uses an AI system on their own initiative in the course of their professional activities or uses a provided AI system beyond its intended purpose, the employee may also be considered the deployer.[5] Personal, i.e. **non-professional, activities** are **excluded.**

1. Use according to the instructions

36 The obligations for deployers of high-risk AI systems are **significantly reduced** compared to those of providers: Art. 26 para. 1 AI Act only obliges them to ensure via technical and organizational measures and to continuously check that the AI system is used exclusively in compliance with its **instructions for use** and in accordance with the requirements of the AI Act, Art. 26. para. 5 AI Act.

37 If the deployer is concerned that even use in accordance with the instructions poses a **risk** to the **health, safety** or **fundamental rights of** persons, he must immediately inform the provider, the distributor and the competent **market surveillance authority** in accordance with Art. 72 of the AI Act and may no longer use the system for the time being.

---

[3] Schuh/Witt EuDIR 2025, 142 (146).
[4] Schuh/Witt EuDIR 2025, 142 (147).
[5] Schwartmann/Zenner EuDIR 2025, 3 (9).

2. Notification in the event of a serious incident

Even in the event of a **serious incident**, the **provider** must be informed first and the importer, distributor and market surveillance authority must be informed in a second step. If the deployer is unable to contact the provider, the communication channel under Art. 73 AI Act goes directly to the **market surveillance authority**. Only law enforcement authorities are exempt from this obligation with regard to sensitive operational data. 38

If the deployer is a **financial institution** (→ mn. 13, 17) that is subject to **internal corporate governance** regulations, the AI Act avoids duplication and considers the monitoring obligation to be fulfilled if the relevant regulations for financial services are complied with. 39

3. Human oversight

Art. 26 para. 2 AI Act sets out further requirements for **human oversight**: The deployer may only delegate this to persons who have the necessary **expertise** in accordance with Art. 4 AI Act. The deployer must provide them with all necessary support. The requirement for AI literacy already arises from the obligation to use the AI system in accordance with the instructions for use pursuant to Art. 26 para. 1 and para. 5 AI Act. A mere "nodding off"[6] of the results of the AI system in the course of a superficial plausibility check does not meet the requirement for monitoring in accordance with Art. 26 para. 5 AI Act.[7] 40

Insofar as the input data in the AI system is subject to their control, the deployers must ensure that they only use **input data** that corresponds to the **purpose of** the **AI system** and is **sufficiently representative.** 41

4. Storage of automatically generated logs

Deployers of high-risk AI systems are also obliged to **maintain** the **logs automatically generated** by the AI system for a period of at least **six months** if they have access to them, Art. 26 para. 6 AI Act. If legal provisions for the **protection of personal data** conflict with the retention, these shall take precedence. Deployers that are subject to internal governance requirements as financial institutions (→ mn. 13, 17) shall retain the logs as part of this documentation, Art. 26 para. 6 subpara. 2 AI Act. 42

5. Further duties

Before using a high-risk AI system in the **workplace**, employers must inform both the employee representatives and the affected employees.[8] According to an initial decision under employment law, the use of ChatGPT and comparable generative AI systems does not immediately constitute a case of **co-determination** pursuant to Section 87 (1) No. 6 BetrVG. The Hamburg Labor Court (ArbG) ruled on 16.1.2024 that the use of AI systems via a private account on a voluntary basis and possibly at the employee's own expense is not subject to co-determination. It is true that the provider of the AI system records employee data. However, the resulting **monitoring pressure** does not come from the employer; the employer cannot even access the information obtained. Accordingly, the Hamburg Labour Court rejected the works council's right 43

[6] Paal/Hüger MMR 20204, 540 (542).
[7] Paal/Hüger MMR 20204, 540 (542).
[8] Kössel DB 2024, 1069 (1070 et seq.); Batista LTZ 2024, 118 (118); Frank/Heine NZA 2024, 433 (433).

of co-determination due to the particularities of the case.[9] However, even minor changes to the facts of the case will presumably lead to different decisions.[10] For example, the works council has a right of co-determination if the employer introduces the systems on its own computers or gains access to the data entered.[11]

44 If the deployer is an **EU** institution or other **body**, **registration** in the new pan-European **database** pursuant to Art. 49 AI Act must be carried out. If the deployer establishes that the high-risk AI system has not been registered in the EU database for high-risk AI systems listed in Annex III in accordance with Art. 71 AI Act, it must refrain from using it and inform the provider or distributor accordingly.

45 The deployers of high-risk AI systems use the information provided under Art. 13 AI Act to comply with their obligation to carry out a **data protection impact assessment** in accordance with Art. 35 GDPR[12] and Art. 27 of the Data Protection in Criminal Matters Directive[13]. The special rules on the **protection of personal data**, in particular the provisions of the GDPR, remain unaffected by the AI Act in connection with the processing of personal data (Art. 2 para. 7 AI Act).[14]

46 Finally, Art. 27 AI Act also contains provisions for deployers who use the AI system for post-remote **biometric identification** (post-remote by automatic identification). This may be used for the targeted search of a person who is suspected or convicted of having committed a criminal offense. Its use requires the **approval of a judicial** or administrative authority, whose decision must in turn be subject to judicial review. The authorization must be obtained before or when the AI system is used – within 48 hours at the latest. An exception to this narrow time window applies if the AI is used to identify a potential suspect for the first time on the basis of objective, verifiable facts that are directly related to the crime. Any **use is limited** to what is **strictly necessary** for the investigation of a specific criminal offense.

47 If the requested **authorization is rejected**, the use of the system for subsequent remote biometric identification must be discontinued with immediate effect. Any **personal data** already collected will be **deleted**.

48 These provisions on retrospective remote biometric identification reveal a **surprising assessment of** the AI Act: While the Council and the EU Parliament argued persistently in the trilogue about the pros and cons of the categorical ban on real-time remote biometric identification (→ § 3 mn. 18), the classification of subsequent remote biometric identification as simply high-risk AI was not up for discussion. So while real-time remote biometric identification was ultimately declared unacceptable and largely prohibited, subsequent remote biometric identification is permitted.[15]

---

[9] ArbG Hamburg of 16.01.2024 – 24 BVGa 1/24, ZIP 2024, 589 = ECLI:DE:ARBGHH:2024:0116.24BVGA1.24.00.

[10] Kössel DB 2024, 1069 (1073); see also Lang/Reinbach NZA 2023, 1273 (1276); Witteler/Moll NZA 2023, 327 (331).

[11] Kössel DB 2024, 1069 (1072).

[12] Regulation (EU) 2016/679 of the European Parliament and of the Council of 27.4.2016 on the protection of natural persons with regard to the processing of personal data and on the free movement of such data, and repealing Directive 95/46/EC (General Data Protection Regulation), OJ L 119, 4.5.2016, pp. 1–88.

[13] Directive (EU) 2016/680 of the European Parliament and of the Council of 27.4.2016 on the protection of natural persons with regard to the processing of personal data by competent authorities for the purposes of the prevention, investigation, detection or prosecution of criminal offenses or the execution of criminal penalties, and on the free movement of such data, and repealing Council Framework Decision 2008/977/JHA, OJ L 119, 4.5.2016, pp. 89–131.

[14] Cf. OLG Köln of 23.5.2025 – 15 UKI 2/25, ECLI:DE:OLGK:2025:0523.15UKL2.25.00.

[15] In this regard in detail. Hahn ZfDR 2023, 142 (144).

49 The AI Act justifies the differentiation in recital 32 by stating that the use of AI systems for real-time remote biometric identification of natural persons in publicly accessible spaces for law enforcement purposes "*is particularly intrusive to the rights and freedoms of the concerned persons, to the extent that it may affect the private life of a large part of the population, evoke a feeling of constant surveillance and indirectly dissuade the exercise of the freedom of assembly and other fundamental rights*".

50 This is certainly correct, but will also apply to subsequent remote identification.[16] After all, this is probably the AI technology that the security authorities actually use in practice to combat terrorism. The cinema image, in which countless officers sit in front of monitors and monitor everything in real time via thousands of cameras, hardly corresponds to reality. AI is more likely to evaluate the images retrospectively, **create movement or personality profiles** and establish systematic correlations, making this category appear **more threatening from a data protection perspective.**[17]

51 Nevertheless, the AI Act only classifies the retrospective use of real-time data as high-risk AI, while real-time biometric remote identification falls under prohibited practices with a few exceptions. **Subsequent remote biometric identification** is therefore **permitted** subject to compliance with data protection law and the performance of a risk assessment and technical documentation and under the supervision of one or two natural persons.

52 It is true that the use of the results of retrospective remote biometric identification is subject to the aforementioned additional requirements, the **judicial reservation** and other **procedural safeguards**. Despite these restrictions, however, the difference between the rigorous prohibition of one practice and the permission subject to conditions of the other practice is an unexpected differentiation of the AI Act. This corresponds to the fact that the AI Act leaves it up to the Member States to enact **stricter legislation** for the use of real-time remote biometric identification systems (→ § 3 mn. 21).

53 The use of AI systems for retrospective remote biometric identification is only prohibited in a non-targeted manner and without any **connection to a criminal offense, criminal proceedings**, the existing or foreseeable risk of a criminal offense or the **search for a missing person**. It must also always be ensured that the law enforcement authorities do not take any decisions against a person that are based solely on subsequent remote biometric identification. This requirement applies in parallel to Art. 9 GDPR[18] for the processing of special categories of personal data and Art. 10 of the Data Protection in Criminal Matters Directive[19] for the processing of biometric data.

54 Any use of an AI system for retrospective remote biometric identification must be **documented** in the police file and made available to the competent **market surveillance authority and** the national **data protection authority** upon request. The only exception to this is the disclosure of sensitive operational data in connection with criminal prosecution.

---

16 Hahn ZfDR 2023, 142 (155).

17 Hahn ZfDR 2023, 142 (155 et seq.).

18 Regulation (EU) 2016/679 of the European Parliament and of the Council of 27.4.2016 on the protection of natural persons with regard to the processing of personal data and on the free movement of such data, and repealing Directive 95/46/EC (General Data Protection Regulation), OJ L 119, 4.5.2016, pp. 1–88.

19 Directive (EU) 2016/680 of the European Parliament and of the Council of 27.4.2016 on the protection of natural persons with regard to the processing of personal data by competent authorities for the purposes of the prevention, investigation, detection or prosecution of criminal offenses or the execution of criminal penalties, and on the free movement of such data, and repealing Council Framework Decision 2008/977/JHA, OJ L 119, 4.5.2016, pp. 89–131.

55 In addition to the event-related reporting obligation, deployers must submit **annual reports** on the use of systems for subsequent remote biometric identification to the competent **market surveillance** and **data protection authorities.** This also excludes the disclosure of sensitive operational data related to criminal prosecution. The reports will typically contain a **summary** of several operations.

56 Parallel to the transparency obligations under Art. 50 AI Act, Art. 27 AI Act also contains information obligations: Deployers of high-risk AI systems listed in Annex III must **inform** natural **persons** as soon as an **AI system makes decisions that affect them.** This also applies even if the AI system merely provides support for such decisions. Art. 13 of the Data Protection in Criminal Matters Directive applies to high-risk AI systems used for law enforcement purposes.[20] Deployers are also obliged to cooperate with the national authorities in all measures they take in connection with the high-risk AI system.

III. Obligations of the importer

57 Value chains for AI systems are regularly complex. In order to ensure legal certainty at all levels of the chain, the AI Act includes other players in its group of addressees in addition to the provider and the deployer.[21] The obligations of importers can be found in Art. 23 AI Act. According to Art. 3 para. 6 AI Act, an importer is a natural or legal person located or established in the EU who places an **AI system from a third country on the market in the EU.**

58 According to Art. 23 AI Act, importers of a high-risk AI system must ensure that providers of the high-risk AI systems they import have complied with their obligations under the AI Act before placing them on the market. In particular, the **conformity assessment** pursuant to Art. 43 AI Act, the preparation of the **technical documentation** pursuant to Art. 11 in conjunction with Annex IV AI Act, the **CE marking** and declaration as well as the attachment of instructions for use, Art. 23 para. 1 lit. a-c AI Act must be checked. In addition, an authorized **representative** based in the EU must **be appointed** who can provide the competent authorities with all necessary information on the conformity of the AI system, Art. 23 para. 1 lit. d AI Act. Otherwise, the AI system must be withdrawn from the market, Art. 23 para. 2 AI Act.[22]

59 If the AI system poses a **risk** within the meaning of Art. 79 para. 1 AI Act, i.e. a risk to the health, safety or fundamental rights of persons, the importer must **inform** the **authorized representative** and the competent **market surveillance authority**.

60 In addition, **contact details** of the importer (name, registered trade name, registered trade mark, address) must **be indicated** on the high-risk AI systems themselves or, if not possible, on the packaging or accompanying documents, Art. 23 para. 3 AI Act.

61 Importers must ensure the **proper storage** and **transportation** of the AI systems under their responsibility, Art. 23 para. 4 AI Act. **Records of conformity** must be kept for ten years after the AI system in question has been placed on the market or put into service, Art. 23 para. 5 AI Act, and must be made available to the competent authority

[20] Directive (EU) 2016/680 of the European Parliament and of the Council of 27.4.2016 on the protection of natural persons with regard to the processing of personal data by competent authorities for the purposes of the prevention, investigation, detection or prosecution of criminal offenses or the execution of criminal penalties, and on the free movement of such data, and repealing Council Framework Decision 2008/977/JHA, OJ L 119 p. 89.

[21] Cf. recital 83 AI Act.

[22] See also Ammann/Pohle CB 5/2024, 137 (141).

in an understandable language upon request, Art. 23 para. 6 AI Act. There is also a general obligation to **cooperate** with the competent **authorities**, Art. 23 para. 7 AI Act.

The requirement for **communication in easily understandable language** can be found in several articles of the AI Act, including in Art. 21 para. 1 AI Act on cooperation with the competent authorities, in Art. 44 para. 1 AI Act on the certificates issued by notified bodies in accordance with Annex VII and in Art. 47 para. 2 AI Act on the EU declaration of conformity. 62

Recital 143 states that Member States should choose a language for the relevant documentation of providers and for communication with deployers that is **understood** by **the largest possible number of deployers, including cross-border deployers.** Of the 24 official languages of the EU, this requirement will certainly apply to the three procedural languages of the EU – French, English and German – which are also statistically spoken by most people within the EU.[23] 63

In certain situations, **the roles of the actors overlap**. For example, it is conceivable that an importer also acts as a distributor. In this case, he is obliged to **fulfill** all **obligations** associated with these roles **cumulatively.**[24] 64

IV. Obligations of the Distributor

Art. 24 of the AI Act obliges **distributors** to **check** whether the high-risk AI system bears the required **CE marking,**[25] a copy of the **declaration of conformity** and **instructions for use** are enclosed and whether the provider or, if applicable, the importer of the system has fulfilled his obligations. The system may only be placed on the market after a positive inspection. 65

If the distributor has reason to believe that the AI system does not comply with the requirements of the AI Act, he is obliged to **withhold** it until compliance with the requirements has been ensured. 66

As long as the high-risk AI system is under its responsibility, the distributor guarantees that the **storage or transportation conditions** do not affect the conformity of the system. 67

If the distributor has at least reason to believe that a high-risk AI system provided by it on the market does not comply with the requirements of the AI Act, it must take the necessary **corrective measures** to ensure compliance. If he cannot do this himself, he must request the provider, the importer or, if applicable, any other relevant actor who is in a position to do so, to make the corrections. If this attempt also fails, the system must be **recalled** from the market. 68

If the AI system poses a **risk to the health, safety or fundamental rights of** persons, the distributor shall **notify** the provider or importer of the system and the competent **authorities** of the Member States in which the system was made available. The notification must be accompanied by detailed information, in particular on the non-compliance and corrective measures already taken. 69

[23] Since Brexit, English is only the native language of 13 % of EU citizens; however, around half of Europeans (47 %) speak English as a foreign or second language. After English, German (native language 20 %, foreign language 10 %) and French (native language 12 %, foreign language 11 %) are the most widely spoken languages in the EU. SEE https://europa.eu/eurobarometer/surveys/detail/2979.

[24] Cf. recital 83 AI Act.

[25] See König/Schanz RDG 2017, 208 (209).

70 Upon request, the distributor must **prove** the **conformity of** the AI system to the national competent authorities. If the authorities take measures to mitigate risks posed by the system, the distributor is obliged to cooperate.

V. Responsibilities along the AI Value Chain

71 AI is rarely developed and brought to market directly by a single company.[26] In most cases, other companies are involved in adapting the general model precisely to specific applications. The legislator must take this structure of **multiple intermediaries** into account. Ideally, it should always impose obligations on the actor who can exert the most effective and cost-efficient influence.[27]

72 The AI Act maps these stages along the value chain. It differentiates between the various actors when defining obligations and imposes **obligations** on them **to varying degrees**. Art. 16 AI Act places the most comprehensive requirements on providers (→ mn. 2).

73 Only in certain circumstances do other actors in the value chain have to meet provider obligations, meaning deployers, distributors, importers, and other third parties are treated as providers, Art. 25 para. 1 AI Act. This is the case if they label a high-risk AI system that has already been placed on the market or put into service **with their name or trademark** or contractually agree on a corresponding distribution of obligations, Art. 25 para. 1 lit. a AI Act.[28]

74 They are also subject to the provider obligations if they make a **substantial modification** to a high-risk AI system or change the purpose of an AI system that was not previously classified as high-risk in such a way that it becomes a high-risk AI system, Art. 25 para. 1 lit. b and c AI Act. Other actors can thus enter the position of the provider if they either label high-risk AI systems on the market with their name or brand and thus show identification with the respective AI system or make significant changes to them or their intended use. In these cases, they take on the role of the provider in relation to the marked or modified system, Art. 25 para. 1 AI Act. The original provider is released from its responsibility in relation to this system, Art. 25 para. 2, sentence 1 AI Act. However, it is obliged to work closely with the "**new providers**" and to provide them with all necessary information, Art. 25 para. 2 AI Act.[29]

75 It is therefore particularly important for deployers not to exceed the threshold of a substantial modification, as otherwise they are subject to the more comprehensive provider obligations. Art. 3 No. 23 AI Act defines a substantial modification as "*a change to an AI system after its placing on the market or putting into service which is not foreseen or planned in the initial conformity assessment carried out by the provider and as a result of which the compliance of the AI system with the requirements set out in Chapter III, Section 2 is affected or results in a modification to the intended purpose for which the AI system has been assessed*".

76 Interpretation aids can also be found outside the AI Act. The concept of substantial change is typical for product safety law, especially for the New Legislative Framework (NLF).[30] Section 2.1 of the Blue Guide to the NLF published by the EU Commission

---

[26] Hacker/Berz ZRP 2023, 226 (228).
[27] Hacker/Berz ZRP 2023, 226 (228).
[28] Ammann/Pohle CB 5/24, 137 (141).
[29] Ammann/Pohle CB 5/24, 137 (142).
[30] Blum/Rappenglück, CR 9/2024, 626 (630).

(Notice of 29.6.2022 – 2002/C 247/01) deals in detail with "substantial change". This is to be understood as any modification to a product that has already been placed on the market, which triggers a product hazard that is **no longer covered by the original conformity assessment.** The new EU Machinery Regulation of 14.6.2023[31] also addresses the concept of "substantial modification" in Art. 3 No. 16 and 18. The basic idea of these constellations is that an approved product is modified after it has been placed on the market in a way that is outside the scope of the initial conformity assessment.[32]

However, it initially remained unclear to what extent Art. 25 AI Act, which sets a norm for high-risk AI systems, could be applied to GPAI models. There was a lack of clarity as to when an actor along the AI value chain must fulfil the obligations for providers of GPAI models. 77

What applies when a GPAI model is integrated into an AI system? According to recital 97, AI models are usually integrated into AI systems and form a part of them. Recital 97 further states that GPAI models can be modified or optimised to create new models. Deep learning models in particular are typically fine-tuned for specific tasks after pre-training, which takes place using a large general data set. During the fine-tuning phase, a specific smaller dataset is used to adjust the pre-trained foundation model to specific tasks. In particular, the weights of the AI model in the rear layers are adjusted to improve its capabilities with regard to the specific objective.[33]

Although the question of the intensity of change involved in fine-tuning generative models is an obvious one, the AI Act does not contain any provisions for GPAI models that correspond to high-risk AI. This is likely due primarily to the fact that the product safety law concept of substantial change cannot be applied one-to-one to AI models, as these are not products but, at most, components thereof.[34] Does the EU Commission therefore consider an actor who modifies a GPAI model to be a provider of that model, such that the provider obligations under the AI Act apply to them?

The interpretation of this extremely important definition was ultimately provided for providers of general-purpose AI models in the EU Commission's GPAI guidelines, which were published on 18.7.2025.[35] 78

In these guidelines, the EU Commission expresses its conviction that not every change to a GPAI model also means that the downstream company is considered the provider of the modified AI model. This is in line with the Blue Guide on the NLF (→ mn. 76), which states that a product that has undergone a substantial modification or revisions to alter its original performance, purpose or nature may be considered a new product. 79

Rather, the Commission considers that a downstream company only becomes a provider of the modified GPAI model if the modification results in a significant change in the generality, capabilities or systemic risk of the model. The GPAI guidelines use the training computing power used for the modification as an indicative criterion for the intensity of the change: If a company retrains a model with more than one-third of the original amount of FLOPs, the AI Office considers the new model to 80

[31] Regulation (EU) 2023/1230 of the European Parliament and of the Council of 14.6.2023 on machinery, and repealing Directive 2006/42/EC of the European Parliament and of the Council and Council Directive 73/361/EEC, OJ L 165, 29.6.2023, p. 1–102.

[32] Blum/Rappenglück, CR 9/2024, 626 (630).

[33] Ebers/Quarch ChatGPT-HdB/Glauner Rn. 20.

[34] Ebers/Quarch ChatGPT-HdB/Glauner Rn. 20.

[35] Annex to the Communication to the Commission Approval of the content of the draft Communication from the Commission – Guidelines on the scope of the obligations for general-purpose AI models established by Regulation (EU) 2024/1689 (AI Act) of 18.7.2025.

be independent. The company making the adaptation is then considered a so-called modifier.[36]

One-third of the original training computing power is an enormous amount for fine-tuning. The bar is set high so that smaller companies and start-ups that only make minor adjustments are not automatically classified as providers.

If the downstream company does not know the value of the original training computing power – e.g. because it was not disclosed by the provider of the original AI model – and cannot estimate it, the threshold value is set as follows: If the original model is a GPAI model with systemic risk, the current 10^{25} FLOPs are used as the baseline. In all other cases, 10^{23} FLOPs are currently used as the baseline.[37]

However, one question remains unanswered: how should the distillation of a model be evaluated? In this process, the knowledge of a large, complex model is transferred to a smaller, more efficient model – one example is Deepseek, which was apparently trained by distilling an OpenAI model.

81 Finally, a change in the **intended purpose of the AI system** also constitutes a substantial modification of the high-risk AI system. Art 3 no. 12 AI Act defines *the* intended purpose as "*the use for which an AI system is intended by the provider, including the specific context and conditions of use, as specified in the information supplied by the provider in the instructions for use, promotional or sales materials and statements as well as in the technical documentation*". A change of intended purpose is therefore likely to occur if the AI system is used in a new area of application or under changed geographical, contextual, behavioral or functional conditions or is assigned a new target group.

82 Conversely, there is no significant change within the meaning of Art. 25 para. 1 lit. b and c AI Act if the modification was already provided for in the original conformity assessment of the high-risk AI system carried out by the provider. Changes to high-risk AI systems that are self-learning after they have been placed on the market or put into operation do not constitute substantial modifications either, provided that they were already specified by the provider at the time of the original conformity assessment and specified in the information in the technical documentation in accordance with Annex IV No. 2 lit. f AI Act, Art. 43 para. 4 subpara. 2 AI Act.

83 Art. 25 para. 2 sentence 1 AI Act **releases the original provider** from its responsibility for the specifically modified or newly labeled AI system. In particular, it is released from the obligations of Art. 16 AI Act in relation to the specific system.

However, the original provider must cooperate with the new provider, in particular **provide the necessary information** and **grant technical access** as well as provide **other support** required for compliance with the AI Act, in particular for the conformity assessment. Here, Art. 25 para. 2 sentence 2 AI Act refers not only to the obligations referenced in Art. 16 AI Act, but to all obligations of the provider.

84 However, the **initial provider can stipulate** that its **AI system** may **not** be **integrated or converted into** a **high-risk AI system**. In this way, it is released from the obligation to cooperate under Art. 25 para. 2 AI Act. It also does not have to hand over its documentation, Art. 25 para. 2 last sentence AI Act.

---

[36] Annex to the Communication to the Commission Approval of the content of the draft Communication from the Commission – Guidelines on the scope of the obligations for general-purpose AI models established by Regulation (EU) 2024/1689 (AI Act) of 18.7.2025.

[37] Annex to the Communication to the Commission Approval of the content of the draft Communication from the Commission – Guidelines on the scope of the obligations for general-purpose AI models established by Regulation (EU) 2024/1689 (AI Act) of 18.7.2025.

85 The **mirror-image problem** is addressed in Art. 25 para. 4 AI Act: If a third party provides instruments, services, procedures or components for a high-risk AI system, the provider of the high-risk AI system must in turn be enabled to fulfill the obligations set out in the AI Act. To this end, it draws up an agreement together with the third party which sets out the information, capabilities and technical access to the integrated tools, components, services and procedures in accordance with the **recognized state of the art**. If the provider requires additional support, this must also be recorded, Art. 25 para. 4 sentence 1 AI Act.

86 For the preparation of the agreement between the provider and the third party, the AI Office may draw up or recommend voluntary model contract terms and conditions, which also take into account any contractual requirements of individual sectors, Art. 25 para. 4 sentence 3 AI Act. The voluntary model contract terms are made available free of charge and electronically, Art. 25 para. 4 last sentence AI Act.

87 Third parties who make tools, services, processes or components available **open source** are exempt from the obligation to conclude an agreement with the provider, unless they are AI models with a general purpose, Art. 25 para. 4 sentence 2 AI Act.

88 It is undeniable that the right to information is in conflict with **intellectual property** rights and **confidential business information**. These must be protected in accordance with Art. 25 para. 5 AI Act. Here, the route will have to be via non-disclosure agreements and non-competition clauses and, if necessary, protective orders from the courts.[38]

89 If the high-risk AI system is not a stand-alone AI, but the **safety component of a product**, it is questionable whether the manufacturer of the product is also considered to be the provider of the AI system. This is the case for products that are covered by one of the twelve directives and regulations of the New Legislative Framework (NLF) according to Annex I Section A of the AI Act (→ § 9 mn. 15) if the **product and the AI system form a unit** and are **marketed together**. Whether the AI system and the product are placed on the market together at the same time or whether the product is placed on the market first and the AI system is subsequently put into operation is not decisive as long as both are marketed under the name or trademark of the product manufacturer, Art. 25 para. 3 AI Act.

VI. Fundamental rights impact assessment for high-risk AI systems

Literature: *Ashkar, Daniel*, Essential requirements of the GDPR for the introduction and operation of AI applications, ZD 2023, 523; *Baumgartner, Ulrich/Brunnbauer, Jonas H./Cross, Samuel*, Requirements of the GDPR for the use of artificial intelligence, MMR 2023, 543; *Buck-Heeb, Petra*: Rechtsrisiken bei automatisierter Kreditwürdigkeitsprüfung und Kreditvergabe, BKR 2023, 137; *Frank, Justus/Heine, Maurice*, KI-Einsatz im Betrieb unter der KI-Verordnung, NZA 2023, 1281; *Hessel, Stefan/Dillschneider, Jeanne*, Datenschutzrechtliche Herausforderungen beim Einsatz von Künstlicher Intelligenz, RDi 2023, 458; *Horstmann, Jan*, KI-VO und Datenschutz: Überblick und ausgewählte Fragen, ZD-Aktuell 2024, 01580; *Janssen, Heleen/Sengh Ah Lee, Michelle/Singh, Jatinder*, Practical fundamental rights impact assessments, International Journal of Law and Information Technology, Volume 30, Issue 2, 200; *Prange, Hans Michael*, Datenschutz- und lauterkeitsrechtliche Kernfragen des Einsatzes Künstlicher Intelligenz im Marketing, WRP 2024, 151; *Roßnagel, Alexander/Geminn, Christian/Johannes, Paul*, Datenschutz-Folgenabschätzung im Zuge der Gesetzgebung, ZD 2019, 435; *Schmitz, Barbara/von Dall'Arm, Jonas*, Datenschutz-Folgenabschätzung – verstehen und anwenden, ZD 2017, 57; *Schultze-Melling, Jyn*, Notwendigkeit einer intelligenten Regulation der KI, ZD 2021, 289; *Schulz-Große, Stefanie/Genske, Anna*, Auswirkungen der neuen KI-Verordnung auf den Behandlungsalltag – Datenschutzrechtliche Anforderungen und Sorgfaltspflichten der Behandelnden beim Einsatz von künstlicher Intelligenz zu Behandlungszwecken, GuP 2023, 81; *Schürrmann, Kathrin*, Data protection impact assessment when

[38] Hacker/Berz ZRP 2023, 226 (228).

using artificial intelligence, ZD 2022, 316; *Schwartmann, Rolf/Keber, Tobias/Zenner, Kai*, KI-Verordnung. Guide for the practice, 2024.

90 The AI Act is committed to a human-centered regulatory approach. AI applications must be in line with European values and legislation for the protection of fundamental rights. The use of high-risk AI systems in particular can have an impact on fundamental rights. In addition, the complexity and opacity of most AI applications run counter to the demand for transparency and accountability. In order to address this conflict, particularly in the use of high-risk AI systems, the AI Act stipulates that **deployers that** are **bodies governed by public law**, but also **private deployers that provide public services**, as well as **deployers of certain high-risk AI systems**, must carry out a fundamental rights impact assessment. According to recital 96, the aim of this so-called fundamental rights impact assessment is for the deployer of an AI system to assess in advance the specific risks that may affect the rights of individuals and to determine **in advance measures** that will be taken if the risks materialize. These may include compliance structures, arrangements for **human oversight** in accordance with the **instructions for use** or procedures for **handling complaints.**[39]

91 The fundamental rights impact assessment was only included in the AI Act **during the trilogue** at the request of the EU Parliament. Critics of the regulation saw it as a requirement without added value.[40] After all, Art. 9 AI Act requires a general risk assessment anyway, which also covers fundamental rights aspects. In addition, Art. 35 GDPR requires a **data protection impact assessment** to be carried out for personal data in critical scenarios.

1. Addressees

92 The addressees of the obligation to carry out the fundamental rights impact assessment are only **selected deployers of high-risk AI systems**, namely institutions under public law and private institutions that provide public services. **Banks and insurance companies** are also covered by a reference to Annex III if they operate high-risk AI systems for **credit assessment** (Annex III No. 5 lit. b AI Act) or for **risk assessment and pricing** in relation to natural persons in the case of **health and life insurance** (Annex III No. 5 lit. c AI Act).[41]

93 The term "public services" is not to be equated with sovereign services. Rather, it refers to services that are linked to **tasks in the public interest,**[42] but which may well be of a private law nature. The understanding is very broad; recital 96 mentions the sectors of **education, healthcare, social services, housing and administration of justice**, for example, and thus also includes hospital services.

94 Just as the obligation to carry out a fundamental rights impact assessment only applies to certain deployers, it is also limited in terms of content to the high-risk AI systems of Art. 6 para. 2 in conjunction with Annex III AI Act:

- Biometrics (No. 1)
- Education and vocational training (No. 3)
- Employment, workers' management and access to self-employment (No. 4)
- Access to and enjoyment of essential private and essential public services and benefits (No. 5)

[39] See Dienes MMR 2024, 456 (456).
[40] Hacker/Berz ZRP 2023, 226 (228).
[41] Buck-Heeb BKR 2023, 137 (137); see also recital 96 AI Act.
[42] Recital 96 AI Act.

- Law enforcement (No. 6)
- Migration, asylum and border control management (No. 7)
- Administration of justice and democratic processes (No. 8).

The area of **critical infrastructure** (No. 2) is **expressly excluded** from the obligation to carry out a fundamental rights impact assessment pursuant to Art. 27 para. 1 AI Act. 95

2. Contents of the impact assessment

In terms of content, the fundamental rights impact assessment must first contain a **description of the procedures** in which the high-risk AI system is used according to its intended purpose, including **information on the period** and **frequency of use**. 96

In addition, categories of natural persons (groups) who could be affected by its use must be listed. The **risks of harm** must then be **determined** with regard to these **specific groups of persons**. The information to be provided by the provider to the deployer in accordance with Art. 13 AI Act and the human oversight as specified in the instructions for use serve as the basis for this. 97

Specifically, the fundamental rights impact assessment pursuant to Art. 27 para. 1 sentence 2 AI Act must include the following points: 98

- Description of the procedures in which the high-risk AI system is used as intended (lit. a),
- Description of the time period and frequency within which and with which each high-risk AI system is to be used (lit. b),
- Categories of natural persons and groups of persons who could be affected by its use in the specific context (lit. c),
- the specific risks of harm that could affect the categories of persons or groups of persons identified in accordance with lit. c, taking into account the information provided by the provider in accordance with Art. 13 AI Act (lit. d),
- Description of the implementation of human oversight measures in accordance with the instructions for use (lit. e),
- Measures to be taken if these risks materialize, including internal governance arrangements and grievance mechanisms (lit. f).

The fundamental rights impact assessment must be carried out prior to commissioning.[43] The results must be submitted to the market surveillance authority. The **questionnaire** currently being developed by the **AI Office** in accordance with Art. 27 para 5 AI Act can be used for this purpose. It is intended to **make it easier** for deployers to fulfill their **reporting obligations**. 99

If fundamental rights impact assessments have already been carried out (by the provider or deployer) prior to the first use of the high-risk AI system, these may be used. However, this presupposes that the AI system has **not** undergone **any changes** in the meantime or that the existing fundamental rights impact assessment **no longer reflects** the **current status** for other reasons. In these cases, it must be repeated. 100

In parallel to the exemption from the conformity assessment procedure under Art. 46 para. 1 AI Act, the deployer may request the market surveillance authority for **exemption from the fundamental rights impact assessment** for exceptional reasons of public safety, the protection of life and health of persons, environmental protection or the protection of important industrial and infrastructure facilities. 101

[43] Kremer/Haar in: Schwartmann/Keber/Zenner, Part 2, Chapter 1, para. 444.

3. Interaction with data protection impact assessment

102 If there is already an obligation to carry out a **data protection impact assessment (DPIA)** under the GDPR or the Data Protection in Criminal Matters Directive, the AI Act makes it possible to **combine** both **impact assessments**: The data protection impact assessment was introduced as a new instrument by Art. 35 GDPR. Even before the start of data processing, the expected risk should be assessed in order to take appropriate measures in good time and to be able to fulfill the responsibility for data processing.[44] Together with Art. 32 and Art. 36 GDPR, Art. 35 GDPR forms a **three-stage mechanism for risk mitigation.**[45] Previously, with Sections 9 and 4d (5) BDSG aF, there were only significantly less detailed predecessor regulations,[46] which provided for requirements for technical and organizational measures as well as reporting obligations.[47]

103 Art. 35 GDPR works in a similar way to the AI Act with a **risk-based regulatory approach.**[48] However, according to the wording, the connecting factor is the **rights and freedoms of natural persons,**[49] not health, safety or fundamental rights. However, there are likely to be overlaps in terms of content. The material impact of the different wording of the risk classification – "significant risk" under the AI Act and "likely high risk" in the wording of the GDPR – is not further specified. Based on the interpretation of the wording, the GDPR's risk threshold appears to be set somewhat lower.

104 The obligation to carry out a data protection impact assessment applies personally to the **controller** who processes data. **Processors** and **manufacturers** therefore do not fall within the scope of application. According to Art. 4 No. 7 GDPR, the controller is basically the natural or legal person, public authority, agency or other body which determines the purposes and means of the processing of personal data.

105 Objectively, a data protection impact assessment must be carried out if a form of processing takes place that is likely to result in a high risk to the rights and freedoms of natural persons.[50] In abstract terms, Art. 35 para. 1 GDPR states that this high risk results in particular from the **use of new technologies**, the nature, scope, context and purposes of the processing. AI is to be understood as a new technology in this context.[51]

106 The probable risk is determined using a **two-stage process**: The first step is to carry out a preparatory check to determine whether a DPIA is necessary at all. The assessment of whether there is a high risk first requires a threshold analysis. This is a kind of rough data protection impact assessment with regard to all data processing operations, which is intended to provide information on whether there is a likely high risk, which makes a full impact assessment necessary in the second step.[52] However, the GDPR does not define what constitutes a high risk to the rights and freedoms of natural persons. To make it easier to decide whether a specific processing operation requires a data protection impact assessment, the supervisory authorities have drawn up so-called **positive and negative lists** in accordance with Art. 35 para. 4 and para. 5

[44] BeckOK DatenschutzR/Hansen GDPR Art. 35 para. 1.
[45] Ehmann/Selmayr/Baumgartner, Art. 35 para. 1.
[46] Roßnagel/Geminn/Johannes ZD 2019, 435 (435).
[47] Schmitz/von Dall'Armi ZD 2017, 57 (57).
[48] Schmitz/von Dall'Armi ZD 2017, 57 (59).
[49] Roßnagel/Geminn/Johannes ZD 2019, 435 (439).
[50] Schürmann ZD 2022, 316 (320).
[51] Kelber, Artificial Intelligence and AI Act, p. 12.
[52] BeckOK DatenschutzR/Hansen GDPR Art. 35 para. 12.

GDPR.[53] If a processing operation is on one of the two lists, a decision can be made immediately on the basis of this list. If, on the other hand, the processing operation is not on any list, the **standard examples** from Art. 35 para. 3 GDPR should make the decision easier. If no reference is possible here either, the controller must make the decision on the "whether" of a data protection impact assessment on their own responsibility,[54] i.e. evaluate in the specific individual case whether there is a high risk to the rights and freedoms of natural persons.

The understanding of the risk to the rights and freedoms of natural persons must first be interpreted in terms of European individual fundamental rights.[55] A **risk** within the meaning of the GDPR can be defined as "the existence of the possibility of the occurrence of an event which may itself result in damage (including unjustified interference with the rights and freedoms of natural persons) or which may result in further damage to one or more natural persons".[56] Recitals 71, 75, 76, 89 and 90 GDPR are useful for interpretation. 107

Two dimensions must then be taken into account: **Likelihood of occurrence** and **severity** of potential harm. Recital 75 lists a number of examples of damage (e.g. if the processing leads to discrimination, identity theft or fraud, financial loss[57]). However, under Art. 35 GDPR, it is in any case necessary that the specific risk in the individual case goes beyond the general risks.[58] According to Art. 35 para. 1 sentence 1 GDPR, such a high risk may result from the type, scope, circumstances and purpose of processing, in particular if new technologies are used. 108

Recital 91 suggests that a data protection impact assessment should always be required if a **large amount of data** is to be **processed by a large number of people** and **using new technologies** and this poses a potentially high risk due to the **sensitivity of the data**. In practice, this will be relevant in the banking and insurance sector, for example, if AI is used here.[59] The guidelines of the European Data Protection Board offer practical guidance.[60] 109

If the controller comes to the conclusion that the processing operation is "likely to result in a high risk to the rights and freedoms of natural persons" and a data protection impact assessment is therefore required, this must be prepared in the second step with the following minimum content in accordance with Art. 35 para. 7 GDPR: 110

- a systematic description of the envisaged processing operations and the purposes of the processing, including, where applicable, the legitimate interest pursued by the controller, lit. a,
- an assessment of the necessity and proportionality of the processing operations in relation to the purposes, lit. b,
- an assessment of the risks to the rights and freedoms of data subjects, lit. c,
- the remedial measures planned to address the risks, including safeguards, security measures and mechanisms to ensure the protection of personal data and to demonstrate compliance with the GDPR taking into account the rights and legitimate interests of data subjects and other persons concerned, lit. d.

[53] For example, the list of the DSK as amended on 18.7.2018 (so-called "must list").
[54] Ehmann/Selmayr/Baumgartner GDPR Art. 35 para. 5.
[55] BeckOK DatenschutzR/Hansen GDPR Art. 35 para. 14.
[56] DSK Brief Paper No. 18, p. 1.
[57] See only Langenbucher BKR 2023, 205 (206) on the granting of consumer loans.
[58] Sydow/Sassenberg/Schwendemann GDPR Art. 35 para 10.
[59] See Laue/Nink/Kremer § 10 para. 42.
[60] Guidelines on the DSFA as amended on 4.10.2017.

111 The data protection impact assessment must be **comprehensively documented**, whereby the specific method of preparation can be freely chosen. Examples of methods recognized throughout the EU can be found, for example, in Annex I of the guidelines of the European Data Protection Board.[61]

112 A single assessment can be carried out for several processing operations with similarly high risks. In addition, in accordance with Art. 35 para. 2 GDPR, the advice of the data protection officer must be obtained during implementation. If a data protection impact assessment shows that processing would result in a high risk unless the controller takes measures to mitigate the risk, the controller must consult the supervisory authority prior to processing in accordance with Art. 36 para. 1 GDPR and provide it with the data protection impact assessment, among other things. The supervisory authority is then authorized to make recommendations or take measures.

113 The **deployers of high-risk AI systems** covered by the requirement to carry out a fundamental rights impact assessment within the meaning of Art. 6 para. 2 AI Act can also be qualified as **controllers within the meaning of the GDPR** because they regularly process data. In particular, AI is to be understood as a "new technology" within the meaning of Art. 35 GDPR.[62] This means that data processing in connection with the operation of a high-risk AI system regularly requires a data protection impact assessment in accordance with Art. 35 para. 1 GDPR, which must then also be carried out by the deployer. In this case, however, Art. 27 para. 4 AI Act provides that the fundamental rights impact assessment to be carried out under the AI Act only has to supplement the data protection impact assessment required under the GDPR if the controller already fulfills the obligations of the fundamental rights impact assessment in the data protection impact assessment. It follows from this that, according to the legislative concept, **double compliance costs** for deployers should be **avoided** and they can at least keep both processes in uniform documentation. It is therefore conceivable that the controller will describe specific processing operations within the AI system and carry out the associated risk assessment in a uniform manner. Since the contents listed in Art. 35 para. 7 GDPR are only minimum contents, a corresponding addition of special contents of the AI risk assessment is also expressly permitted under the GDPR. A practical difficulty could arise in individual cases from the different risk levels in the wording of the AI Act and the GDPR.

114 Overall, the requirement to conduct a fundamental rights impact assessment can entail a significant amount of work for deployers, as they are often not providers and did not develop the AI system. In order to be able to assess the specific risks, an extensive **cooperation between providers and deployers** is required. At the same time, however, some deployers will already have compliance structures in place to carry out the data protection impact assessment and will be able to use these as a starting point.

[61] Guidelines on the DSFA as amended on 4.10.2017.
[62] Kelber, Artificial Intelligence and AI Act, p. 12.

§ 8
Notification

Literature: *Ashkar, Daniel/ Schröder, Christian*, Das Gesetz über künstliche Intelligenz der Europäischen Union (KI-Verordnung), BB 2024, 771; *Schwartmann, Rolf/Keber, Tobias/Zenner, Kai*, KI-Verordnung. Guide for the practice, 2024.

Art. 28 AI Act introduces the section on **notifying authorities** and **notified bodies.** While the term notification generally describes a procedure in which the Member States must inform the EU Commission (and in some cases also the Member States) of a legal act before it can take effect as a national regulation, notification in the context of the AI Act refers to the **conformity assessment bodies to be set up** in the Member States. According to Art. 3 No. 20 AI Act, conformity assessment refers to the process of assessing whether the requirements of the AI Act (especially those in Title III, Section 2) for a high-risk AI system are met.[1] 1

I. Notifying authorities

According to Article 3 No. 19 AI Act, the **national authorities** responsible for the procedure for the assessment, designation and notification of conformity assessment bodies and their surveillance are "notifying" authorities. As notifying authorities are **part of the supervisory system established by the AI Act**, they will be discussed in detail later (→ § 12 mn. 57). 2

II. Notified bodies

A **notified body** is a conformity assessment body that has been notified under the AI Act and other relevant European harmonization legislation in accordance with Art. 3 No. 22 AI Act. It is responsible for **verifying** the **conformity of high-risk AI systems** in accordance with the conformity assessment procedure set out in Art. 43 AI Act, Art. 34 para. 1 AI Act. 3

Notified bodies are subject to **requirements in terms of resources, cybersecurity, governance**, including the allocation of responsibilities and reporting lines, as well as **quality management**, Art. 31 AI Act. It must be ensured at all times that the functioning of the notified body justifies confidence in its performance and in the results of the conformity assessments carried out, Art. 31 para. 3 AI Act. 4

This includes ensuring that the notified bodies carry out their tasks with the highest level of **professional integrity** and **expertise**. Each notified body must have sufficient knowledge not only of the requirements of the AI Act, but also of relevant AI systems and administrative, technical, legal and scientific personnel, Art. 31 para. 11 AI Act. 5

This requirement also extends to third parties – in particular **subcontractors** or **branches** – who act on behalf of and under the responsibility of the notified body, Art. 31 para. 10 AI Act. The transfer of a contract to a branch or subcontractor requires the consent of the provider, Art. 33 para. 3 AI Act. 6

In particular, it must be ensured that the notified bodies are **independent** of the provider of the high-risk AI system whose conformity they are assessing. Independence must also be ensured with regard to all other actors who have an economic 7

[1] Ashkar/Schröder BB 2024, 771 (774).

interest in the AI system to be assessed. This also includes **competitors of the provider**. Furthermore, neither the conformity assessment body itself, its top level management nor the employees responsible for performing its conformity assessment tasks may be directly involved in the design, development, marketing or use of a high-risk AI system or represent parties involved in these activities. In general, they must not engage in any activities that could compromise their objectivity in the assessment or their integrity. This applies in particular to **consultancy services**, Art. 31 para. 5 AI Act.

8 However, it is not excluded that the conformity assessment body **itself uses AI systems that it has assessed** if these are required for its activities. The use of AI systems to be assessed **for personal use** is also not prohibited, Art. 31 para. 4 AI Act.

9 The notified bodies work with **internal procedural guidelines**. The guidelines take into account the complexity of the AI system to be tested, the size of the deployer, the sector in which it operates and its corporate structure.

10 It must be ensured at all times that the **confidentiality of all information** that comes into its sphere in the course of a conformity assessment is maintained in accordance with Art. 78 AI Act. This obligation includes all employees, branches and subcontractors of the notified body as well as employees of external bodies.

11 To ensure the necessary **transparency**, notified bodies shall establish and publish a **list of their subsidiaries**. The documents concerning the assessment of the qualifications of a subcontractor or a subsidiary and the work carried out by them shall be kept for a period of five years from the date of termination of the subcontracting and, where appropriate, **handed over to the notifying authority**.

12 According to Art. 33 para. 1 AI Act, the notified body must ensure that the branch office or subcontractor **fulfills** the **requirements of Art. 31 AI Act**. It has an **inspection function** in this regard; it **is** also **liable** for the work that it has assigned to third parties.

13 Accordingly, notified bodies are obliged to take out appropriate **liability insurance**, Art. 31 para. 9 AI Act. If the liability is covered directly by the Member State on the basis of national law or if the Member State itself is directly responsible for the conformity assessment, this obligation does not apply.

14 According to Art. 45 AI Act, there should be an **active exchange of information** between the notified bodies and the notifying authority: The notified bodies must inform the notifying authority of all Union certificates concerning the assessment of the technical documentation, any additions to these certificates and approvals of quality management systems. They must also inform vice versa about refusals, restrictions, suspensions or withdrawals of Union certificates, Art. 45 para. 1 AI Act. In general, all circumstances that have consequences for the scope or conditions of the notification must be notified – not only in relation to the notifying authority, but also to other notified bodies, Art. 45 para. 2 AI Act. If other notified bodies undertake conformity assessments for comparable AI systems, it shall provide them with relevant information on negative – and on request also positive – conformity assessment results, Art. 45 para. 3 AI Act. **Confidentiality** towards third parties must be guaranteed, Art. 28 para. 6 in conjunction with Art. 78 AI Act.

15 In order to further promote **cooperation** and **consistency in the assessment**, the notified bodies are requested to participate in the coordination activities referred to in Art. 38 AI Act (→ mn. 22). They should **participate** directly or indirectly in the **work of the European standardization organizations** (→ § 9 mn. 2) and must ensure that they are always informed about the status of the relevant standards.

Notified bodies should **take** due **account** of the **size of the provider**, the **sector** in which it operates, its **structure** and the **complexity** of the high-risk AI system concerned when conducting their **compliance assessment** in order to minimize the administrative burden and costs for micro and small enterprises, including start-ups.[2] It is important to find the right level to consistently **ensure** the rigor and **level of protection** necessary for the high-risk AI system to comply with the requirements of the AI Act while avoiding unnecessary burdens on providers, Art. 34 para. 2 AI Act. 16

Where the notified body confirms the **conformity of an AI system**, it shall issue the **certificate** referred to in Annex VII in a language which can be understood by the relevant authorities of the Member State in which the notified body is established, Art. 44 para. 1 AI Act. 17

The certificate contains a **period of validity**. It may not exceed **five years** for AI systems covered by Annex I (= list of EU harmonization legislation) and **four years** for AI systems covered by Annex III (= high-risk AI systems pursuant to Art. 6 para. 2 AI Act). The provider can apply for an extension. Such an extension would also extend to any supplements attached to the certificate, Art. 44 para. 2 AI Act. 18

Where a notified body finds that an AI system no longer meets the requirements of the AI Act, it may **suspend**, **revoke** or **restrict** the certificate issued, unless appropriate corrective action is taken by the provider within a reasonable period of time. The decision of the notified body must be substantiated. The provider may **appeal** against all decisions of the notified bodies, including those on certificates of conformity issued, Art. 44 para. 3 AI Act. 19

If there are reasonable **doubts** about the **competence** or **compliance of** a notified body, the notifying authority is first called upon to investigate the facts of the case. The notified body is given the opportunity to comment. If the investigation reveals a breach of duty, the notifying authority restricts, suspends or withdraws the notification, depending on the severity of the incident. It is also necessary to check whether the certificates issued by the notified body in the past are still compliant. Certificates of conformity that have not been properly issued will be suspended or revoked, Art. 36 para. 4 AI Act. 20

The EU Commission and the other member states must be informed of the procedure. This is also necessary because the **competence to investigate breaches of duty** by notified bodies passes to the EU Commission if necessary, Art. 37 AI Act. The notifying authority must therefore provide the EU Commission with all information about the notified body in question upon request. If the EU Commission comes to the con clusion that a notified body does not (or no longer) meet the requirements of the AI Act, it will request the Member State to take remedial action, for example by **suspending or withdrawing the notification**. If the Member State does not comply with this request, the EU Commission can suspend, restrict or revoke the designation itself by means of an implementing act. The implementing act must be issued in accordance with Art. 98 para. 2 AI Act. 21

In order to ensure uniformity in the **conformity assessment procedures** and to establish proven procedures, the EU Commission promotes **cooperation between notified bodies throughout the EU**. These should form groups that are organized on a sectoral basis to build up specific expertise. Each notifying authority must ensure that the bodies notified by it participate directly or via representatives in the work of the groups, Art. 38 AI Act. 22

---

[2] Within the meaning of the Commission Recommendation of 6.5.2003 concerning the definition of micro, small and medium-sized enterprises (2003/361/EC), OJ No. L 124 p. 36. 36.

23 Conformity assessment bodies **established under the law of a third country** can also be authorized to act as a notified body if a corresponding agreement with the EU exists and the same level of conformity is ensured, Art. 39 AI Act.

§ 9
Harmonized standards and conformity assessment

Literature: *Abend, Kerstin,* Neues Unionsrecht für die Vermarktung von Bauprodukten, EuZW 2013, 611; *von Czettritz,* Peter, Zur Bedeutung der CE-Zertifizierung in wettbewerbsrechtlichen Verfahren – zugleich eine Anmerkung zu Landgericht Hamburg, Urteil vom 19.9.2019, 403 HKO 43/19 und Oberlandesgericht Hamburg, Urteil vom 12.12.2019, 3 U 14/19, MPR 2020, 14; *De la Roza, Rafael,* "Private Labelling" von Medizinprodukten: Fallstricke und Hinweise zur rechtssicheren Vertragsgestaltung zwischen Inverkehrbringer und OEM-Hersteller, MPR 2008, 70; *Frank, Lucia,* Digitale Barrierefreiheit von Produkten und Dienstleistungen, ZfPC 2024, 21; *Gerdemann, Simon,* Harmonisierte Normen und ihre Bedeutung für die Zukunft der KI, MMR 2024, 614; *Hartmannsberger, Roland/Herzig, Andreas,* Wettbewerbsrechtliche Folgen von Verstößen gegen formale Produktanforderungen, GRUR-RR 2016, 433; *Irmer, Franziska,* CE-Kennzeichnung und die Auswirkung einer Unternehmenstransaktion, MPR 2011, 109; *König, Walter/Schanz, Michael,* Die CE-Kennzeichnung – ein genauer Blick lohnt sich, RDG 2017, 208; *Lachenmann, Mattias,* EU Council approves AI Regulation – new obligations for companies, MMR-Aktuell 2024, 01359; *Lötzsch, Markus/Fifka, Matthias,* Einführung einer CE-Kennzeichnung zum vorbeugenden Schutz von Menschenrechten in Wertschöpfungsketten, EuZW 2020, 179; *Schucht, Carsten,* Der Händler im Produktsicherheitsrecht – Rolle, Pflichten, Rechtsrisiken, CCZ 2020, 322; *Schucht, Carsten,* Produkt-Zertifikate beim Warenvertrieb – Risikosteuerung und Rechtspflicht, NJW 2019, 1335; *Schucht, Carsten,* Produktsicherheit durch Kennzeichnung, DÖV 2018, 431; *Schwartmann, Rolf/Keber, Tobias/Zenner, Kai,* KI-Verordnung. Leitfaden für die Praxis, 2024; *Voigt, Paul/Falk, Lucas,* Der Cyber Resilience Act, MMR 2023, 88; *Wagner, Gerhard,* Schadensersatz wegen Verletzung von Unionsrecht – Luxemburg locuta, causa aperta, NJW 2023, 1761; *Wiebe, Gerhard/Daelen, Johannes,* Der Cyber Resilience Act aus produktsicherheitsrechtlicher Perspektive, EuZW 2023, 257; *Wiebe, Gerhard,* Produktsicherheitsrechtliche Betrachtung des Vorschlags für eine KI-Verordnung, BB 2022, 899; *Wilrich, Thomas,* Kein "nachträgliches CE" des Betreibers, sondern nur Compliance mit der BetrSichV bei rechtswidrigen Altmaschinen, CCZ 2020, 294; *Wilrich, Thomas,* Maschinen ohne CE-Kennzeichnung und die Betreiberverantwortung, ARP 2020, 223.

I. Interaction with European standardization organizations

The AI Act is only one building block in the new system for regulating AI. Another major building block is the setting of standards by means of so-called harmonized standards, which is regulated by Art. 40 AI Act. While harmonized standards are still relatively unknown in digital law, they have been a tried and tested tool in product safety law for years, effectively transferring regulatory powers to the European standardization organizations. They have the task of transforming the sometimes vague abstract requirements of the AI Act into a set of concrete technical requirements that can be handled in practice by developing standards, which are also internationally compatible through cooperation with globally active sister organizations.[1] Although the European standardization organizations do not have their own democratic legitimacy, so that the harmonized standards do not have the character of legal standards, 1

[1] Gerdemann MMR 2024, 614 (615).

their practical importance can hardly be overestimated.[2] This is related to the presumption of conformity regulated in Art. 40 para. 1 AI Act, according to which compliance with the legal requirements is presumed if and to the extent that the design and control of a high-risk AI system complies with the standards of the harmonized standards. Voluntary compliance with the harmonized standards therefore appears to be the most legally secure and at the same time most cost-effective approach, which is regularly superior to in-house technical solutions.[3]

2 The harmonized standards for the AI Act are developed by the JTC 21 committee, which was jointly convened by the European standardization organizations **CEN** (European Committee for Standardization) and **CENELEC** (European Committee for Electrotechnical Standardization).[4] The mandate to create the harmonized standards in accordance with Art. 10 of the European Standardization Regulation[5] was given by the EU Commission in May 2023.[6] However, the mandate does not affect the content of the committee's work; the standardization organizations work independently. The harmonized standards are expected by the end of 2025 in order to give companies sufficient time to adapt to the specific requirements before the main date of application of the AI Act on 2.8.2026.

3 According to Art. 40 para. 2 AI Act, the EU Commission's **standardization mandate** for the AI Act contains details on the scope of application, deadlines and legal requirements that the standards must meet. This ensures that the standards developed comply directly with the requirements set out in the AI Act. The EU Commission also stipulated that the standards must be clear and consistent. This requirement relates in particular to consistency with the sectoral specifications for products.

4 In addition, documents were requested on the **reporting and documentation procedures** with regard to improving the resource performance of AI systems – for example, on the energy-efficient development of general-purpose AI models.

5 When the European standardization organizations draft the standards, the **standardization institutes of the member states** (NSB) also provide[7] technical expertise. This is incorporated into the work of the JTC 21 committee, which also includes a selection of interest groups as observers.

6 The JTC 21 committee is a working group of experts from the standardization institutes of the member states and observers. The group does not necessarily have to include one expert per country; the committee **is free to choose its composition**. It prepares a draft on the basis of **consensus**.

7 As a rule, the European standardization organizations are guided by the **international standards of the Organization for International Standardization (ISO)** or the

---

[2] Gerdemann MMR 2024, 614 (615).

[3] Thus Gerdemann MMR 2024, 614 (615).

[4] Guijarro Santos ZfDR 1/2023, 23 (32); on the financing of standardization organizations and the effects of the so-called Malamud decision of the ECJ (ECJ 5.3.2024 – C-588/21 P, ECLI:EU:C:2024:201), cf. Monsees KIR 2025, 263 (265).

[5] Regulation (EU) No 1025/2012 of the European Parliament and of the Council of 25.10.2012 on European standardization, amending Council Directives 89/686/EEC and 93/15/EEC and Directives 94/9/EC, 94/25/EC, 95/16/EC, 97/23/EC, 98/34/EC, 2004/22/EC, 2007/23/EC, 2009/23/EC and 2009/105/EC of the European Parliament and of the Council and repealing Council Decision 87/95/EEC and Decision No 1673/2006/EC of the European Parliament and of the Council, OJ L 316 p. 12.

[6] Commission implementing decision of 22.5.2023 on a standardisation request to the European Committee for Standardisation and the European Committee for Electrotechnical Standardisation in support of Union policy on artificial intelligence, C(2023) 3215 final.

[7] A list of CEN member NSBs can be found here: https://standards.cencenelec.eu/dyn/www/f.?p=CEN:5.

International Electrotechnical Commission (IEC), insofar as these are available. This corresponds to Art. 40 para. 3 of the AI Act, which declares the strengthening of global cooperation in standardization and the consideration of existing international standards in the field of AI as an objective, insofar as these are in line with the values, fundamental rights and interests of the EU. International cooperation is an important part of the WTO Agreement on Technical Barriers to Trade, which prevents countries from using standards to hinder international trade. It serves to ensure international consistency and is also intended to improve multi-stakeholder governance by promoting effective participation of all relevant stakeholders.[8]

8 The **harmonized standards** take on several tasks. On the one hand, they create a greater **level of detail** and thus support a better understanding of the AI Act. At the same time, **they facilitate the conformity assessment procedures**, as they establish a presumption of conformity in Art. 42 AI Act, which applies in the event of compliance with the harmonized standards. Their compliance establishes the "**presumption of conformity**" with the essential requirements: High-risk AI systems or general-purpose AI models that comply with harmonized standards or parts thereof, the references of which have been published in the Official Journal of the EU (OJEU), are presumed to comply with the requirements of the AI Act insofar as they are covered by the standards, Art. 40 para. 1 AI Act.

9 If none of the European standardization organizations had accepted the EU Commission's mandate to develop **harmonized standards** for the requirements and obligations set out in the AI Act, the EU Commission would have had the option of issuing **implementing acts** itself **to define common specifications**, Art. 41 AI Act. The same applies if CEN and CENELEC do not complete the harmonized standards on time or if there are concerns about the content of the result, particularly with regard to conformity with fundamental rights, or if the result simply does not meet the mandate. Immediate action by the EU Commission also presupposes that no references to harmonized standards relating to the AI Act have yet been published in the OJEU. Furthermore, it cannot be expected that the harmonized standards will be published within a reasonable period of time. Before drafting the common specifications, the EU Commission would have to consult the Advisory Forum referred to in Art. 67 AI Act (→ § 13 mn. 30).

10 Member States can also **criticize the common specifications**: If a Member State is of the opinion that a common specification does not reflect the requirements and obligations of the AI Act, it must explain its concerns in detail. The EU Commission evaluates the criticism and amends the implementing act if necessary.

11 The **presumption of conformity** with the requirements and obligations of the AI Act that applies when harmonized standards are complied with also extends to common specifications in accordance with Art. 41 para. 3 AI Act: Where high-risk AI systems and general purpose AI models conform to common specifications, conformity with all requirements and obligations covered by them is presumed.[9] Conversely, providers of high-risk AI systems or general purpose AI models that do not comply with the common specifications must prove that their technical solutions nevertheless meet the requirements and obligations of the AI Act to the same extent, Art. 41 para. 5 AI Act.

12 If a harmonized standard is subsequently drawn up by one of the European standardization organizations and the reference is published in the Official Journal of the

[8] Critical Guijarro Santos ZfDR 1/2023, 23 (32).
[9] Guijarro Santos ZfDR 1/2023, 23 (33).

EU, any implementing acts that have been drawn up by the EU Commission in the meantime must be repealed, Art. 41 para. 4 AI Act.

II. Conformity assessment

13 **Conformity assessment** is the process of checking whether the requirements placed on a high-risk AI system have been met.[10] The AI Act provides for various forms of conformity assessment. The focus is on **internal conformity assessment (internal control)** and **external conformity assessment (third-party conformity assessment)**. Which conformity assessment procedure is used depends on the type of high-risk AI system.

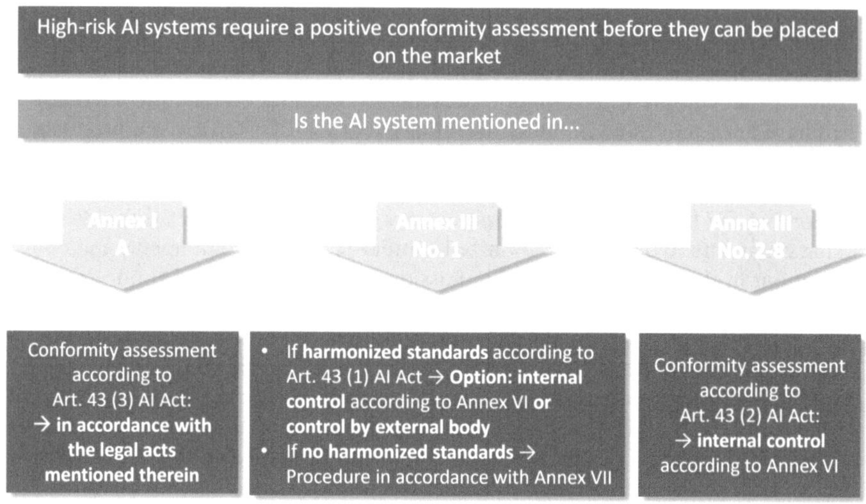

Figure 14: Conformity assessment

1. High-risk AI systems in accordance with Annex I Section A AI Act

14 For high-risk AI systems that fall under Annex I Section A, the conformity assessment procedure of the directive or regulation cited there applies, Art. 43 para. 3 AI Act. As a rule, these provide for a **third-party conformity assessment**.[11] By way of exception, an **internal conformity assessment** is **permissible** if certain technical requirements are met.[12] This procedure corresponds to the regulatory approach of the "New Approach".[13] Annex I Section A refers to the twelve directives and regulations accordingly as the "List of Union harmonization legislation based on the New Legislative Framework".

15 The **New Legislative Framework (NLF)** is made up of directives and regulations of European product safety law. It was introduced in 2015 as a so-called "new uniform legal framework" for conformity legislation for non-food products and replaces the previous version from 2010. The aim of the amendment was to further level the

[10] Fuderer MPR 2022, 121 (121).
[11] Fuderer MPR 2022, 121 (121).
[12] Denga ZfPC 2023, 154 (155).
[13] Denga ZfPC 2023, 154 (155).

playing field in the internal market and increase consumer protection and safety. The New Legislative Framework regulates the stakeholders and their obligations within the supply chain as well as the position of the market surveillance authorities.

The bodies notified under the legal acts from the New Legislative Framework may only verify the conformity of high-risk AI systems with the requirements of the AI Act if they fulfill the requirements pursuant to Art. 31 AI Act. In particular, they must prove their **independence** (para. 4), must **not be subject to conflicts of interest** (para. 5), must have the necessary **expertise** (para. 10) and must have sufficient administrative, technical, legal and scientific **personnel resources** (para. 11). 16

If one of the twelve directives and regulations in Annex I Section A allows the manufacturer of the product to **dispense** with a **conformity assessment by a third party**, provided that he **applies all harmonized standards** and these in turn cover all relevant requirements, the manufacturer may only make use of this option if the harmonized standards according to Art. 41 AI Act are also taken into account, Art. 43 para. 3 AI Act. 17

2. High-risk AI systems in accordance with Annex I Section B AI Act

AI systems that fall under the harmonized legislation listed in Annex I Section B AI Act are not covered by the scope of the AI Act, Art. 2 para. 2 AI Act.[14] The legal acts listed here relate to **civil aviation** (No. 1, 7), **motor vehicles** (No. 2, 3, 6), **shipping** (No. 4) and **rail transport** (No. 5). 18

Only Art. 84 AI Act, which governs the evaluation and revision of the regulation, is applicable to the AI systems covered by these provisions. In contrast to Annex I Section A, Section B follows the **old regulatory framework**, which provides for specific and differentiated regulation that is fundamentally inconsistent with the regulatory approach of the AI Act.[15] The corresponding conformity assessments are therefore not attributable to it.[16] 19

3. High-risk AI systems pursuant to Annex III No. 1 AI Act

Art. 43 para. 1 AI Act provides a separate regulation for **systems for remote biometric identification**. The conformity assessment is carried out either by an internal conformity assessment in accordance with Annex VI of the AI Act or a third-party conformity assessment by a notified body in accordance with Annex VII of the AI Act. However, this only applies if the provider of the system has complied with existing harmonized standards or common specifications, Art. 43 para. 1 sentence 1 AI Act. If this is not the case, for example because such standards do not yet exist, the third-party conformity procedure in accordance with Annex VII, Art. 43 para. 1 sentences 2, 3 AI Act automatically applies.[17] 20

The provider decides which notified body carries out the conformity assessment in accordance with Annex VII; the EU Commission's **NANDO database** can be used for the selection.[18] 21

Only for high-risk AI systems used by law enforcement, immigration or asylum authorities or by EU institutions, bodies, offices or agencies does the AI Act stipulate in 22

[14] Binder/Egli MMR 2024, 626 (627).
[15] Binder/Egli MMR 2024, 626 (627).
[16] Denga ZfPC 2023, 154 (156).
[17] Denga ZfPC 2023, 154 (155).
[18] S. https://webgate.ec.europa.eu/single-market-compliance-space/#/notified-bodies.

Art. 74 para. 8 and 9 that the market surveillance authority assumes the function of the notified body.

4. High-risk AI systems in accordance with Annex III No. 2–8 AI Act

23 For AI systems that are used in areas that are particularly sensitive to fundamental rights, providers only have the option of conformity assessment based on **internal control**. The involvement of a notified body is not provided for here. The particularly sensitive areas are defined in Art. 43 para. 2 AI Act via Annex III No. 2–8. The sectors listed here are critical infrastructure; education; human resources management and access to self-employment; use of public services and benefits; law enforcement; migration, asylum and border control; and administration of justice and democratic processes.

5. Repetition of the conformity assessment

24 A conformity assessment procedure must be **repeated** if the high-risk AI system undergoes a **substantial modification**, Art. 43 para 4 AI Act.[19] This applies regardless of whether it is still to be placed on the market or merely continued to be used by the current deployer.

25 Changes to the system and its performance that the system **acquires through self-learning** are **generally not considered to be significant** and therefore do not trigger an obligation for a new conformity assessment. This applies subject to the restriction that the potential change is already included by the provider in the technical documentation in accordance with Annex IV No. 2 (f) AI Act.

26 In order to ensure the **future viability** of the provisions, the EU Commission may adapt Annexes VI and VII to technological progress by means of a delegated act.

27 It may also amend Art. 43 para. 1 and 2 AI Act itself by means of a delegated act. In this way, the EU Commission can subject AI systems used in sensitive sectors to the conformity assessment procedure based on quality management and technical documentation in accordance with Annex VII (in accordance with Annex III No. 2–8).

28 When adopting delegated acts, the EU Commission must take into account the **effectiveness of the conformity assessment** with regard to the prevention or reduction of risks to health, safety and the protection of fundamental rights as well as the capacities of the notified bodies, Art. 43 para. 6 AI Act.

6. Approval by market surveillance authority

29 In **exceptional circumstances** relating to public safety, the protection of life and health, environmental protection or the protection of important industrial and infrastructure facilities, a high-risk AI system may also be approved by a **market surveillance authority** in exceptional cases.[20]

30 **Approval** by the market surveillance authority is not intended to replace the conformity assessment under Art. 43 AI Act, but only to enable the AI system to be used more quickly. In this respect, Art. 46 AI Act **closes** the **time gap** until the regular assessment procedure has been completed. Accordingly, approvals by the market surveillance authority are always granted for a short period of time; the reasons for the

---

[19] Denga ZfPC 2023, 154 (155).

[20] Only high-risk AI systems according to Annex I Section A cannot make use of this exemption, but are referred to the exemption provisions in their sectoral harmonization legislation, Art. 46 para. 7 AI Act.

exemption are decisive when determining the time limit. The market surveillance authority informs the EU Commission and the other Member States of all approvals that it has granted. If neither the EU Commission nor another Member State raises an objection within 15 calendar days, the authorization is deemed justified, Art. 46 para. 4 AI Act. If an objection is raised, the EU Commission decides after consultation with the Member State concerned. It addresses its decision to the Member State concerned and the stakeholders. If the EU Commission considers the approval to be unjustified, it must be withdrawn by the market surveillance authority of the Member State concerned, Art. 46 para. 6 AI Act.

7. Derogation from conformity assessment

In even more urgent cases, law enforcement or civil protection authorities may 31
even put a high-risk AI system into operation entirely **without authorization** (including from a market surveillance authority). These **exceptional cases** include specific, substantial and imminent threats to the life or physical safety of natural persons or threats to public safety. The approval procedure must also be carried out immediately and applied for during or after use. If approval is refused, the AI system may no longer be used and all results are discarded, Art. 46 para. 2 AI Act.

III. Declaration of conformity

At the end of the conformity assessment procedure is the declaration of conformity 32
in accordance with Art. 47 AI Act. With this declaration, the provider confirms that the high-risk AI system complies with the requirements of the AI Act. The declarations must be in writing and machine-readable. With their physical or electronic signature, the provider assumes responsibility for fulfilling the requirements, especially those in Section II.

Each high-risk AI system requires its own declaration of conformity. The provider 33
must keep the declarations **for ten years** from the date on which the AI system is placed on the market or put into service **and keep them up to date**. The national supervisory authority can request transmission at any time.

The exact **content** of the declaration of conformity can be found in Annex V. The 34
EU Commission is free to amend the Annex by delegated act and adapt it to technological progress, for example by means of extensions, Art. 47 para. 4 AI Act.

If the high-risk AI system is subject to **parallel sector-specific product safety** 35
legislation and this also requires a declaration of conformity, only one declaration needs to be issued that covers all legislation applicable to the high-risk AI system in the EU.

IV. CE marking

While the declaration of conformity describes in detail the compliance of the 36
high-risk AI system with the requirements of the AI Act and serves as proof to the supervisory authorities, the **CE marking** addresses the end user: he should be able to recognize quickly and directly that the AI system has been tested by the provider

and meets all requirements of the AI Act and, if applicable, relevant sector-specific regulations.[21]

37 Accordingly, the CE marking must be affixed **visibly, legibly and indelibly** to the high-risk AI system. If the type of system does not allow this, the provider may exceptionally mark the packaging or accompanying documentation. For purely digitally provided AI systems, Art 48 para. 2 AI Act also provides a **digital CE marking**. However, the use of this requires that the marking can be carried out via an interface or via an easily accessible machine-readable code or similar. If a high-risk AI system has been integrated into a product, a dual physical and digital CE marking is desirable according to recital 129.

38 CE marking is **mandatory** for all products manufactured worldwide and **marketed in the EU**. The CE marking of AI systems is subject to the principles laid down in Art. 30 of the Regulation on the rules for accreditation and market surveillance relating to the marketing of products[22], which form the general legal framework for the surveillance of product safety in the EU. If, in addition to the AI Act, a high-risk AI system is subject to other EU legislation that provides for CE marking, this indicates that the AI system also meets the requirements of this other legislation, Art. 48 para. 5 AI Act.

39 If the conformity assessment of the AI system has been carried out by a notified body, its identification number must be added to the CE marking. It shall also be indicated on any promotional material bearing the CE marking.

V. Inclusion in high-risk database

40 In cooperation with the Member States, the EU Commission creates and maintains an EU-wide accessible **database for high-risk AI systems**, Art. 72 AI Act. The information contained therein should be publicly available in a user-friendly and machine-readable form, Art. 49 para. 4 AI Act. The exception under Art. 60 para. 4 lit. c AI Act must be observed. Only market surveillance authorities and the EU Commission can access the information registered in accordance with Art. 60 AI Act, unless the (future) provider has given its consent to publication. Information on AI systems used in the areas of law enforcement, migration, asylum and border control is excluded from general accessibility. The database has a separate section for them, which can only be accessed by the EU Commission and the national supervisory authorities, Art. 49 para. 4 in conjunction with Art. 74 para. 8 AI Act. The EU Commission is responsible for the database. It is required to provide providers, future providers and deployers with technical and administrative support for registration, Art. 49 para. 6 AI Act.

41 AI systems that fall under Annex III – with the exception of those that are used as safety components in the management and operation of critical digital infrastructure for road traffic or the supply of water, gas, heat or electricity, Art. 49 para. 1 AI Act – are registered. AI systems in accordance with Annex III whose provider has decided to make use of the opting-out clause in accordance with Art. 6 para. 4 AI Act and not to have the system classified as high-risk must also be registered, Art. 49 para. 2 AI Act (→ § 5 mn. 36).

---

[21] Cf. on medical devices, for example König/Schanz RDG 2017, 208 (209).

[22] Regulation (EC) No 765/2008 of the European Parliament and of the Council of 9.7.2008 setting out the requirements for accreditation and market surveillance relating to the marketing of products and repealing Regulation (EEC) No 339/93 (Text with EEA relevance), OJ L 218, 13.8.2008, pp. 30–47.

Annex VIII determines what **information** the database will contain: The provider must provide information about its contact details and any authorized representative. According to Art. 49 para. 5 AI Act, these are the only **personal data** that must be provided for the database. 42

In addition, the provider or authorized representative is required to supply detailed information about the AI system itself. This includes the trade name of the system and, if applicable, other identification features that enable unambiguous assignment and traceability. A description of the intended purpose and the components and functions supported by the AI system is also required, as well as a basic, albeit brief, description of the information used by the system and its operating logic. An electronic operating manual is also included. The status of the AI system – in service, no longer in service, recalled – must also be provided, including information on the Member States in which the AI system is on the market. 43

With regard to the conformity assessment, the type, number and expiration date of the certificate and, if applicable, the name or identification number of the notified body must be stated. A scanned copy of the EU declaration of conformity must also be stored in the database. 44

Providers who make use of the **opting-out clause** of Art. 6 para. 3 AI Act and have their system classified as not high-risk (→ § 5 mn. 36) must also explain their reasons in a brief summary in accordance with Annex VIII Section B, Art. 49 para. 2 AI Act. 45

In addition to the providers, certain deployers are also responsible for entries in the database, namely authorities and institutions, bodies or other entities of the EU or persons acting on their behalf. They must register high-risk AI systems in accordance with Annex III – again with the exception of AI systems for critical infrastructures, Art. 49 para. 3 AI Act. However, they have to provide significantly less information for the database than providers. Section C of Annex VIII only requires the contact details of the deployer and the person from whom they received the information. In addition, the web address (URL) of the entry of the AI system in the EU database by its provider must be provided. It is important that a summary of the results of the fundamental rights impact assessment carried out in accordance with Art. 27 AI Act is also included in the database. 46

When setting up the database for the first time, the EU Commission consults experts, especially when defining the functional specifications. For subsequent updates, it can then consult the AI Board (→ § 13 mn. 22), which has since taken up its work. 47

§ 10
Transparency obligations for providers and deployers

Literature: *Bayer, Judit/Bitiukova, Natalija/Bárd* Petra *u.a.*, Disinformation and propaganda – impact on the functioning of the rule of law in the EU and its Member States, 2019; *Block, Martina*, A Critical Evaluation of Deepfake Regulation Through the AI Act in the European Union, EuCML 2024, 184; *Block, Martina*, Deepfakes und Recht, 2023; *Chesney Robert/Citron, Danielle K.*; A Looming Challenge for Privacy, Democracy and National Security, California Law Review Vol. 107:1753; *Hacker, Philipp*, KI und DMA – Zugang, Transparenz und Fairness für KI-Modelle in der digitalen Wirtschaft, GRUR 2022, 1278; *Hinderks, Tobias*, Die Kennzeichnungspflicht von Deepfakes, ZUM 2022, 110; *Höch, Dominik/Kahl, Jonas*, Anforderungen an eine Kennzeichnungspflicht für KI-Inhalte, K&R 2023, 396; *Johannisbauer, Christoph*, ChatGPT in the legal sector – initial experiences and legal challenges in the use of artificially generated texts, MMR-Aktuell 2023, 455537; *Kalbfus, Michael/Schöberle, Andreas*, Arbeitsrechtliche Fragen beim Einsatz von KI am Beispiel von ChatGPT, ArbRAktuell 2023, 251; *Kalbhenn, Jan Christopher*, Designvorgaben für Chatbots, Deepfakes und Emotionserkennungssysteme: The European Commission's proposal for an AI Regulation as an extension of media law platform regulation, ZUM 2021, 275; *Keber, Tobias/Schwartmann, Rolf*, ChatGPT – Wie reguliert man eine Weltmaschine? MMR-Aktuell 2023, 457196; *King, Christopher*, Complex Contracts in the Era of Chat GPT and Other Generative AI – A German – American View, TLJ 2023, 29; *Konertz, Roman*, Urheberrechtliche Fragen der Textgenerierung durch Künstliche Intelligenz: Insbesondere Schöpfungen und Rechtsverletzungen durch GPT und ChatGPT, WRP 2023, 796; *Krone, Felix*, Urheberrechtlicher Schutz von ChatGPT-Texten? RDi 2023, 117; *Kühling, Jürgen*, Der Einsatz von Künstlicher Intelligenz durch Unternehmen und Aufsichtsbehörden bei der Bekämpfung von Hassrede, ZUM 2023, 566; *Kumkar, Lea Katharina*, Deepfakes – Risiken und Regulierung im europäischen Verordnungsentwurf für künstliche Intelligenz, K&R Beilage 2023, 32; *Kumkar, Lea Katharina/Rapp, Julian Philipp*, Deepfakes, ZfDR 2022, 199; *Labuz, Mateusz*, Regulating Deepfakes in the Artificial Intelligence Act, ACIG 2023, 2(1); *Lantwin, Tobias*, Deep Fakes – Düstere Zeiten für den Persönlichkeitsschutz?, MMR 2019, 574; *Lennartz, Jannis*, "Digitale Puppenspieler" – die Nachbildung von Körper und Stimme durch KI, NJW 2023, 3543; *Linhart, Andrea/Schumacher, Pablo/Zech, Herbert*, Schutz trainierter KI vs. Transparenzpflichten – Ein Spannungsverhältnis, ZUM 2024, 237; *Molavi Vasse'i, Ramak*, Transparenzanforderungen an Künstliche Intelligenz, K&R Beilage 2022, 8; *Rößling, Fabian*, Regulierung von Deep Fakes – Manipulierte Medien in AI Act, DS-GVO und allgemeinem Persönlichkeitsrecht, ZfDR 2024, 187; *Siegel, Dennis/Kaetzer, Christian/Seidlitz, Stefan/Dittmann, Jana*, Media Forensic Considerations of the Usage of Artificial Intelligence Using the Example of DeepFake Detection, J. Imaging 2024, 10, 46; *Song, Xiaokang*, A Study of Ethical Dilemmas and Regulation of AI Chatbots, Journal of Theory and Practice of Social Science 3 (9), 8; *Thiel, Markus*, "Deepfakes" – Sehen heißt glauben, ZRP 2021, 202; *Wach, Krzysztof* et al, The dark side of generative artificial intelligence: A critical analysis of controversies and risks of ChatGPT, Entrepreneurial Business and Economics Review, 11(2), 7; *Wendt, Domenik*, Der AI Act: Compliance-Anforderungen für Anbieter und Betreiber von KI-Systemen, uj 2024, 42.

I. Compliance-by-design

1 The fourth chapter regulates **transparency obligations** in Art. 50 of the AI Act. Specifically, providers must design and develop AI systems intended for direct interaction with natural persons in such a way that the natural persons concerned are aware

that they are interacting with an AI system, Art. 50 para. 1 AI Act.[1] The AI Act thus addresses the **compliance-by-design approach.**[2]

Only in the few cases in which the **context of use** does not allow any other conclusion than that it is an AI is the transparency obligation waived, Art. 50 para. 1 sentence 1 AI Act. The focus here is always on an appropriately informed, attentive and reasonable group of recipients. 2

II. Chatbots

The most common application of Art. 50 of the AI Act is the use of chatbots, i.e. dialogue systems designed for direct interaction with natural persons, which are increasingly acting in a lifelike manner.[3] The launch of ChatGPT showed that development was already more advanced by the end of 2022 than many suspected. It is obvious that this progress is not without risk: AI systems are more successful than natural persons at influencing and manipulating people's views.[4] An AI system can spread false information at high speed and, especially on social media, create the impression that many people share a view.[5] Such an approach can always have serious consequences, especially if the AI is used to collect votes on a large scale.[6] 3

The regulation of AI systems intended for **direct interaction** with natural persons is also intended to protect natural persons from identity fraud and deception.[7] In addition to chatbots, the transparency requirement therefore also includes other interacting AI systems that carry a risk of confusion between humans and machines. In line with the approach of the entire AI Act, the regulation is deliberately technology-neutral. 4

III. Deepfakes

Art. 50 AI Act also comprises **deepfakes** – i.e., AI-generated or manipulated image, audio or video content that resembles existing persons, objects or events and falsely appears to be true to a person, Art. 3 No. 60 AI Act. 5

The **risk of media content being falsified** is nothing new – it has been known for many years that images, at least, can be easily manipulated using various methods.[8] For a long time, however, it was at least still time-consuming to alter dynamic media such as videos or audio recordings in a high-quality manner. Only the rapid advancement of generative AI has made it possible to produce high-quality moving fakes with little effort and expertise. Because **deep neural networks are used** in this process, the term 'deepfakes' has become established for these methods.[9] The AI Act itself defines deepfakes in Art. 3 para. 60 AI Act as image, audio or video content generated or manipulated by AI that resembles real people, objects, places, facilities or events and appears to a person to be genuine or truthful. The AI Act thus focuses on the already 6

[1] Cf. recital 27.
[2] Wendt uj 2/2024, 42 (44).
[3] Kumkar/Rapp ZfDR 2022, 199 (200).
[4] Excerpt on filter bubbles, echo chambers and similar manipulations: Kühling ZUM 2023, 566 (567).
[5] Bayer/Bitiukova/Bárd et al., Disinformation and propaganda 33.
[6] Kühling ZUM 2023, 566 (567); see also Der Standard of 27.5.2024.
[7] Cf. Recital 132.
[8] See Lantwin MMR 2019, 574 (575).
[9] Neologism derived from deep learning and fake, see Kumkar/Rapp ZfDR 2022, 199 (200).

high and rapidly increasing quality of deepfakes: Transparency requirements are necessary because synthetic audio, image, video or text content can often no longer be distinguished from real media content, even by trained eyes.

7 Accordingly, Art. 50 para. 2 AI Act obliges providers of AI systems and GPAI systems that generate **synthetic audio, image, video or text content** to label these results as artificially generated or manipulated. Providers must ensure that their technical solutions are effective, interoperable, resilient and reliable in accordance with the recognized state of the art. What the recognized state of the art requires in each case can be determined by taking into account the current technical standards. For reasons of proportionality, the special features and limitations of the various types of media and the implementation costs must also be taken into account.

8 At present, watermarks are considered one of the most secure methods for identifying AI-generated content. They are an attempt to inextricably link a signature to an AI work, such as an image. Ideally, the signature can only be removed if the content is destroyed. Modern AI watermarks, which are embedded in the work as invisible signatures, are clearly superior to classic markings with a logo, as these only ever cover a small part of a work and are easily 'lost'.

9 Invisible watermarks are embedded in the content without being noticeable to the viewer. The watermark can only be traced using algorithms with a key, such as a token or password. In images, for example, invisible watermarks are integrated by slightly altering the pure noise, i.e., the starting pattern, using mathematical methods. This is then reflected in the composition of the final scene, for example where the trees are located in the depiction of a forest clearing.[10] AI watermarks can also be used in videos and audio recordings.

10 However, AI watermarks do not yet meet the technical interoperability requirement laid down in Art. 50 para. 2 AI Act; they are model-specific – there are as many watermarks as there are models. It is also unclear whether AI watermarks are actually so unremovable that they can withstand all attacks. It is likely that disinformation campaigns and phishing attacks cannot yet be completely prevented with them.

11 At present, many of the major AI providers are still hesitant to integrate AI watermarks into their models and systems. Although Amazon, Anthropic, Google, Inflection, Meta, Microsoft and OpenAI agreed with the then US Biden administration in July 2023 to use AI watermarks in future, implementation is slow. Providers fear a loss of trust if users get the impression that companies are incorporating 'something secret'. On the other hand, users themselves may not want to reveal that content has been generated by AI.

12 At least Google subsidiary Deepmind presented a tool in 2023 that embeds a digital watermark directly into the pixels of an image. The feature, called 'SynthID', was developed for the music generator Lyria, but has since been extended to the image generator Imagen. Texts from the Gemini AI model are also to be marked with it. Finally, in August, the Wall Street Journal reported on a watermarking tool for texts from Open AI that had long been in development but had not yet been rolled out. In a blog post, Open AI explained that the method had 'the potential to disproportionately harm groups'. For example, it could 'stigmatise the use of AI as a useful writing tool for non-native speakers'.[11]

13 In order to do justice to the danger posed by deepfakes, Art. 50 of the AI Act also places an obligation on **deployers**: just like providers, they must disclose if content has

[10] Mohrat, Tagesspiegel of 15.10.2024.

[11] See https://openai.com/index/understanding-the-source-of-what-we-see-and-hear-online/.

been artificially created or manipulated by an AI system in accordance with Art. 50 para. 4 of the AI Act. This also applies to AI systems that generate or modify **texts of public interest**, unless a natural person assumes the final editing and responsibility for the publication of the content. Alternatively, responsibility for the manipulated content may also lie with a legal person, Art. 50 para. 4 sentence 5 AI Act.

The obligation only does not apply if the AI system only performs a **supporting** 14 **function for standard processing** or does not significantly change the input data, Art. 50 para. 2 last sentence AI Act.

IV. Emotion recognition

Deployers of **emotion recognition systems** or **systems for biometric categorization** 15 are also subject to transparency obligations, Art. 50 para. 3 AI Act. According to Art. 3 para. 39 AI Act, emotion recognition systems are AI systems that derive feelings and ultimately intentions of natural persons from biometric data. Biometric categorization systems, on the other hand, are AI systems that categorize natural persons on the basis of their biometric data. According to Art. 3 No. 40 AI Act, the categorization must be an ancillary function of a commercial service that is absolutely necessary for objective, i.e. technical reasons.

Deployers of emotion recognition systems or systems for biometric categorization 16 are obliged to inform data subjects about the operation of their system and the personal data processed. As Art. 50 para. 6 AI Act does not affect parallel transparency obligations under Union or national law, para. 3 refers to the GDPR,[12] the Regulation on the processing of personal data by the Union institutions, bodies, offices and agencies[13] and the Directive on the protection of individuals with regard to the processing of personal data by competent authorities for the purposes of the prevention, investigation, detection or prosecution of criminal offenses or the execution of criminal penalties for the more precise **formulation of the information obligations.**[14] Emotion recognition systems or AI systems for biometric categorization used for the detection, prevention or investigation of criminal offences are again excluded. However, precautions must be taken to protect the rights and freedoms of third parties.

V. Content in creative, satirical, artistic or fictional works

If compliance with the transparency obligation conflicts with the **right to freedom** 17 **of art and science** guaranteed in the Charter and, where applicable, the **right to freedom of expression**, special provisions apply. Content that is obviously part of a cre-

[12] Regulation (EU) 2016/679 of the European Parliament and of the Council of 27.4.2016 on the protection of natural persons with regard to the processing of personal data and on the free movement of such data, and repealing Directive 95/46/EC (General Data Protection Regulation) OJEU L 119, 4.5.2016, p. 1.

[13] Regulation (EU) 2018/1725 of the European Parliament and of the Council of 23.10.2018 on the protection of natural persons with regard to the processing of personal data by the Union institutions, bodies, offices and agencies and on the free movement of such data, and repealing Regulation (EC) No 45/2001 and Decision No 1247/2002/EC, OJEU L 295, 21.11.2018, p. 39.

[14] Directive (EU) 2016/680 of the European Parliament and of the Council of 27.4.2016 on the protection of natural persons with regard to the processing of personal data by competent authorities for the purposes of the prevention, investigation, detection or prosecution of criminal offenses or the execution of criminal penalties, and on the free movement of such data, and repealing Council Framework Decision 2008/977/JHA, OJEU L 119, 4.5.2016, p. 89.

ative, satirical, artistic or fictional work or program and is subject to appropriate safeguards for the rights and freedoms of third parties may be **exempted from the labelling obligation**, Art. 50 para. 4 sentence 3 AI Act. In these cases, the transparency obligation for deepfakes is limited to disclosing the presence of manipulated content in a way that does not impair the presentation or enjoyment of the work and maintains its quality.[15]

VI. Information of public interest

18 Finally, the EU legislator has separately addressed texts created or modified by AI that provide information on **matters of public interest**. Deployers of an AI system that generates or manipulates such a text must disclose that it has been artificially generated or manipulated, Art. 50 para. 4 sentence 4 AI Act. It is doubtful whether this labeling obligation already does justice to the protective purpose. After all, clear names are rarely used when the aim is to influence social discourse.[16]

VII. Exceptions

19 The only exceptions are AI-generated or manipulated texts that are used for the detection, prevention, investigation and prosecution of criminal offenses, Art. 50 para. 4 sentence 5 1st half of the AI Act. However, this **exception** requires that the rights and freedoms of third parties are protected by other means. AI systems that are available to the public to report a criminal offense are even more privileged; they do not require any other protective measures. Also exempt from disclosure is AI-generated content that has undergone human editorial review prior to publication and for which a natural or legal person is responsible, Art. 50 para. 4 sentence 5 second half of the AI Act.[17]

VIII. Implementation and competition

20 The AI Act contains little information on how these transparency obligations can be fulfilled.[18] According to Art. 50 para. 5 AI Act, the information must be provided to the natural person concerned in a **clear and unambiguous manner** at the latest **at the time of the first interaction or suspension.**

21 The transparency obligation under the AI Act does not affect other transparency obligations under EU law, Art. 50 para. 6 AI Act.

IX. Codes of practice

22 In order to facilitate the effective implementation of the obligations relating to the identification and labeling of artificially created or manipulated content, Art. 50 para. 7 AI Act announces the development of **codes of practice** by the AI Office (→ § 13 mn. 13). The guidelines are intended to ensure a **uniform interpretation of the transparency provisions** throughout the EU, which Art. 50 AI Act alone cannot

[15] See examples in Kumkar/Rapp ZfDR 2022, 199 (201 et seq.).
[16] Chibanguza/Steege NJW 2024, 1769 (1773).
[17] Recital 134 AI Act.
[18] See Engelmann/Brunotte/Lütkens RDi 2021, 317 (321); Kumkar/Rapp ZfDR 2022, 199 (224).

achieve due to a lack of detail. To approve the **codes of practice**, the EU Commission adopts implementing acts in accordance with the procedure set out in Art. 98 para. 2 AI Act, Art. 56 para. 6 AI Act. If the EU Commission does not consider a code of practice to be appropriate, it may instead issue an implementing act in accordance with the review procedure specified in Art. 98 para. 2 AI Act and establish common rules for the implementation of these obligations in accordance with Art. 50 para. 7 sentence 3 AI Act.

§ 11
General purpose AI – GPAI

Literature: *Ara, Aftab/Ara, Affreen*, Exploring the Ethical Implications of Generative AI, 2024; *Batista, Patricia*, ChatGPT versus Arbeitsrecht – Leistungserbringung mithilfe von Sprachmodellen, LTZ 2024, 118; *Baumann, Malte*, Generative KI und Urheberrecht – Urheber und Anwender im Spannungsfeld, NJW 2023, 3673; *Bayern, Shawn/Burri, Thomas/Grant, Thomas/Häusermann, Daniel/Möslein, Florian/Williams, Richard*, Company Law and Autonomous Systems: A Blueprint for Lawyers, Entrepreneurs, and Regulators, 9 Hastings Science and Technology Law Journal 2 (Summer 2017), 135; *Berge, Torsten*, IT and more: Generative Künstliche Intelligenz, WPg 2023, 607; *Berz, Amelie/Engel, Andreas/Hacker, Philipp*, Generative KI, Datenschutz, Hassrede und Disinformation – zur Regulierung von KI-Meinungen, ZUM 2023, 586; *Bezold, Vincent/Jasper, Niklas*, Alles eine Frage des richtigen Promptings? Zur Praxistauglichkeit von ChatGPT am Beispiel von zivilgerichtlichen (Verkehrs-)Urteilsentwürfen, InTeR 3/24, 108; *Bomhard, David*, Text und Data Ming auf Grundlage von Webcrawling und Webscraping, InTeR 2023, 174; *Borges, Georg*, Der Begriff des KI-Systems, CR 2023, 706; *Botta, Jonas*, Die Förderung innovativer KI-Systeme in der EU, ZfDR 2022, 391; *Buck-Heeb, Petra/Oppermann, Bernd*, Automatisierte Systeme, 2022; *Burri, Thomas/Trusilo, Daniel*, Ethical Artificial Intelligence: An Approach to Evaluating Disembodied Autonomous Systems, 2021, *Liivoja, Rain/Valjataga, Ann* (eds.), Autonomous Cyber Capabilities in International Law, 2021; *Burri, Thomas/Wildhaber, Isabelle*, Introduction to the Special Issue of the European Journal of Risk Regulation: The Man and the Machine – When Systems Take Decisions Autonomously, EJRR 2, 2016, 295; *Chibanguza, Kuuya/Kuß, Christian/Steege, Hans* (eds.), Künstliche Intelligenz: Recht und Praxis automatisierter und autonomer Systeme, 2022; *Christen, Markus/Burri, Thomas/Chapa, Joseph/Salvi, Raphael/Santoni de Sio, Filippo/Sullins, John*, An Evaluation Schema for the Ethical Use of Autonomous Robotic Systems in Security Applications, University of Zurich Digital Society Initiative White Paper Series, no. 1, 2017; *De la Durantaye, Katharina*, "Garbage in, garbage out" – Die Regulierung generativer KI durch Urheberrecht, ZUM 2023, 645; *Denga, Michael*, Konformitätsbewertung von KI-Systemen, ZfPC 2023, 154; *Dornis, Tim W. /Stober, Sebastian*, Urheberrecht und Training generativer KI-Modelle, 2024, doi.org/10.5771/9783748949558; *Drapatz, Roland/Kureljusic, Marko*, Einsatz von generativen Sprachmodellen ("Large Language Models") in Mergers and Acquisitions, WPg 2024, 391; *Ebers, Martin*, Standardisierung Künstlicher Intelligenz und KI-Verordnungsvorschlag, RDi 2021, 588; *Ebers, Martin/Quarch, Benedikt M.*, Rechtshandbuch ChatGPT, 2024; *Fuderer, Markus*, Doppelte Konformitätsbewertung bei KI-basierten Medizinprodukten? MPR 2022, 121; *Gerecke, Martin*, Social Media und Recht: Einige urheberrechtliche Gedanken zu generativen KI-Modellen, GRUR-Prax 2023, 381; *Glauner, Patrick*, Technical foundations of generative AI models, LTZ 2024, 24; *Hacker, Philipp*, KI und DMA – Zugang, Transparenz und Fairness für KI-Modelle in der digitalen Wirtschaft, GRUR 2022, 1278; *Heine, Robert*, Generative KI: Nutzungsrechte und Nutzungsvorbehalt, GRUR-Prax 2024, 87; *Hofmann, Franz*, Retten Schranken Geschäftsmodelle generativer KI-Systeme?, ZUM 2024, 166; *Käde, Lisa*, When is a reservation of use vis-à-vis text and data mining machine-readable and attributable to the rights holder?, CR 9/2024, 598; *Käde, Lisa*, Do You Remember? – Do AI models contain copies of training data, can they be reconstructed in a targeted manner and what implications does this have for copyright law?, ZUM 2024, 174; *Kainer, Friedemann/Förster, Lydia*, Autonome Systeme im Kontext des Vertragsrechts, ZfPW 2020, 275; *Kalbhenn, Jan Christopher*, Design specifications for chatbots, deepfakes and emotion recognition systems: The European Commission's proposal for an AI Regulation as an extension of media law platform regulation, ZUM 2021, 663; *Kästner, Lena/Schomäcker, Astrid*, KI-Systeme in der modernen Gesellschaft: Potenziale und Grenzen, ZUM 2023, 558; *Klindt, Thomas*, "Fluides" Genehmigungsrecht bei selbstlernenden Systemen? ZRP 2022, 169; *Kögel, Daniel*, Urheberrechtliche Implikationen bei der Verwendung kreativer und generativer künstlicher Intelligenz, InTeR 2023, 179; *Konertz, Roman/Schönhoff, Raoul*, Vervielfältigungen und die Text- und Data-Mining-Schranke beim Training von (generativer) Künstlicher Intelligenz, WRP 2024, 289; *Konertz, Roman/Schönhoff, Raoul*, Rechtsfolgen der Urheberrechtsverletzung bei generativer Künstlicher Intelligenz: Über die Möglichkeit des "Vergessens" in neuronalen Netzen, WRP 2024, 534; *Lobinger, Simon*, (Chat-)GPT in der juristischen Leistungserbringung – Möglichkeiten und Grenzen, LTZ 2023, 187; *Lucchi, Nicola*, ChatGPT: A Case Study on Copyright Challenges for Generative Artificial Intelligence Systems, European Journal of Risk Regulation (2023), 1; *Lucchi, Nicola*, Generative AI and Copyright – Training, Creation, Regulation, Study Requested by the JURI Committee (2025); *Luckett, Jonathan*, Regulating Generative AI: A Pathway to Ethical and Responsible Implementation, International Journal on Cybernetics & Informatics (IJCI) Vol. 12, No. 5, 2023; *Maamar, Niklas*, Urheberrechtliche Fragen beim Einsatz von generativen KI-Systemen, ZUM 2023, 481; *Möllenkamp, Olaf*, ArbG Hamburg: Mitbestimmung bei Anwendung von ChatGPT mit Anm. Möllenkamp, NZA-RR 2024, 137; *Möller-Klapperich, Julia*, ChatGPT und Co. – aus der Perspektive der Rechtswissenschaft, NJ 2023, 144; *Mohn, Matthias*, Dürfen Arbeitnehmer ChatGPT zur Erledigung ihrer Aufgaben einsetzen? NZA 2023, 538; *Moreno,*

Anna, KI-gestützte Systeme – Zur Notwendigkeit von Systemsicht, Evaluation und Interdisziplinarität, GuP 2023, 54; *Müller, Ferdinand/Kirchner, Elsa/Schüßler, Martin*, Ein "KI-TÜV" für Europa? – Eckpunkte einer horizontalen Regulierung algorithmischer Entscheidungssysteme, Intelligente Systeme, Intelligentes Recht, 2021; *Nickl, Afra*, ChatGPT als Rechtsdienstleister, MMR 2023, 328; *Nordemann, Jan*, Generative Künstliche Intelligenz: Urheberrechtsverletzungen und Haftung, GRUR 2024, 1; *Oschinski, Matthias*, Assessing the Impact of Artificial Intelligence on Germany's Labor Market: Insights from a ChatGPT Analysis, MPRA Paper No. 118300, 2023; *Pesch, Paulina/Böhme, Rainer*, Artpocalypse now? – Generative AI and the reproduction of training images, GRUR 2023, 997; *Raue, Benjamin*, Kreativität im Zeitalter ihrer technischen Reproduzierbarkeit: Generative KI als Totengräberin des Urheberrechts? Eine Gedankenskizze, ZUM 2024, 157; *Saidakhrarovich Gulyamov, Said*, Ethische und rechtliche Dimensionen der Regulierung von Quantum Artificial Intelligence-Systemen, MMR 2024, 26; *Schubert, Jens*, Anm. zu ArbG Hamburg: Mitbestimmung beim Einsatz von ChatGPT und anderer Systemen der künstlichen Intelligenz, BRuR 2024, 98; *Schwartmann, Rolf/Keber, Tobias/Zenner, Kai*, KI-Verordnung. Leitfaden für die Praxis, 2024; *Shi, Yuzhuo*, Study on security risks and legal regulations of generative artificial intelligence, Science of Law Journal Vol. 2 Num. 11, 2023; *Spies, Axel*, ChatGPT & Co. – Keine Insellösungen, MMR 2023, 469; *Strowel, Alain*, ChatGPT and Generative AI Tools: Theft of Intellectual Labor? IIC 2023, 491; *Teichmann, Fabian*, Das Hinweisgeberschutzgesetz (HinSchG) im Kontext generativer künstlicher Intelligenz – eine experimentelle Untersuchung möglicher Missbrauchsmöglichkeiten und ihre dogmatischen Implikationen, NZWiSt 2023, 289; *Veale, Michael/Zuiderveen Borgesius, Frederik*, Demystifying the Draft EU Artificial Intelligence Act, CRi 4/2021, 97; *von Welser, Marcus*, ChatGPT und Urheberrecht, GRUR-Prax 2023, 57; *von Welser, Marcus*, Generative KI und Urheberrechtsschranken, GRUR-Prax 2023, 516; *Wagner, Kristina*, Generative KI: A "black box" of copyright liability risks? Balancing act between promoting innovation and effective legal protection for third-party works, MMR 2024, 298; *Werry, Susanne*, Generative AI models in the sights of data protection authorities, MMR 2023, 911; *Woerlein, Andreas*, ChatGPT – "Fortschritt" durch Künstliche Intelligenz auf Kosten des Datenschutz- und Urheberrechts, ZD-Aktuell 2023, 01205; *Wunner, Katharina*, Generative K.I. and copyright law – a complicated relationship, ZUM 2024, 19; *Zhao, Yuan*, The Infringement Risk and Legal Regulation of Generative AI Works, Science of Law Journal Vol. 2 Num. 7, 2023.

The rise of OpenAI's ChatGPT chatbot in November 2022 marks a decisive turning point in the development of artificial intelligence.[1] The general public was suddenly confronted with the realization of how advanced and useful **generative AI** already is in everyday life. In contrast to other types of artificial intelligence, generative AI is designed to create new content – for example in the form of text, audio, images or videos. Since these models can be used in a wide range of applications, there is a large overlap with general-purpose artificial intelligence (GPAI), which the AI Act addresses as a separate category. Nevertheless, the two terms are not synonymous: Generative AI is defined by the creation (= generation) of new data instances, while general-purpose AI is distinguished by its openness to purpose (→ § 1 mn. 11). 1

However, the sudden emergence of generative AI not only raised questions for individual users, but also for European legislators. Even before the ChatGPT moment, the French Council Presidency had proposed imposing high-risk obligations on GPAI sys- 2

[1] Martini/Wiesehöfer NVwZ 2024, 137 (137).

tems. This approach was rejected by the European Parliament, which rightly pointed out that generative applications – especially GPAI models – do not yet have a fixed intended purpose, but that potentially thousands of use cases are conceivable.[2]The compliance requirements for high-risk AI systems, such as the obligation to carry out a conformity assessment or risk management, are therefore simply not feasible for generative AI providers. As general-purpose AI, generative systems therefore do not fit into the regulatory system of the AI Act, which was intended to cover the specific application and not the technology as such (→ § 3 mn. 47).

I. Functionality

3 **Generative AI systems** are currently based on large language **models (LLMs)**. With the help of large amounts of universal data, the models learn to recognize word and sentence patterns in the pre-training phase. They are trained using various methods – such as supervised, unsupervised and reinforcement learning (→ § 2 mn. 35 et seq.) – to find the next appropriate token based on probabilities.[3] Tokens are small groups of characters into which words and texts with which the language model works are broken down. As a rule of thumb, a word in the English language corresponds to around 1.3 tokens, in the German language it is around 1.8 tokens.[4] Although the large language models do not acquire an understanding of the content of the language, in human perception they are able to provide the respective next word in a dialog and thus interact with us.[5] They can also answer technical questions from all disciplines with continuously increasing quality, draft social media posts, scientific papers, school and student assignments or contracts, compose music or program.[6] The pre-training completed in conjunction with the learning ability of the models means that they can be used in a variety of ways as a **foundation model**.

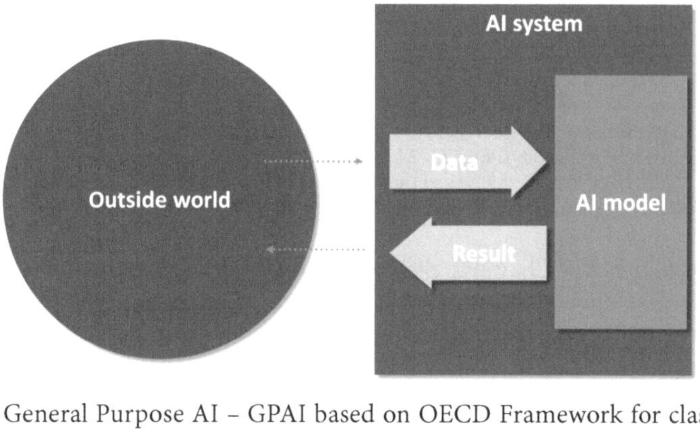

Figure 15: General Purpose AI – GPAI based on OECD Framework for classifying AI Systems

[2] See in detail Zenner/Schwartmann/Hansen: in Schwartmann/Keber/Zenner, Part 2, Chapter 1, para. 488.
[3] Cf. recital 97 AI Act.
[4] Buxmann FAZ 17.5.2024.
[5] Martini/Wiesehöfer NVwZ 2024, 137 (138).
[6] See also Glauner, in: Ebers/Quarch, Technische Grundlagen von generativen KI-Modellen, para. 41.

II. Definition

4 Since the models can even competently perform unexpected tasks, they are referred to as **general purpose AI (GPAI)** or **foundation models.**[7] The AI Act uses the term '**general-purpose AI models**' and calls for these to be clearly and distinctly distinguished from the term (other) AI systems.[8]

However, the AI Act itself does not specify exactly when an AI model is considered to be 'general-purpose '. Art. 3 No. 63 AI Act merely states in its definition that the GPAI model 'displays significant generality and is capable of competently performing a wide range of distinct tasks regardless of the way the model is placed on the market and that can be integrated into a variety of downstream systems or applications [...]'. In addition, Art. 3 No. 63 AI Act points out that this also includes cases 'where such an AI model is trained with a large amount of data using self-supervision at scale

5 A clearer distinction is made in the aforementioned **GPAI guidelines**[9] (→ § 7, mn. 77, 79). They are based on the definition in the AI Act and reiterate that AI has a general purpose if a model can be used for different applications and is capable of performing a wide range of different tasks. To enable reliable classification, the guidelines set a **quantitative threshold**: Whether AI is considered to be for general use is determined by the computing power used to train the model. The threshold is a cumulative amount of more than 10^{23} floating point operations, measured in floating point operations (FLOPs).

The advantage of such a threshold value is that it is concrete and measurable. However, a threshold value is unlikely to remain robust over the long term. Even if it currently correlates with the most consequential models, the value is likely to shift gradually.[10]

6 Information about the computing power that providers use to train their models is scarce: In April 2024, the multidisciplinary research institute Epoch AI published an assessment of the computing power required to train large models.[11] The overview shows that many models exceed the threshold of 10^{23} FLOPs.[12]

7 On a different note, European companies in particular are increasingly using techniques to produce smaller and more efficient models, so that they do not necessarily reach the threshold (→ § 5 mn. 52).

8 The term generative AI, on the other hand, only appears in Recitals 99 and 105: Generative AI models are to be considered a **typical example** of a **general-purpose AI model**, as they generally enable the flexible generation of content – for example, in the form of text, audio, image or video content – which can cover a wide range of different tasks. Recital 105 uses the term generative AI in a very similar way. It appeals to the responsibility of providers of general-purpose AI models, in particular those of large generative AI models that can generate text, images and other content. While these offer unique opportunities for innovation, they also pose challenges for artists, authors and other creative professionals, as well as for the creative content itself. Here, too, generative AI is seen as a prime example of general-purpose AI models.

---

[7] See rec. 97 AI Act and Martini/Wiesehöfer NVwZ 2024, 137 (138).

[8] Rec. 97 AI Act.

[9] Annex to the Communication to the Commission Approval of the content of the draft Communication from the Commission – Guidelines on the scope of the obligations for general-purpose AI models established by Regulation (EU) 2024/1689 (AI Act) 18.7.2025.

[10] In previous draft versions of the GPAI guidelines, a threshold value of 10^{22} FLOPs had initially been discussed.

[11] See https://epoch.ai/blog/tracking-large-scale-ai-models.

[12] While only eleven models exceeded this threshold in 2020, the number had grown to 81 by 2024.

Despite some overlap in content, the meanings differ, so the terms cannot be used synonymously.

9 In fact, the definitions of the individual terms are still unclear. Despite overlapping content, the meanings sometimes differ, meaning that the terms cannot be used entirely synonymously.

III. Differentiation between GPAI models and GPAI systems

10 The AI Act contains specific provisions for GPAI models. In contrast, the regular AI model without a general purpose is neither legally defined nor explicitly addressed in the AI Act.

With regard to GPAI systems, Art. 3 No. 66 AI Act states that these are AI systems that are based on a general-purpose AI model and are capable of serving a wide range of purposes, both for direct use and for integration into other AI systems. This draws an important **line of distinction** between the AI models addressed by the AI Act, which are intended for general use, and the corresponding AI systems.

11 Recital 100 defines that a general-purpose AI system is capable of being used in different scenarios due to the integration of the corresponding model. Although the AI model is an essential component of the AI system, it does not in itself constitute an AI system: For an AI model to become an AI system, the addition of further components, such as a user interface, is required.[13] Conversely, an AI model with a general purpose is regularly integrated into an AI system and is therefore part of it.

12 The path from the model to the system, i.e. placing the model on the market, takes place via libraries, **application programming interfaces (API)**, direct downloading or (hardly anymore) via a physical copy.[14]

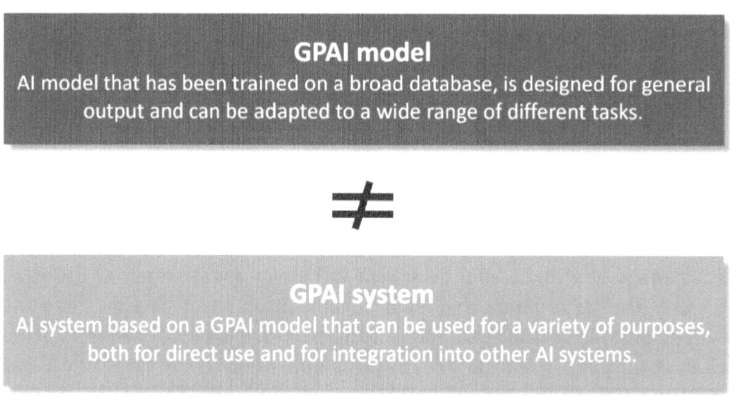

Figure 16: Differentiation between GPAI model and GPAI system

13 How the final AI system, which contains a general-purpose AI model as a building block, is ultimately regulated depends – in line with the regulatory approach of the AI Act – on its individual area of application: general-purpose AI systems can either be used directly or integrated into other AI systems.[15] This means that the general-pur-

[13] Thus Recital 97 AI Act.
[14] Recital 97 AI Act.
[15] RecG 100 AI Act.

pose AI system can also be used in a high-risk sector, as a stand-alone high-risk AI system or as a component of such a system.[16]

In order for the provider of the final high-risk AI system to fulfill its comprehensive obligations under the AI Act, it is dependent on the **information and cooperation** of the provider of the general purpose AI model. Accordingly, the AI Act calls for close cooperation and a fair distribution of responsibilities along the AI value chain.[17] The providers of general-purpose AI models have a particular responsibility in this chain, as downstream systems that are attributed to third-party providers are often based on their models. The third-party providers must have a good understanding of the models and their capabilities – on the one hand, to be able to integrate the models into their products, but also to fulfill their obligations under the AI Act or other laws. Downstream providers are therefore dependent on a certain degree of transparency of the models, including the creation of technical documentation. The EU Commission will define the minimum content of this documentation by means of delegated acts in the light of technological progress.[18] However, many general-purpose AI systems will also be used outside of high-risk applications. Last but not least, they are already being used in numerous industries, for example as chatbots to communicate with customers and enable cost savings. 14

If an AI system with a general purpose is used as a **chatbot**, the risk of disinformation is high – especially as this can also be deliberately disseminated as fake news in search engines, for example.[19] This is where the transparency obligations of Art. 50 AI Act come into play. 15

IV. Market for GPAI systems

With the aim of achieving efficiency gains, many companies are already using general-purpose AI systems. As a rule, companies acquire a general-purpose AI model for this purpose, which they integrate into an AI system according to their own requirements (**custom GenAI**). The AI model can be licensed via a subscription solution or billed based on usage.[20] 16

The advantage of **usage-independent licensing** is the transparency of the costs: an OpenAI Team license, which is required to use the GPT-4 model, is around USD 20 per month and user. In this case, the AI image generator DALL-E is also part of the license. The licenses for the Microsoft Copilot for Office 365 are in a comparable price range. 17

One alternative is **billing via access**. This makes it possible to send requests to the language models directly from in-house software solutions via an API interface and receive the output. Billing is regularly based on the length of the text input and output or on the number of tokens. When using GPT-4, for example, the cost for one million tokens entered is around EUR 60, and around EUR 120 for those issued. 18

In both variants, there are also the costs for **employee training**. However, these costs are manageable and can be easily estimated. Planning is therefore significantly better and easier than in individual use cases. 19

---

[16] Recital 85 AI Act.
[17] See recitals 85 and 101 AI Act.
[18] Recital 101 AI Act.
[19] Martini/Wiesehöfer NVwZ 2024, 137 (139).
[20] Buxmann, Artificial intelligence in companies – the business perspective, FAZ 26.5.2024.

V. Regulation of GPAI models

20 The launch of ChatGPT and the subsequent pervasive spread of AI models for general use made it necessary to intervene in the already advanced negotiations on the AI Act and subject them to regulation as well. To this end, the risk-based regulatory approach, which makes the specific use of AI the starting point for risk evaluation, had to be adapted. After all, AI models with a general purpose **do not have a predefined area of application**, but are nevertheless too influential to be allowed onto the market unregulated.

21 Accordingly, after lengthy negotiations, the EU Commission, the EU Parliament and the Council agreed in the trilogue to take the efficiency of AI models with a general purpose as the starting point for regulation and, in particular, to place normative restrictions on those models that pose a systemic risk.

22 This shows the fundamental system break that the GPAI models required: While the risk of AI systems throughout the AI Act is always measured on the basis of the specific area of application, this yardstick was precisely not available for general purpose AI models. Instead, the European legislator had to define a **new criterion** to determine the level of risk of an AI model.

23 According to Art. 51 AI Act, this criterion is the **impact of the AI model**: According to the legislator's assessment, AI models with a general purpose of use pose a **systemic risk** if they either meet certain indicators and benchmarks that stand for high impact capabilities (para. 1a) or if the EU Commission assumes a correspondingly high impact in an individual case decision (para. 1b). Systemic is defined as the risk that the specific capabilities of the GPAI model, e.g. due to its scope, have actual or foreseeable negative consequences for public health, safety, fundamental rights or society as a whole, which can also spread across the entire value chain.[21]

24 While Art. 51 para. 1a AI Act is therefore based on a general assessment using suitable technical instruments and methods as well as indicators and benchmarks, para. 1b allows for an **ad hoc gap closure** by the EU Commission. With reference to the criteria set out in Annex XIII, the EU Commission may, ex officio or in response to a warning from the scientific panel, individually assign a high degree of effectiveness to an AI model with a general purpose, provided that the model has capabilities that correspond to para. 1a, Art. 52 para. 4 AI Act.

25 The content of the abstract criterion of "**high impact capabilities**" is then defined in Art. 51 para. 2 AI Act: It stipulates that this is to be assumed if the cumulative amount of calculations used for training, measured in **floating point operations**, is more than 10^{25}. AI models are therefore considered to be particularly effective if a cumulative amount of calculations of more than 10^{25} floating point operations (FLOPs) was used for training (→ § 5 mn. 49).

26 Both the reference framework for the calculations made (in floating point operations – FLOPs) and the specific level of the threshold for GPAI models with "systemic risks" were highly controversial in the trilogue. The US, which was the first to define a threshold in the "**Executive Order** on the Safe, Secure and Trustworthy Development and Use of Artificial Intelligence" of 30.10.2023, set the limit at 10^{26} FLOPs.[22] Because no AI model reached this value at the time, the EU Parliament advocated a lower threshold, specifically 10^{24} FLOPs. This would have included the most effective mod-

[21] Recital 65 AI Act.

[22] See https://www.whitehouse.gov/briefing-room/presidential-actions/2023/10/30/executive-order-on-the-safe-secure-and-trustworthy-development-and-use-of-artificial-intelligence/.

els at the time – including GPT-4. The Council, on the other hand, voted in favor of the higher US value. It argued that the rules would apply with a time lag and that it could be expected that the strongest AI models at that time would in any case exceed the threshold. In the end, an agreement was reached on the value in between.[23]

As this value will change continuously in the course of technological progress – for example due to algorithmic improvements or increased hardware efficiency – the EU Commission may amend the **threshold value** and the corresponding benchmarks and indicators by means of a delegated act in accordance with Art. 97 AI Act; Art. 51 para. 3 AI Act. 27

While the EU Commission originally believed that the threshold for AI models with general use and systemic risk could only be revised upwards in the future, model providers such as Deepseek R1 have shown that even a small model can cause systemic risks. The quantitative threshold should therefore not remain the only criterion for classifying a model as a systemic risk.

The EU Commission publishes a **list** of AI models with a general purpose and systemic risk and keeps this list up to date, taking into account any intellectual property rights and/or confidential business information or trade secrets, Art. 52 para. 6 AI Act. 28

VI. Mandatory reporting

If a GPAI model meets the systemic risk conditions, the provider of the model is obliged to notify the EU Commission without delay; Art. 52 para. 1 AI Act. The provider must give the **information** as soon as the AI model reaches the threshold or the provider becomes aware of this. In order to avoid individual arguments and quibbles, the AI Act directly specifies a maximum grace period of two weeks ("in any event within two weeks"). The notification to the EU Commission must be substantiated and contain evidence. If the EU Commission becomes aware of an AI model with a general purpose that poses systemic risks by other means, it will decide whether to classify it as a model with systemic risks, Art. 52 para. 1 AI Act. 29

VII. Opting out

If the provider of a GPAI model that meets the systemic risk impact criterion believes that, due to its specific characteristics, it does not pose such a risk, it may attempt to convince the EU Commission in its notification, Art. 52 para. 2 AI Act. The EU Commission does not have to follow his argumentation and can still assess the AI model as an GPAI model with systemic risk, Art. 52 para. 3 AI Act. 30

If the EU Commission has classified an AI model as a GPAI model with systemic risk on its own initiative or following a warning from the scientific panel (→ § 13 mn. 38), the provider may apply for a **reassessment** after six months at the earliest. The provider must objectively and in detail explain what has changed since the decision was made. If the EU Commission considers the request, it will re-examine whether the AI model still meets the criteria set out in Annex XIII and continues to pose a systemic risk. If the EU Commission maintains its assessment, the provider may again request a reassessment after six months at the earliest, Art. 52 para. 5 AI Act. 31

[23] Zenner/Schwartmann/Hansen in: Schwartmann/Keber/Zenner, Part 2, Chapter 1, para. 494.

VIII. Obligations for providers of GPAI models without systemic risk

32 The division into GPAI models with and without systemic risk is also reflected in the list of obligations for the providers of the models: While Art. 53 AI Act first lists the obligations for providers of GPAI models in Section 2, Art. 55 AI Act then sets out additional obligations for providers of GPAI models with systemic risk in Section 3.

33 Providers of GPAI models are obliged to create **technical documentation** for their model and keep it up to date. The documentation must contain the training and test procedures as well as the results of the assessment, but at least all the information listed in Annex XI, so that the AI Office and the national supervisory authorities can form an opinion if necessary.

34 However, the required documentation does not only serve the purpose of being **accountable** to the supervisory authorities if necessary. The information is also intended for providers of AI systems who intend to integrate the GPAI model into their system. AI system providers need a basic understanding of the capabilities and limitations of the underlying AI model in order to fulfill their own obligations under the AI Act. To this end, the information contained in the documentation must cover at least the elements listed in Annex XII.

IX. Copyright-compliant training of GPAI models

35 Finally, Art. 53 para. 1c AI Act addresses the sensitive issue of **copyright**: any output provided by a general-purpose AI system such as ChatGPT is based on prior training of the inherent AI model, which has taken place with an immeasurable amount of data. The model learns to recognize patterns in the data and to generate new texts based on them, for example.[24] The training data primarily includes publicly accessible texts from the internet.[25] Their extensive use exposes the providers of the models to the accusation that they do not take into account any copyright protection of the works used when selecting the training data.[26]In Germany, it is argued that the training of generative AI models involves various acts of reproduction of copyright-protected works within the meaning of § 16 para. 1 of the German Copyright Act (UrhG).[27] This initially concerns the collection, preparation and storage of the protected works used during training. The AI models simply read everything they can access via an automated process. In addition, during the training process of GPAI models – both during pre-training and fine-tuning[28] – the works used for training are **reproduced** within the model **in** a way **that is relevant to copyright law**. The training data is **memorized.**[29]

36 Although model providers such as OpenAI promise to use texts that are in the public domain, for which a rights clearance has taken place or whose use falls under the US "fair use" principle, this principle is alien to German copyright law.[30] German

[24] For an instructive description of the training process, see Käde ZUM 2024, 174 (175 et seq.).

[25] Wagner MMR 2024, 298 (298).

[26] Kögel InTeR 2023, 179 (180).

[27] Dornis/Stober, Copyright and training of generative AI models 13.

[28] On the differentiation, see Glauner in: Ebers/Quarch, Technische Grundlagen von generativen KI-Modellen, para. 2.para. 18 et seq.; Dornis/Stober, Urheberrecht und Training generativer KI-Modelle 35.

[29] Studies have shown that between 0.1 % and 10 % of the training data is stored directly in the models, see Dornis/Stober, Urheberrecht und Training generativer KI-Modelle 74 mwN.

[30] De la Durantaye ZUM 2023, 645 (648).

copyright law generally requires the author's permission for the use of copyrighted works. Obtaining this in each case is not feasible with the enormous amounts of data that flow into generative AI models.

Therefore, providers of AI models regularly invoke the applicability of a so-called **limitation provision**. The UrhG provides for various limitation provisions under which the use of copyright-protected works is permitted in exceptional cases even without the author's permission. These legally permitted uses include, for example, acts of use for the purpose of quotation (§ 51 UrhG), caricature, parody and pastiche (§ 51a UrhG) and for scientific research (§ 60c UrhG). 37

Providers of generative AI models usually invoke the exception under § 44b UrhG or Art. 4 of the DSM Directive for commercial text and data mining.[31] **Text and data mining (TDM)** refers to processes for the automated extraction of information, patterns and insights from large data collections.[32] However, it is debatable whether the TDM exception, as a neutralising provision, allows interference with exploitation rights.[33] 38

An interdisciplinary scientific opinion commissioned by the Initiative Urheberrecht[34] by Tim Dornis and Sebastian Stober from the Universities of Hanover and Magdeburg comes to the clear conclusion that the training of AI models does not constitute TDM, but rather entails copyright infringement.[35] The classification of AI model training as TDM already fails due to technological and conceptual differences:[36] In its basic idea, TDM always aims to gain more or less abstract knowledge from the analyzed texts. To this end, TDM does not access the creative expression of protected works, but merely processes semantic information. This does not restrict authors in their exploitation rights. Training generative AI models, on the other hand, primarily serves the goal of generating an output that is as similar as possible to the training data.[37] This breaks the boundary of pure information evaluation at the input level: generative AI models also embed elements of syntax, i.e. proprietary components of expression and form, into the vector space of the AI model. More than just semantic information would therefore be compiled during the production of the output. 39

The exception for TDM therefore does not apply to the synthetic nature of generative AI training. Applying it to AI systems risks distorting the purpose and limits of the copyright exception. This conclusion is also confirmed by a study commissioned by the European Parliament's Legal Affairs Committee (JURI) and published in July 2025 by Nicola Lucchi.[38] 40

The scientific opinion and the study have reignited the debate on legally compliant training of generative AI models. The mention of the TDM exception in Art. 53 para. 1 lit. c AI Act was most recently interpreted as an argument that the EU legislature does indeed consider the TDM exception to apply to AI training.

[31] Directive (EU) 2019/790 of the European Parliament and of the Council of 27.4.2019 on copyright and related rights in the Digital Single Market and amending Directives 96/9/EC and 2001/29/EC, OJ L 130, 17.5.2019, pp. 92–125.

[32] Dornis/Stober, Urheberrecht und Training generativer KI-Modelle, 57.

[33] Cf. hierzu Baumann NJW 2023, 3673 (3673); Konertz/Schönhof WRP 2024, 289 (294); Wagner MMR 2024, 298 (299); Käde CR 9/2024, 600.

[34] https://urheber.info/.

[35] Dornis/Stober, Copyright and training of generative AI models.

[36] Dornis/Stober, Copyright and training of generative AI models 87.

[37] Dornis/Stober, Copyright and training of generative AI models 58.

[38] Lucchi, Study Generative AI and Copyright – Training, Creation, Regulation, 2025, 41.

41 This view was supported by a **decision of the Hamburg Regional Court** on 27.9.2024.[39] The Regional Court was the first court in Europe to rule on the admissibility of using copyright-protected content for AI training. The judgment is based on the following facts, summarized below: The plaintiff is professional photographer Robert Kneschke. The defendant is LAION e.V., a non-profit association that, among other things, makes data sets freely available for training AI models. The plaintiff is seeking an injunction against the defendant to prevent the reproduction of his photographs in the context of the creation of AI training data sets. This was preceded by the use of one of the plaintiff's photographs for the AI training data set LAION-5B. The image, which was watermarked by a photo agency, was downloaded by the defendant from the website www.bigstockphoto.com, analyzed and included in the data set with the meta data (URL and image description). The exploitation rights to the photograph in dispute are held by the plaintiff. He himself had uploaded it to a website for stock images. The plaintiff considered that the reproduction of his photograph in the training data set infringed his copyright and invoked the reservation of use stated on the website. The defendant, on the other hand, was of the opinion that the reproduction was permissible under a limitation provision of the UrhG. According to LAION, the LAION-5B training data set contains descriptions of 5.85 billion image-text pairs suitable for AI training – but without the images themselves being included in the data set. Rather, the data set merely contains references to their respective storage locations. The point of reference for the infringement was therefore neither the training of artificial neural networks with the created data set nor its provision by the defendant, but rather the temporary reproduction pursuant to § 16 para. 2 UrhG in the context of data processing, which served to determine the suitability of the image-text pairs for AI training.

42 The Hamburg Regional Court acknowledged that there had been an infringement of the plaintiff's rights of use, but considered this to be covered by the limitation provision in § 60d UrhG, according to which text and data mining for scientific research purposes is permissible under certain conditions. Scientific research is generally understood to mean the methodical and systematic pursuit of new knowledge. It is sufficient that the work step in question is aimed at gaining knowledge. Thus, in the view of the Regional Court, the creation of a data set can also fall under this term if it serves to gain knowledge at a later date, for examplc by being published free of charge, as in the present case, and thus also made available to researchers.

43 Since the Hamburg Regional Court affirmed the applicability of the limitation provision under § 60d UrhG, it did not have to decide whether TDM always applies to AI training. Nevertheless, the court took the opportunity to comment on questions relating to the limitation in § 44b UrhG in the form of an obiter dictum: The court rejected a teleological reduction of the limitation in the form of excluding the reproduction of data for the purpose of AI training from the scope of the TDM limitation. Contrary to the opinion expressed in the above-mentioned expert opinion, 'AI web scraping' does not involve the creation of competing products that are identical or similar in content to the works used. Rather, the court emphasized that a distinction must be made between the creation of the AI training data set, the training of an AI with this data set and the use of the trained AI for the purpose of creating new content. The court also examined the three-step test applicable in European law to the use of protected works and affirmed its requirements. In particular, there was no impairment of the normal

[39] LG Hamburg of 27.9.2024 – 310 O 227/23, NJW 2024, 3383 = ECLI:DE:LGHH:2024:0927.310O227.23.00.

exploitation of the copyright-protected works, as any competing products did not arise solely from the creation of the training data sets.

The Regional Court also commented in detail on the **requirements for the reservation of rights** by the copyright holder: The TDM exception allows reproductions of copyright-protected works for the purpose of text and data mining only if the works are legally accessible and the copyright holder has not expressly reserved the right of use (§ 44b para. 3 UrhG). For works accessible online, the law requires a reservation in machine-readable form. The defendant had argued that the reservation of rights on the website www.bigstockfoto.com was present but not machine-readable because it was not written in the website's code. In this regard, the Hamburg Regional Court held that **machine readability** must be understood in the sense of machine comprehensibility. In interpreting the term, there would be a contradiction in assessment if, on the one hand, the use of works for training AI tools without consent were permitted via the TDM exception, but on the other hand, their capabilities were not included in the reservation of use. In its decision, the court tended to consider a reservation of use written solely in 'natural language' to be machine-understandable, but made this assessment subject to the proviso that the assessment must always be made in dependence on the technical development existing at the time of the relevant use of the work. 44

In this specific case, the court saw clear indications that, at the time the photograph in question was used, the defendant had access to suitable technology to read the reservation of rights on the website, even though it was not included in the website code. However, the court did not ultimately have to make a final decision on the general TDM exception (Section 44a UrhG), as it already considered the use of the image to be lawful on the basis of the TDM exception for scientific research purposes (§ 60d UrhG). This does not provide for any reservation in machine-readable form. With its more general statements, the ruling has the potential to influence future case law and the technical design of AI training. 45

A swift clarification of this controversial issue is desirable. Until now, it seemed unlikely that clarification of the restrictions would be provided before the evaluation of Directive 2019/790 on copyright and related rights in the digital single market, which is due in June 2026. However, the ball is now in the court of the **European Court of Justice (ECJ)**, to which the Budapest District Court (Környéki Törvényszék) has referred questions regarding the legal dispute between **Like Company and Google.**[40] The Hungarian publishing house Like accuses Google of reproducing a copyright-protected article as a largely verbatim summary via its AI chatbot Gemini. The Budapest District Court has asked the ECJ to clarify whether the reproduction of content by a chatbot that is identical to protected texts on a website constitutes reproduction and making available to the public. If so, the Budapest court also aims to determine whether it makes a difference that chatbots predict the next word in their tasks solely on the basis of observed patterns. Even more fundamental is the question of **whether the TDM exception applies.** 46

Until clarification by the ECJ, rights holders retain the option of excluding TDM via a so-called **reservation of use.**[41] In accordance with § 44b para. 3 UrhG, this must be declared in machine-readable form for works accessible online. The Robots Exclusion Standard, established in 1999, could serve as a machine-readable form of the reservation of use, informing web scrapers via a 'robots.txt' file that they are not wel- 47

---

[40] EuGH Rs. C-250/25, request for preliminary ruling of 3.4.2025.

[41] Kögel InTeR 2023, 179 (181); Bomhard InTeR 2023, 174 (177); Käde CR 9/2024, 601 et seq.

come on the site.[42] As the robots.txt solution sometimes has undesirable negative effects on search engine scrapers,[43] it is advisable to implement the new TDM Reservation Protocol as an alternative, which was proposed by a separate community group[44] – and is therefore not (yet) a W3C standard.[45]

48 In line with this framework, Art. 53 para. 1c AI Act requires that providers of general purpose AI models develop a **strategy to comply with** EU **copyright law** and related rights. In particular, this must pursue the goal of ensuring, also by means of state-of-the-art technologies, that a reservation of rights asserted in accordance with Art. 4 para. 3 of the Directive on Copyright and Related Rights in the Digital Single Market[46] is upheld.[47]

49 In this context, providers of AI models must also prepare and publish a sufficiently detailed **summary** of the content used for training the general purpose AI model. In order to facilitate and standardize this, the AI Office provides a corresponding template, Art. 53 para. 1d AI Act.

50 Art. 53 para. 1c and 1d of the AI Act were ultimately a compromise reached in trilogue on the contentious issue of whether copyright issues should become part of the AI Act at all. One side argued that copyright infringement was an important aspect of the regulation of general purpose AI models. The opposing view was that the issue was undoubtedly important, but also large and independent and that the AI Act was a poor location for copyright debates. Moreover, the training of the large AI models was already in the past at the time of the trilogue; the copyrighted rights had already been disregarded. A regulation could only have given rise to further claims. Therefore, the trilogue ultimately decided to only include a **reference to copyright** in the regulations on general purpose AI models in Art. 53 para. 1c and 1d AI Act and to oblige the providers of the models to create and publish a copyright compliance strategy and an overview of the content used for the training of the general purpose AI model. Further regulations are to be included in an amendment to copyright law, which is planned for the current European legislative period.

51 In the meantime, the GPAI Code of practice (→ mn. 53) provides guidance. The code of practice formulates transparency requirements for all GPAI models and security requirements for GPAI models with systemic risk (→ mn. 58). It also contains a separate chapter dealing in detail with copyright issues.[48] The guideline requires all providers of AI models to comply with copyright and related rights. They should establish and implement a copyright policy that is updated as soon as new training data is added to the AI model or other changes are made. Before concluding a contract with a third party on the use of data sets, providers should carry out a copyright due diligence check. In doing so, providers must in particular ensure that they have lawful access to copyright-protected content. Pirated content must be excluded from crawling, including pages listed on the EU Commission's watch list for counterfeiting and piracy. Providers may also only use crawlers that respect a page's robots.txt file. If a provider also controls an online search engine, authors who prohibit crawling must not be penalized by no longer appearing in the search results.

---

[42] Exec. Käde, CR 9/2024, 601 et seq.

[43] Bomhard InTeR 2023, 174 (178).

[44] See https://www.w3.org/community/reports/tdmrep/CG-FINAL-tdmrep-20240202/.

[45] Bomhard InTeR 2023, 174 (179).

[46] Directive (EU) 2019/790 of the European Parliament and of the Council of 27.4.2019 on copyright and related rights in the Digital Single Market and amending Directives 96/9/EC and 2001/29/EC, OJ L 130 p. 92.

[47] Cf. in detail Raue ZUM 2024, 157 (157).

[48] Code of Practice for General-Purpose AI Models – Copyright Chapter, 2025.

In addition, providers should make every effort to observe other machine-readable reservations. The EU Commission will develop machine-readable standards for this purpose in collaboration with interest groups. Until then, providers should transparently disclose how they identify legal reservations. They should list the name of the crawler and the functions of the robots.txt file. In addition, a contact point should be set up where rights holders can lodge complaints. 52

In order to facilitate and standardize the provision of information on what content has been used for model training, the EU Commission made a **training data template** available in summer 2025.[49] Providers must then fill this out in 'sufficient detail' in accordance with Art. 53 para. 1d AI Act in order to provide certainty to rights holders. Finally, providers should also minimize the risk that an AI application already based on their model generates copyright-infringing output.

X. GPAI Code of practice

In parallel with the harmonized European standards, providers of general-purpose AI models can refer to a **code of practice** within the meaning of Art. 56 AI Act. The Code of Practice for General-Purpose AI Models (GPAI Code of practice) was developed by the AI Office (→ § 13 mn. 13) and the national supervisory authorities in four working groups with distinct areas of responsibility. In accordance with Art. 56 para. 9 AI Act, which specified a period of nine months from the entry into force of the Regulation, the guidelines were originally supposed to be available by 2.5.2025. However, they were not completed on time due to the significant differences that had to be overcome in the negotiations. The final version of the code of practice, which consists of three chapters, has been available since 10.7.2025.[50] 53

In order to avoid any **accusations of being impractical**, the GPAI Code of practice was drawn up in accordance with Art. 56 para. 3 AI Act in a complex multi-stakeholder process involving industry, academia, civil society organizations and other relevant stakeholders, including providers and experts.[51] A code of practice ultimately becomes valid upon approval by the EU Commission, which issues an implementing act pursuant to Art. 98 para. 2 AI Act, Art. 56 para. 6 AI Act. 54

The code of practice is a voluntary tool. However, compliance with an approved code of practice, like compliance with a harmonized European standard, gives the **appearance of conformity** (→ § 9 mn. 1). It relieves providers of the burden of having to convince the AI Office, as the supervisory authority, of their compliance with the obligations using individually developed procedures. Conversely, the guide also reduces the burden on supervisory authorities, which can work more efficiently with a uniform approach. 55

Accordingly, the AI Office requests providers to follow the code of practice, Art. 56 para. 1 and 7 AI Act. As an additional incentive, a **grace period** applies: Providers who sign the GPAI Code of practice but are unable to implement all the requirements of the AI Act immediately will not be subject to sanctions by the AI Office within the first year, but will receive support.[52] The signatories of the GPAI Code of practice are 56

---

[49] Cf. Code of Practice for General-Purpose AI Models – Copyright Chapter, 2025, .

[50] Available at: https://digital-strategy.ec.europa.eu/en/policies/contents-code-gpai.

[51] Cf. hierzu statt vieler Guldiman/Spiridonov et al., COMPL-AI Framework, https://doi.org/10.48550/arXiv.2410.07959.

[52] See Q&A on the code of practice for General-Purpose AI: https://digital-strategy.ec.europa.eu/en/faqs/questions-and-answers-code-practice-general-purpose-ai.

listed on the EU Commission's website. As of August 2025, 27 providers had signed the code, including Amazon, Anthropic, Google, Microsoft, Mistral AI, and OpenAI.[53]

57 In terms of content, the code of practice explains the **obligations of providers** of AI models for general use – with and without systemic risk. In three separate chapters on **transparency,**[54] **copyright,**[55] and **security,**[56] it aims to provide **guidance** on how the sometimes vague requirements of the AI Act are to be understood and implemented in concrete terms. While the requirements of the code on transparency and copyright must be followed by all AI model providers,[57] the chapter on security and risk management is aimed exclusively at providers of the most advanced AI models that pose a systemic risk.[58]

58 With regard to the classification of GPAI models into those with and without systemic risk, the code of practice provides for a graded system, i.e., a more differentiated pyramid. It assumes that currently only a handful of GPAI models pose a systemic risk.[59] Those that do will be subject to tailored requirements based on the size and capacity of the provider, which are designed not to overburden small businesses in particular.[60]

59 The requirements include, for example, the **establishment of a risk management system** that assesses the risks of the specific AI model, sets an **acceptability threshold** and provides for **security measures to minimize risk.**[61] The GPAI Code of practice is results-oriented: Compared to earlier drafts, the final version gives providers considerable freedom in implementing risk management. In order to further differentiate systemic risk, some compliance measures are also limited to models with specific systemic risks. The list of specific systemic risks includes those related to chemical, biological, radiological and nuclear accidents, as well as risks related to the loss of human control, large-scale cyber attacks and the harmful manipulation of human behavior.[62] Their compliance must be regularly validated externally, i.e., by qualified third parties – a requirement that remained controversial until the very end. Now, independent experts only need to be consulted if the model exceeds the current state of the art.[63]

[53] See https://digital-strategy.ec.europa.eu/en/policies/contents-code-gpai/.

[54] Code of Practice for General-Purpose AI Models – Transparency Chapter, 2025; Working Group 1: Nuria Oliver (Co-Chair) and Rishi Bommasani (Vice-Chair).

[55] Code of Practice for General-Purpose AI Models – Copyright Chapter, 2025; Working Group 1: Alexander Peukert (Co-Chair) and Céline Castets-Renard (Vice-Chair).

[56] Code of Practice for General-Purpose AI Models – Safety and Security Chapter, 2025; Working Group 2: Matthias Samwald (Chair), Marta Ziosi (Vice-Chair) and Alexander Zacherl (Vice-Chair); Working Group 3: Yoshua Bengio (Chair), Daniel Privitera (Vice-Chair) and Nitarshan Rajkumar (Vice-Chair); Working Group 4: Marietje Schaake (Chair), Anka Reuel (Vice-Chair) and Markus Anderljung (Vice-Chair).

[57] Cf. Code of Practice for General-Purpose AI Models – Transparency Chapter, 2025, 3 et seq.; Code of Practice for General-Purpose AI Models – Copyright Chapter, 2025, 2 et seq.

[58] Cf. Code of Practice for General-Purpose AI Models – Safety and Security Chapter, 2025, 3.

[59] See General-Purpose AI Models in the AI Act – Q&A: https://digital-strategy.ec.europa.eu/en/faqs/general-purpose-ai-models-ai-act-questions-answers.

[60] Code of Practice for General-Purpose AI Models – Safety and Security Chapter, 2025, 4.

[61] Cf. Code of Practice for General-Purpose AI Models – Safety and Security Chapter, 2025, 15 et seq.

[62] Cf. Code of Practice for General-Purpose AI Models – Safety and Security Chapter, 2025, 35.

[63] See Code of Practice for General-Purpose AI Models – Safety and Security Chapter, 2025, 38.

60

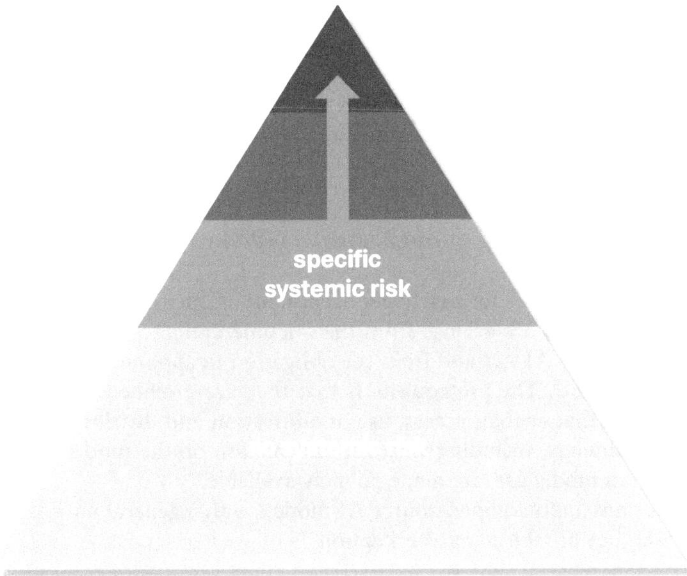

Abbildung 17: Taxonomy of systemic risk

In order to be able to assess the type of systemic risk and thus its correct classification in the pyramid at all times, risk management must be adjusted at least every six months - and whenever the model learns new capabilities.[64] Providers should identify potentially dangerous model capabilities, tendencies and other sources of risk and classify them according to severity.

In the chapter on transparency, the GPAI Code of practice addresses a major point 61 of contention, namely the obligation of providers to disclose information about their training data and training processes.[65] The code differentiates between the recipients of the information: The AI Office, national authorities and operators who integrate GPAI models into their AI systems should, for example, be informed about how the data for these models was collected (through web crawling, data licensing or synthetic generation), processed (was harmful or private information filtered out?) and tested.[66] Other information, on the other hand, is only intended for the AI Office and national authorities.[67] This includes how providers identify unsuitable data sources and biases in the data. They must also describe the core elements of their model training, such as how many stages the training comprises or what targets it is optimized for. Design decisions must also be justified. Providers must also provide the authorities with information on the computing resources required to train and operate their models. This includes information on energy and water consumption and emissions generated. With the growing demand for AI, the environmental impact is also becoming a greater focus. In order to standardize the provision of information, the authors of the GPAI

[64] Code of Practice for General-Purpose AI Models - Safety and Security Chapter, 2025, 21.

[65] Code of Practice for General-Purpose AI Models - Transparency Chapter, 2025, 3; see also the simultaneously applicable data protection law on the right to an explanation of automated decisions as part of the right to information, Kaesling MMR 2025, 403.

[66] See Code of Practice for General-Purpose AI Models - Transparency Chapter, 2025, 5 f, und Model Documentation Form, 7 et seqq.

[67] Cf. Code of Practice for General-Purpose AI Models - Transparency Chapter, 2025, 3.

Code of practice have designed a 'Model Documentation Form' as a template for providers.[68]

62 The AI Office, together with the AI Board (→ § 13 mn. 22), will evaluate whether the GPAI Code of practice fulfills its objectives of specifying the obligations of providers and offering them clear guidance on where they currently stand. The results of the evaluation will be published.

XI. Privileging of open source GPAI models

63 Art. 53 para. 2 AI Act provides for **privileged treatment of open-source AI models with a general purpose**. They are exempt from the documentation obligations under Art. 53 para. 1 lit. a and lit. b AI Act and from the obligation to appoint an authorized representative within the EU. The prerequisite is that they are provided under a free and open source license that enables access, use, modification and distribution of the model and whose parameters, including weights, information on the model architecture and information on model use, are made publicly available.

64 The privilege does not apply to open-source AI models with a general purpose that entail a systemic risk; they are the counter-exception.

XII. Authorized representatives of the providers of GPAI models

65 Only a few GPAI models currently come from providers within the EU. At one point, Luminous from Aleph Alpha (Germany) attracted attention, but did not prevail. This currently leaves only Mistral AI (France) with the Mistral Large model. Art. 54 AI Act takes this fact into account. It requires providers from third countries who wish to place a general purpose AI model on the EU market to appoint an **authorized representative** in writing in advance. The authorized representative must be established in the EU. He serves the supervisory authorities – in addition to or instead of the provider – as a **contact person "on site"**, Art. 54 para. 4 AI Act.

66 The authorized representative has a contractual relationship with the provider of the AI model itself. The tasks covered by the mandate must be recorded in writing and submitted to the AI Office on request, Art. 54 para. 3 AI Act. The provider is obliged to enable the authorized representative to fulfil their duties.

67 One of the tasks of the authorized representative is to check whether the technical documentation has been prepared in accordance with Annex XI and whether the provider fulfils all obligations under Art. 53 AI Act – and, in the case of systemic risk, Art. 55 AI Act. A copy of the technical documentation must be kept and made available to the AI Office or the national authorities on request, together with the provider's contact details.

68 If there is a reasoned request, the authorized representative is obliged to support the AI Office and the national supervisory authorities in all measures they take in connection with a general purpose AI model. This also applies if the AI model has only been integrated into AI systems that are placed on the market or put into service in the Union.

[68] See Code of Practice for General-Purpose AI Models – Transparency Chapter, 2025, Model Documentation Form, 7 et seqq.

If the authorized representative comes to the conclusion or must assume that the provider is in breach of its obligations, it is obliged to terminate the contractual relationship and inform the AI Office accordingly, Art. 54 para. 5 AI Act. 69

Providers of open-source AI models are exempt from the obligation to appoint an authorized representative, provided that they also make their parameters, including weights, information on the model architecture and information on model use publicly available. The counter-exception again covers AI models with a general purpose and systemic risks; they require an authorized representative, Art. 54 para. 6 AI Act. 70

XIII. Obligations of providers of GPAI models with systemic risk

Providers of GPAI models that have **high-impact** capabilities that are considered equivalent to **systemic risk** must fulfill additional obligations. The obligations also apply if the general purpose and systemic risk models are integrated into or form part of an AI system. High impact refers to capabilities that match or exceed the most advanced GPAI models currently available.[69] 71

The additional obligations arise from Art. 55 AI Act. These include carrying out a **model assessment** using **standardized protocols** and **instruments that** correspond to **the current state of the art**. Attack tests on the model should also be carried out and documented as part of the model assessment. They serve the purpose of identifying and preventing or reducing systemic risks. 72

The recording of possible systemic risks resulting from the development, marketing or use of the AI model must not only take place at national level, but must refer to the entire Union. If the providers receive relevant **information about serious incidents**, this information and possible remedial measures must be recorded and reported immediately to the AI Office and, if applicable, to the national competent authorities. 73

Finally, providers of general purpose and systemic risk AI models are also required to ensure an appropriate level of **cybersecurity** and the physical infrastructure of the model. 74

When filling in the undefined legal terms such as "appropriate level of cybersecurity", the providers of AI models with a general purpose and systemic risk can also refer to the codes of practice in accordance with Art. 56 AI Act until a corresponding harmonized standard is published (→ § 13 mn. 13). Compliance with the harmonized European standard also gives rise to a presumption of conformity, provided that the standard covers the respective obligation. Providers of AI models with a general purpose and systemic risk that do not comply with an approved code of practice or the corresponding harmonized European standard must prove compliance using a suitable alternative procedure. 75

[69] Recital 111 AI Act.

§ 12
Measures in support of innovation

Literature: *Bomhard, David/Merkle, Marieke*, Regulation of Artificial Intelligence, EuCML 2021, 257; *Buocz, Thomas/Pfotenhauer, Sebastian/Eisenberger, Iris*, Regulatory sandboxes in the AI Act: reconciling innovation and safety? Law, Innovation and Technology, 15:2 (2023), 357; *Gonzalez Torres, Ana Paula/Sawhney, Nítin*, Role of Regulatory Sandboxes and MLOps for AI-Enabled Public Sector Services, Rev Socionetwork Strat 17 (2023), 297; *Haar, Tobias*, KI-Regulierung: Gelingt die Quadratur des Kreises? MMR 2023, 397; *Micklitz, Hans*, AI Standards, EU Digital Policy Legislation and Stakeholder Participation, EuCML 2023, 212; *Muttach, Jan-Philipp/Link, Hendrik*, Verarbeitung personenbezogener Daten in KI-Reallaboren nach dem KI-VO-E, CR 2023, 725; *Orssich, Irina*, Das europäische Konzept für vertrauenswürdige Künstliche Intelligenz, EuZW 2022, 254; *Philipp, Otmar*, Digitales: Law on Artificial Intelligence, EuZW 2023, 635; *Rostalski, Frauke/Weiss, Erik*, Der KI-Verordnungsentwurf der Europäischen Kommission, ZfDR 2021, 329; *Spindler, Gerald/Büning, Felix*, Einsatz von Reallaboren (Regulatory Sandboxes) – insbesondere im Recht der Künstlichen Intelligenz und der Finanzmärkte, JZ 2023, 799; *Truby, John/Drown, Rafael/Ibrahim, Imad/Parellada, Oriol*, A Sandbox Approach to Regulating High-Risk Artificial Intelligence Applications, EJRR 2022, vol. 13, Iss. 2, 270; *Valta, Matthias/Vasel, Johann*, Commission Proposal for a Regulation on Artificial Intelligence, ZRP 2021, 142.

1 The AI Act has been accused of stifling technical innovation and new business models and placing an excessive burden on small companies in particular, including start-ups.[1] This can be countered by the provisions in Chapter 6, which set out **measures in support of innovation**. The EU legislator has in mind[2] that AI, as a rapidly developing technology, requires scope for testing. These spaces are to be opened up via so-called **real world laboratories**. AI real world laboratories are privileged framework conditions created by the national competent authorities, Art. 57 para. 11 AI Act, which are granted to providers of AI systems for a limited period of time under regulatory supervision. They are primarily intended to make it easier for small companies such as start-ups to develop, train, validate and – if necessary – test innovative AI systems under real conditions,[3] Art. 3 para. 55 AI Act. Ultimately, a real world laboratory is therefore a controlled trial and test environment for the development phase and the phase preceding the placing on the market of an AI system, Art. 57 para. 5 AI Act.[4] Real world laboratories can be set up physically, digitally or hybrid.

I. Objective

2 Real world laboratories have their origins as **regulatory sandboxes** in information technology (IT). Here, they are used in the course of software development to initially test new, potentially unsafe code within a defined framework in order to minimize the risk for users when introducing new products to the market as a whole.[5] Real world

[1] Haar MMR 2023, 397 (398); Frost/Steininger/Vivekens MPR 2024, 4 (12); Ashkar/Schröder BB 2024, 771 (773).
[2] Cf. recital 138 AI Act.
[3] Cf. recital 139.
[4] Ammann/Pohle CB 5/2024, 137 (143).
[5] Global Financial Innovation Network, Consultation document, 2018, 17.

laboratories can also be found in the energy industry and in medicine. What all sectors have in common is the idea of testing innovations within defined limits before market launch in order to identify potential risks and regulatory problems at an early stage.[6] The aim is to give innovators and regulatory authorities time to adapt to each other and learn from each other based on evidence: Within the real world laboratory, the supervisory authority has the freedom to exercise discretion in applying the applicable legislation, Art. 57 para. 11 AI Act. This gives it the opportunity to adapt its supervisory practice to previously unknown possibilities, risks and effects of AI use. The provider in turn receives legal certainty with regard to regulatory expectations, Art. 57 para. 6, 7 and 9 AI Act, and can accelerate its market access accordingly, Art. 57 para. 9e AI Act. In the best case scenario, real world laboratories move the supervisory authority from the position of a purely reactive observer to a preventive co-designer.

II. Obligation to set up regulatory sandboxes

Art. 57 AI Act obliges each **Member State to** establish **at least one AI** regulatory sandbox, which must be operational two years after the AI Act enters into force. Member States may also comply with this obligation by participating in existing regulatory sandboxes or by jointly establishing one with the competent authorities of one or more Member States. It must be ensured that the participation provides equivalent national coverage for the participating Member States. Common rules for the implementation of AI regulatory sandboxes and framework agreements for cooperation between the participating authorities are encouraged in order to ensure uniform implementation across the EU and to achieve economies of scale.[7] Participation in an AI regulatory sandbox established by a Member State shall be mutually recognised and have uniform legal effect throughout the Union, Art. 58 para. 2g AI Act. 3

Upon request, the EU Commission provides **technical support, advice** and **tools** for the establishment and operation of an AI regulatory sandbox. It also sets up its own interface, which contains all relevant information on AI real world laboratories, Art. 57 para. 17 AI Act. The AI Office also maintains an up-to-date list of all planned and existing regulatory sandboxes. 4

The first German AI regulatory sandbox was launched in Osnabrück (Lower Saxony) in spring 2025. Aimed at small and medium-sized enterprises, the CRAI (Centre for Research and Development of Trustworthy AI Applications for Mid-sized Companies) project at the German Research Centre for Artificial Intelligence (DFKI) is intended to facilitate the implementation of trustworthy AI.[8] The first use cases come from four industries: manufacturing, logistics, healthcare and administration. However, the real world laboratory is pursuing a cross-innovation approach so that established practices in one industry can be transferred to others as far as possible

III. Access to the regulatory sandbox

In order to prevent fragmentation within the EU, the European Commission is using implementing acts to lay down detailed rules for the establishment, development, implementation, operation and supervision of AI regulatory sandboxes. In particular, 5

[6] Cf. Ringe/Ruof, Regulating Fintech, 3.
[7] See recital 139 AI Act.
[8] See https://crai-reallabor.de/.

the implementing acts must define the **application** procedure and the requirements to be met by the provider in a transparent and fair manner, while keeping the limited legal and administrative capacities of SMEs, including start-ups, in mind. **In principle,** access to AI regulatory sandboxes should be granted **free of charge**. Only exceptional costs may be proportionately passed on to the provider.

6 The EU Commission must ensure that AI regulatory sandboxes are open to all providers that meet the criteria, Art. 58 para. 2 AI Act. The AI regulatory sandboxes should enable broad and **equal access** and must keep pace with demand.

7 The decision on access to the regulatory sandbox is made by the national competent authority. It must inform the provider within three months of the application.

IV. Implementation of the regulatory sandbox

8 In addition to the procedure for submitting an application, the implementing acts must also contain detailed provisions on the **implementation of the** regulatory sandbox, **monitoring, withdrawal** and **termination,** Art. 58 para. 1 AI Act.

9 The objectives, conditions, timeframe, methodology and requirements for the activities carried out within the regulatory sandbox are defined individually between the provider and the competent supervisory authority as a so-called **sandbox plan,** Art. 3 para. 54 AI Act.

10 The period of participation in the AI regulatory sandbox should be based on the complexity and scope of the project and can be extended by the national authority, Art. 58 para. 2 lit. h AI Act.

11 Where necessary, other actors within the AI ecosystem may be involved - such as standardization organizations, notified bodies or research laboratories, Art. 57 para. 4 AI Act.[9]

12 Any **significant risks** that become apparent during the development and testing of new AI systems must result in **risk mitigation measures**. If necessary, the testing process must be temporarily suspended. If it turns out that a test procedure does not enable effective risk mitigation, the supervisory authority must permanently terminate the AI provider's participation in the regulatory sandbox, Art. 57 para. 11 AI Act. The AI Office is informed of temporary and permanent suspensions.

V. Liability in the regulatory sandbox

13 A provider participating in the regulatory sandbox is liable under national law for damages incurred by a third party as a result of testing in the sandbox. However, any fines for violations of the AI Act are waived if the provider has complied with the plan and the conditions for participation in the regulatory sandbox and followed the guidance of the supervisory authority in good faith, Art. 57 para. 12 AI Act.

VI. Facilitation of conformity assessment

14 Upon request, the supervisory authority will provide the AI provider with **proof** of the activities successfully carried out in the regulatory sandbox. In any case, it submits a final report that also shows the results and findings obtained. Providers can **use** the

[9] Recital 139 AI Act.

evidence and the **final report** to demonstrate compliance with the AI Act in the **conformity assessment procedure** or in relation to a market surveillance activity, Art. 57 para. 7 AI Act.

The market surveillance authorities and the notified bodies (→ § 8 mn. 3) are requested to give the submission of the final report an appropriately positive assessment with a view to **speeding up the conformity assessment**. 15

VII. Testing in real world conditions

Provided that the national supervisory authority agrees, tests under real world conditions may be carried out in the sandbox, Art. 57 para. 5 AI Act.[10] To this end, the supervisory authority shall agree with the parties involved on the conditions for the tests and appropriate safeguards for the fundamental rights, health, and safety of all parties involved. 16

Art. 60 AI Act gives providers of high-risk AI systems the option of accelerating the development of their AI systems through **testing under real world conditions without** having to participate in an AI **regulatory sandbox.** Naturally, certain conditions must be met for this: These include the informed consent of all natural persons to participate in the real world testing. As might be expected, the AI Act also requires that risks be minimized as far as possible. 17

Among other things, the provider must ensure that the **tests** are carried out **under human oversight** and that the supervising persons are **adequately qualified** in the relevant field, Art. 60 para. 4 lit. j AI Act. In addition, the AI system to be tested may only make predictions, recommendations or decisions that can be effectively reversed and disregarded, Art. 60 para. 4 lit. k AI Act. 18

In advance, the provider has to submit a '**real world testing plan**' to the market surveillance authority.The plan must explain the objectives, methodology, geographical and temporal scope as well as the monitoring and execution of the tests, Art. 3 No. 53 AI Act. The period of time is determined by the duration required to achieve the objective. However, it may under no circumstances exceed six months. The period may be extended once, Art. 60 para. 4 lit. f. AI Act. 19

The **market surveillance authority** of the respective member state must **approve** the test under real conditions and the associated **plan**. During the test phase, it is entitled to obtain additional information from the providers and, if necessary, to convince itself of the safe execution of the tests on site without prior notice, Art. 60 para. 6 AI Act. 20

If a serious **incident** occurs during a test under real world conditions, the provider must take **immediate action** to limit the damage and inform the market surveillance authority. A serious incident can be a **malfunction of the AI system** that results in the **death** or **serious harm to a person's health**. However, serious incidents also include major disruptions, such as to critical infrastructure or damage to property and the environment, as well as the infringement of obligations intended to protect fundamental rights, Art. 3 No. 49 AI Act. 21

In the event of a serious incident, the provider must **suspend** the **test** until **damage limitation** has been achieved. If the provider must definitively terminate the test under real conditions, an immediate **recall** of the AI system must be initiated, Art. 60 para. 7 AI Act. The providers are liable for damages, Art. 60 para. 9 AI Act. 22

[10] Ammann/Pohle CB 5/2024, 137 (143).

23 Every test participant may terminate their participation at any time by **withdrawing their consent** and request the immediate and permanent deletion of their personal data without incurring any disadvantages and without having to justify this in any way, Art. 60 para. 5 AI Act. If persons belonging to vulnerable groups are involved, additional protective measures must be taken, Art. 60 para. 4 lit. g AI Act.

24 The **details** of the tests under real conditions will also be determined by the EU Commission **in an implementing act**.

§ 13
Supervisory system

Literature: *Novelli, Claudio/Hacker, Philipp/Morley, Jessica/Trondal, Jarle/Floridi, Luciano*, A Robust Governance for the AI Act: AI Office, AI Board, Scientific Panel, and National Authorities, European Journal of Risk Regulation 2024, 1; *Schwartmann, Rolf/Keber, Tobias/Zenner, Kai*, KI-Verordnung. Leitfaden für die Praxis, 2024; *Wendt, Janine/Wendt, Domenik*, Einigung auf Rechtsrahmen für Künstliche Intelligenz in der EU, ZfPC 2024, 86.

The AI Act provides for a new **supervisory system** for AI systems.[1] The AI Act refers to a "**governance framework**" that "both allows to coordinate and support the application of this Regulation at national level, as well as build capabilities at Union level and integrate stakeholders in the field of AI."[2] This new governance framework is composed of the EU Commission and new bodies at EU level as well as competent authorities at national level. The structure of new supervisory actors created in this way is initially cross-sectoral and will exist alongside already established supervisory systems in markets regulated by product and financial market law. 1

I. Regulatory basis and supervisory actors

Provisions on the new supervisory system for AI systems can be found primarily in Art. 64 et seq. AI Act. These provisions are to be seen in particular in connection with 2

[1] Wendt/Wendt ZfPC 2024, 86 (87).
[2] See recital 148 AI Act.

the EU Commission's decision of 24.1.2024 to establish the European Office (sic!)[3] for Artificial Intelligence (Decision C/2024/1459).[4]

3 The AI Act also refers to **national competent authorities** (Art. 70 AI Act), but provides only few details in this regard. The provisions at EU level therefore had to be supplemented at the national level by requirements designating the national competent authorities and regulating their powers.

II. EU Commission

1. Delegation of power

4 In accordance with Art. 88 para. 1 AI Act, the **EU Commission** transfers the authority to supervise and enforce the regulations in Art. 51–56 AI Act, i.e. the requirements for GPAI (→ § 11 mn. 30 et seq.), to the **AI Office** (→ mn. 9). This means that the EU Commission, as an EU body, is directly responsible in particular for drawing up or updating the delegated acts (see Art. 97 AI Act) and the guidelines (see Art. 96 AI Act).

2. Delegated acts

5 Art. 97 AI Act gives the EU Commission the power to adopt so-called **delegated acts**. This gives it the power to adopt further legal acts outside the ordinary legislative procedure. The annexes to the AI Act are these delegated acts.[5] The EU Parliament and the Council can revoke the delegation of powers at any time in accordance with Art. 97 para. 3 AI Act. In addition, a delegated act pursuant to Art. 97 para. 6 AI Act only enters into force if the EU Parliament or the Council have not vetoed it within a period of three months (can be extended by three months, see Art. 97 para. 6 sentence 2 AI Act) after transmission of the act by the EU Commission. No veto has been declared against the current annexes to the AI Act.

3. Guidelines

6 Art. 96 para. 1 subpara. 1 AI Act empowers the EU Commission to **draw** up and **issue guidelines**. These guidelines are intended to facilitate the practical implementation of the AI Act. They should relate to:

- the application of the requirements and obligations set out in Art. 8–15 AI Act and Art. 25 AI Act, lit. a,
- the prohibited practices listed in Art. 5 AI Act, lit. b,
- the practical implementation of the provisions on material changes (see, for example, Art. 25 para. 1 lit. b AI Act), lit. c,
- the practical implementation of the transparency obligations pursuant to Art. 50 AI Act, lit. d,
- detailed information on the relationship of the AI Act to the harmonization legislation listed in Annex I and to other relevant EU legislation, lit. e,
- the application of the definition of an AI system pursuant to Art. 3 No. 1, lit. f.

---

[3] The German version of the resolution reads "Amt", while the English version uses the term "Office" in line with the terminology in the AI Act, meaning the "AI Office" within the meaning of Art. 64 of the AI Act.

[4] See Decision C/2024/1459, OJEU of 14.2.2024.

[5] See also Zenner in: Schwartmann/Keber/Zenner, Part 3, Chapter 1, para. 6.

Art. 96 para. 1 subpara. 1 AI Act thus gives the EU Commission the competence to discuss particularly relevant aspects of the AI Act by means of supplementary guideline provisions. It can thus define an important **framework for** the interpretation and application of the provisions of the AI Act. 7

The guidelines are intended to provide greater legal clarity by providing insight into the EU Commission's interpretation of the AI Act in order to ensure its consistent, effective, and uniform application. The first guidelines were issued on 4.2.2025, pursuant to Art. 96 para. 1 lit. b AI Act, on prohibited practices of artificial intelligence.[6] Here, it was particularly urgent to obtain clarity regarding applicability, as the prohibitions have been directly applicable since 2.2.2025. On 6.2.2025, the EU Commission also published guidelines on the definition of AI systems,[7] and, on 18.7.2025, guidelines for providers of GPAI models.[8] The guidelines are always formally adopted by the Commission and are applicable from that date.

With regard to the binding effect of corresponding publications by the EU Commission, the limits set by the Court of Justice must be observed in particular.[9]

The list set out in Art. 96 para. 1 AI Act is not exhaustive ("in particular"). Should the EU Commission wish to issue guidelines on further aspects of the AI Act, however, these aspects would have to be of comparable relevance to the standard examples listed in Art. 96 para. 1 subpara. 1 lit. a-f AI Act. Otherwise, the EU Commission would exceed its powers to issue guidelines under the AI Act. A **general competence to issue guidelines** is **not provided for** in Art. 96 AI Act. 8

III. AI Office

According to Art. 64 para. 1 Act, the EU Commission develops the EU's **expertise and capabilities** in the field of AI through the **AI Office**. The AI Office therefore has a central role in the new supervisory system.[10] In addition, the EU Commission transfers the power to supervise and enforce the regulations in Art. 51–56 AI Act to the AI Office in accordance with Art. 88 para. 1 AI Act. 9

1. Composition and organization

The AI Office has been established with effect from 21.2.2024, see Art. 1 and 9 Decision C/2024/1459. It is to be part of the administrative structure of the Directorate-General for Communications Networks, Content and Technology (DG CONNECT) 10

---

[6] Communication to the Commission Approval of the content of the draft Communication from the Commission – Commission Guidelines on prohibited artificial intelligence practices established by Regulation (EU) 2024/1689 (AI Act) and Annex to the Communication to the Commission Approval of the content of the draft Communication from the Commission – Commission Guidelines on prohibited artificial intelligence practices established by Regulation (EU) 2024/1689 (AI Act) from 4.2.2025.

[7] Annex to the Communication to the Commission Approval of the content of the draft Communication from the Commission – Commission Guidelines on the definition of an artificial intelligence system established by Regulation (EU) 2024/1689 (AI Act) of 6.2.2025.

[8] Annex to the Communication to the Commission Approval of the content of the draft Communication from the Commission – Guidelines on the scope of the obligations for general-purpose AI models established by Regulation (EU) 2024/1689 (AI Act) of 18.7.2025.

[9] Cf. for example ECJ judgment of. 13.12.2012 – C-226/11 (para. 27 et seq.), ECLI:EU:C:2012:795; ECJ judgment of. 14.6.2011 – C-360/09 (para. 21 et seq.), ECLI:EU:C:2011:389; ECJ judgment of 20.5.2010 – T-258/06 (para. 28), ECLI:EU:T:2010:214.

[10] Novelli/Hacker/Morley/Trondal/Floridi, 2024.

and subject to its annual management plan.[11] The AI Office is a European office[12] within the meaning of Art. 2 No. 26 of Regulation (EU, Euratom) 2018/1046.[13] It is therefore considered to be an administrative structure created by the EU Commission that performs specific cross-sectoral tasks. These tasks arise, inter alia, from Art. 2 Decision C/2024/1459.

11 The AI Office will employ more than 140 people. The staff will include technology specialists, administrative assistants, lawyers and other experts such as economists.[14] Since 16.6.2024, the **organizational structure** of the AI Office has consisted of five units and two advisors,[15] by name:

- Presentation "Excellence in AI and robotics",
- Unit "Regulation and compliance",
- AI safety" presentation,
- Presentation "AI innovation and policy coordination",
- Unit "AI for the common good",
- the chief scientific advisor and
- the advisor for international affairs.

2. Tasks for the purposes of implementing and enforcing the AI Act

a) Tasks related to general purpose AI models

12 Pursuant to Art. 2 para. 1 Decision C/2024/1459, the AI Office initially performs the tasks specified in Art. 3 para. 1 Decision C/2024/1459 for the purposes of implementing and enforcing the AI Act. These requirements expressly relate solely to general purpose AI models (GPAI models). The tasks in this regard include

- the development of certain instruments, methods and benchmarks, lit. a,
- monitoring the implementation of and compliance with requirements as well as the occurrence of unforeseen risks, lit. b and c, supported by a scientific committee of independent experts,[16]
- the investigation of possible violations of regulations, lit. d,
- ensuring coordinated monitoring and enforcement, lit. e and
- supporting the implementation of regulations relating to prohibited AI practices and high-risk AI systems, lit. f.

13 The tasks are specified in the powers set out in Art. 56 AI Act. The AI Office shall promote and facilitate the development of codes of practice (→ § 11 mn. 53 et seq.), Art. 56 para. 1 AI Act. These codes shall contribute to the proper application of the AI Act, taking into account international approaches. Pursuant to Art. 56 para. 6 sentences 1 and 2 AI Act, the AI Office, together with the AI Board, monitors and evaluates the "achievement of the objectives of the codes of practice by the participants," in particular with regard to the obligations provided for in Art. 53 and 55 AI Act. Recitals

---

[11] See Recital 6 Decision C/2024/1459.

[12] Recital 7 Decision C/2024/1459.

[13] Regulation (EU, Euratom) 2018/1046 of the European Parliament and of the Council of 18.7.2018 on the financial rules applicable to the general budget of the Union, amending Regulations (EU) No. 1296/2013, (EU) No. 1301/2013, (EU) No. 1303/2013, (EU) No 1304/2013, (EU) No 1309/2013, (EU) No 1316/2013, (EU) No 223/2014, (EU) No 283/2014 and Decision No 541/2014/EU and repealing Regulation (EU, Euratom) No 966/2012, OJ L 193, 30.7.2018, pp. 1–222.

[14] See EU Commission press release "Commission establishes AI Office to strengthen EU leadership in safe and trustworthy Artificial Intelligence, 29.5.2024.

[15] See https://digital-strategy.ec.europa.eu/de/policies/ai-office.

[16] Recital 151 AI Act.

116 and 117 address codes of practice and outline their possible content. On 10.7.2025, the AI Office published a first GPAI Code of practice (→ § 11 mn. 53). The codes of practice are to be distinguished from the codes of conduct provided for in Art. 95 AI Act for AI systems with no or minimal risk.

The AI Office can also take **monitoring actions** set out in Art. 89 AI Act. Art. 89 para. 1 AI Act refers to "necessary actions". This general power is specified for 14

- so-called qualified alerts, Art. 90 AI Act,
- requests for documentation and information, Art. 91 AI Act,
- conducting evaluations, Art. 92 AI Act,
- request for measures, Art. 93 AI Act.

In accordance with Art. 94 AI Act, the procedural rights pursuant to Art. 18 Regulation 2019/1020 must be observed mutatis mutandis. 15

b) Additional tasks

Furthermore, with regard to the effective implementation of the AI Act pursuant to Art. 2 para. 1 in conjunction with Art. 3 para. 2 Decision C/2024/1459, the AI Office is tasked with 16

- to assist in the preparation of relevant Commission decisions, implementing acts and delegated acts, lit. a,
- to facilitate the uniform application of the AI Act, lit. b, which should be seen in particular in the systematic context of the following power,
- in the development of orientation aids and guidelines as well as in the development of supporting instruments, lit. c,
- to assist in the development of standardization mandates, the evaluation of existing standards and the development of common specifications for the implementation of the future Regulation, lit. d.

In addition, the AI Office 17

- contributes to the provision of technical support, advice and tools for the establishment and operation of AI living labs and their coordination, lit. e,
- carries out assessments and reviews and prepare reports in connection with the future regulation, lit. f,
- coordinates the establishment of an effective governance system, lit. g,
- provides the secretariat for the AI Committee and its sub-groups as well as administrative support for the consultative forum and, where appropriate, the scientific panel, lit. h, and
- promotes and monitors the development of codes of practice and codes of conduct at Union level, lit. i.

The aforementioned tasks are specified in particular by the competencies regulated in Art. 95 AI Act. 18

3. Further tasks

According to Art. 2 para. 2 Decision C/2024/1459, the AI Office has further tasks; it 19

- contributes to the Union's strategic, coherent and effective approach to international AI initiatives in accordance with Art. 7, in coordination with the Member States and in line with the EU's positions and strategies, lit. a,

- contributes to the promotion of measures and strategies in the Commission that harness the social and economic benefits of AI technology in accordance with Art. 5 AI Act, lit. b,
- supports the accelerated development, deployment and use of trustworthy AI systems and applications that deliver societal and economic benefits and contribute to competitiveness and economic growth in the Union. In particular, the Office shall foster innovation ecosystems by working with relevant public and private stakeholders and the start-up community, lit. c,
- monitors the development of AI markets and technologies, lit. d.

4. Cooperation with other institutions

a) Overview

20 In performing the aforementioned tasks, the AI Office should not act alone, but **cooperate** with various **institutions and interest groups**. Art. 3 para. 3 Decision C/2024/1459 refers to "seeking [...] cooperation" with

- stakeholders, in particular experts from the scientific community and AI developers, Art. 3 para. 3 lit. a Decision C/2024/1459,
- the relevant Directorates-General and departments of the Commission, Art. 3 para. 3 lit. b Decision C/2024/1459,
- all relevant Union institutions, bodies, offices and agencies, including the European High Performance Computing Joint Undertaking (EuroHPC JU), Article 3(3)(c) Decision C/2024/1459, and
- with authorities and other bodies of the Member States on behalf of the EU Commission, Art. 3 para. 3 lit. d Decision C/2024/1459.

b) Coexistence of powers

21 The aforementioned regulations do not affect other powers and responsibilities of national authorities, bodies, institutions and other EU bodies arising from the AI Act and sector-specific requirements;[17] they therefore exist in addition. However, the AI Office should **avoid overlaps** when performing its tasks.[18] In this context, it should be noted that the Member States should facilitate the tasks assigned to the AI Office, Art. 64 para. 2 AI Act. This requirement should also be understood as an expectation on the part of the EU legislator to provide sufficient structural and substantive support at authority level in the Member States.

IV. European Artificial Intelligence Board (AI Board)

22 Pursuant to Art. 65 para. 1 AI Act, a **European Artificial Intelligence Board** (hereinafter "**AI Board**") will be established alongside the AI Office. There is no provision for an establishment resolution as with the AI Office. The sole basis for legitimization is therefore Art. 65 para. 1 AI Act.

[17] See Recital 7 Decision C/2024/1459.
[18] See Recital 7 Decision C/2024/1459.

1. Composition and organization

23 The AI Board is composed of **one representative per member state** in accordance with Art. 65 para. 2 sentence 1 AI Act. These representatives are appointed for a period of three years with the possibility of one extension, Art. 65 para. 3 sentence 1 AI Act. The appointment is made by the member states themselves in accordance with Art. 65 para. 3 sentence 1 AI Act. These representatives may be persons who belong to public institutions.[19] However, the public institutions should have the relevant responsibilities and powers.[20]

24 According to Art. 65 para. 4 AI Act, the Member States must ensure that the representatives have the **competencies and powers** to actively contribute to the accomplishment of the assigned tasks and to act as central points of contact, see Art. 65 para. 4 lit. a and b AI Act. According to Art. 65 para. 4 lit. c AI Act, the representatives should also be authorized to work towards consistency and coordination between the national competent authorities in their Member State in the implementation of the AI Act. The representatives should also be allowed to collect relevant data and information for the purposes of fulfilling their duties on the AI Board. In view of the range of tasks defined in Art. 66 AI Act, the latter presupposes the existence of an infrastructure designed for this purpose.

25 The committee **meets** in **sessions**. The AI Act does not specify how often and to what extent meetings should be held. However, this can be regulated by rules of procedure (arg. ex Art. 65 para. 5 sentences 1 and 2 AI Act). According to Art. 65 para. 5 sentence 2 AI Act, rules of procedure should also ("in particular") regulate this:

- the procedure for the selection process,
- the duration of the mandate,
- the tasks of the Chair,
- the voting regulations,
- the organization of the activities of the AI committee and its subgroups.

26 The aspects regulated in Art. 65 para. 7 and para. 8 AI Act must also be implemented. The **European Data Protection Supervisor** and the AI Office also take part in meetings of the AI Board as observers without voting rights, see Art. 65 para. 2 sentences 2 and 3 AI Act. If necessary, other authorities or bodies of the EU Member States or experts may also be invited to meetings in accordance with Art. 65 para. 2 sentence 4 AI Act. The AI Board must set up at least **two permanent sub-groups** (for market surveillance[21] and for notification), Art. 65 para. 6 AI Act. These should enable the national market surveillance authorities and the national notifying authorities to exchange information on issues relevant to their activities.[22] Further appropriate (permanent or temporary)[23] subgroups are possible in accordance with Art. 65 para. 6 subpara. 3 AI Act.

---

[19] See recital 149; see Zenner in: Schwartmann/Keber/Zenner, Part 3, Chapter 1, para. 7: national supervisory authority or national competent ministry.

[20] Cf. recital 149.

[21] In accordance with Art. 65 para. 6 subpara. 2 AI Act, should act as an administrative cooperation group (ADCO group) within the meaning of Article 30 of Regulation (EU) 2019/1020; see also Recital 149, which provides that the EU Commission -should support the activities of the permanent subgroup for market surveillance by carrying out market assessments or -investigations in accordance with Article 33 of Regulation (EU) 2019/1020-.

[22] Cf. recital 149 AI Act.

[23] Recital 149 AI Act.

2. Tasks

27 In accordance with Art. 66 AI Act, the AI Board advises and supports the EU Commission and the member states. The aim is to facilitate the uniform and effective application of the AI Act. To this end, the AI Board can take numerous measures listed in Art. 66 lit. a-o AI Act.[24] The options for action listed there are not exhaustive ("in particular").

28 According to Art. 66 lit. k AI Act, the AI Board should also expressly support the AI Office. Tasks such as coordinating cooperation between the national competent supervisory authorities (lit. a) and contributing to uniform administrative practice in the Member States (lit. d) are likely to require a common format of exchange.

29 The task under Art. 66 lit. e AI Act to issue recommendations and written opinions at the request of the EU Commission, for example on the development and application of codes of conduct and practice guidelines or on delegated acts and implementing acts as well as on the AI Act itself (amendment of Annex III or revision of Art. 5 AI Act), is an example of the great importance of the AI Board in the new supervisory system.

V. Advisory forum

30 In accordance with Art. 67 para. 1 AI Act, an **advisory forum** will also be established.

1. Composition and organization

31 In accordance with Art. 67 para. 2 sentence 1 AI Act, the advisory forum is made up of **representatives of industry, start-ups, SMEs, civil society and academia**. According to Art. 67 para. 2 sentence 2 of the AI Act, the composition of the advisory forum should ensure a balanced relationship between economic and non-economic interests. This could be achieved, for example, by a representative ratio of 50 % economic and 50 % non-economic interests. In addition, within the category of economic interests, attention should be paid to a balanced relationship between SMEs and other companies. As Art. 67 para. 2 sentence 1 AI Act already differentiates between industry, start-ups and SMEs with regard to representatives of economic interests, a participation of 1/3 each (within the 50 %) could be expedient.

32 The representatives are appointed by the EU Commission for a **period of two years** in accordance with Art. 67 para. 4 1st subpara. 1 AI Act, which can be **extended once for a further two years** in accordance with Art. 67 para. 4 2nd subpara. 2 AI Act.

33 Pursuant to Art. 67 para. 5 AI Act, the following are also **permanent members** of the advisory forum

- the EU Agency for Fundamental Rights (FRA),
- the EU Agency for Cybersecurity (ENISA),
- the European Committee for Standardization (CEN),
- the European Committee for Electrotechnical Standardization (CENELEC) and the
- European Telecommunications Standards Institute (ETSI).

34 All members of the advisory forum elect **two co-chairs** for a **term of office** of **two years** in accordance with Art. 67 para. 6 AI Act; the term of office can be extended

[24] Overview in Zenner in: Schwartmann/Keber/Zenner, Part 3, Chapter 1, para. 9 et seq.

once (i.e. by a further two years). The criteria set out in Art. 67 para. 2 AI Act must be observed during the election. This can only mean a balanced selection of economic and non-economic interests. This means that the chairmanship must be held by one representative of economic interests and one representative of non-economic interests. A chairmanship by permanent representatives within the meaning of Art. 67 para. 5 AI Act is ruled out.

The advisory forum **meets** at least twice a year in accordance with Art. 67 para. 7 sentence 1 AI Act. Experts and stakeholders may be invited to the meetings in accordance with Art. 67 para. 7 sentence 2 AI Act. Further details, including the framework conditions for **permanent or temporary sub-groups** (see Art. 67 para. 9 AI Act) can be regulated by rules of procedure in accordance with Art. 67 para. 6 AI Act. 35

2. Tasks

The advisory forum is to **provide technical expertise** and **advise** the AI Board and the EU Commission, Art. 67 para. 1 AI Act. The AI Office is not explicitly named in Art. 67 para. 1 AI Act, but as an institution of the EU Commission, it is likely to benefit at least indirectly from the technical expertise of the advisory forum. 36

According to Art. 67 para. 9 AI Act, the advisory forum can prepare **statements, recommendations** and **written contributions** at the request of the AI Board or the EU Commission. According to Art. 67 para. 10 AI Act, it must prepare and publish an annual activity report. 37

VI. Scientific panel

The provisions in Art. 68 AI Act deal with the so-called "**Scientific panel**". The EU Commission must lay down provisions on the establishment of the panel by means of an implementing act within the meaning of Art. 291 TFEU, as Art. 68 para. 1 sentence 2 AI Act refers to Art. 98 para. 2 AI Act, which in turn refers to Art. 5 Regulation (EU) No. 182/2011, which applies to implementing acts within the meaning of Art. 291 TFEU. Pursuant to Art. 68 para. 5 AI Act, the implementing act should contain, among other things, detailed rules according to which the scientific panel and its members may issue warnings. In addition, pursuant to Art. 68 para. 5 AI Act, the legal act should regulate how the panel can request support from the AI Office in the performance of its tasks. The implementing act must also regulate the structure and amount of fees as well as the scope and structure of reimbursable costs to be paid by the Member States when experts are consulted, see Art. 69 para. 2 sentences 1 and 2 AI Act. 38

The implementing act was published as Implementing Regulation (EU) 2025/454 (hereinafter: DVO (EU) 2025/454) on 10.3.2025, in the Official Journal of the EU and, pursuant to Art. 20 of the Regulation, it entered into force 20 days later, i.e., on 31.3.2025.[25] Pursuant to Art. 1(a) DVO (EU) 2025/454, the Implementing Regulation regulates the establishment and functioning of the scientific panel in the field of AI. According to Art. 1(a) of the Implementing Regulation (EU) 2025/454, it also contains provisions on the conditions, procedures, and detailed rules under which the scientific panel and its members may issue qualified warnings and request assistance from the

[25] Implementing Regulation (EU) 2025/454 laying down rules for the implementation of Regulation (EU) 2024/1689 of the European Parliament and of the Council with regard to the establishment of a Scientific Body of Independent Experts in the field of artificial intelligence, OJ 2025 L 454, 1.

AI Office. This is in line with the requirements of Art. 68 para. 1 sentence 2 and para. 5 AI Act.

1. Composition and organization

39 Pursuant to Art. 68 para. 2 sentence 1 AI Act, the scientific panel is composed of experts selected by the EU Commission. The number of experts must be determined by the EU Commission in consultation with the AI Board. This is in line with the provision in Art. 3 para. 2 sentence 1 of Delegated Regulation (EU) 2025/454. The maximum number of experts on the scientific panel is set at 60 in Art. 3 para. 2 sentence 2 of Delegated Regulation (EU) 2025/454. When determining the number of experts, the "relevant requirements" must be taken into account in accordance with Art. 68 para. 2 subparagraph 2 AI Act. The EU Commission, in consultation with the AI Board, must ensure a **balanced gender distribution** and a "**fair geographical distribution**." With regard to gender balance, Article 3 para. 5 sentence 2 of the Implementing Regulation (EU) 2025/454 stipulates that the EU Commission shall give preference to the underrepresented gender when choosing between two equally qualified candidates in the selection process. Art. 3 para. 4 of the Implementing Regulation (EU) 2025/454 clarifies what is meant by equitable geographical distribution.

The experts are to be selected on the "basis of current scientific or technical expertise in the field of AI", which is required to fulfill the tasks specified in Art. 68 para. 3 AI Act. Art. 68 para. 2 sentence 1 lit. a-c stipulates that evidence of certain skills must be provided; these are in particular

- scientific or technical expertise and competence in the field of AI, lit. a,
- independence from providers of AI systems or GPAI models, lit. b,
- the ability to carry out activities diligently, accurately and objectively., lit. c.

40 Statements on the selection criteria and composition of the scientific panel can also be found in Art. 3 of Regulation (EU) 2025/454. The provision in Art. 3 para. 1 of Regulation (EU) 2025/454 initially refers only to the call for expressions of interest with regard to the selection criteria. However, Article 3(3) of the Delegated Regulation (EU) 2025/454 then clarifies that certain aspects must be ensured when selecting experts. According to Art. 3 para. 3 lit. a of the Delegated Regulation (EU) 2025/454, it is necessary for the scientific panel to have "appropriate multidisciplinary, interdisciplinary, and up-to-date scientific, technical, or sociotechnical expertise." This expertise should be related to AI, "the impact of AI or other issues relevant to the effective enforcement of Regulation (EU) 2024/1689." This also includes expertise "in areas of application and on fundamental rights and equality." The provision in Art. 3 para. 3 lit. a of the DVO (EU) 2025/454 thus specifies in considerable detail the requirements set out in Art. 68 para. 2 sentence 1 lit. a AI Act, which are still rather general. Article 3 para. 3 lit. d of the DPO (EU) 2025/454 takes up the requirement set out in Art. 68 para. 2 sentence 1 lit. c AI Act.

41 According to the wording of the requirement ("it"), the **evidence** relates to the "scientific body". This means that the **panel as a whole** must be able to provide the required evidence. With regard to the required skills, the individual experts can complement each other. However, all experts must be independent of providers of AI systems or GPAI models (see also Art. 68 (4) AI Act and Art. 3 para. 3 lit. b and Art. 10 para. 2 DVO (EU) 2025/454). According to Art. 10 para. 2 of the EU Delegated Regulation (EU) 2025/454, this is precluded in any case by an employment or contractual relationship with such a provider. The same should apply to employment relationships with associations of providers.

The **term of office** is governed by Art. 4 of Implementing Regulation (EU) 2025/454. It is limited to two years but may be extended. Provisions on the **chair** and **vice-chair** are set out in Art. 5 of Implementing Regulation (EU) 2025/454. According to Art. 6 of Implementing Regulation (EU) 2025/454, the scientific panel is supported by a **secretariat**. The secretariat shall perform the following tasks in particular: 42

- Identifying and addressing potential conflicts of interest;
- Monitoring compliance with the rules of procedure pursuant to Art. 8 of the Implementing Regulation (EU) 2025/454 and with requests for the performance of tasks pursuant to Art. 68 para. 3 AI Act;
- Processing requests for additional opinions addressed to the scientific panel by the market surveillance authorities;
- Processing requests from Member States for assistance from experts for the purposes of enforcing the AI Act at the national level.

2. Tasks

Pursuant to Art. 68 para. 1 AI Act, the body is to support the enforcement activities regulated under the AI Act. This requirement is specified in Art. 68 para. 3 AI Act. Accordingly, the scientific panel expressly advises and supports the AI Office alone, but should also assist authorities at national level (cf. Art. 68 para. 3 lit. b and c AI Act). The provisions in Art. 68 para. 3 lit. a AI Act refer to GPAI models and systems. In this respect, the committee should 43

- warn of potential systemic risks of general purpose AI models at Union level, i),
- contribute to the development of tools and methodologies for assessing the capabilities of GPAI models and systems, including through benchmarks, ii),
- provide advice on the classification of GPAI models with systemic risk, iii),
- provide advice on the classification of different general purpose AI models and systems, iv) and
- contribute to the development of tools and patterns, v).

According to Art. 68 para. 3 lit. d AI Act, the committee should also support the AI Office in performing its tasks within the framework of the **Union safeguard clause procedure** regulated in Art. 81 AI Act. This procedure can be carried out if action is to be taken against measures (in particular bans or restrictions) of the national market surveillance authorities (see also Art. 79 para. 5 AI Act). It is noteworthy that Art. 81 of the AI Act and – as far as can be seen – Decision C/2024/1459 do not provide for the involvement of the AI Office in this procedure, but only name the EU Commission as the acting actor at EU level. 44

Contrary to what the introductory wording in Art. 68 para. 3 AI Act suggests, the panel is also intended to **support the work of the market surveillance authorities** in addition to the AI Office in accordance with Art. 68 para. 3 lit. b and c AI Act.[26] However, Art. 14 of Implementing Regulation (EU) 2025/454 clarifies that this requires a request from the relevant market surveillance authority to the AI Office. 45

Art. 69 para. 1 AI Act also provides that the member states may also consult experts from the scientific panel. According to Art. 69 para. 3, the EU Commission must provide **timely access to the experts**.

[26] See also Zenner in: Schwartmann/Keber/Zenner, Part 3, Chapter 1, para. 12.

46 According to Art. 68 para. 4 sentence 1 AI Act, the **experts** must perform their tasks in accordance with the principles of impartiality and objectivity, cf. also Art. 3 para. 3 lit. c and Art. 10 para. 2 DVO (EU) 2025/454.

The ECB and the ESCB, for example, also derive such principles from Art. 130 TFEU.[27] If these standards are applied accordingly – as far as possible – "**impartiality**" would mean that work results must be developed, produced and disseminated in a neutral manner. Correspondingly, "objectivity" would mean that the work results must be developed, produced and disseminated in a systematic, reliable and unbiased manner, also in compliance with professional and ethical standards. In this sense, Art. 68 para. 4 sentence 2 of the AI Act stipulates that experts may not request or accept instructions when performing their tasks in accordance with Art. 68 para. 3 of the AI Act. The publicly accessible "declaration of interests" required in Art. 68 para. 4 sentence 3 AI Act should be understood in this sense as a "declaration of independence", see also Art. 10 para. 3 of Delegated Regulation (EU) 2025/454. According to Art. 68 para. 4 sentence 4 AI Act, the AI Office must set up systems and procedures with which potential conflicts of interest can be prevented or actively managed.

47 Pursuant to Art. 68 para. 4 sentence 1 AI Act, the experts must also ensure that they treat **information and data confidentially**. Art. 68 para. 4 sentence 1 AI Act refers to information and data that they come into possession of when carrying out their tasks and activities. Art. 78 para. 1 AI Act contains a corresponding requirement. Article 13 para. 1 of Implementing Regulation (EU) 2025/454 adds that experts may not disclose any information of a confidential nature that comes to their knowledge during their work in the scientific panel or as a result of other activities covered by this Regulation. To this end, the experts shall sign a **confidentiality agreement** in accordance with Art. 13 para. 1 sentence 2 of the Delegated Regulation (EU) 2025/454.

The provision will have to be interpreted (restrictively) as meaning that only non-public information that experts receive in the course of their duties and activities for the respective institution declared responsible by the AI Act (in this case the scientific panel) can be meant.

VII. National competent authorities

48 The EU legislator assigns a key role to the Member States in the application and enforcement of the AI Act.[28] The AI Act therefore also contains provisions on the **national competent authorities** and **single points of contact**, see Art. 70 AI Act.

1. Equipment and organization

49 According to Art. 70 para. 1 sentence 1 AI Act, **each Member State** must establish or designate at least one **notifying authority** and at least one **market surveillance authority** as the national competent authorities for the purposes of the AI Act. Member States are free to choose the type of public body.[29] The wording "at least" gives the Member States the option of declaring several national authorities to be competent and – where necessary – establishing or designating them (see also Art. 70 para. 1 sentence 4 AI Act). Art. 74 para. 3 and 7 AI Act also expressly clarifies that, under certain

[27] Cf. the ESCB's public statement with regard to the statistics it compiles; here No. 6.
[28] Cf. recital 153 AI Act.
[29] Cf. recital 154 AI Act.

conditions, other relevant authorities may be designated as market surveillance authorities in relation to high-risk AI systems.

When setting up or appointing the national competent authorities, it should be noted that they must exercise their powers **independently, impartially and without bias** in accordance with Art. 70 para. 1 sentence 2 AI Act. The aim is to guarantee the objectivity of activities and tasks and to ensure the application and implementation of the AI Act. Art. 70 para. 1 sentence 3 AI Act clarifies in this sense that the members of the authorities must refrain from any actions that are incompatible with their duties.[30] 50

The wording of Art. 70 para. 1 sentence 4 AI Act can also be understood as meaning that the activities and tasks (market surveillance and notification) can be carried out by only one national competent authority while complying with the aforementioned provisions. However, this contradicts the provisions in Art. 70 para. 1 sentence 1 AI Act, which refer to at least one authority to be established or designated for each field of activity or task. In each case, the Member States must appoint a market surveillance authority in accordance with Art. 70 para. 2 sentence 3 of the AI Act, which is the single point of contact for the AI Act. The central contact points of the Member States are then listed by the EU Commission in a publicly available list. 51

Notification and information obligations of the Member States can be found in Art. 70 para. 2 AI Act. Noteworthy is the provision in Art. 70 para 2 sentence 2 AI Act, according to which Member States must make information on the competent authorities and the central contact point publicly available twelve months after the AI Act enters into force. This results in the **timeframe for the establishment** or **designation** of the authorities and contact point: no later than twelve months after the AI Act came into force. 52

In Germany, the **Federal Network Agency** (BNetzA) plays a central role in supervising AI systems. It is the competent market surveillance and notifying authority and coordinates cooperation with other authorities. **Coordination** is necessary as authorities that already act as market surveillance authorities and notifying authorities in fully harmonized areas of product regulation will retain their responsibilities under the AI Act. This will avoid duplication of structures and make use of existing sector-specific expertise. The fully harmonized sectors include, in particular, those listed in Annex I, Section A, including machinery, medical devices, toys, elevators, and radio equipment. If further fully harmonized products are added in the future, these will also fall under the single supervisory structure. This future clause could apply in particular to the automotive and aviation sectors and could also affect the Cyber Resilience Act. 53

In the financial services sector, for example, it is not the BNetzA but the Federal Financial Supervisory Authority (Bafin) that is responsible: If the use of an AI system is directly related to the provision of financial services, market surveillance is its responsibility.

According to Art. 70 para. 3 sentence 1 AI Act, the Member States must ensure that their national competent authorities are **adequately equipped**. The provision refers to **technical and financial resources** as well as **suitable personnel**. Art. 70 para. 3 sentence 2 AI Act expressly states that the authorities "shall have a sufficient number of personnel permanently available" whose competences and expertise shall include an in-depth understanding of: 54

- AI technologies,
- data and data computing,

---

[30] See also recital 153 AI Act.

- personal data protection,
- cybersecurity,
- fundamental rights,
- health and safety risks and
- knowledge of existing standards and legal requirements.

Art. 70 para. 3 sentence 1 AI Act specifically regulates for public authorities what Art. 4 AI Act generally provides for. The requirement in Art. 70 para. 3 AI Act is to be understood to mean that not every employee individually, but the employees of an authority as a **group** must fulfill these requirements. The wording "permanently" stipulates that the authorities must maintain a suitable workforce from the outset. The competencies and resources must be reviewed regularly (Art. 70 para. 3 sentence 3 AI Act) and reported to the EU Commission initially one year after the AI Act comes into force and subsequently every two years (Art. 70 para. 6 AI Act). The requirements in Art. 70 AI Act are supplemented by the requirements in Art. 28 AI Act regarding the notifying authorities.

2. Tasks

55 The **range of tasks of** the national supervisory authorities is essentially defined by the AI Act, but must also be considered in the context of the New Legislative Framework (NLF), in particular Regulation (EU) 2019/1020 and the enforcement powers set out therein.[31] Art. 74 para. 1 sentence 1 AI Act expressly states that Regulation (EU) 2019/1020 also applies to AI systems within the meaning of the AI Act.

56 In line with the division into notifying authorities and market surveillance authorities, the areas of responsibility must also be considered separately. In principle, the tasks of the notifying authorities start[32] before the AI system is placed on the market and the tasks of the market surveillance authorities start after the AI system is placed on the market.

a) Notification

57 According to Art. 3 No. 19 AI Act, the notifying authority is a "national authority responsible for setting up and carrying out the necessary procedures for the assessment, designation and notification of conformity assessment bodies and for their monitoring" (→ § 8 mn. 2). Requirements regarding the tasks of the notifying authorities can be found in particular in Art. 30 et seq. AI Act. According to this, the authorities notify so-called conformity assessment bodies, see Art. 30 para. 1 AI Act. According to Art. 3 No. 21 AI Act, these are bodies "that performs third-party conformity assessment activities, including testing, certification and inspection".

58 The AI Act does not define what a **notification** is, but Art. 30 AI Act regulates the notification procedure. Notification by the authority may only take place if conformity assessment bodies fulfill the requirements of Art. 31 AI Act. Under the conditions of Art. 32 AI Act, which are linked to the harmonized standards within the meaning of Art. 40 AI Act, conformity can also be presumed. A conformity assessment body that has been notified in accordance with the AI Act and the other relevant Union harmonization legislation is deemed to be a notified body in accordance with Art. 3 No. 22 AI Act (→ § 8 mn. 3).[33]

---

[31] See also recital 156 AI Act.
[32] But see Art. 76 AI Act, which regulates requirements and powers for tests in regulatory sandboxes.
[33] Cf. Zenner in: Schwartmann/Keber/Zenner, Part 3, Chapter 1, para. 20: e.g. TÜV or DEKRA.

In addition to some notification obligations (see, for example, Art. 30 para. 2 and 36 para. 1 AI Act), the AI Act sets out in detail the range of tasks of the authority, especially in the case of changes to the notification of a notified body, see Art. 36 para. 2–9 AI Act. 59

b) Market surveillance

According to Art. 3 No. 26 AI Act, **a market surveillance authority** is the "national authority carrying out the activities and taking the measures pursuant to Regulation (EU) 2019/1020". Requirements regarding the scope of duties of market surveillance authorities arise in particular from the provisions in Art. 72 et seq. AI Act and from the provisions of Regulation (EU) 2019/1020. 60

Specific tasks of the market surveillance authorities are regulated, for example, in relation to 61

- serious incidents, Art. 73 para. 8 AI Act in conjunction with Art. 19 Regulation (EU) 2019/1020,
- the market surveillance and control of AI systems, Art. 74 AI Act in conjunction with Regulation (EU) 2019/1020,[34]
- administrative assistance and market surveillance and control of GPAI systems, Art. 75 AI Act in conjunction with Regulation (EU) 2019/1020,
- supervision of tests under real conditions, Art. 76 AI Act,
- the procedure at national level for dealing with AI systems presenting a risk, Art. 79 AI Act in conjunction with Art. 3 No. 19 and Art. 18 Regulation (EU) 2019/1020,
- the procedure for dealing with AI systems classified by the provider as non-high-risk in application of Annex III, Art. 80 AI Act in conjunction with Art. 11 Regulation (EU) 2019/1020,
- the Union safeguard procedure, Art. 81 AI Act in conjunction with Art. 11 Regulation (EU) 1025/2012,
- compliant AI systems which present a risk, Art. 82 AI Act,
- formal non-compliance, Art. 83 AI Act.

In addition, there are various reporting and notification obligations in accordance with Art. 74 para. 2 AI Act. 62

[34] For an overview, see Zenner in Schwartmann/Keber/Zenner, Part 3, Chapter 1, para. 32.

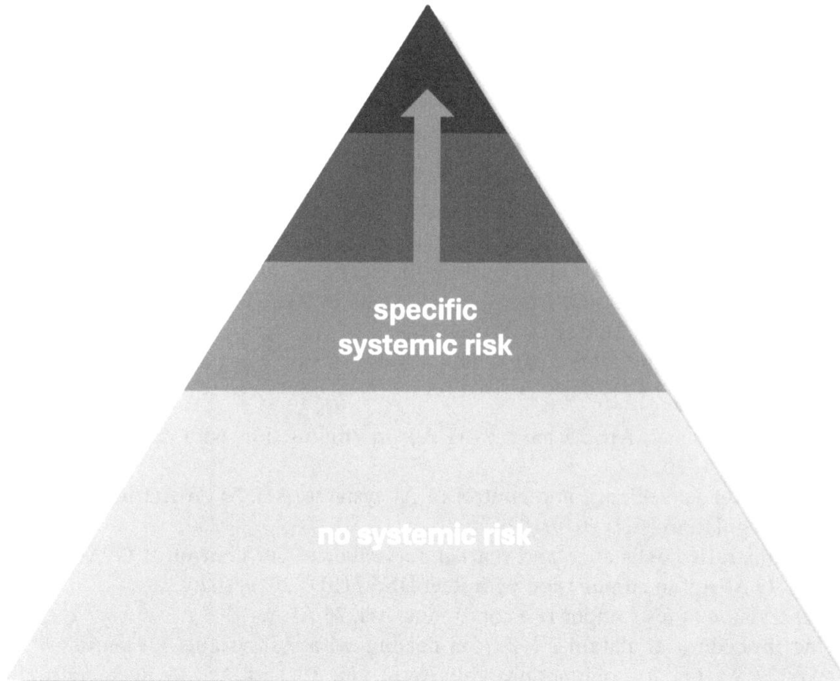

Figure 17: Supervisory system for AI in the EU

c) Penalties

63 The basis for **penalties and other enforcement measures** is set out in particular in Art. 99 of the AI Act. According to Art. 99 para. 1 of the AI Act, the member states lay down the rules on sanctions in the event of violations of the AI Act, which may also include warnings and non-monetary measures.[35] The guidelines yet to be issued by the EU Commission within the meaning of Art. 96 of the AI Act must be taken into account. Art. 99 para. 1 sentence 2 stipulates that the sanctions must be effective, proportionate and dissuasive. The clarification in Art. 99 para. 1 sentence 3 AI Act is significant, according to which the interests of SMEs, including start-ups, and their "economic viability" must be taken into consideration.

64 The penalties that the EU legislator considers appropriate in this sense can be seen in particular in the provisions of Art. 99 para. 3–7 AI Act.[36] If a prohibited AI system is placed on the market or operated, fines of up to EUR 35 million or 7 % of the worldwide annual turnover of the previous financial year[37] (depending on which amount is higher) may be imposed in accordance with Art. 99 para. 3 AI Act. In the event of breaches of the list of obligations in Art. 16, 22–26, 31, 33 para. 1, 3 and 4, 34, 50 AI Act, actors can be sanctioned with fines of up to EUR 15 million or 3 % of annual turnover in accordance with Art. 99 para. 4 AI Act. The same applies to breaches

[35] See Schwartmann/Köhler in Schwartmann/Keber/Zenner, Part 3, Chapter 3, para. 3: no clear allocation of responsibility for the imposition of fines.

[36] See also Wendt uj 2/2024, 42, 45.

[37] Schwartmann/Köhler in Schwartmann/Keber/Zenner, Part 3, Chapter 3, para. 9: annual turnover of the parent company, if applicable.

of obligations for providers of GPAI models, Art. 101 AI Act; however, the EU Commission or the AI Office is the competent authority in this case. In the case of false, incomplete or misleading information, fines of up to EUR 7.5 million or 1 % annual turnover can be imposed in accordance with Art. 99 para. 5 AI Act. Pursuant to Art. 99 para. 6 AI Act, a reduction applies to SMEs, including start-ups. In this case, the lower of the percentages or sums mentioned is applied.[38]

d) Legal remedies

The right to **legal remedies** is only expressly regulated with regard to market surveillance authorities in Art. 85 AI Act (which refers to Regulation (EU) 2019/1020) and Art. 86 AI Act.[39] An appeal procedure in relation to a notification that has not been issued or has been revoked is – as far as can be seen – not regulated. However, Art. 99 para. 10 AI Act generally stipulates for sanctioning powers that the exercise of these powers must be subject to appropriate procedural safeguards in accordance with Union and national law, including effective judicial remedies and due process. **65**

Irrespective of this, all "rights and remedies available to consumers and other persons who may be adversely affected by AI systems" under Union law should remain unaffected and fully applicable, including with regard to possible compensation for damages.[40] **66**

[38] Wendt uj 2/2024, 42, 45.
[39] See Zenner in Schwartmann/Keber/Zenner, Part 3, Chapter 1, para. 58.
[40] See recital 9 AI Act.

§ 14
Codes of conduct

1 Art. 95 AI Act contains provisions on **codes of** conduct. The provisions address providers and deployers of AI systems that do not fall into the category of high-risk AI systems and for which there are therefore no mandatory compliance requirements. For providers and deployers of AI systems with moderate or no risk, the AI Act provides for codes of conduct to be drawn up on a voluntary basis and used as a guide.

2 The codes of conduct should also provide for **governance mechanisms** and promote the voluntary application of some or all of the requirements applicable to high-risk AI systems.[1] Thus, on the one hand, it may be advisable to base the codes on the compliance requirements for providers and deployers of high-risk AI systems. These can then be adapted "in light of the intended purpose of the systems and the lower risk".[2]

3 From the perspective of the EU legislator, additional requirements can also be established voluntarily[3]. Art. 95 para. 2 AI Act provides examples of this in relation to

- the elements of the Union ethical guidelines for trustworthy AI,
- environmental sustainability,
- promoting AI literacy,
- an inclusive and diverse design and development of AI systems,
- the involvement of stakeholders.

4 According to Art. 95 para. 3 sentence 2 AI Act, codes of conduct may extend to one or more AI systems. This is intended to take account of similar purposes of the respective systems.

5 The drawing up of codes of conduct should be promoted by the AI Office and the member states, Art. 95 para. 1 AI Act. According to Art. 95 para. 4 AI Act, the AI Office and the member states should also expressly take into account the special interests and needs of SMEs, including start-ups.

6 The task of structuring is to be assumed by individual AI system providers or deployers or by their interest groups, Art. 95 para. 3 AI Act. Civil society organizations and universities can also be involved according to Art. 95 para. 3 AI Act.

7 The codes of conduct regulated in Art. 95 AI Act must be distinguished from the GPAI codes of practice (→ § 11 mn. 51).

[1] Recital 165 AI Act.
[2] Recital 165 AI Act.
[3] Recital 165 AI Act.

§ 15
Liability

Literature: *Bollweg, Hans-Georg*, Neue Vorschläge aus Brüssel zur KI- und Produkthaftung, ZfPC 2023, 1; *Bomhard, David/Siglmüller, Jonas*, Europäische KI-Haftungsrichtlinie, RDi 2022, 506; *Bommel, Robert*, Künstliche Intelligenz – Haftung für selbstlernende Software, 2023; *Borges, Georg*, Liability for AI Systems Under Current and Future Law, CRi 1/2023, 1; *Bubinger, Phillip*, Die zivilrechtliche Haftung des Herstellers und Händlers für Fahrassistenzsysteme, RAW 2023, 57; *Dany, Jannis*, Haftung beim Einsatz von KI durch den Vorstand, BB 2022, 2056; *Denga, Michael*, Unternehmenshaftung für KI – zur Konformitätsbewertung in Permanenz, CR 2023, 277; *Dietrich, Henrik*, Produzentenhaftung für Künstliche Intelligenz, InTeR 2024, 49; *Durante, Masimo/Floridi, Luciano*, A Legal Principles-Based Framework for AI Liability Regulation, in The 2021 Yearbook of the Digital Ethics Lab, pp. 93; *Eichelberger, Jan*, Arzthaftung beim Einsatz von KI und Robotik, ZfPC 2023, 209; *Eichelberger, Jan*, Der Vorschlag einer "Richtlinie über KI-Haftung", DB 2022, 2783; *Elter, Sven*, Strafrechtliche Produktverantwortung für automatisiertes und autonomes Fahren, 2023; *Frost, Yannick/Steininger, Manuela/Vivekens, Sabrina*, Benefits, Opportunities, Risks and Liability in the Use of Artificial Intelligence in the Context of the AI Regulation and the AI Liability Directive, MPR 2024, 4; *Hacker, Philipp*, The European AI Liability Directive – Critique of a Half-Hearted Approach and Lessons for the Future, Computer Law & Security Review, Volume 51, 2022, 105871; *Hacker, Philipp/Berz, Amelie*, Der AI Act der Europäischen Union – Überblick, Kritik und Ausblick, ZRP 2023, 226; *Haftenberger, Anna*, Die Produkthaftung für künstlich intelligente Medizinprodukte, 2023; *Heiss, Stefan*, Künstliche Intelligenz: Gesetzentwurf für ein europäisches Haftungsrecht beim Einsatz von künstlicher Intelligenz, NZG 2021, 2; *Heiss, Stefan*, Europäische Haftungsregeln für Künstliche Intelligenz, EuZW 2021, 932; *Heiss, Stefan*, Artificial Intelligence meets European Union Law, EuCML 2021, 252; *König, Jochen*, Geschäftsleiterhaftung bei Einsatz von KI aus der Perspektive eines Praktikers, BB 2023, 1923; *Krüger, Daniel/Wagner, Susan*, Das Phänomen "Künstliche Intelligenz" aus regulatorischer und haftungsrechtlicher Sicht, ZfPC 2023, 124; *Kuntz, Thilo*, Künstliche Intelligenz, Wissenszurechnung und Wissensverantwortung, ZfPW 2022, 177; *Lachenmann, Matthias/Meyer, Johanna*, Die Richtlinie über KI-Haftung – Beweiserleichterungen für durch KI-Systeme entstandene Schäden?, MMR-Aktuell 2023, 457000; *Li, Shu/Schütte, Béatrice*, The Proposed EU Artificial Intelligence Liability Directive, Technology & Regulation 2024, 143; *Lohmann, Melinda*, Roboter als Wundertüten – Eine zivilrechtliche Haftungsanalyse, AJP 2017, 152; *Lohmann, Melinda/Müller-Chen, Markus*, Selbstlernende Fahrzeuge – eine Haftungsanalyse, Schweizerische Zeitschrift für Wirtschafts- und Finanzmarktrecht 2017, 48; *Lohsse, Sebastian/Schulze, Reiner/Staudenmayer, Dirk*, Liability for AI, 2023; *May, Claudia*, EU-Politik: Neue Haftungsvorschriften für Produkte und künstliche Intelligenz zum Schutz der Verbraucher, DAR 2022, 719; *Mayrhofer, Ann-Kristin*, Außervertragliche Haftung für fremde Autonomie, 2023; *Mayrhofer, Ann-Kristin*, Produkthaftungsrechtliche Verantwortung des "Trainer-Nutzers" von KI-Systemen, RDi 2023, 20; *Müller-Hengstenberg, Claus/Kirn, Stefan*, Liability of the deployer of autonomous software agents – Possible effects of the European Parliament's resolution on liability for the use of AI, MMR 2021, 376; *Navas, Susana*, Civil liability of legal tech tool developers vis-à-vis end-users – The upcoming EU legal framework, LTZ 2022, 147; *Nordemann, Jan*, Generative Künstliche Intelligenz; Urheberrechtsverletzungen und Haftung, GRUR 2024, 1; *Oechsler, Jürgen*, Die Haftungsverantwortung für selbstlernende KI-Systeme, NJW 2022, 2713; *Pauli, Laura Katharina*, Künstliche Intelligenz und Gefährdungshaftung im öffentlichen Recht, 2023; *Piovano, Christian/Hess, Christian*, Das neue europäische Produkthaftungsrecht, 2024; *Piovano, Christian/Hess, Christian*, Mehr Pflichten, mehr Rechte: Wie die neue EU-Produkthaftungsrichtlinie die Spielregeln für Wirtschaftsakteure und die Verbraucher ändert, ZfPC 3/2004, 90 and 4/2024, 161; *Reus, Katharina*, KI und Haftung – Realisierung erlaubter Risiken, NZG 2024, 369; *Reusch, Philipp*, KI und Software im Kontext von Produkthaftung und Produktsicherheit, RDi 2023, 152; *Rossek, Corvin/Link, Hendrik*, EU-Kommission: Entwurf einer überarbeiteten Produkthaftungs-RL – Relevanz hinsichtlich der Haftung für KI, ZD-Aktuell 2023, 01105; *Schreitmüller, Zeynep/Schucht, Carsten*, Künstliche Intelligenz im Arbeitsschutz – Das künftige EU Haftungsregime für Anbieter, Nutzer und Wirtschaftsakteure, ARP 2023, 226; *Schwartmann, Rolf/Keber, Tobias/Zenner, Kai*, KI-Verordnung. Leitfaden für die Praxis, 2024; *Sedlmaier, Felix/Bogataj, Andreaja Krzic*, Die Haftung beim (teil-)autonomen Fahren, NJW 2022, 2953; *Siglmüller, Jonas/Gassner, Daniel*, Softwareentwicklung durch Open-Source-trainierte KI – Schutz und Haftung, RDi 2023, 124; *Spindler, Gerald*, Die Vorschläge der EU-Kommission zu einer neuen Produkthaftung und zur Haftung von Herstellern und Betreibern Künstlicher Intelligenz, CR 11/2022, 689; *Spittka, Jan*, Haftung in Zeiten der Digitalisierung – EU-Kommission stellt neue Regeln für KI und Software vor, ZfPC 2022, 197; *Staudenmayer, Dirk*, Haftung für Künstliche Intelligenz, NJW 2023, 894; *Steege, Hans*, Haftung für Künstliche Intelligenz im Straßenverkehr, SVR 2023, 9; *Theis, Ricarda*, Auswirkungen der KI-Verordnung und der KI-Haftungs-Richtlinie auf die Haftung beim KI-Einsatz in der Finanzbranche, BKR 2024, 414; *Thiermann, Arne/Böck, Nicole*, Künstliche Intelligenz in Medizinprodukten, RDi 2022, 333; *Wagner, Gerhard*, Produkthaftung für das digitale Zeitalter – ein Paukenschlag aus Brüssel, JZ 2023, 1; *Wagner, Gerhard*, Haftung für Künstliche Intelligenz – Eine Gesetzesinitiative des Europäischen Parlaments, ZEuP 2021, 545; *Wildhaber, Isabelle*, Eine Einführung in die Haftung für Künstliche Intelligenz (KI), HAVE – Haftung und Versicherung 3/2021, 1; *Zech, Herbert*, Empfehl sich Regelungen zu Verantwortung und Haftung beim Einsatz Künstlicher Intelligenz?, NJW-Beil. 2022, 33; *Zech, Herbert*, Haftung für Trainingsdaten Künstlicher Intelligenz, NJW 2022, 502; *Zein, Sarah*, The Civil Liability for Artificial Intelligence, BAU Journal – Journal of Legal Studies, Volume 2022, Article 14.

I. Dual liability structure

1 The AI Act is a central building block in the overall structure of the EU regulatory system for AI. However, it does not stand alone. When considering it, the downstream **civil liability** that applies in the event of a breach of the AI Act must also be taken into account. In line with the dual liability structure[1], it is dealt with in two separate directives, the updated **product liability directive** (2024/2853/EU), hereinafter referred to as PLD,[2] which came into force at the end of 2024, and the draft of a directive on the **adaptation of the rules on non-contractual civil liability to artificial intelligence** (**AI Liability Directive**, hereinafter AILD-D),[3] which has been put on hold for the time being.

Both directives are also intended to set limits on AI, but at the same time increase safety by making liability risks calculable and insurable.[4] In this way, the liability standards also ultimately contribute to the goal of creating trust in AI and promoting the spread of AI systems.[5]

---

[1] Dietrich InTeR 2/24, 49 (50).

[2] See Piovano/Hess Neue ProdHaftRL § 1 para. 7.

[3] EU Commission, Proposal for a Directive of the European Parliament and of the Council on adapting non-contractual civil liability rules to artificial intelligence (AI Liability Directive) of 28.9.2022, COM(2022) 496 final; on 24.7.2024, the Commission services published considerations on the possible substantive amendments to the AILD-D in view of the AI Act, see Proposal for a Directive of the European Parliament and of the Council on adapting non-contractual civil liability rules to artificial intelligence (AI Liability Directive) – Commission Services considerations on the possible substantive amendments to the AILD in view of the AI Act, Council Doc. No. 12517/24.

[4] Hacker/Berz ZRP 2023, 221 (226).

[5] Hacker/Berz ZRP 2023, 221 (226).

Figure 18: Timeline – Product Liability Directive and AI Liability Directive (AILD-D)

2 Both directives provided for new rules on the distribution of the burden of proof (Art. 10 PLD and Art. 4 AILD-D) and the disclosure of evidence (Art. 9 PLD and Art. 3 AILD-D) that were highly relevant in practice and noticeably shifted the balance of power in favor of the injured party.[6]

3 While the updating of the Product Liability Directive,[7] which dates back to 1985, was completed during the last legislative period,[8] the future of AILD is more than uncertain. The EU Commission withdrew the draft directive on 11.2.2025 for the time being. This step came as a surprise. The Commission justified its decision by stating that it did not see any foreseeable agreement on the directive. There is uncertainty about the usefulness of the directive, not least at Council level. A broad front of critical Member States, led by France, Italy, and Denmark, questions the legal loophole that the AILD is attempting to close.

4 Accordingly, the Legal Affairs Committee (JURI), which is responsible for this matter at parliamentary level, commissioned a study from the EU Parliament's Research Service to determine whether there is still a need for the AILD in light of the AI Act and the PLD. The study was published in September 2024 as a supplementary impact assessment of the AILD-D.[9] It identifies areas of regulation (discrimination, hate speech, and fundamental rights) that are covered by the AILD-D but not by the PLD, and therefore generally supports the coexistence of the PLD and the AILD. At the same time, it proposes extending the scope of the AILD to general and other highly effective AI systems as well as to software, and recommends moving from a purely AI-focused directive to a broader software liability regime in order to avoid market fragmentation.

[6] Piavono/Hess ZfPC 4/2024, 161 (162); Lachenmann/Meyer MMR-Aktuell 2023, 457000.

[7] Council Directive 85/374/EEC of 25.7.1985 on the approximation of the laws, regulations and administrative provisions of the Member States concerning liability for defective products, OJ L 210, 7.8.1985, p. 29–33.

RL 85/374/EWG.

[8] Spindler CR 11/2022, 689 (690).

[9] Hacker, Proposal for a directive on adapting non-contractual civil liability rules to artificial intelligence Complementary impact assessment, https://www.europarl.europa.eu/RegData/etudes/STUD/2024/762861/EPRS_STU(2024)762861_EN.pdf.

II. Product liability

5 According to the Product Liability Directive, which was implemented in Germany in the **Product Liability Act**, manufacturers are liable for certain violations of legal interests caused by a defect in their product. The reason for liability is the placing of the defective product on the market, regardless of fault. In order to do justice to the nature of products in the digital age and the risks associated with them, the material scope of application was extended to **AI and software** in the course of updating the directive.[10]

6 In addition, the directive now provides for **a reduction in the burden of proof** for complex cases, including those relating to AI systems. Until now, the injured party has borne the burden of proof for all liability requirements. This will remain the case in the future. However, disclosure obligations and presumptions of causality will apply to simplify the enforcement of a claim for compensation.

7 The special characteristics of AI systems are **complexity, autonomy,** and **opacity** (black box effect).[11] They make it difficult for a person who is harmed as a result of a result (not) produced by a defective AI system to meet the requirements for asserting a claim for compensation. In order to make this easier, the new Product Liability Directive states that both the product defect itself and the causality between the product defect and the damage will in future be (rebuttably) presumed if, despite the disclosure of information and taking into account the circumstances of the individual case, it is "excessively difficult" for the claimant to provide evidence "due to the technical or scientific complexity" (see Recital 48). This may be the case, for example, if the product (medical device) or the technology (AI) or the proof of the causal link is particularly difficult. In addition, the plaintiff must at least have succeeded in demonstrating the probability of the defectiveness of the product and the causality between the defect and the damage.

8 The directive also stipulates that, in future, the defendant must disclose the relevant evidence under its control (e.g. relating to the AI system, the code used or the training or validation data) at the request of the plaintiff in court proceedings. The **obligation to disclose evidence** is intended to lead to a fairer distribution of risk and the compensation of significant disadvantages due to information asymmetries, as injured parties can otherwise hardly obtain sufficient evidence without the cooperation of the manufacturer.[12] Corresponding disclosure obligations are no longer completely alien to European law,[13] but they are in tension with the German and most European rules of civil procedure.[14] In fact, the instrument of disclosure of evidence appears to have been borrowed from the US American disclosure of documents or pre-trial discovery, which has led to the new regulations being accused of a breach of culture.[15]

---

[10] Krüger/Wagner ZfPC 2023, 124 (126); Spindler CR 11/2022, 689 (690).

[11] Kuntz ZfPW 2022, 177 (185).

[12] Piavono/Hess ZfPC 4/2024, 161 (162).

[13] For example, medical device law in Art. 10 para. 14 MDR provides for a right of access to conformity documents for potential plaintiffs, although this is not directed against the manufacturer, but against the competent authority.

[14] Piavono/Hess ZfPC 4/2024, 161 (162).

[15] Piavono/Hess ZfPC 4/2024, 161 (162).

III. Liability in tort

However, the peculiarities of AI systems not only cause difficulties in product liability law, but also in **tortious liability**. After all, this requires human behavior as a connecting factor. However, AI systems act autonomously. They sometimes make decisions that are unforeseeable for humans.[16] In addition, AI systems can change their behavior without external cause by adapting the underlying algorithm. In short, an AI system is not under the (complete) control of the provider or deployer.[17] 9

In **tort law**, however, a **breach of the duty of care** is required to establish liability. The special features of AI systems described above regularly make it difficult for the injured party to meet its burden of presentation and proof with regard to the breach of the duty of care and the causality giving rise to liability.[18] 10

The AILD-D was intended to solve this problem for tortious liability and, in this respect, create a certain degree of legal policy synchronization with the Product Liability Directive. In concrete terms, however, the two directives do not overlap in their areas of application: the new Product Liability Directive regulates the manufacturer's liability for a defective product. It creates a separate, no-fault claim. In contrast, the draft of the AILD was only aimed at the procedural requirements for asserting claims against providers or users of an AI under national law. 11

In terms of content, the EU Commission's proposal of 28.9.2022 also provided for **evidence-based measures** for the benefit of injured parties. Finally, the "large number of persons involved [...] in the design, development, deployment and operation of high-risk AI systems [...] makes it difficult for injured parties to identify the person potentially liable for the damage caused and to prove the conditions for a claim for damages."[19] Both directives are therefore based on the initial assumption that the use of AI requires generic measures to ease the burden of proof. 12

Accordingly, the draft directive provided for the power of national courts to order the **disclosure of** certain **evidence** upon request. This gives the plaintiff a right to disclosure. This was largely structured in the same way as in the new Product Liability Directive.[20] 13

However, it should have been applied only **to high-risk AI systems**, as only these are subject to the corresponding documentation and recording obligations under the AI Act. In contrast to the Product Liability Directive, the claim should also have been open to potential plaintiffs. The purpose of this extension was to make it easier for the injured party to find a claimant in the first place.[21] 14

In addition, the court should have been given the authority to order evidence-protection measures under the AILD-D.[22] As a procedural instrument for enforcing the duty of disclosure, the draft directive provided for the rebuttable presumption that a duty of care has been breached if the defendant does not comply with the court's request. Since the burden of proof of a breach of the duty of care otherwise lies with the claimant, this presumption rule certainly constituted an interference with a cornerstone of civil procedural law, namely the principle of production of evidence under 15

---

[16] Staudenmayer NJW 2023, 894 (895).
[17] Wagner JZ 2023, 1 (2).
[18] Krüger/Wagner ZfPC 2023, 124 (125); Kessen in: Schwartmann/Keber/Zenner, Part 3, Chapter 2, para. 16.
[19] Cf. recital 17 AILD.
[20] Staudenmayer NJW 2023, 894 (900); Spindler CR 2022, 689 (701).
[21] Krüger/Wagner ZfPC 2023, 124 (128).
[22] Staudenmayer NJW 2023, 894 (900).

§ 284 of the German Code of Civil Procedure (ZPO).[23] In practice, the presumption could have become the de facto rule. This is because the question of whether the defendant complies with a claim for information to the necessary and proportionate extent is ultimately subject to an overall assessment by the court.[24] In addition, the legal consequence of the existence of a breach of the duty of care was also a prerequisite for a presumption rule, namely that of causality between fault and the AI result.

16 According to the EU Commission, claims for damages could also fail if the **causal link** between the defendant's breach of duty of care and "the result produced by the AI system" (= AI result) cannot be proven. Therefore, Art. 4 para. 1 AILD-D introduced the **presumption** that such a causal link exists. To this end, Art. 4 para. 1 lit. a AILD-D required that the claimant proves "the fault of the defendant, or of a person for whose behaviour the defendant is responsible, consisting in the non-compliance with a duty of care laid down in Union or national law directly intended to protect against the damage that occurred".

17 There is no equivalent in German law for the **causality between the breach of duty of care and the AI result.**[25] § 823 para. 1 German Civil Code (BGB) recognizes two types of causality – that between breach of duty of care (action or omission) and breach of legal interest (= establishing liability) and that between breach of legal interest and damage (= fulfilling liability). In the absence of human action, the AI result cannot constitute a breach of the duty of care and certainly not a breach of legal interests or damage. In this way, the AILD-D introduced an intermediate step, so to speak, in the causality between a breach of duty of care and the violation of the legal interest, which forms the basis for liability in the German doctrine.

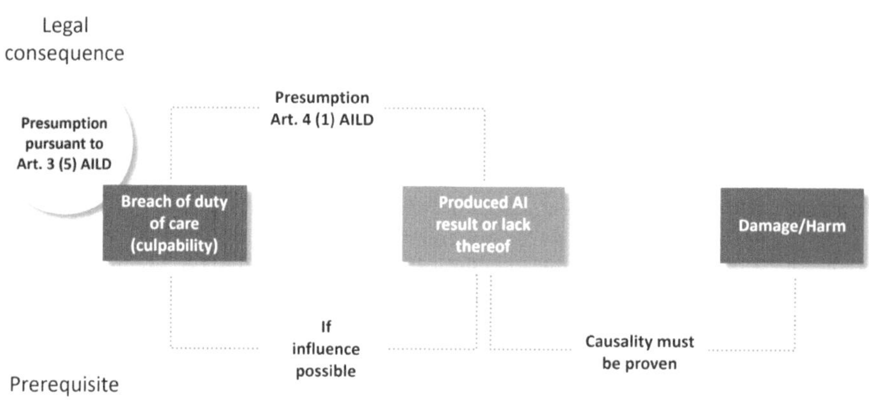

Figure 19: Regulation on liability in the AI Liability Directive (AILD-D), Bomhard/Siglmüller RDi 2022, 506 (510).

18 Overall, the **coupling of the two presumption rules** meant that an incomplete disclosure of evidence automatically leads to the presumption of causality between fault and the AI result. In doing so it set off a **domino effect** which, as a result, presumed the most critical claim prerequisites of a tortious claim – far beyond § 280 para. 1 sentence 2 BGB.[26]

[23] Bomhard/Siglmüller RDi 2022, 506 (507).
[24] Bomhard/Siglmüller RDi 2022, 506 (507).
[25] Bomhard/Siglmüller RDi 2022, 506 (512).
[26] Bomhard/Siglmüller RDi 2022, 506 (507).

This was considered to be quite **excessive**: after all, even if the plaintiff were to provide complete evidence of how the AI system works, he would still have to overcome the enormous hurdle of analyzing this data in order to ultimately establish a breach of duty of care.[27] This will regularly be no easy task, even for experts. The proposed directive exempted the plaintiff from this analysis across the board as soon as evidence is not submitted or not submitted in full. 19

Only the causality between the AI result and the infringement of legal interests as well as the causality fulfilling liability, thus, the causal link between the AI result and the violation of rights, as well as between the violation of rights and the damage, was still to be proven by the injured party according to the draft directive. 20

IV. Further legal policy discussion

The withdrawal of the AILD-D on 11.2.2025, came as a surprise. Not least, the Complementary Impact Assessment had recently identified important gaps in liability law regarding the use of AI systems and created room for further legal policy discussions. The annex to the EU Commission's work program expressly states that the EU Commission will examine whether a further proposal should be submitted or a different approach taken.[28] 21

If the EU Commission does indeed conclude that no further regulations in line with the AILD-D are necessary, this could possibly be explained by the high compliance costs for companies described in Mario Draghi's report on European competitiveness. However, the gaps in EU liability law identified for the use of AI systems would remain unaddressed in this case.[29] This applies, for example, to non-product-related risks such as discrimination, hate speech, and fundamental rights. It would still be possible to resort to existing national liability regulations in the EU member states. However, it is not yet clear whether national provisions can comprehensively answer open liability questions regarding the use of AI systems. In addition, the familiar **patchwork quilt** of different national bases for claims and legal consequences would remain in place. It is also unclear whether the ECJ will build the necessary bridges within the scope of its power to interpret EU law, for example by taking into account the requirements of the Product Liability Directive. This would, of course, also require that the ECJ be given the opportunity to answer relevant questions. 22

It is therefore hoped that the EU Commission will use the findings and develop a **new regulatory solution**. There is likely to be at least some interest in continuing the discussions in the EU Parliament.[30] The idea of the originally planned, coherent AI strategy is certainly worth pursuing in these discussions.[31] 23

27 Bomhard/Siglmüller RDi 2022, 506 (507).

28 Annex IV: Withdrawals on the EU Commission's work programme of 11.2.2025, point 32: „No foreseeable agreement – the Commission will assess whether another proposal should be tabled or another type of approach should be chosen."

29 Wendt ZfPC 2025, 45 (45).

30 Zenner ZfPC 2024, 242.

31 Wendt ZfPC 2025, 45 (45).

Regulation (EU) 2024/1689 of the European Parliament and of the Council of 13 June 2024 laying down harmonised rules on artificial intelligence and amending Regulations (EC) No 300/2008, (EU) No 167/2013, (EU) No 168/2013, (EU) 2018/858, (EU) 2018/1139 and (EU) 2019/2144 and Directives 2014/90/EU, (EU) 2016/797 and (EU) 2020/1828 (Artificial Intelligence Act)

(Text with EEA relevance)

(OJ L, 2024/1689, ELI: http://data.europa.eu/eli/reg/2024/1689/oj)

THE EUROPEAN PARLIAMENT AND THE COUNCIL OF THE EUROPEAN UNION,
Having regard to the Treaty on the Functioning of the European Union, and in particular Articles 16 and 114 thereof,
Having regard to the proposal from the European Commission,
After transmission of the draft legislative act to the national parliaments,
Having regard to the opinion of the European Economic and Social Committee[1],
Having regard to the opinion of the European Central Bank[2],
Having regard to the opinion of the Committee of the Regions[3],
Acting in accordance with the ordinary legislative procedure[4],
Whereas:

(1) The purpose of this Regulation is to improve the functioning of the internal market by laying down a uniform legal framework in particular for the development, the placing on the market, the putting into service and the use of artificial intelligence systems (AI systems) in the Union, in accordance with Union values, to promote the uptake of human centric and trustworthy artificial intelligence (AI) while ensuring a high level of protection of health, safety, fundamental rights as enshrined in the Charter of Fundamental Rights of the European Union (the „Charter"), including democracy, the rule of law and environmental protection, to protect against the harmful effects of AI systems in the Union, and to support innovation. This Regulation ensures the free movement, cross-border, of AI-based goods and services, thus preventing Member States from imposing restrictions on the development, marketing and use of AI systems, unless explicitly authorised by this Regulation.

(2) This Regulation should be applied in accordance with the values of the Union enshrined as in the Charter, facilitating the protection of natural persons, undertakings, democracy, the rule of law and environmental protection, while boosting innovation and employment and making the Union a leader in the uptake of trustworthy AI.

(3) AI systems can be easily deployed in a large variety of sectors of the economy and many parts of society, including across borders, and can easily circulate throughout the Union. Certain Member States have already explored the adop-

[1] **Official note:** OJ C 517, 22.12.2021, p. 56.
[2] **Official note:** OJ C 115, 11.3.2022, p. 5.
[3] **Official note:** OJ C 97, 28.2.2022, p. 60.
[4] **Official note:** Position of the European Parliament of 13 March 2024 (not yet published in the Official Journal) and decision of the Council of 21 May 2024.

tion of national rules to ensure that AI is trustworthy and safe and is developed and used in accordance with fundamental rights obligations. Diverging national rules may lead to the fragmentation of the internal market and may decrease legal certainty for operators that develop, import or use AI systems. A consistent and high level of protection throughout the Union should therefore be ensured in order to achieve trustworthy AI, while divergences hampering the free circulation, innovation, deployment and the uptake of AI systems and related products and services within the internal market should be prevented by laying down uniform obligations for operators and guaranteeing the uniform protection of overriding reasons of public interest and of rights of persons throughout the internal market on the basis of Article 114 of the Treaty on the Functioning of the European Union (TFEU). To the extent that this Regulation contains specific rules on the protection of individuals with regard to the processing of personal data concerning restrictions of the use of AI systems for remote biometric identification for the purpose of law enforcement, of the use of AI systems for risk assessments of natural persons for the purpose of law enforcement and of the use of AI systems of biometric categorisation for the purpose of law enforcement, it is appropriate to base this Regulation, in so far as those specific rules are concerned, on Article 16 TFEU. In light of those specific rules and the recourse to Article 16 TFEU, it is appropriate to consult the European Data Protection Board.

(4) AI is a fast evolving family of technologies that contributes to a wide array of economic, environmental and societal benefits across the entire spectrum of industries and social activities. By improving prediction, optimising operations and resource allocation, and personalising digital solutions available for individuals and organisations, the use of AI can provide key competitive advantages to undertakings and support socially and environmentally beneficial outcomes, for example in healthcare, agriculture, food safety, education and training, media, sports, culture, infrastructure management, energy, transport and logistics, public services, security, justice, resource and energy efficiency, environmental monitoring, the conservation and restoration of biodiversity and ecosystems and climate change mitigation and adaptation.

(5) At the same time, depending on the circumstances regarding its specific application, use, and level of technological development, AI may generate risks and cause harm to public interests and fundamental rights that are protected by Union law. Such harm might be material or immaterial, including physical, psychological, societal or economic harm.

(6) Given the major impact that AI can have on society and the need to build trust, it is vital for AI and its regulatory framework to be developed in accordance with Union values as enshrined in Article 2 of the Treaty on European Union (TEU), the fundamental rights and freedoms enshrined in the Treaties and, pursuant to Article 6 TEU, the Charter. As a prerequisite, AI should be a human-centric technology. It should serve as a tool for people, with the ultimate aim of increasing human well-being.

(7) In order to ensure a consistent and high level of protection of public interests as regards health, safety and fundamental rights, common rules for high-risk AI systems should be established. Those rules should be consistent with the Charter, non-discriminatory and in line with the Union's international trade commitments. They should also take into account the European Declaration on Digital Rights and Principles for the Digital Decade and the Ethics guidelines

for trustworthy AI of the High-Level Expert Group on Artificial Intelligence (AI HLEG).

(8) A Union legal framework laying down harmonised rules on AI is therefore needed to foster the development, use and uptake of AI in the internal market that at the same time meets a high level of protection of public interests, such as health and safety and the protection of fundamental rights, including democracy, the rule of law and environmental protection as recognised and protected by Union law. To achieve that objective, rules regulating the placing on the market, the putting into service and the use of certain AI systems should be laid down, thus ensuring the smooth functioning of the internal market and allowing those systems to benefit from the principle of free movement of goods and services. Those rules should be clear and robust in protecting fundamental rights, supportive of new innovative solutions, enabling a European ecosystem of public and private actors creating AI systems in line with Union values and unlocking the potential of the digital transformation across all regions of the Union. By laying down those rules as well as measures in support of innovation with a particular focus on small and medium enterprises (SMEs), including startups, this Regulation supports the objective of promoting the European human-centric approach to AI and being a global leader in the development of secure, trustworthy and ethical AI as stated by the European Council[5], and it ensures the protection of ethical principles, as specifically requested by the European Parliament[6].

(9) Harmonised rules applicable to the placing on the market, the putting into service and the use of high-risk AI systems should be laid down consistently with Regulation (EC) No 765/2008 of the European Parliament and of the Council[7], Decision No 768/2008/EC of the European Parliament and of the Council[8] and Regulation (EU) 2019/1020 of the European Parliament and of the Council[9] (New Legislative Framework). The harmonised rules laid down in this Regulation should apply across sectors and, in line with the New Legislative Framework, should be without prejudice to existing Union law, in particular on data protection, consumer protection, fundamental rights, employment, and protection of workers, and product safety, to which this Regulation is complementary. As a consequence, all rights and remedies provided for by such Union law to consumers, and other persons on whom AI systems may have a negative impact, including as regards the compensation of possible damages

---

[5] **Official note:** European Council, Special meeting of the European Council (1 and 2 October 2020) – Conclusions, EUCO 13/20, 2020, p. 6.

[6] **Official note:** European Parliament resolution of 20 October 2020 with recommendations to the Commission on a framework of ethical aspects of artificial intelligence, robotics and related technologies, 2020/2012(INL).

[7] **Official note:** Regulation (EC) No 765/2008 of the European Parliament and of the Council of 9 July 2008 setting out the requirements for accreditation and repealing Regulation (EEC) No 339/93 (OJ L 218, 13.8.2008, p. 30).

[8] **Official note:** Decision No 768/2008/EC of the European Parliament and of the Council of 9 July 2008 on a common framework for the marketing of products, and repealing Council Decision 93/465/EEC (OJ L 218, 13.8.2008, p. 82).

[9] **Official note:** Regulation (EU) 2019/1020 of the European Parliament and of the Council of 20 June 2019 on market surveillance and compliance of products and amending Directive 2004/42/EC and Regulations (EC) No 765/2008 and (EU) No 305/2011 (OJ L 169, 25.6.2019, p. 1).

pursuant to Council Directive 85/374/EEC[10] remain unaffected and fully applicable. Furthermore, in the context of employment and protection of workers, this Regulation should therefore not affect Union law on social policy and national labour law, in compliance with Union law, concerning employment and working conditions, including health and safety at work and the relationship between employers and workers. This Regulation should also not affect the exercise of fundamental rights as recognised in the Member States and at Union level, including the right or freedom to strike or to take other action covered by the specific industrial relations systems in Member States as well as the right to negotiate, to conclude and enforce collective agreements or to take collective action in accordance with national law. This Regulation should not affect the provisions aiming to improve working conditions in platform work laid down in a Directive of the European Parliament and of the Council on improving working conditions in platform work. Moreover, this Regulation aims to strengthen the effectiveness of such existing rights and remedies by establishing specific requirements and obligations, including in respect of the transparency, technical documentation and record-keeping of AI systems. Furthermore, the obligations placed on various operators involved in the AI value chain under this Regulation should apply without prejudice to national law, in compliance with Union law, having the effect of limiting the use of certain AI systems where such law falls outside the scope of this Regulation or pursues legitimate public interest objectives other than those pursued by this Regulation. For example, national labour law and law on the protection of minors, namely persons below the age of 18, taking into account the UNCRC General Comment No 25 (2021) on children's rights in relation to the digital environment, insofar as they are not specific to AI systems and pursue other legitimate public interest objectives, should not be affected by this Regulation.

(10) The fundamental right to the protection of personal data is safeguarded in particular by Regulations (EU) 2016/679[11] and (EU) 2018/1725[12] of the European Parliament and of the Council and Directive (EU) 2016/680 of the European Parliament and of the Council[13]. Directive 2002/58/EC of the European Parliament and of the Council[14] additionally protects private life and the confidentiality of communications, including by way of providing conditions for any storing of personal and non-personal data in, and access from, terminal

[10] **Official note:** Council Directive 85/374/EEC of 25 July 1985 on the approximation of the laws, regulations and administrative provisions of the Member States concerning liability for defective products (OJ L 210, 7.8.1985, p. 29).

[11] **Official note:** Regulation (EU) 2016/679 of the European Parliament and of the Council of 27 April 2016 on the protection of natural persons with regard to the processing of personal data and on the free movement of such data, and repealing Directive 95/46/EC (General Data Protection Regulation) (OJ L 119, 4.5.2016, p. 1).

[12] **Official note:** Regulation (EU) 2018/1725 of the European Parliament and of the Council of 23 October 2018 on the protection of natural persons with regard to the processing of personal data by the Union institutions, bodies, offices and agencies and on the free movement of such data, and repealing Regulation (EC) No 45/2001 and Decision No 1247/2002/EC (OJ L 295, 21.11.2018, p. 39).

[13] **Official note:** Directive (EU) 2016/680 of the European Parliament and of the Council of 27 April 2016 on the protection of natural persons with regard to the processing of personal data by competent authorities for the purposes of the prevention, investigation, detection or prosecution of criminal offences or the execution of criminal penalties, and on the free movement of such data, and repealing Council Framework Decision 2008/977/JHA (OJ L 119, 4.5.2016, p. 89).

[14] **Official note:** Directive 2002/58/EC of the European Parliament and of the Council of 12 July 2002 concerning the processing of personal data and the protection of privacy in the electronic communications sector (Directive on privacy and electronic communications) (OJ L 201, 31.7.2002, p. 37).

equipment. Those Union legal acts provide the basis for sustainable and responsible data processing, including where data sets include a mix of personal and non-personal data. This Regulation does not seek to affect the application of existing Union law governing the processing of personal data, including the tasks and powers of the independent supervisory authorities competent to monitor compliance with those instruments. It also does not affect the obligations of providers and deployers of AI systems in their role as data controllers or processors stemming from Union or national law on the protection of personal data in so far as the design, the development or the use of AI systems involves the processing of personal data. It is also appropriate to clarify that data subjects continue to enjoy all the rights and guarantees awarded to them by such Union law, including the rights related to solely automated individual decision-making, including profiling. Harmonised rules for the placing on the market, the putting into service and the use of AI systems established under this Regulation should facilitate the effective implementation and enable the exercise of the data subjects' rights and other remedies guaranteed under Union law on the protection of personal data and of other fundamental rights.

(11) This Regulation should be without prejudice to the provisions regarding the liability of providers of intermediary services as set out in Regulation (EU) 2022/2065 of the European Parliament and of the Council[15].

(12) The notion of „AI system" in this Regulation should be clearly defined and should be closely aligned with the work of international organisations working on AI to ensure legal certainty, facilitate international convergence and wide acceptance, while providing the flexibility to accommodate the rapid technological developments in this field. Moreover, the definition should be based on key characteristics of AI systems that distinguish it from simpler traditional software systems or programming approaches and should not cover systems that are based on the rules defined solely by natural persons to automatically execute operations. A key characteristic of AI systems is their capability to infer. This capability to infer refers to the process of obtaining the outputs, such as predictions, content, recommendations, or decisions, which can influence physical and virtual environments, and to a capability of AI systems to derive models or algorithms, or both, from inputs or data. The techniques that enable inference while building an AI system include machine learning approaches that learn from data how to achieve certain objectives, and logic- and knowledge-based approaches that infer from encoded knowledge or symbolic representation of the task to be solved. The capacity of an AI system to infer transcends basic data processing by enabling learning, reasoning or modelling. The term „machine-based" refers to the fact that AI systems run on machines. The reference to explicit or implicit objectives underscores that AI systems can operate according to explicit defined objectives or to implicit objectives. The objectives of the AI system may be different from the intended purpose of the AI system in a specific context. For the purposes of this Regulation, environments should be understood to be the contexts in which the AI systems operate, whereas outputs generated by the AI system reflect different functions performed by AI systems and include predictions, content, recommendations or decisions. AI systems are designed to operate with varying levels of auton-

[15] **Official note:** Regulation (EU) 2022/2065 of the European Parliament and of the Council of 19 October 2022 on a Single Market For Digital Services and amending Directive 2000/31/EC (Digital Services Act) (OJ L 277, 27.10.2022, p. 1).

omy, meaning that they have some degree of independence of actions from human involvement and of capabilities to operate without human intervention. The adaptiveness that an AI system could exhibit after deployment, refers to self-learning capabilities, allowing the system to change while in use. AI systems can be used on a stand-alone basis or as a component of a product, irrespective of whether the system is physically integrated into the product (embedded) or serves the functionality of the product without being integrated therein (non-embedded).

(13) The notion of „deployer“ referred to in this Regulation should be interpreted as any natural or legal person, including a public authority, agency or other body, using an AI system under its authority, except where the AI system is used in the course of a personal non-professional activity. Depending on the type of AI system, the use of the system may affect persons other than the deployer.

(14) The notion of „biometric data“ used in this Regulation should be interpreted in light of the notion of biometric data as defined in Article 4, point (14) of Regulation (EU) 2016/679, Article 3, point (18) of Regulation (EU) 2018/1725 and Article 3, point (13) of Directive (EU) 2016/680. Biometric data can allow for the authentication, identification or categorisation of natural persons and for the recognition of emotions of natural persons.

(15) The notion of „biometric identification“ referred to in this Regulation should be defined as the automated recognition of physical, physiological and behavioural human features such as the face, eye movement, body shape, voice, prosody, gait, posture, heart rate, blood pressure, odour, keystrokes characteristics, for the purpose of establishing an individual's identity by comparing biometric data of that individual to stored biometric data of individuals in a reference database, irrespective of whether the individual has given its consent or not. This excludes AI systems intended to be used for biometric verification, which includes authentication, whose sole purpose is to confirm that a specific natural person is the person he or she claims to be and to confirm the identity of a natural person for the sole purpose of having access to a service, unlocking a device or having security access to premises.

(16) The notion of „biometric categorisation“ referred to in this Regulation should be defined as assigning natural persons to specific categories on the basis of their biometric data. Such specific categories can relate to aspects such as sex, age, hair colour, eye colour, tattoos, behavioural or personality traits, language, religion, membership of a national minority, sexual or political orientation. This does not include biometric categorisation systems that are a purely ancillary feature intrinsically linked to another commercial service, meaning that the feature cannot, for objective technical reasons, be used without the principal service, and the integration of that feature or functionality is not a means to circumvent the applicability of the rules of this Regulation. For example, filters categorising facial or body features used on online marketplaces could constitute such an ancillary feature as they can be used only in relation to the principal service which consists in selling a product by allowing the consumer to preview the display of the product on him or herself and help the consumer to make a purchase decision. Filters used on online social network services which categorise facial or body features to allow users to add or modify pictures or videos could also be considered to be ancillary feature as such filter cannot be used without the principal service of the social network services consisting in the sharing of content online.

(17) The notion of „remote biometric identification system" referred to in this Regulation should be defined functionally, as an AI system intended for the identification of natural persons without their active involvement, typically at a distance, through the comparison of a person's biometric data with the biometric data contained in a reference database, irrespectively of the particular technology, processes or types of biometric data used. Such remote biometric identification systems are typically used to perceive multiple persons or their behaviour simultaneously in order to facilitate significantly the identification of natural persons without their active involvement. This excludes AI systems intended to be used for biometric verification, which includes authentication, the sole purpose of which is to confirm that a specific natural person is the person he or she claims to be and to confirm the identity of a natural person for the sole purpose of having access to a service, unlocking a device or having security access to premises. That exclusion is justified by the fact that such systems are likely to have a minor impact on fundamental rights of natural persons compared to the remote biometric identification systems which may be used for the processing of the biometric data of a large number of persons without their active involvement. In the case of „real-time" systems, the capturing of the biometric data, the comparison and the identification occur all instantaneously, near-instantaneously or in any event without a significant delay. In this regard, there should be no scope for circumventing the rules of this Regulation on the „real-time" use of the AI systems concerned by providing for minor delays. „Real-time" systems involve the use of „live" or „near-live" material, such as video footage, generated by a camera or other device with similar functionality. In the case of „post" systems, in contrast, the biometric data has already been captured and the comparison and identification occur only after a significant delay. This involves material, such as pictures or video footage generated by closed circuit television cameras or private devices, which has been generated before the use of the system in respect of the natural persons concerned.

(18) The notion of „emotion recognition system" referred to in this Regulation should be defined as an AI system for the purpose of identifying or inferring emotions or intentions of natural persons on the basis of their biometric data. The notion refers to emotions or intentions such as happiness, sadness, anger, surprise, disgust, embarrassment, excitement, shame, contempt, satisfaction and amusement. It does not include physical states, such as pain or fatigue, including, for example, systems used in detecting the state of fatigue of professional pilots or drivers for the purpose of preventing accidents. This does also not include the mere detection of readily apparent expressions, gestures or movements, unless they are used for identifying or inferring emotions. Those expressions can be basic facial expressions, such as a frown or a smile, or gestures such as the movement of hands, arms or head, or characteristics of a person's voice, such as a raised voice or whispering.

(19) For the purposes of this Regulation the notion of „publicly accessible space" should be understood as referring to any physical space that is accessible to an undetermined number of natural persons, and irrespective of whether the space in question is privately or publicly owned, irrespective of the activity for which the space may be used, such as for commerce, for example, shops, restaurants, cafés; for services, for example, banks, professional activities, hospitality; for sport, for example, swimming pools, gyms, stadiums; for transport, for example, bus, metro and railway stations, airports, means of transport; for

entertainment, for example, cinemas, theatres, museums, concert and conference halls; or for leisure or otherwise, for example, public roads and squares, parks, forests, playgrounds. A space should also be classified as being publicly accessible if, regardless of potential capacity or security restrictions, access is subject to certain predetermined conditions which can be fulfilled by an undetermined number of persons, such as the purchase of a ticket or title of transport, prior registration or having a certain age. In contrast, a space should not be considered to be publicly accessible if access is limited to specific and defined natural persons through either Union or national law directly related to public safety or security or through the clear manifestation of will by the person having the relevant authority over the space. The factual possibility of access alone, such as an unlocked door or an open gate in a fence, does not imply that the space is publicly accessible in the presence of indications or circumstances suggesting the contrary, such as. signs prohibiting or restricting access. Company and factory premises, as well as offices and workplaces that are intended to be accessed only by relevant employees and service providers, are spaces that are not publicly accessible. Publicly accessible spaces should not include prisons or border control. Some other spaces may comprise both publicly accessible and non-publicly accessible spaces, such as the hallway of a private residential building necessary to access a doctor's office or an airport. Online spaces are not covered, as they are not physical spaces. Whether a given space is accessible to the public should however be determined on a case-by-case basis, having regard to the specificities of the individual situation at hand.

(20) In order to obtain the greatest benefits from AI systems while protecting fundamental rights, health and safety and to enable democratic control, AI literacy should equip providers, deployers and affected persons with the necessary notions to make informed decisions regarding AI systems. Those notions may vary with regard to the relevant context and can include understanding the correct application of technical elements during the AI system's development phase, the measures to be applied during its use, the suitable ways in which to interpret the AI system's output, and, in the case of affected persons, the knowledge necessary to understand how decisions taken with the assistance of AI will have an impact on them. In the context of the application this Regulation, AI literacy should provide all relevant actors in the AI value chain with the insights required to ensure the appropriate compliance and its correct enforcement. Furthermore, the wide implementation of AI literacy measures and the introduction of appropriate follow-up actions could contribute to improving working conditions and ultimately sustain the consolidation, and innovation path of trustworthy AI in the Union. The European Artificial Intelligence Board (the „Board") should support the Commission, to promote AI literacy tools, public awareness and understanding of the benefits, risks, safeguards, rights and obligations in relation to the use of AI systems. In cooperation with the relevant stakeholders, the Commission and the Member States should facilitate the drawing up of voluntary codes of conduct to advance AI literacy among persons dealing with the development, operation and use of AI.

(21) In order to ensure a level playing field and an effective protection of rights and freedoms of individuals across the Union, the rules established by this Regulation should apply to providers of AI systems in a non-discriminatory manner, irrespective of whether they are established within the Union or in a third country, and to deployers of AI systems established within the Union.

(22) In light of their digital nature, certain AI systems should fall within the scope of this Regulation even when they are not placed on the market, put into service, or used in the Union. This is the case, for example, where an operator established in the Union contracts certain services to an operator established in a third country in relation to an activity to be performed by an AI system that would qualify as high-risk. In those circumstances, the AI system used in a third country by the operator could process data lawfully collected in and transferred from the Union, and provide to the contracting operator in the Union the output of that AI system resulting from that processing, without that AI system being placed on the market, put into service or used in the Union. To prevent the circumvention of this Regulation and to ensure an effective protection of natural persons located in the Union, this Regulation should also apply to providers and deployers of AI systems that are established in a third country, to the extent the output produced by those systems is intended to be used in the Union. Nonetheless, to take into account existing arrangements and special needs for future cooperation with foreign partners with whom information and evidence is exchanged, this Regulation should not apply to public authorities of a third country and international organisations when acting in the framework of cooperation or international agreements concluded at Union or national level for law enforcement and judicial cooperation with the Union or the Member States, provided that the relevant third country or international organisation provides adequate safeguards with respect to the protection of fundamental rights and freedoms of individuals. Where relevant, this may cover activities of entities entrusted by the third countries to carry out specific tasks in support of such law enforcement and judicial cooperation. Such framework for cooperation or agreements have been established bilaterally between Member States and third countries or between the European Union, Europol and other Union agencies and third countries and international organisations. The authorities competent for supervision of the law enforcement and judicial authorities under this Regulation should assess whether those frameworks for cooperation or international agreements include adequate safeguards with respect to the protection of fundamental rights and freedoms of individuals. Recipient national authorities and Union institutions, bodies, offices and agencies making use of such outputs in the Union remain accountable to ensure their use complies with Union law. When those international agreements are revised or new ones are concluded in the future, the contracting parties should make utmost efforts to align those agreements with the requirements of this Regulation.

(23) This Regulation should also apply to Union institutions, bodies, offices and agencies when acting as a provider or deployer of an AI system.

(24) If, and insofar as, AI systems are placed on the market, put into service, or used with or without modification of such systems for military, defence or national security purposes, those should be excluded from the scope of this Regulation regardless of which type of entity is carrying out those activities, such as whether it is a public or private entity. As regards military and defence purposes, such exclusion is justified both by Article 4(2) TEU and by the specificities of the Member States' and the common Union defence policy covered by Chapter 2 of Title V TEU that are subject to public international law, which is therefore the more appropriate legal framework for the regulation of AI systems in the context of the use of lethal force and other AI systems in the context of military and defence activities. As regards national security

purposes, the exclusion is justified both by the fact that national security remains the sole responsibility of Member States in accordance with Article 4(2) TEU and by the specific nature and operational needs of national security activities and specific national rules applicable to those activities. Nonetheless, if an AI system developed, placed on the market, put into service or used for military, defence or national security purposes is used outside those temporarily or permanently for other purposes, for example, civilian or humanitarian purposes, law enforcement or public security purposes, such a system would fall within the scope of this Regulation. In that case, the entity using the AI system for other than military, defence or national security purposes should ensure the compliance of the AI system with this Regulation, unless the system is already compliant with this Regulation. AI systems placed on the market or put into service for an excluded purpose, namely military, defence or national security, and one or more non-excluded purposes, such as civilian purposes or law enforcement, fall within the scope of this Regulation and providers of those systems should ensure compliance with this Regulation. In those cases, the fact that an AI system may fall within the scope of this Regulation should not affect the possibility of entities carrying out national security, defence and military activities, regardless of the type of entity carrying out those activities, to use AI systems for national security, military and defence purposes, the use of which is excluded from the scope of this Regulation. An AI system placed on the market for civilian or law enforcement purposes which is used with or without modification for military, defence or national security purposes should not fall within the scope of this Regulation, regardless of the type of entity carrying out those activities.

(25) This Regulation should support innovation, should respect freedom of science, and should not undermine research and development activity. It is therefore necessary to exclude from its scope AI systems and models specifically developed and put into service for the sole purpose of scientific research and development. Moreover, it is necessary to ensure that this Regulation does not otherwise affect scientific research and development activity on AI systems or models prior to being placed on the market or put into service. As regards product-oriented research, testing and development activity regarding AI systems or models, the provisions of this Regulation should also not apply prior to those systems and models being put into service or placed on the market. That exclusion is without prejudice to the obligation to comply with this Regulation where an AI system falling into the scope of this Regulation is placed on the market or put into service as a result of such research and development activity and to the application of provisions on AI regulatory sandboxes and testing in real world conditions. Furthermore, without prejudice to the exclusion of AI systems specifically developed and put into service for the sole purpose of scientific research and development, any other AI system that may be used for the conduct of any research and development activity should remain subject to the provisions of this Regulation. In any event, any research and development activity should be carried out in accordance with recognised ethical and professional standards for scientific research and should be conducted in accordance with applicable Union law.

(26) In order to introduce a proportionate and effective set of binding rules for AI systems, a clearly defined risk-based approach should be followed. That approach should tailor the type and content of such rules to the intensity

and scope of the risks that AI systems can generate. It is therefore necessary to prohibit certain unacceptable AI practices, to lay down requirements for high-risk AI systems and obligations for the relevant operators, and to lay down transparency obligations for certain AI systems.

(27) While the risk-based approach is the basis for a proportionate and effective set of binding rules, it is important to recall the 2019 Ethics guidelines for trustworthy AI developed by the independent AI HLEG appointed by the Commission. In those guidelines, the AI HLEG developed seven non-binding ethical principles for AI which are intended to help ensure that AI is trustworthy and ethically sound. The seven principles include human agency and oversight; technical robustness and safety; privacy and data governance; transparency; diversity, non-discrimination and fairness; societal and environmental well-being and accountability. Without prejudice to the legally binding requirements of this Regulation and any other applicable Union law, those guidelines contribute to the design of coherent, trustworthy and human-centric AI, in line with the Charter and with the values on which the Union is founded. According to the guidelines of the AI HLEG, human agency and oversight means that AI systems are developed and used as a tool that serves people, respects human dignity and personal autonomy, and that is functioning in a way that can be appropriately controlled and overseen by humans. Technical robustness and safety means that AI systems are developed and used in a way that allows robustness in the case of problems and resilience against attempts to alter the use or performance of the AI system so as to allow unlawful use by third parties, and minimise unintended harm. Privacy and data governance means that AI systems are developed and used in accordance with privacy and data protection rules, while processing data that meets high standards in terms of quality and integrity. Transparency means that AI systems are developed and used in a way that allows appropriate traceability and explainability, while making humans aware that they communicate or interact with an AI system, as well as duly informing deployers of the capabilities and limitations of that AI system and affected persons about their rights. Diversity, non-discrimination and fairness means that AI systems are developed and used in a way that includes diverse actors and promotes equal access, gender equality and cultural diversity, while avoiding discriminatory impacts and unfair biases that are prohibited by Union or national law. Social and environmental well-being means that AI systems are developed and used in a sustainable and environmentally friendly manner as well as in a way to benefit all human beings, while monitoring and assessing the long-term impacts on the individual, society and democracy. The application of those principles should be translated, when possible, in the design and use of AI models. They should in any case serve as a basis for the drafting of codes of conduct under this Regulation. All stakeholders, including industry, academia, civil society and standardisation organisations, are encouraged to take into account, as appropriate, the ethical principles for the development of voluntary best practices and standards.

(28) Aside from the many beneficial uses of AI, it can also be misused and provide novel and powerful tools for manipulative, exploitative and social control practices. Such practices are particularly harmful and abusive and should be prohibited because they contradict Union values of respect for human dignity, freedom, equality, democracy and the rule of law and fundamental rights

enshrined in the Charter, including the right to non-discrimination, to data protection and to privacy and the rights of the child.

(29) AI-enabled manipulative techniques can be used to persuade persons to engage in unwanted behaviours, or to deceive them by nudging them into decisions in a way that subverts and impairs their autonomy, decision-making and free choices. The placing on the market, the putting into service or the use of certain AI systems with the objective to or the effect of materially distorting human behaviour, whereby significant harms, in particular having sufficiently important adverse impacts on physical, psychological health or financial interests are likely to occur, are particularly dangerous and should therefore be prohibited. Such AI systems deploy subliminal components such as audio, image, video stimuli that persons cannot perceive, as those stimuli are beyond human perception, or other manipulative or deceptive techniques that subvert or impair person's autonomy, decision-making or free choice in ways that people are not consciously aware of those techniques or, where they are aware of them, can still be deceived or are not able to control or resist them. This could be facilitated, for example, by machine-brain interfaces or virtual reality as they allow for a higher degree of control of what stimuli are presented to persons, insofar as they may materially distort their behaviour in a significantly harmful manner. In addition, AI systems may also otherwise exploit the vulnerabilities of a person or a specific group of persons due to their age, disability within the meaning of Directive (EU) 2019/882 of the European Parliament and of the Council[16], or a specific social or economic situation that is likely to make those persons more vulnerable to exploitation such as persons living in extreme poverty, ethnic or religious minorities. Such AI systems can be placed on the market, put into service or used with the objective to or the effect of materially distorting the behaviour of a person and in a manner that causes or is reasonably likely to cause significant harm to that or another person or groups of persons, including harms that may be accumulated over time and should therefore be prohibited. It may not be possible to assume that there is an intention to distort behaviour where the distortion results from factors external to the AI system which are outside the control of the provider or the deployer, namely factors that may not be reasonably foreseeable and therefore not possible for the provider or the deployer of the AI system to mitigate. In any case, it is not necessary for the provider or the deployer to have the intention to cause significant harm, provided that such harm results from the manipulative or exploitative AI-enabled practices. The prohibitions for such AI practices are complementary to the provisions contained in Directive 2005/29/EC of the European Parliament and of the Council[17], in particular unfair commercial practices leading to economic or financial harms to consumers are prohibited under all circumstances, irrespective of whether they are put in place through AI systems or otherwise. The prohibitions of manipulative and exploitative practices in this Regulation should not affect lawful practices in the context

[16] **Official note:** Directive (EU) 2019/882 of the European Parliament and of the Council of 17 April 2019 on the accessibility requirements for products and services (OJ L 151, 7.6.2019, p. 70).

[17] **Official note:** Directive 2005/29/EC of the European Parliament and of the Council of 11 May 2005 concerning unfair business-to-consumer commercial practices in the internal market and amending Council Directive 84/450/EEC, Directives 97/7/EC, 98/27/EC and 2002/65/EC of the European Parliament and of the Council and Regulation (EC) No 2006/2004 of the European Parliament and of the Council („Unfair Commercial Practices Directive") (OJ L 149, 11.6.2005, p. 22).

of medical treatment such as psychological treatment of a mental disease or physical rehabilitation, when those practices are carried out in accordance with the applicable law and medical standards, for example explicit consent of the individuals or their legal representatives. In addition, common and legitimate commercial practices, for example in the field of advertising, that comply with the applicable law should not, in themselves, be regarded as constituting harmful manipulative AI-enabled practices.

(30) Biometric categorisation systems that are based on natural persons' biometric data, such as an individual person's face or fingerprint, to deduce or infer an individuals' political opinions, trade union membership, religious or philosophical beliefs, race, sex life or sexual orientation should be prohibited. That prohibition should not cover the lawful labelling, filtering or categorisation of biometric data sets acquired in line with Union or national law according to biometric data, such as the sorting of images according to hair colour or cye colour, which can for example be used in the area of law enforcement.

(31) AI systems providing social scoring of natural persons by public or private actors may lead to discriminatory outcomes and the exclusion of certain groups. They may violate the right to dignity and non-discrimination and the values of equality and justice. Such AI systems evaluate or classify natural persons or groups thereof on the basis of multiple data points related to their social behaviour in multiple contexts or known, inferred or predicted personal or personality characteristics over certain periods of time. The social score obtained from such AI systems may lead to the detrimental or unfavourable treatment of natural persons or whole groups thereof in social contexts, which are unrelated to the context in which the data was originally generated or collected or to a detrimental treatment that is disproportionate or unjustified to the gravity of their social behaviour. AI systems entailing such unacceptable scoring practices and leading to such detrimental or unfavourable outcomes should therefore be prohibited. That prohibition should not affect lawful evaluation practices of natural persons that are carried out for a specific purpose in accordance with Union and national law.

(32) The use of AI systems for „real-time" remote biometric identification of natural persons in publicly accessible spaces for the purpose of law enforcement is particularly intrusive to the rights and freedoms of the concerned persons, to the extent that it may affect the private life of a large part of the population, evoke a feeling of constant surveillance and indirectly dissuade the exercise of the freedom of assembly and other fundamental rights. Technical inaccuracies of AI systems intended for the remote biometric identification of natural persons can lead to biased results and entail discriminatory effects. Such possible biased results and discriminatory effects are particularly relevant with regard to age, ethnicity, race, sex or disabilities. In addition, the immediacy of the impact and the limited opportunities for further checks or corrections in relation to the use of such systems operating in real-time carry heightened risks for the rights and freedoms of the persons concerned in the context of, or impacted by, law enforcement activities.

(33) The use of those systems for the purpose of law enforcement should therefore be prohibited, except in exhaustively listed and narrowly defined situations, where the use is strictly necessary to achieve a substantial public interest, the importance of which outweighs the risks. Those situations involve the search for certain victims of crime including missing persons; certain threats to the

life or to the physical safety of natural persons or of a terrorist attack; and the localisation or identification of perpetrators or suspects of the criminal offences listed in an annex to this Regulation, where those criminal offences are punishable in the Member State concerned by a custodial sentence or a detention order for a maximum period of at least four years and as they are defined in the law of that Member State. Such a threshold for the custodial sentence or detention order in accordance with national law contributes to ensuring that the offence should be serious enough to potentially justify the use of „real-time" remote biometric identification systems. Moreover, the list of criminal offences provided in an annex to this Regulation is based on the 32 criminal offences listed in the Council Framework Decision 2002/584/JHA[18], taking into account that some of those offences are, in practice, likely to be more relevant than others, in that the recourse to „real-time" remote biometric identification could, foreseeably, be necessary and proportionate to highly varying degrees for the practical pursuit of the localisation or identification of a perpetrator or suspect of the different criminal offences listed and having regard to the likely differences in the seriousness, probability and scale of the harm or possible negative consequences. An imminent threat to life or the physical safety of natural persons could also result from a serious disruption of critical infrastructure, as defined in Article 2, point (4) of Directive (EU) 2022/2557 of the European Parliament and of the Council[19], where the disruption or destruction of such critical infrastructure would result in an imminent threat to life or the physical safety of a person, including through serious harm to the provision of basic supplies to the population or to the exercise of the core function of the State. In addition, this Regulation should preserve the ability for law enforcement, border control, immigration or asylum authorities to carry out identity checks in the presence of the person concerned in accordance with the conditions set out in Union and national law for such checks. In particular, law enforcement, border control, immigration or asylum authorities should be able to use information systems, in accordance with Union or national law, to identify persons who, during an identity check, either refuse to be identified or are unable to state or prove their identity, without being required by this Regulation to obtain prior authorisation. This could be, for example, a person involved in a crime, being unwilling, or unable due to an accident or a medical condition, to disclose their identity to law enforcement authorities.

(34) In order to ensure that those systems are used in a responsible and proportionate manner, it is also important to establish that, in each of those exhaustively listed and narrowly defined situations, certain elements should be taken into account, in particular as regards the nature of the situation giving rise to the request and the consequences of the use for the rights and freedoms of all persons concerned and the safeguards and conditions provided for with the use. In addition, the use of „real-time" remote biometric identification systems in publicly accessible spaces for the purpose of law enforcement should be deployed only to confirm the specifically targeted individual's identity and should be limited to what is strictly necessary concerning the period of time, as well as

[18] **Official note:** Council Framework Decision 2002/584/JHA of 13 June 2002 on the European arrest warrant and the surrender procedures between Member States (OJ L 190, 18.7.2002, p. 1).

[19] **Official note:** Directive (EU) 2022/2557 of the European Parliament and of the Council of 14 December 2022 on the resilience of critical entities and repealing Council Directive 2008/114/EC (OJ L 333, 27.12.2022, p. 164).

the geographic and personal scope, having regard in particular to the evidence or indications regarding the threats, the victims or perpetrator. The use of the real-time remote biometric identification system in publicly accessible spaces should be authorised only if the relevant law enforcement authority has completed a fundamental rights impact assessment and, unless provided otherwise in this Regulation, has registered the system in the database as set out in this Regulation. The reference database of persons should be appropriate for each use case in each of the situations mentioned above.

(35) Each use of a „real-time" remote biometric identification system in publicly accessible spaces for the purpose of law enforcement should be subject to an express and specific authorisation by a judicial authority or by an independent administrative authority of a Member State whose decision is binding. Such authorisation should, in principle, be obtained prior to the use of the AI system with a view to identifying a person or persons. Exceptions to that rule should be allowed in duly justified situations on grounds of urgency, namely in situations where the need to use the systems concerned is such as to make it effectively and objectively impossible to obtain an authorisation before commencing the use of the AI system. In such situations of urgency, the use of the AI system should be restricted to the absolute minimum necessary and should be subject to appropriate safeguards and conditions, as determined in national law and specified in the context of each individual urgent use case by the law enforcement authority itself. In addition, the law enforcement authority should in such situations request such authorisation while providing the reasons for not having been able to request it earlier, without undue delay and at the latest within 24 hours. If such an authorisation is rejected, the use of real-time biometric identification systems linked to that authorisation should cease with immediate effect and all the data related to such use should be discarded and deleted. Such data includes input data directly acquired by an AI system in the course of the use of such system as well as the results and outputs of the use linked to that authorisation. It should not include input that is legally acquired in accordance with another Union or national law. In any case, no decision producing an adverse legal effect on a person should be taken based solely on the output of the remote biometric identification system.

(36) In order to carry out their tasks in accordance with the requirements set out in this Regulation as well as in national rules, the relevant market surveillance authority and the national data protection authority should be notified of each use of the real-time biometric identification system. Market surveillance authorities and the national data protection authorities that have been notified should submit to the Commission an annual report on the use of real-time biometric identification systems.

(37) Furthermore, it is appropriate to provide, within the exhaustive framework set by this Regulation that such use in the territory of a Member State in accordance with this Regulation should only be possible where and in as far as the Member State concerned has decided to expressly provide for the possibility to authorise such use in its detailed rules of national law. Consequently, Member States remain free under this Regulation not to provide for such a possibility at all or to only provide for such a possibility in respect of some of the objectives capable of justifying authorised use identified in this Regulation. Such national rules should be notified to the Commission within 30 days of their adoption.

(38) The use of AI systems for real-time remote biometric identification of natural persons in publicly accessible spaces for the purpose of law enforcement necessarily involves the processing of biometric data. The rules of this Regulation that prohibit, subject to certain exceptions, such use, which are based on Article 16 TFEU, should apply as *lex specialis* in respect of the rules on the processing of biometric data contained in Article 10 of Directive (EU) 2016/680, thus regulating such use and the processing of biometric data involved in an exhaustive manner. Therefore, such use and processing should be possible only in as far as it is compatible with the framework set by this Regulation, without there being scope, outside that framework, for the competent authorities, where they act for purpose of law enforcement, to use such systems and process such data in connection thereto on the grounds listed in Article 10 of Directive (EU) 2016/680. In that context, this Regulation is not intended to provide the legal basis for the processing of personal data under Article 8 of Directive (EU) 2016/680. However, the use of real-time remote biometric identification systems in publicly accessible spaces for purposes other than law enforcement, including by competent authorities, should not be covered by the specific framework regarding such use for the purpose of law enforcement set by this Regulation. Such use for purposes other than law enforcement should therefore not be subject to the requirement of an authorisation under this Regulation and the applicable detailed rules of national law that may give effect to that authorisation.

(39) Any processing of biometric data and other personal data involved in the use of AI systems for biometric identification, other than in connection to the use of real-time remote biometric identification systems in publicly accessible spaces for the purpose of law enforcement as regulated by this Regulation, should continue to comply with all requirements resulting from Article 10 of Directive (EU) 2016/680. For purposes other than law enforcement, Article 9(1) of Regulation (EU) 2016/679 and Article 10(1) of Regulation (EU) 2018/1725 prohibit the processing of biometric data subject to limited exceptions as provided in those Articles. In the application of Article 9(1) of Regulation (EU) 2016/679, the use of remote biometric identification for purposes other than law enforcement has already been subject to prohibition decisions by national data protection authorities.

(40) In accordance with Article 6a of Protocol No 21 on the position of the United Kingdom and Ireland in respect of the area of freedom, security and justice, as annexed to the TEU and to the TFEU, Ireland is not bound by the rules laid down in Article 5(1), first subparagraph, point (g), to the extent it applies to the use of biometric categorisation systems for activities in the field of police cooperation and judicial cooperation in criminal matters, Article 5(1), first subparagraph, point (d), to the extent it applies to the use of AI systems covered by that provision, Article 5(1), first subparagraph, point (h), Article 5(2) to (6) and Article 26(10) of this Regulation adopted on the basis of Article 16 TFEU which relate to the processing of personal data by the Member States when carrying out activities falling within the scope of Chapter 4 or Chapter 5 of Title V of Part Three of the TFEU, where Ireland is not bound by the rules governing the forms of judicial cooperation in criminal matters or police cooperation which require compliance with the provisions laid down on the basis of Article 16 TFEU.

(41) In accordance with Articles 2 and 2a of Protocol No 22 on the position of Denmark, annexed to the TEU and to the TFEU, Denmark is not bound by rules laid down in Article 5(1), first subparagraph, point (g), to the extent it applies to the use of biometric categorisation systems for activities in the field of police cooperation and judicial cooperation in criminal matters, Article 5(1), first subparagraph, point (d), to the extent it applies to the use of AI systems covered by that provision, Article 5(1), first subparagraph, point (h), (2) to (6) and Article 26(10) of this Regulation adopted on the basis of Article 16 TFEU, or subject to their application, which relate to the processing of personal data by the Member States when carrying out activities falling within the scope of Chapter 4 or Chapter 5 of Title V of Part Three of the TFEU.

(42) In line with the presumption of innocence, natural persons in the Union should always be judged on their actual behaviour. Natural persons should never be judged on AI-predicted behaviour based solely on their profiling, personality traits or characteristics, such as nationality, place of birth, place of residence, number of children, level of debt or type of car, without a reasonable suspicion of that person being involved in a criminal activity based on objective verifiable facts and without human assessment thereof. Therefore, risk assessments carried out with regard to natural persons in order to assess the likelihood of their offending or to predict the occurrence of an actual or potential criminal offence based solely on profiling them or on assessing their personality traits and characteristics should be prohibited. In any case, that prohibition does not refer to or touch upon risk analytics that are not based on the profiling of individuals or on the personality traits and characteristics of individuals, such as AI systems using risk analytics to assess the likelihood of financial fraud by undertakings on the basis of suspicious transactions or risk analytic tools to predict the likelihood of the localisation of narcotics or illicit goods by customs authorities, for example on the basis of known trafficking routes.

(43) The placing on the market, the putting into service for that specific purpose, or the use of AI systems that create or expand facial recognition databases through the untargeted scraping of facial images from the internet or CCTV footage, should be prohibited because that practice adds to the feeling of mass surveillance and can lead to gross violations of fundamental rights, including the right to privacy.

(44) There are serious concerns about the scientific basis of AI systems aiming to identify or infer emotions, particularly as expression of emotions vary considerably across cultures and situations, and even within a single individual. Among the key shortcomings of such systems are the limited reliability, the lack of specificity and the limited generalisability. Therefore, AI systems identifying or inferring emotions or intentions of natural persons on the basis of their biometric data may lead to discriminatory outcomes and can be intrusive to the rights and freedoms of the concerned persons. Considering the imbalance of power in the context of work or education, combined with the intrusive nature of these systems, such systems could lead to detrimental or unfavourable treatment of certain natural persons or whole groups thereof. Therefore, the placing on the market, the putting into service, or the use of AI systems intended to be used to detect the emotional state of individuals in situations related to the workplace and education should be prohibited. That prohibition should not cover AI systems placed on the market strictly for medical or safety reasons, such as systems intended for therapeutical use.

(45) Practices that are prohibited by Union law, including data protection law, non-discrimination law, consumer protection law, and competition law, should not be affected by this Regulation.

(46) High-risk AI systems should only be placed on the Union market, put into service or used if they comply with certain mandatory requirements. Those requirements should ensure that high-risk AI systems available in the Union or whose output is otherwise used in the Union do not pose unacceptable risks to important Union public interests as recognised and protected by Union law. On the basis of the New Legislative Framework, as clarified in the Commission notice „The ‚Blue Guide' on the implementation of EU product rules 2022"[20], the general rule is that more than one legal act of Union harmonisation legislation, such as Regulations (EU) 2017/745[21] and (EU) 2017/746[22] of the European Parliament and of the Council or Directive 2006/42/EC of the European Parliament and of the Council[23], may be applicable to one product, since the making available or putting into service can take place only when the product complies with all applicable Union harmonisation legislation. To ensure consistency and avoid unnecessary administrative burdens or costs, providers of a product that contains one or more high-risk AI systems, to which the requirements of this Regulation and of the Union harmonisation legislation listed in an annex to this Regulation apply, should have flexibility with regard to operational decisions on how to ensure compliance of a product that contains one or more AI systems with all applicable requirements of the Union harmonisation legislation in an optimal manner. AI systems identified as high-risk should be limited to those that have a significant harmful impact on the health, safety and fundamental rights of persons in the Union and such limitation should minimise any potential restriction to international trade.

(47) AI systems could have an adverse impact on the health and safety of persons, in particular when such systems operate as safety components of products. Consistent with the objectives of Union harmonisation legislation to facilitate the free movement of products in the internal market and to ensure that only safe and otherwise compliant products find their way into the market, it is important that the safety risks that may be generated by a product as a whole due to its digital components, including AI systems, are duly prevented and mitigated. For instance, increasingly autonomous robots, whether in the context of manufacturing or personal assistance and care should be able to safely operate and performs their functions in complex environments. Similarly, in the health sector where the stakes for life and health are particularly high, increasingly sophisticated diagnostics systems and systems supporting human decisions should be reliable and accurate.

(48) The extent of the adverse impact caused by the AI system on the fundamental rights protected by the Charter is of particular relevance when classifying an

[20] **Official note:** OJ C 247, 29.6.2022, p. 1.

[21] **Official note:** Regulation (EU) 2017/745 of the European Parliament and of the Council of 5 April 2017 on medical devices, amending Directive 2001/83/EC, Regulation (EC) No 178/2002 and Regulation (EC) No 1223/2009 and repealing Council Directives 90/385/EEC and 93/42/EEC (OJ L 117, 5.5.2017, p. 1).

[22] **Official note:** Regulation (EU) 2017/746 of the European Parliament and of the Council of 5 April 2017 on *in vitro* diagnostic medical devices and repealing Directive 98/79/EC and Commission Decision 2010/227/EU (OJ L 117, 5.5.2017, p. 176).

[23] **Official note:** Directive 2006/42/EC of the European Parliament and of the Council of 17 May 2006 on machinery, and amending Directive 95/16/EC (OJ L 157, 9.6.2006, p. 24).

AI system as high risk. Those rights include the right to human dignity, respect for private and family life, protection of personal data, freedom of expression and information, freedom of assembly and of association, the right to non-discrimination, the right to education, consumer protection, workers' rights, the rights of persons with disabilities, gender equality, intellectual property rights, the right to an effective remedy and to a fair trial, the right of defence and the presumption of innocence, and the right to good administration. In addition to those rights, it is important to highlight the fact that children have specific rights as enshrined in Article 24 of the Charter and in the United Nations Convention on the Rights of the Child, further developed in the UNCRC General Comment No 25 as regards the digital environment, both of which require consideration of the children's vulnerabilities and provision of such protection and care as necessary for their well-being. The fundamental right to a high level of environmental protection enshrined in the Charter and implemented in Union policies should also be considered when assessing the severity of the harm that an AI system can cause, including in relation to the health and safety of persons.

(49) As regards high-risk AI systems that are safety components of products or systems, or which are themselves products or systems falling within the scope of Regulation (EC) No 300/2008 of the European Parliament and of the Council[24], Regulation (EU) No 167/2013 of the European Parliament and of the Council[25], Regulation (EU) No 168/2013 of the European Parliament and of the Council[26], Directive 2014/90/EU of the European Parliament and of the Council[27], Directive (EU) 2016/797 of the European Parliament and of the Council[28], Regulation (EU) 2018/858 of the European Parliament and of the Council[29], Regulation (EU) 2018/1139 of the European Parliament and of the Council[30], and Regulation (EU) 2019/2144 of the European Parliament and of the Coun-

[24] **Official note:** Regulation (EC) No 300/2008 of the European Parliament and of the Council of 11 March 2008 on common rules in the field of civil aviation security and repealing Regulation (EC) No 2320/2002 (OJ L 97, 9.4.2008, p. 72).

[25] **Official note:** Regulation (EU) No 167/2013 of the European Parliament and of the Council of 5 February 2013 on the approval and market surveillance of agricultural and forestry vehicles (OJ L 60, 2.3.2013, p. 1).

[26] **Official note:** Regulation (EU) No 168/2013 of the European Parliament and of the Council of 15 January 2013 on the approval and market surveillance of two- or three-wheel vehicles and quadricycles (OJ L 60, 2.3.2013, p. 52).

[27] **Official note:** Directive 2014/90/EU of the European Parliament and of the Council of 23 July 2014 on marine equipment and repealing Council Directive 96/98/EC (OJ L 257, 28.8.2014, p. 146).

[28] **Official note:** Directive (EU) 2016/797 of the European Parliament and of the Council of 11 May 2016 on the interoperability of the rail system within the European Union (OJ L 138, 26.5.2016, p. 44).

[29] **Official note:** Regulation (EU) 2018/858 of the European Parliament and of the Council of 30 May 2018 on the approval and market surveillance of motor vehicles and their trailers, and of systems, components and separate technical units intended for such vehicles, amending Regulations (EC) No 715/2007 and (EC) No 595/2009 and repealing Directive 2007/46/EC (OJ L 151, 14.6.2018, p. 1).

[30] **Official note:** Regulation (EU) 2018/1139 of the European Parliament and of the Council of 4 July 2018 on common rules in the field of civil aviation and establishing a European Union Aviation Safety Agency, and amending Regulations (EC) No 2111/2005, (EC) No 1008/2008, (EU) No 996/2010, (EU) No 376/2014 and Directives 2014/30/EU and 2014/53/EU of the European Parliament and of the Council, and repealing Regulations (EC) No 552/2004 and (EC) No 216/2008 of the European Parliament and of the Council and Council Regulation (EEC) No 3922/91 (OJ L 212, 22.8.2018, p. 1).

cil[31], it is appropriate to amend those acts to ensure that the Commission takes into account, on the basis of the technical and regulatory specificities of each sector, and without interfering with existing governance, conformity assessment and enforcement mechanisms and authorities established therein, the mandatory requirements for high-risk AI systems laid down in this Regulation when adopting any relevant delegated or implementing acts on the basis of those acts.

(50) As regards AI systems that are safety components of products, or which are themselves products, falling within the scope of certain Union harmonisation legislation listed in an annex to this Regulation, it is appropriate to classify them as high-risk under this Regulation if the product concerned undergoes the conformity assessment procedure with a third-party conformity assessment body pursuant to that relevant Union harmonisation legislation. In particular, such products are machinery, toys, lifts, equipment and protective systems intended for use in potentially explosive atmospheres, radio equipment, pressure equipment, recreational craft equipment, cableway installations, appliances burning gaseous fuels, medical devices, *in vitro* diagnostic medical devices, automotive and aviation.

(51) The classification of an AI system as high-risk pursuant to this Regulation should not necessarily mean that the product whose safety component is the AI system, or the AI system itself as a product, is considered to be high-risk under the criteria established in the relevant Union harmonisation legislation that applies to the product. This is, in particular, the case for Regulations (EU) 2017/745 and (EU) 2017/746, where a third-party conformity assessment is provided for medium-risk and high-risk products.

(52) As regards stand-alone AI systems, namely high-risk AI systems other than those that are safety components of products, or that are themselves products, it is appropriate to classify them as high-risk if, in light of their intended purpose, they pose a high risk of harm to the health and safety or the fundamental rights of persons, taking into account both the severity of the possible harm and its probability of occurrence and they are used in a number of specifically predefined areas specified in this Regulation. The identification of those systems is based on the same methodology and criteria envisaged also for any future amendments of the list of high-risk AI systems that the Commission should be empowered to adopt, via delegated acts, to take into account the rapid pace of technological development, as well as the potential changes in the use of AI systems.

(53) It is also important to clarify that there may be specific cases in which AI systems referred to in pre-defined areas specified in this Regulation do not lead to a significant risk of harm to the legal interests protected under those areas because they do not materially influence the decision-making or do not harm those interests substantially. For the purposes of this Regulation, an AI system

[31] **Official note:** Regulation (EU) 2019/2144 of the European Parliament and of the Council of 27 November 2019 on type-approval requirements for motor vehicles and their trailers, and systems, components and separate technical units intended for such vehicles, as regards their general safety and the protection of vehicle occupants and vulnerable road users, amending Regulation (EU) 2018/858 of the European Parliament and of the Council and repealing Regulations (EC) No 78/2009, (EC) No 79/2009 and (EC) No 661/2009 of the European Parliament and of the Council and Commission Regulations (EC) No 631/2009, (EU) No 406/2010, (EU) No 672/2010, (EU) No 1003/2010, (EU) No 1005/2010, (EU) No 1008/2010, (EU) No 1009/2010, (EU) No 19/2011, (EU) No 109/2011, (EU) No 458/2011, (EU) No 65/2012, (EU) No 130/2012, (EU) No 347/2012, (EU) No 351/2012, (EU) No 1230/2012 and (EU) 2015/166 (OJ L 325, 16.12.2019, p. 1).

that does not materially influence the outcome of decision-making should be understood to be an AI system that does not have an impact on the substance, and thereby the outcome, of decision-making, whether human or automated. An AI system that does not materially influence the outcome of decision-making could include situations in which one or more of the following conditions are fulfilled. The first such condition should be that the AI system is intended to perform a narrow procedural task, such as an AI system that transforms unstructured data into structured data, an AI system that classifies incoming documents into categories or an AI system that is used to detect duplicates among a large number of applications. Those tasks are of such narrow and limited nature that they pose only limited risks which are not increased through the use of an AI system in a context that is listed as a high-risk use in an annex to this Regulation. The second condition should be that the task performed by the AI system is intended to improve the result of a previously completed human activity that may be relevant for the purposes of the high-risk uses listed in an annex to this Regulation. Considering those characteristics, the AI system provides only an additional layer to a human activity with consequently lowered risk. That condition would, for example, apply to AI systems that are intended to improve the language used in previously drafted documents, for example in relation to professional tone, academic style of language or by aligning text to a certain brand messaging. The third condition should be that the AI system is intended to detect decision-making patterns or deviations from prior decision-making patterns. The risk would be lowered because the use of the AI system follows a previously completed human assessment which it is not meant to replace or influence, without proper human review. Such AI systems include for instance those that, given a certain grading pattern of a teacher, can be used to check *ex post* whether the teacher may have deviated from the grading pattern so as to flag potential inconsistencies or anomalies. The fourth condition should be that the AI system is intended to perform a task that is only preparatory to an assessment relevant for the purposes of the AI systems listed in an annex to this Regulation, thus making the possible impact of the output of the system very low in terms of representing a risk for the assessment to follow. That condition covers, inter alia, smart solutions for file handling, which include various functions from indexing, searching, text and speech processing or linking data to other data sources, or AI systems used for translation of initial documents. In any case, AI systems used in high-risk use-cases listed in an annex to this Regulation should be considered to pose significant risks of harm to the health, safety or fundamental rights if the AI system implies profiling within the meaning of Article 4, point (4) of Regulation (EU) 2016/679 or Article 3, point (4) of Directive (EU) 2016/680 or Article 3, point (5) of Regulation (EU) 2018/1725. To ensure traceability and transparency, a provider who considers that an AI system is not high-risk on the basis of the conditions referred to above should draw up documentation of the assessment before that system is placed on the market or put into service and should provide that documentation to national competent authorities upon request. Such a provider should be obliged to register the AI system in the EU database established under this Regulation. With a view to providing further guidance for the practical implementation of the conditions under which the AI systems listed in an annex to this Regulation are, on an exceptional basis, non-high-risk, the Commission should, after consulting the Board, provide guidelines specifying that practical implementation, completed by a comprehensive list of practical examples of use cases of AI systems that are high-risk and use cases that are not.

(54) As biometric data constitutes a special category of personal data, it is appropriate to classify as high-risk several critical-use cases of biometric systems, insofar as their use is permitted under relevant Union and national law. Technical inaccuracies of AI systems intended for the remote biometric identification of natural persons can lead to biased results and entail discriminatory effects. The risk of such biased results and discriminatory effects is particularly relevant with regard to age, ethnicity, race, sex or disabilities. Remote biometric identification systems should therefore be classified as high-risk in view of the risks that they pose. Such a classification excludes AI systems intended to be used for biometric verification, including authentication, the sole purpose of which is to confirm that a specific natural person is who that person claims to be and to confirm the identity of a natural person for the sole purpose of having access to a service, unlocking a device or having secure access to premises. In addition, AI systems intended to be used for biometric categorisation according to sensitive attributes or characteristics protected under Article 9(1) of Regulation (EU) 2016/679 on the basis of biometric data, in so far as these are not prohibited under this Regulation, and emotion recognition systems that are not prohibited under this Regulation, should be classified as high-risk. Biometric systems which are intended to be used solely for the purpose of enabling cybersecurity and personal data protection measures should not be considered to be high-risk AI systems.

(55) As regards the management and operation of critical infrastructure, it is appropriate to classify as high-risk the AI systems intended to be used as safety components in the management and operation of critical digital infrastructure as listed in point (8) of the Annex to Directive (EU) 2022/2557, road traffic and the supply of water, gas, heating and electricity, since their failure or malfunctioning may put at risk the life and health of persons at large scale and lead to appreciable disruptions in the ordinary conduct of social and economic activities. Safety components of critical infrastructure, including critical digital infrastructure, are systems used to directly protect the physical integrity of critical infrastructure or the health and safety of persons and property but which are not necessary in order for the system to function. The failure or malfunctioning of such components might directly lead to risks to the physical integrity of critical infrastructure and thus to risks to health and safety of persons and property. Components intended to be used solely for cybersecurity purposes should not qualify as safety components. Examples of safety components of such critical infrastructure may include systems for monitoring water pressure or fire alarm controlling systems in cloud computing centres.

(56) The deployment of AI systems in education is important to promote high-quality digital education and training and to allow all learners and teachers to acquire and share the necessary digital skills and competences, including media literacy, and critical thinking, to take an active part in the economy, society, and in democratic processes. However, AI systems used in education or vocational training, in particular for determining access or admission, for assigning persons to educational and vocational training institutions or programmes at all levels, for evaluating learning outcomes of persons, for assessing the appropriate level of education for an individual and materially influencing the level of education and training that individuals will receive or will be able to access

or for monitoring and detecting prohibited behaviour of students during tests should be classified as high-risk AI systems, since they may determine the educational and professional course of a person's life and therefore may affect that person's ability to secure a livelihood. When improperly designed and used, such systems may be particularly intrusive and may violate the right to education and training as well as the right not to be discriminated against and perpetuate historical patterns of discrimination, for example against women, certain age groups, persons with disabilities, or persons of certain racial or ethnic origins or sexual orientation.

(57) AI systems used in employment, workers management and access to self-employment, in particular for the recruitment and selection of persons, for making decisions affecting terms of the work-related relationship, promotion and termination of work-related contractual relationships, for allocating tasks on the basis of individual behaviour, personal traits or characteristics and for monitoring or evaluation of persons in work-related contractual relationships, should also be classified as high-risk, since those systems may have an appreciable impact on future career prospects, livelihoods of those persons and workers' rights. Relevant work-related contractual relationships should, in a meaningful manner, involve employees and persons providing services through platforms as referred to in the Commission Work Programme 2021. Throughout the recruitment process and in the evaluation, promotion, or retention of persons in work-related contractual relationships, such systems may perpetuate historical patterns of discrimination, for example against women, certain age groups, persons with disabilities, or persons of certain racial or ethnic origins or sexual orientation. AI systems used to monitor the performance and behaviour of such persons may also undermine their fundamental rights to data protection and privacy.

(58) Another area in which the use of AI systems deserves special consideration is the access to and enjoyment of certain essential private and public services and benefits necessary for people to fully participate in society or to improve one's standard of living. In particular, natural persons applying for or receiving essential public assistance benefits and services from public authorities namely healthcare services, social security benefits, social services providing protection in cases such as maternity, illness, industrial accidents, dependency or old age and loss of employment and social and housing assistance, are typically dependent on those benefits and services and in a vulnerable position in relation to the responsible authorities. If AI systems are used for determining whether such benefits and services should be granted, denied, reduced, revoked or reclaimed by authorities, including whether beneficiaries are legitimately entitled to such benefits or services, those systems may have a significant impact on persons' livelihood and may infringe their fundamental rights, such as the right to social protection, non-discrimination, human dignity or an effective remedy and should therefore be classified as high-risk. Nonetheless, this Regulation should not hamper the development and use of innovative approaches in the public administration, which would stand to benefit from a wider use of compliant and safe AI systems, provided that those systems do not entail a high risk to legal and natural persons. In addition, AI systems used to evaluate the credit score or creditworthiness of natural persons should be classified as high-risk AI systems, since they determine those persons' access to financial resources or essential services such as housing, electricity, and telecommunication services.

AI systems used for those purposes may lead to discrimination between persons or groups and may perpetuate historical patterns of discrimination, such as that based on racial or ethnic origins, gender, disabilities, age or sexual orientation, or may create new forms of discriminatory impacts. However, AI systems provided for by Union law for the purpose of detecting fraud in the offering of financial services and for prudential purposes to calculate credit institutions' and insurance undertakings' capital requirements should not be considered to be high-risk under this Regulation. Moreover, AI systems intended to be used for risk assessment and pricing in relation to natural persons for health and life insurance can also have a significant impact on persons' livelihood and if not duly designed, developed and used, can infringe their fundamental rights and can lead to serious consequences for people's life and health, including financial exclusion and discrimination. Finally, AI systems used to evaluate and classify emergency calls by natural persons or to dispatch or establish priority in the dispatching of emergency first response services, including by police, firefighters and medical aid, as well as of emergency healthcare patient triage systems, should also be classified as high-risk since they make decisions in very critical situations for the life and health of persons and their property.

(59) Given their role and responsibility, actions by law enforcement authorities involving certain uses of AI systems are characterised by a significant degree of power imbalance and may lead to surveillance, arrest or deprivation of a natural person's liberty as well as other adverse impacts on fundamental rights guaranteed in the Charter. In particular, if the AI system is not trained with high-quality data, does not meet adequate requirements in terms of its performance, its accuracy or robustness, or is not properly designed and tested before being put on the market or otherwise put into service, it may single out people in a discriminatory or otherwise incorrect or unjust manner. Furthermore, the exercise of important procedural fundamental rights, such as the right to an effective remedy and to a fair trial as well as the right of defence and the presumption of innocence, could be hampered, in particular, where such AI systems are not sufficiently transparent, explainable and documented. It is therefore appropriate to classify as high-risk, insofar as their use is permitted under relevant Union and national law, a number of AI systems intended to be used in the law enforcement context where accuracy, reliability and transparency is particularly important to avoid adverse impacts, retain public trust and ensure accountability and effective redress. In view of the nature of the activities and the risks relating thereto, those high-risk AI systems should include in particular AI systems intended to be used by or on behalf of law enforcement authorities or by Union institutions, bodies, offices, or agencies in support of law enforcement authorities for assessing the risk of a natural person to become a victim of criminal offences, as polygraphs and similar tools, for the evaluation of the reliability of evidence in in the course of investigation or prosecution of criminal offences, and, insofar as not prohibited under this Regulation, for assessing the risk of a natural person offending or reoffending not solely on the basis of the profiling of natural persons or the assessment of personality traits and characteristics or the past criminal behaviour of natural persons or groups, for profiling in the course of detection, investigation or prosecution of criminal offences. AI systems specifically intended to be used for administrative proceedings by tax and customs authorities as well as by financial intelligence units carrying out administrative tasks analysing informa-

tion pursuant to Union anti-money laundering law should not be classified as high-risk AI systems used by law enforcement authorities for the purpose of prevention, detection, investigation and prosecution of criminal offences. The use of AI tools by law enforcement and other relevant authorities should not become a factor of inequality, or exclusion. The impact of the use of AI tools on the defence rights of suspects should not be ignored, in particular the difficulty in obtaining meaningful information on the functioning of those systems and the resulting difficulty in challenging their results in court, in particular by natural persons under investigation.

(60) AI systems used in migration, asylum and border control management affect persons who are often in particularly vulnerable position and who are dependent on the outcome of the actions of the competent public authorities. The accuracy, non-discriminatory nature and transparency of the AI systems used in those contexts are therefore particularly important to guarantee respect for the fundamental rights of the affected persons, in particular their rights to free movement, non-discrimination, protection of private life and personal data, international protection and good administration. It is therefore appropriate to classify as high-risk, insofar as their use is permitted under relevant Union and national law, AI systems intended to be used by or on behalf of competent public authorities or by Union institutions, bodies, offices or agencies charged with tasks in the fields of migration, asylum and border control management as polygraphs and similar tools, for assessing certain risks posed by natural persons entering the territory of a Member State or applying for visa or asylum, for assisting competent public authorities for the examination, including related assessment of the reliability of evidence, of applications for asylum, visa and residence permits and associated complaints with regard to the objective to establish the eligibility of the natural persons applying for a status, for the purpose of detecting, recognising or identifying natural persons in the context of migration, asylum and border control management, with the exception of verification of travel documents. AI systems in the area of migration, asylum and border control management covered by this Regulation should comply with the relevant procedural requirements set by the Regulation (EC) No 810/2009 of the European Parliament and of the Council[32], the Directive 2013/32/EU of the European Parliament and of the Council[33], and other relevant Union law. The use of AI systems in migration, asylum and border control management should, in no circumstances, be used by Member States or Union institutions, bodies, offices or agencies as a means to circumvent their international obligations under the UN Convention relating to the Status of Refugees done at Geneva on 28 July 1951 as amended by the Protocol of 31 January 1967. Nor should they be used to in any way infringe on the principle of non-refoulement, or to deny safe and effective legal avenues into the territory of the Union, including the right to international protection.

(61) Certain AI systems intended for the administration of justice and democratic processes should be classified as high-risk, considering their potentially significant impact on democracy, the rule of law, individual freedoms as well as

---

[32] **Official note:** Regulation (EC) No 810/2009 of the European Parliament and of the Council of 13 July 2009 establishing a Community Code on Visas (Visa Code) (OJ L 243, 15.9.2009, p. 1).

[33] **Official note:** Directive 2013/32/EU of the European Parliament and of the Council of 26 June 2013 on common procedures for granting and withdrawing international protection (OJ L 180, 29.6.2013, p. 60).

the right to an effective remedy and to a fair trial. In particular, to address the risks of potential biases, errors and opacity, it is appropriate to qualify as high-risk AI systems intended to be used by a judicial authority or on its behalf to assist judicial authorities in researching and interpreting facts and the law and in applying the law to a concrete set of facts. AI systems intended to be used by alternative dispute resolution bodies for those purposes should also be considered to be high-risk when the outcomes of the alternative dispute resolution proceedings produce legal effects for the parties. The use of AI tools can support the decision-making power of judges or judicial independence, but should not replace it: the final decision-making must remain a human-driven activity. The classification of AI systems as high-risk should not, however, extend to AI systems intended for purely ancillary administrative activities that do not affect the actual administration of justice in individual cases, such as anonymisation or pseudonymisation of judicial decisions, documents or data, communication between personnel, administrative tasks.

(62) Without prejudice to the rules provided for in Regulation (EU) 2024/900 of the European Parliament and of the Council[34], and in order to address the risks of undue external interference with the right to vote enshrined in Article 39 of the Charter, and of adverse effects on democracy and the rule of law, AI systems intended to be used to influence the outcome of an election or referendum or the voting behaviour of natural persons in the exercise of their vote in elections or referenda should be classified as high-risk AI systems with the exception of AI systems whose output natural persons are not directly exposed to, such as tools used to organise, optimise and structure political campaigns from an administrative and logistical point of view.

(63) The fact that an AI system is classified as a high-risk AI system under this Regulation should not be interpreted as indicating that the use of the system is lawful under other acts of Union law or under national law compatible with Union law, such as on the protection of personal data, on the use of polygraphs and similar tools or other systems to detect the emotional state of natural persons. Any such use should continue to occur solely in accordance with the applicable requirements resulting from the Charter and from the applicable acts of secondary Union law and national law. This Regulation should not be understood as providing for the legal ground for processing of personal data, including special categories of personal data, where relevant, unless it is specifically otherwise provided for in this Regulation.

(64) To mitigate the risks from high-risk AI systems placed on the market or put into service and to ensure a high level of trustworthiness, certain mandatory requirements should apply to high-risk AI systems, taking into account the intended purpose and the context of use of the AI system and according to the risk-management system to be established by the provider. The measures adopted by the providers to comply with the mandatory requirements of this Regulation should take into account the generally acknowledged state of the art on AI, be proportionate and effective to meet the objectives of this Regulation. Based on the New Legislative Framework, as clarified in Commission notice „The ‚Blue Guide' on the implementation of EU product rules 2022", the general rule is that more than one legal act of Union harmonisation

[34] **Official note:** Regulation (EU) 2024/900 of the European parliament and of the Council of 13 March 2024 on the transparency and targeting of political advertising (OJ L, 2024/900, 20.3.2024, ELI: http://data.europa.eu/eli/reg/2024/900/oj).

legislation may be applicable to one product, since the making available or putting into service can take place only when the product complies with all applicable Union harmonisation legislation. The hazards of AI systems covered by the requirements of this Regulation concern different aspects than the existing Union harmonisation legislation and therefore the requirements of this Regulation would complement the existing body of the Union harmonisation legislation. For example, machinery or medical devices products incorporating an AI system might present risks not addressed by the essential health and safety requirements set out in the relevant Union harmonised legislation, as that sectoral law does not deal with risks specific to AI systems. This calls for a simultaneous and complementary application of the various legislative acts. To ensure consistency and to avoid an unnecessary administrative burden and unnecessary costs, providers of a product that contains one or more high-risk AI system, to which the requirements of this Regulation and of the Union harmonisation legislation based on the New Legislative Framework and listed in an annex to this Regulation apply, should have flexibility with regard to operational decisions on how to ensure compliance of a product that contains one or more AI systems with all the applicable requirements of that Union harmonised legislation in an optimal manner. That flexibility could mean, for example a decision by the provider to integrate a part of the necessary testing and reporting processes, information and documentation required under this Regulation into already existing documentation and procedures required under existing Union harmonisation legislation based on the New Legislative Framework and listed in an annex to this Regulation. This should not, in any way, undermine the obligation of the provider to comply with all the applicable requirements.

(65) The risk-management system should consist of a continuous, iterative process that is planned and run throughout the entire lifecycle of a high-risk AI system. That process should be aimed at identifying and mitigating the relevant risks of AI systems on health, safety and fundamental rights. The risk-management system should be regularly reviewed and updated to ensure its continuing effectiveness, as well as justification and documentation of any significant decisions and actions taken subject to this Regulation. This process should ensure that the provider identifies risks or adverse impacts and implements mitigation measures for the known and reasonably foreseeable risks of AI systems to the health, safety and fundamental rights in light of their intended purpose and reasonably foreseeable misuse, including the possible risks arising from the interaction between the AI system and the environment within which it operates. The risk-management system should adopt the most appropriate risk-management measures in light of the state of the art in AI. When identifying the most appropriate risk-management measures, the provider should document and explain the choices made and, when relevant, involve experts and external stakeholders. In identifying the reasonably foreseeable misuse of high-risk AI systems, the provider should cover uses of AI systems which, while not directly covered by the intended purpose and provided for in the instruction for use may nevertheless be reasonably expected to result from readily predictable human behaviour in the context of the specific characteristics and use of a particular AI system. Any known or foreseeable circumstances related to the use of the high-risk AI system in accordance with its intended purpose or under conditions of reasonably foreseeable misuse, which may lead to risks to the

health and safety or fundamental rights should be included in the instructions for use that are provided by the provider. This is to ensure that the deployer is aware and takes them into account when using the high-risk AI system. Identifying and implementing risk mitigation measures for foreseeable misuse under this Regulation should not require specific additional training for the high-risk AI system by the provider to address foreseeable misuse. The providers however are encouraged to consider such additional training measures to mitigate reasonable foreseeable misuses as necessary and appropriate.

(66) Requirements should apply to high-risk AI systems as regards risk management, the quality and relevance of data sets used, technical documentation and record-keeping, transparency and the provision of information to deployers, human oversight, and robustness, accuracy and cybersecurity. Those requirements are necessary to effectively mitigate the risks for health, safety and fundamental rights. As no other less trade restrictive measures are reasonably available those requirements are not unjustified restrictions to trade.

(67) High-quality data and access to high-quality data plays a vital role in providing structure and in ensuring the performance of many AI systems, especially when techniques involving the training of models are used, with a view to ensure that the high-risk AI system performs as intended and safely and it does not become a source of discrimination prohibited by Union law. High-quality data sets for training, validation and testing require the implementation of appropriate data governance and management practices. Data sets for training, validation and testing, including the labels, should be relevant, sufficiently representative, and to the best extent possible free of errors and complete in view of the intended purpose of the system. In order to facilitate compliance with Union data protection law, such as Regulation (EU) 2016/679, data governance and management practices should include, in the case of personal data, transparency about the original purpose of the data collection. The data sets should also have the appropriate statistical properties, including as regards the persons or groups of persons in relation to whom the high-risk AI system is intended to be used, with specific attention to the mitigation of possible biases in the data sets, that are likely to affect the health and safety of persons, have a negative impact on fundamental rights or lead to discrimination prohibited under Union law, especially where data outputs influence inputs for future operations (feedback loops). Biases can for example be inherent in underlying data sets, especially when historical data is being used, or generated when the systems are implemented in real world settings. Results provided by AI systems could be influenced by such inherent biases that are inclined to gradually increase and thereby perpetuate and amplify existing discrimination, in particular for persons belonging to certain vulnerable groups, including racial or ethnic groups. The requirement for the data sets to be to the best extent possible complete and free of errors should not affect the use of privacy-preserving techniques in the context of the development and testing of AI systems. In particular, data sets should take into account, to the extent required by their intended purpose, the features, characteristics or elements that are particular to the specific geographical, contextual, behavioural or functional setting which the AI system is intended to be used. The requirements related to data governance can be complied with by having recourse to third parties that offer certified compliance services including verification of data governance, data set integrity,

and data training, validation and testing practices, as far as compliance with the data requirements of this Regulation are ensured.

(68) For the development and assessment of high-risk AI systems, certain actors, such as providers, notified bodies and other relevant entities, such as European Digital Innovation Hubs, testing experimentation facilities and researchers, should be able to access and use high-quality data sets within the fields of activities of those actors which are related to this Regulation. European common data spaces established by the Commission and the facilitation of data sharing between businesses and with government in the public interest will be instrumental to provide trustful, accountable and non-discriminatory access to high-quality data for the training, validation and testing of AI systems. For example, in health, the European health data space will facilitate non-discriminatory access to health data and the training of AI algorithms on those data sets, in a privacy-preserving, secure, timely, transparent and trustworthy manner, and with an appropriate institutional governance. Relevant competent authorities, including sectoral ones, providing or supporting the access to data may also support the provision of high-quality data for the training, validation and testing of AI systems.

(69) The right to privacy and to protection of personal data must be guaranteed throughout the entire lifecycle of the AI system. In this regard, the principles of data minimisation and data protection by design and by default, as set out in Union data protection law, are applicable when personal data are processed. Measures taken by providers to ensure compliance with those principles may include not only anonymisation and encryption, but also the use of technology that permits algorithms to be brought to the data and allows training of AI systems without the transmission between parties or copying of the raw or structured data themselves, without prejudice to the requirements on data governance provided for in this Regulation.

(70) In order to protect the right of others from the discrimination that might result from the bias in AI systems, the providers should, exceptionally, to the extent that it is strictly necessary for the purpose of ensuring bias detection and correction in relation to the high-risk AI systems, subject to appropriate safeguards for the fundamental rights and freedoms of natural persons and following the application of all applicable conditions laid down under this Regulation in addition to the conditions laid down in Regulations (EU) 2016/679 and (EU) 2018/1725 and Directive (EU) 2016/680, be able to process also special categories of personal data, as a matter of substantial public interest within the meaning of Article 9(2), point (g) of Regulation (EU) 2016/679 and Article 10(2), point (g) of Regulation (EU) 2018/1725.

(71) Having comprehensible information on how high-risk AI systems have been developed and how they perform throughout their lifetime is essential to enable traceability of those systems, verify compliance with the requirements under this Regulation, as well as monitoring of their operations and post market monitoring. This requires keeping records and the availability of technical documentation, containing information which is necessary to assess the compliance of the AI system with the relevant requirements and facilitate post market monitoring. Such information should include the general characteristics, capabilities and limitations of the system, algorithms, data, training, testing and validation processes used as well as documentation on the relevant risk-management system and drawn in a clear and comprehensive form. The technical

documentation should be kept up to date, appropriately throughout the lifetime of the AI system. Furthermore, high-risk AI systems should technically allow for the automatic recording of events, by means of logs, over the duration of the lifetime of the system.

(72) To address concerns related to opacity and complexity of certain AI systems and help deployers to fulfil their obligations under this Regulation, transparency should be required for high-risk AI systems before they are placed on the market or put it into service. High-risk AI systems should be designed in a manner to enable deployers to understand how the AI system works, evaluate its functionality, and comprehend its strengths and limitations. High-risk AI systems should be accompanied by appropriate information in the form of instructions of use. Such information should include the characteristics, capabilities and limitations of performance of the AI system. Those would cover information on possible known and foreseeable circumstances related to the use of the high-risk AI system, including deployer action that may influence system behaviour and performance, under which the AI system can lead to risks to health, safety, and fundamental rights, on the changes that have been pre-determined and assessed for conformity by the provider and on the relevant human oversight measures, including the measures to facilitate the interpretation of the outputs of the AI system by the deployers. Transparency, including the accompanying instructions for use, should assist deployers in the use of the system and support informed decision making by them. Deployers should, inter alia, be in a better position to make the correct choice of the system that they intend to use in light of the obligations applicable to them, be educated about the intended and precluded uses, and use the AI system correctly and as appropriate. In order to enhance legibility and accessibility of the information included in the instructions of use, where appropriate, illustrative examples, for instance on the limitations and on the intended and precluded uses of the AI system, should be included. Providers should ensure that all documentation, including the instructions for use, contains meaningful, comprehensive, accessible and understandable information, taking into account the needs and foreseeable knowledge of the target deployers. Instructions for use should be made available in a language which can be easily understood by target deployers, as determined by the Member State concerned.

(73) High-risk AI systems should be designed and developed in such a way that natural persons can oversee their functioning, ensure that they are used as intended and that their impacts are addressed over the system's lifecycle. To that end, appropriate human oversight measures should be identified by the provider of the system before its placing on the market or putting into service. In particular, where appropriate, such measures should guarantee that the system is subject to in-built operational constraints that cannot be overridden by the system itself and is responsive to the human operator, and that the natural persons to whom human oversight has been assigned have the necessary competence, training and authority to carry out that role. It is also essential, as appropriate, to ensure that high-risk AI systems include mechanisms to guide and inform a natural person to whom human oversight has been assigned to make informed decisions if, when and how to intervene in order to avoid negative consequences or risks, or stop the system if it does not perform as intended. Considering the significant consequences for persons in the case of an incorrect match by certain biometric identification systems, it is appropriate

to provide for an enhanced human oversight requirement for those systems so that no action or decision may be taken by the deployer on the basis of the identification resulting from the system unless this has been separately verified and confirmed by at least two natural persons. Those persons could be from one or more entities and include the person operating or using the system. This requirement should not pose unnecessary burden or delays and it could be sufficient that the separate verifications by the different persons are automatically recorded in the logs generated by the system. Given the specificities of the areas of law enforcement, migration, border control and asylum, this requirement should not apply where Union or national law considers the application of that requirement to be disproportionate.

(74) High-risk AI systems should perform consistently throughout their lifecycle and meet an appropriate level of accuracy, robustness and cybersecurity, in light of their intended purpose and in accordance with the generally acknowledged state of the art. The Commission and relevant organisations and stakeholders are encouraged to take due consideration of the mitigation of risks and the negative impacts of the AI system. The expected level of performance metrics should be declared in the accompanying instructions of use. Providers are urged to communicate that information to deployers in a clear and easily understandable way, free of misunderstandings or misleading statements. Union law on legal metrology, including Directives 2014/31/EU[35] and 2014/32/EU[36] of the European Parliament and of the Council, aims to ensure the accuracy of measurements and to help the transparency and fairness of commercial transactions. In that context, in cooperation with relevant stakeholders and organisation, such as metrology and benchmarking authorities, the Commission should encourage, as appropriate, the development of benchmarks and measurement methodologies for AI systems. In doing so, the Commission should take note and collaborate with international partners working on metrology and relevant measurement indicators relating to AI.

(75) Technical robustness is a key requirement for high-risk AI systems. They should be resilient in relation to harmful or otherwise undesirable behaviour that may result from limitations within the systems or the environment in which the systems operate (e.g. errors, faults, inconsistencies, unexpected situations). Therefore, technical and organisational measures should be taken to ensure robustness of high-risk AI systems, for example by designing and developing appropriate technical solutions to prevent or minimise harmful or otherwise undesirable behaviour. Those technical solution may include for instance mechanisms enabling the system to safely interrupt its operation (fail-safe plans) in the presence of certain anomalies or when operation takes place outside certain predetermined boundaries. Failure to protect against these risks could lead to safety impacts or negatively affect the fundamental rights, for example due to erroneous decisions or wrong or biased outputs generated by the AI system.

(76) Cybersecurity plays a crucial role in ensuring that AI systems are resilient against attempts to alter their use, behaviour, performance or compromise their

---

[35] **Official note:** Directive 2014/31/EU of the European Parliament and of the Council of 26 February 2014 on the harmonisation of the laws of the Member States relating to the making available on the market of non-automatic weighing instruments (OJ L 96, 29.3.2014, p. 107).

[36] **Official note:** Directive 2014/32/EU of the European Parliament and of the Council of 26 February 2014 on the harmonisation of the laws of the Member States relating to the making available on the market of measuring instruments (OJ L 96, 29.3.2014, p. 149).

security properties by malicious third parties exploiting the system's vulnerabilities. Cyberattacks against AI systems can leverage AI specific assets, such as training data sets (e.g. data poisoning) or trained models (e.g. adversarial attacks or membership inference), or exploit vulnerabilities in the AI system's digital assets or the underlying ICT infrastructure. To ensure a level of cybersecurity appropriate to the risks, suitable measures, such as security controls, should therefore be taken by the providers of high-risk AI systems, also taking into account as appropriate the underlying ICT infrastructure.

(77) Without prejudice to the requirements related to robustness and accuracy set out in this Regulation, high-risk AI systems which fall within the scope of a regulation of the European Parliament and of the Council on horizontal cybersecurity requirements for products with digital elements, in accordance with that regulation may demonstrate compliance with the cybersecurity requirements of this Regulation by fulfilling the essential cybersecurity requirements set out in that regulation. When high-risk AI systems fulfil the essential requirements of a regulation of the European Parliament and of the Council on horizontal cybersecurity requirements for products with digital elements, they should be deemed compliant with the cybersecurity requirements set out in this Regulation in so far as the achievement of those requirements is demonstrated in the EU declaration of conformity or parts thereof issued under that regulation. To that end, the assessment of the cybersecurity risks, associated to a product with digital elements classified as high-risk AI system according to this Regulation, carried out under a regulation of the European Parliament and of the Council on horizontal cybersecurity requirements for products with digital elements, should consider risks to the cyber resilience of an AI system as regards attempts by unauthorised third parties to alter its use, behaviour or performance, including AI specific vulnerabilities such as data poisoning or adversarial attacks, as well as, as relevant, risks to fundamental rights as required by this Regulation.

(78) The conformity assessment procedure provided by this Regulation should apply in relation to the essential cybersecurity requirements of a product with digital elements covered by a regulation of the European Parliament and of the Council on horizontal cybersecurity requirements for products with digital elements and classified as a high-risk AI system under this Regulation. However, this rule should not result in reducing the necessary level of assurance for critical products with digital elements covered by a regulation of the European Parliament and of the Council on horizontal cybersecurity requirements for products with digital elements. Therefore, by way of derogation from this rule, high-risk AI systems that fall within the scope of this Regulation and are also qualified as important and critical products with digital elements pursuant to a regulation of the European Parliament and of the Council on horizontal cybersecurity requirements for products with digital elements and to which the conformity assessment procedure based on internal control set out in an annex to this Regulation applies, are subject to the conformity assessment provisions of a regulation of the European Parliament and of the Council on horizontal cybersecurity requirements for products with digital elements insofar as the essential cybersecurity requirements of that regulation are concerned. In this case, for all the other aspects covered by this Regulation the respective provisions on conformity assessment based on internal control set out in an annex to this Regulation should apply. Building on the knowledge and expertise of ENISA

on the cybersecurity policy and tasks assigned to ENISA under the Regulation (EU) 2019/881 of the European Parliament and of the Council[37], the Commission should cooperate with ENISA on issues related to cybersecurity of AI systems.

(79) It is appropriate that a specific natural or legal person, defined as the provider, takes responsibility for the placing on the market or the putting into service of a high-risk AI system, regardless of whether that natural or legal person is the person who designed or developed the system.

(80) As signatories to the United Nations Convention on the Rights of Persons with Disabilities, the Union and the Member States are legally obliged to protect persons with disabilities from discrimination and promote their equality, to ensure that persons with disabilities have access, on an equal basis with others, to information and communications technologies and systems, and to ensure respect for privacy for persons with disabilities. Given the growing importance and use of AI systems, the application of universal design principles to all new technologies and services should ensure full and equal access for everyone potentially affected by or using AI technologies, including persons with disabilities, in a way that takes full account of their inherent dignity and diversity. It is therefore essential that providers ensure full compliance with accessibility requirements, including Directive (EU) 2016/2102 of the European Parliament and of the Council[38] and Directive (EU) 2019/882. Providers should ensure compliance with these requirements by design. Therefore, the necessary measures should be integrated as much as possible into the design of the high-risk AI system.

(81) The provider should establish a sound quality management system, ensure the accomplishment of the required conformity assessment procedure, draw up the relevant documentation and establish a robust post-market monitoring system. Providers of high-risk AI systems that are subject to obligations regarding quality management systems under relevant sectoral Union law should have the possibility to include the elements of the quality management system provided for in this Regulation as part of the existing quality management system provided for in that other sectoral Union law. The complementarity between this Regulation and existing sectoral Union law should also be taken into account in future standardisation activities or guidance adopted by the Commission. Public authorities which put into service high-risk AI systems for their own use may adopt and implement the rules for the quality management system as part of the quality management system adopted at a national or regional level, as appropriate, taking into account the specificities of the sector and the competences and organisation of the public authority concerned.

(82) To enable enforcement of this Regulation and create a level playing field for operators, and, taking into account the different forms of making available of digital products, it is important to ensure that, under all circumstances, a person established in the Union can provide authorities with all the necessary

[37] **Official note:** Regulation (EU) 2019/881 of the European Parliament and of the Council of 17 April 2019 on ENISA (the European Union Agency for Cybersecurity) and on information and communications technology cybersecurity certification and repealing Regulation (EU) No 526/2013 (Cybersecurity Act) (OJ L 151, 7.6.2019, p. 15).

[38] **Official note:** Directive (EU) 2016/2102 of the European Parliament and of the Council of 26 October 2016 on the accessibility of the websites and mobile applications of public sector bodies (OJ L 327, 2.12.2016, p. 1).

information on the compliance of an AI system. Therefore, prior to making their AI systems available in the Union, providers established in third countries should, by written mandate, appoint an authorised representative established in the Union. This authorised representative plays a pivotal role in ensuring the compliance of the high-risk AI systems placed on the market or put into service in the Union by those providers who are not established in the Union and in serving as their contact person established in the Union.

(83) In light of the nature and complexity of the value chain for AI systems and in line with the New Legislative Framework, it is essential to ensure legal certainty and facilitate the compliance with this Regulation. Therefore, it is necessary to clarify the role and the specific obligations of relevant operators along that value chain, such as importers and distributors who may contribute to the development of AI systems. In certain situations those operators could act in more than one role at the same time and should therefore fulfil cumulatively all relevant obligations associated with those roles. For example, an operator could act as a distributor and an importer at the same time.

(84) To ensure legal certainty, it is necessary to clarify that, under certain specific conditions, any distributor, importer, deployer or other third-party should be considered to be a provider of a high-risk AI system and therefore assume all the relevant obligations. This would be the case if that party puts its name or trademark on a high-risk AI system already placed on the market or put into service, without prejudice to contractual arrangements stipulating that the obligations are allocated otherwise. This would also be the case if that party makes a substantial modification to a high-risk AI system that has already been placed on the market or has already been put into service in a way that it remains a high-risk AI system in accordance with this Regulation, or if it modifies the intended purpose of an AI system, including a general-purpose AI system, which has not been classified as high-risk and has already been placed on the market or put into service, in a way that the AI system becomes a high-risk AI system in accordance with this Regulation. Those provisions should apply without prejudice to more specific provisions established in certain Union harmonisation legislation based on the New Legislative Framework, together with which this Regulation should apply. For example, Article 16(2) of Regulation (EU) 2017/745, establishing that certain changes should not be considered to be modifications of a device that could affect its compliance with the applicable requirements, should continue to apply to high-risk AI systems that are medical devices within the meaning of that Regulation.

(85) General-purpose AI systems may be used as high-risk AI systems by themselves or be components of other high-risk AI systems. Therefore, due to their particular nature and in order to ensure a fair sharing of responsibilities along the AI value chain, the providers of such systems should, irrespective of whether they may be used as high-risk AI systems as such by other providers or as components of high-risk AI systems and unless provided otherwise under this Regulation, closely cooperate with the providers of the relevant high-risk AI systems to enable their compliance with the relevant obligations under this Regulation and with the competent authorities established under this Regulation.

(86) Where, under the conditions laid down in this Regulation, the provider that initially placed the AI system on the market or put it into service should no longer be considered to be the provider for the purposes of this Regulation, and when that provider has not expressly excluded the change of the AI system

into a high-risk AI system, the former provider should nonetheless closely cooperate and make available the necessary information and provide the reasonably expected technical access and other assistance that are required for the fulfilment of the obligations set out in this Regulation, in particular regarding the compliance with the conformity assessment of high-risk AI systems.

(87) In addition, where a high-risk AI system that is a safety component of a product which falls within the scope of Union harmonisation legislation based on the New Legislative Framework is not placed on the market or put into service independently from the product, the product manufacturer defined in that legislation should comply with the obligations of the provider established in this Regulation and should, in particular, ensure that the AI system embedded in the final product complies with the requirements of this Regulation.

(88) Along the AI value chain multiple parties often supply AI systems, tools and services but also components or processes that are incorporated by the provider into the AI system with various objectives, including the model training, model retraining, model testing and evaluation, integration into software, or other aspects of model development. Those parties have an important role to play in the value chain towards the provider of the high-risk AI system into which their AI systems, tools, services, components or processes are integrated, and should provide by written agreement this provider with the necessary information, capabilities, technical access and other assistance based on the generally acknowledged state of the art, in order to enable the provider to fully comply with the obligations set out in this Regulation, without compromising their own intellectual property rights or trade secrets.

(89) Third parties making accessible to the public tools, services, processes, or AI components other than general-purpose AI models, should not be mandated to comply with requirements targeting the responsibilities along the AI value chain, in particular towards the provider that has used or integrated them, when those tools, services, processes, or AI components are made accessible under a free and open-source licence. Developers of free and open-source tools, services, processes, or AI components other than general-purpose AI models should be encouraged to implement widely adopted documentation practices, such as model cards and data sheets, as a way to accelerate information sharing along the AI value chain, allowing the promotion of trustworthy AI systems in the Union.

(90) The Commission could develop and recommend voluntary model contractual terms between providers of high-risk AI systems and third parties that supply tools, services, components or processes that are used or integrated in high-risk AI systems, to facilitate the cooperation along the value chain. When developing voluntary model contractual terms, the Commission should also take into account possible contractual requirements applicable in specific sectors or business cases.

(91) Given the nature of AI systems and the risks to safety and fundamental rights possibly associated with their use, including as regards the need to ensure proper monitoring of the performance of an AI system in a real-life setting, it is appropriate to set specific responsibilities for deployers. Deployers should in particular take appropriate technical and organisational measures to ensure they use high-risk AI systems in accordance with the instructions of use and certain other obligations should be provided for with regard to monitoring of the functioning of the AI systems and with regard to record-keeping, as

appropriate. Furthermore, deployers should ensure that the persons assigned to implement the instructions for use and human oversight as set out in this Regulation have the necessary competence, in particular an adequate level of AI literacy, training and authority to properly fulfil those tasks. Those obligations should be without prejudice to other deployer obligations in relation to high-risk AI systems under Union or national law.

(92) This Regulation is without prejudice to obligations for employers to inform or to inform and consult workers or their representatives under Union or national law and practice, including Directive 2002/14/EC of the European Parliament and of the Council[39], on decisions to put into service or use AI systems. It remains necessary to ensure information of workers and their representatives on the planned deployment of high-risk AI systems at the workplace where the conditions for those information or information and consultation obligations in other legal instruments are not fulfilled. Moreover, such information right is ancillary and necessary to the objective of protecting fundamental rights that underlies this Regulation. Therefore, an information requirement to that effect should be laid down in this Regulation, without affecting any existing rights of workers.

(93) Whilst risks related to AI systems can result from the way such systems are designed, risks can as well stem from how such AI systems are used. Deployers of high-risk AI system therefore play a critical role in ensuring that fundamental rights are protected, complementing the obligations of the provider when developing the AI system. Deployers are best placed to understand how the high-risk AI system will be used concretely and can therefore identify potential significant risks that were not foreseen in the development phase, due to a more precise knowledge of the context of use, the persons or groups of persons likely to be affected, including vulnerable groups. Deployers of high-risk AI systems listed in an annex to this Regulation also play a critical role in informing natural persons and should, when they make decisions or assist in making decisions related to natural persons, where applicable, inform the natural persons that they are subject to the use of the high-risk AI system. This information should include the intended purpose and the type of decisions it makes. The deployer should also inform the natural persons about their right to an explanation provided under this Regulation. With regard to high-risk AI systems used for law enforcement purposes, that obligation should be implemented in accordance with Article 13 of Directive (EU) 2016/680.

(94) Any processing of biometric data involved in the use of AI systems for biometric identification for the purpose of law enforcement needs to comply with Article 10 of Directive (EU) 2016/680, that allows such processing only where strictly necessary, subject to appropriate safeguards for the rights and freedoms of the data subject, and where authorised by Union or Member State law. Such use, when authorised, also needs to respect the principles laid down in Article 4(1) of Directive (EU) 2016/680 including lawfulness, fairness and transparency, purpose limitation, accuracy and storage limitation.

(95) Without prejudice to applicable Union law, in particular Regulation (EU) 2016/679 and Directive (EU) 2016/680, considering the intrusive nature of post-remote biometric identification systems, the use of post-remote biometric

[39] **Official note:** Directive 2002/14/EC of the European Parliament and of the Council of 11 March 2002 establishing a general framework for informing and consulting employees in the European Community (OJ L 80, 23.3.2002, p. 29).

identification systems should be subject to safeguards. Post-remote biometric identification systems should always be used in a way that is proportionate, legitimate and strictly necessary, and thus targeted, in terms of the individuals to be identified, the location, temporal scope and based on a closed data set of legally acquired video footage. In any case, post-remote biometric identification systems should not be used in the framework of law enforcement to lead to indiscriminate surveillance. The conditions for post-remote biometric identification should in any case not provide a basis to circumvent the conditions of the prohibition and strict exceptions for real time remote biometric identification.

(96) In order to efficiently ensure that fundamental rights are protected, deployers of high-risk AI systems that are bodies governed by public law, or private entities providing public services and deployers of certain high-risk AI systems listed in an annex to this Regulation, such as banking or insurance entities, should carry out a fundamental rights impact assessment prior to putting it into use. Services important for individuals that are of public nature may also be provided by private entities. Private entities providing such public services are linked to tasks in the public interest such as in the areas of education, healthcare, social services, housing, administration of justice. The aim of the fundamental rights impact assessment is for the deployer to identify the specific risks to the rights of individuals or groups of individuals likely to be affected, identify measures to be taken in the case of a materialisation of those risks. The impact assessment should be performed prior to deploying the high-risk AI system, and should be updated when the deployer considers that any of the relevant factors have changed. The impact assessment should identify the deployer's relevant processes in which the high-risk AI system will be used in line with its intended purpose, and should include a description of the period of time and frequency in which the system is intended to be used as well as of specific categories of natural persons and groups who are likely to be affected in the specific context of use. The assessment should also include the identification of specific risks of harm likely to have an impact on the fundamental rights of those persons or groups. While performing this assessment, the deployer should take into account information relevant to a proper assessment of the impact, including but not limited to the information given by the provider of the high-risk AI system in the instructions for use. In light of the risks identified, deployers should determine measures to be taken in the case of a materialisation of those risks, including for example governance arrangements in that specific context of use, such as arrangements for human oversight according to the instructions of use or, complaint handling and redress procedures, as they could be instrumental in mitigating risks to fundamental rights in concrete use-cases. After performing that impact assessment, the deployer should notify the relevant market surveillance authority. Where appropriate, to collect relevant information necessary to perform the impact assessment, deployers of high-risk AI system, in particular when AI systems are used in the public sector, could involve relevant stakeholders, including the representatives of groups of persons likely to be affected by the AI system, independent experts, and civil society organisations in conducting such impact assessments and designing measures to be taken in the case of materialisation of the risks. The European Artificial Intelligence Office (AI Office) should develop a template for a questionnaire

in order to facilitate compliance and reduce the administrative burden for deployers.

(97) The notion of general-purpose AI models should be clearly defined and set apart from the notion of AI systems to enable legal certainty. The definition should be based on the key functional characteristics of a general-purpose AI model, in particular the generality and the capability to competently perform a wide range of distinct tasks. These models are typically trained on large amounts of data, through various methods, such as self-supervised, unsupervised or reinforcement learning. General-purpose AI models may be placed on the market in various ways, including through libraries, application programming interfaces (APIs), as direct download, or as physical copy. These models may be further modified or fine-tuned into new models. Although AI models are essential components of AI systems, they do not constitute AI systems on their own. AI models require the addition of further components, such as for example a user interface, to become AI systems. AI models are typically integrated into and form part of AI systems. This Regulation provides specific rules for general-purpose AI models and for general-purpose AI models that pose systemic risks, which should apply also when these models are integrated or form part of an AI system. It should be understood that the obligations for the providers of general-purpose AI models should apply once the general-purpose AI models are placed on the market. When the provider of a general-purpose AI model integrates an own model into its own AI system that is made available on the market or put into service, that model should be considered to be placed on the market and, therefore, the obligations in this Regulation for models should continue to apply in addition to those for AI systems. The obligations laid down for models should in any case not apply when an own model is used for purely internal processes that are not essential for providing a product or a service to third parties and the rights of natural persons are not affected. Considering their potential significantly negative effects, the general-purpose AI models with systemic risk should always be subject to the relevant obligations under this Regulation. The definition should not cover AI models used before their placing on the market for the sole purpose of research, development and prototyping activities. This is without prejudice to the obligation to comply with this Regulation when, following such activities, a model is placed on the market.

(98) Whereas the generality of a model could, inter alia, also be determined by a number of parameters, models with at least a billion of parameters and trained with a large amount of data using self-supervision at scale should be considered to display significant generality and to competently perform a wide range of distinctive tasks.

(99) Large generative AI models are a typical example for a general-purpose AI model, given that they allow for flexible generation of content, such as in the form of text, audio, images or video, that can readily accommodate a wide range of distinctive tasks.

(100) When a general-purpose AI model is integrated into or forms part of an AI system, this system should be considered to be general-purpose AI system when, due to this integration, this system has the capability to serve a variety of purposes. A general-purpose AI system can be used directly, or it may be integrated into other AI systems.

(101) Providers of general-purpose AI models have a particular role and responsibility along the AI value chain, as the models they provide may form the basis

for a range of downstream systems, often provided by downstream providers that necessitate a good understanding of the models and their capabilities, both to enable the integration of such models into their products, and to fulfil their obligations under this or other regulations. Therefore, proportionate transparency measures should be laid down, including the drawing up and keeping up to date of documentation, and the provision of information on the general-purpose AI model for its usage by the downstream providers. Technical documentation should be prepared and kept up to date by the general-purpose AI model provider for the purpose of making it available, upon request, to the AI Office and the national competent authorities. The minimal set of elements to be included in such documentation should be set out in specific annexes to this Regulation. The Commission should be empowered to amend those annexes by means of delegated acts in light of evolving technological developments.

(102) Software and data, including models, released under a free and open-source licence that allows them to be openly shared and where users can freely access, use, modify and redistribute them or modified versions thereof, can contribute to research and innovation in the market and can provide significant growth opportunities for the Union economy. General-purpose AI models released under free and open-source licences should be considered to ensure high levels of transparency and openness if their parameters, including the weights, the information on the model architecture, and the information on model usage are made publicly available. The licence should be considered to be free and open-source also when it allows users to run, copy, distribute, study, change and improve software and data, including models under the condition that the original provider of the model is credited, the identical or comparable terms of distribution are respected.

(103) Free and open-source AI components covers the software and data, including models and general-purpose AI models, tools, services or processes of an AI system. Free and open-source AI components can be provided through different channels, including their development on open repositories. For the purposes of this Regulation, AI components that are provided against a price or otherwise monetised, including through the provision of technical support or other services, including through a software platform, related to the AI component, or the use of personal data for reasons other than exclusively for improving the security, compatibility or interoperability of the software, with the exception of transactions between microenterprises, should not benefit from the exceptions provided to free and open-source AI components. The fact of making AI components available through open repositories should not, in itself, constitute a monetisation.

(104) The providers of general-purpose AI models that are released under a free and open-source licence, and whose parameters, including the weights, the information on the model architecture, and the information on model usage, are made publicly available should be subject to exceptions as regards the transparency-related requirements imposed on general-purpose AI models, unless they can be considered to present a systemic risk, in which case the circumstance that the model is transparent and accompanied by an open-source license should not be considered to be a sufficient reason to exclude compliance with the obligations under this Regulation. In any case, given that the release of general-purpose AI models under free and open-source licence does not necessarily reveal substantial information on the data set used for the training

or fine-tuning of the model and on how compliance of copyright law was thereby ensured, the exception provided for general-purpose AI models from compliance with the transparency-related requirements should not concern the obligation to produce a summary about the content used for model training and the obligation to put in place a policy to comply with Union copyright law, in particular to identify and comply with the reservation of rights pursuant to Article 4(3) of Directive (EU) 2019/790 of the European Parliament and of the Council[40].

(105) General-purpose AI models, in particular large generative AI models, capable of generating text, images, and other content, present unique innovation opportunities but also challenges to artists, authors, and other creators and the way their creative content is created, distributed, used and consumed. The development and training of such models require access to vast amounts of text, images, videos and other data. Text and data mining techniques may be used extensively in this context for the retrieval and analysis of such content, which may be protected by copyright and related rights. Any use of copyright protected content requires the authorisation of the rightsholder concerned unless relevant copyright exceptions and limitations apply. Directive (EU) 2019/790 introduced exceptions and limitations allowing reproductions and extractions of works or other subject matter, for the purpose of text and data mining, under certain conditions. Under these rules, rightsholders may choose to reserve their rights over their works or other subject matter to prevent text and data mining, unless this is done for the purposes of scientific research. Where the rights to opt out has been expressly reserved in an appropriate manner, providers of general-purpose AI models need to obtain an authorisation from rightsholders if they want to carry out text and data mining over such works.

(106) Providers that place general-purpose AI models on the Union market should ensure compliance with the relevant obligations in this Regulation. To that end, providers of general-purpose AI models should put in place a policy to comply with Union law on copyright and related rights, in particular to identify and comply with the reservation of rights expressed by rightsholders pursuant to Article 4(3) of Directive (EU) 2019/790. Any provider placing a general-purpose AI model on the Union market should comply with this obligation, regardless of the jurisdiction in which the copyright-relevant acts underpinning the training of those general-purpose AI models take place. This is necessary to ensure a level playing field among providers of general-purpose AI models where no provider should be able to gain a competitive advantage in the Union market by applying lower copyright standards than those provided in the Union.

(107) In order to increase transparency on the data that is used in the pre-training and training of general-purpose AI models, including text and data protected by copyright law, it is adequate that providers of such models draw up and make publicly available a sufficiently detailed summary of the content used for training the general-purpose AI model. While taking into due account the need to protect trade secrets and confidential business information, this summary should be generally comprehensive in its scope instead of technically detailed to facilitate parties with legitimate interests, including copyright holders, to ex-

[40] **Official note:** Directive (EU) 2019/790 of the European Parliament and of the Council of 17 April 2019 on copyright and related rights in the Digital Single Market and amending Directives 96/9/EC and 2001/29/EC (OJ L 130, 17.5.2019, p. 92).

ercise and enforce their rights under Union law, for example by listing the main data collections or sets that went into training the model, such as large private or public databases or data archives, and by providing a narrative explanation about other data sources used. It is appropriate for the AI Office to provide a template for the summary, which should be simple, effective, and allow the provider to provide the required summary in narrative form.

(108) With regard to the obligations imposed on providers of general-purpose AI models to put in place a policy to comply with Union copyright law and make publicly available a summary of the content used for the training, the AI Office should monitor whether the provider has fulfilled those obligations without verifying or proceeding to a work-by-work assessment of the training data in terms of copyright compliance. This Regulation does not affect the enforcement of copyright rules as provided for under Union law.

(109) Compliance with the obligations applicable to the providers of general-purpose AI models should be commensurate and proportionate to the type of model provider, excluding the need for compliance for persons who develop or use models for non-professional or scientific research purposes, who should nevertheless be encouraged to voluntarily comply with these requirements. Without prejudice to Union copyright law, compliance with those obligations should take due account of the size of the provider and allow simplified ways of compliance for SMEs, including start-ups, that should not represent an excessive cost and not discourage the use of such models. In the case of a modification or fine-tuning of a model, the obligations for providers of general-purpose AI models should be limited to that modification or fine-tuning, for example by complementing the already existing technical documentation with information on the modifications, including new training data sources, as a means to comply with the value chain obligations provided in this Regulation.

(110) General-purpose AI models could pose systemic risks which include, but are not limited to, any actual or reasonably foreseeable negative effects in relation to major accidents, disruptions of critical sectors and serious consequences to public health and safety; any actual or reasonably foreseeable negative effects on democratic processes, public and economic security; the dissemination of illegal, false, or discriminatory content. Systemic risks should be understood to increase with model capabilities and model reach, can arise along the entire lifecycle of the model, and are influenced by conditions of misuse, model reliability, model fairness and model security, the level of autonomy of the model, its access to tools, novel or combined modalities, release and distribution strategies, the potential to remove guardrails and other factors. In particular, international approaches have so far identified the need to pay attention to risks from potential intentional misuse or unintended issues of control relating to alignment with human intent; chemical, biological, radiological, and nuclear risks, such as the ways in which barriers to entry can be lowered, including for weapons development, design acquisition, or use; offensive cyber capabilities, such as the ways in vulnerability discovery, exploitation, or operational use can be enabled; the effects of interaction and tool use, including for example the capacity to control physical systems and interfere with critical infrastructure; risks from models of making copies of themselves or „self-replicating“ or training other models; the ways in which models can give rise to harmful bias and discrimination with risks to individuals, communities or societies; the facilitation of disinformation or harming privacy with threats to democratic values

and human rights; risk that a particular event could lead to a chain reaction with considerable negative effects that could affect up to an entire city, an entire domain activity or an entire community.

(111) It is appropriate to establish a methodology for the classification of general-purpose AI models as general-purpose AI model with systemic risks. Since systemic risks result from particularly high capabilities, a general-purpose AI model should be considered to present systemic risks if it has high-impact capabilities, evaluated on the basis of appropriate technical tools and methodologies, or significant impact on the internal market due to its reach. High-impact capabilities in general-purpose AI models means capabilities that match or exceed the capabilities recorded in the most advanced general-purpose AI models. The full range of capabilities in a model could be better understood after its placing on the market or when deployers interact with the model. According to the state of the art at the time of entry into force of this Regulation, the cumulative amount of computation used for the training of the general-purpose AI model measured in floating point operations is one of the relevant approximations for model capabilities. The cumulative amount of computation used for training includes the computation used across the activities and methods that are intended to enhance the capabilities of the model prior to deployment, such as pre-training, synthetic data generation and fine-tuning. Therefore, an initial threshold of floating point operations should be set, which, if met by a general-purpose AI model, leads to a presumption that the model is a general-purpose AI model with systemic risks. This threshold should be adjusted over time to reflect technological and industrial changes, such as algorithmic improvements or increased hardware efficiency, and should be supplemented with benchmarks and indicators for model capability. To inform this, the AI Office should engage with the scientific community, industry, civil society and other experts. Thresholds, as well as tools and benchmarks for the assessment of high-impact capabilities, should be strong predictors of generality, its capabilities and associated systemic risk of general-purpose AI models, and could take into account the way the model will be placed on the market or the number of users it may affect. To complement this system, there should be a possibility for the Commission to take individual decisions designating a general-purpose AI model as a general-purpose AI model with systemic risk if it is found that such model has capabilities or an impact equivalent to those captured by the set threshold. That decision should be taken on the basis of an overall assessment of the criteria for the designation of a general-purpose AI model with systemic risk set out in an annex to this Regulation, such as quality or size of the training data set, number of business and end users, its input and output modalities, its level of autonomy and scalability, or the tools it has access to. Upon a reasoned request of a provider whose model has been designated as a general-purpose AI model with systemic risk, the Commission should take the request into account and may decide to reassess whether the general-purpose AI model can still be considered to present systemic risks.

(112) It is also necessary to clarify a procedure for the classification of a general-purpose AI model with systemic risks. A general-purpose AI model that meets the applicable threshold for high-impact capabilities should be presumed to be a general-purpose AI models with systemic risk. The provider should notify the AI Office at the latest two weeks after the requirements are met or it becomes known that a general-purpose AI model will meet the requirements that lead

to the presumption. This is especially relevant in relation to the threshold of floating point operations because training of general-purpose AI models takes considerable planning which includes the upfront allocation of compute resources and, therefore, providers of general-purpose AI models are able to know if their model would meet the threshold before the training is completed. In the context of that notification, the provider should be able to demonstrate that, because of its specific characteristics, a general-purpose AI model exceptionally does not present systemic risks, and that it thus should not be classified as a general-purpose AI model with systemic risks. That information is valuable for the AI Office to anticipate the placing on the market of general-purpose AI models with systemic risks and the providers can start to engage with the AI Office early on. That information is especially important with regard to general-purpose AI models that are planned to be released as open-source, given that, after the open-source model release, necessary measures to ensure compliance with the obligations under this Regulation may be more difficult to implement.

(113) If the Commission becomes aware of the fact that a general-purpose AI model meets the requirements to classify as a general-purpose AI model with systemic risk, which previously had either not been known or of which the relevant provider has failed to notify the Commission, the Commission should be empowered to designate it so. A system of qualified alerts should ensure that the AI Office is made aware by the scientific panel of general-purpose AI models that should possibly be classified as general-purpose AI models with systemic risk, in addition to the monitoring activities of the AI Office.

(114) The providers of general-purpose AI models presenting systemic risks should be subject, in addition to the obligations provided for providers of general-purpose AI models, to obligations aimed at identifying and mitigating those risks and ensuring an adequate level of cybersecurity protection, regardless of whether it is provided as a standalone model or embedded in an AI system or a product. To achieve those objectives, this Regulation should require providers to perform the necessary model evaluations, in particular prior to its first placing on the market, including conducting and documenting adversarial testing of models, also, as appropriate, through internal or independent external testing. In addition, providers of general-purpose AI models with systemic risks should continuously assess and mitigate systemic risks, including for example by putting in place risk-management policies, such as accountability and governance processes, implementing post-market monitoring, taking appropriate measures along the entire model's lifecycle and cooperating with relevant actors along the AI value chain.

(115) Providers of general-purpose AI models with systemic risks should assess and mitigate possible systemic risks. If, despite efforts to identify and prevent risks related to a general-purpose AI model that may present systemic risks, the development or use of the model causes a serious incident, the general-purpose AI model provider should without undue delay keep track of the incident and report any relevant information and possible corrective measures to the Commission and national competent authorities. Furthermore, providers should ensure an adequate level of cybersecurity protection for the model and its physical infrastructure, if appropriate, along the entire model lifecycle. Cybersecurity protection related to systemic risks associated with malicious use or attacks should duly consider accidental model leakage, unauthorised releases, circum-

vention of safety measures, and defence against cyberattacks, unauthorised access or model theft. That protection could be facilitated by securing model weights, algorithms, servers, and data sets, such as through operational security measures for information security, specific cybersecurity policies, adequate technical and established solutions, and cyber and physical access controls, appropriate to the relevant circumstances and the risks involved.

(116) The AI Office should encourage and facilitate the drawing up, review and adaptation of codes of practice, taking into account international approaches. All providers of general-purpose AI models could be invited to participate. To ensure that the codes of practice reflect the state of the art and duly take into account a diverse set of perspectives, the AI Office should collaborate with relevant national competent authorities, and could, where appropriate, consult with civil society organisations and other relevant stakeholders and experts, including the Scientific Panel, for the drawing up of such codes. Codes of practice should cover obligations for providers of general-purpose AI models and of general-purpose AI models presenting systemic risks. In addition, as regards systemic risks, codes of practice should help to establish a risk taxonomy of the type and nature of the systemic risks at Union level, including their sources. Codes of practice should also be focused on specific risk assessment and mitigation measures.

(117) The codes of practice should represent a central tool for the proper compliance with the obligations provided for under this Regulation for providers of general-purpose AI models. Providers should be able to rely on codes of practice to demonstrate compliance with the obligations. By means of implementing acts, the Commission may decide to approve a code of practice and give it a general validity within the Union, or, alternatively, to provide common rules for the implementation of the relevant obligations, if, by the time this Regulation becomes applicable, a code of practice cannot be finalised or is not deemed adequate by the AI Office. Once a harmonised standard is published and assessed as suitable to cover the relevant obligations by the AI Office, compliance with a European harmonised standard should grant providers the presumption of conformity. Providers of general-purpose AI models should furthermore be able to demonstrate compliance using alternative adequate means, if codes of practice or harmonised standards are not available, or they choose not to rely on those.

(118) This Regulation regulates AI systems and AI models by imposing certain requirements and obligations for relevant market actors that are placing them on the market, putting into service or use in the Union, thereby complementing obligations for providers of intermediary services that embed such systems or models into their services regulated by Regulation (EU) 2022/2065. To the extent that such systems or models are embedded into designated very large online platforms or very large online search engines, they are subject to the risk-management framework provided for in Regulation (EU) 2022/2065. Consequently, the corresponding obligations of this Regulation should be presumed to be fulfilled, unless significant systemic risks not covered by Regulation (EU) 2022/2065 emerge and are identified in such models. Within this framework, providers of very large online platforms and very large online search engines are obliged to assess potential systemic risks stemming from the design, functioning and use of their services, including how the design of algorithmic systems used in the service may contribute to such risks, as well as systemic

risks stemming from potential misuses. Those providers are also obliged to take appropriate mitigating measures in observance of fundamental rights.

(119) Considering the quick pace of innovation and the technological evolution of digital services in scope of different instruments of Union law in particular having in mind the usage and the perception of their recipients, the AI systems subject to this Regulation may be provided as intermediary services or parts thereof within the meaning of Regulation (EU) 2022/2065, which should be interpreted in a technology-neutral manner. For example, AI systems may be used to provide online search engines, in particular, to the extent that an AI system such as an online chatbot performs searches of, in principle, all websites, then incorporates the results into its existing knowledge and uses the updated knowledge to generate a single output that combines different sources of information.

(120) Furthermore, obligations placed on providers and deployers of certain AI systems in this Regulation to enable the detection and disclosure that the outputs of those systems are artificially generated or manipulated are particularly relevant to facilitate the effective implementation of Regulation (EU) 2022/2065. This applies in particular as regards the obligations of providers of very large online platforms or very large online search engines to identify and mitigate systemic risks that may arise from the dissemination of content that has been artificially generated or manipulated, in particular risk of the actual or foreseeable negative effects on democratic processes, civic discourse and electoral processes, including through disinformation.

(121) Standardisation should play a key role to provide technical solutions to providers to ensure compliance with this Regulation, in line with the state of the art, to promote innovation as well as competitiveness and growth in the single market. Compliance with harmonised standards as defined in Article 2, point (1)(c), of Regulation (EU) No 1025/2012 of the European Parliament and of the Council[41], which are normally expected to reflect the state of the art, should be a means for providers to demonstrate conformity with the requirements of this Regulation. A balanced representation of interests involving all relevant stakeholders in the development of standards, in particular SMEs, consumer organisations and environmental and social stakeholders in accordance with Articles 5 and 6 of Regulation (EU) No 1025/2012 should therefore be encouraged. In order to facilitate compliance, the standardisation requests should be issued by the Commission without undue delay. When preparing the standardisation request, the Commission should consult the advisory forum and the Board in order to collect relevant expertise. However, in the absence of relevant references to harmonised standards, the Commission should be able to establish, via implementing acts, and after consultation of the advisory forum, common specifications for certain requirements under this Regulation. The common specification should be an exceptional fall back solution to facilitate the provider's obligation to comply with the requirements of this Regulation, when the standardisation request has not been accepted by any of the European

[41] **Official note:** Regulation (EU) No 1025/2012 of the European Parliament and of the Council of 25 October 2012 on European standardisation, amending Council Directives 89/686/EEC and 93/15/EEC and Directives 94/9/EC, 94/25/EC, 95/16/EC, 97/23/EC, 98/34/EC, 2004/22/EC, 2007/23/EC, 2009/23/EC and 2009/105/EC of the European Parliament and of the Council and repealing Council Decision 87/95/EEC and Decision No 1673/2006/EC of the European Parliament and of the Council (OJ L 316, 14.11.2012, p. 12).

standardisation organisations, or when the relevant harmonised standards insufficiently address fundamental rights concerns, or when the harmonised standards do not comply with the request, or when there are delays in the adoption of an appropriate harmonised standard. Where such a delay in the adoption of a harmonised standard is due to the technical complexity of that standard, this should be considered by the Commission before contemplating the establishment of common specifications. When developing common specifications, the Commission is encouraged to cooperate with international partners and international standardisation bodies.

(122) It is appropriate that, without prejudice to the use of harmonised standards and common specifications, providers of a high-risk AI system that has been trained and tested on data reflecting the specific geographical, behavioural, contextual or functional setting within which the AI system is intended to be used, should be presumed to comply with the relevant measure provided for under the requirement on data governance set out in this Regulation. Without prejudice to the requirements related to robustness and accuracy set out in this Regulation, in accordance with Article 54(3) of Regulation (EU) 2019/881, high-risk AI systems that have been certified or for which a statement of conformity has been issued under a cybersecurity scheme pursuant to that Regulation and the references of which have been published in the *Official Journal of the European Union* should be presumed to comply with the cybersecurity requirement of this Regulation in so far as the cybersecurity certificate or statement of conformity or parts thereof cover the cybersecurity requirement of this Regulation. This remains without prejudice to the voluntary nature of that cybersecurity scheme.

(123) In order to ensure a high level of trustworthiness of high-risk AI systems, those systems should be subject to a conformity assessment prior to their placing on the market or putting into service.

(124) It is appropriate that, in order to minimise the burden on operators and avoid any possible duplication, for high-risk AI systems related to products which are covered by existing Union harmonisation legislation based on the New Legislative Framework, the compliance of those AI systems with the requirements of this Regulation should be assessed as part of the conformity assessment already provided for in that law. The applicability of the requirements of this Regulation should thus not affect the specific logic, methodology or general structure of conformity assessment under the relevant Union harmonisation legislation.

(125) Given the complexity of high-risk AI systems and the risks that are associated with them, it is important to develop an adequate conformity assessment procedure for high-risk AI systems involving notified bodies, so-called third party conformity assessment. However, given the current experience of professional pre-market certifiers in the field of product safety and the different nature of risks involved, it is appropriate to limit, at least in an initial phase of application of this Regulation, the scope of application of third-party conformity assessment for high-risk AI systems other than those related to products. Therefore, the conformity assessment of such systems should be carried out as a general rule by the provider under its own responsibility, with the only exception of AI systems intended to be used for biometrics.

(126) In order to carry out third-party conformity assessments when so required, notified bodies should be notified under this Regulation by the national competent authorities, provided that they comply with a set of requirements, in particular on independence, competence, absence of conflicts of interests and suitable

cybersecurity requirements. Notification of those bodies should be sent by national competent authorities to the Commission and the other Member States by means of the electronic notification tool developed and managed by the Commission pursuant to Article R23 of Annex I to Decision No 768/2008/EC.

(127) In line with Union commitments under the World Trade Organization Agreement on Technical Barriers to Trade, it is adequate to facilitate the mutual recognition of conformity assessment results produced by competent conformity assessment bodies, independent of the territory in which they are established, provided that those conformity assessment bodies established under the law of a third country meet the applicable requirements of this Regulation and the Union has concluded an agreement to that extent. In this context, the Commission should actively explore possible international instruments for that purpose and in particular pursue the conclusion of mutual recognition agreements with third countries.

(128) In line with the commonly established notion of substantial modification for products regulated by Union harmonisation legislation, it is appropriate that whenever a change occurs which may affect the compliance of a high-risk AI system with this Regulation (e.g. change of operating system or software architecture), or when the intended purpose of the system changes, that AI system should be considered to be a new AI system which should undergo a new conformity assessment. However, changes occurring to the algorithm and the performance of AI systems which continue to „learn“ after being placed on the market or put into service, namely automatically adapting how functions are carried out, should not constitute a substantial modification, provided that those changes have been pre-determined by the provider and assessed at the moment of the conformity assessment.

(129) High-risk AI systems should bear the CE marking to indicate their conformity with this Regulation so that they can move freely within the internal market. For high-risk AI systems embedded in a product, a physical CE marking should be affixed, and may be complemented by a digital CE marking. For high-risk AI systems only provided digitally, a digital CE marking should be used. Member States should not create unjustified obstacles to the placing on the market or the putting into service of high-risk AI systems that comply with the requirements laid down in this Regulation and bear the CE marking.

(130) Under certain conditions, rapid availability of innovative technologies may be crucial for health and safety of persons, the protection of the environment and climate change and for society as a whole. It is thus appropriate that under exceptional reasons of public security or protection of life and health of natural persons, environmental protection and the protection of key industrial and infrastructural assets, market surveillance authorities could authorise the placing on the market or the putting into service of AI systems which have not undergone a conformity assessment. In duly justified situations, as provided for in this Regulation, law enforcement authorities or civil protection authorities may put a specific high-risk AI system into service without the authorisation of the market surveillance authority, provided that such authorisation is requested during or after the use without undue delay.

(131) In order to facilitate the work of the Commission and the Member States in the AI field as well as to increase the transparency towards the public, providers of high-risk AI systems other than those related to products falling within the scope of relevant existing Union harmonisation legislation, as well as providers

who consider that an AI system listed in the high-risk use cases in an annex to this Regulation is not high-risk on the basis of a derogation, should be required to register themselves and information about their AI system in an EU database, to be established and managed by the Commission. Before using an AI system listed in the high-risk use cases in an annex to this Regulation, deployers of high-risk AI systems that are public authorities, agencies or bodies, should register themselves in such database and select the system that they envisage to use. Other deployers should be entitled to do so voluntarily. This section of the EU database should be publicly accessible, free of charge, the information should be easily navigable, understandable and machine-readable. The EU database should also be user-friendly, for example by providing search functionalities, including through keywords, allowing the general public to find relevant information to be submitted upon the registration of high-risk AI systems and on the use case of high-risk AI systems, set out in an annex to this Regulation, to which the high-risk AI systems correspond. Any substantial modification of high-risk AI systems should also be registered in the EU database. For high-risk AI systems in the area of law enforcement, migration, asylum and border control management, the registration obligations should be fulfilled in a secure non-public section of the EU database. Access to the secure non-public section should be strictly limited to the Commission as well as to market surveillance authorities with regard to their national section of that database. High-risk AI systems in the area of critical infrastructure should only be registered at national level. The Commission should be the controller of the EU database, in accordance with Regulation (EU) 2018/1725. In order to ensure the full functionality of the EU database, when deployed, the procedure for setting the database should include the development of functional specifications by the Commission and an independent audit report. The Commission should take into account cybersecurity risks when carrying out its tasks as data controller on the EU database. In order to maximise the availability and use of the EU database by the public, the EU database, including the information made available through it, should comply with requirements under the Directive (EU) 2019/882.

(132) Certain AI systems intended to interact with natural persons or to generate content may pose specific risks of impersonation or deception irrespective of whether they qualify as high-risk or not. In certain circumstances, the use of these systems should therefore be subject to specific transparency obligations without prejudice to the requirements and obligations for high-risk AI systems and subject to targeted exceptions to take into account the special need of law enforcement. In particular, natural persons should be notified that they are interacting with an AI system, unless this is obvious from the point of view of a natural person who is reasonably well-informed, observant and circumspect taking into account the circumstances and the context of use. When implementing that obligation, the characteristics of natural persons belonging to vulnerable groups due to their age or disability should be taken into account to the extent the AI system is intended to interact with those groups as well. Moreover, natural persons should be notified when they are exposed to AI systems that, by processing their biometric data, can identify or infer the emotions or intentions of those persons or assign them to specific categories. Such specific categories can relate to aspects such as sex, age, hair colour, eye colour, tattoos, personal traits, ethnic origin, personal preferences and interests. Such information and

notifications should be provided in accessible formats for persons with disabilities.

(133) A variety of AI systems can generate large quantities of synthetic content that becomes increasingly hard for humans to distinguish from human-generated and authentic content. The wide availability and increasing capabilities of those systems have a significant impact on the integrity and trust in the information ecosystem, raising new risks of misinformation and manipulation at scale, fraud, impersonation and consumer deception. In light of those impacts, the fast technological pace and the need for new methods and techniques to trace origin of information, it is appropriate to require providers of those systems to embed technical solutions that enable marking in a machine readable format and detection that the output has been generated or manipulated by an AI system and not a human. Such techniques and methods should be sufficiently reliable, interoperable, effective and robust as far as this is technically feasible, taking into account available techniques or a combination of such techniques, such as watermarks, metadata identifications, cryptographic methods for proving provenance and authenticity of content, logging methods, fingerprints or other techniques, as may be appropriate. When implementing this obligation, providers should also take into account the specificities and the limitations of the different types of content and the relevant technological and market developments in the field, as reflected in the generally acknowledged state of the art. Such techniques and methods can be implemented at the level of the AI system or at the level of the AI model, including general-purpose AI models generating content, thereby facilitating fulfilment of this obligation by the downstream provider of the AI system. To remain proportionate, it is appropriate to envisage that this marking obligation should not cover AI systems performing primarily an assistive function for standard editing or AI systems not substantially altering the input data provided by the deployer or the semantics thereof.

(134) Further to the technical solutions employed by the providers of the AI system, deployers who use an AI system to generate or manipulate image, audio or video content that appreciably resembles existing persons, objects, places, entities or events and would falsely appear to a person to be authentic or truthful (deep fakes), should also clearly and distinguishably disclose that the content has been artificially created or manipulated by labelling the AI output accordingly and disclosing its artificial origin. Compliance with this transparency obligation should not be interpreted as indicating that the use of the AI system or its output impedes the right to freedom of expression and the right to freedom of the arts and sciences guaranteed in the Charter, in particular where the content is part of an evidently creative, satirical, artistic, fictional or analogous work or programme, subject to appropriate safeguards for the rights and freedoms of third parties. In those cases, the transparency obligation for deep fakes set out in this Regulation is limited to disclosure of the existence of such generated or manipulated content in an appropriate manner that does not hamper the display or enjoyment of the work, including its normal exploitation and use, while maintaining the utility and quality of the work. In addition, it is also appropriate to envisage a similar disclosure obligation in relation to AI-generated or manipulated text to the extent it is published with the purpose of informing the public on matters of public interest unless the AI-generated content has undergone a process of human review or editorial control and a

natural or legal person holds editorial responsibility for the publication of the content.

(135) Without prejudice to the mandatory nature and full applicability of the transparency obligations, the Commission may also encourage and facilitate the drawing up of codes of practice at Union level to facilitate the effective implementation of the obligations regarding the detection and labelling of artificially generated or manipulated content, including to support practical arrangements for making, as appropriate, the detection mechanisms accessible and facilitating cooperation with other actors along the value chain, disseminating content or checking its authenticity and provenance to enable the public to effectively distinguish AI-generated content.

(136) The obligations placed on providers and deployers of certain AI systems in this Regulation to enable the detection and disclosure that the outputs of those systems are artificially generated or manipulated are particularly relevant to facilitate the effective implementation of Regulation (EU) 2022/2065. This applies in particular as regards the obligations of providers of very large online platforms or very large online search engines to identify and mitigate systemic risks that may arise from the dissemination of content that has been artificially generated or manipulated, in particular the risk of the actual or foreseeable negative effects on democratic processes, civic discourse and electoral processes, including through disinformation. The requirement to label content generated by AI systems under this Regulation is without prejudice to the obligation in Article 16(6) of Regulation (EU) 2022/2065 for providers of hosting services to process notices on illegal content received pursuant to Article 16(1) of that Regulation and should not influence the assessment and the decision on the illegality of the specific content. That assessment should be performed solely with reference to the rules governing the legality of the content.

(137) Compliance with the transparency obligations for the AI systems covered by this Regulation should not be interpreted as indicating that the use of the AI system or its output is lawful under this Regulation or other Union and Member State law and should be without prejudice to other transparency obligations for deployers of AI systems laid down in Union or national law.

(138) AI is a rapidly developing family of technologies that requires regulatory oversight and a safe and controlled space for experimentation, while ensuring responsible innovation and integration of appropriate safeguards and risk mitigation measures. To ensure a legal framework that promotes innovation, is future-proof and resilient to disruption, Member States should ensure that their national competent authorities establish at least one AI regulatory sandbox at national level to facilitate the development and testing of innovative AI systems under strict regulatory oversight before these systems are placed on the market or otherwise put into service. Member States could also fulfil this obligation through participating in already existing regulatory sandboxes or establishing jointly a sandbox with one or more Member States' competent authorities, insofar as this participation provides equivalent level of national coverage for the participating Member States. AI regulatory sandboxes could be established in physical, digital or hybrid form and may accommodate physical as well as digital products. Establishing authorities should also ensure that the AI regulatory sandboxes have the adequate resources for their functioning, including financial and human resources.

(139) The objectives of the AI regulatory sandboxes should be to foster AI innovation by establishing a controlled experimentation and testing environment in the development and pre-marketing phase with a view to ensuring compliance of the innovative AI systems with this Regulation and other relevant Union and national law. Moreover, the AI regulatory sandboxes should aim to enhance legal certainty for innovators and the competent authorities' oversight and understanding of the opportunities, emerging risks and the impacts of AI use, to facilitate regulatory learning for authorities and undertakings, including with a view to future adaptions of the legal framework, to support cooperation and the sharing of best practices with the authorities involved in the AI regulatory sandbox, and to accelerate access to markets, including by removing barriers for SMEs, including start-ups. AI regulatory sandboxes should be widely available throughout the Union, and particular attention should be given to their accessibility for SMEs, including start-ups. The participation in the AI regulatory sandbox should focus on issues that raise legal uncertainty for providers and prospective providers to innovate, experiment with AI in the Union and contribute to evidence-based regulatory learning. The supervision of the AI systems in the AI regulatory sandbox should therefore cover their development, training, testing and validation before the systems are placed on the market or put into service, as well as the notion and occurrence of substantial modification that may require a new conformity assessment procedure. Any significant risks identified during the development and testing of such AI systems should result in adequate mitigation and, failing that, in the suspension of the development and testing process. Where appropriate, national competent authorities establishing AI regulatory sandboxes should cooperate with other relevant authorities, including those supervising the protection of fundamental rights, and could allow for the involvement of other actors within the AI ecosystem such as national or European standardisation organisations, notified bodies, testing and experimentation facilities, research and experimentation labs, European Digital Innovation Hubs and relevant stakeholder and civil society organisations. To ensure uniform implementation across the Union and economies of scale, it is appropriate to establish common rules for the AI regulatory sandboxes' implementation and a framework for cooperation between the relevant authorities involved in the supervision of the sandboxes. AI regulatory sandboxes established under this Regulation should be without prejudice to other law allowing for the establishment of other sandboxes aiming to ensure compliance with law other than this Regulation. Where appropriate, relevant competent authorities in charge of those other regulatory sandboxes should consider the benefits of using those sandboxes also for the purpose of ensuring compliance of AI systems with this Regulation. Upon agreement between the national competent authorities and the participants in the AI regulatory sandbox, testing in real world conditions may also be operated and supervised in the framework of the AI regulatory sandbox.

(140) This Regulation should provide the legal basis for the providers and prospective providers in the AI regulatory sandbox to use personal data collected for other purposes for developing certain AI systems in the public interest within the AI regulatory sandbox, only under specified conditions, in accordance with Article 6(4) and Article 9(2), point (g), of Regulation (EU) 2016/679, and Articles 5, 6 and 10 of Regulation (EU) 2018/1725, and without prejudice to Article 4(2) and Article 10 of Directive (EU) 2016/680. All other obligations of

data controllers and rights of data subjects under Regulations (EU) 2016/679 and (EU) 2018/1725 and Directive (EU) 2016/680 remain applicable. In particular, this Regulation should not provide a legal basis in the meaning of Article 22(2), point (b) of Regulation (EU) 2016/679 and Article 24(2), point (b) of Regulation (EU) 2018/1725. Providers and prospective providers in the AI regulatory sandbox should ensure appropriate safeguards and cooperate with the competent authorities, including by following their guidance and acting expeditiously and in good faith to adequately mitigate any identified significant risks to safety, health, and fundamental rights that may arise during the development, testing and experimentation in that sandbox.

(141) In order to accelerate the process of development and the placing on the market of the high-risk AI systems listed in an annex to this Regulation, it is important that providers or prospective providers of such systems may also benefit from a specific regime for testing those systems in real world conditions, without participating in an AI regulatory sandbox. However, in such cases, taking into account the possible consequences of such testing on individuals, it should be ensured that appropriate and sufficient guarantees and conditions are introduced by this Regulation for providers or prospective providers. Such guarantees should include, inter alia, requesting informed consent of natural persons to participate in testing in real world conditions, with the exception of law enforcement where the seeking of informed consent would prevent the AI system from being tested. Consent of subjects to participate in such testing under this Regulation is distinct from, and without prejudice to, consent of data subjects for the processing of their personal data under the relevant data protection law. It is also important to minimise the risks and enable oversight by competent authorities and therefore require prospective providers to have a real-world testing plan submitted to competent market surveillance authority, register the testing in dedicated sections in the EU database subject to some limited exceptions, set limitations on the period for which the testing can be done and require additional safeguards for persons belonging to certain vulnerable groups, as well as a written agreement defining the roles and responsibilities of prospective providers and deployers and effective oversight by competent personnel involved in the real world testing. Furthermore, it is appropriate to envisage additional safeguards to ensure that the predictions, recommendations or decisions of the AI system can be effectively reversed and disregarded and that personal data is protected and is deleted when the subjects have withdrawn their consent to participate in the testing without prejudice to their rights as data subjects under the Union data protection law. As regards transfer of data, it is also appropriate to envisage that data collected and processed for the purpose of testing in real-world conditions should be transferred to third countries only where appropriate and applicable safeguards under Union law are implemented, in particular in accordance with bases for transfer of personal data under Union law on data protection, while for non-personal data appropriate safeguards are

put in place in accordance with Union law, such as Regulations (EU) 2022/868[42] and (EU) 2023/2854[43] of the European Parliament and of the Council.

(142) To ensure that AI leads to socially and environmentally beneficial outcomes, Member States are encouraged to support and promote research and development of AI solutions in support of socially and environmentally beneficial outcomes, such as AI-based solutions to increase accessibility for persons with disabilities, tackle socio-economic inequalities, or meet environmental targets, by allocating sufficient resources, including public and Union funding, and, where appropriate and provided that the eligibility and selection criteria are fulfilled, considering in particular projects which pursue such objectives. Such projects should be based on the principle of interdisciplinary cooperation between AI developers, experts on inequality and non-discrimination, accessibility, consumer, environmental, and digital rights, as well as academics.

(143) In order to promote and protect innovation, it is important that the interests of SMEs, including start-ups, that are providers or deployers of AI systems are taken into particular account. To that end, Member States should develop initiatives, which are targeted at those operators, including on awareness raising and information communication. Member States should provide SMEs, including start-ups, that have a registered office or a branch in the Union, with priority access to the AI regulatory sandboxes provided that they fulfil the eligibility conditions and selection criteria and without precluding other providers and prospective providers to access the sandboxes provided the same conditions and criteria are fulfilled. Member States should utilise existing channels and where appropriate, establish new dedicated channels for communication with SMEs, including start-ups, deployers, other innovators and, as appropriate, local public authorities, to support SMEs throughout their development path by providing guidance and responding to queries about the implementation of this Regulation. Where appropriate, these channels should work together to create synergies and ensure homogeneity in their guidance to SMEs, including start-ups, and deployers. Additionally, Member States should facilitate the participation of SMEs and other relevant stakeholders in the standardisation development processes. Moreover, the specific interests and needs of providers that are SMEs, including start-ups, should be taken into account when notified bodies set conformity assessment fees. The Commission should regularly assess the certification and compliance costs for SMEs, including start-ups, through transparent consultations and should work with Member States to lower such costs. For example, translation costs related to mandatory documentation and communication with authorities may constitute a significant cost for providers and other operators, in particular those of a smaller scale. Member States should possibly ensure that one of the languages determined and accepted by them for relevant providers' documentation and for communication with operators is one which is broadly understood by the largest possible number of cross-border deployers. In order to address the specific needs of SMEs, including start-ups,

---

[42] **Official note:** Regulation (EU) 2022/868 of the European Parliament and of the Council of 30 May 2022 on European data governance and amending Regulation (EU) 2018/1724 (Data Governance Act) (OJ L 152, 3.6.2022, p. 1).

[43] **Official note:** Regulation (EU) 2023/2854 of the European Parliament and of the Council of 13 December 2023 on harmonised rules on fair access to and use of data and amending Regulation (EU) 2017/2394 and Directive (EU) 2020/1828 (Data Act) (OJ L, 2023/2854, 22.12.2023, ELI: http://data.europa.eu/eli/reg/2023/2854/oj).

the Commission should provide standardised templates for the areas covered by this Regulation, upon request of the Board. Additionally, the Commission should complement Member States' efforts by providing a single information platform with easy-to-use information with regards to this Regulation for all providers and deployers, by organising appropriate communication campaigns to raise awareness about the obligations arising from this Regulation, and by evaluating and promoting the convergence of best practices in public procurement procedures in relation to AI systems. Medium-sized enterprises which until recently qualified as small enterprises within the meaning of the Annex to Commission Recommendation 2003/361/EC[44] should have access to those support measures, as those new medium-sized enterprises may sometimes lack the legal resources and training necessary to ensure proper understanding of, and compliance with, this Regulation.

(144) In order to promote and protect innovation, the AI-on-demand platform, all relevant Union funding programmes and projects, such as Digital Europe Programme, Horizon Europe, implemented by the Commission and the Member States at Union or national level should, as appropriate, contribute to the achievement of the objectives of this Regulation.

(145) In order to minimise the risks to implementation resulting from lack of knowledge and expertise in the market as well as to facilitate compliance of providers, in particular SMEs, including start-ups, and notified bodies with their obligations under this Regulation, the AI-on-demand platform, the European Digital Innovation Hubs and the testing and experimentation facilities established by the Commission and the Member States at Union or national level should contribute to the implementation of this Regulation. Within their respective mission and fields of competence, the AI-on-demand platform, the European Digital Innovation Hubs and the testing and experimentation Facilities are able to provide in particular technical and scientific support to providers and notified bodies.

(146) Moreover, in light of the very small size of some operators and in order to ensure proportionality regarding costs of innovation, it is appropriate to allow microenterprises to fulfil one of the most costly obligations, namely to establish a quality management system, in a simplified manner which would reduce the administrative burden and the costs for those enterprises without affecting the level of protection and the need for compliance with the requirements for high-risk AI systems. The Commission should develop guidelines to specify the elements of the quality management system to be fulfilled in this simplified manner by microenterprises.

(147) It is appropriate that the Commission facilitates, to the extent possible, access to testing and experimentation facilities to bodies, groups or laboratories established or accredited pursuant to any relevant Union harmonisation legislation and which fulfil tasks in the context of conformity assessment of products or devices covered by that Union harmonisation legislation. This is, in particular, the case as regards expert panels, expert laboratories and reference laboratories in the field of medical devices pursuant to Regulations (EU) 2017/745 and (EU) 2017/746.

---

[44] **Official note:** Commission Recommendation of 6 May 2003 concerning the definition of micro, small and medium-sized enterprises (OJ L 124, 20.5.2003, p. 36).

(148) This Regulation should establish a governance framework that both allows to coordinate and support the application of this Regulation at national level, as well as build capabilities at Union level and integrate stakeholders in the field of AI. The effective implementation and enforcement of this Regulation require a governance framework that allows to coordinate and build up central expertise at Union level. The AI Office was established by Commission Decision[45] and has as its mission to develop Union expertise and capabilities in the field of AI and to contribute to the implementation of Union law on AI. Member States should facilitate the tasks of the AI Office with a view to support the development of Union expertise and capabilities at Union level and to strengthen the functioning of the digital single market. Furthermore, a Board composed of representatives of the Member States, a scientific panel to integrate the scientific community and an advisory forum to contribute stakeholder input to the implementation of this Regulation, at Union and national level, should be established. The development of Union expertise and capabilities should also include making use of existing resources and expertise, in particular through synergies with structures built up in the context of the Union level enforcement of other law and synergies with related initiatives at Union level, such as the EuroHPC Joint Undertaking and the AI testing and experimentation facilities under the Digital Europe Programme.

(149) In order to facilitate a smooth, effective and harmonised implementation of this Regulation a Board should be established. The Board should reflect the various interests of the AI eco-system and be composed of representatives of the Member States. The Board should be responsible for a number of advisory tasks, including issuing opinions, recommendations, advice or contributing to guidance on matters related to the implementation of this Regulation, including on enforcement matters, technical specifications or existing standards regarding the requirements established in this Regulation and providing advice to the Commission and the Member States and their national competent authorities on specific questions related to AI. In order to give some flexibility to Member States in the designation of their representatives in the Board, such representatives may be any persons belonging to public entities who should have the relevant competences and powers to facilitate coordination at national level and contribute to the achievement of the Board's tasks. The Board should establish two standing sub-groups to provide a platform for cooperation and exchange among market surveillance authorities and notifying authorities on issues related, respectively, to market surveillance and notified bodies. The standing subgroup for market surveillance should act as the administrative cooperation group (ADCO) for this Regulation within the meaning of Article 30 of Regulation (EU) 2019/1020. In accordance with Article 33 of that Regulation, the Commission should support the activities of the standing subgroup for market surveillance by undertaking market evaluations or studies, in particular with a view to identifying aspects of this Regulation requiring specific and urgent coordination among market surveillance authorities. The Board may establish other standing or temporary sub-groups as appropriate for the purpose of examining specific issues. The Board should also cooperate, as appropriate, with relevant Union bodies, experts groups and networks active in the context

[45] **Official note:** Commission Decision of 24.1.2024 establishing the European Artificial Intelligence Office C(2024) 390.

of relevant Union law, including in particular those active under relevant Union law on data, digital products and services.

(150) With a view to ensuring the involvement of stakeholders in the implementation and application of this Regulation, an advisory forum should be established to advise and provide technical expertise to the Board and the Commission. To ensure a varied and balanced stakeholder representation between commercial and non-commercial interest and, within the category of commercial interests, with regards to SMEs and other undertakings, the advisory forum should comprise inter alia industry, start-ups, SMEs, academia, civil society, including the social partners, as well as the Fundamental Rights Agency, ENISA, the European Committee for Standardization (CEN), the European Committee for Electrotechnical Standardization (CENELEC) and the European Telecommunications Standards Institute (ETSI).

(151) To support the implementation and enforcement of this Regulation, in particular the monitoring activities of the AI Office as regards general-purpose AI models, a scientific panel of independent experts should be established. The independent experts constituting the scientific panel should be selected on the basis of up-to-date scientific or technical expertise in the field of AI and should perform their tasks with impartiality, objectivity and ensure the confidentiality of information and data obtained in carrying out their tasks and activities. To allow the reinforcement of national capacities necessary for the effective enforcement of this Regulation, Member States should be able to request support from the pool of experts constituting the scientific panel for their enforcement activities.

(152) In order to support adequate enforcement as regards AI systems and reinforce the capacities of the Member States, Union AI testing support structures should be established and made available to the Member States.

(153) Member States hold a key role in the application and enforcement of this Regulation. In that respect, each Member State should designate at least one notifying authority and at least one market surveillance authority as national competent authorities for the purpose of supervising the application and implementation of this Regulation. Member States may decide to appoint any kind of public entity to perform the tasks of the national competent authorities within the meaning of this Regulation, in accordance with their specific national organisational characteristics and needs. In order to increase organisation efficiency on the side of Member States and to set a single point of contact vis-à-vis the public and other counterparts at Member State and Union levels, each Member State should designate a market surveillance authority to act as a single point of contact.

(154) The national competent authorities should exercise their powers independently, impartially and without bias, so as to safeguard the principles of objectivity of their activities and tasks and to ensure the application and implementation of this Regulation. The members of these authorities should refrain from any action incompatible with their duties and should be subject to confidentiality rules under this Regulation.

(155) In order to ensure that providers of high-risk AI systems can take into account the experience on the use of high-risk AI systems for improving their systems and the design and development process or can take any possible corrective action in a timely manner, all providers should have a post-market monitoring system in place. Where relevant, post-market monitoring should include an

analysis of the interaction with other AI systems including other devices and software. Post-market monitoring should not cover sensitive operational data of deployers which are law enforcement authorities. This system is also key to ensure that the possible risks emerging from AI systems which continue to „learn" after being placed on the market or put into service can be more efficiently and timely addressed. In this context, providers should also be required to have a system in place to report to the relevant authorities any serious incidents resulting from the use of their AI systems, meaning incident or malfunctioning leading to death or serious damage to health, serious and irreversible disruption of the management and operation of critical infrastructure, infringements of obligations under Union law intended to protect fundamental rights or serious damage to property or the environment.

(156) In order to ensure an appropriate and effective enforcement of the requirements and obligations set out by this Regulation, which is Union harmonisation legislation, the system of market surveillance and compliance of products established by Regulation (EU) 2019/1020 should apply in its entirety. Market surveillance authorities designated pursuant to this Regulation should have all enforcement powers laid down in this Regulation and in Regulation (EU) 2019/1020 and should exercise their powers and carry out their duties independently, impartially and without bias. Although the majority of AI systems are not subject to specific requirements and obligations under this Regulation, market surveillance authorities may take measures in relation to all AI systems when they present a risk in accordance with this Regulation. Due to the specific nature of Union institutions, agencies and bodies falling within the scope of this Regulation, it is appropriate to designate the European Data Protection Supervisor as a competent market surveillance authority for them. This should be without prejudice to the designation of national competent authorities by the Member States. Market surveillance activities should not affect the ability of the supervised entities to carry out their tasks independently, when such independence is required by Union law.

(157) This Regulation is without prejudice to the competences, tasks, powers and independence of relevant national public authorities or bodies which supervise the application of Union law protecting fundamental rights, including equality bodies and data protection authorities. Where necessary for their mandate, those national public authorities or bodies should also have access to any documentation created under this Regulation. A specific safeguard procedure should be set for ensuring adequate and timely enforcement against AI systems presenting a risk to health, safety and fundamental rights. The procedure for such AI systems presenting a risk should be applied to high-risk AI systems presenting a risk, prohibited systems which have been placed on the market, put into service or used in violation of the prohibited practices laid down in this Regulation and AI systems which have been made available in violation of the transparency requirements laid down in this Regulation and present a risk.

(158) Union financial services law includes internal governance and risk-management rules and requirements which are applicable to regulated financial institutions in the course of provision of those services, including when they make use of AI systems. In order to ensure coherent application and enforcement of the obligations under this Regulation and relevant rules and requirements of the Union financial services legal acts, the competent authorities for the supervision and enforcement of those legal acts, in particular competent authorities as defined

in Regulation (EU) No 575/2013 of the European Parliament and of the Council[46] and Directives 2008/48/EC[47], 2009/138/EC[48], 2013/36/EU[49], 2014/17/EU[50] and (EU) 2016/97[51] of the European Parliament and of the Council, should be designated, within their respective competences, as competent authorities for the purpose of supervising the implementation of this Regulation, including for market surveillance activities, as regards AI systems provided or used by regulated and supervised financial institutions unless Member States decide to designate another authority to fulfil these market surveillance tasks. Those competent authorities should have all powers under this Regulation and Regulation (EU) 2019/1020 to enforce the requirements and obligations of this Regulation, including powers to carry our *ex post* market surveillance activities that can be integrated, as appropriate, into their existing supervisory mechanisms and procedures under the relevant Union financial services law. It is appropriate to envisage that, when acting as market surveillance authorities under this Regulation, the national authorities responsible for the supervision of credit institutions regulated under Directive 2013/36/EU, which are participating in the Single Supervisory Mechanism established by Council Regulation (EU) No 1024/2013[52], should report, without delay, to the European Central Bank any information identified in the course of their market surveillance activities that may be of potential interest for the European Central Bank's prudential supervisory tasks as specified in that Regulation. To further enhance the consistency between this Regulation and the rules applicable to credit institutions regulated under Directive 2013/36/EU, it is also appropriate to integrate some of the providers' procedural obligations in relation to risk management, post marketing monitoring and documentation into the existing obligations and procedures under Directive 2013/36/EU. In order to avoid overlaps, limited derogations should also be envisaged in relation to the quality management system of providers and the monitoring obligation placed on deployers of high-risk AI systems to the extent that these apply to credit institutions regulated by Directive 2013/36/EU. The same regime should apply to insurance and re-insurance undertakings and insurance holding companies under Directive 2009/138/EC and the insurance intermediaries under Directive (EU) 2016/97 and other types

[46] **Official note:** Regulation (EU) No 575/2013 of the European Parliament and of the Council of 26 June 2013 on prudential requirements for credit institutions and investment firms and amending Regulation (EU) No 648/2012 (OJ L 176, 27.6.2013, p. 1).

[47] **Official note:** Directive 2008/48/EC of the European Parliament and of the Council of 23 April 2008 on credit agreements for consumers and repealing Council Directive 87/102/EEC (OJ L 133, 22.5.2008, p. 66).

[48] **Official note:** Directive 2009/138/EC of the European Parliament and of the Council of 25 November 2009 on the taking-up and pursuit of the business of Insurance and Reinsurance (Solvency II) (OJ L 335, 17.12.2009, p. 1).

[49] **Official note:** Directive 2013/36/EU of the European Parliament and of the Council of 26 June 2013 on access to the activity of credit institutions and the prudential supervision of credit institutions and investment firms, amending Directive 2002/87/EC and repealing Directives 2006/48/EC and 2006/49/EC (OJ L 176, 27.6.2013, p. 338).

[50] **Official note:** Directive 2014/17/EU of the European Parliament and of the Council of 4 February 2014 on credit agreements for consumers relating to residential immovable property and amending Directives 2008/48/EC and 2013/36/EU and Regulation (EU) No 1093/2010 (OJ L 60, 28.2.2014, p. 34).

[51] **Official note:** Directive (EU) 2016/97 of the European Parliament and of the Council of 20 January 2016 on insurance distribution (OJ L 26, 2.2.2016, p. 19).

[52] **Official note:** Council Regulation (EU) No 1024/2013 of 15 October 2013 conferring specific tasks on the European Central Bank concerning policies relating to the prudential supervision of credit institutions (OJ L 287, 29.10.2013, p. 63).

of financial institutions subject to requirements regarding internal governance, arrangements or processes established pursuant to the relevant Union financial services law to ensure consistency and equal treatment in the financial sector.

(159) Each market surveillance authority for high-risk AI systems in the area of biometrics, as listed in an annex to this Regulation insofar as those systems are used for the purposes of law enforcement, migration, asylum and border control management, or the administration of justice and democratic processes, should have effective investigative and corrective powers, including at least the power to obtain access to all personal data that are being processed and to all information necessary for the performance of its tasks. The market surveillance authorities should be able to exercise their powers by acting with complete independence. Any limitations of their access to sensitive operational data under this Regulation should be without prejudice to the powers conferred to them by Directive (EU) 2016/680. No exclusion on disclosing data to national data protection authorities under this Regulation should affect the current or future powers of those authorities beyond the scope of this Regulation.

(160) The market surveillance authorities and the Commission should be able to propose joint activities, including joint investigations, to be conducted by market surveillance authorities or market surveillance authorities jointly with the Commission, that have the aim of promoting compliance, identifying non-compliance, raising awareness and providing guidance in relation to this Regulation with respect to specific categories of high-risk AI systems that are found to present a serious risk across two or more Member States. Joint activities to promote compliance should be carried out in accordance with Article 9 of Regulation (EU) 2019/1020. The AI Office should provide coordination support for joint investigations.

(161) It is necessary to clarify the responsibilities and competences at Union and national level as regards AI systems that are built on general-purpose AI models. To avoid overlapping competences, where an AI system is based on a general-purpose AI model and the model and system are provided by the same provider, the supervision should take place at Union level through the AI Office, which should have the powers of a market surveillance authority within the meaning of Regulation (EU) 2019/1020 for this purpose. In all other cases, national market surveillance authorities remain responsible for the supervision of AI systems. However, for general-purpose AI systems that can be used directly by deployers for at least one purpose that is classified as high-risk, market surveillance authorities should cooperate with the AI Office to carry out evaluations of compliance and inform the Board and other market surveillance authorities accordingly. Furthermore, market surveillance authorities should be able to request assistance from the AI Office where the market surveillance authority is unable to conclude an investigation on a high-risk AI system because of its inability to access certain information related to the general-purpose AI model on which the high-risk AI system is built. In such cases, the procedure regarding mutual assistance in cross-border cases in Chapter VI of Regulation (EU) 2019/1020 should apply *mutatis mutandis*.

(162) To make best use of the centralised Union expertise and synergies at Union level, the powers of supervision and enforcement of the obligations on providers of general-purpose AI models should be a competence of the Commission. The AI Office should be able to carry out all necessary actions to monitor the effective implementation of this Regulation as regards general-purpose AI

models. It should be able to investigate possible infringements of the rules on providers of general-purpose AI models both on its own initiative, following the results of its monitoring activities, or upon request from market surveillance authorities in line with the conditions set out in this Regulation. To support effective monitoring of the AI Office, it should provide for the possibility that downstream providers lodge complaints about possible infringements of the rules on providers of general-purpose AI models and systems.

(163) With a view to complementing the governance systems for general-purpose AI models, the scientific panel should support the monitoring activities of the AI Office and may, in certain cases, provide qualified alerts to the AI Office which trigger follow-ups, such as investigations. This should be the case where the scientific panel has reason to suspect that a general-purpose AI model poses a concrete and identifiable risk at Union level. Furthermore, this should be the case where the scientific panel has reason to suspect that a general-purpose AI model meets the criteria that would lead to a classification as general-purpose AI model with systemic risk. To equip the scientific panel with the information necessary for the performance of those tasks, there should be a mechanism whereby the scientific panel can request the Commission to require documentation or information from a provider.

(164) The AI Office should be able to take the necessary actions to monitor the effective implementation of and compliance with the obligations for providers of general-purpose AI models laid down in this Regulation. The AI Office should be able to investigate possible infringements in accordance with the powers provided for in this Regulation, including by requesting documentation and information, by conducting evaluations, as well as by requesting measures from providers of general-purpose AI models. When conducting evaluations, in order to make use of independent expertise, the AI Office should be able to involve independent experts to carry out the evaluations on its behalf. Compliance with the obligations should be enforceable, inter alia, through requests to take appropriate measures, including risk mitigation measures in the case of identified systemic risks as well as restricting the making available on the market, withdrawing or recalling the model. As a safeguard, where needed beyond the procedural rights provided for in this Regulation, providers of general-purpose AI models should have the procedural rights provided for in Article 18 of Regulation (EU) 2019/1020, which should apply *mutatis mutandis*, without prejudice to more specific procedural rights provided for by this Regulation.

(165) The development of AI systems other than high-risk AI systems in accordance with the requirements of this Regulation may lead to a larger uptake of ethical and trustworthy AI in the Union. Providers of AI systems that are not high-risk should be encouraged to create codes of conduct, including related governance mechanisms, intended to foster the voluntary application of some or all of the mandatory requirements applicable to high-risk AI systems, adapted in light of the intended purpose of the systems and the lower risk involved and taking into account the available technical solutions and industry best practices such as model and data cards. Providers and, as appropriate, deployers of all AI systems, high-risk or not, and AI models should also be encouraged to apply on a voluntary basis additional requirements related, for example, to the elements of the Union's Ethics Guidelines for Trustworthy AI, environmental sustainability, AI literacy measures, inclusive and diverse design and development of AI systems, including attention to vulnerable persons and accessibility to persons with

disability, stakeholders' participation with the involvement, as appropriate, of relevant stakeholders such as business and civil society organisations, academia, research organisations, trade unions and consumer protection organisations in the design and development of AI systems, and diversity of the development teams, including gender balance. To ensure that the voluntary codes of conduct are effective, they should be based on clear objectives and key performance indicators to measure the achievement of those objectives. They should also be developed in an inclusive way, as appropriate, with the involvement of relevant stakeholders such as business and civil society organisations, academia, research organisations, trade unions and consumer protection organisation. The Commission may develop initiatives, including of a sectoral nature, to facilitate the lowering of technical barriers hindering cross-border exchange of data for AI development, including on data access infrastructure, semantic and technical interoperability of different types of data.

(166) It is important that AI systems related to products that are not high-risk in accordance with this Regulation and thus are not required to comply with the requirements set out for high-risk AI systems are nevertheless safe when placed on the market or put into service. To contribute to this objective, Regulation (EU) 2023/988 of the European Parliament and of the Council[53] would apply as a safety net.

(167) In order to ensure trustful and constructive cooperation of competent authorities on Union and national level, all parties involved in the application of this Regulation should respect the confidentiality of information and data obtained in carrying out their tasks, in accordance with Union or national law. They should carry out their tasks and activities in such a manner as to protect, in particular, intellectual property rights, confidential business information and trade secrets, the effective implementation of this Regulation, public and national security interests, the integrity of criminal and administrative proceedings, and the integrity of classified information.

(168) Compliance with this Regulation should be enforceable by means of the imposition of penalties and other enforcement measures. Member States should take all necessary measures to ensure that the provisions of this Regulation are implemented, including by laying down effective, proportionate and dissuasive penalties for their infringement, and to respect the *ne bis in idem* principle. In order to strengthen and harmonise administrative penalties for infringement of this Regulation, the upper limits for setting the administrative fines for certain specific infringements should be laid down. When assessing the amount of the fines, Member States should, in each individual case, take into account all relevant circumstances of the specific situation, with due regard in particular to the nature, gravity and duration of the infringement and of its consequences and to the size of the provider, in particular if the provider is an SME, including a start-up. The European Data Protection Supervisor should have the power to impose fines on Union institutions, agencies and bodies falling within the scope of this Regulation.

---

[53] **Official note:** Regulation (EU) 2023/988 of the European Parliament and of the Council of 10 May 2023 on general product safety, amending Regulation (EU) No 1025/2012 of the European Parliament and of the Council and Directive (EU) 2020/1828 of the European Parliament and the Council, and repealing Directive 2001/95/EC of the European Parliament and of the Council and Council Directive 87/357/EEC (OJ L 135, 23.5.2023, p. 1).

(169) Compliance with the obligations on providers of general-purpose AI models imposed under this Regulation should be enforceable, inter alia, by means of fines. To that end, appropriate levels of fines should also be laid down for infringement of those obligations, including the failure to comply with measures requested by the Commission in accordance with this Regulation, subject to appropriate limitation periods in accordance with the principle of proportionality. All decisions taken by the Commission under this Regulation are subject to review by the Court of Justice of the European Union in accordance with the TFEU, including the unlimited jurisdiction of the Court of Justice with regard to penalties pursuant to Article 261 TFEU.

(170) Union and national law already provide effective remedies to natural and legal persons whose rights and freedoms are adversely affected by the use of AI systems. Without prejudice to those remedies, any natural or legal person that has grounds to consider that there has been an infringement of this Regulation should be entitled to lodge a complaint to the relevant market surveillance authority.

(171) Affected persons should have the right to obtain an explanation where a deployer's decision is based mainly upon the output from certain high-risk AI systems that fall within the scope of this Regulation and where that decision produces legal effects or similarly significantly affects those persons in a way that they consider to have an adverse impact on their health, safety or fundamental rights. That explanation should be clear and meaningful and should provide a basis on which the affected persons are able to exercise their rights. The right to obtain an explanation should not apply to the use of AI systems for which exceptions or restrictions follow from Union or national law and should apply only to the extent this right is not already provided for under Union law.

(172) Persons acting as whistleblowers on the infringements of this Regulation should be protected under the Union law. Directive (EU) 2019/1937 of the European Parliament and of the Council[54] should therefore apply to the reporting of infringements of this Regulation and the protection of persons reporting such infringements.

(173) In order to ensure that the regulatory framework can be adapted where necessary, the power to adopt acts in accordance with Article 290 TFEU should be delegated to the Commission to amend the conditions under which an AI system is not to be considered to be high-risk, the list of high-risk AI systems, the provisions regarding technical documentation, the content of the EU declaration of conformity the provisions regarding the conformity assessment procedures, the provisions establishing the high-risk AI systems to which the conformity assessment procedure based on assessment of the quality management system and assessment of the technical documentation should apply, the threshold, benchmarks and indicators, including by supplementing those benchmarks and indicators, in the rules for the classification of general-purpose AI models with systemic risk, the criteria for the designation of general-purpose AI models with systemic risk, the technical documentation for providers of general-purpose AI models and the transparency information for providers of general-purpose AI models. It is of particular importance that the Commission carry out appropriate consultations during its preparatory work, including at

[54] **Official note:** Directive (EU) 2019/1937 of the European Parliament and of the Council of 23 October 2019 on the protection of persons who report breaches of Union law (OJ L 305, 26.11.2019, p. 17).

expert level, and that those consultations be conducted in accordance with the principles laid down in the Interinstitutional Agreement of 13 April 2016 on Better Law-Making[55]. In particular, to ensure equal participation in the preparation of delegated acts, the European Parliament and the Council receive all documents at the same time as Member States' experts, and their experts systematically have access to meetings of Commission expert groups dealing with the preparation of delegated acts.

(174) Given the rapid technological developments and the technical expertise required to effectively apply this Regulation, the Commission should evaluate and review this Regulation by 2 August 2029 and every four years thereafter and report to the European Parliament and the Council. In addition, taking into account the implications for the scope of this Regulation, the Commission should carry out an assessment of the need to amend the list of high-risk AI systems and the list of prohibited practices once a year. Moreover, by 2 August 2028 and every four years thereafter, the Commission should evaluate and report to the European Parliament and to the Council on the need to amend the list of high-risk areas headings in the annex to this Regulation, the AI systems within the scope of the transparency obligations, the effectiveness of the supervision and governance system and the progress on the development of standardisation deliverables on energy efficient development of general-purpose AI models, including the need for further measures or actions. Finally, by 2 August 2028 and every three years thereafter, the Commission should evaluate the impact and effectiveness of voluntary codes of conduct to foster the application of the requirements provided for high-risk AI systems in the case of AI systems other than high-risk AI systems and possibly other additional requirements for such AI systems.

(175) In order to ensure uniform conditions for the implementation of this Regulation, implementing powers should be conferred on the Commission. Those powers should be exercised in accordance with Regulation (EU) No 182/2011 of the European Parliament and of the Council[56].

(176) Since the objective of this Regulation, namely to improve the functioning of the internal market and to promote the uptake of human centric and trustworthy AI, while ensuring a high level of protection of health, safety, fundamental rights enshrined in the Charter, including democracy, the rule of law and environmental protection against harmful effects of AI systems in the Union and supporting innovation, cannot be sufficiently achieved by the Member States and can rather, by reason of the scale or effects of the action, be better achieved at Union level, the Union may adopt measures in accordance with the principle of subsidiarity as set out in Article 5 TEU. In accordance with the principle of proportionality as set out in that Article, this Regulation does not go beyond what is necessary in order to achieve that objective.

(177) In order to ensure legal certainty, ensure an appropriate adaptation period for operators and avoid disruption to the market, including by ensuring continuity of the use of AI systems, it is appropriate that this Regulation applies to the high-risk AI systems that have been placed on the market or put into service before the general date of application thereof, only if, from that date, those

---

[55] **Official note:** OJ L 123, 12.5.2016, p. 1.

[56] **Official note:** Regulation (EU) No 182/2011 of the European Parliament and of the Council of 16 February 2011 laying down the rules and general principles concerning mechanisms for control by Member States of the Commission's exercise of implementing powers (OJ L 55, 28.2.2011, p. 13).

systems are subject to significant changes in their design or intended purpose. It is appropriate to clarify that, in this respect, the concept of significant change should be understood as equivalent in substance to the notion of substantial modification, which is used with regard only to high-risk AI systems pursuant to this Regulation. On an exceptional basis and in light of public accountability, operators of AI systems which are components of the large-scale IT systems established by the legal acts listed in an annex to this Regulation and operators of high-risk AI systems that are intended to be used by public authorities should, respectively, take the necessary steps to comply with the requirements of this Regulation by end of 2030 and by 2 August 2030.

(178) Providers of high-risk AI systems are encouraged to start to comply, on a voluntary basis, with the relevant obligations of this Regulation already during the transitional period.

(179) This Regulation should apply from 2 August 2026. However, taking into account the unacceptable risk associated with the use of AI in certain ways, the prohibitions as well as the general provisions of this Regulation should already apply from 2 February 2025. While the full effect of those prohibitions follows with the establishment of the governance and enforcement of this Regulation, anticipating the application of the prohibitions is important to take account of unacceptable risks and to have an effect on other procedures, such as in civil law. Moreover, the infrastructure related to the governance and the conformity assessment system should be operational before 2 August 2026, therefore the provisions on notified bodies and governance structure should apply from 2 August 2025. Given the rapid pace of technological advancements and adoption of general-purpose AI models, obligations for providers of general-purpose AI models should apply from 2 August 2025. Codes of practice should be ready by 2 May 2025 in view of enabling providers to demonstrate compliance on time. The AI Office should ensure that classification rules and procedures are up to date in light of technological developments. In addition, Member States should lay down and notify to the Commission the rules on penalties, including administrative fines, and ensure that they are properly and effectively implemented by the date of application of this Regulation. Therefore the provisions on penalties should apply from 2 August 2025.

(180) The European Data Protection Supervisor and the European Data Protection Board were consulted in accordance with Article 42(1) and (2) of Regulation (EU) 2018/1725 and delivered their joint opinion on 18 June 2021,

HAVE ADOPTED THIS REGULATION:

CHAPTER I
GENERAL PROVISIONS

Article 1
Subject matter

1. The purpose of this Regulation is to improve the functioning of the internal market and promote the uptake of human-centric and trustworthy artificial intelligence (AI), while ensuring a high level of protection of health, safety, fundamental rights enshrined in the Charter, including democracy, the rule of law and environmental

protection, against the harmful effects of AI systems in the Union and supporting innovation.
2. This Regulation lays down:

(a) harmonised rules for the placing on the market, the putting into service, and the use of AI systems in the Union;
(b) prohibitions of certain AI practices;
(c) specific requirements for high-risk AI systems and obligations for operators of such systems;
(d) harmonised transparency rules for certain AI systems;
(e) harmonised rules for the placing on the market of general-purpose AI models;
(f) rules on market monitoring, market surveillance, governance and enforcement;
(g) measures to support innovation, with a particular focus on SMEs, including start-ups.

Article 2
Scope

1. This Regulation applies to:

(a) providers placing on the market or putting into service AI systems or placing on the market general-purpose AI models in the Union, irrespective of whether those providers are established or located within the Union or in a third country;
(b) deployers of AI systems that have their place of establishment or are located within the Union;
(c) providers and deployers of AI systems that have their place of establishment or are located in a third country, where the output produced by the AI system is used in the Union;
(d) importers and distributors of AI systems;
(e) product manufacturers placing on the market or putting into service an AI system together with their product and under their own name or trademark;
(f) authorised representatives of providers, which are not established in the Union;
(g) affected persons that are located in the Union.

2. [1]For AI systems classified as high-risk AI systems in accordance with Article 6(1) related to products covered by the Union harmonisation legislation listed in Section B of Annex I, only Article 6(1), Articles 102 to 109 and Article 112 apply. [2]Article 57 applies only in so far as the requirements for high-risk AI systems under this Regulation have been integrated in that Union harmonisation legislation.
3.

(1) This Regulation does not apply to areas outside the scope of Union law, and shall not, in any event, affect the competences of the Member States concerning national security, regardless of the type of entity entrusted by the Member States with carrying out tasks in relation to those competences.
(2) This Regulation does not apply to AI systems where and in so far they are placed on the market, put into service, or used with or without modification exclusively for military, defence or national security purposes, regardless of the type of entity carrying out those activities.
(3) This Regulation does not apply to AI systems which are not placed on the market or put into service in the Union, where the output is used in the Union exclusively

for military, defence or national security purposes, regardless of the type of entity carrying out those activities.

4. This Regulation applies neither to public authorities in a third country nor to international organisations falling within the scope of this Regulation pursuant to paragraph 1, where those authorities or organisations use AI systems in the framework of international cooperation or agreements for law enforcement and judicial cooperation with the Union or with one or more Member States, provided that such a third country or international organisation provides adequate safeguards with respect to the protection of fundamental rights and freedoms of individuals.
5. This Regulation shall not affect the application of the provisions on the liability of providers of intermediary services as set out in Chapter II of Regulation (EU) 2022/2065.
6. This Regulation does not apply to AI systems or AI models, including their output, specifically developed and put into service for the sole purpose of scientific research and development.
7. [1]Union law on the protection of personal data, privacy and the confidentiality of communications applies to personal data processed in connection with the rights and obligations laid down in this Regulation. [2]This Regulation shall not affect Regulation (EU) 2016/679 or (EU) 2018/1725, or Directive 2002/58/EC or (EU) 2016/680, without prejudice to Article 10(5) and Article 59 of this Regulation.
8. [1]This Regulation does not apply to any research, testing or development activity regarding AI systems or AI models prior to their being placed on the market or put into service. [2]Such activities shall be conducted in accordance with applicable Union law. [3]Testing in real world conditions shall not be covered by that exclusion.
9. This Regulation is without prejudice to the rules laid down by other Union legal acts related to consumer protection and product safety.
10. This Regulation does not apply to obligations of deployers who are natural persons using AI systems in the course of a purely personal non-professional activity.
11. This Regulation does not preclude the Union or Member States from maintaining or introducing laws, regulations or administrative provisions which are more favourable to workers in terms of protecting their rights in respect of the use of AI systems by employers, or from encouraging or allowing the application of collective agreements which are more favourable to workers.
12. This Regulation does not apply to AI systems released under free and open-source licences, unless they are placed on the market or put into service as high-risk AI systems or as an AI system that falls under Article 5 or 50.

Article 3
Definitions

For the purposes of this Regulation, the following definitions apply:

(1) „AI system" means a machine-based system that is designed to operate with varying levels of autonomy and that may exhibit adaptiveness after deployment, and that, for explicit or implicit objectives, infers, from the input it receives, how to generate outputs such as predictions, content, recommendations, or decisions that can influence physical or virtual environments;
(2) „risk" means the combination of the probability of an occurrence of harm and the severity of that harm;

(3) „provider" means a natural or legal person, public authority, agency or other body that develops an AI system or a general-purpose AI model or that has an AI system or a general-purpose AI model developed and places it on the market or puts the AI system into service under its own name or trademark, whether for payment or free of charge;
(4) „deployer" means a natural or legal person, public authority, agency or other body using an AI system under its authority except where the AI system is used in the course of a personal non-professional activity;
(5) „authorised representative" means a natural or legal person located or established in the Union who has received and accepted a written mandate from a provider of an AI system or a general-purpose AI model to, respectively, perform and carry out on its behalf the obligations and procedures established by this Regulation;
(6) „importer" means a natural or legal person located or established in the Union that places on the market an AI system that bears the name or trademark of a natural or legal person established in a third country;
(7) „distributor" means a natural or legal person in the supply chain, other than the provider or the importer, that makes an AI system available on the Union market;
(8) „operator" means a provider, product manufacturer, deployer, authorised representative, importer or distributor;
(9) „placing on the market" means the first making available of an AI system or a general-purpose AI model on the Union market;
(10) „making available on the market" means the supply of an AI system or a general-purpose AI model for distribution or use on the Union market in the course of a commercial activity, whether in return for payment or free of charge;
(11) „putting into service" means the supply of an AI system for first use directly to the deployer or for own use in the Union for its intended purpose;
(12) „intended purpose" means the use for which an AI system is intended by the provider, including the specific context and conditions of use, as specified in the information supplied by the provider in the instructions for use, promotional or sales materials and statements, as well as in the technical documentation;
(13) „reasonably foreseeable misuse" means the use of an AI system in a way that is not in accordance with its intended purpose, but which may result from reasonably foreseeable human behaviour or interaction with other systems, including other AI systems;
(14) „safety component" means a component of a product or of an AI system which fulfils a safety function for that product or AI system, or the failure or malfunctioning of which endangers the health and safety of persons or property;
(15) „instructions for use" means the information provided by the provider to inform the deployer of, in particular, an AI system's intended purpose and proper use;
(16) „recall of an AI system" means any measure aiming to achieve the return to the provider or taking out of service or disabling the use of an AI system made available to deployers;
(17) „withdrawal of an AI system" means any measure aiming to prevent an AI system in the supply chain being made available on the market;
(18) „performance of an AI system" means the ability of an AI system to achieve its intended purpose;
(19) „notifying authority" means the national authority responsible for setting up and carrying out the necessary procedures for the assessment, designation and notification of conformity assessment bodies and for their monitoring;

(20) „conformity assessment" means the process of demonstrating whether the requirements set out in Chapter III, Section 2 relating to a high-risk AI system have been fulfilled;
(21) „conformity assessment body" means a body that performs third-party conformity assessment activities, including testing, certification and inspection;
(22) „notified body" means a conformity assessment body notified in accordance with this Regulation and other relevant Union harmonisation legislation;
(23) „substantial modification" means a change to an AI system after its placing on the market or putting into service which is not foreseen or planned in the initial conformity assessment carried out by the provider and as a result of which the compliance of the AI system with the requirements set out in Chapter III, Section 2 is affected or results in a modification to the intended purpose for which the AI system has been assessed;
(24) „CE marking" means a marking by which a provider indicates that an AI system is in conformity with the requirements set out in Chapter III, Section 2 and other applicable Union harmonisation legislation providing for its affixing;
(25) „post-market monitoring system" means all activities carried out by providers of AI systems to collect and review experience gained from the use of AI systems they place on the market or put into service for the purpose of identifying any need to immediately apply any necessary corrective or preventive actions;
(26) „market surveillance authority" means the national authority carrying out the activities and taking the measures pursuant to Regulation (EU) 2019/1020;
(27) „harmonised standard" means a harmonised standard as defined in Article 2(1), point (c), of Regulation (EU) No 1025/2012;
(28) „common specification" means a set of technical specifications as defined in Article 2, point (4) of Regulation (EU) No 1025/2012, providing means to comply with certain requirements established under this Regulation;
(29) „training data" means data used for training an AI system through fitting its learnable parameters;
(30) „validation data" means data used for providing an evaluation of the trained AI system and for tuning its non-learnable parameters and its learning process in order, inter alia, to prevent underfitting or overfitting;
(31) „validation data set" means a separate data set or part of the training data set, either as a fixed or variable split;
(32) „testing data" means data used for providing an independent evaluation of the AI system in order to confirm the expected performance of that system before its placing on the market or putting into service;
(33) „input data" means data provided to or directly acquired by an AI system on the basis of which the system produces an output;
(34) „biometric data" means personal data resulting from specific technical processing relating to the physical, physiological or behavioural characteristics of a natural person, such as facial images or dactyloscopic data;
(35) „biometric identification" means the automated recognition of physical, physiological, behavioural, or psychological human features for the purpose of establishing the identity of a natural person by comparing biometric data of that individual to biometric data of individuals stored in a database;
(36) „biometric verification" means the automated, one-to-one verification, including authentication, of the identity of natural persons by comparing their biometric data to previously provided biometric data;

(37) „special categories of personal data" means the categories of personal data referred to in Article 9(1) of Regulation (EU) 2016/679, Article 10 of Directive (EU) 2016/680 and Article 10(1) of Regulation (EU) 2018/1725;
(38) „sensitive operational data" means operational data related to activities of prevention, detection, investigation or prosecution of criminal offences, the disclosure of which could jeopardise the integrity of criminal proceedings;
(39) „emotion recognition system" means an AI system for the purpose of identifying or inferring emotions or intentions of natural persons on the basis of their biometric data;
(40) „biometric categorisation system" means an AI system for the purpose of assigning natural persons to specific categories on the basis of their biometric data, unless it is ancillary to another commercial service and strictly necessary for objective technical reasons;
(41) „remote biometric identification system" means an AI system for the purpose of identifying natural persons, without their active involvement, typically at a distance through the comparison of a person's biometric data with the biometric data contained in a reference database;
(42) „real-time remote biometric identification system" means a remote biometric identification system, whereby the capturing of biometric data, the comparison and the identification all occur without a significant delay, comprising not only instant identification, but also limited short delays in order to avoid circumvention;
(43) „post-remote biometric identification system" means a remote biometric identification system other than a real-time remote biometric identification system;
(44) „publicly accessible space" means any publicly or privately owned physical place accessible to an undetermined number of natural persons, regardless of whether certain conditions for access may apply, and regardless of the potential capacity restrictions;
(45) „law enforcement authority" means:
   (a) any public authority competent for the prevention, investigation, detection or prosecution of criminal offences or the execution of criminal penalties, including the safeguarding against and the prevention of threats to public security; or
   (b) any other body or entity entrusted by Member State law to exercise public authority and public powers for the purposes of the prevention, investigation, detection or prosecution of criminal offences or the execution of criminal penalties, including the safeguarding against and the prevention of threats to public security;
(46) „law enforcement" means activities carried out by law enforcement authorities or on their behalf for the prevention, investigation, detection or prosecution of criminal offences or the execution of criminal penalties, including safeguarding against and preventing threats to public security;
(47) „AI Office" means the Commission's function of contributing to the implementation, monitoring and supervision of AI systems and general-purpose AI models, and AI governance, provided for in Commission Decision of 24 January 2024; references in this Regulation to the AI Office shall be construed as references to the Commission;
(48) „national competent authority" means a notifying authority or a market surveillance authority; as regards AI systems put into service or used by Union institutions, agencies, offices and bodies, references to national competent authorities or

market surveillance authorities in this Regulation shall be construed as references to the European Data Protection Supervisor;

(49) „serious incident“ means an incident or malfunctioning of an AI system that directly or indirectly leads to any of the following:
 (a) the death of a person, or serious harm to a person's health;
 (b) a serious and irreversible disruption of the management or operation of critical infrastructure;
 (c) the infringement of obligations under Union law intended to protect fundamental rights;
 (d) serious harm to property or the environment;

(50) „personal data“ means personal data as defined in Article 4, point (1), of Regulation (EU) 2016/679;

(51) „non-personal data“ means data other than personal data as defined in Article 4, point (1), of Regulation (EU) 2016/679;

(52) „profiling“ means profiling as defined in Article 4, point (4), of Regulation (EU) 2016/679;

(53) „real-world testing plan“ means a document that describes the objectives, methodology, geographical, population and temporal scope, monitoring, organisation and conduct of testing in real-world conditions;

(54) „sandbox plan“ means a document agreed between the participating provider and the competent authority describing the objectives, conditions, timeframe, methodology and requirements for the activities carried out within the sandbox;

(55) „AI regulatory sandbox“ means a controlled framework set up by a competent authority which offers providers or prospective providers of AI systems the possibility to develop, train, validate and test, where appropriate in real-world conditions, an innovative AI system, pursuant to a sandbox plan for a limited time under regulatory supervision;

(56) „AI literacy“ means skills, knowledge and understanding that allow providers, deployers and affected persons, taking into account their respective rights and obligations in the context of this Regulation, to make an informed deployment of AI systems, as well as to gain awareness about the opportunities and risks of AI and possible harm it can cause;

(57) „testing in real-world conditions“ means the temporary testing of an AI system for its intended purpose in real-world conditions outside a laboratory or otherwise simulated environment, with a view to gathering reliable and robust data and to assessing and verifying the conformity of the AI system with the requirements of this Regulation and it does not qualify as placing the AI system on the market or putting it into service within the meaning of this Regulation, provided that all the conditions laid down in Article 57 or 60 are fulfilled;

(58) „subject“, for the purpose of real-world testing, means a natural person who participates in testing in real-world conditions;

(59) „informed consent“ means a subject's freely given, specific, unambiguous and voluntary expression of his or her willingness to participate in a particular testing in real-world conditions, after having been informed of all aspects of the testing that are relevant to the subject's decision to participate;

(60) „deep fake“ means AI-generated or manipulated image, audio or video content that resembles existing persons, objects, places, entities or events and would falsely appear to a person to be authentic or truthful;

(61) „widespread infringement“ means any act or omission contrary to Union law protecting the interest of individuals, which:

(a) has harmed or is likely to harm the collective interests of individuals residing in at least two Member States other than the Member State in which:
    (i) the act or omission originated or took place;
    (ii) the provider concerned, or, where applicable, its authorised representative is located or established; or
    (iii) the deployer is established, when the infringement is committed by the deployer;
(b) has caused, causes or is likely to cause harm to the collective interests of individuals and has common features, including the same unlawful practice or the same interest being infringed, and is occurring concurrently, committed by the same operator, in at least three Member States;

(62) „critical infrastructure" means critical infrastructure as defined in Article 2, point (4), of Directive (EU) 2022/2557;

(63) „general-purpose AI model" means an AI model, including where such an AI model is trained with a large amount of data using self-supervision at scale, that displays significant generality and is capable of competently performing a wide range of distinct tasks regardless of the way the model is placed on the market and that can be integrated into a variety of downstream systems or applications, except AI models that are used for research, development or prototyping activities before they are placed on the market;

(64) „high-impact capabilities" means capabilities that match or exceed the capabilities recorded in the most advanced general-purpose AI models;

(65) „systemic risk" means a risk that is specific to the high-impact capabilities of general-purpose AI models, having a significant impact on the Union market due to their reach, or due to actual or reasonably foreseeable negative effects on public health, safety, public security, fundamental rights, or the society as a whole, that can be propagated at scale across the value chain;

(66) „general-purpose AI system" means an AI system which is based on a general-purpose AI model and which has the capability to serve a variety of purposes, both for direct use as well as for integration in other AI systems;

(67) „floating-point operation" means any mathematical operation or assignment involving floating-point numbers, which are a subset of the real numbers typically represented on computers by an integer of fixed precision scaled by an integer exponent of a fixed base;

(68) „downstream provider" means a provider of an AI system, including a general-purpose AI system, which integrates an AI model, regardless of whether the AI model is provided by themselves and vertically integrated or provided by another entity based on contractual relations.

Article 4
AI literacy

Providers and deployers of AI systems shall take measures to ensure, to their best extent, a sufficient level of AI literacy of their staff and other persons dealing with the operation and use of AI systems on their behalf, taking into account their technical knowledge, experience, education and training and the context the AI systems are to be used in, and considering the persons or groups of persons on whom the AI systems are to be used.

CHAPTER II
PROHIBITED AI PRACTICES

Article 5
Prohibited AI practices

1. [1]The following AI practices shall be prohibited:

(a) the placing on the market, the putting into service or the use of an AI system that deploys subliminal techniques beyond a person's consciousness or purposefully manipulative or deceptive techniques, with the objective, or the effect of materially distorting the behaviour of a person or a group of persons by appreciably impairing their ability to make an informed decision, thereby causing them to take a decision that they would not have otherwise taken in a manner that causes or is reasonably likely to cause that person, another person or group of persons significant harm;
(b) the placing on the market, the putting into service or the use of an AI system that exploits any of the vulnerabilities of a natural person or a specific group of persons due to their age, disability or a specific social or economic situation, with the objective, or the effect, of materially distorting the behaviour of that person or a person belonging to that group in a manner that causes or is reasonably likely to cause that person or another person significant harm;
(c) the placing on the market, the putting into service or the use of AI systems for the evaluation or classification of natural persons or groups of persons over a certain period of time based on their social behaviour or known, inferred or predicted personal or personality characteristics, with the social score leading to either or both of the following:
  (i) detrimental or unfavourable treatment of certain natural persons or groups of persons in social contexts that are unrelated to the contexts in which the data was originally generated or collected;
  (ii) detrimental or unfavourable treatment of certain natural persons or groups of persons that is unjustified or disproportionate to their social behaviour or its gravity;
(d) the placing on the market, the putting into service for this specific purpose, or the use of an AI system for making risk assessments of natural persons in order to assess or predict the risk of a natural person committing a criminal offence, based solely on the profiling of a natural person or on assessing their personality traits and characteristics; this prohibition shall not apply to AI systems used to support the human assessment of the involvement of a person in a criminal activity, which is already based on objective and verifiable facts directly linked to a criminal activity;
(e) the placing on the market, the putting into service for this specific purpose, or the use of AI systems that create or expand facial recognition databases through the untargeted scraping of facial images from the internet or CCTV footage;
(f) the placing on the market, the putting into service for this specific purpose, or the use of AI systems to infer emotions of a natural person in the areas of workplace and education institutions, except where the use of the AI system is intended to be put in place or into the market for medical or safety reasons;
(g) the placing on the market, the putting into service for this specific purpose, or the use of biometric categorisation systems that categorise individually natural

persons based on their biometric data to deduce or infer their race, political opinions, trade union membership, religious or philosophical beliefs, sex life or sexual orientation; this prohibition does not cover any labelling or filtering of lawfully acquired biometric datasets, such as images, based on biometric data or categorizing of biometric data in the area of law enforcement;

(h) the use of „real-time“ remote biometric identification systems in publicly accessible spaces for the purposes of law enforcement, unless and in so far as such use is strictly necessary for one of the following objectives:
   (i) the targeted search for specific victims of abduction, trafficking in human beings or sexual exploitation of human beings, as well as the search for missing persons;
   (ii) the prevention of a specific, substantial and imminent threat to the life or physical safety of natural persons or a genuine and present or genuine and foreseeable threat of a terrorist attack;
   (iii) the localisation or identification of a person suspected of having committed a criminal offence, for the purpose of conducting a criminal investigation or prosecution or executing a criminal penalty for offences referred to in Annex II and punishable in the Member State concerned by a custodial sentence or a detention order for a maximum period of at least four years.

[2]Point (h) of the first subparagraph is without prejudice to Article 9 of Regulation (EU) 2016/679 for the processing of biometric data for purposes other than law enforcement.

2. [1]The use of „real-time“ remote biometric identification systems in publicly accessible spaces for the purposes of law enforcement for any of the objectives referred to in paragraph 1, first subparagraph, point (h), shall be deployed for the purposes set out in that point only to confirm the identity of the specifically targeted individual, and it shall take into account the following elements:

(a) the nature of the situation giving rise to the possible use, in particular the seriousness, probability and scale of the har m that would be caused if the system were not used;
(b) the consequences of the use of the system for the rights and freedoms of all persons concerned, in particular the seriousness, probability and scale of those consequences.

[2]In addition, the use of „real-time“ remote biometric identification systems in publicly accessible spaces for the purposes of law enforcement for any of the objectives referred to in paragraph 1, first subparagraph, point (h), of this Article shall comply with necessary and proportionate safeguards and conditions in relation to the use in accordance with the national law authorising the use thereof, in particular as regards the temporal, geographic and personal limitations. [3]The use of the „real-time“ remote biometric identification system in publicly accessible spaces shall be authorised only if the law enforcement authority has completed a fundamental rights impact assessment as provided for in Article 27 and has registered the system in the EU database according to Article 49. [4]However, in duly justified cases of urgency, the use of such systems may be commenced without the registration in the EU database, provided that such registration is completed without undue delay.

3.

(1) [1]For the purposes of paragraph 1, first subparagraph, point (h) and paragraph 2, each use for the purposes of law enforcement of a „real-time“ remote biometric

identification system in publicly accessible spaces shall be subject to a prior authorisation granted by a judicial authority or an independent administrative authority whose decision is binding of the Member State in which the use is to take place, issued upon a reasoned request and in accordance with the detailed rules of national law referred to in paragraph 5. [2]However, in a duly justified situation of urgency, the use of such system may be commenced without an authorisation provided that such authorisation is requested without undue delay, at the latest within 24 hours. [3]If such authorisation is rejected, the use shall be stopped with immediate effect and all the data, as well as the results and outputs of that use shall be immediately discarded and deleted.

(2) [1]The competent judicial authority or an independent administrative authority whose decision is binding shall grant the authorisation only where it is satisfied, on the basis of objective evidence or clear indications presented to it, that the use of the „real-time" remote biometric identification system concerned is necessary for, and proportionate to, achieving one of the objectives specified in paragraph 1, first subparagraph, point (h), as identified in the request and, in particular, remains limited to what is strictly necessary concerning the period of time as well as the geographic and personal scope. [2]In deciding on the request, that authority shall take into account the elements referred to in paragraph 2. [3]No decision that produces an adverse legal effect on a person may be taken based solely on the output of the „real-time" remote biometric identification system.

4. [1]Without prejudice to paragraph 3, each use of a „real-time" remote biometric identification system in publicly accessible spaces for law enforcement purposes shall be notified to the relevant market surveillance authority and the national data protection authority in accordance with the national rules referred to in paragraph 5. [2]The notification shall, as a minimum, contain the information specified under paragraph 6 and shall not include sensitive operational data.

5. [1]A Member State may decide to provide for the possibility to fully or partially authorise the use of „real-time" remote biometric identification systems in publicly accessible spaces for the purposes of law enforcement within the limits and under the conditions listed in paragraph 1, first subparagraph, point (h), and paragraphs 2 and 3. [2]Member States concerned shall lay down in their national law the necessary detailed rules for the request, issuance and exercise of, as well as supervision and reporting relating to, the authorisations referred to in paragraph 3. [3]Those rules shall also specify in respect of which of the objectives listed in paragraph 1, first subparagraph, point (h), including which of the criminal offences referred to in point (h)(iii) thereof, the competent authorities may be authorised to use those systems for the purposes of law enforcement. [4]Member States shall notify those rules to the Commission at the latest 30 days following the adoption thereof. [5]Member States may introduce, in accordance with Union law, more restrictive laws on the use of remote biometric identification systems.

6. [1]National market surveillance authorities and the national data protection authorities of Member States that have been notified of the use of „real-time" remote biometric identification systems in publicly accessible spaces for law enforcement purposes pursuant to paragraph 4 shall submit to the Commission annual reports on such use. [2]For that purpose, the Commission shall provide Member States and national market surveillance and data protection authorities with a template, including information on the number of the decisions taken by competent judicial authorities or an independent administrative authority whose decision is binding upon requests for authorisations in accordance with paragraph 3 and their result.

7. [1]The Commission shall publish annual reports on the use of real-time remote biometric identification systems in publicly accessible spaces for law enforcement purposes, based on aggregated data in Member States on the basis of the annual reports referred to in paragraph 6. [2]Those annual reports shall not include sensitive operational data of the related law enforcement activities.
8. This Article shall not affect the prohibitions that apply where an AI practice infringes other Union law.

CHAPTER III
HIGH-RISK AI SYSTEMS

Section 1
Classification of AI systems as high-risk

Article 6
Classification rules for high-risk AI systems

1. Irrespective of whether an AI system is placed on the market or put into service independently of the products referred to in points (a) and (b), that AI system shall be considered to be high-risk where both of the following conditions are fulfilled:

(a) the AI system is intended to be used as a safety component of a product, or the AI system is itself a product, covered by the Union harmonisation legislation listed in Annex I;
(b) the product whose safety component pursuant to point (a) is the AI system, or the AI system itself as a product, is required to undergo a third-party conformity assessment, with a view to the placing on the market or the putting into service of that product pursuant to the Union harmonisation legislation listed in Annex I.

2. In addition to the high-risk AI systems referred to in paragraph 1, AI systems referred to in Annex III shall be considered to be high-risk.
3.

(1) By derogation from paragraph 2, an AI system referred to in Annex III shall not be considered to be high-risk where it does not pose a significant risk of harm to the health, safety or fundamental rights of natural persons, including by not materially influencing the outcome of decision making.
(2) [1]The first subparagraph shall apply where any of the following conditions is fulfilled:
   (a) the AI system is intended to perform a narrow procedural task;
   (b) the AI system is intended to improve the result of a previously completed human activity;
   (c) the AI system is intended to detect decision-making patterns or deviations from prior decision-making patterns and is not meant to replace or influence the previously completed human assessment, without proper human review; or
   (d) the AI system is intended to perform a preparatory task to an assessment relevant for the purposes of the use cases listed in Annex III.

[2]Notwithstanding the first subparagraph, an AI system referred to in Annex III shall always be considered to be high-risk where the AI system performs profiling of natural persons.
4. [1]A provider who considers that an AI system referred to in Annex III is not high-risk shall document its assessment before that system is placed on the market or put into service. [2]Such provider shall be subject to the registration obligation set out in Article 49(2). [3]Upon request of national competent authorities, the provider shall provide the documentation of the assessment.
5. The Commission shall, after consulting the European Artificial Intelligence Board (the „Board"), and no later than 2 February 2026, provide guidelines specifying the practical implementation of this Article in line with Article 96 together with a comprehensive list of practical examples of use cases of AI systems that are high-risk and not high-risk.
6. The Commission is empowered to adopt delegated acts in accordance with Article 97 in order to amend paragraph 3, second subparagraph, of this Article by adding new conditions to those laid down therein, or by modifying them, where there is concrete and reliable evidence of the existence of AI systems that fall under the scope of Annex III, but do not pose a significant risk of harm to the health, safety or fundamental rights of natural persons.
7. The Commission shall adopt delegated acts in accordance with Article 97 in order to amend paragraph 3, second subparagraph, of this Article by deleting any of the conditions laid down therein, where there is concrete and reliable evidence that this is necessary to maintain the level of protection of health, safety and fundamental rights provided for by this Regulation.
8. Any amendment to the conditions laid down in paragraph 3, second subparagraph, adopted in accordance with paragraphs 6 and 7 of this Article shall not decrease the overall level of protection of health, safety and fundamental rights provided for by this Regulation and shall ensure consistency with the delegated acts adopted pursuant to Article 7(1), and take account of market and technological developments.

Article 7
Amendments to Annex III

1. The Commission is empowered to adopt delegated acts in accordance with Article 97 to amend Annex III by adding or modifying use-cases of high-risk AI systems where both of the following conditions are fulfilled:

(a) the AI systems are intended to be used in any of the areas listed in Annex III;
(b) the AI systems pose a risk of harm to health and safety, or an adverse impact on fundamental rights, and that risk is equivalent to, or greater than, the risk of harm or of adverse impact posed by the high-risk AI systems already referred to in Annex III.

2. When assessing the condition under paragraph 1, point (b), the Commission shall take into account the following criteria:

(a) the intended purpose of the AI system;
(b) the extent to which an AI system has been used or is likely to be used;
(c) the nature and amount of the data processed and used by the AI system, in particular whether special categories of personal data are processed;

(d) the extent to which the AI system acts autonomously and the possibility for a human to override a decision or recommendations that may lead to potential harm;
(e) the extent to which the use of an AI system has already caused harm to health and safety, has had an adverse impact on fundamental rights or has given rise to significant concerns in relation to the likelihood of such harm or adverse impact, as demonstrated, for example, by reports or documented allegations submitted to national competent authorities or by other reports, as appropriate;
(f) the potential extent of such harm or such adverse impact, in particular in terms of its intensity and its ability to affect multiple persons or to disproportionately affect a particular group of persons;
(g) the extent to which persons who are potentially harmed or suffer an adverse impact are dependent on the outcome produced with an AI system, in particular because for practical or legal reasons it is not reasonably possible to opt-out from that outcome;
(h) the extent to which there is an imbalance of power, or the persons who are potentially harmed or suffer an adverse impact are in a vulnerable position in relation to the deployer of an AI system, in particular due to status, authority, knowledge, economic or social circumstances, or age;
(i) the extent to which the outcome produced involving an AI system is easily corrigible or reversible, taking into account the technical solutions available to correct or reverse it, whereby outcomes having an adverse impact on health, safety or fundamental rights, shall not be considered to be easily corrigible or reversible;
(j) the magnitude and likelihood of benefit of the deployment of the AI system for individuals, groups, or society at large, including possible improvements in product safety;
(k) the extent to which existing Union law provides for:
    (i) effective measures of redress in relation to the risks posed by an AI system, with the exclusion of claims for damages;
    (ii) effective measures to prevent or substantially minimise those risks.

3. The Commission is empowered to adopt delegated acts in accordance with Article 97 to amend the list in Annex III by removing high-risk AI systems where both of the following conditions are fulfilled:

(a) the high-risk AI system concerned no longer poses any significant risks to fundamental rights, health or safety, taking into account the criteria listed in paragraph 2;
(b) the deletion does not decrease the overall level of protection of health, safety and fundamental rights under Union law.

Section 2
Requirements for high-risk AI systems

Article 8
Compliance with the requirements

1. [1]High-risk AI systems shall comply with the requirements laid down in this Section, taking into account their intended purpose as well as the generally acknowledged state of the art on AI and AI-related technologies. [2]The risk management system referred

to in Article 9 shall be taken into account when ensuring compliance with those requirements.
2. [1]Where a product contains an AI system, to which the requirements of this Regulation as well as requirements of the Union harmonisation legislation listed in Section A of Annex I apply, providers shall be responsible for ensuring that their product is fully compliant with all applicable requirements under applicable Union harmonisation legislation. [2]In ensuring the compliance of high-risk AI systems referred to in paragraph 1 with the requirements set out in this Section, and in order to ensure consistency, avoid duplication and minimise additional burdens, providers shall have a choice of integrating, as appropriate, the necessary testing and reporting processes, information and documentation they provide with regard to their product into documentation and procedures that already exist and are required under the Union harmonisation legislation listed in Section A of Annex I.

Article 9
Risk management system

1. A risk management system shall be established, implemented, documented and maintained in relation to high-risk AI systems.
2. [1]The risk management system shall be understood as a continuous iterative process planned and run throughout the entire lifecycle of a high-risk AI system, requiring regular systematic review and updating. [2]It shall comprise the following steps:

(a) the identification and analysis of the known and the reasonably foreseeable risks that the high-risk AI system can pose to health, safety or fundamental rights when the high-risk AI system is used in accordance with its intended purpose;
(b) the estimation and evaluation of the risks that may emerge when the high-risk AI system is used in accordance with its intended purpose, and under conditions of reasonably foreseeable misuse;
(c) the evaluation of other risks possibly arising, based on the analysis of data gathered from the post-market monitoring system referred to in Article 72;
(d) the adoption of appropriate and targeted risk management measures designed to address the risks identified pursuant to point (a).

3. The risks referred to in this Article shall concern only those which may be reasonably mitigated or eliminated through the development or design of the high-risk AI system, or the provision of adequate technical information.
4. The risk management measures referred to in paragraph 2, point (d), shall give due consideration to the effects and possible interaction resulting from the combined application of the requirements set out in this Section, with a view to minimising risks more effectively while achieving an appropriate balance in implementing the measures to fulfil those requirements.
5.

(1) The risk management measures referred to in paragraph 2, point (d), shall be such that the relevant residual risk associated with each hazard, as well as the overall residual risk of the high-risk AI systems is judged to be acceptable.
(2) [1]In identifying the most appropriate risk management measures, the following shall be ensured:

(a) elimination or reduction of risks identified and evaluated pursuant to paragraph 2 in as far as technically feasible through adequate design and development of the high-risk AI system;
(b) where appropriate, implementation of adequate mitigation and control measures addressing risks that cannot be eliminated;
(c) provision of information required pursuant to Article 13 and, where appropriate, training to deployers.

[2]With a view to eliminating or reducing risks related to the use of the high-risk AI system, due consideration shall be given to the technical knowledge, experience, education, the training to be expected by the deployer, and the presumable context in which the system is intended to be used.
6. [1]High-risk AI systems shall be tested for the purpose of identifying the most appropriate and targeted risk management measures. [2]Testing shall ensure that high-risk AI systems perform consistently for their intended purpose and that they are in compliance with the requirements set out in this Section.
7. Testing procedures may include testing in real-world conditions in accordance with Article 60.
8. [1]The testing of high-risk AI systems shall be performed, as appropriate, at any time throughout the development process, and, in any event, prior to their being placed on the market or put into service. [2]Testing shall be carried out against prior defined metrics and probabilistic thresholds that are appropriate to the intended purpose of the high-risk AI system.
9. When implementing the risk management system as provided for in paragraphs 1 to 7, providers shall give consideration to whether in view of its intended purpose the high-risk AI system is likely to have an adverse impact on persons under the age of 18 and, as appropriate, other vulnerable groups.
10. For providers of high-risk AI systems that are subject to requirements regarding internal risk management processes under other relevant provisions of Union law, the aspects provided in paragraphs 1 to 9 may be part of, or combined with, the risk management procedures established pursuant to that law.

Article 10
Data and data governance

1. High-risk AI systems which make use of techniques involving the training of AI models with data shall be developed on the basis of training, validation and testing data sets that meet the quality criteria referred to in paragraphs 2 to 5 whenever such data sets are used.
2. [1]Training, validation and testing data sets shall be subject to data governance and management practices appropriate for the intended purpose of the high-risk AI system. [2]Those practices shall concern in particular:

(a) the relevant design choices;
(b) data collection processes and the origin of data, and in the case of personal data, the original purpose of the data collection;
(c) relevant data-preparation processing operations, such as annotation, labelling, cleaning, updating, enrichment and aggregation;
(d) the formulation of assumptions, in particular with respect to the information that the data are supposed to measure and represent;

(e) an assessment of the availability, quantity and suitability of the data sets that are needed;
(f) examination in view of possible biases that are likely to affect the health and safety of persons, have a negative impact on fundamental rights or lead to discrimination prohibited under Union law, especially where data outputs influence inputs for future operations;
(g) appropriate measures to detect, prevent and mitigate possible biases identified according to point (f);
(h) the identification of relevant data gaps or shortcomings that prevent compliance with this Regulation, and how those gaps and shortcomings can be addressed.

3. [1]Training, validation and testing data sets shall be relevant, sufficiently representative, and to the best extent possible, free of errors and complete in view of the intended purpose. [2]They shall have the appropriate statistical properties, including, where applicable, as regards the persons or groups of persons in relation to whom the high-risk AI system is intended to be used. [3]Those characteristics of the data sets may be met at the level of individual data sets or at the level of a combination thereof.
4. Data sets shall take into account, to the extent required by the intended purpose, the characteristics or elements that are particular to the specific geographical, contextual, behavioural or functional setting within which the high-risk AI system is intended to be used.
5. [1]To the extent that it is strictly necessary for the purpose of ensuring bias detection and correction in relation to the high-risk AI systems in accordance with paragraph (2), points (f) and (g) of this Article, the providers of such systems may exceptionally process special categories of personal data, subject to appropriate safeguards for the fundamental rights and freedoms of natural persons. [2]In addition to the provisions set out in Regulations (EU) 2016/679 and (EU) 2018/1725 and Directive (EU) 2016/680, all the following conditions must be met in order for such processing to occur:

(a) the bias detection and correction cannot be effectively fulfilled by processing other data, including synthetic or anonymised data;
(b) the special categories of personal data are subject to technical limitations on the re-use of the personal data, and state-of-the-art security and privacy-preserving measures, including pseudonymisation;
(c) the special categories of personal data are subject to measures to ensure that the personal data processed are secured, protected, subject to suitable safeguards, including strict controls and documentation of the access, to avoid misuse and ensure that only authorised persons have access to those personal data with appropriate confidentiality obligations;
(d) the special categories of personal data are not to be transmitted, transferred or otherwise accessed by other parties;
(e) the special categories of personal data are deleted once the bias has been corrected or the personal data has reached the end of its retention period, whichever comes first;
(f) the records of processing activities pursuant to Regulations (EU) 2016/679 and (EU) 2018/1725 and Directive (EU) 2016/680 include the reasons why the processing of special categories of personal data was strictly necessary to detect and correct biases, and why that objective could not be achieved by processing other data.

6. For the development of high-risk AI systems not using techniques involving the training of AI models, paragraphs 2 to 5 apply only to the testing data sets.

Article 11
Technical documentation

1.

(1) The technical documentation of a high-risk AI system shall be drawn up before that system is placed on the market or put into service and shall be kept up-to date.

(2) [1]The technical documentation shall be drawn up in such a way as to demonstrate that the high-risk AI system complies with the requirements set out in this Section and to provide national competent authorities and notified bodies with the necessary information in a clear and comprehensive form to assess the compliance of the AI system with those requirements. [2]It shall contain, at a minimum, the elements set out in Annex IV. SMEs, including start-ups, may provide the elements of the technical documentation specified in Annex IV in a simplified manner. [3]To that end, the Commission shall establish a simplified technical documentation form targeted at the needs of small and microenterprises. [4]Where an SME, including a start-up, opts to provide the information required in Annex IV in a simplified manner, it shall use the form referred to in this paragraph. [5]Notified bodies shall accept the form for the purposes of the conformity assessment.

2. Where a high-risk AI system related to a product covered by the Union harmonisation legislation listed in Section A of Annex I is placed on the market or put into service, a single set of technical documentation shall be drawn up containing all the information set out in paragraph 1, as well as the information required under those legal acts.
3. The Commission is empowered to adopt delegated acts in accordance with Article 97 in order to amend Annex IV, where necessary, to ensure that, in light of technical progress, the technical documentation provides all the information necessary to assess the compliance of the system with the requirements set out in this Section.

Article 12
Record-keeping

1. High-risk AI systems shall technically allow for the automatic recording of events (logs) over the lifetime of the system.
2. In order to ensure a level of traceability of the functioning of a high-risk AI system that is appropriate to the intended purpose of the system, logging capabilities shall enable the recording of events relevant for:

(a) identifying situations that may result in the high-risk AI system presenting a risk within the meaning of Article 79(1) or in a substantial modification;
(b) facilitating the post-market monitoring referred to in Article 72; and
(c) monitoring the operation of high-risk AI systems referred to in Article 26(5).

3. For high-risk AI systems referred to in point 1 (a), of Annex III, the logging capabilities shall provide, at a minimum:

(a) recording of the period of each use of the system (start date and time and end date and time of each use);
(b) the reference database against which input data has been checked by the system;
(c) the input data for which the search has led to a match;
(d) the identification of the natural persons involved in the verification of the results, as referred to in Article 14(5).

Article 13
Transparency and provision of information to deployers

1. [1]High-risk AI systems shall be designed and developed in such a way as to ensure that their operation is sufficiently transparent to enable deployers to interpret a system's output and use it appropriately. [2]An appropriate type and degree of transparency shall be ensured with a view to achieving compliance with the relevant obligations of the provider and deployer set out in Section 3.
2. High-risk AI systems shall be accompanied by instructions for use in an appropriate digital format or otherwise that include concise, complete, correct and clear information that is relevant, accessible and comprehensible to deployers.
3. The instructions for use shall contain at least the following information:

(a) the identity and the contact details of the provider and, where applicable, of its authorised representative;
(b) the characteristics, capabilities and limitations of performance of the high-risk AI system, including:
    (i) its intended purpose;
    (ii) the level of accuracy, including its metrics, robustness and cybersecurity referred to in Article 15 against which the high-risk AI system has been tested and validated and which can be expected, and any known and foreseeable circumstances that may have an impact on that expected level of accuracy, robustness and cybersecurity;
    (iii) any known or foreseeable circumstance, related to the use of the high-risk AI system in accordance with its intended purpose or under conditions of reasonably foreseeable misuse, which may lead to risks to the health and safety or fundamental rights referred to in Article 9(2);
    (iv) where applicable, the technical capabilities and characteristics of the high-risk AI system to provide information that is relevant to explain its output;
    (v) when appropriate, its performance regarding specific persons or groups of persons on which the system is intended to be used;
    (vi) when appropriate, specifications for the input data, or any other relevant information in terms of the training, validation and testing data sets used, taking into account the intended purpose of the high-risk AI system;
    (vii) where applicable, information to enable deployers to interpret the output of the high-risk AI system and use it appropriately;
(c) the changes to the high-risk AI system and its performance which have been pre-determined by the provider at the moment of the initial conformity assessment, if any;
(d) the human oversight measures referred to in Article 14, including the technical measures put in place to facilitate the interpretation of the outputs of the high-risk AI systems by the deployers;

(e) the computational and hardware resources needed, the expected lifetime of the high-risk AI system and any necessary maintenance and care measures, including their frequency, to ensure the proper functioning of that AI system, including as regards software updates;
(f) where relevant, a description of the mechanisms included within the high-risk AI system that allows deployers to properly collect, store and interpret the logs in accordance with Article 12.

Article 14
Human oversight

1. High-risk AI systems shall be designed and developed in such a way, including with appropriate human-machine interface tools, that they can be effectively overseen by natural persons during the period in which they are in use.
2. Human oversight shall aim to prevent or minimise the risks to health, safety or fundamental rights that may emerge when a high-risk AI system is used in accordance with its intended purpose or under conditions of reasonably foreseeable misuse, in particular where such risks persist despite the application of other requirements set out in this Section.
3. The oversight measures shall be commensurate with the risks, level of autonomy and context of use of the high-risk AI system, and shall be ensured through either one or both of the following types of measures:

(a) measures identified and built, when technically feasible, into the high-risk AI system by the provider before it is placed on the market or put into service;
(b) measures identified by the provider before placing the high-risk AI system on the market or putting it into service and that are appropriate to be implemented by the deployer.

4. For the purpose of implementing paragraphs 1, 2 and 3, the high-risk AI system shall be provided to the deployer in such a way that natural persons to whom human oversight is assigned are enabled, as appropriate and proportionate:

(a) to properly understand the relevant capacities and limitations of the high-risk AI system and be able to duly monitor its operation, including in view of detecting and addressing anomalies, dysfunctions and unexpected performance;
(b) to remain aware of the possible tendency of automatically relying or over-relying on the output produced by a high-risk AI system (automation bias), in particular for high-risk AI systems used to provide information or recommendations for decisions to be taken by natural persons;
(c) to correctly interpret the high-risk AI system's output, taking into account, for example, the interpretation tools and methods available;
(d) to decide, in any particular situation, not to use the high-risk AI system or to otherwise disregard, override or reverse the output of the high-risk AI system;
(e) to intervene in the operation of the high-risk AI system or interrupt the system through a „stop" button or a similar procedure that allows the system to come to a halt in a safe state.

5.

(1) For high-risk AI systems referred to in point 1(a) of Annex III, the measures referred to in paragraph 3 of this Article shall be such as to ensure that, in addition,

no action or decision is taken by the deployer on the basis of the identification resulting from the system unless that identification has been separately verified and confirmed by at least two natural persons with the necessary competence, training and authority.

(2) The requirement for a separate verification by at least two natural persons shall not apply to high-risk AI systems used for the purposes of law enforcement, migration, border control or asylum, where Union or national law considers the application of this requirement to be disproportionate.

Article 15
Accuracy, robustness and cybersecurity

1. High-risk AI systems shall be designed and developed in such a way that they achieve an appropriate level of accuracy, robustness, and cybersecurity, and that they perform consistently in those respects throughout their lifecycle.
2. To address the technical aspects of how to measure the appropriate levels of accuracy and robustness set out in paragraph 1 and any other relevant performance metrics, the Commission shall, in cooperation with relevant stakeholders and organisations such as metrology and benchmarking authorities, encourage, as appropriate, the development of benchmarks and measurement methodologies.
3. The levels of accuracy and the relevant accuracy metrics of high-risk AI systems shall be declared in the accompanying instructions of use.
4.

(1) [1]High-risk AI systems shall be as resilient as possible regarding errors, faults or inconsistencies that may occur within the system or the environment in which the system operates, in particular due to their interaction with natural persons or other systems. [2]Technical and organisational measures shall be taken in this regard.

(2) The robustness of high-risk AI systems may be achieved through technical redundancy solutions, which may include backup or fail-safe plans.

(3) High-risk AI systems that continue to learn after being placed on the market or put into service shall be developed in such a way as to eliminate or reduce as far as possible the risk of possibly biased outputs influencing input for future operations (feedback loops), and as to ensure that any such feedback loops are duly addressed with appropriate mitigation measures.

5.

(1) High-risk AI systems shall be resilient against attempts by unauthorised third parties to alter their use, outputs or performance by exploiting system vulnerabilities.

(2) The technical solutions aiming to ensure the cybersecurity of high-risk AI systems shall be appropriate to the relevant circumstances and the risks.

(3) The technical solutions to address AI specific vulnerabilities shall include, where appropriate, measures to prevent, detect, respond to, resolve and control for attacks trying to manipulate the training data set (data poisoning), or pre-trained components used in training (model poisoning), inputs designed to cause the AI model to make a mistake (adversarial examples or model evasion), confidentiality attacks or model flaws.

Section 3
Obligations of providers and deployers of high-risk AI systems and other parties

Article 16
Obligations of providers of high-risk AI systems

Providers of high-risk AI systems shall:

(a) ensure that their high-risk AI systems are compliant with the requirements set out in Section 2;
(b) indicate on the high-risk AI system or, where that is not possible, on its packaging or its accompanying documentation, as applicable, their name, registered trade name or registered trade mark, the address at which they can be contacted;
(c) have a quality management system in place which complies with Article 17;
(d) keep the documentation referred to in Article 18;
(e) when under their control, keep the logs automatically generated by their high-risk AI systems as referred to in Article 19;
(f) ensure that the high-risk AI system undergoes the relevant conformity assessment procedure as referred to in Article 43, prior to its being placed on the market or put into service;
(g) draw up an EU declaration of conformity in accordance with Article 47;
(h) affix the CE marking to the high-risk AI system or, where that is not possible, on its packaging or its accompanying documentation, to indicate conformity with this Regulation, in accordance with Article 48;
(i) comply with the registration obligations referred to in Article 49(1);
(j) take the necessary corrective actions and provide information as required in Article 20;
(k) upon a reasoned request of a national competent authority, demonstrate the conformity of the high-risk AI system with the requirements set out in Section 2;
(l) ensure that the high-risk AI system complies with accessibility requirements in accordance with Directives (EU) 2016/2102 and (EU) 2019/882.

Article 17
Quality management system

1. [1]Providers of high-risk AI systems shall put a quality management system in place that ensures compliance with this Regulation. [2]That system shall be documented in a systematic and orderly manner in the form of written policies, procedures and instructions, and shall include at least the following aspects:

(a) a strategy for regulatory compliance, including compliance with conformity assessment procedures and procedures for the management of modifications to the high-risk AI system;
(b) techniques, procedures and systematic actions to be used for the design, design control and design verification of the high-risk AI system;
(c) techniques, procedures and systematic actions to be used for the development, quality control and quality assurance of the high-risk AI system;

(d) examination, test and validation procedures to be carried out before, during and after the development of the high-risk AI system, and the frequency with which they have to be carried out;
(e) technical specifications, including standards, to be applied and, where the relevant harmonised standards are not applied in full or do not cover all of the relevant requirements set out in Section 2, the means to be used to ensure that the high-risk AI system complies with those requirements;
(f) systems and procedures for data management, including data acquisition, data collection, data analysis, data labelling, data storage, data filtration, data mining, data aggregation, data retention and any other operation regarding the data that is performed before and for the purpose of the placing on the market or the putting into service of high-risk AI systems;
(g) the risk management system referred to in Article 9;
(h) the setting-up, implementation and maintenance of a post-market monitoring system, in accordance with Article 72;
(i) procedures related to the reporting of a serious incident in accordance with Article 73;
(j) the handling of communication with national competent authorities, other relevant authorities, including those providing or supporting the access to data, notified bodies, other operators, customers or other interested parties;
(k) systems and procedures for record-keeping of all relevant documentation and information;
(l) resource management, including security-of-supply related measures;
(m) an accountability framework setting out the responsibilities of the management and other staff with regard to all the aspects listed in this paragraph.

2. [1]The implementation of the aspects referred to in paragraph 1 shall be proportionate to the size of the provider's organisation. [2]Providers shall, in any event, respect the degree of rigour and the level of protection required to ensure the compliance of their high-risk AI systems with this Regulation.
3. Providers of high-risk AI systems that are subject to obligations regarding quality management systems or an equivalent function under relevant sectoral Union law may include the aspects listed in paragraph 1 as part of the quality management systems pursuant to that law.
4. [1]For providers that are financial institutions subject to requirements regarding their internal governance, arrangements or processes under Union financial services law, the obligation to put in place a quality management system, with the exception of paragraph 1, points (g), (h) and (i) of this Article, shall be deemed to be fulfilled by complying with the rules on internal governance arrangements or processes pursuant to the relevant Union financial services law. [2]To that end, any harmonised standards referred to in Article 40 shall be taken into account.

Article 18
Documentation keeping

1. The provider shall, for a period ending 10 years after the high-risk AI system has been placed on the market or put into service, keep at the disposal of the national competent authorities:

(a) the technical documentation referred to in Article 11;
(b) the documentation concerning the quality management system referred to in Article 17;
(c) the documentation concerning the changes approved by notified bodies, where applicable;
(d) the decisions and other documents issued by the notified bodies, where applicable;
(e) the EU declaration of conformity referred to in Article 47.

2. Each Member State shall determine conditions under which the documentation referred to in paragraph 1 remains at the disposal of the national competent authorities for the period indicated in that paragraph for the cases when a provider or its authorised representative established on its territory goes bankrupt or ceases its activity prior to the end of that period.
3. Providers that are financial institutions subject to requirements regarding their internal governance, arrangements or processes under Union financial services law shall maintain the technical documentation as part of the documentation kept under the relevant Union financial services law.

Article 19
Automatically generated logs

1. [1]Providers of high-risk AI systems shall keep the logs referred to in Article 12(1), automatically generated by their high-risk AI systems, to the extent such logs are under their control. [2]Without prejudice to applicable Union or national law, the logs shall be kept for a period appropriate to the intended purpose of the high-risk AI system, of at least six months, unless provided otherwise in the applicable Union or national law, in particular in Union law on the protection of personal data.
2. Providers that are financial institutions subject to requirements regarding their internal governance, arrangements or processes under Union financial services law shall maintain the logs automatically generated by their high-risk AI systems as part of the documentation kept under the relevant financial services law.

Article 20
Corrective actions and duty of information

1. [1]Providers of high-risk AI systems which consider or have reason to consider that a high-risk AI system that they have placed on the market or put into service is not in conformity with this Regulation shall immediately take the necessary corrective actions to bring that system into conformity, to withdraw it, to disable it, or to recall it, as appropriate. [2]They shall inform the distributors of the high-risk AI system concerned and, where applicable, the deployers, the authorised representative and importers accordingly.
2. Where the high-risk AI system presents a risk within the meaning of Article 79(1) and the provider becomes aware of that risk, it shall immediately investigate the causes, in collaboration with the reporting deployer, where applicable, and inform the market surveillance authorities competent for the high-risk AI system concerned and, where applicable, the notified body that issued a certificate for that high-risk AI sys-

tem in accordance with Article 44, in particular, of the nature of the non-compliance and of any relevant corrective action taken.

Article 21
Cooperation with competent authorities

1. Providers of high-risk AI systems shall, upon a reasoned request by a competent authority, provide that authority all the information and documentation necessary to demonstrate the conformity of the high-risk AI system with the requirements set out in Section 2, in a language which can be easily understood by the authority in one of the official languages of the institutions of the Union as indicated by the Member State concerned.
2. Upon a reasoned request by a competent authority, providers shall also give the requesting competent authority, as applicable, access to the automatically generated logs of the high-risk AI system referred to in Article 12(1), to the extent such logs are under their control.
3. Any information obtained by a competent authority pursuant to this Article shall be treated in accordance with the confidentiality obligations set out in Article 78.

Article 22
Authorised representatives of providers of high-risk AI systems

1. Prior to making their high-risk AI systems available on the Union market, providers established in third countries shall, by written mandate, appoint an authorised representative which is established in the Union.
2. The provider shall enable its authorised representative to perform the tasks specified in the mandate received from the provider.
3. [1]The authorised representative shall perform the tasks specified in the mandate received from the provider. [2]It shall provide a copy of the mandate to the market surveillance authorities upon request, in one of the official languages of the institutions of the Union, as indicated by the competent authority. [3]For the purposes of this Regulation, the mandate shall empower the authorised representative to carry out the following tasks:

(a) verify that the EU declaration of conformity referred to in Article 47 and the technical documentation referred to in Article 11 have been drawn up and that an appropriate conformity assessment procedure has been carried out by the provider;
(b) keep at the disposal of the competent authorities and national authorities or bodies referred to in Article 74(10), for a period of 10 years after the high-risk AI system has been placed on the market or put into service, the contact details of the provider that appointed the authorised representative, a copy of the EU declaration of conformity referred to in Article 47, the technical documentation and, if applicable, the certificate issued by the notified body;
(c) provide a competent authority, upon a reasoned request, with all the information and documentation, including that referred to in point (b) of this subparagraph, necessary to demonstrate the conformity of a high-risk AI system with the requirements set out in Section 2, including access to the logs, as referred to in

Article 12(1), automatically generated by the high-risk AI system, to the extent such logs are under the control of the provider;
(d) cooperate with competent authorities, upon a reasoned request, in any action the latter take in relation to the high-risk AI system, in particular to reduce and mitigate the risks posed by the high-risk AI system;
(e) where applicable, comply with the registration obligations referred to in Article 49(1), or, if the registration is carried out by the provider itself, ensure that the information referred to in point 3 of Section A of Annex VIII is correct.

[4]The mandate shall empower the authorised representative to be addressed, in addition to or instead of the provider, by the competent authorities, on all issues related to ensuring compliance with this Regulation.
4. [1]The authorised representative shall terminate the mandate if it considers or has reason to consider the provider to be acting contrary to its obligations pursuant to this Regulation. [2]In such a case, it shall immediately inform the relevant market surveillance authority, as well as, where applicable, the relevant notified body, about the termination of the mandate and the reasons therefor.

Article 23
Obligations of importers

1. Before placing a high-risk AI system on the market, importers shall ensure that the system is in conformity with this Regulation by verifying that:

(a) the relevant conformity assessment procedure referred to in Article 43 has been carried out by the provider of the high-risk AI system;
(b) the provider has drawn up the technical documentation in accordance with Article 11 and Annex IV;
(c) the system bears the required CE marking and is accompanied by the EU declaration of conformity referred to in Article 47 and instructions for use;
(d) the provider has appointed an authorised representative in accordance with Article 22(1).

2. [1]Where an importer has sufficient reason to consider that a high-risk AI system is not in conformity with this Regulation, or is falsified, or accompanied by falsified documentation, it shall not place the system on the market until it has been brought into conformity. [2]Where the high risk AI system presents a risk within the meaning of Article 79(1), the importer shall inform the provider of the system, the authorised representative and the market surveillance authorities to that effect.
3. Importers shall indicate their name, registered trade name or registered trade mark, and the address at which they can be contacted on the high-risk AI system and on its packaging or its accompanying documentation, where applicable.
4. Importers shall ensure that, while a high-risk AI system is under their responsibility, storage or transport conditions, where applicable, do not jeopardise its compliance with the requirements set out in Section 2.
5. Importers shall keep, for a period of 10 years after the high-risk AI system has been placed on the market or put into service, a copy of the certificate issued by the notified body, where applicable, of the instructions for use, and of the EU declaration of conformity referred to in Article 47.
6. [1]Importers shall provide the relevant competent authorities, upon a reasoned request, with all the necessary information and documentation, including that referred

to in paragraph 5, to demonstrate the conformity of a high-risk AI system with the requirements set out in Section 2 in a language which can be easily understood by them. [2]For this purpose, they shall also ensure that the technical documentation can be made available to those authorities.
7. Importers shall cooperate with the relevant competent authorities in any action those authorities take in relation to a high-risk AI system placed on the market by the importers, in particular to reduce and mitigate the risks posed by it.

Article 24
Obligations of distributors

1. Before making a high-risk AI system available on the market, distributors shall verify that it bears the required CE marking, that it is accompanied by a copy of the EU declaration of conformity referred to in Article 47 and instructions for use, and that the provider and the importer of that system, as applicable, have complied with their respective obligations as laid down in Article 16, points (b) and (c) and Article 23(3).
2. [1]Where a distributor considers or has reason to consider, on the basis of the information in its possession, that a high-risk AI system is not in conformity with the requirements set out in Section 2, it shall not make the high-risk AI system available on the market until the system has been brought into conformity with those requirements. [2]Furthermore, where the high-risk AI system presents a risk within the meaning of Article 79(1), the distributor shall inform the provider or the importer of the system, as applicable, to that effect.
3. Distributors shall ensure that, while a high-risk AI system is under their responsibility, storage or transport conditions, where applicable, do not jeopardise the compliance of the system with the requirements set out in Section 2.
4. [1]A distributor that considers or has reason to consider, on the basis of the information in its possession, a high-risk AI system which it has made available on the market not to be in conformity with the requirements set out in Section 2, shall take the corrective actions necessary to bring that system into conformity with those requirements, to withdraw it or recall it, or shall ensure that the provider, the importer or any relevant operator, as appropriate, takes those corrective actions. [2]Where the high-risk AI system presents a risk within the meaning of Article 79(1), the distributor shall immediately inform the provider or importer of the system and the authorities competent for the high-risk AI system concerned, giving details, in particular, of the non-compliance and of any corrective actions taken.
5. Upon a reasoned request from a relevant competent authority, distributors of a high-risk AI system shall provide that authority with all the information and documentation regarding their actions pursuant to paragraphs 1 to 4 necessary to demonstrate the conformity of that system with the requirements set out in Section 2.
6. Distributors shall cooperate with the relevant competent authorities in any action those authorities take in relation to a high-risk AI system made available on the market by the distributors, in particular to reduce or mitigate the risk posed by it.

Article 25
Responsibilities along the AI value chain

1. Any distributor, importer, deployer or other third-party shall be considered to be a provider of a high-risk AI system for the purposes of this Regulation and shall be subject to the obligations of the provider under Article 16, in any of the following circumstances:

(a) they put their name or trademark on a high-risk AI system already placed on the market or put into service, without prejudice to contractual arrangements stipulating that the obligations are otherwise allocated;
(b) they make a substantial modification to a high-risk AI system that has already been placed on the market or has already been put into service in such a way that it remains a high-risk AI system pursuant to Article 6;
(c) they modify the intended purpose of an AI system, including a general-purpose AI system, which has not been classified as high-risk and has already been placed on the market or put into service in such a way that the AI system concerned becomes a high-risk AI system in accordance with Article 6.

2. [1]Where the circumstances referred to in paragraph 1 occur, the provider that initially placed the AI system on the market or put it into service shall no longer be considered to be a provider of that specific AI system for the purposes of this Regulation. [2]That initial provider shall closely cooperate with new providers and shall make available the necessary information and provide the reasonably expected technical access and other assistance that are required for the fulfilment of the obligations set out in this Regulation, in particular regarding the compliance with the conformity assessment of high-risk AI systems. [3]This paragraph shall not apply in cases where the initial provider has clearly specified that its AI system is not to be changed into a high-risk AI system and therefore does not fall under the obligation to hand over the documentation.
3. In the case of high-risk AI systems that are safety components of products covered by the Union harmonisation legislation listed in Section A of Annex I, the product manufacturer shall be considered to be the provider of the high-risk AI system, and shall be subject to the obligations under Article 16 under either of the following circumstances:

(a) the high-risk AI system is placed on the market together with the product under the name or trademark of the product manufacturer;
(b) the high-risk AI system is put into service under the name or trademark of the product manufacturer after the product has been placed on the market.

4.

(1) [1]The provider of a high-risk AI system and the third party that supplies an AI system, tools, services, components, or processes that are used or integrated in a high-risk AI system shall, by written agreement, specify the necessary information, capabilities, technical access and other assistance based on the generally acknowledged state of the art, in order to enable the provider of the high-risk AI system to fully comply with the obligations set out in this Regulation. [2]This paragraph shall not apply to third parties making accessible to the public tools, services, processes, or components, other than general-purpose AI models, under a free and open-source licence.

(2) [1]The AI Office may develop and recommend voluntary model terms for contracts between providers of high-risk AI systems and third parties that supply tools, services, components or processes that are used for or integrated into high-risk AI systems. [2]When developing those voluntary model terms, the AI Office shall take into account possible contractual requirements applicable in specific sectors or business cases. [3]The voluntary model terms shall be published and be available free of charge in an easily usable electronic format.

5. Paragraphs 2 and 3 are without prejudice to the need to observe and protect intellectual property rights, confidential business information and trade secrets in accordance with Union and national law.

Article 26
Obligations of deployers of high-risk AI systems

1. Deployers of high-risk AI systems shall take appropriate technical and organisational measures to ensure they use such systems in accordance with the instructions for use accompanying the systems, pursuant to paragraphs 3 and 6.
2. Deployers shall assign human oversight to natural persons who have the necessary competence, training and authority, as well as the necessary support.
3. The obligations set out in paragraphs 1 and 2, are without prejudice to other deployer obligations under Union or national law and to the deployer's freedom to organise its own resources and activities for the purpose of implementing the human oversight measures indicated by the provider.
4. Without prejudice to paragraphs 1 and 2, to the extent the deployer exercises control over the input data, that deployer shall ensure that input data is relevant and sufficiently representative in view of the intended purpose of the high-risk AI system.
5.

(1) [1]Deployers shall monitor the operation of the high-risk AI system on the basis of the instructions for use and, where relevant, inform providers in accordance with Article 72. [2]Where deployers have reason to consider that the use of the high-risk AI system in accordance with the instructions may result in that AI system presenting a risk within the meaning of Article 79(1), they shall, without undue delay, inform the provider or distributor and the relevant market surveillance authority, and shall suspend the use of that system. [3]Where deployers have identified a serious incident, they shall also immediately inform first the provider, and then the importer or distributor and the relevant market surveillance authorities of that incident. [4]If the deployer is not able to reach the provider, Article 73 shall apply *mutatis mutandis*. [5]This obligation shall not cover sensitive operational data of deployers of AI systems which are law enforcement authorities.

(2) For deployers that are financial institutions subject to requirements regarding their internal governance, arrangements or processes under Union financial services law, the monitoring obligation set out in the first subparagraph shall be deemed to be fulfilled by complying with the rules on internal governance arrangements, processes and mechanisms pursuant to the relevant financial service law.

6.

(1) Deployers of high-risk AI systems shall keep the logs automatically generated by that high-risk AI system to the extent such logs are under their control, for a period appropriate to the intended purpose of the high-risk AI system, of at least six months, unless provided otherwise in applicable Union or national law, in particular in Union law on the protection of personal data.
(2) Deployers that are financial institutions subject to requirements regarding their internal governance, arrangements or processes under Union financial services law shall maintain the logs as part of the documentation kept pursuant to the relevant Union financial service law.

7. [1]Before putting into service or using a high-risk AI system at the workplace, deployers who are employers shall inform workers' representatives and the affected workers that they will be subject to the use of the high-risk AI system. [2]This information shall be provided, where applicable, in accordance with the rules and procedures laid down in Union and national law and practice on information of workers and their representatives.
8. [1]Deployers of high-risk AI systems that are public authorities, or Union institutions, bodies, offices or agencies shall comply with the registration obligations referred to in Article 49. [2]When such deployers find that the high-risk AI system that they envisage using has not been registered in the EU database referred to in Article 71, they shall not use that system and shall inform the provider or the distributor.
9. Where applicable, deployers of high-risk AI systems shall use the information provided under Article 13 of this Regulation to comply with their obligation to carry out a data protection impact assessment under Article 35 of Regulation (EU) 2016/679 or Article 27 of Directive (EU) 2016/680.
10.

(1) [1]Without prejudice to Directive (EU) 2016/680, in the framework of an investigation for the targeted search of a person suspected or convicted of having committed a criminal offence, the deployer of a high-risk AI system for post-remote biometric identification shall request an authorisation, *ex ante*, or without undue delay and no later than 48 hours, by a judicial authority or an administrative authority whose decision is binding and subject to judicial review, for the use of that system, except when it is used for the initial identification of a potential suspect based on objective and verifiable facts directly linked to the offence. [2]Each use shall be limited to what is strictly necessary for the investigation of a specific criminal offence.
(2) If the authorisation requested pursuant to the first subparagraph is rejected, the use of the post-remote biometric identification system linked to that requested authorisation shall be stopped with immediate effect and the personal data linked to the use of the high-risk AI system for which the authorisation was requested shall be deleted.
(3) [1]In no case shall such high-risk AI system for post-remote biometric identification be used for law enforcement purposes in an untargeted way, without any link to a criminal offence, a criminal proceeding, a genuine and present or genuine and foreseeable threat of a criminal offence, or the search for a specific missing person. [2]It shall be ensured that no decision that produces an adverse legal effect on a person may be taken by the law enforcement authorities based solely on the output of such post-remote biometric identification systems.

(4) This paragraph is without prejudice to Article 9 of Regulation (EU) 2016/679 and Article 10 of Directive (EU) 2016/680 for the processing of biometric data.

(5) [1]Regardless of the purpose or deployer, each use of such high-risk AI systems shall be documented in the relevant police file and shall be made available to the relevant market surveillance authority and the national data protection authority upon request, excluding the disclosure of sensitive operational data related to law enforcement. [2]This subparagraph shall be without prejudice to the powers conferred by Directive (EU) 2016/680 on supervisory authorities.

(6) [1]Deployers shall submit annual reports to the relevant market surveillance and national data protection authorities on their use of post-remote biometric identification systems, excluding the disclosure of sensitive operational data related to law enforcement. [2]The reports may be aggregated to cover more than one deployment.

(7) Member States may introduce, in accordance with Union law, more restrictive laws on the use of post-remote biometric identification systems.

11. [1]Without prejudice to Article 50 of this Regulation, deployers of high-risk AI systems referred to in Annex III that make decisions or assist in making decisions related to natural persons shall inform the natural persons that they are subject to the use of the high-risk AI system. [2]For high-risk AI systems used for law enforcement purposes Article 13 of Directive (EU) 2016/680 shall apply.

12. Deployers shall cooperate with the relevant competent authorities in any action those authorities take in relation to the high-risk AI system in order to implement this Regulation.

Article 27
Fundamental rights impact assessment for high-risk AI systems

1. [1]Prior to deploying a high-risk AI system referred to in Article 6(2), with the exception of high-risk AI systems intended to be used in the area listed in point 2 of Annex III, deployers that are bodies governed by public law, or are private entities providing public services, and deployers of high-risk AI systems referred to in points 5 (b) and (c) of Annex III, shall perform an assessment of the impact on fundamental rights that the use of such system may produce. [2]For that purpose, deployers shall perform an assessment consisting of:

(a) a description of the deployer's processes in which the high-risk AI system will be used in line with its intended purpose;
(b) a description of the period of time within which, and the frequency with which, each high-risk AI system is intended to be used;
(c) the categories of natural persons and groups likely to be affected by its use in the specific context;
(d) the specific risks of harm likely to have an impact on the categories of natural persons or groups of persons identified pursuant to point (c) of this paragraph, taking into account the information given by the provider pursuant to Article 13;
(e) a description of the implementation of human oversight measures, according to the instructions for use;
(f) the measures to be taken in the case of the materialisation of those risks, including the arrangements for internal governance and complaint mechanisms.

2. [1]The obligation laid down in paragraph 1 applies to the first use of the high-risk AI system. [2]The deployer may, in similar cases, rely on previously conducted fundamental rights impact assessments or existing impact assessments carried out by provider. [3]If, during the use of the high-risk AI system, the deployer considers that any of the elements listed in paragraph 1 has changed or is no longer up to date, the deployer shall take the necessary steps to update the information.
3. [1]Once the assessment referred to in paragraph 1 of this Article has been performed, the deployer shall notify the market surveillance authority of its results, submitting the filled-out template referred to in paragraph 5 of this Article as part of the notification. [2]In the case referred to in Article 46(1), deployers may be exempt from that obligation to notify.
4. If any of the obligations laid down in this Article is already met through the data protection impact assessment conducted pursuant to Article 35 of Regulation (EU) 2016/679 or Article 27 of Directive (EU) 2016/680, the fundamental rights impact assessment referred to in paragraph 1 of this Article shall complement that data protection impact assessment.
5. The AI Office shall develop a template for a questionnaire, including through an automated tool, to facilitate deployers in complying with their obligations under this Article in a simplified manner.

Section 4
Notifying authorities and notified bodies

Article 28
Notifying authorities

1. [1]Each Member State shall designate or establish at least one notifying authority responsible for setting up and carrying out the necessary procedures for the assessment, designation and notification of conformity assessment bodies and for their monitoring. [2]Those procedures shall be developed in cooperation between the notifying authorities of all Member States.
2. Member States may decide that the assessment and monitoring referred to in paragraph 1 is to be carried out by a national accreditation body within the meaning of, and in accordance with, Regulation (EC) No 765/2008.
3. Notifying authorities shall be established, organised and operated in such a way that no conflict of interest arises with conformity assessment bodies, and that the objectivity and impartiality of their activities are safeguarded.
4. Notifying authorities shall be organised in such a way that decisions relating to the notification of conformity assessment bodies are taken by competent persons different from those who carried out the assessment of those bodies.
5. Notifying authorities shall offer or provide neither any activities that conformity assessment bodies perform, nor any consultancy services on a commercial or competitive basis.
6. Notifying authorities shall safeguard the confidentiality of the information that they obtain, in accordance with Article 78.
7. [1]Notifying authorities shall have an adequate number of competent personnel at their disposal for the proper performance of their tasks. [2]Competent personnel shall have the necessary expertise, where applicable, for their function, in fields such as information technologies, AI and law, including the supervision of fundamental rights.

Article 29
Application of a conformity assessment body for notification

1. Conformity assessment bodies shall submit an application for notification to the notifying authority of the Member State in which they are established.
2.

(1) The application for notification shall be accompanied by a description of the conformity assessment activities, the conformity assessment module or modules and the types of AI systems for which the conformity assessment body claims to be competent, as well as by an accreditation certificate, where one exists, issued by a national accreditation body attesting that the conformity assessment body fulfils the requirements laid down in Article 31.
(2) Any valid document related to existing designations of the applicant notified body under any other Union harmonisation legislation shall be added.

3. Where the conformity assessment body concerned cannot provide an accreditation certificate, it shall provide the notifying authority with all the documentary evidence necessary for the verification, recognition and regular monitoring of its compliance with the requirements laid down in Article 31.
4. [1]For notified bodies which are designated under any other Union harmonisation legislation, all documents and certificates linked to those designations may be used to support their designation procedure under this Regulation, as appropriate. [2]The notified body shall update the documentation referred to in paragraphs 2 and 3 of this Article whenever relevant changes occur, in order to enable the authority responsible for notified bodies to monitor and verify continuous compliance with all the requirements laid down in Article 31.

Article 30
Notification procedure

1. Notifying authorities may notify only conformity assessment bodies which have satisfied the requirements laid down in Article 31.
2. Notifying authorities shall notify the Commission and the other Member States, using the electronic notification tool developed and managed by the Commission, of each conformity assessment body referred to in paragraph 1.
3. [1]The notification referred to in paragraph 2 of this Article shall include full details of the conformity assessment activities, the conformity assessment module or modules, the types of AI systems concerned, and the relevant attestation of competence. [2]Where a notification is not based on an accreditation certificate as referred to in Article 29(2), the notifying authority shall provide the Commission and the other Member States with documentary evidence which attests to the competence of the conformity assessment body and to the arrangements in place to ensure that that body will be monitored regularly and will continue to satisfy the requirements laid down in Article 31.
4. The conformity assessment body concerned may perform the activities of a notified body only where no objections are raised by the Commission or the other Member States within two weeks of a notification by a notifying authority where it includes an accreditation certificate referred to in Article 29(2), or within two months of a notifi-

cation by the notifying authority where it includes documentary evidence referred to in Article 29(3).
5. [1]Where objections are raised, the Commission shall, without delay, enter into consultations with the relevant Member States and the conformity assessment body. [2]In view thereof, the Commission shall decide whether the authorisation is justified. [3]The Commission shall address its decision to the Member State concerned and to the relevant conformity assessment body.

Article 31
Requirements relating to notified bodies

1. A notified body shall be established under the national law of a Member State and shall have legal personality.
2. Notified bodies shall satisfy the organisational, quality management, resources and process requirements that are necessary to fulfil their tasks, as well as suitable cybersecurity requirements.
3. The organisational structure, allocation of responsibilities, reporting lines and operation of notified bodies shall ensure confidence in their performance, and in the results of the conformity assessment activities that the notified bodies conduct.
4. [1]Notified bodies shall be independent of the provider of a high-risk AI system in relation to which they perform conformity assessment activities. [2]Notified bodies shall also be independent of any other operator having an economic interest in high-risk AI systems assessed, as well as of any competitors of the provider. [3]This shall not preclude the use of assessed high-risk AI systems that are necessary for the operations of the conformity assessment body, or the use of such high-risk AI systems for personal purposes.
5. [1]Neither a conformity assessment body, its top-level management nor the personnel responsible for carrying out its conformity assessment tasks shall be directly involved in the design, development, marketing or use of high-risk AI systems, nor shall they represent the parties engaged in those activities. [2]They shall not engage in any activity that might conflict with their independence of judgement or integrity in relation to conformity assessment activities for which they are notified. [3]This shall, in particular, apply to consultancy services.
6. [1]Notified bodies shall be organised and operated so as to safeguard the independence, objectivity and impartiality of their activities. [2]Notified bodies shall document and implement a structure and procedures to safeguard impartiality and to promote and apply the principles of impartiality throughout their organisation, personnel and assessment activities.
7. [1]Notified bodies shall have documented procedures in place ensuring that their personnel, committees, subsidiaries, subcontractors and any associated body or personnel of external bodies maintain, in accordance with Article 78, the confidentiality of the information which comes into their possession during the performance of conformity assessment activities, except when its disclosure is required by law. [2]The staff of notified bodies shall be bound to observe professional secrecy with regard to all information obtained in carrying out their tasks under this Regulation, except in relation to the notifying authorities of the Member State in which their activities are carried out.

8. Notified bodies shall have procedures for the performance of activities which take due account of the size of a provider, the sector in which it operates, its structure, and the degree of complexity of the AI system concerned.
9. Notified bodies shall take out appropriate liability insurance for their conformity assessment activities, unless liability is assumed by the Member State in which they are established in accordance with national law or that Member State is itself directly responsible for the conformity assessment.
10. Notified bodies shall be capable of carrying out all their tasks under this Regulation with the highest degree of professional integrity and the requisite competence in the specific field, whether those tasks are carried out by notified bodies themselves or on their behalf and under their responsibility.
11. [1]Notified bodies shall have sufficient internal competences to be able effectively to evaluate the tasks conducted by external parties on their behalf. [2]The notified body shall have permanent availability of sufficient administrative, technical, legal and scientific personnel who possess experience and knowledge relating to the relevant types of AI systems, data and data computing, and relating to the requirements set out in Section 2.
12. [1]Notified bodies shall participate in coordination activities as referred to in Article 38. [2]They shall also take part directly, or be represented in, European standardisation organisations, or ensure that they are aware and up to date in respect of relevant standards.

Article 32
Presumption of conformity with requirements relating to notified bodies

Where a conformity assessment body demonstrates its conformity with the criteria laid down in the relevant harmonised standards or parts thereof, the references of which have been published in the *Official Journal of the European Union*, it shall be presumed to comply with the requirements set out in Article 31 in so far as the applicable harmonised standards cover those requirements.

Article 33
Subsidiaries of notified bodies and subcontracting

1. Where a notified body subcontracts specific tasks connected with the conformity assessment or has recourse to a subsidiary, it shall ensure that the subcontractor or the subsidiary meets the requirements laid down in Article 31, and shall inform the notifying authority accordingly.
2. Notified bodies shall take full responsibility for the tasks performed by any subcontractors or subsidiaries.
3. [1]Activities may be subcontracted or carried out by a subsidiary only with the agreement of the provider. [2]Notified bodies shall make a list of their subsidiaries publicly available.
4. The relevant documents concerning the assessment of the qualifications of the subcontractor or the subsidiary and the work carried out by them under this Regulation shall be kept at the disposal of the notifying authority for a period of five years from the termination date of the subcontracting.

Article 34
Operational obligations of notified bodies

1. Notified bodies shall verify the conformity of high-risk AI systems in accordance with the conformity assessment procedures set out in Article 43.
2. [1]Notified bodies shall avoid unnecessary burdens for providers when performing their activities, and take due account of the size of the provider, the sector in which it operates, its structure and the degree of complexity of the high-risk AI system concerned, in particular in view of minimising administrative burdens and compliance costs for micro- and small enterprises within the meaning of Recommendation 2003/361/EC. [2]The notified body shall, nevertheless, respect the degree of rigour and the level of protection required for the compliance of the high-risk AI system with the requirements of this Regulation.
3. Notified bodies shall make available and submit upon request all relevant documentation, including the providers' documentation, to the notifying authority referred to in Article 28 to allow that authority to conduct its assessment, designation, notification and monitoring activities, and to facilitate the assessment outlined in this Section.

Article 35
Identification numbers and lists of notified bodies

1. The Commission shall assign a single identification number to each notified body, even where a body is notified under more than one Union act.
2. [1]The Commission shall make publicly available the list of the bodies notified under this Regulation, including their identification numbers and the activities for which they have been notified. [2]The Commission shall ensure that the list is kept up to date.

Article 36
Changes to notifications

1. The notifying authority shall notify the Commission and the other Member States of any relevant changes to the notification of a notified body via the electronic notification tool referred to in Article 30(2).
2.

(1) The procedures laid down in Articles 29 and 30 shall apply to extensions of the scope of the notification.
(2) For changes to the notification other than extensions of its scope, the procedures laid down in paragraphs (3) to (9) shall apply.

3. [1]Where a notified body decides to cease its conformity assessment activities, it shall inform the notifying authority and the providers concerned as soon as possible and, in the case of a planned cessation, at least one year before ceasing its activities. [2]The certificates of the notified body may remain valid for a period of nine months after cessation of the notified body's activities, on condition that another notified body has confirmed in writing that it will assume responsibilities for the high-risk AI systems covered by those certificates. [3]The latter notified body shall complete a full assessment of the high-risk AI systems affected by the end of that nine-month-period before issuing new certificates for those systems. [4]Where the notified body has ceased its activity, the notifying authority shall withdraw the designation.

4. [1]Where a notifying authority has sufficient reason to consider that a notified body no longer meets the requirements laid down in Article 31, or that it is failing to fulfil its obligations, the notifying authority shall without delay investigate the matter with the utmost diligence. [2]In that context, it shall inform the notified body concerned about the objections raised and give it the possibility to make its views known. [3]If the notifying authority comes to the conclusion that the notified body no longer meets the requirements laid down in Article 31 or that it is failing to fulfil its obligations, it shall restrict, suspend or withdraw the designation as appropriate, depending on the seriousness of the failure to meet those requirements or fulfil those obligations. [4]It shall immediately inform the Commission and the other Member States accordingly.
5. Where its designation has been suspended, restricted, or fully or partially withdrawn, the notified body shall inform the providers concerned within 10 days.
6. In the event of the restriction, suspension or withdrawal of a designation, the notifying authority shall take appropriate steps to ensure that the files of the notified body concerned are kept, and to make them available to notifying authorities in other Member States and to market surveillance authorities at their request.
7. In the event of the restriction, suspension or withdrawal of a designation, the notifying authority shall:

(a) assess the impact on the certificates issued by the notified body;
(b) submit a report on its findings to the Commission and the other Member States within three months of having notified the changes to the designation;
(c) require the notified body to suspend or withdraw, within a reasonable period of time determined by the authority, any certificates which were unduly issued, in order to ensure the continuing conformity of high-risk AI systems on the market;
(d) inform the Commission and the Member States about certificates the suspension or withdrawal of which it has required;
(e) provide the national competent authorities of the Member State in which the provider has its registered place of business with all relevant information about the certificates of which it has required the suspension or withdrawal; that authority shall take the appropriate measures, where necessary, to avoid a potential risk to health, safety or fundamental rights.

8. With the exception of certificates unduly issued, and where a designation has been suspended or restricted, the certificates shall remain valid in one of the following circumstances:

(a) the notifying authority has confirmed, within one month of the suspension or restriction, that there is no risk to health, safety or fundamental rights in relation to certificates affected by the suspension or restriction, and the notifying authority has outlined a timeline for actions to remedy the suspension or restriction; or
(b) the notifying authority has confirmed that no certificates relevant to the suspension will be issued, amended or re-issued during the course of the suspension or restriction, and states whether the notified body has the capability of continuing to monitor and remain responsible for existing certificates issued for the period of the suspension or restriction; in the event that the notifying authority determines that the notified body does not have the capability to support existing certificates issued, the provider of the system covered by the certificate shall confirm in writing to the national competent authorities of the Member State in which it has its registered place of business, within three months of the suspension or restriction, that another qualified notified body is temporarily assuming the functions of the

notified body to monitor and remain responsible for the certificates during the period of suspension or restriction.

9.

(1) [1]With the exception of certificates unduly issued, and where a designation has been withdrawn, the certificates shall remain valid for a period of nine months under the following circumstances:

(a) the national competent authority of the Member State in which the provider of the high-risk AI system covered by the certificate has its registered place of business has confirmed that there is no risk to health, safety or fundamental rights associated with the high-risk AI systems concerned; and

(b) another notified body has confirmed in writing that it will assume immediate responsibility for those AI systems and completes its assessment within 12 months of the withdrawal of the designation.

[2]In the circumstances referred to in the first subparagraph, the national competent authority of the Member State in which the provider of the system covered by the certificate has its place of business may extend the provisional validity of the certificates for additional periods of three months, which shall not exceed 12 months in total.

(2) The national competent authority or the notified body assuming the functions of the notified body affected by the change of designation shall immediately inform the Commission, the other Member States and the other notified bodies thereof.

Article 37
Challenge to the competence of notified bodies

1. The Commission shall, where necessary, investigate all cases where there are reasons to doubt the competence of a notified body or the continued fulfilment by a notified body of the requirements laid down in Article 31 and of its applicable responsibilities.

2. The notifying authority shall provide the Commission, on request, with all relevant information relating to the notification or the maintenance of the competence of the notified body concerned.

3. The Commission shall ensure that all sensitive information obtained in the course of its investigations pursuant to this Article is treated confidentially in accordance with Article 78.

4. [1]Where the Commission ascertains that a notified body does not meet or no longer meets the requirements for its notification, it shall inform the notifying Member State accordingly and request it to take the necessary corrective measures, including the suspension or withdrawal of the notification if necessary. [2]Where the Member State fails to take the necessary corrective measures, the Commission may, by means of an implementing act, suspend, restrict or withdraw the designation. [3]That implementing act shall be adopted in accordance with the examination procedure referred to in Article 98(2).

Article 38
Coordination of notified bodies

1. The Commission shall ensure that, with regard to high-risk AI systems, appropriate coordination and cooperation between notified bodies active in the conformity assessment procedures pursuant to this Regulation are put in place and properly operated in the form of a sectoral group of notified bodies.
2. Each notifying authority shall ensure that the bodies notified by it participate in the work of a group referred to in paragraph 1, directly or through designated representatives.
3. The Commission shall provide for the exchange of knowledge and best practices between notifying authorities.

Article 39
Conformity assessment bodies of third countries

Conformity assessment bodies established under the law of a third country with which the Union has concluded an agreement may be authorised to carry out the activities of notified bodies under this Regulation, provided that they meet the requirements laid down in Article 31 or they ensure an equivalent level of compliance.

Section 5
Standards, conformity assessment, certificates, registration

Article 40
Harmonised standards and standardisation deliverables

1. High-risk AI systems or general-purpose AI models which are in conformity with harmonised standards or parts thereof the references of which have been published in the *Official Journal of the European Union* in accordance with Regulation (EU) No 1025/2012 shall be presumed to be in conformity with the requirements set out in Section 2 of this Chapter or, as applicable, with the obligations set out in of Chapter V, Sections 2 and 3, of this Regulation, to the extent that those standards cover those requirements or obligations.
2.

(1) [1]In accordance with Article 10 of Regulation (EU) No 1025/2012, the Commission shall issue, without undue delay, standardisation requests covering all requirements set out in Section 2 of this Chapter and, as applicable, standardisation requests covering obligations set out in Chapter V, Sections 2 and 3, of this Regulation. [2]The standardisation request shall also ask for deliverables on reporting and documentation processes to improve AI systems' resource performance, such as reducing the high-risk AI system's consumption of energy and of other resources during its lifecycle, and on the energy-efficient development of general-purpose AI models. [3]When preparing a standardisation request, the Commission shall consult the Board and relevant stakeholders, including the advisory forum.

(2) When issuing a standardisation request to European standardisation organisations, the Commission shall specify that standards have to be clear, consistent, including with the standards developed in the various sectors for products covered by the existing Union harmonisation legislation listed in Annex I, and aiming

to ensure that high-risk AI systems or general-purpose AI models placed on the market or put into service in the Union meet the relevant requirements or obligations laid down in this Regulation.

(3) The Commission shall request the European standardisation organisations to provide evidence of their best efforts to fulfil the objectives referred to in the first and the second subparagraph of this paragraph in accordance with Article 24 of Regulation (EU) No 1025/2012.

3. The participants in the standardisation process shall seek to promote investment and innovation in AI, including through increasing legal certainty, as well as the competitiveness and growth of the Union market, to contribute to strengthening global cooperation on standardisation and taking into account existing international standards in the field of AI that are consistent with Union values, fundamental rights and interests, and to enhance multi-stakeholder governance ensuring a balanced representation of interests and the effective participation of all relevant stakeholders in accordance with Articles 5, 6, and 7 of Regulation (EU) No 1025/2012.

Article 41
Common specifications

1.

(1) [1]The Commission may adopt, implementing acts establishing common specifications for the requirements set out in Section 2 of this Chapter or, as applicable, for the obligations set out in Sections 2 and 3 of Chapter V where the following conditions have been fulfilled:

(a) the Commission has requested, pursuant to Article 10(1) of Regulation (EU) No 1025/2012, one or more European standardisation organisations to draft a harmonised standard for the requirements set out in Section 2 of this Chapter, or, as applicable, for the obligations set out in Sections 2 and 3 of Chapter V, and:

(i) the request has not been accepted by any of the European standardisation organisations; or

(ii) the harmonised standards addressing that request are not delivered within the deadline set in accordance with Article 10(1) of Regulation (EU) No 1025/2012; or

(iii) the relevant harmonised standards insufficiently address fundamental rights concerns; or

(iv) the harmonised standards do not comply with the request; and

(b) no reference to harmonised standards covering the requirements referred to in Section 2 of this Chapter or, as applicable, the obligations referred to in Sections 2 and 3 of Chapter V has been published in the *Official Journal of the European Union* in accordance with Regulation (EU) No 1025/2012, and no such reference is expected to be published within a reasonable period.

[2]When drafting the common specifications, the Commission shall consult the advisory forum referred to in Article 67.

(2) The implementing acts referred to in the first subparagraph of this paragraph shall be adopted in accordance with the examination procedure referred to in Article 98(2).

2. Before preparing a draft implementing act, the Commission shall inform the committee referred to in Article 22 of Regulation (EU) No 1025/2012 that it considers the conditions laid down in paragraph 1 of this Article to be fulfilled.
3. High-risk AI systems or general-purpose AI models which are in conformity with the common specifications referred to in paragraph 1, or parts of those specifications, shall be presumed to be in conformity with the requirements set out in Section 2 of this Chapter or, as applicable, to comply with the obligations referred to in Sections 2 and 3 of Chapter V, to the extent those common specifications cover those requirements or those obligations.
4. [1]Where a harmonised standard is adopted by a European standardisation organisation and proposed to the Commission for the publication of its reference in the *Official Journal of the European Union*, the Commission shall assess the harmonised standard in accordance with Regulation (EU) No 1025/2012. [2]When reference to a harmonised standard is published in the *Official Journal of the European Union*, the Commission shall repeal the implementing acts referred to in paragraph 1, or parts thereof which cover the same requirements set out in Section 2 of this Chapter or, as applicable, the same obligations set out in Sections 2 and 3 of Chapter V.
5. Where providers of high-risk AI systems or general-purpose AI models do not comply with the common specifications referred to in paragraph 1, they shall duly justify that they have adopted technical solutions that meet the requirements referred to in Section 2 of this Chapter or, as applicable, comply with the obligations set out in Sections 2 and 3 of Chapter V to a level at least equivalent thereto.
6. [1]Where a Member State considers that a common specification does not entirely meet the requirements set out in Section 2 or, as applicable, comply with obligations set out in Sections 2 and 3 of Chapter V, it shall inform the Commission thereof with a detailed explanation. [2]The Commission shall assess that information and, if appropriate, amend the implementing act establishing the common specification concerned.

Article 42
Presumption of conformity with certain requirements

1. High-risk AI systems that have been trained and tested on data reflecting the specific geographical, behavioural, contextual or functional setting within which they are intended to be used shall be presumed to comply with the relevant requirements laid down in Article 10(4).
2. High-risk AI systems that have been certified or for which a statement of conformity has been issued under a cybersecurity scheme pursuant to Regulation (EU) 2019/881 and the references of which have been published in the *Official Journal of the European Union* shall be presumed to comply with the cybersecurity requirements set out in Article 15 of this Regulation in so far as the cybersecurity certificate or statement of conformity or parts thereof cover those requirements.

Article 43
Conformity assessment

1. [1]For high-risk AI systems listed in point 1 of Annex III, where, in demonstrating the compliance of a high-risk AI system with the requirements set out in Section 2, the provider has applied harmonised standards referred to in Article 40, or, where

applicable, common specifications referred to in Article 41, the provider shall opt for one of the following conformity assessment procedures based on:

(a) the internal control referred to in Annex VI; or
(b) the assessment of the quality management system and the assessment of the technical documentation, with the involvement of a notified body, referred to in Annex VII.

[2]In demonstrating the compliance of a high-risk AI system with the requirements set out in Section 2, the provider shall follow the conformity assessment procedure set out in Annex VII where:

(a) harmonised standards referred to in Article 40 do not exist, and common specifications referred to in Article 41 are not available;
(b) the provider has not applied, or has applied only part of, the harmonised standard;
(c) the common specifications referred to in point (a) exist, but the provider has not applied them;
(d) one or more of the harmonised standards referred to in point (a) has been published with a restriction, and only on the part of the standard that was restricted.

[3]For the purposes of the conformity assessment procedure referred to in Annex VII, the provider may choose any of the notified bodies. [4]However, where the high-risk AI system is intended to be put into service by law enforcement, immigration or asylum authorities or by Union institutions, bodies, offices or agencies, the market surveillance authority referred to in Article 74(8) or (9), as applicable, shall act as a notified body.
2. For high-risk AI systems referred to in points 2 to 8 of Annex III, providers shall follow the conformity assessment procedure based on internal control as referred to in Annex VI, which does not provide for the involvement of a notified body.
3.

(1) [1]For high-risk AI systems covered by the Union harmonisation legislation listed in Section A of Annex I, the provider shall follow the relevant conformity assessment procedure as required under those legal acts. [2]The requirements set out in Section 2 of this Chapter shall apply to those high-risk AI systems and shall be part of that assessment. [3]Points 4.3., 4.4., 4.5. and the fifth paragraph of point 4.6 of Annex VII shall also apply.
(2) For the purposes of that assessment, notified bodies which have been notified under those legal acts shall be entitled to control the conformity of the high-risk AI systems with the requirements set out in Section 2, provided that the compliance of those notified bodies with requirements laid down in Article 31(4), (5), (10) and (11) has been assessed in the context of the notification procedure under those legal acts.
(3) Where a legal act listed in Section A of Annex I enables the product manufacturer to opt out from a third-party conformity assessment, provided that that manufacturer has applied all harmonised standards covering all the relevant requirements, that manufacturer may use that option only if it has also applied harmonised standards or, where applicable, common specifications referred to in Article 41, covering all requirements set out in Section 2 of this Chapter.

4.

(1) High-risk AI systems that have already been subject to a conformity assessment procedure shall undergo a new conformity assessment procedure in the event of a substantial modification, regardless of whether the modified system is intended to be further distributed or continues to be used by the current deployer.
(2) For high-risk AI systems that continue to learn after being placed on the market or put into service, changes to the high-risk AI system and its performance that have been pre-determined by the provider at the moment of the initial conformity assessment and are part of the information contained in the technical documentation referred to in point 2(f) of Annex IV, shall not constitute a substantial modification.

5. The Commission is empowered to adopt delegated acts in accordance with Article 97 in order to amend Annexes VI and VII by updating them in light of technical progress.
6. [1]The Commission is empowered to adopt delegated acts in accordance with Article 97 in order to amend paragraphs 1 and 2 of this Article in order to subject high-risk AI systems referred to in points 2 to 8 of Annex III to the conformity assessment procedure referred to in Annex VII or parts thereof. [2]The Commission shall adopt such delegated acts taking into account the effectiveness of the conformity assessment procedure based on internal control referred to in Annex VI in preventing or minimising the risks to health and safety and protection of fundamental rights posed by such systems, as well as the availability of adequate capacities and resources among notified bodies.

Article 44
Certificates

1. Certificates issued by notified bodies in accordance with Annex VII shall be drawn-up in a language which can be easily understood by the relevant authorities in the Member State in which the notified body is established.
2. [1]Certificates shall be valid for the period they indicate, which shall not exceed five years for AI systems covered by Annex I, and four years for AI systems covered by Annex III. At the request of the provider, the validity of a certificate may be extended for further periods, each not exceeding five years for AI systems covered by Annex I, and four years for AI systems covered by Annex III, based on a re-assessment in accordance with the applicable conformity assessment procedures. [2]Any supplement to a certificate shall remain valid, provided that the certificate which it supplements is valid.
3.

(1) [1]Where a notified body finds that an AI system no longer meets the requirements set out in Section 2, it shall, taking account of the principle of proportionality, suspend or withdraw the certificate issued or impose restrictions on it, unless compliance with those requirements is ensured by appropriate corrective action taken by the provider of the system within an appropriate deadline set by the notified body. [2]The notified body shall give reasons for its decision.
(2) An appeal procedure against decisions of the notified bodies, including on conformity certificates issued, shall be available.

Article 45
Information obligations of notified bodies

1. Notified bodies shall inform the notifying authority of the following:

(a) any Union technical documentation assessment certificates, any supplements to those certificates, and any quality management system approvals issued in accordance with the requirements of Annex VII;
(b) any refusal, restriction, suspension or withdrawal of a Union technical documentation assessment certificate or a quality management system approval issued in accordance with the requirements of Annex VII;
(c) any circumstances affecting the scope of or conditions for notification;
(d) any request for information which they have received from market surveillance authorities regarding conformity assessment activities;
(e) on request, conformity assessment activities performed within the scope of their notification and any other activity performed, including cross-border activities and subcontracting.

2. Each notified body shall inform the other notified bodies of:

(a) quality management system approvals which it has refused, suspended or withdrawn, and, upon request, of quality system approvals which it has issued;
(b) Union technical documentation assessment certificates or any supplements thereto which it has refused, withdrawn, suspended or otherwise restricted, and, upon request, of the certificates and/or supplements thereto which it has issued.

3. Each notified body shall provide the other notified bodies carrying out similar conformity assessment activities covering the same types of AI systems with relevant information on issues relating to negative and, on request, positive conformity assessment results.
4. Notified bodies shall safeguard the confidentiality of the information that they obtain, in accordance with Article 78.

Article 46
Derogation from conformity assessment procedure

1. [1]By way of derogation from Article 43 and upon a duly justified request, any market surveillance authority may authorise the placing on the market or the putting into service of specific high-risk AI systems within the territory of the Member State concerned, for exceptional reasons of public security or the protection of life and health of persons, environmental protection or the protection of key industrial and infrastructural assets. [2]That authorisation shall be for a limited period while the necessary conformity assessment procedures are being carried out, taking into account the exceptional reasons justifying the derogation. [3]The completion of those procedures shall be undertaken without undue delay.
2. [1]In a duly justified situation of urgency for exceptional reasons of public security or in the case of specific, substantial and imminent threat to the life or physical safety of natural persons, law-enforcement authorities or civil protection authorities may put a specific high-risk AI system into service without the authorisation referred to in paragraph 1, provided that such authorisation is requested during or after the use without undue delay. [2]If the authorisation referred to in paragraph 1 is refused, the use

of the high-risk AI system shall be stopped with immediate effect and all the results and outputs of such use shall be immediately discarded.
3. [1]The authorisation referred to in paragraph 1 shall be issued only if the market surveillance authority concludes that the high-risk AI system complies with the requirements of Section 2. [2]The market surveillance authority shall inform the Commission and the other Member States of any authorisation issued pursuant to paragraphs 1 and 2. [3]This obligation shall not cover sensitive operational data in relation to the activities of law-enforcement authorities.
4. Where, within 15 calendar days of receipt of the information referred to in paragraph 3, no objection has been raised by either a Member State or the Commission in respect of an authorisation issued by a market surveillance authority of a Member State in accordance with paragraph 1, that authorisation shall be deemed justified.
5. [1]Where, within 15 calendar days of receipt of the notification referred to in paragraph 3, objections are raised by a Member State against an authorisation issued by a market surveillance authority of another Member State, or where the Commission considers the authorisation to be contrary to Union law, or the conclusion of the Member States regarding the compliance of the system as referred to in paragraph 3 to be unfounded, the Commission shall, without delay, enter into consultations with the relevant Member State. [2]The operators concerned shall be consulted and have the possibility to present their views. [3]Having regard thereto, the Commission shall decide whether the authorisation is justified. [4]The Commission shall address its decision to the Member State concerned and to the relevant operators.
6. Where the Commission considers the authorisation unjustified, it shall be withdrawn by the market surveillance authority of the Member State concerned.
7. For high-risk AI systems related to products covered by Union harmonisation legislation listed in Section A of Annex I, only the derogations from the conformity assessment established in that Union harmonisation legislation shall apply.

Article 47
EU declaration of conformity

1. [1]The provider shall draw up a written machine readable, physical or electronically signed EU declaration of conformity for each high-risk AI system, and keep it at the disposal of the national competent authorities for 10 years after the high-risk AI system has been placed on the market or put into service. [2]The EU declaration of conformity shall identify the high-risk AI system for which it has been drawn up. [3]A copy of the EU declaration of conformity shall be submitted to the relevant national competent authorities upon request.
2. [1]The EU declaration of conformity shall state that the high-risk AI system concerned meets the requirements set out in Section 2. [2]The EU declaration of conformity shall contain the information set out in Annex V, and shall be translated into a language that can be easily understood by the national competent authorities of the Member States in which the high-risk AI system is placed on the market or made available.
3. [1]Where high-risk AI systems are subject to other Union harmonisation legislation which also requires an EU declaration of conformity, a single EU declaration of conformity shall be drawn up in respect of all Union law applicable to the high-risk AI system. [2]The declaration shall contain all the information required to identify the Union harmonisation legislation to which the declaration relates.

4. [1]By drawing up the EU declaration of conformity, the provider shall assume responsibility for compliance with the requirements set out in Section 2. [2]The provider shall keep the EU declaration of conformity up-to-date as appropriate.
5. The Commission is empowered to adopt delegated acts in accordance with Article 97 in order to amend Annex V by updating the content of the EU declaration of conformity set out in that Annex, in order to introduce elements that become necessary in light of technical progress.

Article 48
CE marking

1. The CE marking shall be subject to the general principles set out in Article 30 of Regulation (EC) No 765/2008.
2. For high-risk AI systems provided digitally, a digital CE marking shall be used, only if it can easily be accessed via the interface from which that system is accessed or via an easily accessible machine-readable code or other electronic means.
3. [1]The CE marking shall be affixed visibly, legibly and indelibly for high-risk AI systems. [2]Where that is not possible or not warranted on account of the nature of the high-risk AI system, it shall be affixed to the packaging or to the accompanying documentation, as appropriate.
4. [1]Where applicable, the CE marking shall be followed by the identification number of the notified body responsible for the conformity assessment procedures set out in Article 43. [2]The identification number of the notified body shall be affixed by the body itself or, under its instructions, by the provider or by the provider's authorised representative. [3]The identification number shall also be indicated in any promotional material which mentions that the high-risk AI system fulfils the requirements for CE marking.
5. Where high-risk AI systems are subject to other Union law which also provides for the affixing of the CE marking, the CE marking shall indicate that the high-risk AI system also fulfil the requirements of that other law.

Article 49
Registration

1. Before placing on the market or putting into service a high-risk AI system listed in Annex III, with the exception of high-risk AI systems referred to in point 2 of Annex III, the provider or, where applicable, the authorised representative shall register themselves and their system in the EU database referred to in Article 71.
2. Before placing on the market or putting into service an AI system for which the provider has concluded that it is not high-risk according to Article 6(3), that provider or, where applicable, the authorised representative shall register themselves and that system in the EU database referred to in Article 71.
3. Before putting into service or using a high-risk AI system listed in Annex III, with the exception of high-risk AI systems listed in point 2 of Annex III, deployers that are public authorities, Union institutions, bodies, offices or agencies or persons acting on their behalf shall register themselves, select the system and register its use in the EU database referred to in Article 71.
4. [1]For high-risk AI systems referred to in points 1, 6 and 7 of Annex III, in the areas of law enforcement, migration, asylum and border control management, the

registration referred to in paragraphs 1, 2 and 3 of this Article shall be in a secure non-public section of the EU database referred to in Article 71 and shall include only the following information, as applicable, referred to in:

(a) Section A, points 1 to 10, of Annex VIII, with the exception of points 6, 8 and 9;
(b) Section B, points 1 to 5, and points 8 and 9 of Annex VIII;
(c) Section C, points 1 to 3, of Annex VIII;
(d) points 1, 2, 3 and 5, of Annex IX.

[2]Only the Commission and national authorities referred to in Article 74(8) shall have access to the respective restricted sections of the EU database listed in the first subparagraph of this paragraph.
5. High-risk AI systems referred to in point 2 of Annex III shall be registered at national level.

CHAPTER IV
TRANSPARENCY OBLIGATIONS FOR PROVIDERS AND DEPLOYERS OF CERTAIN AI SYSTEMS

Article 50
Transparency obligations for providers and deployers of certain AI systems

1. [1]Providers shall ensure that AI systems intended to interact directly with natural persons are designed and developed in such a way that the natural persons concerned are informed that they are interacting with an AI system, unless this is obvious from the point of view of a natural person who is reasonably well-informed, observant and circumspect, taking into account the circumstances and the context of use. [2]This obligation shall not apply to AI systems authorised by law to detect, prevent, investigate or prosecute criminal offences, subject to appropriate safeguards for the rights and freedoms of third parties, unless those systems are available for the public to report a criminal offence.
2. [1]Providers of AI systems, including general-purpose AI systems, generating synthetic audio, image, video or text content, shall ensure that the outputs of the AI system are marked in a machine-readable format and detectable as artificially generated or manipulated. [2]Providers shall ensure their technical solutions are effective, interoperable, robust and reliable as far as this is technically feasible, taking into account the specificities and limitations of various types of content, the costs of implementation and the generally acknowledged state of the art, as may be reflected in relevant technical standards. [3]This obligation shall not apply to the extent the AI systems perform an assistive function for standard editing or do not substantially alter the input data provided by the deployer or the semantics thereof, or where authorised by law to detect, prevent, investigate or prosecute criminal offences.
3. [1]Deployers of an emotion recognition system or a biometric categorisation system shall inform the natural persons exposed thereto of the operation of the system, and shall process the personal data in accordance with Regulations (EU) 2016/679 and (EU) 2018/1725 and Directive (EU) 2016/680, as applicable. [2]This obligation shall not apply to AI systems used for biometric categorisation and emotion recognition, which are permitted by law to detect, prevent or investigate criminal offences, subject to

appropriate safeguards for the rights and freedoms of third parties, and in accordance with Union law.

4.

(1) [1]Deployers of an AI system that generates or manipulates image, audio or video content constituting a deep fake, shall disclose that the content has been artificially generated or manipulated. [2]This obligation shall not apply where the use is authorised by law to detect, prevent, investigate or prosecute criminal offence. [3]Where the content forms part of an evidently artistic, creative, satirical, fictional or analogous work or programme, the transparency obligations set out in this paragraph are limited to disclosure of the existence of such generated or manipulated content in an appropriate manner that does not hamper the display or enjoyment of the work.

(2) [1]Deployers of an AI system that generates or manipulates text which is published with the purpose of informing the public on matters of public interest shall disclose that the text has been artificially generated or manipulated. [2]This obligation shall not apply where the use is authorised by law to detect, prevent, investigate or prosecute criminal offences or where the AI-generated content has undergone a process of human review or editorial control and where a natural or legal person holds editorial responsibility for the publication of the content.

5. [1]The information referred to in paragraphs 1 to 4 shall be provided to the natural persons concerned in a clear and distinguishable manner at the latest at the time of the first interaction or exposure. [2]The information shall conform to the applicable accessibility requirements.

6. Paragraphs 1 to 4 shall not affect the requirements and obligations set out in Chapter III, and shall be without prejudice to other transparency obligations laid down in Union or national law for deployers of AI systems.

7. [1]The AI Office shall encourage and facilitate the drawing up of codes of practice at Union level to facilitate the effective implementation of the obligations regarding the detection and labelling of artificially generated or manipulated content. [2]The Commission may adopt implementing acts to approve those codes of practice in accordance with the procedure laid down in Article 56 (6). [3]If it deems the code is not adequate, the Commission may adopt an implementing act specifying common rules for the implementation of those obligations in accordance with the examination procedure laid down in Article 98(2).

CHAPTER V
GENERAL-PURPOSE AI MODELS

Section 1
Classification rules

Article 51
Classification of general-purpose AI models as general-purpose AI models with systemic risk

1. A general-purpose AI model shall be classified as a general-purpose AI model with systemic risk if it meets any of the following conditions:

(a) it has high impact capabilities evaluated on the basis of appropriate technical tools and methodologies, including indicators and benchmarks;
(b) based on a decision of the Commission, *ex officio* or following a qualified alert from the scientific panel, it has capabilities or an impact equivalent to those set out in point (a) having regard to the criteria set out in Annex XIII.

2. A general-purpose AI model shall be presumed to have high impact capabilities pursuant to paragraph 1, point (a), when the cumulative amount of computation used for its training measured in floating point operations is greater than 10^{25}.
3. The Commission shall adopt delegated acts in accordance with Article 97 to amend the thresholds listed in paragraphs 1 and 2 of this Article, as well as to supplement benchmarks and indicators in light of evolving technological developments, such as algorithmic improvements or increased hardware efficiency, when necessary, for these thresholds to reflect the state of the art.

Article 52
Procedure

1. [1]Where a general-purpose AI model meets the condition referred to in Article 51(1), point (a), the relevant provider shall notify the Commission without delay and in any event within two weeks after that requirement is met or it becomes known that it will be met. [2]That notification shall include the information necessary to demonstrate that the relevant requirement has been met. [3]If the Commission becomes aware of a general-purpose AI model presenting systemic risks of which it has not been notified, it may decide to designate it as a model with systemic risk.
2. The provider of a general-purpose AI model that meets the condition referred to in Article 51(1), point (a), may present, with its notification, sufficiently substantiated arguments to demonstrate that, exceptionally, although it meets that requirement, the general-purpose AI model does not present, due to its specific characteristics, systemic risks and therefore should not be classified as a general-purpose AI model with systemic risk.
3. Where the Commission concludes that the arguments submitted pursuant to paragraph 2 are not sufficiently substantiated and the relevant provider was not able to demonstrate that the general-purpose AI model does not present, due to its specific characteristics, systemic risks, it shall reject those arguments, and the general-purpose AI model shall be considered to be a general-purpose AI model with systemic risk.
4.

(1) The Commission may designate a general-purpose AI model as presenting systemic risks, *ex officio* or following a qualified alert from the scientific panel pursuant to Article 90(1), point (a), on the basis of criteria set out in Annex XIII.
(2) The Commission is empowered to adopt delegated acts in accordance with Article 97 in order to amend Annex XIII by specifying and updating the criteria set out in that Annex.

5. [1]Upon a reasoned request of a provider whose model has been designated as a general-purpose AI model with systemic risk pursuant to paragraph 4, the Commission shall take the request into account and may decide to reassess whether the general-purpose AI model can still be considered to present systemic risks on the basis of the criteria set out in Annex XIII. Such a request shall contain objective, detailed and new reasons that have arisen since the designation decision. [2]Providers may

request reassessment at the earliest six months after the designation decision. [3]Where the Commission, following its reassessment, decides to maintain the designation as a general-purpose AI model with systemic risk, providers may request reassessment at the earliest six months after that decision.
6. The Commission shall ensure that a list of general-purpose AI models with systemic risk is published and shall keep that list up to date, without prejudice to the need to observe and protect intellectual property rights and confidential business information or trade secrets in accordance with Union and national law.

Section 2
Obligations for providers of general-purpose AI models

Article 53
Obligations for providers of general-purpose AI models

1. Providers of general-purpose AI models shall:

(a) draw up and keep up-to-date the technical documentation of the model, including its training and testing process and the results of its evaluation, which shall contain, at a minimum, the information set out in Annex XI for the purpose of providing it, upon request, to the AI Office and the national competent authorities;
(b) draw up, keep up-to-date and make available information and documentation to providers of AI systems who intend to integrate the general-purpose AI model into their AI systems. Without prejudice to the need to observe and protect intellectual property rights and confidential business information or trade secrets in accordance with Union and national law, the information and documentation shall:
    (i) enable providers of AI systems to have a good understanding of the capabilities and limitations of the general-purpose AI model and to comply with their obligations pursuant to this Regulation; and
    (ii) contain, at a minimum, the elements set out in Annex XII;
(c) put in place a policy to comply with Union law on copyright and related rights, and in particular to identify and comply with, including through state-of-the-art technologies, a reservation of rights expressed pursuant to Article 4(3) of Directive (EU) 2019/790;
(d) draw up and make publicly available a sufficiently detailed summary about the content used for training of the general-purpose AI model, according to a template provided by the AI Office.

2. [1]The obligations set out in paragraph 1, points (a) and (b), shall not apply to providers of AI models that are released under a free and open-source licence that allows for the access, usage, modification, and distribution of the model, and whose parameters, including the weights, the information on the model architecture, and the information on model usage, are made publicly available. [2]This exception shall not apply to general-purpose AI models with systemic risks.
3. Providers of general-purpose AI models shall cooperate as necessary with the Commission and the national competent authorities in the exercise of their competences and powers pursuant to this Regulation.
4. [1]Providers of general-purpose AI models may rely on codes of practice within the meaning of Article 56 to demonstrate compliance with the obligations set out in para-

graph 1 of this Article, until a harmonised standard is published. [2]Compliance with European harmonised standards grants providers the presumption of conformity to the extent that those standards cover those obligations. [3]Providers of general-purpose AI models who do not adhere to an approved code of practice or do not comply with a European harmonised standard shall demonstrate alternative adequate means of compliance for assessment by the Commission.
5. For the purpose of facilitating compliance with Annex XI, in particular points 2 (d) and (e) thereof, the Commission is empowered to adopt delegated acts in accordance with Article 97 to detail measurement and calculation methodologies with a view to allowing for comparable and verifiable documentation.
6. The Commission is empowered to adopt delegated acts in accordance with Article 97(2) to amend Annexes XI and XII in light of evolving technological developments.
7. Any information or documentation obtained pursuant to this Article, including trade secrets, shall be treated in accordance with the confidentiality obligations set out in Article 78.

Article 54
Authorised representatives of providers of general-purpose AI models

1. Prior to placing a general-purpose AI model on the Union market, providers established in third countries shall, by written mandate, appoint an authorised representative which is established in the Union.
2. The provider shall enable its authorised representative to perform the tasks specified in the mandate received from the provider.
3. [1]The authorised representative shall perform the tasks specified in the mandate received from the provider. [2]It shall provide a copy of the mandate to the AI Office upon request, in one of the official languages of the institutions of the Union. [3]For the purposes of this Regulation, the mandate shall empower the authorised representative to carry out the following tasks:

(a) verify that the technical documentation specified in Annex XI has been drawn up and all obligations referred to in Article 53 and, where applicable, Article 55 have been fulfilled by the provider;
(b) keep a copy of the technical documentation specified in Annex XI at the disposal of the AI Office and national competent authorities, for a period of 10 years after the general-purpose AI model has been placed on the market, and the contact details of the provider that appointed the authorised representative;
(c) provide the AI Office, upon a reasoned request, with all the information and documentation, including that referred to in point (b), necessary to demonstrate compliance with the obligations in this Chapter;
(d) cooperate with the AI Office and competent authorities, upon a reasoned request, in any action they take in relation to the general-purpose AI model, including when the model is integrated into AI systems placed on the market or put into service in the Union.

4. The mandate shall empower the authorised representative to be addressed, in addition to or instead of the provider, by the AI Office or the competent authorities, on all issues related to ensuring compliance with this Regulation.

5. [1]The authorised representative shall terminate the mandate if it considers or has reason to consider the provider to be acting contrary to its obligations pursuant to this Regulation. [2]In such a case, it shall also immediately inform the AI Office about the termination of the mandate and the reasons therefor.
6. The obligation set out in this Article shall not apply to providers of general-purpose AI models that are released under a free and open-source licence that allows for the access, usage, modification, and distribution of the model, and whose parameters, including the weights, the information on the model architecture, and the information on model usage, are made publicly available, unless the general-purpose AI models present systemic risks.

Section 3
Obligations of providers of general-purpose AI models with systemic risk

Article 55
Obligations of providers of general-purpose AI models with systemic risk

1. In addition to the obligations listed in Articles 53 and 54, providers of general-purpose AI models with systemic risk shall:

(a) perform model evaluation in accordance with standardised protocols and tools reflecting the state of the art, including conducting and documenting adversarial testing of the model with a view to identifying and mitigating systemic risks;
(b) assess and mitigate possible systemic risks at Union level, including their sources, that may stem from the development, the placing on the market, or the use of general-purpose AI models with systemic risk;
(c) keep track of, document, and report, without undue delay, to the AI Office and, as appropriate, to national competent authorities, relevant information about serious incidents and possible corrective measures to address them;
(d) ensure an adequate level of cybersecurity protection for the general-purpose AI model with systemic risk and the physical infrastructure of the model.

2. [1]Providers of general-purpose AI models with systemic risk may rely on codes of practice within the meaning of Article 56 to demonstrate compliance with the obligations set out in paragraph 1 of this Article, until a harmonised standard is published. [2]Compliance with European harmonised standards grants providers the presumption of conformity to the extent that those standards cover those obligations. [3]Providers of general-purpose AI models with systemic risks who do not adhere to an approved code of practice or do not comply with a European harmonised standard shall demonstrate alternative adequate means of compliance for assessment by the Commission.
3. Any information or documentation obtained pursuant to this Article, including trade secrets, shall be treated in accordance with the confidentiality obligations set out in Article 78.

Section 4
Codes of practice

Article 56
Codes of practice

1. The AI Office shall encourage and facilitate the drawing up of codes of practice at Union level in order to contribute to the proper application of this Regulation, taking into account international approaches.
2. The AI Office and the Board shall aim to ensure that the codes of practice cover at least the obligations provided for in Articles 53 and 55, including the following issues:

(a) the means to ensure that the information referred to in Article 53(1), points (a) and (b), is kept up to date in light of market and technological developments;
(b) the adequate level of detail for the summary about the content used for training;
(c) the identification of the type and nature of the systemic risks at Union level, including their sources, where appropriate;
(d) the measures, procedures and modalities for the assessment and management of the systemic risks at Union level, including the documentation thereof, which shall be proportionate to the risks, take into consideration their severity and probability and take into account the specific challenges of tackling those risks in light of the possible ways in which such risks may emerge and materialise along the AI value chain.

3. [1]The AI Office may invite all providers of general-purpose AI models, as well as relevant national competent authorities, to participate in the drawing-up of codes of practice. [2]Civil society organisations, industry, academia and other relevant stakeholders, such as downstream providers and independent experts, may support the process.
4. The AI Office and the Board shall aim to ensure that the codes of practice clearly set out their specific objectives and contain commitments or measures, including key performance indicators as appropriate, to ensure the achievement of those objectives, and that they take due account of the needs and interests of all interested parties, including affected persons, at Union level.
5. [1]The AI Office shall aim to ensure that participants to the codes of practice report regularly to the AI Office on the implementation of the commitments and the measures taken and their outcomes, including as measured against the key performance indicators as appropriate. [2]Key performance indicators and reporting commitments shall reflect differences in size and capacity between various participants.
6.

(1) [1]The AI Office and the Board shall regularly monitor and evaluate the achievement of the objectives of the codes of practice by the participants and their contribution to the proper application of this Regulation. [2]The AI Office and the Board shall assess whether the codes of practice cover the obligations provided for in Articles 53 and 55, and shall regularly monitor and evaluate the achievement of their objectives. [3]They shall publish their assessment of the adequacy of the codes of practice.
(2) [1]The Commission may, by way of an implementing act, approve a code of practice and give it a general validity within the Union. [2]That implementing act shall be adopted in accordance with the examination procedure referred to in Article 98(2).

7. [1]The AI Office may invite all providers of general-purpose AI models to adhere to the codes of practice. [2]For providers of general-purpose AI models not presenting systemic risks this adherence may be limited to the obligations provided for in Article 53, unless they declare explicitly their interest to join the full code.
8. [1]The AI Office shall, as appropriate, also encourage and facilitate the review and adaptation of the codes of practice, in particular in light of emerging standards. [2]The AI Office shall assist in the assessment of available standards.
9.

(1) [1]Codes of practice shall be ready at the latest by 2 May 2025. [2]The AI Office shall take the necessary steps, including inviting providers pursuant to paragraph 7.
(2) [1]If, by 2 August 2025, a code of practice cannot be finalised, or if the AI Office deems it is not adequate following its assessment under paragraph 6 of this Article, the Commission may provide, by means of implementing acts, common rules for the implementation of the obligations provided for in Articles 53 and 55, including the issues set out in paragraph 2 of this Article. [2]Those implementing acts shall be adopted in accordance with the examination procedure referred to in Article 98(2).

CHAPTER VI
MEASURES IN SUPPORT OF INNOVATION

Article 57
AI regulatory sandboxes

1.

(1) [1]Member States shall ensure that their competent authorities establish at least one AI regulatory sandbox at national level, which shall be operational by 2 August 2026. [2]That sandbox may also be established jointly with the competent authorities of other Member States. [3]The Commission may provide technical support, advice and tools for the establishment and operation of AI regulatory sandboxes.
(2) The obligation under the first subparagraph may also be fulfilled by participating in an existing sandbox in so far as that participation provides an equivalent level of national coverage for the participating Member States.

2. Additional AI regulatory sandboxes at regional or local level, or established jointly with the competent authorities of other Member States may also be established.
3. The European Data Protection Supervisor may also establish an AI regulatory sandbox for Union institutions, bodies, offices and agencies, and may exercise the roles and the tasks of national competent authorities in accordance with this Chapter.
4. [1]Member States shall ensure that the competent authorities referred to in paragraphs 1 and 2 allocate sufficient resources to comply with this Article effectively and in a timely manner. [2]Where appropriate, national competent authorities shall cooperate with other relevant authorities, and may allow for the involvement of other actors within the AI ecosystem. [3]This Article shall not affect other regulatory sandboxes established under Union or national law. [4]Member States shall ensure an appropriate level of cooperation between the authorities supervising those other sandboxes and the national competent authorities.
5. [1]AI regulatory sandboxes established under paragraph 1 shall provide for a controlled environment that fosters innovation and facilitates the development, training,

testing and validation of innovative AI systems for a limited time before their being placed on the market or put into service pursuant to a specific sandbox plan agreed between the providers or prospective providers and the competent authority. [2]Such sandboxes may include testing in real world conditions supervised therein.
6. Competent authorities shall provide, as appropriate, guidance, supervision and support within the AI regulatory sandbox with a view to identifying risks, in particular to fundamental rights, health and safety, testing, mitigation measures, and their effectiveness in relation to the obligations and requirements of this Regulation and, where relevant, other Union and national law supervised within the sandbox.
7.

(1) Competent authorities shall provide providers and prospective providers participating in the AI regulatory sandbox with guidance on regulatory expectations and how to fulfil the requirements and obligations set out in this Regulation.
(2) [1]Upon request of the provider or prospective provider of the AI system, the competent authority shall provide a written proof of the activities successfully carried out in the sandbox. [2]The competent authority shall also provide an exit report detailing the activities carried out in the sandbox and the related results and learning outcomes. [3]Providers may use such documentation to demonstrate their compliance with this Regulation through the conformity assessment process or relevant market surveillance activities. [4]In this regard, the exit reports and the written proof provided by the national competent authority shall be taken positively into account by market surveillance authorities and notified bodies, with a view to accelerating conformity assessment procedures to a reasonable extent.

8. [1]Subject to the confidentiality provisions in Article 78, and with the agreement of the provider or prospective provider, the Commission and the Board shall be authorised to access the exit reports and shall take them into account, as appropriate, when exercising their tasks under this Regulation. [2]If both the provider or prospective provider and the national competent authority explicitly agree, the exit report may be made publicly available through the single information platform referred to in this Article.
9. The establishment of AI regulatory sandboxes shall aim to contribute to the following objectives:

(a) improving legal certainty to achieve regulatory compliance with this Regulation or, where relevant, other applicable Union and national law;
(b) supporting the sharing of best practices through cooperation with the authorities involved in the AI regulatory sandbox;
(c) fostering innovation and competitiveness and facilitating the development of an AI ecosystem;
(d) contributing to evidence-based regulatory learning;
(e) facilitating and accelerating access to the Union market for AI systems, in particular when provided by SMEs, including start-ups.

10. National competent authorities shall ensure that, to the extent the innovative AI systems involve the processing of personal data or otherwise fall under the supervisory remit of other national authorities or competent authorities providing or supporting access to data, the national data protection authorities and those other national or competent authorities are associated with the operation of the AI regulatory sandbox

and involved in the supervision of those aspects to the extent of their respective tasks and powers.
11. [1]The AI regulatory sandboxes shall not affect the supervisory or corrective powers of the competent authorities supervising the sandboxes, including at regional or local level. [2]Any significant risks to health and safety and fundamental rights identified during the development and testing of such AI systems shall result in an adequate mitigation. [3]National competent authorities shall have the power to temporarily or permanently suspend the testing process, or the participation in the sandbox if no effective mitigation is possible, and shall inform the AI Office of such decision. [4]National competent authorities shall exercise their supervisory powers within the limits of the relevant law, using their discretionary powers when implementing legal provisions in respect of a specific AI regulatory sandbox project, with the objective of supporting innovation in AI in the Union.
12. [1]Providers and prospective providers participating in the AI regulatory sandbox shall remain liable under applicable Union and national liability law for any damage inflicted on third parties as a result of the experimentation taking place in the sandbox. [2]However, provided that the prospective providers observe the specific plan and the terms and conditions for their participation and follow in good faith the guidance given by the national competent authority, no administrative fines shall be imposed by the authorities for infringements of this Regulation. [3]Where other competent authorities responsible for other Union and national law were actively involved in the supervision of the AI system in the sandbox and provided guidance for compliance, no administrative fines shall be imposed regarding that law.
13. The AI regulatory sandboxes shall be designed and implemented in such a way that, where relevant, they facilitate cross-border cooperation between national competent authorities.
14. National competent authorities shall coordinate their activities and cooperate within the framework of the Board.
15. [1]National competent authorities shall inform the AI Office and the Board of the establishment of a sandbox, and may ask them for support and guidance. [2]The AI Office shall make publicly available a list of planned and existing sandboxes and keep it up to date in order to encourage more interaction in the AI regulatory sandboxes and cross-border cooperation.
16. [1]National competent authorities shall submit annual reports to the AI Office and to the Board, from one year after the establishment of the AI regulatory sandbox and every year thereafter until its termination, and a final report. [2]Those reports shall provide information on the progress and results of the implementation of those sandboxes, including best practices, incidents, lessons learnt and recommendations on their setup and, where relevant, on the application and possible revision of this Regulation, including its delegated and implementing acts, and on the application of other Union law supervised by the competent authorities within the sandbox. [3]The national competent authorities shall make those annual reports or abstracts thereof available to the public, online. [4]The Commission shall, where appropriate, take the annual reports into account when exercising its tasks under this Regulation.
17. [1]The Commission shall develop a single and dedicated interface containing all relevant information related to AI regulatory sandboxes to allow stakeholders to interact with AI regulatory sandboxes and to raise enquiries with competent authorities, and to seek non-binding guidance on the conformity of innovative products, services, business models embedding AI technologies, in accordance with Article 62(1), point

(c). [2]The Commission shall proactively coordinate with national competent authorities, where relevant.

Article 58
Detailed arrangements for, and functioning of, AI regulatory sandboxes

1. [1]In order to avoid fragmentation across the Union, the Commission shall adopt implementing acts specifying the detailed arrangements for the establishment, development, implementation, operation and supervision of the AI regulatory sandboxes. [2]The implementing acts shall include common principles on the following issues:

(a) eligibility and selection criteria for participation in the AI regulatory sandbox;
(b) procedures for the application, participation, monitoring, exiting from and termination of the AI regulatory sandbox, including the sandbox plan and the exit report;
(c) the terms and conditions applicable to the participants.

[3]Those implementing acts shall be adopted in accordance with the examination procedure referred to in Article 98(2).
2. The implementing acts referred to in paragraph 1 shall ensure:

(a) that AI regulatory sandboxes are open to any applying provider or prospective provider of an AI system who fulfils eligibility and selection criteria, which shall be transparent and fair, and that national competent authorities inform applicants of their decision within three months of the application;
(b) that AI regulatory sandboxes allow broad and equal access and keep up with demand for participation; providers and prospective providers may also submit applications in partnerships with deployers and other relevant third parties;
(c) that the detailed arrangements for, and conditions concerning AI regulatory sandboxes support, to the best extent possible, flexibility for national competent authorities to establish and operate their AI regulatory sandboxes;
(d) that access to the AI regulatory sandboxes is free of charge for SMEs, including start-ups, without prejudice to exceptional costs that national competent authorities may recover in a fair and proportionate manner;
(e) that they facilitate providers and prospective providers, by means of the learning outcomes of the AI regulatory sandboxes, in complying with conformity assessment obligations under this Regulation and the voluntary application of the codes of conduct referred to in Article 95;
(f) that AI regulatory sandboxes facilitate the involvement of other relevant actors within the AI ecosystem, such as notified bodies and standardisation organisations, SMEs, including start-ups, enterprises, innovators, testing and experimentation facilities, research and experimentation labs and European Digital Innovation Hubs, centres of excellence, individual researchers, in order to allow and facilitate cooperation with the public and private sectors;
(g) that procedures, processes and administrative requirements for application, selection, participation and exiting the AI regulatory sandbox are simple, easily intelligible, and clearly communicated in order to facilitate the participation of SMEs, including start-ups, with limited legal and administrative capacities and are streamlined across the Union, in order to avoid fragmentation and that participation in an AI regulatory sandbox established by a Member State, or by the

European Data Protection Supervisor is mutually and uniformly recognised and carries the same legal effects across the Union;

(h) that participation in the AI regulatory sandbox is limited to a period that is appropriate to the complexity and scale of the project and that may be extended by the national competent authority;

(i) that AI regulatory sandboxes facilitate the development of tools and infrastructure for testing, benchmarking, assessing and explaining dimensions of AI systems relevant for regulatory learning, such as accuracy, robustness and cybersecurity, as well as measures to mitigate risks to fundamental rights and society at large.

3. Prospective providers in the AI regulatory sandboxes, in particular SMEs and start-ups, shall be directed, where relevant, to pre-deployment services such as guidance on the implementation of this Regulation, to other value-adding services such as help with standardisation documents and certification, testing and experimentation facilities, European Digital Innovation Hubs and centres of excellence.

4. [1]Where national competent authorities consider authorising testing in real world conditions supervised within the framework of an AI regulatory sandbox to be established under this Article, they shall specifically agree the terms and conditions of such testing and, in particular, the appropriate safeguards with the participants, with a view to protecting fundamental rights, health and safety. [2]Where appropriate, they shall cooperate with other national competent authorities with a view to ensuring consistent practices across the Union.

Article 59
Further processing of personal data for developing certain AI systems in the public interest in the AI regulatory sandbox

1. In the AI regulatory sandbox, personal data lawfully collected for other purposes may be processed solely for the purpose of developing, training and testing certain AI systems in the sandbox when all of the following conditions are met:

(a) AI systems shall be developed for safeguarding substantial public interest by a public authority or another natural or legal person and in one or more of the following areas:
   (i) public safety and public health, including disease detection, diagnosis prevention, control and treatment and improvement of health care systems;
   (ii) a high level of protection and improvement of the quality of the environment, protection of biodiversity, protection against pollution, green transition measures, climate change mitigation and adaptation measures;
   (iii) energy sustainability;
   (iv) safety and resilience of transport systems and mobility, critical infrastructure and networks;
   (v) efficiency and quality of public administration and public services;

(b) the data processed are necessary for complying with one or more of the requirements referred to in Chapter III, Section 2 where those requirements cannot effectively be fulfilled by processing anonymised, synthetic or other non-personal data;

(c) there are effective monitoring mechanisms to identify if any high risks to the rights and freedoms of the data subjects, as referred to in Article 35 of Regulation (EU) 2016/679 and in Article 39 of Regulation (EU) 2018/1725, may arise during the sandbox experimentation, as well as response mechanisms to promptly mitigate those risks and, where necessary, stop the processing;

(d) any personal data to be processed in the context of the sandbox are in a functionally separate, isolated and protected data processing environment under the control of the prospective provider and only authorised persons have access to those data;

(e) providers can further share the originally collected data only in accordance with Union data protection law; any personal data created in the sandbox cannot be shared outside the sandbox;

(f) any processing of personal data in the context of the sandbox neither leads to measures or decisions affecting the data subjects nor does it affect the application of their rights laid down in Union law on the protection of personal data;

(g) any personal data processed in the context of the sandbox are protected by means of appropriate technical and organisational measures and deleted once the participation in the sandbox has terminated or the personal data has reached the end of its retention period;

(h) the logs of the processing of personal data in the context of the sandbox are kept for the duration of the participation in the sandbox, unless provided otherwise by Union or national law;

(i) a complete and detailed description of the process and rationale behind the training, testing and validation of the AI system is kept together with the testing results as part of the technical documentation referred to in Annex IV;

(j) a short summary of the AI project developed in the sandbox, its objectives and expected results is published on the website of the competent authorities; this obligation shall not cover sensitive operational data in relation to the activities of law enforcement, border control, immigration or asylum authorities.

2. For the purposes of the prevention, investigation, detection or prosecution of criminal offences or the execution of criminal penalties, including safeguarding against and preventing threats to public security, under the control and responsibility of law enforcement authorities, the processing of personal data in AI regulatory sandboxes shall be based on a specific Union or national law and subject to the same cumulative conditions as referred to in paragraph 1.

3. Paragraph 1 is without prejudice to Union or national law which excludes processing of personal data for other purposes than those explicitly mentioned in that law, as well as to Union or national law laying down the basis for the processing of personal data which is necessary for the purpose of developing, testing or training of innovative AI systems or any other legal basis, in compliance with Union law on the protection of personal data.

Article 60
Testing of high-risk AI systems in real world conditions outside AI regulatory sandboxes

1.

(1) [1]Testing of high-risk AI systems in real world conditions outside AI regulatory sandboxes may be conducted by providers or prospective providers of high-risk AI systems listed in Annex III, in accordance with this Article and the real-world testing plan referred to in this Article, without prejudice to the prohibitions under

Article 5. [2]The Commission shall, by means of implementing acts, specify the detailed elements of the real-world testing plan.

(2) Those implementing acts shall be adopted in accordance with the examination procedure referred to in Article 98(2).

(3) This paragraph shall be without prejudice to Union or national law on the testing in real world conditions of high-risk AI systems related to products covered by Union harmonisation legislation listed in Annex I.

2. Providers or prospective providers may conduct testing of high-risk AI systems referred to in Annex III in real world conditions at any time before the placing on the market or the putting into service of the AI system on their own or in partnership with one or more deployers or prospective deployers.
3. The testing of high-risk AI systems in real world conditions under this Article shall be without prejudice to any ethical review that is required by Union or national law.
4. Providers or prospective providers may conduct the testing in real world conditions only where all of the following conditions are met:

(a) the provider or prospective provider has drawn up a real-world testing plan and submitted it to the market surveillance authority in the Member State where the testing in real world conditions is to be conducted;
(b) the market surveillance authority in the Member State where the testing in real world conditions is to be conducted has approved the testing in real world conditions and the real-world testing plan; where the market surveillance authority has not provided an answer within 30 days, the testing in real world conditions and the real-world testing plan shall be understood to have been approved; where national law does not provide for a tacit approval, the testing in real world conditions shall remain subject to an authorisation;
(c) the provider or prospective provider, with the exception of providers or prospective providers of high-risk AI systems referred to in points 1, 6 and 7 of Annex III in the areas of law enforcement, migration, asylum and border control management, and high-risk AI systems referred to in point 2 of Annex III has registered the testing in real world conditions in accordance with Article 71(4) with a Union-wide unique single identification number and with the information specified in Annex IX; the provider or prospective provider of high-risk AI systems referred to in points 1, 6 and 7 of Annex III in the areas of law enforcement, migration, asylum and border control management, has registered the testing in real-world conditions in the secure non-public section of the EU database according to Article 49(4), point (d), with a Union-wide unique single identification number and with the information specified therein; the provider or prospective provider of high-risk AI systems referred to in point 2 of Annex III has registered the testing in real-world conditions in accordance with Article 49(5);
(d) the provider or prospective provider conducting the testing in real world conditions is established in the Union or has appointed a legal representative who is established in the Union;
(e) data collected and processed for the purpose of the testing in real world conditions shall be transferred to third countries only provided that appropriate and applicable safeguards under Union law are implemented;
(f) the testing in real world conditions does not last longer than necessary to achieve its objectives and in any case not longer than six months, which may be extended for an additional period of six months, subject to prior notification by the

provider or prospective provider to the market surveillance authority, accompanied by an explanation of the need for such an extension;
(g) the subjects of the testing in real world conditions who are persons belonging to vulnerable groups due to their age or disability, are appropriately protected;
(h) where a provider or prospective provider organises the testing in real world conditions in cooperation with one or more deployers or prospective deployers, the latter have been informed of all aspects of the testing that are relevant to their decision to participate, and given the relevant instructions for use of the AI system referred to in Article 13; the provider or prospective provider and the deployer or prospective deployer shall conclude an agreement specifying their roles and responsibilities with a view to ensuring compliance with the provisions for testing in real world conditions under this Regulation and under other applicable Union and national law;
(i) the subjects of the testing in real world conditions have given informed consent in accordance with Article 61, or in the case of law enforcement, where the seeking of informed consent would prevent the AI system from being tested, the testing itself and the outcome of the testing in the real world conditions shall not have any negative effect on the subjects, and their personal data shall be deleted after the test is performed;
(j) the testing in real world conditions is effectively overseen by the provider or prospective provider, as well as by deployers or prospective deployers through persons who are suitably qualified in the relevant field and have the necessary capacity, training and authority to perform their tasks;
(k) the predictions, recommendations or decisions of the AI system can be effectively reversed and disregarded.

5. [1]Any subjects of the testing in real world conditions, or their legally designated representative, as appropriate, may, without any resulting detriment and without having to provide any justification, withdraw from the testing at any time by revoking their informed consent and may request the immediate and permanent deletion of their personal data. [2]The withdrawal of the informed consent shall not affect the activities already carried out.
6. [1]In accordance with Article 75, Member States shall confer on their market surveillance authorities the powers of requiring providers and prospective providers to provide information, of carrying out unannounced remote or on-site inspections, and of performing checks on the conduct of the testing in real world conditions and the related high-risk AI systems. [2]Market surveillance authorities shall use those powers to ensure the safe development of testing in real world conditions.
7. [1]Any serious incident identified in the course of the testing in real world conditions shall be reported to the national market surveillance authority in accordance with Article 73. [2]The provider or prospective provider shall adopt immediate mitigation measures or, failing that, shall suspend the testing in real world conditions until such mitigation takes place, or otherwise terminate it. [3]The provider or prospective provider shall establish a procedure for the prompt recall of the AI system upon such termination of the testing in real world conditions.
8. Providers or prospective providers shall notify the national market surveillance authority in the Member State where the testing in real world conditions is to be conducted of the suspension or termination of the testing in real world conditions and of the final outcomes.

9. The provider or prospective provider shall be liable under applicable Union and national liability law for any damage caused in the course of their testing in real world conditions.

Article 61
Informed consent to participate in testing in real world conditions outside AI regulatory sandboxes

1. For the purpose of testing in real world conditions under Article 60, freely-given informed consent shall be obtained from the subjects of testing prior to their participation in such testing and after their having been duly informed with concise, clear, relevant, and understandable information regarding:

(a) the nature and objectives of the testing in real world conditions and the possible inconvenience that may be linked to their participation;
(b) the conditions under which the testing in real world conditions is to be conducted, including the expected duration of the subject or subjects' participation;
(c) their rights, and the guarantees regarding their participation, in particular their right to refuse to participate in, and the right to withdraw from, testing in real world conditions at any time without any resulting detriment and without having to provide any justification;
(d) the arrangements for requesting the reversal or the disregarding of the predictions, recommendations or decisions of the AI system;
(e) the Union-wide unique single identification number of the testing in real world conditions in accordance with Article 60(4) point (c), and the contact details of the provider or its legal representative from whom further information can be obtained.

2. The informed consent shall be dated and documented and a copy shall be given to the subjects of testing or their legal representative.

Article 62
Measures for providers and deployers, in particular SMEs, including start-ups

1. Member States shall undertake the following actions:

(a) provide SMEs, including start-ups, having a registered office or a branch in the Union, with priority access to the AI regulatory sandboxes, to the extent that they fulfil the eligibility conditions and selection criteria; the priority access shall not preclude other SMEs, including start-ups, other than those referred to in this paragraph from access to the AI regulatory sandbox, provided that they also fulfil the eligibility conditions and selection criteria;
(b) organise specific awareness raising and training activities on the application of this Regulation tailored to the needs of SMEs including start-ups, deployers and, as appropriate, local public authorities;
(c) utilise existing dedicated channels and where appropriate, establish new ones for communication with SMEs including start-ups, deployers, other innovators and, as appropriate, local public authorities to provide advice and respond to queries

about the implementation of this Regulation, including as regards participation in AI regulatory sandboxes;
(d) facilitate the participation of SMEs and other relevant stakeholders in the standardisation development process.

2. The specific interests and needs of the SME providers, including start-ups, shall be taken into account when setting the fees for conformity assessment under Article 43, reducing those fees proportionately to their size, market size and other relevant indicators.
3. The AI Office shall undertake the following actions:

(a) provide standardised templates for areas covered by this Regulation, as specified by the Board in its request;
(b) develop and maintain a single information platform providing easy to use information in relation to this Regulation for all operators across the Union;
(c) organise appropriate communication campaigns to raise awareness about the obligations arising from this Regulation;
(d) evaluate and promote the convergence of best practices in public procurement procedures in relation to AI systems.

Article 63
Derogations for specific operators

1. [1]Microenterprises within the meaning of Recommendation 2003/361/EC may comply with certain elements of the quality management system required by Article 17 of this Regulation in a simplified manner, provided that they do not have partner enterprises or linked enterprises within the meaning of that Recommendation. [2]For that purpose, the Commission shall develop guidelines on the elements of the quality management system which may be complied with in a simplified manner considering the needs of microenterprises, without affecting the level of protection or the need for compliance with the requirements in respect of high-risk AI systems.
2. Paragraph 1 of this Article shall not be interpreted as exempting those operators from fulfilling any other requirements or obligations laid down in this Regulation, including those established in Articles 9, 10, 11, 12, 13, 14, 15, 72 and 73.

CHAPTER VII
GOVERNANCE

Section 1
Governance at Union level

Article 64
AI Office

1. The Commission shall develop Union expertise and capabilities in the field of AI through the AI Office.
2. Member States shall facilitate the tasks entrusted to the AI Office, as reflected in this Regulation.

Article 65
Establishment and structure of the European Artificial Intelligence Board

1. A European Artificial Intelligence Board (the „Board") is hereby established.
2. [1]The Board shall be composed of one representative per Member State. [2]The European Data Protection Supervisor shall participate as observer. [3]The AI Office shall also attend the Board's meetings, without taking part in the votes. [4]Other national and Union authorities, bodies or experts may be invited to the meetings by the Board on a case by case basis, where the issues discussed are of relevance for them.
3. Each representative shall be designated by their Member State for a period of three years, renewable once.
4. Member States shall ensure that their representatives on the Board:

(a) have the relevant competences and powers in their Member State so as to contribute actively to the achievement of the Board's tasks referred to in Article 66;
(b) are designated as a single contact point vis-à-vis the Board and, where appropriate, taking into account Member States' needs, as a single contact point for stakeholders;
(c) are empowered to facilitate consistency and coordination between national competent authorities in their Member State as regards the implementation of this Regulation, including through the collection of relevant data and information for the purpose of fulfilling their tasks on the Board.

5. [1]The designated representatives of the Member States shall adopt the Board's rules of procedure by a two-thirds majority. [2]The rules of procedure shall, in particular, lay down procedures for the selection process, the duration of the mandate of, and specifications of the tasks of, the Chair, detailed arrangements for voting, and the organisation of the Board's activities and those of its sub-groups.
6.

(1) The Board shall establish two standing sub-groups to provide a platform for cooperation and exchange among market surveillance authorities and notifying authorities about issues related to market surveillance and notified bodies respectively.
(2) The standing sub-group for market surveillance should act as the administrative cooperation group (ADCO) for this Regulation within the meaning of Article 30 of Regulation (EU) 2019/1020.
(3) [1]The Board may establish other standing or temporary sub-groups as appropriate for the purpose of examining specific issues. [2]Where appropriate, representatives of the advisory forum referred to in Article 67 may be invited to such sub-groups or to specific meetings of those subgroups as observers.

7. The Board shall be organised and operated so as to safeguard the objectivity and impartiality of its activities.
8. [1]The Board shall be chaired by one of the representatives of the Member States. [2]The AI Office shall provide the secretariat for the Board, convene the meetings upon request of the Chair, and prepare the agenda in accordance with the tasks of the Board pursuant to this Regulation and its rules of procedure.

Article 66
Tasks of the Board

[1]The Board shall advise and assist the Commission and the Member States in order to facilitate the consistent and effective application of this Regulation. [2]To that end, the Board may in particular:

(a) contribute to the coordination among national competent authorities responsible for the application of this Regulation and, in cooperation with and subject to the agreement of the market surveillance authorities concerned, support joint activities of market surveillance authorities referred to in Article 74(11);
(b) collect and share technical and regulatory expertise and best practices among Member States;
(c) provide advice on the implementation of this Regulation, in particular as regards the enforcement of rules on general-purpose AI models;
(d) contribute to the harmonisation of administrative practices in the Member States, including in relation to the derogation from the conformity assessment procedures referred to in Article 46, the functioning of AI regulatory sandboxes, and testing in real world conditions referred to in Articles 57, 59 and 60;
(e) at the request of the Commission or on its own initiative, issue recommendations and written opinions on any relevant matters related to the implementation of this Regulation and to its consistent and effective application, including:
    (i) on the development and application of codes of conduct and codes of practice pursuant to this Regulation, as well as of the Commission's guidelines;
    (ii) the evaluation and review of this Regulation pursuant to Article 112, including as regards the serious incident reports referred to in Article 73, and the functioning of the EU database referred to in Article 71, the preparation of the delegated or implementing acts, and as regards possible alignments of this Regulation with the Union harmonisation legislation listed in Annex I;
    (iii) on technical specifications or existing standards regarding the requirements set out in Chapter III, Section 2;
    (iv) on the use of harmonised standards or common specifications referred to in Articles 40 and 41;
    (v) trends, such as European global competitiveness in AI, the uptake of AI in the Union, and the development of digital skills;
    (vi) trends on the evolving typology of AI value chains, in particular on the resulting implications in terms of accountability;
    (vii) on the potential need for amendment to Annex III in accordance with Article 7, and on the potential need for possible revision of Article 5 pursuant to Article 112, taking into account relevant available evidence and the latest developments in technology;
(f) support the Commission in promoting AI literacy, public awareness and understanding of the benefits, risks, safeguards and rights and obligations in relation to the use of AI systems;
(g) facilitate the development of common criteria and a shared understanding among market operators and competent authorities of the relevant concepts provided for in this Regulation, including by contributing to the development of benchmarks;
(h) cooperate, as appropriate, with other Union institutions, bodies, offices and agencies, as well as relevant Union expert groups and networks, in particular in the fields of product safety, cybersecurity, competition, digital and media services, financial services, consumer protection, data and fundamental rights protection;

(i) contribute to effective cooperation with the competent authorities of third countries and with international organisations;
(j) assist national competent authorities and the Commission in developing the organisational and technical expertise required for the implementation of this Regulation, including by contributing to the assessment of training needs for staff of Member States involved in implementing this Regulation;
(k) assist the AI Office in supporting national competent authorities in the establishment and development of AI regulatory sandboxes, and facilitate cooperation and information-sharing among AI regulatory sandboxes;
(l) contribute to, and provide relevant advice on, the development of guidance documents;
(m) advise the Commission in relation to international matters on AI;
(n) provide opinions to the Commission on the qualified alerts regarding general-purpose AI models;
(o) receive opinions by the Member States on qualified alerts regarding general-purpose AI models, and on national experiences and practices on the monitoring and enforcement of AI systems, in particular systems integrating the general-purpose AI models.

Article 67
Advisory forum

1. An advisory forum shall be established to provide technical expertise and advise the Board and the Commission, and to contribute to their tasks under this Regulation.
2. [1]The membership of the advisory forum shall represent a balanced selection of stakeholders, including industry, start-ups, SMEs, civil society and academia. [2]The membership of the advisory forum shall be balanced with regard to commercial and non-commercial interests and, within the category of commercial interests, with regard to SMEs and other undertakings.
3. The Commission shall appoint the members of the advisory forum, in accordance with the criteria set out in paragraph 2, from amongst stakeholders with recognised expertise in the field of AI.
4. The term of office of the members of the advisory forum shall be two years, which may be extended by up to no more than four years.
5. The Fundamental Rights Agency, ENISA, the European Committee for Standardization (CEN), the European Committee for Electrotechnical Standardization (CENELEC), and the European Telecommunications Standards Institute (ETSI) shall be permanent members of the advisory forum.
6. [1]The advisory forum shall draw up its rules of procedure. [2]It shall elect two co-chairs from among its members, in accordance with criteria set out in paragraph 2. [3]The term of office of the co-chairs shall be two years, renewable once.
7. [1]The advisory forum shall hold meetings at least twice a year. [2]The advisory forum may invite experts and other stakeholders to its meetings.
8. The advisory forum may prepare opinions, recommendations and written contributions at the request of the Board or the Commission.
9. The advisory forum may establish standing or temporary sub-groups as appropriate for the purpose of examining specific questions related to the objectives of this Regulation.

10. [1]The advisory forum shall prepare an annual report on its activities. [2]That report shall be made publicly available.

Article 68
Scientific panel of independent experts

1. [1]The Commission shall, by means of an implementing act, make provisions on the establishment of a scientific panel of independent experts (the „scientific panel") intended to support the enforcement activities under this Regulation. [2]That implementing act shall be adopted in accordance with the examination procedure referred to in Article 98(2).
2. [1]The scientific panel shall consist of experts selected by the Commission on the basis of up-to-date scientific or technical expertise in the field of AI necessary for the tasks set out in paragraph 3, and shall be able to demonstrate meeting all of the following conditions:

(a) having particular expertise and competence and scientific or technical expertise in the field of AI;
(b) independence from any provider of AI systems or general-purpose AI models;
(c) an ability to carry out activities diligently, accurately and objectively.

[2]The Commission, in consultation with the Board, shall determine the number of experts on the panel in accordance with the required needs and shall ensure fair gender and geographical representation.
3. The scientific panel shall advise and support the AI Office, in particular with regard to the following tasks:

(a) supporting the implementation and enforcement of this Regulation as regards general-purpose AI models and systems, in particular by:
    (i) alerting the AI Office of possible systemic risks at Union level of general-purpose AI models, in accordance with Article 90;
    (ii) contributing to the development of tools and methodologies for evaluating capabilities of general-purpose AI models and systems, including through benchmarks;
    (iii) providing advice on the classification of general-purpose AI models with systemic risk;
    (iv) providing advice on the classification of various general-purpose AI models and systems;
    (v) contributing to the development of tools and templates;
(b) supporting the work of market surveillance authorities, at their request;
(c) supporting cross-border market surveillance activities as referred to in Article 74(11), without prejudice to the powers of market surveillance authorities;
(d) supporting the AI Office in carrying out its duties in the context of the Union safeguard procedure pursuant to Article 81.

4. [1]The experts on the scientific panel shall perform their tasks with impartiality and objectivity, and shall ensure the confidentiality of information and data obtained in carrying out their tasks and activities. [2]They shall neither seek nor take instructions from anyone when exercising their tasks under paragraph 3. [3]Each expert shall draw up a declaration of interests, which shall be made publicly available. [4]The AI Office

shall establish systems and procedures to actively manage and prevent potential conflicts of interest.
5. The implementing act referred to in paragraph 1 shall include provisions on the conditions, procedures and detailed arrangements for the scientific panel and its members to issue alerts, and to request the assistance of the AI Office for the performance of the tasks of the scientific panel.

Article 69
Access to the pool of experts by the Member States

1. Member States may call upon experts of the scientific panel to support their enforcement activities under this Regulation.
2. [1]The Member States may be required to pay fees for the advice and support provided by the experts. [2]The structure and the level of fees as well as the scale and structure of recoverable costs shall be set out in the implementing act referred to in Article 68(1), taking into account the objectives of the adequate implementation of this Regulation, cost-effectiveness and the necessity of ensuring effective access to experts for all Member States.
3. The Commission shall facilitate timely access to the experts by the Member States, as needed, and ensure that the combination of support activities carried out by Union AI testing support pursuant to Article 84 and experts pursuant to this Article is efficiently organised and provides the best possible added value.

Section 2
National competent authorities

Article 70
Designation of national competent authorities and single points of contact

1. [1]Each Member State shall establish or designate as national competent authorities at least one notifying authority and at least one market surveillance authority for the purposes of this Regulation. [2]Those national competent authorities shall exercise their powers independently, impartially and without bias so as to safeguard the objectivity of their activities and tasks, and to ensure the application and implementation of this Regulation. [3]The members of those authorities shall refrain from any action incompatible with their duties. [4]Provided that those principles are observed, such activities and tasks may be performed by one or more designated authorities, in accordance with the organisational needs of the Member State.
2. [1]Member States shall communicate to the Commission the identity of the notifying authorities and the market surveillance authorities and the tasks of those authorities, as well as any subsequent changes thereto. [2]Member States shall make publicly available information on how competent authorities and single points of contact can be contacted, through electronic communication means by 2 August 2025. [3]Member States shall designate a market surveillance authority to act as the single point of contact for this Regulation, and shall notify the Commission of the identity of the single point of contact. [4]The Commission shall make a list of the single points of contact publicly available.

3. [1]Member States shall ensure that their national competent authorities are provided with adequate technical, financial and human resources, and with infrastructure to fulfil their tasks effectively under this Regulation. [2]In particular, the national competent authorities shall have a sufficient number of personnel permanently available whose competences and expertise shall include an in-depth understanding of AI technologies, data and data computing, personal data protection, cybersecurity, fundamental rights, health and safety risks and knowledge of existing standards and legal requirements. [3]Member States shall assess and, if necessary, update competence and resource requirements referred to in this paragraph on an annual basis.
4. National competent authorities shall take appropriate measures to ensure an adequate level of cybersecurity.
5. When performing their tasks, the national competent authorities shall act in accordance with the confidentiality obligations set out in Article 78.
6. [1]By 2 August 2025, and once every two years thereafter, Member States shall report to the Commission on the status of the financial and human resources of the national competent authorities, with an assessment of their adequacy. [2]The Commission shall transmit that information to the Board for discussion and possible recommendations.
7. The Commission shall facilitate the exchange of experience between national competent authorities.
8. [1]National competent authorities may provide guidance and advice on the implementation of this Regulation, in particular to SMEs including start-ups, taking into account the guidance and advice of the Board and the Commission, as appropriate. [2]Whenever national competent authorities intend to provide guidance and advice with regard to an AI system in areas covered by other Union law, the national competent authorities under that Union law shall be consulted, as appropriate.
9. Where Union institutions, bodies, offices or agencies fall within the scope of this Regulation, the European Data Protection Supervisor shall act as the competent authority for their supervision.

CHAPTER VIII
EU DATABASE FOR HIGH-RISK AI SYSTEMS

Article 71
EU database for high-risk AI systems listed in Annex III

1. [1]The Commission shall, in collaboration with the Member States, set up and maintain an EU database containing information referred to in paragraphs 2 and 3 of this Article concerning high-risk AI systems referred to in Article 6(2) which are registered in accordance with Articles 49 and 60 and AI systems that are not considered as high-risk pursuant to Article 6(3) and which are registered in accordance with Article 6(4) and Article 49. [2]When setting the functional specifications of such database, the Commission shall consult the relevant experts, and when updating the functional specifications of such database, the Commission shall consult the Board.
2. The data listed in Sections A and B of Annex VIII shall be entered into the EU database by the provider or, where applicable, by the authorised representative.
3. The data listed in Section C of Annex VIII shall be entered into the EU database by the deployer who is, or who acts on behalf of, a public authority, agency or body, in accordance with Article 49(3) and (4).
4. [1]With the exception of the section referred to in Article 49(4) and Article 60(4), point (c), the information contained in the EU database registered in accordance

with Article 49 shall be accessible and publicly available in a user-friendly manner. [2]The information should be easily navigable and machine-readable. [3]The information registered in accordance with Article 60 shall be accessible only to market surveillance authorities and the Commission, unless the prospective provider or provider has given consent for also making the information accessible the public.
5. [1]The EU database shall contain personal data only in so far as necessary for collecting and processing information in accordance with this Regulation. [2]That information shall include the names and contact details of natural persons who are responsible for registering the system and have the legal authority to represent the provider or the deployer, as applicable.
6. [1]The Commission shall be the controller of the EU database. [2]It shall make available to providers, prospective providers and deployers adequate technical and administrative support. [3]The EU database shall comply with the applicable accessibility requirements.

CHAPTER IX
POST-MARKET MONITORING, INFORMATION SHARING AND MARKET SURVEILLANCE

Section 1
Post-market monitoring

Article 72
Post-market monitoring by providers and post-market monitoring plan for high-risk AI systems

1. Providers shall establish and document a post-market monitoring system in a manner that is proportionate to the nature of the AI technologies and the risks of the high-risk AI system.
2. [1]The post-market monitoring system shall actively and systematically collect, document and analyse relevant data which may be provided by deployers or which may be collected through other sources on the performance of high-risk AI systems throughout their lifetime, and which allow the provider to evaluate the continuous compliance of AI systems with the requirements set out in Chapter III, Section 2. [2]Where relevant, post-market monitoring shall include an analysis of the interaction with other AI systems. [3]This obligation shall not cover sensitive operational data of deployers which are law-enforcement authorities.
3. [1]The post-market monitoring system shall be based on a post-market monitoring plan. [2]The post-market monitoring plan shall be part of the technical documentation referred to in Annex IV. The Commission shall adopt an implementing act laying down detailed provisions establishing a template for the post-market monitoring plan and the list of elements to be included in the plan by 2 February 2026. [3]That implementing act shall be adopted in accordance with the examination procedure referred to in Article 98(2).
4.

(1) For high-risk AI systems covered by the Union harmonisation legislation listed in Section A of Annex I, where a post-market monitoring system and plan are already established under that legislation, in order to ensure consistency, avoid duplications and minimise additional burdens, providers shall have a choice of

integrating, as appropriate, the necessary elements described in paragraphs 1, 2 and 3 using the template referred in paragraph 3 into systems and plans already existing under that legislation, provided that it achieves an equivalent level of protection.

(2) The first subparagraph of this paragraph shall also apply to high-risk AI systems referred to in point 5 of Annex III placed on the market or put into service by financial institutions that are subject to requirements under Union financial services law regarding their internal governance, arrangements or processes.

Section 2
Sharing of information on serious incidents

Article 73
Reporting of serious incidents

1. Providers of high-risk AI systems placed on the Union market shall report any serious incident to the market surveillance authorities of the Member States where that incident occurred.

2.

(1) The report referred to in paragraph 1 shall be made immediately after the provider has established a causal link between the AI system and the serious incident or the reasonable likelihood of such a link, and, in any event, not later than 15 days after the provider or, where applicable, the deployer, becomes aware of the serious incident.

(2) The period for the reporting referred to in the first subparagraph shall take account of the severity of the serious incident.

3. Notwithstanding paragraph 2 of this Article, in the event of a widespread infringement or a serious incident as defined in Article 3, point (49)(b), the report referred to in paragraph 1 of this Article shall be provided immediately, and not later than two days after the provider or, where applicable, the deployer becomes aware of that incident.

4. Notwithstanding paragraph 2, in the event of the death of a person, the report shall be provided immediately after the provider or the deployer has established, or as soon as it suspects, a causal relationship between the high-risk AI system and the serious incident, but not later than 10 days after the date on which the provider or, where applicable, the deployer becomes aware of the serious incident.

5. Where necessary to ensure timely reporting, the provider or, where applicable, the deployer, may submit an initial report that is incomplete, followed by a complete report.

6.

(1) [1]Following the reporting of a serious incident pursuant to paragraph 1, the provider shall, without delay, perform the necessary investigations in relation to the serious incident and the AI system concerned. [2]This shall include a risk assessment of the incident, and corrective action.

(2) The provider shall cooperate with the competent authorities, and where relevant with the notified body concerned, during the investigations referred to in the first subparagraph, and shall not perform any investigation which involves altering the AI system concerned in a way which may affect any subsequent evaluation of

the causes of the incident, prior to informing the competent authorities of such action.

7. [1]Upon receiving a notification related to a serious incident referred to in Article 3, point (49)(c), the relevant market surveillance authority shall inform the national public authorities or bodies referred to in Article 77(1). [2]The Commission shall develop dedicated guidance to facilitate compliance with the obligations set out in paragraph 1 of this Article. [3]That guidance shall be issued by 2 August 2025, and shall be assessed regularly.
8. The market surveillance authority shall take appropriate measures, as provided for in Article 19 of Regulation (EU) 2019/1020, within seven days from the date it received the notification referred to in paragraph 1 of this Article, and shall follow the notification procedures as provided in that Regulation.
9. For high-risk AI systems referred to in Annex III that are placed on the market or put into service by providers that are subject to Union legislative instruments laying down reporting obligations equivalent to those set out in this Regulation, the notification of serious incidents shall be limited to those referred to in Article 3, point (49)(c).
10. For high-risk AI systems which are safety components of devices, or are themselves devices, covered by Regulations (EU) 2017/745 and (EU) 2017/746, the notification of serious incidents shall be limited to those referred to in Article 3, point (49)(c) of this Regulation, and shall be made to the national competent authority chosen for that purpose by the Member States where the incident occurred.
11. National competent authorities shall immediately notify the Commission of any serious incident, whether or not they have taken action on it, in accordance with Article 20 of Regulation (EU) 2019/1020.

Section 3
Enforcement

Article 74
Market surveillance and control of AI systems in the Union market

1. [1]Regulation (EU) 2019/1020 shall apply to AI systems covered by this Regulation. [2]For the purposes of the effective enforcement of this Regulation:

(a) any reference to an economic operator under Regulation (EU) 2019/1020 shall be understood as including all operators identified in Article 2(1) of this Regulation;
(b) any reference to a product under Regulation (EU) 2019/1020 shall be understood as including all AI systems falling within the scope of this Regulation.

2. [1]As part of their reporting obligations under Article 34(4) of Regulation (EU) 2019/1020, the market surveillance authorities shall report annually to the Commission and relevant national competition authorities any information identified in the course of market surveillance activities that may be of potential interest for the application of Union law on competition rules. [2]They shall also annually report to the Commission about the use of prohibited practices that occurred during that year and about the measures taken.
3.

(1) For high-risk AI systems related to products covered by the Union harmonisation legislation listed in Section A of Annex I, the market surveillance authority for

the purposes of this Regulation shall be the authority responsible for market surveillance activities designated under those legal acts.

(2) By derogation from the first subparagraph, and in appropriate circumstances, Member States may designate another relevant authority to act as a market surveillance authority, provided they ensure coordination with the relevant sectoral market surveillance authorities responsible for the enforcement of the Union harmonisation legislation listed in Annex I.

4. [1]The procedures referred to in Articles 79 to 83 of this Regulation shall not apply to AI systems related to products covered by the Union harmonisation legislation listed in section A of Annex I, where such legal acts already provide for procedures ensuring an equivalent level of protection and having the same objective. [2]In such cases, the relevant sectoral procedures shall apply instead.
5. Without prejudice to the powers of market surveillance authorities under Article 14 of Regulation (EU) 2019/1020, for the purpose of ensuring the effective enforcement of this Regulation, market surveillance authorities may exercise the powers referred to in Article 14(4), points (d) and (j), of that Regulation remotely, as appropriate.
6. For high-risk AI systems placed on the market, put into service, or used by financial institutions regulated by Union financial services law, the market surveillance authority for the purposes of this Regulation shall be the relevant national authority responsible for the financial supervision of those institutions under that legislation in so far as the placing on the market, putting into service, or the use of the AI system is in direct connection with the provision of those financial services.
7.

(1) By way of derogation from paragraph 6, in appropriate circumstances, and provided that coordination is ensured, another relevant authority may be identified by the Member State as market surveillance authority for the purposes of this Regulation.

(2) National market surveillance authorities supervising regulated credit institutions regulated under Directive 2013/36/EU, which are participating in the Single Supervisory Mechanism established by Regulation (EU) No 1024/2013, should report, without delay, to the European Central Bank any information identified in the course of their market surveillance activities that may be of potential interest for the prudential supervisory tasks of the European Central Bank specified in that Regulation.

8. [1]For high-risk AI systems listed in point 1 of Annex III to this Regulation, in so far as the systems are used for law enforcement purposes, border management and justice and democracy, and for high-risk AI systems listed in points 6, 7 and 8 of Annex III to this Regulation, Member States shall designate as market surveillance authorities for the purposes of this Regulation either the competent data protection supervisory authorities under Regulation (EU) 2016/679 or Directive (EU) 2016/680, or any other authority designated pursuant to the same conditions laid down in Articles 41 to 44 of Directive (EU) 2016/680. [2]Market surveillance activities shall in no way affect the independence of judicial authorities, or otherwise interfere with their activities when acting in their judicial capacity.
9. Where Union institutions, bodies, offices or agencies fall within the scope of this Regulation, the European Data Protection Supervisor shall act as their market surveillance authority, except in relation to the Court of Justice of the European Union acting in its judicial capacity.

10. Member States shall facilitate coordination between market surveillance authorities designated under this Regulation and other relevant national authorities or bodies which supervise the application of Union harmonisation legislation listed in Annex I, or in other Union law, that might be relevant for the high-risk AI systems referred to in Annex III.
11. [1]Market surveillance authorities and the Commission shall be able to propose joint activities, including joint investigations, to be conducted by either market surveillance authorities or market surveillance authorities jointly with the Commission, that have the aim of promoting compliance, identifying non-compliance, raising awareness or providing guidance in relation to this Regulation with respect to specific categories of high-risk AI systems that are found to present a serious risk across two or more Member States in accordance with Article 9 of Regulation (EU) 2019/1020. [2]The AI Office shall provide coordination support for joint investigations.
12. Without prejudice to the powers provided for under Regulation (EU) 2019/1020, and where relevant and limited to what is necessary to fulfil their tasks, the market surveillance authorities shall be granted full access by providers to the documentation as well as the training, validation and testing data sets used for the development of high-risk AI systems, including, where appropriate and subject to security safeguards, through application programming interfaces (API) or other relevant technical means and tools enabling remote access.
13. Market surveillance authorities shall be granted access to the source code of the high-risk AI system upon a reasoned request and only when both of the following conditions are fulfilled:

(a) access to source code is necessary to assess the conformity of a high-risk AI system with the requirements set out in Chapter III, Section 2; and
(b) testing or auditing procedures and verifications based on the data and documentation provided by the provider have been exhausted or proved insufficient.

14. Any information or documentation obtained by market surveillance authorities shall be treated in accordance with the confidentiality obligations set out in Article 78.

Article 75
Mutual assistance, market surveillance and control of general-purpose AI systems

1. [1]Where an AI system is based on a general-purpose AI model, and the model and the system are developed by the same provider, the AI Office shall have powers to monitor and supervise compliance of that AI system with obligations under this Regulation. [2]To carry out its monitoring and supervision tasks, the AI Office shall have all the powers of a market surveillance authority provided for in this Section and Regulation (EU) 2019/1020.
2. Where the relevant market surveillance authorities have sufficient reason to consider general-purpose AI systems that can be used directly by deployers for at least one purpose that is classified as high-risk pursuant to this Regulation to be non-compliant with the requirements laid down in this Regulation, they shall cooperate with the AI Office to carry out compliance evaluations, and shall inform the Board and other market surveillance authorities accordingly.
3. [1]Where a market surveillance authority is unable to conclude its investigation of the high-risk AI system because of its inability to access certain information related to the

general-purpose AI model despite having made all appropriate efforts to obtain that information, it may submit a reasoned request to the AI Office, by which access to that information shall be enforced. [2]In that case, the AI Office shall supply to the applicant authority without delay, and in any event within 30 days, any information that the AI Office considers to be relevant in order to establish whether a high-risk AI system is non-compliant. [3]Market surveillance authorities shall safeguard the confidentiality of the information that they obtain in accordance with Article 78 of this Regulation. [4]The procedure provided for in Chapter VI of Regulation (EU) 2019/1020 shall apply *mutatis mutandis.*

Article 76
Supervision of testing in real world conditions by market surveillance authorities

1. Market surveillance authorities shall have competences and powers to ensure that testing in real world conditions is in accordance with this Regulation.
2. [1]Where testing in real world conditions is conducted for AI systems that are supervised within an AI regulatory sandbox under Article 58, the market surveillance authorities shall verify the compliance with Article 60 as part of their supervisory role for the AI regulatory sandbox. [2]Those authorities may, as appropriate, allow the testing in real world conditions to be conducted by the provider or prospective provider, in derogation from the conditions set out in Article 60(4), points (f) and (g).
3. Where a market surveillance authority has been informed by the prospective provider, the provider or any third party of a serious incident or has other grounds for considering that the conditions set out in Articles 60 and 61 are not met, it may take either of the following decisions on its territory, as appropriate:

(a) to suspend or terminate the testing in real world conditions;
(b) to require the provider or prospective provider and the deployer or prospective deployer to modify any aspect of the testing in real world conditions.

4. Where a market surveillance authority has taken a decision referred to in paragraph 3 of this Article, or has issued an objection within the meaning of Article 60(4), point (b), the decision or the objection shall indicate the grounds therefor and how the provider or prospective provider can challenge the decision or objection.
5. Where applicable, where a market surveillance authority has taken a decision referred to in paragraph 3, it shall communicate the grounds therefor to the market surveillance authorities of other Member States in which the AI system has been tested in accordance with the testing plan.

Article 77
Powers of authorities protecting fundamental rights

1. [1]National public authorities or bodies which supervise or enforce the respect of obligations under Union law protecting fundamental rights, including the right to non-discrimination, in relation to the use of high-risk AI systems referred to in Annex III shall have the power to request and access any documentation created or maintained under this Regulation in accessible language and format when access to that documentation is necessary for effectively fulfilling their mandates within the

limits of their jurisdiction. [2]The relevant public authority or body shall inform the market surveillance authority of the Member State concerned of any such request.
2. [1]By 2 November 2024, each Member State shall identify the public authorities or bodies referred to in paragraph 1 and make a list of them publicly available. [2]Member States shall notify the list to the Commission and to the other Member States, and shall keep the list up to date.
3. [1]Where the documentation referred to in paragraph 1 is insufficient to ascertain whether an infringement of obligations under Union law protecting fundamental rights has occurred, the public authority or body referred to in paragraph 1 may make a reasoned request to the market surveillance authority, to organise testing of the high-risk AI system through technical means. [2]The market surveillance authority shall organise the testing with the close involvement of the requesting public authority or body within a reasonable time following the request.
4. Any information or documentation obtained by the national public authorities or bodies referred to in paragraph 1 of this Article pursuant to this Article shall be treated in accordance with the confidentiality obligations set out in Article 78.

Article 78
Confidentiality

1. The Commission, market surveillance authorities and notified bodies and any other natural or legal person involved in the application of this Regulation shall, in accordance with Union or national law, respect the confidentiality of information and data obtained in carrying out their tasks and activities in such a manner as to protect, in particular:

(a) the intellectual property rights and confidential business information or trade secrets of a natural or legal person, including source code, except in the cases referred to in Article 5 of Directive (EU) 2016/943 of the European Parliament and of the Council[1];
(b) the effective implementation of this Regulation, in particular for the purposes of inspections, investigations or audits;
(c) public and national security interests;
(d) the conduct of criminal or administrative proceedings;
(e) information classified pursuant to Union or national law.

2. [1]The authorities involved in the application of this Regulation pursuant to paragraph 1 shall request only data that is strictly necessary for the assessment of the risk posed by AI systems and for the exercise of their powers in accordance with this Regulation and with Regulation (EU) 2019/1020. [2]They shall put in place adequate and effective cybersecurity measures to protect the security and confidentiality of the information and data obtained, and shall delete the data collected as soon as it is no longer needed for the purpose for which it was obtained, in accordance with applicable Union or national law.

[1] **Official note:** Directive (EU) 2016/943 of the European Parliament and of the Council of 8 June 2016 on the protection of undisclosed know-how and business information (trade secrets) against their unlawful acquisition, use and disclosure (OJ L 157, 15.6.2016, p. 1).

3.

(1) [1]Without prejudice to paragraphs 1 and 2, information exchanged on a confidential basis between the national competent authorities or between national competent authorities and the Commission shall not be disclosed without prior consultation of the originating national competent authority and the deployer when high-risk AI systems referred to in point 1, 6 or 7 of Annex III are used by law enforcement, border control, immigration or asylum authorities and when such disclosure would jeopardise public and national security interests. [2]This exchange of information shall not cover sensitive operational data in relation to the activities of law enforcement, border control, immigration or asylum authorities.

(2) [1]When the law enforcement, immigration or asylum authorities are providers of high-risk AI systems referred to in point 1, 6 or 7 of Annex III, the technical documentation referred to in Annex IV shall remain within the premises of those authorities. [2]Those authorities shall ensure that the market surveillance authorities referred to in Article 74(8) and (9), as applicable, can, upon request, immediately access the documentation or obtain a copy thereof. [3]Only staff of the market surveillance authority holding the appropriate level of security clearance shall be allowed to access that documentation or any copy thereof.

4. Paragraphs 1, 2 and 3 shall not affect the rights or obligations of the Commission, Member States and their relevant authorities, as well as those of notified bodies, with regard to the exchange of information and the dissemination of warnings, including in the context of cross-border cooperation, nor shall they affect the obligations of the parties concerned to provide information under criminal law of the Member States.
5. The Commission and Member States may exchange, where necessary and in accordance with relevant provisions of international and trade agreements, confidential information with regulatory authorities of third countries with which they have concluded bilateral or multilateral confidentiality arrangements guaranteeing an adequate level of confidentiality.

Article 79
Procedure at national level for dealing with AI systems presenting a risk

1. AI systems presenting a risk shall be understood as a „product presenting a risk“ as defined in Article 3, point 19 of Regulation (EU) 2019/1020, in so far as they present risks to the health or safety, or to fundamental rights, of persons.
2.

(1) [1]Where the market surveillance authority of a Member State has sufficient reason to consider an AI system to present a risk as referred to in paragraph 1 of this Article, it shall carry out an evaluation of the AI system concerned in respect of its compliance with all the requirements and obligations laid down in this Regulation. [2]Particular attention shall be given to AI systems presenting a risk to vulnerable groups. [3]Where risks to fundamental rights are identified, the market surveillance authority shall also inform and fully cooperate with the relevant national public authorities or bodies referred to in Article 77(1). [4]The relevant operators shall cooperate as necessary with the market surveillance authority and with the other national public authorities or bodies referred to in Article 77(1).

(2) Where, in the course of that evaluation, the market surveillance authority or, where applicable the market surveillance authority in cooperation with the national public authority referred to in Article 77(1), finds that the AI system does not comply with the requirements and obligations laid down in this Regulation, it shall without undue delay require the relevant operator to take all appropriate corrective actions to bring the AI system into compliance, to withdraw the AI system from the market, or to recall it within a period the market surveillance authority may prescribe, and in any event within the shorter of 15 working days, or as provided for in the relevant Union harmonisation legislation.

(3) [1]The market surveillance authority shall inform the relevant notified body accordingly. [2]Article 18 of Regulation (EU) 2019/1020 shall apply to the measures referred to in the second subparagraph of this paragraph.

3. Where the market surveillance authority considers that the non-compliance is not restricted to its national territory, it shall inform the Commission and the other Member States without undue delay of the results of the evaluation and of the actions which it has required the operator to take.
4. The operator shall ensure that all appropriate corrective action is taken in respect of all the AI systems concerned that it has made available on the Union market.
5. [1]Where the operator of an AI system does not take adequate corrective action within the period referred to in paragraph 2, the market surveillance authority shall take all appropriate provisional measures to prohibit or restrict the AI system's being made available on its national market or put into service, to withdraw the product or the standalone AI system from that market or to recall it. [2]That authority shall without undue delay notify the Commission and the other Member States of those measures.
6. [1]The notification referred to in paragraph 5 shall include all available details, in particular the information necessary for the identification of the non-compliant AI system, the origin of the AI system and the supply chain, the nature of the non-compliance alleged and the risk involved, the nature and duration of the national measures taken and the arguments put forward by the relevant operator. [2]In particular, the market surveillance authorities shall indicate whether the non-compliance is due to one or more of the following:

(a) non-compliance with the prohibition of the AI practices referred to in Article 5;
(b) a failure of a high-risk AI system to meet requirements set out in Chapter III, Section 2;
(c) shortcomings in the harmonised standards or common specifications referred to in Articles 40 and 41 conferring a presumption of conformity;
(d) non-compliance with Article 50.

7. The market surveillance authorities other than the market surveillance authority of the Member State initiating the procedure shall, without undue delay, inform the Commission and the other Member States of any measures adopted and of any additional information at their disposal relating to the non-compliance of the AI system concerned, and, in the event of disagreement with the notified national measure, of their objections.
8. [1]Where, within three months of receipt of the notification referred to in paragraph 5 of this Article, no objection has been raised by either a market surveillance authority of a Member State or by the Commission in respect of a provisional measure taken by a market surveillance authority of another Member State, that measure shall be deemed justified. [2]This shall be without prejudice to the procedural rights of the

concerned operator in accordance with Article 18 of Regulation (EU) 2019/1020. [3]The three-month period referred to in this paragraph shall be reduced to 30 days in the event of non-compliance with the prohibition of the AI practices referred to in Article 5 of this Regulation.
9. The market surveillance authorities shall ensure that appropriate restrictive measures are taken in respect of the product or the AI system concerned, such as withdrawal of the product or the AI system from their market, without undue delay.

Article 80
Procedure for dealing with AI systems classified by the provider as non-high-risk in application of Annex III

1. Where a market surveillance authority has sufficient reason to consider that an AI system classified by the provider as non-high-risk pursuant to Article 6(3) is indeed high-risk, the market surveillance authority shall carry out an evaluation of the AI system concerned in respect of its classification as a high-risk AI system based on the conditions set out in Article 6 and the Commission guidelines.
2. Where, in the course of that evaluation, the market surveillance authority finds that the AI system concerned is high-risk, it shall without undue delay require the relevant provider to take all necessary actions to bring the AI system into compliance with the requirements and obligations laid down in this Regulation, as well as take appropriate corrective action within a period the market surveillance authority may prescribe.
3. Where the market surveillance authority considers that the use of the AI system concerned is not restricted to its national territory, it shall inform the Commission and the other Member States without undue delay of the results of the evaluation and of the actions which it has required the provider to take.
4. [1]The provider shall ensure that all necessary action is taken to bring the AI system into compliance with the requirements and obligations laid down in this Regulation. [2]Where the provider of an AI system concerned does not bring the AI system into compliance with those requirements and obligations within the period referred to in paragraph 2 of this Article, the provider shall be subject to fines in accordance with Article 99.
5. The provider shall ensure that all appropriate corrective action is taken in respect of all the AI systems concerned that it has made available on the Union market.
6. Where the provider of the AI system concerned does not take adequate corrective action within the period referred to in paragraph 2 of this Article, Article 79(5) to (9) shall apply.
7. Where, in the course of the evaluation pursuant to paragraph 1 of this Article, the market surveillance authority establishes that the AI system was misclassified by the provider as non-high-risk in order to circumvent the application of requirements in Chapter III, Section 2, the provider shall be subject to fines in accordance with Article 99.
8. In exercising their power to monitor the application of this Article, and in accordance with Article 11 of Regulation (EU) 2019/1020, market surveillance authorities may perform appropriate checks, taking into account in particular information stored in the EU database referred to in Article 71 of this Regulation.

Article 81
Union safeguard procedure

1. [1]Where, within three months of receipt of the notification referred to in Article 79(5), or within 30 days in the case of non-compliance with the prohibition of the AI practices referred to in Article 5, objections are raised by the market surveillance authority of a Member State to a measure taken by another market surveillance authority, or where the Commission considers the measure to be contrary to Union law, the Commission shall without undue delay enter into consultation with the market surveillance authority of the relevant Member State and the operator or operators, and shall evaluate the national measure. [2]On the basis of the results of that evaluation, the Commission shall, within six months, or within 60 days in the case of non-compliance with the prohibition of the AI practices referred to in Article 5, starting from the notification referred to in Article 79(5), decide whether the national measure is justified and shall notify its decision to the market surveillance authority of the Member State concerned. [3]The Commission shall also inform all other market surveillance authorities of its decision.
2. [1]Where the Commission considers the measure taken by the relevant Member State to be justified, all Member States shall ensure that they take appropriate restrictive measures in respect of the AI system concerned, such as requiring the withdrawal of the AI system from their market without undue delay, and shall inform the Commission accordingly. [2]Where the Commission considers the national measure to be unjustified, the Member State concerned shall withdraw the measure and shall inform the Commission accordingly.
3. Where the national measure is considered justified and the non-compliance of the AI system is attributed to shortcomings in the harmonised standards or common specifications referred to in Articles 40 and 41 of this Regulation, the Commission shall apply the procedure provided for in Article 11 of Regulation (EU) No 1025/2012.

Article 82
Compliant AI systems which present a risk

1. Where, having performed an evaluation under Article 79, after consulting the relevant national public authority referred to in Article 77(1), the market surveillance authority of a Member State finds that although a high-risk AI system complies with this Regulation, it nevertheless presents a risk to the health or safety of persons, to fundamental rights, or to other aspects of public interest protection, it shall require the relevant operator to take all appropriate measures to ensure that the AI system concerned, when placed on the market or put into service, no longer presents that risk without undue delay, within a period it may prescribe.
2. The provider or other relevant operator shall ensure that corrective action is taken in respect of all the AI systems concerned that it has made available on the Union market within the timeline prescribed by the market surveillance authority of the Member State referred to in paragraph 1.
3. [1]The Member States shall immediately inform the Commission and the other Member States of a finding under paragraph 1. [2]That information shall include all available details, in particular the data necessary for the identification of the AI system concerned, the origin and the supply chain of the AI system, the nature of the risk involved and the nature and duration of the national measures taken.

4. [1]The Commission shall without undue delay enter into consultation with the Member States concerned and the relevant operators, and shall evaluate the national measures taken. [2]On the basis of the results of that evaluation, the Commission shall decide whether the measure is justified and, where necessary, propose other appropriate measures.
5. [1]The Commission shall immediately communicate its decision to the Member States concerned and to the relevant operators. [2]It shall also inform the other Member States.

Article 83
Formal non-compliance

1. Where the market surveillance authority of a Member State makes one of the following findings, it shall require the relevant provider to put an end to the non-compliance concerned, within a period it may prescribe:

(a) the CE marking has been affixed in violation of Article 48;
(b) the CE marking has not been affixed;
(c) the EU declaration of conformity referred to in Article 47 has not been drawn up;
(d) the EU declaration of conformity referred to in Article 47 has not been drawn up correctly;
(e) the registration in the EU database referred to in Article 71 has not been carried out;
(f) where applicable, no authorised representative has been appointed;
(g) technical documentation is not available.

2. Where the non-compliance referred to in paragraph 1 persists, the market surveillance authority of the Member State concerned shall take appropriate and proportionate measures to restrict or prohibit the high-risk AI system being made available on the market or to ensure that it is recalled or withdrawn from the market without delay.

Article 84
Union AI testing support structures

1. The Commission shall designate one or more Union AI testing support structures to perform the tasks listed under Article 21(6) of Regulation (EU) 2019/1020 in the area of AI.
2. Without prejudice to the tasks referred to in paragraph 1, Union AI testing support structures shall also provide independent technical or scientific advice at the request of the Board, the Commission, or of market surveillance authorities.

Section 4
Remedies

Article 85
Right to lodge a complaint with a market surveillance authority

(1) Without prejudice to other administrative or judicial remedies, any natural or legal person having grounds to consider that there has been an infringement of

the provisions of this Regulation may submit complaints to the relevant market surveillance authority.

(2) In accordance with Regulation (EU) 2019/1020, such complaints shall be taken into account for the purpose of conducting market surveillance activities, and shall be handled in line with the dedicated procedures established therefor by the market surveillance authorities.

Article 86
Right to explanation of individual decision-making

1. Any affected person subject to a decision which is taken by the deployer on the basis of the output from a high-risk AI system listed in Annex III, with the exception of systems listed under point 2 thereof, and which produces legal effects or similarly significantly affects that person in a way that they consider to have an adverse impact on their health, safety or fundamental rights shall have the right to obtain from the deployer clear and meaningful explanations of the role of the AI system in the decision-making procedure and the main elements of the decision taken.
2. Paragraph 1 shall not apply to the use of AI systems for which exceptions from, or restrictions to, the obligation under that paragraph follow from Union or national law in compliance with Union law.
3. This Article shall apply only to the extent that the right referred to in paragraph 1 is not otherwise provided for under Union law.

Article 87
Reporting of infringements and protection of reporting persons

Directive (EU) 2019/1937 shall apply to the reporting of infringements of this Regulation and the protection of persons reporting such infringements.

Section 5
Supervision, investigation, enforcement and monitoring in respect of providers of general-purpose AI models

Article 88
Enforcement of the obligations of providers of general-purpose AI models

1. [1]The Commission shall have exclusive powers to supervise and enforce Chapter V, taking into account the procedural guarantees under Article 94. [2]The Commission shall entrust the implementation of these tasks to the AI Office, without prejudice to the powers of organisation of the Commission and the division of competences between Member States and the Union based on the Treaties.
2. Without prejudice to Article 75(3), market surveillance authorities may request the Commission to exercise the powers laid down in this Section, where that is necessary and proportionate to assist with the fulfilment of their tasks under this Regulation.

Article 89
Monitoring actions

1. For the purpose of carrying out the tasks assigned to it under this Section, the AI Office may take the necessary actions to monitor the effective implementation and compliance with this Regulation by providers of general-purpose AI models, including their adherence to approved codes of practice.
2. [1]Downstream providers shall have the right to lodge a complaint alleging an infringement of this Regulation. [2]A complaint shall be duly reasoned and indicate at least:

(a) the point of contact of the provider of the general-purpose AI model concerned;
(b) a description of the relevant facts, the provisions of this Regulation concerned, and the reason why the downstream provider considers that the provider of the general-purpose AI model concerned infringed this Regulation;
(c) any other information that the downstream provider that sent the request considers relevant, including, where appropriate, information gathered on its own initiative.

Article 90
Alerts of systemic risks by the scientific panel

1. The scientific panel may provide a qualified alert to the AI Office where it has reason to suspect that:

(a) a general-purpose AI model poses concrete identifiable risk at Union level; or
(b) a general-purpose AI model meets the conditions referred to in Article 51.

2. [1]Upon such qualified alert, the Commission, through the AI Office and after having informed the Board, may exercise the powers laid down in this Section for the purpose of assessing the matter. [2]The AI Office shall inform the Board of any measure according to Articles 91 to 94.
3. A qualified alert shall be duly reasoned and indicate at least:

(a) the point of contact of the provider of the general-purpose AI model with systemic risk concerned;
(b) a description of the relevant facts and the reasons for the alert by the scientific panel;
(c) any other information that the scientific panel considers to be relevant, including, where appropriate, information gathered on its own initiative.

Article 91
Power to request documentation and information

1. The Commission may request the provider of the general-purpose AI model concerned to provide the documentation drawn up by the provider in accordance with Articles 53 and 55, or any additional information that is necessary for the purpose of assessing compliance of the provider with this Regulation.
2. Before sending the request for information, the AI Office may initiate a structured dialogue with the provider of the general-purpose AI model.

3. Upon a duly substantiated request from the scientific panel, the Commission may issue a request for information to a provider of a general-purpose AI model, where the access to information is necessary and proportionate for the fulfilment of the tasks of the scientific panel under Article 68(2).
4. The request for information shall state the legal basis and the purpose of the request, specify what information is required, set a period within which the information is to be provided, and indicate the fines provided for in Article 101 for supplying incorrect, incomplete or misleading information.
5. [1]The provider of the general-purpose AI model concerned, or its representative shall supply the information requested. [2]In the case of legal persons, companies or firms, or where the provider has no legal personality, the persons authorised to represent them by law or by their statutes, shall supply the information requested on behalf of the provider of the general-purpose AI model concerned. [3]Lawyers duly authorised to act may supply information on behalf of their clients. [4]The clients shall nevertheless remain fully responsible if the information supplied is incomplete, incorrect or misleading.

Article 92
Power to conduct evaluations

1. The AI Office, after consulting the Board, may conduct evaluations of the general-purpose AI model concerned:

(a) to assess compliance of the provider with obligations under this Regulation, where the information gathered pursuant to Article 91 is insufficient; or
(b) to investigate systemic risks at Union level of general-purpose AI models with systemic risk, in particular following a qualified alert from the scientific panel in accordance with Article 90(1), point (a).

2. [1]The Commission may decide to appoint independent experts to carry out evaluations on its behalf, including from the scientific panel established pursuant to Article 68. [2]Independent experts appointed for this task shall meet the criteria outlined in Article 68(2).
3. For the purposes of paragraph 1, the Commission may request access to the general-purpose AI model concerned through APIs or further appropriate technical means and tools, including source code.
4. The request for access shall state the legal basis, the purpose and reasons of the request and set the period within which the access is to be provided, and the fines provided for in Article 101 for failure to provide access.
5. [1]The providers of the general-purpose AI model concerned or its representative shall supply the information requested. [2]In the case of legal persons, companies or firms, or where the provider has no legal personality, the persons authorised to represent them by law or by their statutes, shall provide the access requested on behalf of the provider of the general-purpose AI model concerned.
6. [1]The Commission shall adopt implementing acts setting out the detailed arrangements and the conditions for the evaluations, including the detailed arrangements for involving independent experts, and the procedure for the selection thereof. [2]Those implementing acts shall be adopted in accordance with the examination procedure referred to in Article 98(2).

7. Prior to requesting access to the general-purpose AI model concerned, the AI Office may initiate a structured dialogue with the provider of the general-purpose AI model to gather more information on the internal testing of the model, internal safeguards for preventing systemic risks, and other internal procedures and measures the provider has taken to mitigate such risks.

Article 93
Power to request measures

1. Where necessary and appropriate, the Commission may request providers to:

(a) take appropriate measures to comply with the obligations set out in Articles 53 and 54;
(b) implement mitigation measures, where the evaluation carried out in accordance with Article 92 has given rise to serious and substantiated concern of a systemic risk at Union level;
(c) restrict the making available on the market, withdraw or recall the model.

2. Before a measure is requested, the AI Office may initiate a structured dialogue with the provider of the general-purpose AI model.
3. If, during the structured dialogue referred to in paragraph 2, the provider of the general-purpose AI model with systemic risk offers commitments to implement mitigation measures to address a systemic risk at Union level, the Commission may, by decision, make those commitments binding and declare that there are no further grounds for action.

Article 94
Procedural rights of economic operators of the general-purpose AI model

Article 18 of Regulation (EU) 2019/1020 shall apply *mutatis mutandis* to the providers of the general-purpose AI model, without prejudice to more specific procedural rights provided for in this Regulation.

CHAPTER X
CODES OF CONDUCT AND GUIDELINES

Article 95
Codes of conduct for voluntary application of specific requirements

1. The AI Office and the Member States shall encourage and facilitate the drawing up of codes of conduct, including related governance mechanisms, intended to foster the voluntary application to AI systems, other than high-risk AI systems, of some or all of the requirements set out in Chapter III, Section 2 taking into account the available technical solutions and industry best practices allowing for the application of such requirements.
2. The AI Office and the Member States shall facilitate the drawing up of codes of conduct concerning the voluntary application, including by deployers, of specific requirements to all AI systems, on the basis of clear objectives and key performance

indicators to measure the achievement of those objectives, including elements such as, but not limited to:

(a) applicable elements provided for in Union ethical guidelines for trustworthy AI;
(b) assessing and minimising the impact of AI systems on environmental sustainability, including as regards energy-efficient programming and techniques for the efficient design, training and use of AI;
(c) promoting AI literacy, in particular that of persons dealing with the development, operation and use of AI;
(d) facilitating an inclusive and diverse design of AI systems, including through the establishment of inclusive and diverse development teams and the promotion of stakeholders' participation in that process;
(e) assessing and preventing the negative impact of AI systems on vulnerable persons or groups of vulnerable persons, including as regards accessibility for persons with a disability, as well as on gender equality.

3. [1]Codes of conduct may be drawn up by individual providers or deployers of AI systems or by organisations representing them or by both, including with the involvement of any interested stakeholders and their representative organisations, including civil society organisations and academia. [2]Codes of conduct may cover one or more AI systems taking into account the similarity of the intended purpose of the relevant systems.
4. The AI Office and the Member States shall take into account the specific interests and needs of SMEs, including start-ups, when encouraging and facilitating the drawing up of codes of conduct.

Article 96
Guidelines from the Commission on the implementation of this Regulation

1.

(1) [1]The Commission shall develop guidelines on the practical implementation of this Regulation, and in particular on:
   (a) the application of the requirements and obligations referred to in Articles 8 to 15 and in Article 25;
   (b) the prohibited practices referred to in Article 5;
   (c) the practical implementation of the provisions related to substantial modification;
   (d) the practical implementation of transparency obligations laid down in Article 50;
   (e) detailed information on the relationship of this Regulation with the Union harmonisation legislation listed in Annex I, as well as with other relevant Union law, including as regards consistency in their enforcement;
   (f) the application of the definition of an AI system as set out in Article 3, point (1).

   [2]When issuing such guidelines, the Commission shall pay particular attention to the needs of SMEs including start-ups, of local public authorities and of the sectors most likely to be affected by this Regulation.

(2) The guidelines referred to in the first subparagraph of this paragraph shall take due account of the generally acknowledged state of the art on AI, as well as of relevant harmonised standards and common specifications that are referred to in Articles 40 and 41, or of those harmonised standards or technical specifications that are set out pursuant to Union harmonisation law.

2. At the request of the Member States or the AI Office, or on its own initiative, the Commission shall update guidelines previously adopted when deemed necessary.

CHAPTER XI
DELEGATION OF POWER AND COMMITTEE PROCEDURE

Article 97
Exercise of the delegation

1. The power to adopt delegated acts is conferred on the Commission subject to the conditions laid down in this Article.
2. [1]The power to adopt delegated acts referred to in Article 6(6) and (7), Article 7(1) and (3), Article 11(3), Article 43(5) and (6), Article 47(5), Article 51(3), Article 52(4) and Article 53(5) and (6) shall be conferred on the Commission for a period of five years from 1 August 2024. [2]The Commission shall draw up a report in respect of the delegation of power not later than nine months before the end of the five-year period. [3]The delegation of power shall be tacitly extended for periods of an identical duration, unless the European Parliament or the Council opposes such extension not later than three months before the end of each period.
3. [1]The delegation of power referred to in Article 6(6)and (7), Article 7(1) and (3), Article 11(3), Article 43(5) and (6), Article 47(5), Article 51(3), Article 52(4) and Article 53(5) and (6)may be revoked at any time by the European Parliament or by the Council. [2]A decision of revocation shall put an end to the delegation of power specified in that decision. [3]It shall take effect the day following that of its publication in the *Official Journal of the European Union* or at a later date specified therein. [4]It shall not affect the validity of any delegated acts already in force.
4. Before adopting a delegated act, the Commission shall consult experts designated by each Member State in accordance with the principles laid down in the Interinstitutional Agreement of 13 April 2016 on Better Law-Making.
5. As soon as it adopts a delegated act, the Commission shall notify it simultaneously to the European Parliament and to the Council.
6. [1]Any delegated act adopted pursuant to Article 6(6) or (7), Article 7(1) or (3), Article 11(3), Article 43(5) or (6), Article 47(5), Article 51(3), Article 52(4) or Article 53(5) or (6) shall enter into force only if no objection has been expressed by either the European Parliament or the Council within a period of three months of notification of that act to the European Parliament and the Council or if, before the expiry of that period, the European Parliament and the Council have both informed the Commission that they will not object. [2]That period shall be extended by three months at the initiative of the European Parliament or of the Council.

Article 98
Committee procedure

1. [1]The Commission shall be assisted by a committee. [2]That committee shall be a committee within the meaning of Regulation (EU) No 182/2011.
2. Where reference is made to this paragraph, Article 5 of Regulation (EU) No 182/2011 shall apply.

CHAPTER XII
PENALTIES

Article 99
Penalties

1. [1]In accordance with the terms and conditions laid down in this Regulation, Member States shall lay down the rules on penalties and other enforcement measures, which may also include warnings and non-monetary measures, applicable to infringements of this Regulation by operators, and shall take all measures necessary to ensure that they are properly and effectively implemented, thereby taking into account the guidelines issued by the Commission pursuant to Article 96. [2]The penalties provided for shall be effective, proportionate and dissuasive. [3]They shall take into account the interests of SMEs, including start-ups, and their economic viability.
2. The Member States shall, without delay and at the latest by the date of entry into application, notify the Commission of the rules on penalties and of other enforcement measures referred to in paragraph 1, and shall notify it, without delay, of any subsequent amendment to them.
3. Non-compliance with the prohibition of the AI practices referred to in Article 5 shall be subject to administrative fines of up to EUR 35 000 000 or, if the offender is an undertaking, up to 7 % of its total worldwide annual turnover for the preceding financial year, whichever is higher.
4. Non-compliance with any of the following provisions related to operators or notified bodies, other than those laid down in Articles 5, shall be subject to administrative fines of up to EUR 15 000 000 or, if the offender is an undertaking, up to 3 % of its total worldwide annual turnover for the preceding financial year, whichever is higher:

(a) obligations of providers pursuant to Article 16;
(b) obligations of authorised representatives pursuant to Article 22;
(c) obligations of importers pursuant to Article 23;
(d) obligations of distributors pursuant to Article 24;
(e) obligations of deployers pursuant to Article 26;
(f) requirements and obligations of notified bodies pursuant to Article 31, Article 33(1), (3) and (4) or Article 34;
(g) transparency obligations for providers and deployers pursuant to Article 50.

5. The supply of incorrect, incomplete or misleading information to notified bodies or national competent authorities in reply to a request shall be subject to administrative fines of up to EUR 7 500 000 or, if the offender is an undertaking, up to 1 % of its total worldwide annual turnover for the preceding financial year, whichever is higher.
6. In the case of SMEs, including start-ups, each fine referred to in this Article shall be up to the percentages or amount referred to in paragraphs 3, 4 and 5, whichever thereof is lower.

7. When deciding whether to impose an administrative fine and when deciding on the amount of the administrative fine in each individual case, all relevant circumstances of the specific situation shall be taken into account and, as appropriate, regard shall be given to the following:

(a) the nature, gravity and duration of the infringement and of its consequences, taking into account the purpose of the AI system, as well as, where appropriate, the number of affected persons and the level of damage suffered by them;
(b) whether administrative fines have already been applied by other market surveillance authorities to the same operator for the same infringement;
(c) whether administrative fines have already been applied by other authorities to the same operator for infringements of other Union or national law, when such infringements result from the same activity or omission constituting a relevant infringement of this Regulation;
(d) the size, the annual turnover and market share of the operator committing the infringement;
(e) any other aggravating or mitigating factor applicable to the circumstances of the case, such as financial benefits gained, or losses avoided, directly or indirectly, from the infringement;
(f) the degree of cooperation with the national competent authorities, in order to remedy the infringement and mitigate the possible adverse effects of the infringement;
(g) the degree of responsibility of the operator taking into account the technical and organisational measures implemented by it;
(h) the manner in which the infringement became known to the national competent authorities, in particular whether, and if so to what extent, the operator notified the infringement;
(i) the intentional or negligent character of the infringement;
(j) any action taken by the operator to mitigate the harm suffered by the affected persons.

8. Each Member State shall lay down rules on to what extent administrative fines may be imposed on public authorities and bodies established in that Member State.
9. [1]Depending on the legal system of the Member States, the rules on administrative fines may be applied in such a manner that the fines are imposed by competent national courts or by other bodies, as applicable in those Member States. [2]The application of such rules in those Member States shall have an equivalent effect.
10. The exercise of powers under this Article shall be subject to appropriate procedural safeguards in accordance with Union and national law, including effective judicial remedies and due process.
11. Member States shall, on an annual basis, report to the Commission about the administrative fines they have issued during that year, in accordance with this Article, and about any related litigation or judicial proceedings.

Article 100
Administrative fines on Union institutions, bodies, offices and agencies

1. [1]The European Data Protection Supervisor may impose administrative fines on Union institutions, bodies, offices and agencies falling within the scope of this Regu-

lation. [2]When deciding whether to impose an administrative fine and when deciding on the amount of the administrative fine in each individual case, all relevant circumstances of the specific situation shall be taken into account and due regard shall be given to the following:

(a) the nature, gravity and duration of the infringement and of its consequences, taking into account the purpose of the AI system concerned, as well as, where appropriate, the number of affected persons and the level of damage suffered by them;
(b) the degree of responsibility of the Union institution, body, office or agency, taking into account technical and organisational measures implemented by them;
(c) any action taken by the Union institution, body, office or agency to mitigate the damage suffered by affected persons;
(d) the degree of cooperation with the European Data Protection Supervisor in order to remedy the infringement and mitigate the possible adverse effects of the infringement, including compliance with any of the measures previously ordered by the European Data Protection Supervisor against the Union institution, body, office or agency concerned with regard to the same subject matter;
(e) any similar previous infringements by the Union institution, body, office or agency;
(f) the manner in which the infringement became known to the European Data Protection Supervisor, in particular whether, and if so to what extent, the Union institution, body, office or agency notified the infringement;
(g) the annual budget of the Union institution, body, office or agency.

2. Non-compliance with the prohibition of the AI practices referred to in Article 5 shall be subject to administrative fines of up to EUR 1 500 000.
3. The non-compliance of the AI system with any requirements or obligations under this Regulation, other than those laid down in Article 5, shall be subject to administrative fines of up to EUR 750 000.
4. [1]Before taking decisions pursuant to this Article, the European Data Protection Supervisor shall give the Union institution, body, office or agency which is the subject of the proceedings conducted by the European Data Protection Supervisor the opportunity of being heard on the matter regarding the possible infringement. [2]The European Data Protection Supervisor shall base his or her decisions only on elements and circumstances on which the parties concerned have been able to comment. [3]Complainants, if any, shall be associated closely with the proceedings.
5. [1]The rights of defence of the parties concerned shall be fully respected in the proceedings. [2]They shall be entitled to have access to the European Data Protection Supervisor's file, subject to the legitimate interest of individuals or undertakings in the protection of their personal data or business secrets.
6. [1]Funds collected by imposition of fines in this Article shall contribute to the general budget of the Union. [2]The fines shall not affect the effective operation of the Union institution, body, office or agency fined.
7. The European Data Protection Supervisor shall, on an annual basis, notify the Commission of the administrative fines it has imposed pursuant to this Article and of any litigation or judicial proceedings it has initiated.

Article 101
Fines for providers of general-purpose AI models

1. [1]The Commission may impose on providers of general-purpose AI models fines not exceeding 3 % of their annual total worldwide turnover in the preceding financial year or EUR 15 000 000, whichever is higher., when the Commission finds that the provider intentionally or negligently:

(a) infringed the relevant provisions of this Regulation;
(b) failed to comply with a request for a document or for information pursuant to Article 91, or supplied incorrect, incomplete or misleading information;
(c) failed to comply with a measure requested under Article 93;
(d) failed to make available to the Commission access to the general-purpose AI model or general-purpose AI model with systemic risk with a view to conducting an evaluation pursuant to Article 92.

[2]In fixing the amount of the fine or periodic penalty payment, regard shall be had to the nature, gravity and duration of the infringement, taking due account of the principles of proportionality and appropriateness. [3]The Commission shall also into account commitments made in accordance with Article 93(3) or made in relevant codes of practice in accordance with Article 56.
2. Before adopting the decision pursuant to paragraph 1, the Commission shall communicate its preliminary findings to the provider of the general-purpose AI model and give it an opportunity to be heard.
3. Fines imposed in accordance with this Article shall be effective, proportionate and dissuasive.
4. Information on fines imposed under this Article shall also be communicated to the Board as appropriate.
5. [1]The Court of Justice of the European Union shall have unlimited jurisdiction to review decisions of the Commission fixing a fine under this Article. [2]It may cancel, reduce or increase the fine imposed.
6. [1]The Commission shall adopt implementing acts containing detailed arrangements and procedural safeguards for proceedings in view of the possible adoption of decisions pursuant to paragraph 1 of this Article. [2]Those implementing acts shall be adopted in accordance with the examination procedure referred to in Article 98(2).

CHAPTER XIII
FINAL PROVISIONS

Article 102
Amendment to Regulation (EC) No 300/2008

In Article 4(3) of Regulation (EC) No 300/2008, the following subparagraph is added: When adopting detailed measures related to technical specifications and procedures for approval and use of security equipment concerning Artificial Intelligence systems within the meaning of Regulation (EU) 2024/1689 of the European Parliament and of the Council[1], the requirements set out in Chapter III, Section 2, of that Regulation shall be taken into account.

Article 103
Amendment to Regulation (EU) No 167/2013

In Article 17(5) of Regulation (EU) No 167/2013, the following subparagraph is added:
When adopting delegated acts pursuant to the first subparagraph concerning artificial intelligence systems which are safety components within the meaning of Regulation (EU) 2024/1689 of the European Parliament and of the Council[1], the requirements set out in Chapter III, Section 2, of that Regulation shall be taken into account.

Article 104
Amendment to Regulation (EU) No 168/2013

In Article 22(5) of Regulation (EU) No 168/2013, the following subparagraph is added:
When adopting delegated acts pursuant to the first subparagraph concerning Artificial Intelligence systems which are safety components within the meaning of Regulation (EU) 2024/1689 of the European Parliament and of the Council[1], the requirements set out in Chapter III, Section 2, of that Regulation shall be taken into account.

Article 105
Amendment to Directive 2014/90/EU

In Article 8 of Directive 2014/90/EU, the following paragraph is added:
5. For Artificial Intelligence systems which are safety components within the meaning of Regulation (EU) 2024/1689 of the European Parliament and of the Council[1], when carrying out its activities pursuant to paragraph 1 and when adopting technical specifications and testing standards in accordance with paragraphs 2 and 3, the Com-

[1] **Official note:** Regulation (EU) 2024/1689 of the European Parliament and of the Council of 13 June 2024 laying down harmonised rules on artificial intelligence and amending Regulations (EC) No 300/2008, (EU) No 167/2013, (EU) No 168/2013, (EU) 2018/858, (EU) 2018/1139 and (EU) 2019/2144 and Directives 2014/90/EU, (EU) 2016/797 and (EU) 2020/1828 (Artificial Intelligence Act) (OJ L, 2024/1689, 12.7.2024, ELI: http://data.europa.eu/eli/reg/2024/1689/oj).

[1] **Official note:** Regulation (EU) 2024/1689 of the European Parliament and of the Council of 13 June 2024 laying down harmonised rules on artificial intelligence and amending Regulations (EC) No 300/2008, (EU) No 167/2013, (EU) No 168/2013, (EU) 2018/858, (EU) 2018/1139 and (EU) 2019/2144 and Directives 2014/90/EU, (EU) 2016/797 and (EU) 2020/1828 (Artificial Intelligence Act) (OJ L, 2024/1689, 12.7.2024, ELI: http://data.europa.eu/eli/reg/2024/1689/oj).

[1] **Official note:** Regulation (EU) 2024/1689 of the European Parliament and of the Council of 13 June 2024 laying down harmonised rules on artificial intelligence and amending Regulations (EC) No 300/2008, (EU) No 167/2013, (EU) No 168/2013, (EU) 2018/858, (EU) 2018/1139 and (EU) 2019/2144 and Directives 2014/90/EU, (EU) 2016/797 and (EU) 2020/1828 (Artificial Intelligence Act) (OJ L, 2024/1689, 12.7.2024, ELI: http://data.europa.eu/eli/reg/2024/1689/oj).

[1] **Official note:** Regulation (EU) 2024/1689 of the European Parliament and of the Council of 13 June 2024 laying down harmonised rules on artificial intelligence and amending Regulations (EC) No 300/2008, (EU) No 167/2013, (EU) No 168/2013, (EU) 2018/858, (EU) 2018/1139 and (EU) 2019/2144 and Directives 2014/90/EU, (EU) 2016/797 and (EU) 2020/1828 (Artificial Intelligence Act) (OJ L, 2024/1689, 12.7.2024, ELI: http://data.europa.eu/eli/reg/2024/1689/oj).

mission shall take into account the requirements set out in Chapter III, Section 2, of that Regulation.

Article 106
Amendment to Directive (EU) 2016/797

In Article 5 of Directive (EU) 2016/797, the following paragraph is added:
12. When adopting delegated acts pursuant to paragraph 1 and implementing acts pursuant to paragraph 11 concerning Artificial Intelligence systems which are safety components within the meaning of Regulation (EU) 2024/1689 of the European Parliament and of the Council[1], the requirements set out in Chapter III, Section 2, of that Regulation shall be taken into account.

Article 107
Amendment to Regulation (EU) 2018/858

In Article 5 of Regulation (EU) 2018/858 the following paragraph is added:
4. When adopting delegated acts pursuant to paragraph 3 concerning Artificial Intelligence systems which are safety components within the meaning of Regulation (EU) 2024/1689 of the European Parliament and of the Council[1], the requirements set out in Chapter III, Section 2, of that Regulation shall be taken into account.

Article 108
Amendments to Regulation (EU) 2018/1139

Regulation (EU) 2018/1139 is amended as follows:

(1) in Article 17, the following paragraph is added:

3. Without prejudice to paragraph 2, when adopting implementing acts pursuant to paragraph 1 concerning Artificial Intelligence systems which are safety components within the meaning of Regulation (EU) 2024/1689 of the European Parliament and of the Council[1], the requirements set out in Chapter III, Section 2, of that Regulation shall be taken into account.

---

[1] **Official note:** Regulation (EU) 2024/1689 of the European Parliament and of the Council of 13 June 2024 laying down harmonised rules on artificial intelligence and amending Regulations (EC) No 300/2008, (EU) No 167/2013, (EU) No 168/2013, (EU) 2018/858, (EU) 2018/1139 and (EU) 2019/2144 and Directives 2014/90/EU, (EU) 2016/797 and (EU) 2020/1828 (Artificial Intelligence Act) (OJ L, 2024/1689, 12.7.2024, ELI: http://data.europa.eu/eli/reg/2024/1689/oj).

[1] **Official note:** Regulation (EU) 2024/1689 of the European Parliament and of the Council of 13 June 2024 laying down harmonised rules on artificial intelligence and amending Regulations (EC) No 300/2008, (EU) No 167/2013, (EU) No 168/2013, (EU) 2018/858, (EU) 2018/1139 and (EU) 2019/2144 and Directives 2014/90/EU, (EU) 2016/797 and (EU) 2020/1828 (Artificial Intelligence Act) (OJ L, 2024/1689, 12.7.2024, ELI: http://data.europa.eu/eli/reg/2024/1689/oj).

[1] **Official note:** Regulation (EU) 2024/1689 of the European Parliament and of the Council of 13 June 2024 laying down harmonised rules on artificial intelligence and amending Regulations (EC) No 300/2008, (EU) No 167/2013, (EU) No 168/2013, (EU) 2018/858, (EU) 2018/1139 and (EU) 2019/2144 and Directives 2014/90/EU, (EU) 2016/797 and (EU) 2020/1828 (Artificial Intelligence Act) (OJ L, 2024/1689, 12.7.2024, ELI: http://data.europa.eu/eli/reg/2024/1689/oj).

(2) in Article 19, the following paragraph is added:

4. When adopting delegated acts pursuant to paragraphs 1 and 2 concerning Artificial Intelligence systems which are safety components within the meaning of Regulation (EU) 2024/1689, the requirements set out in Chapter III, Section 2, of that Regulation shall be taken into account.

(3) in Article 43, the following paragraph is added:

4. When adopting implementing acts pursuant to paragraph 1 concerning Artificial Intelligence systems which are safety components within the meaning of Regulation (EU) 2024/1689, the requirements set out in Chapter III, Section 2, of that Regulation shall be taken into account.

(4) in Article 47, the following paragraph is added:

3. When adopting delegated acts pursuant to paragraphs 1 and 2 concerning Artificial Intelligence systems which are safety components within the meaning of Regulation (EU) 2024/1689, the requirements set out in Chapter III, Section 2, of that Regulation shall be taken into account.

(5) in Article 57, the following subparagraph is added:

When adopting those implementing acts concerning Artificial Intelligence systems which are safety components within the meaning of Regulation (EU) 2024/1689, the requirements set out in Chapter III, Section 2, of that Regulation shall be taken into account.

(6) in Article 58, the following paragraph is added:

3. When adopting delegated acts pursuant to paragraphs 1 and 2 concerning Artificial Intelligence systems which are safety components within the meaning of Regulation (EU) 2024/1689, the requirements set out in Chapter III, Section 2, of that Regulation shall be taken into account.

Article 109
Amendment to Regulation (EU) 2019/2144

In Article 11 of Regulation (EU) 2019/2144, the following paragraph is added:
3. When adopting the implementing acts pursuant to paragraph 2, concerning artificial intelligence systems which are safety components within the meaning of Regulation (EU) 2024/1689 of the European Parliament and of the Council[1], the requirements set out in Chapter III, Section 2, of that Regulation shall be taken into account.

[1] **Official note:** Regulation (EU) 2024/1689 of the European Parliament and of the Council of 13 June 2024 laying down harmonised rules on artificial intelligence and amending Regulations (EC) No 300/2008, (EU) No 167/2013, (EU) No 168/2013, (EU) 2018/858, (EU) 2018/1139 and (EU) 2019/2144 and Directives 2014/90/EU, (EU) 2016/797 and (EU) 2020/1828 (Artificial Intelligence Act) (OJ L, 2024/1689, 12.7.2024, ELI: http://data.europa.eu/eli/reg/2024/1689/oj).

Article 110
Amendment to Directive (EU) 2020/1828

In Annex I to Directive (EU) 2020/1828 of the European Parliament and of the Council[1], the following point is added:

(68) Regulation (EU) 2024/1689 of the European Parliament and of the Council of 13 June 2024 laying down harmonised rules on artificial intelligence and amending Regulations (EC) No 300/2008, (EU) No 167/2013, (EU) No 168/2013, (EU) 2018/858, (EU) 2018/1139 and (EU) 2019/2144 and Directives 2014/90/EU, (EU) 2016/797 and (EU) 2020/1828 (Artificial Intelligence Act) (OJ L, 2024/1689, 12.7.2024, ELI: http://data.europa.eu/eli/reg/2024/1689/oj).

Article 111
AI systems already placed on the market or put into service and general-purpose AI models already placed on the marked

1.

(1) Without prejudice to the application of Article 5 as referred to in Article 113(3), point (a), AI systems which are components of the large-scale IT systems established by the legal acts listed in Annex X that have been placed on the market or put into service before 2 August 2027 shall be brought into compliance with this Regulation by 31 December 2030.

(2) The requirements laid down in this Regulation shall be taken into account in the evaluation of each large-scale IT system established by the legal acts listed in Annex X to be undertaken as provided for in those legal acts and where those legal acts are replaced or amended.

2. [1]Without prejudice to the application of Article 5 as referred to in Article 113(3), point (a), this Regulation shall apply to operators of high-risk AI systems, other than the systems referred to in paragraph 1 of this Article, that have been placed on the market or put into service before 2 August 2026, only if, as from that date, those systems are subject to significant changes in their designs. [2]In any case, the providers and deployers of high-risk AI systems intended to be used by public authorities shall take the necessary steps to comply with the requirements and obligations of this Regulation by 2 August 2030.

3. Providers of general-purpose AI models that have been placed on the market before 2 August 2025 shall take the necessary steps in order to comply with the obligations laid down in this Regulation by 2 August 2027.

Article 112
Evaluation and review

1. [1]The Commission shall assess the need for amendment of the list set out in Annex III and of the list of prohibited AI practices laid down in Article 5, once a year

[1] **Official note:** Directive (EU) 2020/1828 of the European Parliament and of the Council of 25 November 2020 on representative actions for the protection of the collective interests of consumers and repealing Directive 2009/22/EC (OJ L 409, 4.12.2020, p. 1).

following the entry into force of this Regulation, and until the end of the period of the delegation of power laid down in Article 97. [2]The Commission shall submit the findings of that assessment to the European Parliament and the Council.
2. By 2 August 2028 and every four years thereafter, the Commission shall evaluate and report to the European Parliament and to the Council on the following:

(a) the need for amendments extending existing area headings or adding new area headings in Annex III;
(b) amendments to the list of AI systems requiring additional transparency measures in Article 50;
(c) amendments enhancing the effectiveness of the supervision and governance system.

3. [1]By 2 August 2029 and every four years thereafter, the Commission shall submit a report on the evaluation and review of this Regulation to the European Parliament and to the Council. [2]The report shall include an assessment with regard to the structure of enforcement and the possible need for a Union agency to resolve any identified shortcomings. [3]On the basis of the findings, that report shall, where appropriate, be accompanied by a proposal for amendment of this Regulation. [4]The reports shall be made public.
4. The reports referred to in paragraph 2 shall pay specific attention to the following:

(a) the status of the financial, technical and human resources of the national competent authorities in order to effectively perform the tasks assigned to them under this Regulation;
(b) the state of penalties, in particular administrative fines as referred to in Article 99(1), applied by Member States for infringements of this Regulation;
(c) adopted harmonised standards and common specifications developed to support this Regulation;
(d) the number of undertakings that enter the market after the entry into application of this Regulation, and how many of them are SMEs.

5. [1]By 2 August 2028, the Commission shall evaluate the functioning of the AI Office, whether the AI Office has been given sufficient powers and competences to fulfil its tasks, and whether it would be relevant and needed for the proper implementation and enforcement of this Regulation to upgrade the AI Office and its enforcement competences and to increase its resources. [2]The Commission shall submit a report on its evaluation to the European Parliament and to the Council.
6. [1]By 2 August 2028 and every four years thereafter, the Commission shall submit a report on the review of the progress on the development of standardisation deliverables on the energy-efficient development of general-purpose AI models, and asses the need for further measures or actions, including binding measures or actions. [2]The report shall be submitted to the European Parliament and to the Council, and it shall be made public.
7. By 2 August 2028 and every three years thereafter, the Commission shall evaluate the impact and effectiveness of voluntary codes of conduct to foster the application of the requirements set out in Chapter III, Section 2 for AI systems other than high-risk AI systems and possibly other additional requirements for AI systems other than high-risk AI systems, including as regards environmental sustainability.
8. For the purposes of paragraphs 1 to 7, the Board, the Member States and national competent authorities shall provide the Commission with information upon its request and without undue delay.

9. In carrying out the evaluations and reviews referred to in paragraphs 1 to 7, the Commission shall take into account the positions and findings of the Board, of the European Parliament, of the Council, and of other relevant bodies or sources.
10. The Commission shall, if necessary, submit appropriate proposals to amend this Regulation, in particular taking into account developments in technology, the effect of AI systems on health and safety, and on fundamental rights, and in light of the state of progress in the information society.
11. To guide the evaluations and reviews referred to in paragraphs 1 to 7 of this Article, the AI Office shall undertake to develop an objective and participative methodology for the evaluation of risk levels based on the criteria outlined in the relevant Articles and the inclusion of new systems in:

(a) the list set out in Annex III, including the extension of existing area headings or the addition of new area headings in that Annex;
(b) the list of prohibited practices set out in Article 5; and
(c) the list of AI systems requiring additional transparency measures pursuant to Article 50.

12. Any amendment to this Regulation pursuant to paragraph 10, or relevant delegated or implementing acts, which concerns sectoral Union harmonisation legislation listed in Section B of Annex I shall take into account the regulatory specificities of each sector, and the existing governance, conformity assessment and enforcement mechanisms and authorities established therein.
13. [1]By 2 August 2031, the Commission shall carry out an assessment of the enforcement of this Regulation and shall report on it to the European Parliament, the Council and the European Economic and Social Committee, taking into account the first years of application of this Regulation. [2]On the basis of the findings, that report shall, where appropriate, be accompanied by a proposal for amendment of this Regulation with regard to the structure of enforcement and the need for a Union agency to resolve any identified shortcomings.

Article 113
Entry into force and application

(1) This Regulation shall enter into force on the twentieth day following that of its publication in the *Official Journal of the European Union*.
(2) It shall apply from 2 August 2026.
(3) However:
   (a) Chapters I and II shall apply from 2 February 2025;
   (b) Chapter III Section 4, Chapter V, Chapter VII and Chapter XII and Article 78 shall apply from 2 August 2025, with the exception of Article 101;
   (c) Article 6(1) and the corresponding obligations in this Regulation shall apply from 2 August 2027.

This Regulation shall be binding in its entirety and directly applicable in all Member States.

Done at Brussels, 13 June 2024.

For the European Parliament	*For the Council*
The President	*The President*
R. METSOLA	M. MICHEL

Annex I
List of Union harmonisation legislation

Section A.
List of Union harmonisation legislation based on the New Legislative Framework

1. Directive 2006/42/EC of the European Parliament and of the Council of 17 May 2006 on machinery, and amending Directive 95/16/EC (OJ L 157, 9.6.2006, p. 24);
2. Directive 2009/48/EC of the European Parliament and of the Council of 18 June 2009 on the safety of toys (OJ L 170, 30.6.2009, p. 1);
3. Directive 2013/53/EU of the European Parliament and of the Council of 20 November 2013 on recreational craft and personal watercraft and repealing Directive 94/25/EC (OJ L 354, 28.12.2013, p. 90);
4. Directive 2014/33/EU of the European Parliament and of the Council of 26 February 2014 on the harmonisation of the laws of the Member States relating to lifts and safety components for lifts (OJ L 96, 29.3.2014, p. 251);
5. Directive 2014/34/EU of the European Parliament and of the Council of 26 February 2014 on the harmonisation of the laws of the Member States relating to equipment and protective systems intended for use in potentially explosive atmospheres (OJ L 96, 29.3.2014, p. 309);
6. Directive 2014/53/EU of the European Parliament and of the Council of 16 April 2014 on the harmonisation of the laws of the Member States relating to the making available on the market of radio equipment and repealing Directive 1999/5/EC (OJ L 153, 22.5.2014, p. 62);
7. Directive 2014/68/EU of the European Parliament and of the Council of 15 May 2014 on the harmonisation of the laws of the Member States relating to the making available on the market of pressure equipment (OJ L 189, 27.6.2014, p. 164);
8. Regulation (EU) 2016/424 of the European Parliament and of the Council of 9 March 2016 on cableway installations and repealing Directive 2000/9/EC (OJ L 81, 31.3.2016, p. 1);
9. Regulation (EU) 2016/425 of the European Parliament and of the Council of 9 March 2016 on personal protective equipment and repealing Council Directive 89/686/EEC (OJ L 81, 31.3.2016, p. 51);
10. Regulation (EU) 2016/426 of the European Parliament and of the Council of 9 March 2016 on appliances burning gaseous fuels and repealing Directive 2009/142/EC (OJ L 81, 31.3.2016, p. 99);
11. Regulation (EU) 2017/745 of the European Parliament and of the Council of 5 April 2017 on medical devices, amending Directive 2001/83/EC, Regulation (EC) No 178/2002 and Regulation (EC) No 1223/2009 and repealing Council Directives 90/385/EEC and 93/42/EEC (OJ L 117, 5.5.2017, p. 1);
12. Regulation (EU) 2017/746 of the European Parliament and of the Council of 5 April 2017 on *in vitro* diagnostic medical devices and repealing Directive 98/79/EC and Commission Decision 2010/227/EU (OJ L 117, 5.5.2017, p. 176).

Section B.
List of other Union harmonisation legislation

13. Regulation (EC) No 300/2008 of the European Parliament and of the Council of 11 March 2008 on common rules in the field of civil aviation security and repealing Regulation (EC) No 2320/2002 (OJ L 97, 9.4.2008, p. 72);
14. Regulation (EU) No 168/2013 of the European Parliament and of the Council of 15 January 2013 on the approval and market surveillance of two- or three-wheel vehicles and quadricycles (OJ L 60, 2.3.2013, p. 52);
15. Regulation (EU) No 167/2013 of the European Parliament and of the Council of 5 February 2013 on the approval and market surveillance of agricultural and forestry vehicles (OJ L 60, 2.3.2013, p. 1);
16. Directive 2014/90/EU of the European Parliament and of the Council of 23 July 2014 on marine equipment and repealing Council Directive 96/98/EC (OJ L 257, 28.8.2014, p. 146);
17. Directive (EU) 2016/797 of the European Parliament and of the Council of 11 May 2016 on the interoperability of the rail system within the European Union (OJ L 138, 26.5.2016, p. 44);
18. Regulation (EU) 2018/858 of the European Parliament and of the Council of 30 May 2018 on the approval and market surveillance of motor vehicles and their trailers, and of systems, components and separate technical units intended for such vehicles, amending Regulations (EC) No 715/2007 and (EC) No 595/2009 and repealing Directive 2007/46/EC (OJ L 151, 14.6.2018, p. 1);
19. Regulation (EU) 2019/2144 of the European Parliament and of the Council of 27 November 2019 on type-approval requirements for motor vehicles and their trailers, and systems, components and separate technical units intended for such vehicles, as regards their general safety and the protection of vehicle occupants and vulnerable road users, amending Regulation (EU) 2018/858 of the European Parliament and of the Council and repealing Regulations (EC) No 78/2009, (EC) No 79/2009 and (EC) No 661/2009 of the European Parliament and of the Council and Commission Regulations (EC) No 631/2009, (EU) No 406/2010, (EU) No 672/2010, (EU) No 1003/2010, (EU) No 1005/2010, (EU) No 1008/2010, (EU) No 1009/2010, (EU) No 19/2011, (EU) No 109/2011, (EU) No 458/2011, (EU) No 65/2012, (EU) No 130/2012, (EU) No 347/2012, (EU) No 351/2012, (EU) No 1230/2012 and (EU) 2015/166 (OJ L 325, 16.12.2019, p. 1);
20. Regulation (EU) 2018/1139 of the European Parliament and of the Council of 4 July 2018 on common rules in the field of civil aviation and establishing a European Union Aviation Safety Agency, and amending Regulations (EC) No 2111/2005, (EC) No 1008/2008, (EU) No 996/2010, (EU) No 376/2014 and Directives 2014/30/EU and 2014/53/EU of the European Parliament and of the Council, and repealing Regulations (EC) No 552/2004 and (EC) No 216/2008 of the European Parliament and of the Council and Council Regulation (EEC) No 3922/91 (OJ L 212, 22.8.2018, p. 1), in so far as the design, production and placing on the market of aircrafts referred to in Article 2(1), points (a) and (b) thereof, where it concerns unmanned aircraft and their engines, propellers, parts and equipment to control them remotely, are concerned.

Annex II
List of criminal offences referred to in Article 5(1), first subparagraph, point (h)(iii)

Criminal offences referred to in Article 5(1), first subparagraph, point (h)(iii):

- terrorism,
- trafficking in human beings,
- sexual exploitation of children, and child pornography,
- illicit trafficking in narcotic drugs or psychotropic substances,
- illicit trafficking in weapons, munitions or explosives,
- murder, grievous bodily injury,
- illicit trade in human organs or tissue,
- illicit trafficking in nuclear or radioactive materials,
- kidnapping, illegal restraint or hostage-taking,
- crimes within the jurisdiction of the International Criminal Court,
- unlawful seizure of aircraft or ships,
- rape,
- environmental crime,
- organised or armed robbery,
- sabotage,
- participation in a criminal organisation involved in one or more of the offences listed above.

Annex III
High-risk AI systems referred to in Article 6(2)

High-risk AI systems pursuant to Article 6(2) are the AI systems listed in any of the following areas:

1. Biometrics, in so far as their use is permitted under relevant Union or national law:
   (a) remote biometric identification systems.
   This shall not include AI systems intended to be used for biometric verification the sole purpose of which is to confirm that a specific natural person is the person he or she claims to be;
   (b) AI systems intended to be used for biometric categorisation, according to sensitive or protected attributes or characteristics based on the inference of those attributes or characteristics;
   (c) AI systems intended to be used for emotion recognition.
2. Critical infrastructure: AI systems intended to be used as safety components in the management and operation of critical digital infrastructure, road traffic, or in the supply of water, gas, heating or electricity.
3. Education and vocational training:
   (a) AI systems intended to be used to determine access or admission or to assign natural persons to educational and vocational training institutions at all levels;
   (b) AI systems intended to be used to evaluate learning outcomes, including when those outcomes are used to steer the learning process of natural persons in educational and vocational training institutions at all levels;

(c) AI systems intended to be used for the purpose of assessing the appropriate level of education that an individual will receive or will be able to access, in the context of or within educational and vocational training institutions at all levels;
(d) AI systems intended to be used for monitoring and detecting prohibited behaviour of students during tests in the context of or within educational and vocational training institutions at all levels.

4. Employment, workers' management and access to self-employment:
(a) AI systems intended to be used for the recruitment or selection of natural persons, in particular to place targeted job advertisements, to analyse and filter job applications, and to evaluate candidates;
(b) AI systems intended to be used to make decisions affecting terms of work-related relationships, the promotion or termination of work-related contractual relationships, to allocate tasks based on individual behaviour or personal traits or characteristics or to monitor and evaluate the performance and behaviour of persons in such relationships.

5. Access to and enjoyment of essential private services and essential public services and benefits:
(a) AI systems intended to be used by public authorities or on behalf of public authorities to evaluate the eligibility of natural persons for essential public assistance benefits and services, including healthcare services, as well as to grant, reduce, revoke, or reclaim such benefits and services;
(b) AI systems intended to be used to evaluate the creditworthiness of natural persons or establish their credit score, with the exception of AI systems used for the purpose of detecting financial fraud;
(c) AI systems intended to be used for risk assessment and pricing in relation to natural persons in the case of life and health insurance;
(d) AI systems intended to evaluate and classify emergency calls by natural persons or to be used to dispatch, or to establish priority in the dispatching of, emergency first response services, including by police, firefighters and medical aid, as well as of emergency healthcare patient triage systems.

6. Law enforcement, in so far as their use is permitted under relevant Union or national law:
(a) AI systems intended to be used by or on behalf of law enforcement authorities, or by Union institutions, bodies, offices or agencies in support of law enforcement authorities or on their behalf to assess the risk of a natural person becoming the victim of criminal offences;
(b) AI systems intended to be used by or on behalf of law enforcement authorities or by Union institutions, bodies, offices or agencies in support of law enforcement authorities as polygraphs or similar tools;
(c) AI systems intended to be used by or on behalf of law enforcement authorities, or by Union institutions, bodies, offices or agencies, in support of law enforcement authorities to evaluate the reliability of evidence in the course of the investigation or prosecution of criminal offences;
(d) AI systems intended to be used by law enforcement authorities or on their behalf or by Union institutions, bodies, offices or agencies in support of law enforcement authorities for assessing the risk of a natural person offending or re-offending not solely on the basis of the profiling of natural persons as referred to in Article 3(4) of Directive (EU) 2016/680, or to assess personality

traits and characteristics or past criminal behaviour of natural persons or groups;

(e) AI systems intended to be used by or on behalf of law enforcement authorities or by Union institutions, bodies, offices or agencies in support of law enforcement authorities for the profiling of natural persons as referred to in Article 3(4) of Directive (EU) 2016/680 in the course of the detection, investigation or prosecution of criminal offences.

7. Migration, asylum and border control management, in so far as their use is permitted under relevant Union or national law:

(a) AI systems intended to be used by or on behalf of competent public authorities or by Union institutions, bodies, offices or agencies as polygraphs or similar tools;

(b) AI systems intended to be used by or on behalf of competent public authorities or by Union institutions, bodies, offices or agencies to assess a risk, including a security risk, a risk of irregular migration, or a health risk, posed by a natural person who intends to enter or who has entered into the territory of a Member State;

(c) AI systems intended to be used by or on behalf of competent public authorities or by Union institutions, bodies, offices or agencies to assist competent public authorities for the examination of applications for asylum, visa or residence permits and for associated complaints with regard to the eligibility of the natural persons applying for a status, including related assessments of the reliability of evidence;

(d) AI systems intended to be used by or on behalf of competent public authorities, or by Union institutions, bodies, offices or agencies, in the context of migration, asylum or border control management, for the purpose of detecting, recognising or identifying natural persons, with the exception of the verification of travel documents.

8. Administration of justice and democratic processes:

(a) AI systems intended to be used by a judicial authority or on their behalf to assist a judicial authority in researching and interpreting facts and the law and in applying the law to a concrete set of facts, or to be used in a similar way in alternative dispute resolution;

(b) AI systems intended to be used for influencing the outcome of an election or referendum or the voting behaviour of natural persons in the exercise of their vote in elections or referenda. This does not include AI systems to the output of which natural persons are not directly exposed, such as tools used to organise, optimise or structure political campaigns from an administrative or logistical point of view.

Annex IV
Technical documentation referred to in Article 11(1)

The technical documentation referred to in Article 11(1) shall contain at least the following information, as applicable to the relevant AI system:

1. A general description of the AI system including:

(a) its intended purpose, the name of the provider and the version of the system reflecting its relation to previous versions;

(b) how the AI system interacts with, or can be used to interact with, hardware or software, including with other AI systems, that are not part of the AI system itself, where applicable;
(c) the versions of relevant software or firmware, and any requirements related to version updates;
(d) the description of all the forms in which the AI system is placed on the market or put into service, such as software packages embedded into hardware, downloads, or APIs;
(e) the description of the hardware on which the AI system is intended to run;
(f) where the AI system is a component of products, photographs or illustrations showing external features, the marking and internal layout of those products;
(g) a basic description of the user-interface provided to the deployer;
(h) instructions for use for the deployer, and a basic description of the user-interface provided to the deployer, where applicable;

2. A detailed description of the elements of the AI system and of the process for its development, including:
(a) the methods and steps performed for the development of the AI system, including, where relevant, recourse to pre-trained systems or tools provided by third parties and how those were used, integrated or modified by the provider;
(b) the design specifications of the system, namely the general logic of the AI system and of the algorithms; the key design choices including the rationale and assumptions made, including with regard to persons or groups of persons in respect of who, the system is intended to be used; the main classification choices; what the system is designed to optimise for, and the relevance of the different parameters; the description of the expected output and output quality of the system; the decisions about any possible trade-off made regarding the technical solutions adopted to comply with the requirements set out in Chapter III, Section 2;
(c) the description of the system architecture explaining how software components build on or feed into each other and integrate into the overall processing; the computational resources used to develop, train, test and validate the AI system;
(d) where relevant, the data requirements in terms of datasheets describing the training methodologies and techniques and the training data sets used, including a general description of these data sets, information about their provenance, scope and main characteristics; how the data was obtained and selected; labelling procedures (e.g. for supervised learning), data cleaning methodologies (e.g. outliers detection);
(e) assessment of the human oversight measures needed in accordance with Article 14, including an assessment of the technical measures needed to facilitate the interpretation of the outputs of AI systems by the deployers, in accordance with Article 13(3), point (d);
(f) where applicable, a detailed description of pre-determined changes to the AI system and its performance, together with all the relevant information related to the technical solutions adopted to ensure continuous compliance of the AI system with the relevant requirements set out in Chapter III, Section 2;
(g) the validation and testing procedures used, including information about the validation and testing data used and their main characteristics; metrics used to measure accuracy, robustness and compliance with other relevant require-

ments set out in Chapter III, Section 2, as well as potentially discriminatory impacts; test logs and all test reports dated and signed by the responsible persons, including with regard to pre-determined changes as referred to under point (f);

(h) cybersecurity measures put in place;

3. Detailed information about the monitoring, functioning and control of the AI system, in particular with regard to: its capabilities and limitations in performance, including the degrees of accuracy for specific persons or groups of persons on which the system is intended to be used and the overall expected level of accuracy in relation to its intended purpose; the foreseeable unintended outcomes and sources of risks to health and safety, fundamental rights and discrimination in view of the intended purpose of the AI system; the human oversight measures needed in accordance with Article 14, including the technical measures put in place to facilitate the interpretation of the outputs of AI systems by the deployers; specifications on input data, as appropriate;
4. A description of the appropriateness of the performance metrics for the specific AI system;
5. A detailed description of the risk management system in accordance with Article 9;
6. A description of relevant changes made by the provider to the system through its lifecycle;
7. A list of the harmonised standards applied in full or in part the references of which have been published in the *Official Journal of the European Union*; where no such harmonised standards have been applied, a detailed description of the solutions adopted to meet the requirements set out in Chapter III, Section 2, including a list of other relevant standards and technical specifications applied;
8. A copy of the EU declaration of conformity referred to in Article 47;
9. A detailed description of the system in place to evaluate the AI system performance in the post-market phase in accordance with Article 72, including the post-market monitoring plan referred to in Article 72(3).

Annex V
EU declaration of conformity

The EU declaration of conformity referred to in Article 47, shall contain all of the following information:

1. AI system name and type and any additional unambiguous reference allowing the identification and traceability of the AI system;
2. The name and address of the provider or, where applicable, of their authorised representative;
3. A statement that the EU declaration of conformity referred to in Article 47 is issued under the sole responsibility of the provider;
4. A statement that the AI system is in conformity with this Regulation and, if applicable, with any other relevant Union law that provides for the issuing of the EU declaration of conformity referred to in Article 47;
5. Where an AI system involves the processing of personal data, a statement that that AI system complies with Regulations (EU) 2016/679 and (EU) 2018/1725 and Directive (EU) 2016/680;
6. References to any relevant harmonised standards used or any other common specification in relation to which conformity is declared;

7. Where applicable, the name and identification number of the notified body, a description of the conformity assessment procedure performed, and identification of the certificate issued;
8. The place and date of issue of the declaration, the name and function of the person who signed it, as well as an indication for, or on behalf of whom, that person signed, a signature.

Annex VI
Conformity assessment procedure based on internal control

1. The conformity assessment procedure based on internal control is the conformity assessment procedure based on points 2, 3 and 4.
2. The provider verifies that the established quality management system is in compliance with the requirements of Article 17.
3. The provider examines the information contained in the technical documentation in order to assess the compliance of the AI system with the relevant essential requirements set out in Chapter III, Section 2.
4. The provider also verifies that the design and development process of the AI system and its post-market monitoring as referred to in Article 72 is consistent with the technical documentation.

Annex VII
Conformity based on an assessment of the quality management system and an assessment of the technical documentation

1.
Introduction

Conformity based on an assessment of the quality management system and an assessment of the technical documentation is the conformity assessment procedure based on points 2 to 5.

2.
Overview

The approved quality management system for the design, development and testing of AI systems pursuant to Article 17 shall be examined in accordance with point 3 and shall be subject to surveillance as specified in point 5. The technical documentation of the AI system shall be examined in accordance with point 4.

3.
Quality management system

3.1.

The application of the provider shall include:

(a) the name and address of the provider and, if the application is lodged by an authorised representative, also their name and address;
(b) the list of AI systems covered under the same quality management system;
(c) the technical documentation for each AI system covered under the same quality management system;
(d) the documentation concerning the quality management system which shall cover all the aspects listed under Article 17;
(e) a description of the procedures in place to ensure that the quality management system remains adequate and effective;
(f) a written declaration that the same application has not been lodged with any other notified body.

3.2.

The quality management system shall be assessed by the notified body, which shall determine whether it satisfies the requirements referred to in Article 17.
The decision shall be notified to the provider or its authorised representative.
The notification shall contain the conclusions of the assessment of the quality management system and the reasoned assessment decision.

3.3.

The quality management system as approved shall continue to be implemented and maintained by the provider so that it remains adequate and efficient.

3.4.

Any intended change to the approved quality management system or the list of AI systems covered by the latter shall be brought to the attention of the notified body by the provider.
The proposed changes shall be examined by the notified body, which shall decide whether the modified quality management system continues to satisfy the requirements referred to in point 3.2 or whether a reassessment is necessary.
The notified body shall notify the provider of its decision. The notification shall contain the conclusions of the examination of the changes and the reasoned assessment decision.

4.

Control of the technical documentation.

4.1.

In addition to the application referred to in point 3, an application with a notified body of their choice shall be lodged by the provider for the assessment of the technical documentation relating to the AI system which the provider intends to place on the market or put into service and which is covered by the quality management system referred to under point 3.

4.2.

The application shall include:

(a) the name and address of the provider;
(b) a written declaration that the same application has not been lodged with any other notified body;
(c) the technical documentation referred to in Annex IV.

4.3.

The technical documentation shall be examined by the notified body. Where relevant, and limited to what is necessary to fulfil its tasks, the notified body shall be granted full access to the training, validation, and testing data sets used, including, where appropriate and subject to security safeguards, through API or other relevant technical means and tools enabling remote access.

4.4.

In examining the technical documentation, the notified body may require that the provider supply further evidence or carry out further tests so as to enable a proper assessment of the conformity of the AI system with the requirements set out in Chapter III, Section 2. Where the notified body is not satisfied with the tests carried out by the provider, the notified body shall itself directly carry out adequate tests, as appropriate.

4.5.

Where necessary to assess the conformity of the high-risk AI system with the requirements set out in Chapter III, Section 2, after all other reasonable means to verify conformity have been exhausted and have proven to be insufficient, and upon a reasoned request, the notified body shall also be granted access to the training and trained models of the AI system, including its relevant parameters. Such access shall be subject to existing Union law on the protection of intellectual property and trade secrets.

4.6.

The decision of the notified body shall be notified to the provider or its authorised representative. The notification shall contain the conclusions of the assessment of the technical documentation and the reasoned assessment decision.

Where the AI system is in conformity with the requirements set out in Chapter III, Section 2, the notified body shall issue a Union technical documentation assessment certificate. The certificate shall indicate the name and address of the provider, the conclusions of the examination, the conditions (if any) for its validity and the data necessary for the identification of the AI system.
The certificate and its annexes shall contain all relevant information to allow the conformity of the AI system to be evaluated, and to allow for control of the AI system while in use, where applicable.
Where the AI system is not in conformity with the requirements set out in Chapter III, Section 2, the notified body shall refuse to issue a Union technical documentation assessment certificate and shall inform the applicant accordingly, giving detailed reasons for its refusal.
Where the AI system does not meet the requirement relating to the data used to train it, re-training of the AI system will be needed prior to the application for a new conformity assessment. In this case, the reasoned assessment decision of the notified body refusing to issue the Union technical documentation assessment certificate shall contain specific considerations on the quality data used to train the AI system, in particular on the reasons for non-compliance.

4.7.

Any change to the AI system that could affect the compliance of the AI system with the requirements or its intended purpose shall be assessed by the notified body which issued the Union technical documentation assessment certificate. The provider shall inform such notified body of its intention to introduce any of the abovementioned changes, or if it otherwise becomes aware of the occurrence of such changes. The intended changes shall be assessed by the notified body, which shall decide whether those changes require a new conformity assessment in accordance with Article 43(4) or whether they could be addressed by means of a supplement to the Union technical documentation assessment certificate. In the latter case, the notified body shall assess the changes, notify the provider of its decision and, where the changes are approved, issue to the provider a supplement to the Union technical documentation assessment certificate.

5.

Surveillance of the approved quality management system.

5.1.

The purpose of the surveillance carried out by the notified body referred to in Point 3 is to make sure that the provider duly complies with the terms and conditions of the approved quality management system.

5.2.

For assessment purposes, the provider shall allow the notified body to access the premises where the design, development, testing of the AI systems is taking place. The provider shall further share with the notified body all necessary information.

5.3.

The notified body shall carry out periodic audits to make sure that the provider maintains and applies the quality management system and shall provide the provider with an audit report. In the context of those audits, the notified body may carry out additional tests of the AI systems for which a Union technical documentation assessment certificate was issued.

Annex VIII
Information to be submitted upon the registration of high-risk AI systems in accordance with Article 49

Section A
- Information to be submitted by providers of high-risk AI systems in accordance with Article 49(1)

The following information shall be provided and thereafter kept up to date with regard to high-risk AI systems to be registered in accordance with Article 49(1):

1. The name, address and contact details of the provider;
2. Where submission of information is carried out by another person on behalf of the provider, the name, address and contact details of that person;
3. The name, address and contact details of the authorised representative, where applicable;
4. The AI system trade name and any additional unambiguous reference allowing the identification and traceability of the AI system;
5. A description of the intended purpose of the AI system and of the components and functions supported through this AI system;
6. A basic and concise description of the information used by the system (data, inputs) and its operating logic;
7. The status of the AI system (on the market, or in service; no longer placed on the market/in service, recalled);
8. The type, number and expiry date of the certificate issued by the notified body and the name or identification number of that notified body, where applicable;
9. A scanned copy of the certificate referred to in point 8, where applicable;
10. Any Member States in which the AI system has been placed on the market, put into service or made available in the Union;
11. A copy of the EU declaration of conformity referred to in Article 47;
12. Electronic instructions for use; this information shall not be provided for high-risk AI systems in the areas of law enforcement or migration, asylum and border control management referred to in Annex III, points 1, 6 and 7;
13. A URL for additional information (optional).

Section B
- Information to be submitted by providers of high-risk AI systems in accordance with Article 49(2)

The following information shall be provided and thereafter kept up to date with regard to AI systems to be registered in accordance with Article 49(2):

1. The name, address and contact details of the provider;
2. Where submission of information is carried out by another person on behalf of the provider, the name, address and contact details of that person;
3. The name, address and contact details of the authorised representative, where applicable;
4. The AI system trade name and any additional unambiguous reference allowing the identification and traceability of the AI system;
5. A description of the intended purpose of the AI system;
6. The condition or conditions under Article 6(3)based on which the AI system is considered to be not-high-risk;
7. A short summary of the grounds on which the AI system is considered to be not-high-risk in application of the procedure under Article 6(3);
8. The status of the AI system (on the market, or in service; no longer placed on the market/in service, recalled);
9. Any Member States in which the AI system has been placed on the market, put into service or made available in the Union.

Section C
– Information to be submitted by deployers of high-risk AI systems in accordance with Article 49(3)

The following information shall be provided and thereafter kept up to date with regard to high-risk AI systems to be registered in accordance with Article 49(3):

1. The name, address and contact details of the deployer;
2. The name, address and contact details of the person submitting information on behalf of the deployer;
3. The URL of the entry of the AI system in the EU database by its provider;
4. A summary of the findings of the fundamental rights impact assessment conducted in accordance with Article 27;
5. A summary of the data protection impact assessment carried out in accordance with Article 35 of Regulation (EU) 2016/679 or Article 27 of Directive (EU) 2016/680 as specified in Article 26(8) of this Regulation, where applicable.

Annex IX
Information to be submitted upon the registration of high-risk AI systems listed in Annex III in relation to testing in real world conditions in accordance with Article 60

The following information shall be provided and thereafter kept up to date with regard to testing in real world conditions to be registered in accordance with Article 60:

1. A Union-wide unique single identification number of the testing in real world conditions;
2. The name and contact details of the provider or prospective provider and of the deployers involved in the testing in real world conditions;
3. A brief description of the AI system, its intended purpose, and other information necessary for the identification of the system;

4. A summary of the main characteristics of the plan for testing in real world conditions;
5. Information on the suspension or termination of the testing in real world conditions.

Annex X
Union legislative acts on large-scale IT systems in the area of Freedom, Security and Justice

1.
Schengen Information System

(a) Regulation (EU) 2018/1860 of the European Parliament and of the Council of 28 November 2018 on the use of the Schengen Information System for the return of illegally staying third-country nationals (OJ L 312, 7.12.2018, p. 1).
(b) Regulation (EU) 2018/1861 of the European Parliament and of the Council of 28 November 2018 on the establishment, operation and use of the Schengen Information System (SIS) in the field of border checks, and amending the Convention implementing the Schengen Agreement, and amending and repealing Regulation (EC) No 1987/2006 (OJ L 312, 7.12.2018, p. 14).
(c) Regulation (EU) 2018/1862 of the European Parliament and of the Council of 28 November 2018 on the establishment, operation and use of the Schengen Information System (SIS) in the field of police cooperation and judicial cooperation in criminal matters, amending and repealing Council Decision 2007/533/JHA, and repealing Regulation (EC) No 1986/2006 of the European Parliament and of the Council and Commission Decision 2010/261/EU (OJ L 312, 7.12.2018, p. 56).

2.
Visa Information System

(a) Regulation (EU) 2021/1133 of the European Parliament and of the Council of 7 July 2021 amending Regulations (EU) No 603/2013, (EU) 2016/794, (EU) 2018/1862, (EU) 2019/816 and (EU) 2019/818 as regards the establishment of the conditions for accessing other EU information systems for the purposes of the Visa Information System (OJ L 248, 13.7.2021, p. 1).
(b) Regulation (EU) 2021/1134 of the European Parliament and of the Council of 7 July 2021 amending Regulations (EC) No 767/2008, (EC) No 810/2009, (EU) 2016/399, (EU) 2017/2226, (EU) 2018/1240, (EU) 2018/1860, (EU) 2018/1861, (EU) 2019/817 and (EU) 2019/1896 of the European Parliament and of the Council and repealing Council Decisions 2004/512/EC and 2008/633/JHA, for the purpose of reforming the Visa Information System (OJ L 248, 13.7.2021, p. 11).

3.
Eurodac

Regulation (EU) 2024/1358 of the European Parliament and of the Council of 14 May 2024 on the establishment of „Eurodac" for the comparison of biometric data in order to effectively apply Regulations (EU) 2024/1315 and (EU) 2024/1350 of the

European Parliament and of the Council and Council Directive 2001/55/EC and to identify illegally staying third-country nationals and stateless persons and on requests for the comparison with Eurodac data by Member States' law enforcement authorities and Europol for law enforcement purposes, amending Regulations (EU) 2018/1240 and (EU) 2019/818 of the European Parliament and of the Council and repealing Regulation (EU) No 603/2013 of the European Parliament and of the Council (OJ L, 2024/1358, 22.5.2024, ELI: http://data.europa.eu/eli/reg/2024/1358/oj).

4.
Entry/Exit System

Regulation (EU) 2017/2226 of the European Parliament and of the Council of 30 November 2017 establishing an Entry/Exit System (EES) to register entry and exit data and refusal of entry data of third-country nationals crossing the external borders of the Member States and determining the conditions for access to the EES for law enforcement purposes, and amending the Convention implementing the Schengen Agreement and Regulations (EC) No 767/2008 and (EU) No 1077/2011 (OJ L 327, 9.12.2017, p. 20).

5.
European Travel Information and Authorisation System

(a) Regulation (EU) 2018/1240 of the European Parliament and of the Council of 12 September 2018 establishing a European Travel Information and Authorisation System (ETIAS) and amending Regulations (EU) No 1077/2011, (EU) No 515/2014, (EU) 2016/399, (EU) 2016/1624 and (EU) 2017/2226 (OJ L 236, 19.9.2018, p. 1).
(b) Regulation (EU) 2018/1241 of the European Parliament and of the Council of 12 September 2018 amending Regulation (EU) 2016/794 for the purpose of establishing a European Travel Information and Authorisation System (ETIAS) (OJ L 236, 19.9.2018, p. 72).

6.
European Criminal Records Information System on third-country nationals and stateless persons

Regulation (EU) 2019/816 of the European Parliament and of the Council of 17 April 2019 establishing a centralised system for the identification of Member States holding conviction information on third-country nationals and stateless persons (ECRIS-TCN) to supplement the European Criminal Records Information System and amending Regulation (EU) 2018/1726 (OJ L 135, 22.5.2019, p. 1).

7.
Interoperability

(a) Regulation (EU) 2019/817 of the European Parliament and of the Council of 20 May 2019 on establishing a framework for interoperability between EU information systems in the field of borders and visa and amending Regulations (EC)

No 767/2008, (EU) 2016/399, (EU) 2017/2226, (EU) 2018/1240, (EU) 2018/1726 and (EU) 2018/1861 of the European Parliament and of the Council and Council Decisions 2004/512/EC and 2008/633/JHA (OJ L 135, 22.5.2019, p. 27).

(b) Regulation (EU) 2019/818 of the European Parliament and of the Council of 20 May 2019 on establishing a framework for interoperability between EU information systems in the field of police and judicial cooperation, asylum and migration and amending Regulations (EU) 2018/1726, (EU) 2018/1862 and (EU) 2019/816 (OJ L 135, 22.5.2019, p. 85).

Annex XI
Technical documentation referred to in Article 53(1), point (a) – technical documentation for providers of general-purpose AI models

Section 1
Information to be provided by all providers of general-purpose AI models

The technical documentation referred to in Article 53(1), point (a) shall contain at least the following information as appropriate to the size and risk profile of the model:

1.

A general description of the general-purpose AI model including:

(a) the tasks that the model is intended to perform and the type and nature of AI systems in which it can be integrated;
(b) the acceptable use policies applicable;
(c) the date of release and methods of distribution;
(d) the architecture and number of parameters;
(e) the modality (e.g. text, image) and format of inputs and outputs;
(f) the licence.

2.

A detailed description of the elements of the model referred to in point 1, and relevant information of the process for the development, including the following elements:

(a) the technical means (e.g. instructions of use, infrastructure, tools) required for the general-purpose AI model to be integrated in AI systems;
(b) the design specifications of the model and training process, including training methodologies and techniques, the key design choices including the rationale and assumptions made; what the model is designed to optimise for and the relevance of the different parameters, as applicable;
(c) information on the data used for training, testing and validation, where applicable, including the type and provenance of data and curation methodologies (e.g. cleaning, filtering, etc.), the number of data points, their scope and main characteristics; how the data was obtained and selected as well as all other measures to detect the unsuitability of data sources and methods to detect identifiable biases, where applicable;

(d) the computational resources used to train the model (e.g. number of floating point operations), training time, and other relevant details related to the training;
(e) known or estimated energy consumption of the model.

With regard to point (e), where the energy consumption of the model is unknown, the energy consumption may be based on information about computational resources used.

Section 2
Additional information to be provided by providers of general-purpose AI models with systemic risk

1.

A detailed description of the evaluation strategies, including evaluation results, on the basis of available public evaluation protocols and tools or otherwise of other evaluation methodologies. Evaluation strategies shall include evaluation criteria, metrics and the methodology on the identification of limitations.

2.

Where applicable, a detailed description of the measures put in place for the purpose of conducting internal and/or external adversarial testing (e.g. red teaming), model adaptations, including alignment and fine-tuning.

3.

Where applicable, a detailed description of the system architecture explaining how software components build or feed into each other and integrate into the overall processing.

Annex XII
Transparency information referred to in Article 53(1), point (b) – technical documentation for providers of general-purpose AI models to downstream providers that integrate the model into their AI system

The information referred to in Article 53(1), point (b) shall contain at least the following:

1.

A general description of the general-purpose AI model including:

(a) the tasks that the model is intended to perform and the type and nature of AI systems into which it can be integrated;
(b) the acceptable use policies applicable;
(c) the date of release and methods of distribution;

(d) how the model interacts, or can be used to interact, with hardware or software that is not part of the model itself, where applicable;
(e) the versions of relevant software related to the use of the general-purpose AI model, where applicable;
(f) the architecture and number of parameters;
(g) the modality (e.g. text, image) and format of inputs and outputs;
(h) the licence for the model.

2.

A description of the elements of the model and of the process for its development, including:

(a) the technical means (e.g. instructions for use, infrastructure, tools) required for the general-purpose AI model to be integrated into AI systems;
(b) the modality (e.g. text, image, etc.) and format of the inputs and outputs and their maximum size (e.g. context window length, etc.);
(c) information on the data used for training, testing and validation, where applicable, including the type and provenance of data and curation methodologies.

Annex XIII
Criteria for the designation of general-purpose AI models with systemic risk referred to in Article 51

For the purpose of determining that a general-purpose AI model has capabilities or an impact equivalent to those set out in Article 51(1), point (a), the Commission shall take into account the following criteria:

(a) the number of parameters of the model;
(b) the quality or size of the data set, for example measured through tokens;
(c) the amount of computation used for training the model, measured in floating point operations or indicated by a combination of other variables such as estimated cost of training, estimated time required for the training, or estimated energy consumption for the training;
(d) the input and output modalities of the model, such as text to text (large language models), text to image, multi-modality, and the state of the art thresholds for determining high-impact capabilities for each modality, and the specific type of inputs and outputs (e.g. biological sequences);
(e) the benchmarks and evaluations of capabilities of the model, including considering the number of tasks without additional training, adaptability to learn new, distinct tasks, its level of autonomy and scalability, the tools it has access to;
(f) whether it has a high impact on the internal market due to its reach, which shall be presumed when it has been made available to at least 10 000 registered business users established in the Union;
(g) the number of registered end-users.

Overview: Legal Sources, Administrative Practice, Standards

The legal sources (specific to AI), publications on administrative practice and the standards developed by CEN-CENELEC Joint Technical Committee 21 that are particularly relevant to the regulatory framework for AI systems an AI models in the EU can be found under the following links (as of 20.8.2025):

- Regulation (EU) 2024/1689 of the European Parliament and of the Council of 13.6.2024 laying down harmonized rules on artificial intelligence and amending Regulations (EC) No. 300/2008, (EU) No. 167/2013, (EU) No. 168/2013, (EU) 2018/858, (EU) 2018/1139 and (EU) 2019/2144 and Directives 2014/90/EU, (EU) 2016/797 and (EU) 2020/1828 (Artificial Intelligence Act) including recitals and Annexes I-XIII
  - https://eur-lex.europa.eu/legal-content/EN/TXT/HTML/?uri=OJ:L_202401689
- Commission implementing Regulation (EU) 2025/454 of 7.3.2025 laying down rules for the application of Regulation (EU) 2024/1689 of the European Parliament and of the Council with regard to the establishment of a scientific panel of independent experts in the field of artificial intelligence
  - https://eur-lex.europa.eu/legal-content/EN/TXT/HTML/?uri=OJ:L_202500454
- Commission Implementing Decision (EU) 2023/2392 of 3.10.2023 amending Implementing Decision (EU) 2022/2191 as regards harmonised standards for international mobile telecommunications cellular network equipment, transmitting equipment for digital audio broadcasting and digital radio mondiale services, very high frequency maritime survivor locating devices, and satellite earth stations and systems, C/2023/6582
  - Commission Implementing Decision of 22.5.2023 on a standardisation request to the European Committee for Standardisation and the European Committee for Electrotechnical Standardisation in support of Union policy on artificial intelligence, C(2023) 3215 final
    https://ec.europa.eu/transparency/documents-register/api/files/C(2023)3215_0/de00000001048942?rendition=false
  - Annexes of the Commission Implementing Decision of 22.5.2023 on a standardisation request to the European Committee for Standardisation and the European Committee for Electrotechnical Standardisation in support of Union policy on artificial intelligence, C(2023) 3215 final – Annexes 1 to 2
    https://ec.europa.eu/transparency/documents-register/api/files/C(2023)3215_1/de00000001048943?rendition=false
- Commission decision of 24.1.2024 establishing the European Artificial Intelligence Office (C/2024/1459)
  - https://eur-lex.europa.eu/legal-content/EN/TXT/HTML/?uri=OJ:C_202401459
- EU Commission guidelines:
  - Guidelines on the definition of AI systems dated 6.2.2025:
    - Guidelines on the definition of an artificial intelligence system established by Regulation (EU) 2024/1689 (AI Act) – C(2025) 924 final:
      https://ec.europa.eu/newsroom/dae/redirection/document/112455

- Guidelines on prohibited practices dated 4.2.2025:
  - Approval of the content of the draft Communication from the Commission – Commission Guidelines on prohibited artificial intelligence practices established by Regulation (EU) 2024/1689 (AI Act) – C(2025) 884 final: https://ec.europa.eu/newsroom/dae/redirection/document/112366
  - Commission Guidelines on prohibited artificial intelligence practices established by Regulation (EU) 2024/1689 (AI Act) – C(2024) 884 final, ANNEX: https://ec.europa.eu/newsroom/dae/redirection/document/112367
- Guidelines on general-purpose AI:
  - Communication to the Commission – Approval of the content of the draft Communication from the Commission – Guidelines on the scope of the obligations for general-purpose AI models established by Regulation (EU) 2024/1689 (AI Act), C(2025) 5045 final: https://ec.europa.eu/newsroom/dae/redirection/document/118343
  - Annex to the Communication to the Commission – Approval of the content of the draft Communication from the Commission – Guidelines on the scope of the obligations for general-purpose AI models established by Regulation (EU) 2024/1689 (AI Act), C(2025) 5045 final – Annex: https://ec.europa.eu/newsroom/dae/redirection/document/118340
  - Annex to the Communication to the Commission – Approval of the content of the draft Communication from the Commission – Explanatory Notice and Template for the Public Summary of Training Content for general-purpose AI models required by Article 53 (1)(d) of Regulation (EU) 2024/1689 (AI Act): https://ec.europa.eu/newsroom/dae/redirection/document/118480
  - Template for the Public Summary of Training Content for General-Purpose AI models (DOC) https://ec.europa.eu/newsroom/dae/redirection/document/118578

– Practice guide from the AI Office:
  - Practice guide for providers of general-purpose AI models (General Purpose AI Code of Practice) dated 10.7.2025:
    - General information and FAQ: https://digital-strategy.ec.europa.eu/en/policies/contents-code-gpai
    - Transparency Chapter: https://ec.europa.eu/newsroom/dae/redirection/document/118120
    - Model Documentation Form: https://ec.europa.eu/newsroom/dae/redirection/document/118118
    - Copyright Chapter https://ec.europa.eu/newsroom/dae/redirection/document/118115
    - Safety and Security Chapter: https://ec.europa.eu/newsroom/dae/redirection/document/118119

– Living Repository of the AI Office:
  - Living Repository of AI Literacy Practices (16.4.2025): https://digital-strategy.ec.europa.eu/en/library/living-repository-foster-learnin g-and-exchange-ai-literacy

- CEN/CLC/JTC 21: Published standards
  - **CEN/CLC ISO/IEC/TR 24027:2023** (WI=JT021017)
    https://standards.cencenelec.eu/dyn/www/f?p=205:110:0::::FSP_PROJECT:77588&cs=117D63AEABBD08BA3E8BB52AB13F068A7
    Information technology – Artificial intelligence (AI) – Bias in AI systems and AI aided decision making (ISO/IEC TR 24027:2021) – 20.12.2023
  - **CEN/CLC ISO/IEC/TR 24029-1:2023** (WI=JT021018)
    https://standards.cencenelec.eu/dyn/www/f?p=205:110:0::::FSP_PROJECT:77589&cs=13B9138672720A0BFC6C96E2347DCED3D
    Artificial Intelligence (AI) – Assessment of the robustness of neural networks – Part 1: Overview (ISO/IEC TR 24029-1:2021) – 20.12.2023
  - **CEN/CLC ISO/IEC/TS 12791:2024** (WI=JT021013)
    https://standards.cencenelec.eu/dyn/www/f?p=205:110:0::::FSP_PROJECT:77584&cs=1E214F6BC71236253AFF8B30589A6C311
    Information technology – Artificial intelligence – Treatment of unwanted bias in classification and regression machine learning tasks (ISO/IEC TS 12791:2024) – 13.11.2024
  - **CEN/CLC/TR 17894:2024** (WI=JT021001)
    https://standards.cencenelec.eu/dyn/www/f?p=205:110:0::::FSP_PROJECT:75934&cs=10B2A1B084FDE6267DECE6BA7E73F12E7
    Artificial Intelligence – Artificial Intelligence Conformity Assessment – 18.12.2024
  - **CEN/CLC/TR 18115:2024** (WI=JT021007)
    https://standards.cencenelec.eu/dyn/www/f?p=205:110:0::::FSP_PROJECT:76985&cs=1FABC1F0C75ADEAE0A97642046C3ECC73
    Data governance and quality for AI within the European context – 11.6.2024
  - **CEN/CLC/TR 18145:2025** (WI=JT021010)
    https://standards.cencenelec.eu/dyn/www/f?p=205:110:0::::FSP_PROJECT:77083&cs=1054B264D0EF20E09D46DF443839650AD
    Environmentally sustainable Artificial Intelligence – 26.2.2025
  - **EN ISO/IEC 22989:2023** (WI=JT021004)
    https://standards.cencenelec.eu/dyn/www/f?p=205:110:0::::FSP_PROJECT:76616&cs=1FC9F8736D37756142133B45CBA3175BB
    Information technology – Artificial intelligence – Artificial intelligence concepts and terminology (ISO/IEC 22989:2022) – 28.6.2023
  - **EN ISO/IEC 23053:2023** (WI=JT021005)
    https://standards.cencenelec.eu/dyn/www/f?p=205:110:0::::FSP_PROJECT:76617&cs=1FCEB21AB2D7F31FF059BA598B7A5E8EC
    Framework for Artificial Intelligence (AI) Systems Using Machine Learning (ML) (ISO/IEC 23053:2022) – 28.6.2023
  - **EN ISO/IEC 23894:2024** (WI=JT021016)
    https://standards.cencenelec.eu/dyn/www/f?p=205:110:0::::FSP_PROJECT:77587&cs=1FF7382F3EB5F150C3F496A589DF9D20C
    Information technology – Artificial intelligence – Guidance on risk management (ISO/IEC 23894:2023) – 21.2.2024

- **EN ISO/IEC 25059:2024** (WI=JT021014)
https://standards.cencenelec.eu/dyn/www/f?p=205:110:0::::FSP_PROJECT:77585&cs=1C084C5DA531C7AA08AD58E2C35AD47EB
Software engineering – Systems and software Quality Requirements and Evaluation (SQuaRE) – Quality model for AI systems (ISO/IEC 25059:2023) – 7.8.2024
- **EN ISO/IEC 5259-1:2025** (WI=JT021040)
https://standards.cencenelec.eu/dyn/www/f?p=205:110:0::::FSP_PROJECT:80654&cs=1B45768D225CC1F85C2850661EE32E086
Artificial intelligence – Data quality for analytics and machine learning (ML) – Part 1: Overview, terminology, and examples (ISO/IEC 5259-1:2024) – 21.5.2025
- **EN ISO/IEC 5259-2:2025** (WI=JT021041)
https://standards.cencenelec.eu/dyn/www/f?p=205:110:0::::FSP_PROJECT:80655&cs=1F34C857041BE17A0BE0AA19DF793D0E3
Artificial intelligence – Data quality for analytics and machine learning (ML) – Part 2: Data quality measures (ISO/IEC 5259-2:2024) – 21.5.2025
- **EN ISO/IEC 5259-3:2025** (WI=JT021042)
https://standards.cencenelec.eu/dyn/www/f?p=205:110:0::::FSP_PROJECT:80659&cs=1BF1623046F961F1302AA88CFEE335710
Artificial intelligence – Data quality for analytics and machine learning (ML) – Part 3: Data quality management requirements and guidelines (ISO/IEC 5259-3:2024) – 21.5.2025
- **EN ISO/IEC 5259-4:2025** (WI=JT021043)
https://standards.cencenelec.eu/dyn/www/f?p=205:110:0::::FSP_PROJECT:80660&cs=12B09AB8E0BE3FFE3DABDAE85EEA2D2A6
Artificial intelligence – Data quality for analytics and machine learning (ML) – Part 4: Data quality process framework (ISO/IEC 5259-4:2024) – 21.5.2025
- **EN ISO/IEC 8183:2024** (WI=JT021020)
https://standards.cencenelec.eu/dyn/www/f?p=205:110:0::::FSP_PROJECT:78503&cs=195331FD5415AFDF34F05E6F54723CF90
Information technology – Artificial intelligence – Data life cycle framework (ISO/IEC 8183:2023) – 12.6.2024

This chapter is also available digitally at
https://nomosverlag.info/New-AI-Act
It is regularly updated online.

Index

Bold numbers refer to articles, normal ones to margin numbers.